Contemporary Asian America

Contemporary Asian America

A Multidisciplinary Reader

SECOND EDITION

EDITED BY

Min Zhou and J. V. Gatewood

New York University Press

NEW YORK AND LONDON

NEW YORK UNIVERSITY PRESS
New York and London
www.nyupress.org

Library of Congress Cataloging-in-Publication Data
Contemporary Asian America : a multidisciplinary reader / edited by Min Zhou
and James V. Gatewood. — 2nd ed.
p. cm.
Includes bibliographical references and index.
ISBN-13: 978-0-8147-9712-9 (cloth : alk. paper)
ISBN-10: 0-8147-9712-1 (cloth : alk. paper)
ISBN-13: 978-0-8147-9713-6 (pbk. : alk. paper)
ISBN-10: 0-8147-9713-X (pbk. : alk. paper)
1. Asian Americans. 2. Asian Americans—Study and teaching.
I. Zhou, Min, 1956–   II. Gatewood, James V., 1972–   III. Zhou, Min.
IV. Gatewood, James V.
E184.O6C66 2007
973'.0495—dc22   2007015674

New York University Press books are printed on acid-free paper,
and their binding materials are chosen for strength and durability.

Manufactured in the United States of America
c 10 9 8 7 6 5 4 3 2
p 10 9 8 7 6 5 4 3 2

Contents

Preface to the Second Edition

It was no small coincidence that the U.S. population hit the 300-million mark just as we were putting the finishing touches on the second edition of *Contemporary Asian America* in October 2006. For most Americans, this unique historical moment was fairly anticlimactic. There were no visible signs of celebration—no parades with colorful floats and marching bands, no fireworks, not even a public gathering. President Bush—a politician who has an unusual way of speaking to the moment—delivered what could only be described as a tepid response to the demographic change. In a press release issued by the White House, the president lauded the fact that people were "America's greatest asset" and praised the American people for their confidence, ingenuity, hopes, and love of freedom. He concluded that "we welcome this milestone as further proof that the American Dream remains as bright and hopeful as ever."[1] This brief blip in the news cycle disappeared almost as suddenly as it appeared. To be certain, any celebrations that might have occurred were dampened by an ongoing debate in the United States about immigration and its impact on the environment, natural resources, public services, and quality of life.

By contrast, the arrival of the 200–millionth American in November 1967 was a more splendid affair, marked by celebrations and extensive news coverage. Addressing the nation while standing before a giant census clock, President Lyndon Johnson delivered his own message of hope and caution for the future. As Haya Al Nasser recounts, President Johnson's words were broken on several occasions by the sounds of applause from the crowd of onlookers who had converged on the Department of Commerce to hear the president speak.[2] Among the many events that celebrated the 200-million mark was a contest of sorts, sponsored by *Life* magazine. The editors at *Life* sent teams of photographers to twenty-two cities across the United States to find the baby who arrived closest to the hour appointed by the U.S. Census Bureau when the 200-millionth American would arrive. The winning baby was a fourth-generation Chinese American, Robert Ken Woo, Jr., born at Atlanta's Crawford Long Hospital at 11:03 A.M., November 20, 1967, to Robert and Sally Woo. Woo's story was—to paraphrase the writer Gish Gen—"typically Asian American." Bobby's great-grandfather had come to Georgia after the Civil War to work on the Augusta Canal. His mother's family had fled the Communist Revolution in China and settled in Augusta in 1959 after several years of waiting for permission to emigrate. Both of Bobby's parents were college graduates; his father worked as a certified public accountant in Georgia. Bobby Woo was one of a small number of Asian Americans growing up in the suburb of Tucker. He attended Harvard University as an undergraduate and as a law student. Today, he is a practicing attorney (and the first Asian American partner at King &

Spalding, one of the most prestigious law firms in America), an advocate for immigrant rights, and the father of three children.[3]

Woo's story is both fascinating and symbolically appropriate. Even though it was by happenstance, Woo's selection as the 200-millionth American anticipated drastic changes that had altered the country's demographic, social, and political landscape since his ancestors first arrived in America nearly a hundred year before his birth. Woo's parents and Woo himself were beneficiaries of the growing educational and economic opportunities that were made available to them and other racial/ethnic minorities only within a relatively short span of time—by the repeal of the Chinese Exclusion Act in 1943, the Immigration and Nationality Act of 1952 (also known as the McCarran-Walter Act), the Civil Rights Act of 1964, and subsequent changes in public policies and public attitudes toward racial/ethnic minorities as a result of the civil rights movement. The passage of the 1965 Amendments to Immigration and Nationality Act (Hart-Celler Act), two years before Woo's birth, made possible hundreds and thousands of immigrants from all over the world, especially from countries in Asia and Latin America that had legally been excluded. Consequently, the face of America has changed dramatically. Asian Americans, barely visible on the American scene in the 1960s, have experienced unparalleled growth, largely through immigration, from 1.5 million in 1970 to 14.3 million as of today.

At a time when the United States is now the third most populous country on earth after China and India, one wonders what the future of Asian America will look like. With the exception of Woo's story, Asian Americans and their contributions to American life were hardly mentioned by the American public either at the 200-million celebration in November 1967 or at the quiet passing of the 300-million milestone during the third week of October 2006. This absence is a glaring one. Since the arrival of the first immigrants from Asia in the mid-nineteenth century, Asian Americans have played and will continue to play a critical role in this country's future. Their American stories need to be unfolded further and understood more deeply. The second edition of *Contemporary Asian America: A Multidisciplinary Reader* grows out of this urgent need. We have thus worked assiduously to compile a new reader that delves into contemporary Asian America in its fullness and complexity; to assemble a selection of readings and documentary films that offer an excellent grounding for understanding many of the emerging trends, issues, and debates in the community and in Asian American studies; and to organize topics that lend insight into the future of this ethnically diverse Asian American community.

Listening to students, instructors, researchers, and others who have used the first edition of our reader for their studies, teaching, and research, we aimed to make the second edition of *Contemporary Asian America* more user friendly by reducing its size and revamping it with the best and most up-to-date works that reflect contributions—and changes—that have occurred within the field of Asian American Studies since 2000. Our goal proved challenging: How do you reduce the number of articles and yet retain the breadth and depth? How do you retain the "classic" works most utilized by survey courses in Asian American Studies and at the same time introduce new topics, concepts, and perspectives that are sensitive to the changing terrains of contemporary Asian America and essential for the continual development of Asian American Studies today? We have addressed these questions rather substantively through a reconfiguration of certain sections from the original volume and the incorporation of original and recently published works that concern twenty-first-century Asian America, including the impact of September 11th on Asian American identity, citizenship, and civil liberties; globalization as a dynamic force shaping the contemporary Asian American community; theoretical debates that continue to inform Asian American Studies; and an emphasis on the diversity of Asian American experiences along lines of class, ethnicity, nativity, gender, and sexuality. Of particular importance to the new edition is the movement away from nation-centered models of identity formation (a core component of Asian American Studies as it existed in the 1960s through the 1990s) to a model governed by fluidity, cosmopolitanism, and flexible identities rooted in global citizenship.

Of course, our interpretation of Asian American Studies is just an interpretation, and perhaps a limited one at that. While no reader can be all things to all people, this new edition strives to achieve a balanced coverage with the range and depth that reflects our commitment to multiple interpretations of the Asian American experience(s) and the shared vision of the many possibilities and promises that is one of the defining features of Asian American Studies. Along the way, we ask more questions than we answer, offering what we hope will be the framework for a larger discussion within and beyond the classroom. We believe that this second edition has met our intended goals. It also meets the growing expectations of our users. Instructors who have used the original edition of *Contemporary Asian America* should be able to comfortably adopt this new edition whether they choose to teach their courses the same way or differently. Those who have not used *Contemporary Asian America* before may now consider adopting it as it will surely stimulate much intellectual and personally reflexive discussion in classrooms.

We, as coeditors, are appreciative of the encouragement and support of so many individuals who made the original edition of *Contemporary Asian America* a great success and this second edition a real possibility. First and foremost, we thank our editor, Jennifer Hammer, at New York University Press (NYUP). Hammer has been a champion of this edition. Her enthusiasm, encouragement, and editorial insight have made this project as intellectually challenging as it was fun. We thank Eric Zinner, the editor-in-chief at NYUP, for his steadfast support and for his vision of the possibilities of Asian American studies. We thank the managing editor at NYUP, Despina Papazoglou Gimbel, for her hard work in guiding the project to fruition. We also thank our copyeditor, Emily Wright, for her careful reading and meticulous editing of the entire manuscript. We are especially grateful to NYUP's anonymous reviewers, who offered additional suggestions after carefully reading our second edition prospectus.

We are much indebted to many of our colleagues, friends, and students, who offered invaluable feedback, insightful comments, thoughtful ideas, and copious suggestions for our second edition based on their own research and classroom experiences using the original edition of *Contemporary Asian America*. Among these are Christina Chin, Meera Deo, Lane Ryo Hirabayashi, Russell Leong, Valerie Matsumoto, Don Nakanishi, Kyeyoung Park, and Nancy Yuen at the University of California, Los Angeles; Robert Lee, Evelyn Hu-DeHart, and Karen Inouye at Brown University; Carl

L. Bankston III, Yen Le Espiritu, Demetrius Eudell, Matt Guterl, Danielle Antoinette Hidalgo, Christopher Lee, Lynn Mie Itagaki, Elaine Kim, Susan S. Kim, Jennifer Lee, Sunaina Maira, Edward Melillo, Gary Okihiro, Rhacel Salazar Parreñas, Edward Park, John Park, Paul Spickcard and his students, Leti Volpp, Ellen Wu, and Judy Wu at other institutions. We are extremely fortunate to work with our authors, whose contributions were absolutely first-rate and whose cooperation was incredibly generous and timely. We thank Jason Gonzales, Hey-young Kwon, Ly P. Lam, Jesse Lewis, Ravi Shivanna, Tritia Soto, and Yang Sao Xiong, who provided tremendous technical support and research assistance.

We would like to acknowledge the institutional support from the Department of Sociology, Department of Asian American Studies, and Asian American Studies Center at UCLA, and the Department of American Civilization and the Center for the Study of Race and Ethnicity in the Americas at Brown University. The Asian American Studies Center, the Social Sciences Division of the College of Letters and Sciences, and the Academic Senate at UCLA provided partial funding for the project. The Center for Advanced Studies in the Behavioral Sciences at Stanford awarded a fellowship to Min Zhou during the academic year 2005–2006, which freed up much time for her to concentrate on developing this project.

Last—but certainly not least—we thank our wonderful families, who continue to inspire us and our endeavors. Min Zhou dedicates this book to her husband, Sam Nan Guo, and son, Philip Jia Guo. Jim Gatewood dedicates this book to his wife, Jules, to his mum, June Gatewood, and to his pugs, Boo and Moses.

Min Zhou and J. V. Gatewood
October 2006

NOTES

1. Office of the Press Secretary, "Statement by the President on U.S. Reaching 300 Million Population Milestone," News Release (October 17, 2006) http://www.whitehouse.gov/news/releases/2006/10/20061017-8.html [accessed November 1st, 2006 at 10:00 A.M.]

2. Haya El Nasser, "Little Fanfare Expected to Mark Population Milestone," *USA Today* (October 13, 2006), http://www.usatoday.com/printedition/news/20061013/a_300million13.art.html [accessed on November 11, 2006 at 12:44 P.M.]

3. Woo's story appeared in several publications. See for example the following: Jonathan Tilove and Stan Freeman, "U.S. Count Set to Hit 300 Million," *The Republican* (October 16, 2006), http://www.masslive.com/printer/printer.ssf?/base/news-6/1160985918185220.xml [accessed November 3, 2006 at 11:51 A.M.]; Mary Lou Pickel, "Atlanta Baby Named 200,000,000 American in 1967; The Growth of America: A Profile of Robert Woo," *Atlanta Journal-Constitution* (October 9, 2006), http://www.ajc.com/news/content/metro/stories/2006/10/09/1010woo.html [accessed on November 3, 2006 at 11:54 A.M.]

IL 60154; (3) describe the nature of your Claim; and (4) specify the damages or other relief you seek. You must provide the Notice within one year after your Claim accrues; otherwise, you waive the Claim and agree that you are forever barred from asserting it in any jurisdiction. If, following your provision of the Notice, we and you do not resolve the Claim within 30 days after our receipt of your Notice, either you or we may commence an arbitration or file a small claims court action to resolve the Claim.

Any arbitration commenced under this provision shall be administered by the American Arbitration Association and be conducted in accordance with its Consumer Arbitration Rules (the "Rules"). Contact information for the American Arbitration Association, as well as copies of the Rules and applicable forms are available at www.adr.org or by calling the American Arbitration Association at (800) 778-7879. In circumstances in which the Rules provide for an in-person hearing, such hearing will, at your request, take place in the U.S. county (or parish) of your residence, or otherwise in Chicago, Illinois. For any Claim that does not exceed $50,000, we will pay all filing and arbitrator's fees, unless the arbitrator finds the arbitration was frivolous or brought for an improper purpose. If the arbitrator awards you damages that are greater than our last written settlement offer communicated before commencement of the arbitration, we will pay you the greater of $1,000 or the amount of the award. For the avoidance of doubt, no unilateral amendment or modification to this Agreement by Follett shall retroactively modify this agreed upon dispute resolution provision, unless the parties expressly agree otherwise.

8. Governing Law. You and we agree that the terms and conditions of this Agreement, including any Claims asserted in accordance with the arbitration provision set forth in Section 7, shall be interpreted in accordance with the laws of the State of Illinois and the United States of America, without regard to conflict-of-law provisions.

9. Refund. Follett's standard refund policies apply.

10. Tax. Normal tax rates will apply, and vary, depending on State.

11. Severability. In the event any portion of this Agreement is found to be unenforceable or unlawful for any reason, (1) the unenforceable or unlawful provision shall be severed from this Agreement; (2) severance of the unenforceable or unlawful provision shall have no impact whatsoever on the remainder of this Agreement or the parties' ability to compel arbitration of any Claims brought on an individual basis pursuant to Section 7; and (3) to the extent that any Claims must therefore proceed on a class, collective, consolidated, or representative basis, such Claims shall be litigated in a civil court of competent jurisdiction, and not in arbitration, and the parties agree that litigation of those claims shall be stayed pending the outcome of any individual claims in arbitration.

12. Conflict of Terms. With respect to any Service or Rented Materials under this Agreement, in the event of any conflict or inconsistency between the terms and provisions of this Agreement and the terms and provisions of our privacy policy, our terms of use, or any other documents incorporated into the Website, the terms and provisions of this Agreement shall control.

13. Indemnification. You agree to defend, indemnify and hold us harmless against any and all third party claims, damages, costs and expenses, including attorneys' fees, arising from or related to your use or misuse of the Service or Rented Materials and/or your breach of these terms. We reserve the right to assume the exclusive defense and control of any claim subject to indemnification, and in such cases you agree to cooperate with us to defend such claim. You may not settle any claim covered by this section without our prior written approval.

14. Follett's Disclaimer and Limitation of Liability. WE DO NOT WARRANT THAT THE SERVICE OR THE RENTED MATERIALS SHALL BE FREE OF ERRORS OR OMISSIONS. WE SHALL HAVE NO LIABILITY FOR ANY SUCH ISSUES. WE DISCLAIM ANY EXPRESS OR IMPLIED WARRANTIES AS TO THE SERVICE OR RENTED MATERIALS, INCLUDING, WITHOUT LIMITATION, NONINFRINGEMENT, MERCHANTABILITY, FITNESS FOR A PARTICULAR PURPOSE, TITLE, AND AS TO QUALITY, AVAILABILITY AND SUBJECT MATTER OF CONTENT. THE RENTED MATERIALS AND THEIR CONTENT ARE PROVIDED "AS IS," "AS AVAILABLE," AND "WITH ALL FAULTS."

YOUR USE OF THE SERVICE AND RENTED MATERIALS IS AT YOUR RISK. IF YOU ARE DISSATISFIED WITH THE SERVICE OR RENTED MATERIALS, YOUR SOLE AND EXCLUSIVE REMEDY IS TO DISCONTINUE USING THE SERVICE OR RENTED MATERIALS.

WE WILL NOT BE LIABLE TO YOU OR ANYONE ELSE FOR ANY SPECIAL, INDIRECT, INCIDENTAL, EXEMPLARY, PUNITIVE OR CONSEQUENTIAL DAMAGES IN CONNECTION WITH THE SERVICE OR RENTED MATERIALS OR YOUR USE OR INABILITY TO USE THE SERVICE OR RENTED MATERIALS, EVEN IF FORESEEABLE OR EVEN IF WE HAVE BEEN ADVISED OF THE POSSIBILITY OF SUCH DAMAGES. IN NO EVENT WILL OUR LIABILITY FOR OTHER DAMAGES EXCEED THE AMOUNT PAID BY YOU TO US IN CONNECTION WITH YOUR USE OF THE SERVICE OR RENTED MATERIALS IN THE TWELVE MONTHS PRECEDING THE CLAIM.

Rental Agreement

Agreement: 3.0

Agreement Terms and Conditions

This Textbook Rental Agreement (the "Agreement") is a contract between you and Follett and applies to your use of Follett products and services (collectively the "Service" or the "Rented Materials"). This Agreement sets forth your rights and obligations and should be read carefully. In this Agreement, "I", "you" or "your" means any person or entity using the Service or Rented Materials (the "User" or "Users"). Unless otherwise stated, "Follett," the "Company," "we," or "our" will refer collectively to Follett Higher Education Group, Inc.

By clicking "I Agree", "I Accept," or by using the Service, the Rented Materials, or the Follett website (the "Website"), you agree to the terms and conditions of this Agreement, our privacy policy, our terms of use, the receipt, and any other documents incorporated into the Website. You agree that this Agreement constitutes the entire agreement between you and the Company, and is legally binding between you and the Company.

Please note: Section 7 of this Agreement contains an arbitration clause and class action waiver that applies to any dispute with or claim against Follett you may have arising out of or relating to the Service or the Agreement. This clause affects how disputes with Follett are resolved. By accepting the terms and conditions of this Agreement, you agree to be bound by the arbitration clause and class action waiver. Please read it carefully.

Except as provided in Section 7, the Company may modify this Agreement from time to time and such modification shall be effective upon posting by the Company on the Website. You agree to be bound to any changes to this Agreement when you use the Website, the Service, or the Rented Materials after any such modification is posted. It is therefore important that you review this Agreement and the Website regularly to ensure you are aware of any changes.

1. I am at least 18 years of age or the age of majority in the state in which I am conducting this transaction.

2. I am entering this Agreement with Follett of my own free will. I will return the Rented Materials to the Follett campus bookstore from which I rented the materials.

3. I will pay for the materials as specified at the time of order. If I decide to buy any rented book at any time after the time provided for in the standard refund policy and before the check-in date (the "Rental Return Date"), I will pay the difference between the rental fee and the purchase price (based off of purchased condition) as outlined on the transaction receipt provided to me. The charge will be applied to the credit or debit card which is on file. I acknowledge that some rental books are "rental-only" and may not be purchased.

4. Failure to Return. Follett is not responsible for reminding me of the Rental Return Date. If I fail to return the Rented Materials by the Rental Return Date (either in store or post-marked by the Rental Return Date), or if I return them in damaged or unsalable condition, I understand that my patron rental account may be suspended and I may incur charges. I authorize Follett to charge non-return charges and processing fees, which consist of the replacement cost of the Rented Materials plus applicable fees as identified on my transaction receipt to my credit card or debit card on file. I acknowledge that, independent of the purchase price of replacement materials, Follett incurs expenses sourcing replacement materials and other business and logistical costs as a result of late returns. Those costs can be difficult to calculate at the time this Agreement goes into effect. Consequently, I agree that it is reasonable and appropriate for Follett to charge me processing fees associated with any failure on my part to return Rented Materials by the Rental Return Date. All books returned to Follett will be processed and disposed of at Follett's discretion. "Rental only" books must be returned.

5. Conditions upon Return. Highlighting and writing in rented textbooks is permitted and acceptable. However, Rented Materials must be returned in complete and salable condition. This means the spine of the book is intact, there is no damage to the book, and all component parts of the book and any related materials must be present. I am responsible for any loss or theft of the Rented Materials. If the rental is deemed damaged, reported lost or stolen, I am responsible for the replacement cost of the Rented Materials plus applicable fees.

6. Card as Security. I will not cancel or exceed the purchasing limits of the credit or debit card on file until the Rented Materials are either returned to Follett or all applicable fees are paid. If my credit or debit card is declined, I understand that my patron account will be suspended and any amounts due to Follett may be sent to a third party collection agency for collection. I will be responsible for paying all collection fees assessed by the third party collection agency. Follett will make reasonable efforts to process transactions in a timely manner. I agree not to hold Follett responsible in the event Follett does not credit or debit my credit or debit card for a period of time due to circumstances beyond Follett's control. Follett makes no guarantees regarding the processing time for charges. I agree, in order for Follett to service my account or to collect any amount I may owe, unless otherwise prohibited by applicable law, Follett or a designated third party collection agency are authorized to (i) contact me by telephone at the telephone number(s) in my patron contact account, including wireless telephone numbers, which could result in charges to me, (ii) contact me by sending text messages (message and data rates may apply) or emails, using any email address I provide, and/or (iii) contact me using pre-recorded/artificial voice messages and/or by use of an automatic dialing device, as applicable. I have read this disclosure and agree that Follett or any designated third party collection agency may contact me as described above.

7. Arbitration. If you have any dispute with or claim against Follett (a "Claim") arising out of or relating to the Service, the Rented Materials, or the Agreement, including any Claim relating to your rental of books or materials from Follett, you and we each agree to resolve such disputes through an individual binding arbitration or an individual action in small claims court. Class arbitrations and class actions are not permitted, and your Claim may not be consolidated with any other person's claim. You and we agree that the U.S. Federal Arbitration Act governs the interpretation and enforcement of this provision, and that you and we are each waiving the right to a trial by jury or to participate in a class action. This section shall survive termination of your use of the Service or Rented Materials.

    Before you commence an arbitration or file a small claims court action with respect to your Claim, you must first send to Follett a written notice of your claim (the "Notice"). The Notice must (1) be sent by certified mail; (2) be addressed to Follett Corporation Attn: General Counsel, 3 Westbrook Corporate Center, Suite 200, Westchester,

Preface to the First Edition

The purpose of this anthology is to provide undergraduate and graduate students and all those interested in the Asian American community with some of the most central readings informing Asian America and Asian American Studies today. Of critical importance in selecting the readings is our goal of making the entire project a reflexive undertaking. The readings, while important in and of themselves to the evolution of Asian American Studies and the development of the community, have been selected on the basis of what they can tell our readers about themselves or their own lives and, essentially, about the ways in which our readers' experiences may resonate within the larger framework of what we call "Asian American experience."

We feel that it is important at the outset to state the limitations of an anthology such as this one. No one reader can capture the diversity of voices, experiences, and people that compose different Asian American communities today. In privileging one topic of discussion, we must necessarily exclude another. It would be disingenuous for us to state otherwise. One of the most noticeable absences readily apparent to students and teachers is that of literary works produced by Asian American authors—the novels, short stories, poetry, and plays. These literary works have played a fundamental role both in defining the curriculum in Asian American Studies and in providing a valuable window through which to evaluate identity formation within the community itself. Our decision not to include literary works as such is not a matter of happenstance. Initially, we agreed to include these works but found it extremely difficult to devise ways to excerpt pieces without losing sight of their original meaning and context. It is disingenuous to the writers of these literary works to break apart chapters in their books or even short stories in a selection that cannot be fully understood when isolated from their other parts. We feel that most of the excellent literary works that exist in Asian American Studies should be read and experienced in their entirety. Another reason underlying our motivations is that this anthology is meant to accompany a college-level introductory course in Asian American Studies. It has been our experience from teaching Asian American Studies courses that many classes have almost always included a number of monographs and novels by Asian American authors that frame the discussion of certain historical, cultural, and social themes in the community. We thus decided to provide a focus that frames these discussions in a social science context.

Although there have been a number of anthologies in the past that have focused on Asian American immigration, community development, and socialization, none really attempts to integrate the intersection of these themes and their effects on the contemporary Asian American community. The basis on which each section of this anthology is devised has come about through our own introspection into those issues that students find meaningful in Asian American Studies classes today. The issue of identity is a central concept in these classes, and we have made a conscious effort to include various abstractions of Asian American identity—abstractions that deal with the intersections among generation, class, gender, sexuality, religion, and the cultural reconstruction of identity. The sections are meant to read not as merely chronological but rather as different themes framing the reflexive bent that we assume. To compromise on spatial limitations, we have also included in each section's suggested reading list a number of excellent works that have emerged in recent years as well as some of the "classic" readings in Asian American studies.

A project of this scope is never a solitary undertaking. We gratefully acknowledge the support and assistance of all those individuals who offered their precious time and invaluable help in shaping this anthology and making it better. First, we would like to thank Tim Bartlett, former editor at NYU Press, who initiated the project and pushed it through with his keen foresight and enthusiasm. Jennifer Hammer, our current editor at NYU Press, has graciously offered her unlimited support for this project as well as her own commitment to its underlying goals, which greatly facilitated our ability to make this project happen. We would also like to acknowledge the four anonymous reviewers who at an early stage read carefully and critiqued the works we originally selected and the manner in which we organized this reader. Their critical comments greatly strengthened the theoretical framework that we ultimately employed for the reader.

This project was partially supported by a research grant from the Asian American Studies Center at the University of California, Los Angeles. We are particularly indebted to the Center Director, Don Nakanishi, who has always been committed to supporting faculty and students in teaching and research. We would like to thank our colleagues in both the Department of Sociology and the Asian American Studies Center at UCLA for their insightful ideas, helpful comments, constructive critiques, and moral support; particularly, we thank Shirley Hune, Yuji Ichioka, Jennifer Lee, Russell Leong, David Lopez, Valerie Matsumoto, Bob Nakamura, Don Nakanishi, Glenn Omatsu, Henry Yu, and Roger Waldinger. At other academic institutions, we specially thank Carlos Chan, Carla Tengan, and Horacio Chiong. We also thank our colleagues at the Japanese American National Museum for their support, especially Karin Higa, Darcie Iki, Sojin Kim, Eiichiro Azuma, Karen Ishizuka, Cameron Trowbridge, Debbie Henderson, Nikki Chang, and Grace Murakami. A special thanks goes to Krissy Kim for her friendship and encouragement. We send a special note of appreciation to all the students in Asian American Studies, among them, Teresa Ejanda, Lakandiwa M. de Leon, Derek Mateo, Randall Park, Steven Wong, and many others, with whom we have worked and who gave us the incentive to compile this anthology. Diana Lee provided tremendous research and editorial assistance for this project.

Finally, we would like to express our deepest gratitude to our families, who sacrificed a considerable amount of time with us to enable us to see this project through to completion.

Min Zhou
J. V. Gatewood

Introduction

Revisiting Contemporary Asian America

Min Zhou and J. V. Gatewood

As the new millennium unfolds, one cannot help but notice dramatic changes that have transformed contemporary Asian America. Most significantly, the rapid pace of globalization and September 11th have altered the contours of our national identity while creating new challenges for Asian Americans. What is the current state of Asian America? How has it evolved and developed since the 1960s, a turbulent decade in America's history that witnessed the birth of the nation's ethnic-consciousness movements? How have Americans of Asian ancestries constructed ethnic and national identities and how has identity formation changed over time? To what extent has the Asian American community asserted itself socially and politically in American society? How are Asian Americans related to other racial/ethnic groups in the United States and to the people in their ancestral homelands and in other parts of the Third World? These are but a few of the questions posed by this anthology, an introductory reader for those interested in the urgent issues facing contemporary Asian America. We have selected a number of themes that critically inform the current state of the community. We intend to make this anthology personally meaningful to our readers —to incorporate ideas that expose Americans to the struggles and triumphs of a racial minority group, the evolution of Asian American Studies, and the broader social transformations in American society that have historically affected, and continue to affect, people of Asian ancestries and their communities.

Activism, the Movement, and the Development of Asian American Studies

> For Asian Americans, the struggles transformed our communities. They spawned numerous grassroots organizations. They created an extensive network of student organizations and Asian American Studies classes. They recovered a buried cultural tradition as well as produced a new generation of writers, poets, and artists. But most importantly, the struggles profoundly altered Asian American consciousness. They redefined racial and ethnic identity, promoted new ways of thinking about communities, and challenged prevailing notions of power and authority. (Glenn Omatsu, this volume)

The Legacy of Political Activism

The birth of the Asian American Movement coincided with the largest student strike in the nation's history. At San Francisco State College, members of the Third World Liberation Front (TWLF), a coalition of African Americans, Latino Americans/Chicanos, Native Americans, and Asian Americans, launched a student strike in November 1968. The strike made demands on the university for curricular reform, initially aimed at three specific goals. First, student strikers sought to redefine education and to make their curriculum at once more meaningful to their own lives, experiences, and histories and more reflective of the communities in which they lived. Second, they demanded that racial/ethnic minorities play a more active role in the decision-making process and that university administrators institute an admissions policy to give racial/ethnic minorities equal access to advanced education. Third, they attempted to effect larger change in the institutional practices by urging administrators to institutionalize ethnic studies at San Francisco State College. The strike, in which Asian Americans played an integral role, brought about significant institutional changes; in particular, it led to the establishment of the nation's first School of Ethnic Studies at San Francisco State College. More than just a token concession to the students, the School began to implement the students' objectives of curricular reform and equal access to education.

In his seminal article, "The 'Four Prisons' and the Movements of Liberation" (this volume), Glenn Omatsu, a veteran activist of the Movement, contends that the San Francisco student strike not only marked the beginning of the Asian American Movement but also set the agenda for the articulation of an Asian American "consciousness." Omatsu argues that those involved in the Movement were not simply seeking to promote their own legitimacy or representation in mainstream society. Rather, the Movement raised questions about subverting ideals and practices that rewarded racial or ethnic minorities for conforming to white mainstream values. The active involvement of Asian Americans extended well beyond college campuses on which many of these issues were being raised; it reached the working-class communities from which many students originated. Omatsu highlights several emerging themes that exerted a profound impact on the Asian American struggles in the 1970s: (1) building a coalition between activists and the community, (2) reclaiming the heritage of resistance, (3) forming a new ideology that manifested in self-determination and the legitimization of oppositional practices as a means of bringing about change to the racist structures inherent to American society, (4) demanding equal rights and minority power, and (5) urging mass mobilization and militant action. For Omatsu, the Asian American Movement was a grassroots, working-class, community struggle for liberation and self-determination.

The political activism of the 1960s unleashed shock waves that have continued to reverberate in the larger Asian American community today. As both Karen Umemoto and Glenn Omatsu recount in their articles on the Movement (this volume), the spirit that initially infused the period carried over into the next two decades, despite a changing political climate that marked the onset of what Omatsu deems "the winter of civil rights and the rise of neo-conservatism." The Movement has evolved to incorporate a broader range of diverse viewpoints and voices, helping frame the way in which many students approach Asian American Studies today. Not only does the Movement provide students with an understanding of the strategies employed by racial and ethnic minorities in their fight against racism and oppression in American society; it also suggests specific ways in which these strategies can be effectively used for minority empowerment.

Institutional Development

Shortly after the founding of the first ethnic studies program at San Francisco State College in 1968, other universities across the United States set to work on developing their own academic programs. According to a survey conducted by Don Nakanishi and Russell Leong in 1978, at least fourteen universities established Asian American Studies programs, including the Berkeley, Los Angeles, Davis, and Santa Barbara campuses of the University of California; the San Francisco, Fresno, San Jose, Sacramento, and Long Beach campuses of the California State University; the University of Southern California; the University of Washington; the University of Colorado; the University of Hawaii; and City College of New York. The programs at UC Berkeley and San Francisco State University had the largest enrollment with fifteen hundred each, and offered sixty and forty-nine courses respectively. The programs on other campuses offered four to sixty courses per academic year and enrolled one hundred to 650 students. All Asian American Studies programs, with the exception of UCLA, listed teaching as their top priority with community work and research ranked as second and third priorities. UCLA, in contrast, made research and publications its primary goal, with teaching ranked second. By 1978, at least three universities, UCLA, San Francisco State University, and the University of Washington, offered graduate courses (Nakanishi and Leong 1978).

Since the Movement of the later 1960s, Asian American Studies has experienced unparalleled growth as Asian American student enrollment has increased at unprecedented rates at American universities. Today, Asian Americans account for 4 percent of the U.S. population, but Asian American students represent more than 6 percent of total college enrollment and a significantly larger proportion at prestigious public and private universities. In 1995, for example, Asian American students represented more than 10 percent of the student populations at all nine UC campuses and in twelve of the twenty CSU campuses, as well as at Harvard, Yale, the Massachusetts Institute of Technology, Columbia, and other top-ranked universities. These regional and national enrollment trends have continued to grow, with no signs of slowing down, since the mid-1990s. The campuses of the UC system, in particular, have seen their Asian American populations grow rapidly. For example, Asian Americans make up roughly 12 percent of California's population but make up 38 percent of the undergraduates at the University of California system-wide, and 43 percent at Berkeley, 40 percent at Los Angeles, 41 percent at Davis, 51 percent at Irvine, 43 percent at San Diego, and 43 percent at Riverside (University of California 2005). The nation's leading universities have also reported a dramatic increase in enrollment of Asian Americans, who made up 28 percent of the undergraduates at the Massachusetts Institute of Technology, 25 percent at

Stanford, 19 percent at Harvard, and 17 percent at Yale (GoldSea 2005). The 2000 U.S. Census shows that about one-third of Asian Americans are U.S.-born and that 50 percent of U.S.-born Asian Americans between the ages of twenty-five and thirty-four have at least a bachelor's degree—a rate more than twenty percentage points higher than that of non-Hispanic whites (Xie & Goyette 2004).

In response to these demographic changes, major public universities and a growing number of private universities in which Asian American student enrollments are disproportionately large have established Asian American Studies departments or interdepartmental programs. Today, all of the University of California and the California State University campuses have established Asian American Studies programs, some of which have evolved into Asian American Studies departments. Outside California, many universities and colleges have established similar programs, often in response to student protests, even hunger strikes, and pure enrollment numbers (Monaghan 1999). The current directory of the Association for Asian American Studies, compiled at Cornell University, shows an incomplete count of thirty Asian American Studies departments and interdepartmental programs, twenty Asian American Studies programs within social sciences or humanities departments, and nineteen other universities and colleges that offer Asian American Studies courses. These departments and interdepartmental or interdisciplinary programs offer a wide range of courses on the diversity of Asian American experiences and greatly enrich academic curricula on college campuses.[1]

Despite the current boom, however, institutional development has often met with obstacles, ranging from the loss of faculty and staff positions to the retirement of veteran or founding faculty to budget cuts arbitrarily imposed on relatively young but growing departments. Although continued expansion of programs and departments is not inevitable, and is likely to be a matter of ongoing conflict, demographic pressures, and the political weight of the Asian American community, as well as the continuing intellectual development of Asian American Studies as a field, make the prospects for growth very promising.

Asian American Studies as an Interdisciplinary Field

What is Asian American Studies? Is it an academic field with its own unique perspective and with intellectually cohesive themes, or is it a field that brings together people of different disciplines who share common interests and who work on similar topics? According to the Association for Asian American Studies,

> Asian American Studies examines, through multidisciplinary lenses, the experiences of Asians in the United States. It is a field of study, creative and critical, interpretive and analytical, grounded in experience and theory. It is located in the academy and therewith shares some of the assumptions and values of intellectual production and pedagogy, but it is also rooted in the extra-academic community and therewith shares some of the assumptions and values of the prevailing and contested social and cultural relations. Its subject matter is the diverse (but united by "racial" construction, historical experience, political ends) peoples from Asia—from West to East Asia, South to

Southeast Asia—who live(d) and work(ed) in the United States. But its subject matter is also comparative and expansive, inclusive of America's Africans, Europeans, Latinos, and native peoples, and its geographic range is transnational, extending beyond the borders of the United States.[2]

In the early stage of its development, Asian American Studies understood itself as the offspring of the social movement from which it emerged. Thus, in its self conceptualization, Asian American Studies sought to reproduce central aspects of the broader movement for social change in which it started out as an oppositional orientation, preoccupied with refuting the prevailing theoretical paradigm of assimilation and fostering self-determination through a Third-World consciousness (Chan 1978; Nakanishi and Leong 1978; Omatsu, this volume; Umemoto, this volume). Both curricular development and research in the field focused on history, identity, and community (Tachiki et al. 1971). Meanwhile, Asian American Studies explicitly served as an institutionalized training center for future community leaders, trying to connect scholars and students with grassroots working-class communities. Since the students and Asian American faculty of the 1960s and 1970s were mostly Japanese Americans and Chinese Americans, with a smaller number of Filipino Americans, most of the teaching and research was focused on these ethnic populations.

Of course, the guiding theoretical principles and self-understanding of the founders themselves, still present and influential in the field, cannot be accepted without question. The founders' views carry the characteristic traces of the baby boom generation of which the founders are a part: namely, the sense of constituting a unique group whose actions mark a rupture with the past. Indeed, in the late 1960s and the 1970s, both the Asian American Movement and the academic field were intent on distancing themselves from the traditional academic disciplines and the more established, or "assimilated," components of the Asian American community. For example, the ethnic-consciousness movements of the 1960s also fundamentally changed the way historians and other social scientists interpreted Asian American history. The pre-Movement historiography of the wartime incarceration of Japanese Americans tended to interpret this experience as a grave national mistake, but one that had been corrected by the postwar acceptance of Japanese Americans into American society. The Movement challenged this established interpretation and influenced Japanese Americans and others to reexamine the internment experience within the context of the ongoing debate over past and present racism in American society. Although redress was successfully obtained, the issue of Japanese American internment continues to be linked with contemporary issues of racial justice.[3]

In retrospect, it is clear that contemporary Asian American Studies stands in continuity with earlier attempts by Asian American intellectuals, within and outside the academy, to rethink their own experience and to link it to the broader sweep of American history. The connection is most evident in sociology: Paul Siu, Rose Hum Lee, and Frank Miyamoto, who were members of an older cohort, and Tamotsu Shibutani, Harry Kitano, James Sakoda, Eugene Uyeki, Netsuko Nishi, John Kitsuse, and many others, who were members of a younger cohort, all made important contributions to the study of Asian America, as well as to broader areas in sociology. To the extent that

Asian American Studies involves activities that derive from an attempt at self-under-standing, one also needs to point out the crucial literary, autobiographical, and polemical works of an earlier period: we note the writings of Jade Snow Wong, Mon-ica Sone, Carlos Bulosan, Louis Chu, and John Okada, among others, who produced a corpus that has now become the subject of considerable academic work within Asian American Studies. Also noticeable is a small group of Euro-American researchers who work within the mainstream disciplines, but without the assimilatory, condescending assumptions that mar earlier work and who made significant contributions to the study of Asian America *prior* to the advent of the Movement, providing notice to the disciplines that this was a topic worthy of their attention. The historians Alexander Saxton, Roger Daniels, and John Modell and the sociologist Stanford Lyman deserve particular mention.

In its recent development, Asian American Studies is facing a new reality that is at odds with the Asian America community of the 1960s and 1970s. Asian American scholars have keenly observed several significant trends that have transformed Asian America, with attendant effects on Asian American Studies within the academy: an unparalleled demographic transformation from relative homogeneity to increased di-versity; an overall political shift from progressive goals of making societal changes to-ward more individualistic orientations of occupational achievement; unprecedented rates of socioeconomic mobility and residential desegregation of native-born genera-tions; and a greater separation between academia and the community (Fong 1998; Hirabayashi 1995; Kang 1998; Wat 1998). These trends mirror the broader structural changes that have occurred in American society since the late 1970s, which we shall discuss in greater detail shortly, and create both opportunities and challenges for the field.

To a large extent, Asian American Studies has been energized by the interdisci-plinary dynamism that exists not only in history, literature and literary works, and cultural studies but also in anthropology, sociology, psychology, education, politi-cal science, social welfare, and public policy. The field has traditionally been guided by varying theoretical concerns—Marxism, internal colonialism, racial formation, postmodernism, and postcolonialism, among others—and has widened its purview of topics and subject matters. Interdisciplinary course offerings and research have touched on the daily experiences of the internally diverse ethnic populations: course subjects range from the histories and experiences of specific national origin groups to Asian-American literature, film and art, and religion, as well as to special topics such as gender studies, gay and lesbian studies, immigration, and health. The field has also expanded into comparative areas of racial and ethnic relations in America, diasporic experiences, transnational communities, and the interconnectedness of Asians and Asian Americans, while maintaining a community focus through extensive internship and leadership development programs. These interdisciplinary and comparative ap-proaches allow Asian American scholars and students to get beyond the simple as-sumption that, because people look similar, they must also share the same experi-ences, values, and beliefs. Asian American Studies has also injected historical and ethnic sensibility into various academic disciplines and prevented itself from being trapped as an isolated elective subdiscipline.

On the academic front, however, there has been a debate over the relationship between theory and practice. Michael Omi and Dana Takagi voice a central concern over the lack of a sustained and coherent radical theory of social transformation, arguing that this absence may lead to a retreat to "more mainstream, discipline-based paradigmatic orientations." These scholars see the "professionalization" of the field at universities, the demands of tenure and promotion for faculty, and new faculty's lack of exposure to and experience of the Movement of the earlier period as the main contributing factors to this trend of retreat. They suggest that the field should be "transdisciplinary" rather than "interdisciplinary" and that it should be revisited, rethought, and redefined according to three main themes—the scope and domain of theory, the definition of core theoretical problems and issues, and the significance of Asian American Studies as a political project (Omi and Takagi 1995).

Meanwhile, some scholars and students express concern that Asian American Studies is being diverted from its original mission of activism, oppositional ideology, and community-oriented practices (Endo and Wei 1988; Hirabayashi 1995; Kiang 1995; Loo and Mar 1985–1986). As the field gains legitimacy at universities, it is increasingly uprooted from the community. Although students have continued to involve themselves in community affairs, their activities tend to be framed in terms of service provision, since the social infrastructure in many Asian American communities is almost always in need of volunteers, as one might expect. But volunteering is all too often a part-time event, in which students may pass through the community and then ultimately maintain a distance from it. Lane Ryo Hirabayashi (1995) points out that the divergence goes beyond the institutional "reward structure" that prioritizes theoretical contributions over applied research. He alludes to the problems of essentialized notions of race and ethnicity, the presumed unity of the community, and the impacts of poststructural and postmodern critiques aiming at deconstructing academic dominance. He believes that these concerns can be effectively addressed by redefining the community as a multidimensional entity with ongoing internal class, generational, political, gender, and sexual divisions, reconceptualizing Asian American communities as a dynamic social construct, and incorporating new theories and methodologies into community-based research. More recently, Kent A. Ono points out that the risk of dissociation from community struggles is of particularly critical concern, because September 11th has fundamentally redefined race in America (Ono 2005). He argues that, in the post-9/11 context, Asian American Studies must reconfigure itself to become more conversant about the connections with Arab and Arab American, and Muslim, and other marginalized cultural communities.

Finding a common ground from which to approach issues in Asian American Studies is a challenging task. Many scholars have made concerted efforts to develop alternative paradigms and perspectives to deal with issues confronting a new Asian America that has become more dynamic and diverse. For example, to capture the material contradictions among Asian Americans, Lisa Lowe (this volume) reconceptualizes contemporary Asian America in terms of heterogeneity, hybridity, and multiplicity. L. Ling-chi Wang (1995) proposes a dual-domination model for understanding Asian American experiences that takes into account the diplomatic relations between the United States and Asian countries and the extraterritorial interaction between

Asian American communities and their respective homelands. Sau-Ling C. Wong (1995) uses the term "denationalization" to address transnational concerns that have emerged from the intrinsic relations between Asia and Asian America. Sylvia Yanagisako (1995) advances the idea of contextualizing meanings, social relations, and social action and of liberalizing the confines of social borders that cut across nation, gender, ethnicity, kinship, and social class in Asian American history. Shirley Hune (2000) calls for the rethinking of race. She suggests that theoretical paradigms be shifted to articulate the multiplicity of racial dynamics that has moved the black-white dichotomy and that more attention be paid to the differential power and agency of minority communities in the United States and to the situation of Asian America in connection to diasporic communities around the globe. In recent years, Asian American Studies publications have flourished. For example, Sucheng Chan's edited volume, *Remapping Asian American History* (2003), offers new theoretical perspectives and analytical frameworks, such as transnationalism, the politics of international migrations, and interracial/interethnic relations, pointing to new directions in Asian American historiography.

While the ongoing discussion of goals and methodologies is at once refreshing and evidence of the field's continuing vitality, it also testifies to the degree to which intellectual and organizational tensions are built into the field. On the one hand, the very language of the debate, often filled with jargon and trendy concepts, stands in conflict with the self-professed orientation toward the community and its needs. On the other hand, there is a certain nostalgia among veteran activists, now mainly tenured professors, for the spirit of the 1960s and, to some extent, that yearning for the past ironically threatens to produce a divide between U.S.-born (and/or U.S.-raised) scholars and some of their Asian-born counterparts, especially those whose education in the United States was more likely to begin at the college and graduate level, and who may not share the same connections to a history that they never experienced.[4] Moreover, the ideological presuppositions of the scholars oriented toward the Movement has the potential to create distance between them and the growing number of Asian American (often Asian-born) scholars who work on Asian American topics, but from the standpoint of the more traditional disciplines of history, sociology, demography, economics, political science, and so on. Of course, work in the traditional disciplines is by no means value free, but the ideological presuppositions do not preclude the potential for expanding our understanding of the Asian American experience. Finally, we note the irony in the unspoken consensus about which groups are eligible for consideration as "Asian American," namely, everyone with origins east of Afghanistan. As Henry Yu has pointed out, the very definition of Chinese and Japanese as an "Asian American community" was itself the product of earlier externally imposed definitions of America's "Oriental Problem" (Yu 1998). The field has indeed initially organized itself around the study of peoples of East Asian descent, leaving others who are no less eligible on intellectual grounds nor, for that matter, any less vulnerable to discrimination or stigmatization than the "official" Asian American categories, to different schools of "Oriental" studies.[5]

In our view, Asian American Studies is best construed in the broadest possible terms, understood as that body of scholarship devoted to the study of Asian American populations, conducted from any number of standpoints, from within the frameworks most commonly found among scholars affiliated with Asian American Studies as well as from a standpoint more closely connected to the traditional disciplines. Just as we reject the conventional disciplinary boundaries, we also opt for an expanded view of the field's geographical scope, in particular emphasizing a transnational framework that enables us to "better understand the ways that flows of people, money, labor, obligations, and goods between nations and continents have shaped the Asian American experience" (Gupta and Ferguson 1992, see also Lowe, this volume).

The first edition of *Contemporary Asian America* (2000) was the first volume to integrate a broad range of multidisciplinary research in assessing the effects of immigration, community development, socialization, and politics on Asian American communities. It aimed to expose readers to contemporary developments in the field of Asian American Studies and to highlight the changes that the field has undergone since its inception in the 1960s. The range of issues—the Asian American Movement, historical interpretations of the Asian American experience, immigration, family and community issues, religion, gender, sexuality, the construction of identity among Asian Americans, representation, and the future direction of Asian American Studies—that it covered are clearly of contemporary significance. It enjoyed great success precisely because of the range and depth of its coverage. In this second edition, we reaffirm our commitment to providing historical readings on the birth and development of Asian American Studies, Asian American community formation, new immigrant and refugee populations, queer Asian America, multiethnic Asian Americans, interracial and interethnic politics, and citizenship and identity, among many important topics. While it is impossible to cover every new and significant development of the entire field, we hope that this second edition continues to expose our readers to multiple interpretations of the multifaceted Asian American experience(s) and to serve as a valuable reference guide to illuminating some of the most groundbreaking scholarship in the history and contemporary development of the field.

The Contents of This Volume

Toward the end of the millennium's first decade, Asian America is as diverse as ever, full of promises and possibilities for the future. The broad themes covered in this second edition speak to the nature of these transitions and some of the core debates about the future of Asian American Studies as both a political process and an academic discipline. More importantly, these issues are some of the subject matters with which students must contend if they are to have an informed knowledge of the field's development and continued importance.

The chapters in the selection vary in content and information. Some are meant to raise larger issues pertinent to Asian American Studies and to provoke critical thinking, while others provide substantial data to enlighten students about the makeup of the community and its evolution over time. We hope that these two kinds of sources provide students with the background to raise their own questions, to respond to the readings, and to generally make up their own minds about the contemporary issues

facing Asian America today. At the end of each section, we provide a list of reading response questions for use in conjunction with course material to enable students to
seek out the most important information from each article and evoke other questions
for discussion.

Claiming Visibility: The Asian American Movement and Politics

Part 1 introduces the two most important articles ever written about the genesis of
Asian American Studies and the underlying ideologies that were instrumental in its
early guidance, along with a more recent essay that considers the effects of the movement on Asian American masculinity. Karen Umemoto's piece surveys the history
of the 1968 San Francisco State strike and its importance to the development of the
Asian American Movement. She underscores the multifarious dimensions in which
Asian Americans were part of the 1960s struggles, arguing that the student strike did
not occur in a political vacuum but rather was centrally informed by other ethnic-
consciousness movements and international Third World movements for liberation
and self-determination. She asserts that the Asian American Movement, specifically
the outcome of the San Francisco State strike for Asian American students, has left a
legacy for the Asian American community and has continued to influence Asian
American student life on college campuses.

Framing his discussion in a much larger historical context, Glenn Omatsu recuper-
ates the Asian American Movement as a phenomenon centrally informed by the militant struggles against war, racism, and the multiple oppressions with which many
Americans were only beginning to grapple during the 1960s. He contends that the
Asian American Movement, while born of these struggles in the early 1960s, is composed of diverse segments of the community and worked toward one clear goal: liberation from oppression. He acknowledges the decline of the Movement's vitality during
the 1970s and '80s with the rise of neoconservatism but nonetheless argues that the future of Asian American Studies hinges upon the community's ability to "forge a new
moral vision, reclaiming the militancy and moral urgency of past generations and
reaffirming the commitment to participatory democracy, community building, and
collective style of leadership."

Daryl J. Maeda's chapter attempts to explain the ways in which Asian American
radicals and cultural workers of the late 1960s and early 1970s turned to blackness to
reconstruct Asian American identity as a way to resist assimilation into whiteness and
build multiethnic solidarity. Maeda points out that the cross-identifications between
Asians and blacks are mutual. While African Americans often draw inspiration from
Asian resistance to Western imperialism, Asian Americans encountered blackness socially and intellectually and through direct participation in black struggles. This is exemplified in the experiences of the Red Guard in San Francisco's Chinatown and in
the work of Frank Chin. It was the actual performance of blackness, Maeda argues,
that is critical to articulations of multiethnic Asian American racial identity. Instead of
reproducing blackness, these radicals constructed a new form of Asian American subjectivity, one organized around racial commonality among Asians. Maeda also demonstrates limitations in such endeavors. For example, while performing blackness to

recuperate their masculinity, cultural workers ultimately find blackness to be an unsatisfactory model for Asian American identity. Since 1965, new migrants have radically altered its ethnic composition and immigrant status, and technological innovations have made its national boundaries more porous. Yet Maeda predicts that the challenge to twenty-first-century Asian American identity remains the same as it was in 1969: how to make sense of a landscape marked by diversity along the lines of ethnicity, class, gender, and sexuality and how to build political solidarities that bridge these rifts.

Traversing Borders: Contemporary Asian Immigration to the United States

Part 2 examines the effects of contemporary Asian immigration on Asian American demographics and communities. Our chapter on "Transforming Asian America" provides readers with an overview of the profound changes that have taken place in the last four decades and a survey of the terrain that makes up contemporary Asian America. We locate our analysis as a mapping of ethnic diversity to raise questions about how the steady influx of Asian immigrants impacts the Asian American community at present and in the future and what challenges the community currently faces as it is claiming America. We predict that as the community grows in number and heterogeneity, so too will its representation in the broader socioeconomic, cultural, and political milieu that we typify as "mainstream America."

Carl L. Bankston and Danielle Antoinette Hidalgo highlight unique aspects of international migration from Southeast Asia. By illustrating the unusual forces that bring refugees to the United States from Southeast Asia, the authors deftly suggest the differences—both subtle and overt—between refugees and their immigrant counterparts. Significant intragroup and intergroup differences exist among refugees from Vietnam, Laos, and Cambodia and nonrefugees from the Philippines and Thailand in the varied contexts of exit and reception. Bankston and Hidalgo argue that the differential starting points, especially the internal socioeconomic diversity of particular waves and "vintages" within the same nationalities over time, augur differential modes of incorporation and assimilation outcomes that cannot be extrapolated simply from the experience of earlier immigrant groups of the same nationality, let alone from immigrants as an undifferentiated whole.

Indian Americans have been present in small numbers in the United States since the turn of the nineteenth century. It is only in the last twenty years, however, that they have become the third largest national-origin group in the Asian American community. Ajantha Subramanian's chapter provides a case study of Indian immigrants in North Carolina, most of whom arrived in the United States as "knowledge workers" between the 1970s and the 1990s. Subramanina's chapter explores both the social conditions (state developmental priorities, corporate demand for labor, geopolitics) that have enabled the mobility of Indian immigrant professionals and the way Indian migrants have constituted themselves socially, culturally, and politically in a new, First-World home. The lives and narratives of Subramanina's Indian transnationals juxtapose the developmental strategies of the Indian and U.S. states over the latter half of the twentieth century, and social status in both national contexts in ways that illuminate the nuances of globalization. The study shows that, as highly skilled Indian immigrants incorporate into American society, they use multiculturalism as a new hegemonic discourse that enables them to distance themselves from more plebeian solidarities that may cut across ethnic and class lines. The post-civil-rights shift from a racial to a cultural model of citizenship has also allowed for a rearticulation of minority identity in cultural terms that secures class privilege.

Ties That Bind: The Immigrant Family and the Ethnic Community

Part 3 focuses on the family and the ethnic community. Tuyet-Lan Pho and Anne Mulvey's chapter explores the ways in which Southeast Asian refugees cope with the challenges of adapting to their new homeland while navigating the slippery terrain of cultural values. Through a case study of Southeast Asian women in Lowell, Massachusetts, the authors show that the American lives of refugee women from Cambodia, Laos, and Vietnam are intertwined with losses and gains, linguistic and cultural conflicts, changing family relations and gender roles, as well as economic barriers and social marginality in their own community and in the larger American society. Nevertheless, Southeast Asian women in Lowell are actively seeking to assert control over their fates. They are going to school, are employed outside their homes, are appreciating their new roles and opportunities, and, most significantly, are working together to fight domestic violence and to pursue their own interests. In the process, they contribute to enriching their community socially, economically, and culturally.

Rhacel Salazar Parreñas deals with transnational Filipino households, broadly defined as "famil[ies] whose core members are located in at least two or more nation-states." Drawing upon interviews with Filipina domestic workers in Los Angeles and Rome, she documents the formation and reproduction of transnational households among Filipino labor immigrants as one of many mechanisms available to immigrants as they cope with the exigencies of their new lives. She argues that transnational households have long existed among Filipino migrant workers who have historically faced legal and economic barriers to full incorporation into the host society. The recuperation of this immigrant tradition by contemporary Filipino immigrants is the result of intersecting structural and cultural forces.

Wei Li and Emily Skop's chapter examines new patterns of community formation. Since the late 1960s, the combination of global economic restructuring, changing geopolitical contexts, and shifting American immigration policies has set in motion significant flows of new and diverse immigrant influxes from Asia to the United States. While the number of family-sponsored immigrants continues to grow, record numbers of highly skilled, professional immigrants and wealthy investors have also joined the flow as a result of the economic boom in China and other nations in Asia. As a result, patterns of immigrant settlement have also changed. Li and Skop show that traditional inner-city enclaves still exist to receive newcomers but can no longer meet the social and economic needs of these newcomers. Affluent middle-class Asian immigrants tend to bypass inner-city ethnic enclaves to settle directly in suburbs that offer decent housing, high-performing schools, superior living conditions, and public amenities. As more and more immigrants settle away from urban enclaves, ethnoburbs have come into existence. The transformation of American suburbs into multi-racial, multiethnic, multilingual, multicultural, and multinational communities challenges both the widely accepted characterization of the suburbs as the citadel of the white middle class and the traditional notion of residential assimilation.

Struggling to Get Ahead: Economy and Work

Part 4 delves into the question of how immigrants set foot in their new land. Jennifer Lee's chapter focuses on Korean immigrant entrepreneurship and race/ethnic relations. Lee sets out to answer four comprehensive questions about the nature of Korean immigrant entrepreneurship in the United States: Why are Korean immigrants employed at a rate higher than that of any other ethnic group? What resources do Korean immigrants utilize to start their businesses and sustain them over time? What retail niches do Korean immigrants occupy, and why do they concentrate their businesses in economically depressed regions of the inner city? And, finally, what are the structural forces affecting the nature of tensions that have developed between African Americans and Korean immigrants? Lee states that self-employment is a symbol of downward mobility for many Korean immigrants who are educated and trained as white-collar professionals. However, their inability to transfer their pre-immigrant skills to the United States makes entrepreneurship the most effective means of achieving the American dream of upward mobility for Korean immigrants. This dream was shattered after the Los Angeles riots in 1992, placing black-Korean conflict in the fore. Although the media has focused on the conflict between the two communities, Lee illustrates that most encounters between Korean merchants and black customers are not fraught with racial animosity but instead with customary civility. Further, she explains that against the backdrop of inner-city poverty, simple economic arguments sometimes become racially coded and in only a few cases lead to interethnic conflict such as boycotts or urban riots.

Yen Le Espiritu's chapter focuses on Filipina health-care professionals, a much sought after group among U.S. immigrants. In Espiritu's view, U.S. colonial training of nurses in the Philippines highlights the complex intersections of gender ideologies with those of race and class in shaping U.S. colonial agendas and practices. The over-representation of health professionals among contemporary Filipino immigrants is not solely the result of contemporary global restructuring, the "liberalization" of U.S. immigration rules, or individual economic desires, but rather are the product of historical outcomes of early-twentieth-century U.S. colonial rule in the Philippines. Espiritu also provides a detailed analysis of the way migration processes, labor recruitment practices, and employment conditions have reconfigured gender and family relations. She shows that professional women, like most other working women, have to juggle full-time work outside the home with the responsibilities of child care and housework. In the context of migration, Filipina nurses often work in higher-paid jobs but lead lower-status lives; their labor-market advantage does not automatically or uniformly lead to more egalitarian relations in the family.

Lynn H. Fujiwara's chapter examines the impact of food-stamp cuts for Asian immigrants and refugees through the Personal Responsibility Work Opportunity Reconciliation Act of 1996. Drawing from field work conducted from 1996 to 1998 in the bay area of Northern California in Asian immigrant community organizations allowed for a more nuanced examination of Asian immigrant families negotiating poverty. Fujiwara argues that the targeting of noncitizens as undeserving of public benefits not only jeopardized immigrants' human rights; it also reflects the existing and persistent devaluation of immigrant families, who experienced higher levels of hunger and food insecurity due to welfare reform. This focused analysis of the impact of loss of food stamps on immigrant families highlights the intersecting forces of race, gender, class, and citizenship formed through social policy that reinforces the persistence of poverty within immigrant communities.

Sexuality in Asian America

Part 5 looks into an important subject area that has only recently begun to receive its due attention in Asian American Studies—the experiences of gay and lesbian Asian Americans. Alice Y. Hom's chapter brings new insight into the realm of the unspoken in Asian America—the response of Asian American parents to the sexual identities of their children. Based on personal interviews with fathers and mothers, Hom assesses the attitudes of parents towards gays and lesbians prior to their knowing their children's sexual identities. She finds that by and large the response of these Asian American parents is contingent upon the level of experience that these individuals have with gays, lesbians, and transgendered people before their arrival in the United States. Most parents are aware of the gender role reversals in their children's growing up but tend to distance themselves from the phenomenon because it is "not their problem." Upon finding out that their own children were gay or lesbian, the parents experienced a number of different feelings: shame, guilt, surprise, shock, disbelief, and one common theme, a sense of alienation from their children. Only one interviewee in Hom's study mentioned the loss of "Asian values," but for most there was a sense that in some manner they had failed their children. The road to acceptance was neither uniform nor without difficulties. In relating their children's sexualities to individuals within the ethnic community, the interviewees shared mixed feelings. A number of parents decided not to relate any information about their children to friends or anyone outside of the immediate family, while others shared their feelings with friends in and out of the gay and lesbian community.

Martin F. Manalansan's chapter focuses upon immigrant lives in a community of gay Filipino Americans in New York City. Manalansan employs a fluid definition of community, which is both an "imagined" place where people organize around symbols and practices reminiscent of other symbolic communities, and a place of dissent where forces of oppression also unite people toward common goals. The confluence of these seemingly contradictory definitions of community is critical to the way in which Filipino homosexuals, many of whom are recent immigrants to the United States, construct their own identities. According to the author, the differences among this group are substantial and the kinds of homosexual traditions adopted by these men are relative to their life circumstances and the contexts in which they grew up in the Philippines (for native-born Filipino Americans, whether or not they were exposed to these traditions at some point in their lives). Manalansan points to other elements that reflect the diversity of the Filipino gay community he surveys, such as social class and ethnic/racial/national identities. Most of these gay Filipino immigrants possessed any number of regional, ethnic, and linguistic differences that also made a shared sense of community difficult to foster. In spite of these variances, Manalansan provides examples of certain events—the Broadway production of *Miss Saigon*, the AIDS pandemic ('Tita Aida), and the reproduction of Filipino cultural traditions in America —that have reduced barriers to group unity, while not necessarily galvanizing this shared sense of community. This article, in sum, is an early attempt to address both the obstacles that render community among gay Filipino Americans a seemingly impossible construction and a confluence of moments and events that foster the shared sense of needing and the rearticulation of the community.

Race and Asian American Identity

Part 6 examines issues of race and identity. The civil rights movement and the Asian American Movement have challenged the American racial stratification system and shaken its foundation. However, post-1965 Asian immigration has greatly complicated race relations. Janine Young Kim's chapter focuses on the (uneasy) relationship between the black/white paradigm and the Asian American civil rights agenda. Kim argues that the current race discourse oversimplifies the black/white paradigm and that the seemingly unproblematic discussion of the paradigm fails to articulate the full cost of its abandonment. She sees the black/white paradigm as retaining contemporary significance despite demographic changes in American society and as having direct relevance for the Asian American civil rights movement as well as for a deeper understanding of ever changing and racially stratified society today.

Asian Americans have been labeled a "model minority" for their high rates of socioeconomic achievement, and they appear on track to being accepted as "white." Min Zhou argues that the new stereotype serves to thwart other racial minorities' demands for social justice by pitting minority groups against each other while also pitting Asian Americans against whites. Thus, whitening is both premature, given the "foreigner" image Americans still have of Asians, and a heavy burden upon Asian Americans themselves. Zhou shows that even though Asian Americans as a group have achieved parity with whites as measured by observable group-level socioeconomic characteristics such as education, occupation, and income, they are by no means fully viewed as "American," which is oftentimes synonymous with "white." In the end, whitening is a lived cultural phenomenon that has to do with the ideological dynamics of white America, rather than with the actual situation of Asian Americans. Speaking perfect English, effortlessly practicing mainstream cultural values, and even intermarrying members of the dominant group may help reduce this "otherness" at the individual level, but have little effect on the group as a whole. Like the model-minority image that is imposed upon them, new stereotypes can un-whiten Asian Americans anytime and anywhere, no matter how "successful" and "assimilated" they have become.

Helen J. Lee's chapter focuses on the complex process of self-identification undergone by Korean American youth in Philadelphia, offering insight into the fluidity and complexity of identity formation. Drawing from ethnographic participant observation and in-depth interviews, Lee illustrates the intersection of ethnic and religious identities among second-generation Korean American teenagers in a Korean Protestant church. She found that, in one particular religious setting, three types of identity paths emerge among Korean American youths: a group who views ethnic and religious identities as intertwined and develops a strong sense of both identities, another group who views ethnic identity as distinct from religious identity and develops strong ethnic identity with relatively weak attachment to Protestant Christianity, and still a third group who does not have a strong sense of either ethnic or religious identity. Lee cautions that second-generation young adult (college-age and older) congregations are apt to miss the third type of youths as they most likely discontinue participation in an ethnic/religious institution once they leave their parental homes.

The Complexity of Ethnicity

Part 7 delves into the phenomenon of intermarriages and multiracial/ethnic identities. Jennifer Lee and Frank D. Bean's chapter adds another level of complexity to the current Asian American population dynamics, calling attention to the increasing number of people who claim a multiracial background. Based on the analysis of the 2000 Census data, the authors find that more than one out of every four Asian Americans intermarry and that one in eight Asian Americans is racially mixed, which is more than five times the national average in the United States. Today's high rates of Asian intermarriage would cause a substantial growth in the Asian multiracial population, which is projected to be at least one in three by 2050. Lee and Bean also discuss the implications of multiracial identification for the Asian American population and for America's changing color lines, which revolve around a black-nonblack divide in the contexts of diversity and immigration.

Paul R. Spickard's chapter addresses two crucial and interrelated questions: Why has Asian American Studies failed to include the life experiences of biracial Asian Americans, and how can the field make the subject relevant to the needs of this group? In answering the first question, Spickard maps out the complexity of identity formation and its evolution among biracial Asian Americans. According to Spickard, three trends are at work in the process of identity formation among multiracial Asian Americans. The first stems from the dominant society, which tends to categorize and identify multiracial Asian Americans as weak, inferior, promiscuous, and perverse. The net effect of this process is to demoralize these multicultural peoples as well as to ostracize them from the white community proper. A second trend derives from the Asian American community, which, in a fashion similar to that of the dominant society, has also worked to identify and categorize multiracial Asian Americans in often derogatory terms. It is only within the past three decades that a different trend has emerged in the identity-formation process of multiracial Asian Americans, a trend that stems from these multiracial people themselves. Spickard's article raises the critical point: demographics will no longer allow us to think of Asian American Studies as the realm of Japanese Americans, Chinese Americans, and Filipino Americans alone. Asian American communities throughout the United States are in a state of great transformation as new immigrants redefine the parameters of ethnicity/solidarity. The incorporation of diverse constituencies, among them multicultural Asians, will only enhance our understanding of Asian American history and the evolution of this community in the twenty-first century.

Teresa Kay Williams and Michael C. Thornton's chapter investigates the process of multiracial identity construction through the case of Afro-Amerasians. The authors point out the limitations of prior research that focuses on black-white, Asian-white, and minority-majority combinations and on the problematic social and psychological adjustments of Amerasians and their families as results of war, military occupation, poverty, and social and ecological dislocations. They use the case of Afro-Amerasians to examine the complexity of social and psychological marginality, showing that Afro-Amerasians are estranged in that they are situated between two profound forces—the contrasting push of society to identify as only black, and the pull of their own personal and unique experience. As a result, they choose to situate themselves on the traditional boundaries of racial groups rather than deny important parts of who they are; and thus, they choose to be marginal.

Confronting Adversity: Racism, Stereotyping, and Exclusion

Part 8 touches on several aspects of adversity confronting Asian Americans—racism, stereotyping, and exclusion. Lisa Park's chapter speaks to difficulties encountered by two sisters as they struggle to find their own place in American life. Confronting her sister's suicide in a meaningful way forces the narrator to consider the emotional toll that societal double standards inflict on Asian Americans, especially those growing up in immigrant families. Park points out that racism, the perpetual drive to assimilate racial minorities to a white norm, the pressures placed upon the family and individual to live up to the model-minority image, the family's frustration with downward mobility, and the community's reluctance in accepting her mental health problem all play a part in her sister's suicide. She exposes the detrimental effects of the model-minority stereotype—"Do you see what a lie it is and how it is used to reinforce the American Dream and punish those of us who don't 'succeed' or succeed 'too much'?" Park suggests that the model-minority image places unrealistic and harmful expectations not only on Asian Americans who do not achieve the affluence and success associated with the image but also on other racial minorities, specifically African Americans and Latino Americans, who are asked why they cannot do the same.

Sunaina Maira lends her insights into the challenges faced by South Asian Americans in the wake of September 11th. Drawing upon the experiences of young people in Boston, she assesses the way racial stereotyping and the War on Terror have complicated identities and fostered an antagonism among men and women who see their opportunities constrained as a result of blatant stereotyping. The effect, Maira explains, is that 9/11 has strengthened interethnic solidarity among Asians but reduced the desire for assimilation into mainstream American society.

The chapter by Christina B. Chin and her colleagues explores the representation of Asian Americans and Pacific Islanders (AAPIs) on television, on the basis of data collected for the fall 2004 and fall 2005 seasons of prime-time television. This study pays close attention to numerical representation on prime-time shows by race, gender, network, program, and geographic setting, focusing only on those shows featuring AAPI actors. This pioneer study provides powerful evidence to demonstrate that AAPIs continue to be marginalized both in terms of numbers and in terms of the quality of characters. AAPIs are consistently underrepresented numerically compared to their population percentage, particularly in shows set in heavily AAPI-populated cities such as Los Angeles, San Francisco, and New York. Furthermore, AAPI actors feature less prominently than non-AAPI actors as indicated by their comparatively lower amount of time on screen. Chin et al. also find that, over the two-year study period, there were some improvements in character complexity, such as the increased depiction of AAPIs in intimate relationships, and that this improvement resulted in several award nominations and winnings by AAPI actors and in some prime-time programs that showcase complex AAPI actors and characters. Despite the growing recognition of AAPI actors and characters among audience and industry members, however, AAPIs still remain marginalized due to their invisibility in prime-time television.

Behind the Model Minority

Part 9 examines what lies behind the model-minority stereotype. The publication of William Petersen's article on the virtues of Japanese American in the *New York Times Magazine* in January 1966 marked a significant departure from the ways in which Asian immigrants and their succeeding generations had been traditionally depicted in popular culture. A few months later, another article, similar in tone, extolled Chinese Americans for their persistence and success. However, the celebration of the model minority buttresses the myth that the United States is devoid of racism, that it accords equal opportunity to all, and that those who lag behind do so because of their own poor choices and inferior culture (see Zhou in this volume). Robert G. Lee's historical treatment of the model-minority myth suggests that it is a byproduct of the Cold War, constructed during a period of political hysteria when differences of all types became a form of subversion to national consensus. Asian Americans became "model" citizens because the mainstream press and social scientists like William Petersen held them up as models of civic virtue—"good" minorities who advanced in American society by playing by the rules. This myth was held out to other racialized minorities—most specifically, African Americans who were advocating for civil rights—as a symbol of what might be accomplished through hard work. As Lee argues, however, it completely disregarded the vastly different historical experiences of African Americans and other groups.

David Tokiharu Mayeda's chapter examines American media portrayals of two Japanese pitchers now playing American major league baseball: Hideo Nomo and Hideki Irabu. Analyzing data compiled from the sports sections of the *Los Angeles Times,* the *New York Times,* and popular sports magazines, Mayeda finds that journalistic portrayals of Nomo and Irabu have perpetuated stereotypes of Asian Americans and Asian nationals both as model minorities and as economic threats. He contends that, if this positional racialization goes on without scrutiny, unproven and false images of both Asian and African Americans will be further essentialized in American minds.

Thus, journalists should be equipped with a greater cultural awareness and sensitivity when writing sports articles that cover athletes from various ethnic and national backgrounds.

Multiplicity, Citizenship, and Interracial Politics

Part 10 discusses the complexity of citizenship and interracial politics. Lisa Lowe's chapter is a challenging piece to read in its entirety, since it may be open to multiple interpretations. Her purpose is twofold: first, to disrupt the common tropes of generational conflict and filial relationships that permeate the Asian American experience, and, second, to reconceptualize Asian American identity as an entity in a continual state of flux. "Rather than considering 'Asian American identity' as a fixed, established 'given,'" Lowe writes, "perhaps we can consider instead 'Asian American cultural practices' that produce identity; the processes that produce such identity are never complete." The main point underlying her work is that Asian American culture is neither immutable nor vertically transmitted from one generation to the next. Asian American culture is as much a production of identities as it is a reception of traditions. As Lowe contends, "[t]he boundaries and definitions of Asian American culture are continually shifting and being contested from pressures both inside and outside the Asian-origin community." It is these shifting constructions of identity that constitute the heterogeneity, hybridity, and multiplicity of contemporary Asian American community.

Leti Volpp's chapter examines the curious juxtaposition of the terms "Asian American" and "American citizenship." She contends that, while American citizenship seems to easily embrace Asian Americans, historical and recent events suggest that there still exists a contradictory relationship between Asian American racialization and the idea of citizenship. By examining four different discourses of citizenship—citizenship as legal status, citizenship as rights, citizenship as political activity, and citizenship as identity/solidarity—Volpp shows how race fractures the promise of each of these discourses. She finds that the racialization of Asian Americans as disloyal and politically corrupt contradicts the idea of citizenship as produced through political activity. The fact that Asian Americans are not thought to represent the U.S. citizenry suggests that citizenship as identity is ontologically separate from citizenship as a legal matter. That is, access to citizenship in the form of formal legal status, or in the form of rights, does not guarantee full citizenship.

Claire Jean Kim and Taeku Lee's chapter on interracial politics addresses the relationship between Asian Americans and members of other communities of color. Kim and Lee show that the 1992 Los Angeles civil unrest demonstrates the limitations of the black-white framework for explaining race relations in the United States. The authors believe that the rapid growth of Asian American population and Latino population has created both the likelihood of intense intergroup tensions and the possibility of political coalition. They provide a thoughtful analysis of the way ideology, power dynamics, and racial hierarchy shape patterns of conflict and cooperation among Asian Americans and other racial minority groups, particularly outside of formal political institutions. They conclude that the development of a strong racial identity can politicize people and awaken them to their shared interests with members of other racial groups but can also prevent people from seeing past their own group boundaries.

The chapters taken as a whole illustrate some of the prospects, possibilities, and problems currently faced by Asian Americans and their communities and by the field of Asian American Studies. It is our hope that our readers approach these issues in a critical and reflexive manner, one that draws heavily from their own experiences, histories, and interpretations. This anthology is by no means a definitive end to the complexity and range of issues confronting contemporary Asian America. In fact, it only begins to raise questions that may not necessarily have clear or definitive answers. For some people, the resolution may be simple. For many others, however, the solution may require compromise. We are excited by the prospects for the future of Asian American Studies but add a note of caution—one that is cognizant of how far the field has come from those early days at San Francisco State College. Our greatest successes—legitimacy in the academy, recognition by mainstream departments at universities across the United States, and publication of works by major university presses—seem to have distanced us further from the original goals of the Asian American Movement. Nonetheless, we are moving forward in the new millennium. There are no clear answers, only prospects and possibilities.

NOTES

1. Retrieved on August 31, 2006, from http://www.aaastudies.org/directory.tpl?action=start.

2. Retrieved on August 31, 2006, from http://aaastudies.org/directory.tpl?action=showdata& name=Asian%20American%20Studies.

3. The author gained insight from Yuji Ichioka's comments. See also Yamamoto 1999 for detail.

4. See the special issue (vols. 1 & 2, 1995) of *Amerasia Journal* and part 2 of Hirabayashi (1995) for detail.

5. Indeed, all persons born in Asia, including those emanating from that area arbitrarily (and Eurocentrically) designated as the Middle East, were excluded from citizenship, until the 1952 Immigration Act. For details, see Haney López 1996.

REFERENCES

Chan, Sucheng (ed.). 2003. *Remapping Asian American History.* Walnut Creek, CA: AltaMira Press.

———. 1978. Contextual Framework for Reading, Counterpoint. *Amerasia Journal* 5(1): 115–129.

Endo, Russell and William Wei. 1988. On the Development of Asian American Studies Programs. Pp. 5–15 in Gary Y. Okihiro, Shirley Hune, Arthur A. Hansen, and John M. Liu (eds.), *Reflection on Shattered Windows: Promises and Prospects for Asian American Studies.* Pullman: Washington State University Press.

Fong, Timothy P. 1998. Reflections on Teaching about Asian American Communities. Pp. 143–59 in Lane Ryo Harabayashi (ed.), *Teaching Asian America: Diversity and the Problem of the Community.* Lanham, MD: Rowman and Littlefield.

GoldSea. 2005. *Twenty-Five Great Asian American Universities.* Retrieved March 13, 2005, from goldsea.com/AAU/25/25.html.

Gupta, A. and J. Ferguson. 1992. Beyond "Culture": Space, Identity, and the Politics of Difference. *Cultural Anthropology* 7(1): 6–23.

Haney López, Ian F. 1996. *White by Law: The Legal Construction of Race.* New York: New York University Press.

Hirabayashi, Lane Ryo. 1995. Back to the Future: Re-Framing Community-Based Research. *Amerasia Journal* 21: 103–18.

Hune, Shirley. 2000. Doing Gender with a Feminist Gaze: Toward a Historical Reconstruction of Asian America. Pp. 413–30 in Min Zhou and J. V. Gatewood (eds.), *Contemporary Asian America: A Multidisciplinary Reader* (1st ed.). New York: New York University Press.

Kang, Laura Hyun Yi. 1998. A Contending Pedagogy: Asian American Studies as Extracurricular Praxis. Pp. 123–41 in Lane Ryo Harabayashi (ed.), *Teaching Asian America: Diversity and the Problem of the Community.* Lanham, MD: Rowman and Littlefield.

Kiang, Peter Nien-chu. 1995. The New Waves: Developing Asian American Studies on the East Coast. Pp. 305–14 in Gary Y. Okihiro, Marilyn Alquizola, Dorothy Fujita Rony, and K. Scott Wong (ed.), *Privileging Positions: The Sites of Asian American Studies.* Pullman: Washington State University Press.

Loo, Chalsa and Don Mar. 1985–1986. Research and Asian Americans: Social Change or Empty Prize? *Amerasia Journal* 12(2): 85–93.

Monaghan, Peter. 1999. A New Momentum in Asian-American Studies: Many Colleges Create New Programs; Many Programs Broaden Their Courses and Research. *The Chronicle of Higher Education,* March 29.

Nakanishi, Don T. and Russell Leong. 1978. Toward the Second Decade: A National Survey of Asian American Studies Programs in 1978. *Amerasia Journal* 5(1): 1–19.

Omi, Michael and Dana Takagi. 1995. Thinking Theory in Asian American Studies. *Amerasia Journal* 21(1&2): xi–xv.

Ono, Kent A. 2005. Asian American Studies after 9/11. Pp. 439–51 in Cameron McCarthy C. Richlow, Greg Dimitriadis, and Nadine Dolby (eds.), *Race, Identity, and Representation in Education* (2nd ed.). New York: Routledge.

Tachiki, Amy, Eddie Wong, Franklin Odo, with Buck Wong (eds.). 1971. *Roots: An Asian American Studies Reader.* Los Angeles: UCLA Asian American Studies Center.

University of California. 2005. *Statistical Summary of Students and Staff: Fall 2004.* Department of Information Resources and Communications, Office of the President, University of California, p. 27, retrieved on August 29, 2006, from http://www.ucop.edu/ucophome/uwnews/stat/statsum/fall2004/statsumm2004.pdf.

Wang, L. Ling-chi. 1995. The Structure of Dual Domination: Toward a Paradigm for the Study of the Chinese Diaspora in the United States. *Amerasia Journal* 12(1&2): 149–69.

Wat, Eric C. 1998. Beyond the Missionary Position: Student Activism from the Bottom Up. Pp. 161–74 in Lane Ryo Harabayashi (ed.), *Teaching Asian America: Diversity and the Problem of the Community.* Lanham, MD: Rowman and Littlefield.

Wong, Sau-Ling C. 1995. Denationalization Reconsidered: Asian American Cultural Criticism at a Theoretical Crossroads. *Amerasia Journal* 21(1&2): 1–27.

Xie, Y., & K. S. Goyette. 2004. *The American People, Census 2000: A Demographic Portrait of Asian Americans.* New York: Russell Sage Foundation Press; and Washington, DC: Population Reference Bureau.

Yamamoto, Eric. 1999. *Interracial Justice: Conflict and Reconciliation in Post–Civil Rights America.* New York: New York University Press.

Yanagisako, Sylvia. 1995. Transforming Orientalism: Gender, Nationality, and Class in Asian American Studies. Pp. 275–98 in Sylvia Yanagisako and Carol Delaney (eds.), *Naturalizing Power: Essays in Feminist Cultural Analysis*. New York: Routledge.

Yu, Henry. 1998. The "Oriental Problem" in America, 1920–1960: Linking the Identities of Chinese American and Japanese American Intellectuals. Pp. 191–214 in K. Scott Wong and Sucheng Chan (eds.), *Claiming America: Constructing Chinese American Identities during the Exclusion Era*. Philadelphia: Temple University Press.

Claiming Visibility

The Asian American Movement and Politics

Chapter 1

"On Strike!"

San Francisco State College Strike, 1968 1969:
The Role of Asian American Students

Karen Umemoto

The sixth of November, nineteen hundred and sixty-eight. Few thought this would mark the first day of the longest student strike in American history. Student leaders of the San Francisco State College Third World Liberation Front marched with their demands for an education more relevant and accessible to their communities. Their tenacity engaged the university, the police, and politicians in a five-month battle giving birth to the first School of Ethnic Studies in the nation. Batons were swung and blood was shed in the heat of conflict. But this violence was only symptomatic of the challenge made by activists to fundamental tenets of dominant culture as manifested in the university. African American, Asian American, Chicano, Latino, and Native American students called for ethnic studies and open admissions under the slogan of self-determination. They fought for the right to determine their own futures. They believed that they could shape the course of history and define a "new consciousness." For Asian American students in particular, this also marked a "shedding of silence" and an affirmation of identity.

The strike took place against the backdrop of nationwide Third World movements which had profound impact on the culture and ideology of America. Never before had a convergence of struggles—civil rights, antiwar, women, student and oppressed nationality—so sharply redefined the social norms of our society. Originating from the call for basic rights, protestors moved on to demand power and self-determination. When the State resisted, activists held to their convictions "by any means necessary." Though these movements did not produce major changes in the economic or political structure, they strongly affected popular ideology and social relations. They also resulted in the formation of mass organizations and produced a cadre of activists who would continue to pursue their ideals.

The San Francisco State strike was a microcosm of this struggle over cultural hegemony. The focus of the strike was a redefinition of education, which in turn was linked to a larger redefinition of American society. Activists believed that education should be "relevant" and serve the needs of their communities, not the corporations. The redefinition of education evolved from the early 1960s when students initiated programs to broaden the college curriculum and challenge admission standards. They supported the hiring and retention of minority faculty. They demanded power in the institution. When they were met with resistance, activists organized a campus-wide movement with community support for their demands. They built organizations, planned strategies and tactics, and published educational literature. Their activities were rooted in and also shaped more egalitarian relationships based on mutual respect. While this doctrine was not always fully understood nor always put into practice, it was the beginning of a new set of values and beliefs, a "New World Consciousness."

The emergence of this alternative vision is important to study today for several reasons. First, by understanding the beginnings of this vision, today's generation of students can revive certain "counterhegemonic" concepts that have been usurped and redefined by those in power. For example, campus administrators have revamped the concept of "self-determination" to the more benign ones of "diversity" and "cultural pluralism." Thus, the right of a group to decision-making power over institutions affecting their lives has been gutted to the level of "student input" by campus administrators.

Second, studying the strike can deepen our understanding of the process through which ideological currents develop among oppressed groups. Organizers are constantly trying to "raise political consciousness" among the people. But in what ways do the nature of the conflict, methods of organizing, strategy and tactics, propaganda and agitation, and historical factors influence mass consciousness within these movements?

This study will analyze the growth of political consciousness among Asian American students during the San Francisco State strike. I will analyze the development of the strike in four stages from 1964 to 1969, defined according to dominant concepts within the movement. They are: (1) 1964–66—end of the civil rights era marked by the ideals of "racial harmony" and "participatory democracy"; (2) 1966–67—implementation of programs under the banner of "serve the people" and "self-determination"; (3) Fall 1968/Winter 1969—struggle "by any means necessary"; and (4) Spring/Summer 1969—repression of protest and continued "commitment to the community." These concepts signify trends in ideological development and provide a means of understanding the strike as a seed of a revolutionary transformation in America.

1964–1966: "Racial Harmony" and "Participatory Democracy" and the Civil Rights Era

The civil rights era profoundly impacted the racial ideology of the nation, particularly Third World youth. The dreams of Martin Luther King, Jr., and unsung heroes inspired actions for equality, dignity, and self-respect. The African American movement clearly revealed the deep-rooted, institutionalized nature of racial oppression. Although protests resulted in reforms limited to the legal arena, their impact was felt in all other sectors of society.

Many Asian American students who were later to become active in the strike were moved by the protests. One Pilipino activist, R. Q., volunteered for a federal program on the East Coast:

When I was in VISTA and worked in a black neighborhood. . . . They had riots in New Haven. . . . I came back to State College in '67, and the black students were at the forefront in wanting programs. . . . I think the black students and the Black Movement of the sixties made a major impact. They laid the groundwork, which made it a lot easier for us.[1]

The civil rights movement reshaped popular thinking about one's role in society. One student, R. I., described the impact on him:

It had a very heavy impact because I found that to have anyone listen to you, you had to be forceful, expressing yourself, not being quiet. If you know you are in the right, you have every right to speak up and organize your people to a just cause. So that brought home to me the necessity of organized action, and to verbalize your feelings about what is going on.[2]

The protests forced President Kennedy to publicly support civil rights. His entrance into the historic March on Washington in 1963 lent federal legitimacy to the idea of racial harmony through integration. The enacting of legislation provided legal sanction for racial equality. Kennedy's slogan of a "New Frontier" also encouraged youth to participate in American democracy and transform society. This idealism contributed to formations of Students for a Democratic Society and Third World student organizations nationwide.[3] Faith in democracy led to initial acceptance of nonviolent protest and to the reform-oriented goals within mass movements.

This idealism manifested itself in experimentation in all aspects of life. What was called "counterculture" was indeed a reshaping of traditional goals, values, and behavior. One activist, I. C., explained this shift:

There was all this emphasis on doing things for other people, such as the Peace Corps. All those ideas were instilled in us . . . "doing something, giving back to society." You couldn't just live for yourself. And I think that influenced my participation in the strike more than anything."[4]

Prior to 1963, student activism at San Francisco State centered around these themes. Students joined a 1960 walk to San Quentin prison against capital punishment, protested at the 1960 House Un-American Activities Committee (HUAC) hearings, established an outdoor free speech area, joined the 1962 Freedom Rides, and organized lunch counter sit-ins at a local Mel's Drive-in. But 1963–64 also saw the assassination of Medgar Evers, the murder of four black children in an Alabama church bombing, the murder of three Student Nonviolent Coordinating Committee (SNCC) workers, and preparation for an escalation in the war in Vietnam. These and other conflicts provided the context for a growing student movement.

Meanwhile, the slogan of racial harmony clashed with the reality of racial conflict. Asian Americans faced discrimination, especially in the areas of education, employment and housing. A. S. described going to school in Stockton, California:

I went to Franklin because of where I lived. But Edison was . . . [a] minority school, our kissing cousin school—many Chinese, Japanese, Filipinos, Mexicans, and Blacks. Franklin had more poor Whites. . . . You were told where to go. . . . There was a strict code that was enforced.[5]

For J. M., a growing awareness of racism caused conflicts within herself which altered life goals:

I was going with a white man whom I met at Berkeley, whom I eventually married. And so I don't know how to explain this to you, it seems very disorganized and very chaotic, but at the same time I was aspiring to be White, wanting a white child, wanting to marry a white man, I was simultaneously being impacted by all of these events that were challenging me as an Asian woman.[6]

B. I. was like the vast majority of students at San Francisco State who came from the ranks of the working class. He was a farmworker while in high school:

I spent some time in Fairfield, stoop labor, so I knew what they were saying about the low wages, and the twelve to fourteen-hour day. . . . I learned later on that Pilipinos were involved in organizing the first farmworkers' strike. And that made me very proud. . . .[7]

Several strike activists were with the U.S. armed forces in Asia and faced racial hostilities. E. D. C., who became involved with Pilipinos in the strike, described an instance where he was used to "play an agent enemy, in other words, a gook or whatever."[8]

Although it is difficult to determine if those who understood racism were more disposed to strike involvement or if their involvement sensitized them to racial issues or both, it is clear that racial cleavages were at the center of the Asian American experience.

Student-Initiated Programs

The period 1964–66 saw the development of student-run programs to address racial issues and other social concerns. These programs functioned within the university as alternative schools or "counterhegemonic sites" through which many students developed ideas running counter to prevailing paradigms.

The initial programs included the Fillmore Tutorial, the Community Involvement Program, the Experimental College, and the Work-Study Program. They were initiated with Associated Student government monies under its president, Tom Ramsey, a socialist, who wanted to use the $400,000 budget for community work.[9]

The Fillmore Tutorial was an African American–initiated program which tutored youth in the Fillmore District of San Francisco. The Community Involvement Program was an outgrowth of this. Students organized community activities including graphic arts workshops, a housing and job co-op, and support activities for the National Farmworkers Association and the Delano strike.[10]

The Experimental College offered alternative courses on topics including "Perspective on Revolution," "Urban Action," and "Competition and Violence." One outgrowth was the Work-Study Program, which was later renamed the Community Services Institute in 1968. A 1968 statement stated that education should be redesigned to be relevant to community needs, to equip people to control their lives, and to teach that knowledge came from work in the community.[11]

These programs became increasingly popular. By fall 1966, the college had approximately fifteen courses with 300 students; by spring 1967, there were sixty courses with 800 students[12] and by fall 1968, nine experimental colleges existed in the eighteen-campus university system.[13]

A Master Plan for Future Confrontation

The foundation for growing contradictions between students and administrators was the 1960 Master Plan for Higher Education in California. The plan restructured education to meet the changing needs of industry and the growing student population. Projections estimated that by 1975, more than 1 million students would be enrolled in California higher education, nearly triple the full-time enrollment of 1958. Technically skilled and managerial workers were needed for developing high-tech and defense industries. The California Master Plan was preceded by the 1958 National Defense Education Act (NDEA), major federal legislation which provided aid to all levels of public and private education with particular support for the math, science, and foreign language fields. The linking of defense and education coincided with developments in the Cold War, including the 1957 Soviet lift-off of Sputnik, which launched the "space race."

The Master Plan established three tiers: University of California, California State College, and junior college systems, each with target student populations, specialized functions, and centralized governing boards. The UC system for the top 12.5 percent of high school graduates was provided "exclusive jurisdiction over training for professions and the sole authority in public higher education to award the doctor's degree."[14] The state college system was to provide "instruction in the liberal arts and sciences and in professions and applied fields . . . and teacher education." Previously open to 70 percent of high school graduates, it was now reserved for the top 33 percent.[15] The junior colleges were to provide vocational training, general liberal arts background, and preparation for transfer to a four-year institution.

The Master Plan's "solution" to the increasing numbers of students was the "diversion" of students from state colleges and UC campuses to junior colleges.[16] To improve the "quality" of students, the UC system and state colleges were directed to develop new admissions requirements for the fall 1962.[17] Thus, instead of expanding the four-year institutions, the Master Plan restricted admissions. The net result was the decline of minority enrollments. At San Francisco State, African American enrollment dropped from an estimated 11 percent in 1960 to 3.6 percent by 1968.[18]

The Master Plan centralized decision making in the hands of business and political figures. A twenty-one-member Board of Trustees was established to govern the state college system with the system-wide chancellor and board holding absolute control over all academic programs, distribution of allocated funds, and major personnel decisions.

Corporate spokespersons backed the Master Plan. In a 1969 speech entitled "Business and Campus Unrest" to the Education Section Meeting in Sacramento, E. Hornsby Wasson, the board chairman of the Pacific Telephone and Telegraph Company, stated:

> The best we in business can do is to try and work with you . . . furnishing the most clear-cut guidelines . . . to produce the type of young man and woman we need to keep our state and our national economy moving in the years ahead. The interest stems from what I already have expressed: business depends on education *to produce young men and women capable of meeting the demands of our free enterprise system and thus living full, economically independent life.* [Italics added][19]

Business concerns received strong political support with Ronald Reagan's rise to the governorship in 1966. Under his leadership, a collision course was set with growing student radicalism on the issues of university access, relevancy, and control.

1966–May 1968: "Serve the People" and "Self-Determination"

> As I got involved, I saw what happened [on campus] in terms of a microcosm . . . of what was going on in the city and the larger picture of inequality. You can stay neutral and let it slide by you, or you can walk away from it and deny those problems, or you can become a participant. To me, I was going to become a participant.[20]
> —B. L., student government and ICSA member

The process through which action gave rise to new ideas and new ideas shaped action was dialectical. For Asian American students, this process took many forms. Some were involved in the Experimental College, the Tutorial Program, and other Associated Student activities. Some became involved through friendships or contact with other activists. Others literally walked into the strike. Regardless of how they got involved, their actions led to greater questioning and understanding, which in turn shaped later actions.

International events had profound impact on the Third World movements in the United States. Anti-imperialist wars were raging in Asia, Africa, and Latin America. Works of revolutionary intellectuals like Frantz Fanon, Amilcar Cabral, Che Guevara, and Mao Zedong were studied by activists in the United States. The concept of "internal colonialism" became popular to depict the oppressed status of minorities in America. For those who used the colonial analogy, liberation movements abroad suggested that freedom also could be won at home. Anti-imperialism challenged fundamental tenets from the civil rights era. Instead of racial integration, anti-imperialist movements argued for national independence. Instead of nonviolence, they initiated armed struggle. And instead of shared power, they called for "self-determination."

Events abroad were coupled with a growing discontent at the limitations of civil rights programs. The discontent was felt most deeply by working class sectors of Third World communities, those least affected by legislation. An influential figure who clearly represented this sector was Malcolm X, who was killed in 1965 but whose message was popularized for years later. He called for African Americans to control the resources and institutions of their communities "by any means necessary" and to identify their primary enemies as established institutions and those who supported the status quo.[21] These themes are evident in the formation of Asian American organizations during this period. Although these groups were influenced by the African American movement, their development was unique to their cultures and respective experiences in the United States. These groups promoted pride in national heritage; they sought "self-determination" and "power to the people." These slogans captured the diverse life experiences of the activists who were conscious of racism and their lack of political power.

Intercollegiate Chinese for Social Action (ICSA)

ICSA was formed in October 1967 by Chinese students who were mainly interested in social, cultural, and community activities. They worked as volunteers for Chinatown social service agencies including the War on Poverty office, taught immigrant teenagers English language skills, and later solicited monies from the Associated Student government to expand the tutorial project and to study the Chinatown power structure.[22]

As campus conflicts intensified with a May 1968 sit-in, a new leadership arose and eventually steered ICSA toward the strike. By July 1968, the group established an office in Chinatown at 737 Clay Street. Though the organization was community-oriented from its founding, the new leadership was more militant. It immediately joined the Third World Liberation Front (TWLF). It also challenged the traditional Chinatown power brokers, particularly the Six Companies, over the use of Economic Opportunity Council monies and over problems of youth and working-class Chinese.

For the new ICSA leader, A. W., "power to the people" meant "a piece of the pie," since his experience showed him that poor people were rarely given anything. A. W. described himself as being a "playboy" and a "hippie." He accidentally walked into the May 1968 sit-in when he attempted to pay his fees in the administration building and "got busted" by the police.[23]

Following that incident, he and M. W were approached by a member of the Black Students Union (BSU). They were impressed by his militancy and suggested joining forces, but A. W. initially saw it as benefiting only African Americans. He described his change of mind:

And I said, "Okay fine, you Blacks need to go to school, so you guys fight it, and I won't go against it. But I'm not for it because what am I getting out of this?" And he said, "What about all your Chinese who can't get into school?" . . . And I said, "Okay you convince me what you can give me and my people." . . . And he said, "We've got coun-

seling, tutoring service, we have special admission." . . . So I said, "All right, I'm in."
That was the first time in my life that somebody, not Asian, was willing to share with
me their pot of gold. So I had nothing to lose, and all to gain, and then I got involved.[24]

Other ICSA members got involved through community issues. I. C. worked in Chinatown and was aware of the difficulties of immigrant youth. She helped to coordi-
nate ICSA's tutorial program. In reflecting on the reasons for her involvement, she discussed the strong influence of her family who "taught you that you had to do what
was right, do what was fair. And when you would see things that were not right, were
not fair, [it] just upsets you."[25]

Others like J. C., who came from a middle-class family and grew up for most of his
life in a predominantly white Bay Area suburb, experienced a cultural and political
awakening through his participation in ICSA. His involvement in the strike "was the
process of constructing an identity."[26] In high school, he felt competition between
peers over "who was whiter than who." But the strike was different:

> We came together, I think, a little more comfortable with who we were. . . . We found
> issues we felt [were] lack[ing] in our lives. So we could organize ourselves. We could
> socialize with one another. We could actually sacrifice part of our egos. So we could
> join a movement towards some objective that we all thought was correct. I think the
> one thing you can't do when you are trying to melt into the white world is to complain
> about it. But if you join with others of your own kind, you have the opportunity to
> trade stories . . . and articulate your hostility.[27]

This quest to validate the ethnic experience fit squarely with the ICSA demand for
Chinese American Studies under the authority of the people themselves.

M. W. and A. W. proceeded to involve the ICSA in the TWLF. M. W. described the
conflict within ICSA:

> And so we had two factions. One faction that wanted to get more involved in the Third
> World group, because we figured that's where the power was. . . . There was another
> group that said, "No, we don't need that; we can go by ourselves" . . . and so we had
> elections, and all of a sudden I won . . . and we became part of the Third World Liber-
> ation Front, and became very active in the strike . . . which was radical for a lot of peo-
> ple at that time. They thought we were crazy.[28]

This was a major turning point for the organization and brought to power those
who saw the importance of unity with other nationalities for the benefit of Chinese
Americans.

Although joining with other Third World groups, the new ICSA leaders drew from
figures in Chinese history, including Sun Tzu:[29]

> During the strike we read *The Art of War.* . . . All the Chinese in military history are
> raised on this . . . [which] says the main goal of war is to win . . . and the true leader
> doesn't lose lives. . . . The key to win victories is "know thyself."[30]

"Power to the people" for ICSA implicitly meant power to the working class of Chinatown. This is clear from their attacks on the landlords and power brokers, including the Six Companies. Frustrations had mounted over the latter's resistance to youth programs, including those of Leways and the Hwa Ching to develop jobs and programs. On 17 August 1968, ICSA members and community leaders including Reverends Larry Jack Wong, Ed Suo, and Harry Chuck led a peaceful march through Chinatown in support of "education, employment, health, housing, youth, senior citizens, and immigration."[31] ICSA members participated in a coalition called Concerned Chinese for Action and Change. The coalition held a press conference to present several demands, including those for a senior center, a full investigation of the Chinatown North Beach Equal Opportunity Commission office, immediate action for a community youth center, and the future establishment of a multiservice center, educational program, and low cost housing.[32] Students also attended many of the EOC meetings to demand seats on the board and programs to serve youth and low-income residents.

A. W. sat on a community board to the police department. He joined discussions about youth "problems" in the public schools. He pointed to the need for institutions to speak to the needs of immigrant youth:

> At that time, I think that Galileo [High School] was about 80 percent Chinese and 50 percent were non-English speaking. I said, "You need bilingual classes, and you need to give the students some pride." Their argument was that [the students] didn't want to participate. I said "How do you expect them to participate? . . . Give them something to be proud of and they will, in turn, turn Galileo into a good school." They thought it was horse shit. . . . Now they have all those things.[33]

Just as ICSA participation in Chinatown helped build opposition to the Six Companies, their increased understanding of Chinatown's problems strengthened their resolve to fight for ethnic studies. In a position paper, the group stated:

> Chinatown is a GHETTO. In San Francisco there are approximately 80,000 Chinese of whom the vast majority live in Chinatown. It is an area of old buildings, narrow streets and alleys and the effluvia of a great deal of people packed into a very small space. . . . Tuberculosis is endemic, rents are high and constantly rising . . . and space is at such a premium as to resemble the Malthusian ratio at its most extreme conclusion.[34]

The position paper advocated ethnic studies. It stated, "There are not adequate courses in any department or school at San Francisco State that even begin to deal with problems of the Chinese people in this exclusionary and racist environment."[35]

Community efforts converged with that of students. For example, G. W., who worked with Hwa Ching youth, returned to school after the strike began. He and others initiated the Free University for Chinatown Kids, Unincorporated, "to find ways to merge the college students and street kids together and hopefully share the best of their experiences."[36] The acronym, F.U.C.K.U., was a statement: "You guys [the university] don't like us? Well, we don't like you either."[37] F.U.C.K.U. met for several sessions with films, speakers, and discussion on problems and solutions for Chinatown youth.

An organization which actively supported the strike was Leways. Short for "legitimate ways," it set up a pool hall and soda fountain at 615 Jackson Street called the "Fountain of Youth." Leways member Alex Hing wrote, "Because the strike was aimed precisely at giving oppressed Third World people access to college, Leways became the staunchest supporters of the TWLF in Chinatown."[38] Leways assisted in educational, fund-raising, and picket activity during the strike. Through the strike and community involvement, Leways became increasingly political, and later some members formed the revolutionary Red Guards.

Supporters came from many political persuasions. Despite differences, important alliances were built over strike demands. The Equal Opportunity Council board in Chinatown, dominated by members of the Six Companies, held more conservative views as compared with those of strike organizers. However, they shared concern over educational access. G. W. described an exchange which began as a board member responded to students' appeal for support:

"How dare you people make such a racket! My grandson's trying to apply for the university and couldn't get in!" I said in Chinese to him. "Read our demand carefully. We're doing this for your grandson. It is precisely people like your grandson who feel that they have been kept out . . . and we want to get him in." And he said, "Oh, is that right? I'm for it!" And he turned around and looked at everybody. And since he's for it, the rest of the people said "for," and we got a majority. So we had EOC in Chinatown voting to support the San Francisco State Third World strike.[39]

Philippine-American Collegiate Endeavor (PACE)

PACE was established in spring 1968 by P. S. to organize and fight for the rights of Pilipino youth. He had learned about the efforts of Third World students through Professor Juan Martinez. PACE organized counseling programs, tutorial programs, tutor training, study centers, high school recruitment drives, newsletters, fund-raising dances, ethnic studies curricula, community outreach, and liaison with student government.

The backgrounds of PACE members were as diverse as those of other groups. However, most were foreign-born. A number came from military family backgrounds as well as farmworker families. A. S. remarked that "you had multidiverse types of Pilipinos who started PACE, which was really a miracle we even stuck together." But he added, "We had common backgrounds, we had common goals. And we really had a common thought . . . that there really had to be something better in life than what we were used to."[40]

PACE saw the inequality they faced as rooted in racism. It felt that uniting Third World people to create a new consciousness would enable them to control their own destinies. This viewpoint was expressed in the statement of goals and principles, which read:

We seek . . . simply to function as human beings, to control our own lives. Initially, following the myth of the American Dream, we worked to attend predominantly white colleges, but we have learned through direct analysis that it is impossible for our people, so-called minorities, to function as human beings, in a racist society in which white always comes first. . . . So we have decided to fuse ourselves with the masses of Third World people, which are the majority of the world's peoples, to create, through struggle, a new humanity, a new humanism, a New World Consciousness, and within that context collectively control our own destinies.[41]

One of the ways this "New World Consciousness" would develop was through ethnic studies. These courses would educate people to the Pilipino American experience, thus lessening racist attitudes.

Some PACE members organized support for their demands within the community through explaining the concept of "self-determination" with concrete illustrations. P. S. explained:

Self-determination was probably the closest [term] to making other people understand what we were trying to express. Because when you had to explain self-determination, you had to explain the other side, against what? . . . So that buzzword was just convenient to open up . . . discussions. . . . I thought it better to express how what we were doing was going to help. I would say it in different forms . . . how what we were doing would help kids get in school, get jobs . . . very visual things that they could relate to.[42]

Like ICSA members, PACE members saw "self-determination" as taking control over one's life. They initiated community programs through an off-campus office at 829 Cortland. The purpose was fourfold: to encourage and aid low-income Pilipino-American students in the Mission area to enter college; to establish communication channels between youth organizations in the Bay Area; to research socioeconomic problems and their solutions; and to serve as a referral agency for employment, medical, housing, recreation, and counseling services.[43]

PACE worked with youth groups at schools and churches like Mission High School and St. Patrick's. One focus was to recruit Pilipino high school youth to college through the Educational Opportunity Program. Once in college, PACE worked with students to "make sure they stayed on campus" and completed their education. E. I. helped to recruit students and described:

Yeah, particularly on the south of Market . . . they played basketball to keep off the street. If they were out on the street, they would get busted . . . or they wound up in the Army. A lot of people got drafted. You know that the rank and file in the army was Third World. . . . So there was a better alternative: to get them onto campus.[44]

One issue in Manilatown and Chinatown concerned the eviction of elderly residents, community organizations, and small businesses from the International Hotel due to the encroaching financial district. Tenants and supporters resisted evictions for over ten years. Pilipino and other Asian students were active participants throughout the period of the campus strike. E. I. continued:

Sometime in November, mid-December, there were eviction notices posted on the International Hotel door. It said, "You who live here are hereby notified . . . that the Hotel is going to be demolished and you have to leave." . . . And I enlisted the support of (M. W.) and (G. W. of ICSA) and they marched with us. And we had 120 Pilipinos out there, senior citizens, residents of that building. We picketed down Montgomery. . . . These were elderly people, retired veterans. . . . I got appointed to the board of that association. And it was then becoming an issue that totally involved me, and I was a student.[45]

The community programs not only enabled a large number of students to participate in PACE, but they involved students in an implicit challenge to the individualistic pursuits promoted by the university. PACE's activities captured the sentiments of students to uplift their people. The membership roster included almost seventy out of an estimated 125 Pilipino students on campus.[46]

Asian American Political Alliance (AAPA)

AAPA was formed in late summer 1968 at San Francisco State College by mainly Japanese American women. It was a vehicle for students to share political concerns in a pan-Asian organization. One founder, P. N., had worked in the Experimental College and had participated in the May sit-in. During that summer, she met a woman whose brother was a member of AAPA at the University of California, Berkeley. She and others attended those meetings and by fall organized an AAPA at San Francisco State:

I felt a lot of need to do something about racism. Also, there was a need to do something about the lack of political involvement of Asians. . . . [There] was also this amorphous sense of wanting to build a sense of Asian American identity and . . . overcome what I saw as nationalistic kinds of trends. I wanted to see Asians from different ethnic backgrounds working together.[47]

The ideological development of San Francisco State AAPA was influenced by the movement at UC Berkeley. P. N. recalled that many of their concepts "were developed as a result of meetings and discussions, trying to get a sense of what AAPA should be and what its goals should be, what kinds of interests it should address."[48] In one of the first issues of the UC Berkeley AAPA newspaper in fall 1968, an article described the group as a "people's alliance to effect social and political changes."

We believe that the American society is historically racist and is one which has systematically employed social discrimination and economic imperialism both domestically and internationally to exploit all people, but especially nonwhites.[49]

AAPA saw the problems facing Asian people as rooted in racism and imperialism; thus, it was important to build alliances based on race as well as common oppression; political organization should not only effect change but build new nonhierarchical social relationships; therefore, AAPA was only a transition to generate ideas "to effect fundamental social, economical, political changes." A parallel was drawn to the movements against imperialism in the Third World. "We Asian Americans support all oppressed peoples and their struggles for Liberation and believe that Third World People must have complete control over the political, economic, and educational institutions within their communities."[50]

At San Francisco State, AAPA attempted to organize political study which offered critical perspectives for its activity. One founding member stated that activists studied the "Red Book," which contained writings of Mao Zedong. They also read writings of Frantz Fanon and Black Power leaders, including the Black Panther Party newspaper. She described the impact of these readings:

> I think they helped to provide me with a conceptual framework within which I could look at how my involvement fit in with other events: the Vietnam war in particular and the connections between the strike, domestic issues, property, and international issues.[51]

Though AAPA did not have an off-campus office, there were informal gatherings at a house in the Richmond district, several miles west of Japantown. P. Y. explained how this house became a congregating point for AAPA activities, "like an extended family":

> Towards the end of the strike, they found us a big house on 4th and California, 4th and Cornwall actually. . . . They got the whole house, it was three stories, two big flats. There were about eight people living there, seven of them were AAPA members. And it became the meeting place. There was a [mimeo] machine in there, and all of our stuff was printed out of there, all the meetings were held there, all the parties were held there. If anybody came in from out of town—a lot of people from L.A. used to come up—and that's where they would come. So that became a real home for AAPA.[52]

Cultural activities strengthened the closeness that P. Y. and many others spoke about during this period. One artist was Francis Oka, who was killed in an accident shortly after the strike. M. O. described his influence:

> We were like brother and sister. And he would always be the theoretical one; we kind of balanced each other off. And he was trying, struggling to be a writer and a poet and a songwriter. His idol was Dylan, Dylan Thomas. . . . because of our friendship, he always opened my mind up and made me read things. . . . He was the foremost idealist in my life.[53]

The strike unleashed a creative spirit. AAPA member Janice Mirikitani became a leading figure in the Asian American arts movement. The strike provided a focus for her creative expression. She and others created the Third World Communications Collective, a Third World Women's Collective, and published one of the first Asian American journals, *Aion*.

The appointment in late 1968 of S. I. Hayakawa as San Francisco State College president stirred up controversy in the Japanese American community. Public protest against Hayakawa challenged social codes within the community which discouraged confrontation. However, a minority of Nisei publicly supported the students. The director of the YMCA office in Japantown, Y. W., explained this viewpoint:

> It could be that we had more contact with the younger generation in the course of our work. It could also be that we were far more interested in civil liberties, and in the question of freedom of speech, the freedom of assemblage. . . . It could also be that we really didn't feel that restrained to rock the boat, to challenge the status quo. I think it might have been the lessons learned from the evacuation. If there is a wrong, you don't keep quiet about it. . . . I think the evacuation was wrong, and this was one way to say so many years later.[54]

His sentiments may have been shared by some 100 Japanese Americans who expressed support and even pride for striking students at a community meeting at Christ United Presbyterian Church on 6 December 1968. The program consisted of student presentations followed by discussion. A statement by an elderly woman marked a turning point as she expressed her joy that young people were standing up for their rights.

On the evening of 21 February 1969, 125 Japanese Americans picketed a dinner featuring Hayakawa as a speaker. The dinner was sponsored by the Community Interest Committee of Nihonmachi, organized by several individuals affiliated with the Japanese American Citizen's League. AAPA members along with community leaders, including Yori Wada and Rev. Lloyd Wake of Glide Memorial Church, organized the protest and a press conference.

Third World Liberation Front (TWLF)

Closer relations among Third World students impacted the ideological development of Asian Americans by emphasizing the commonalities among "people of color" and creating a forum which facilitated a "cross-pollenization of ideas." The demands of the coalition set a foundation for unity and defined the political issues and struggles which occurred through the course of the strike. Due to the development of the African American movement and the participation of relatively experienced members of the BSU and Black Panther Party, African American students played an influential role in the TWLF.

One individual who was influential in the formation of the TWLF was Juan Martinez, a lecturer in the history department and the faculty advisor of the Mexican American Students Confederation (MASC). The TWLF coalition was formed with his encouragement in spring 1968. He had earlier encouraged P. S. to organize Pilipino students and when PACE was formed, it joined the TWLF. ICSA joined in spring. AAPA joined in summer 1968.

The themes of freedom and self-determination are evident in the "Third World Liberation Front Philosophy and Goals," which stated:

The TWLF . . . has its purpose to aid in further developing politically, economically, and culturally the revolutionary Third World consciousness of racist oppressed peoples both on and off campus. As Third World students, as Third World people, as so-called minorities, we are being exploited to the fullest extent in this racist white America, and we are therefore preparing ourselves and our people for a prolonged struggle for freedom from this yoke of oppression.[55]

The TWLF saw immediate reforms in the context of radical, long-term change. A change in consciousness was seen as necessary to eliminate exploitation and racism.

Racism had been traditionally defined as a set of bigoted assumptions held by individuals. But in this period, racism was redefined as being "institutionalized" into all realms of society. The concept put emphasis on the structure of the economic and political system. Students began to deepen their analysis of society by merging this concept with their own life experiences.

In the immediate work, these ideas manifested themselves in three main demands made to the administration. First, the TWLF advocated the right of all Third World students to an education. They highlighted the existence of "institutionalized racism" as manifested in culturally biased "standardized" tests used as admissions criteria. They demanded open admissions and an expanded special admissions program.

In March and April 1968, TWLF members recruited many high school students to apply for admission to the university. On 30 April, they sponsored an orientation at which several hundred students presented their applications to President Summerskill's office. They later called for the college to use all special admissions slots for disadvantaged students. In 1966 and 1967, the state colleges had admitted only .27 and .85 percent "disadvantaged" respectively, even though 2 percent were allowed through the "exception rule."[56]

Second, the TWLF challenged the fundamental purpose of education by demanding a School of Ethnic Area Studies. This demand stressed that education should be relevant to their lives and communities. Relevancy in education was clarified by students in their stated purpose of a School of Ethnic Area Studies:

The school clearly intends to be involved in confronting racism, poverty and misrepresentation imposed on minority peoples by the formally recognized institutions and organizations operating in the State of California.[57]

This perspective represented a fundamental challenge to the underpinnings of the Master Plan. While the Master Plan called for restructuring the university based largely upon the priorities of the corporate sector, students advocated a redefinition of education to serve their communities. I. C., who was tutoring in Chinatown, stated that "the community had so many needs, and there were so few people that participated. We always hoped that when these courses came about, more people would be encouraged to go back and help the community."[58] PACE member R. Q. also stated, "I know nothing about my background, nothing historically about the people here in this country, and less about the Philippines."[59] Students wanted an education which would help them retrieve their historical legacy as well as contribute to social change in their communities.

Third, the TWLF demanded the right to have ethnic studies classes taught and run by Third World peoples. "Self-determination" meant that each nationality had the right to determine its own curriculum and hire its own faculty. Students argued that those who had lived a particular ethnic experience were best able to teach it to others. ICSA's M. W. added that "the winners are the ones who write the history books"[60] and that oppressed people had their own version of history. The TWLF also recognized that the existing criteria to evaluate ethnic studies and Third World faculty would be biased by racism. Thus, the TWLF demanded programmatic autonomy. The BSU had the most developed curricular philosophy. In their newspaper, *Black Fire,* they listed six goals for teaching:

> (1) a cultural identity, because we live in a society that is racist, that degrades and de-nies cultural heritage of Third World people, specifically black people; (2) to educate our people to understand that the only culture we can have is one that is revolutionary (directed toward our freedom and a complete change in our living conditions), and that this will never be endorsed by our enemy; (3) to build a revolutionary perspective and to understand the need for using the knowledge and skills we have and get only for our liberation and the destruction of all the oppressive conditions surrounding us; (4) to educate ourselves to the necessity of relating to the collective and not the individual; (5) to strive to build a socialist society; (6) to redistribute the wealth, the knowledge, the technology, the natural resources, the food, land, housing, and all of the material resources necessary for a society and its people to function.[61]

The politics of the TWLF were not as overtly revolutionary as those of the BSU but nonetheless were influenced by them. For example, in the TWLF's demand for a School for Ethnic Area Studies, a similar rationale was put forward:

> As assurance against the reoccurrence of education's traditional distortion and misrep-resentation of Third World people's cultures and histories, the School of Ethnic Area Studies is to be developed, implemented, and controlled by Third World people. Whether an area study is at a developmental or a departmental level within the school, the people of an area study will have sole responsibility and control for the staffing and curriculum of their ethnic area study.[62]

Resistance to the Challenge

DeVere Pentony, who had served as chairman of the Department of International Relations, dean of the School of Behavioral and Social Sciences, and deputy president at San Francisco State, wrote:

> The more promising the programs became in exploring and modifying basic as-sumptions, the more resistance grew. As student programs moved away from strictly academic problems toward direct action, problems of budget, propriety, the role of

the university and the place of students in the scheme of things came sharply into view.[63]

As early as June 1967, students had pushed the Council of Academic Deans to authorize a special "task force" to establish Black Studies, but nothing had resulted from it. And by summer 1968, there was still no Black Studies program. When President John Summerskill resigned after the May sit-in, Robert Smith took over the presidency. In his co-authored book, he attributes the delays in the establishment of Black Studies to the fact that "the college did not sense the urgency of the demand; the black students did not trust the world of the honkies."[64] In his view, both sides were being unreasonable; the strike could have been avoided. But he fails to recognize the fundamental contradictions underlying the conflict: student demands ran totally contrary to those who held greatest power in the university and the state. Smith's position was eventually overridden by the trustees; he was forced to resign after the strike began.

Some trustees objected to Experimental College courses and ethnic studies on the grounds that they were not "objective" or had introduced politics into the curriculum. Chancellor Dumke opposed partisan stands of students and faculty on social issues. "If the campus enters politics no force under heaven can keep politics from entering campus . . . the university must remain pure and unsullied and above the battle." Nor did Dumke believe there was a need to expand special admissions. In a letter of transmittal on the question of expanding the 2 percent special admit limit, he stated that "programs for the disadvantaged are a relatively recent development, and that the actual number of students admitted as exceptions . . . is not at present sufficient in itself to justify either expansion or maintenance of present limitations."[65]

The resistance by administrators and trustees led students to use different tactics. In May 1968, Third World students and the Students for a Democratic Society (SDS) staged a sit-in at President Summerskill's office. This resulted in the granting of 412 slots for Third World students over the next two semesters, the creation of at least ten faculty positions for Third World professors with student voice in the hirings, and the rehiring of Juan Martinez in the history department.[66] SDS's demand for ROTC to be expelled from campus was the only demand denied. During the May sit-in, police responded with their first major act of violence against student protesters. One policeman charged a woman. Terrence Hallinan, an attorney, intervened. He was clubbed on the head. Ten were injured and taken to the hospital[67] and twenty-six were arrested. Conflicts heightened when Summerskill resigned a few months later without fulfilling the promises he had made in a signed agreement with the students.

P. N., who participated in this sit-in and later founded AAPA, felt that the administration's resistance to students' demands was rooted in a racially biased understanding of history. "The hardest thing for a lot of administrators to comprehend was the notion [that] there was an existing deficit in the way history brings us [knowledge]—there are subjects we weren't taught." Institutional racism, she continued, "was a very, very difficult thing for people to comprehend, and not just white people."[68]

The resistance of the administration, along with police violence, led greater numbers of students to challenge traditional protest channels. The sentiment to use more militant tactics rose as frustration and anger mounted.

Structure and Organization of the TWLF

During this period, there were many efforts to split the ranks of the student coalition by administrators, media, and others. There were also efforts to learn from these events. In one instance, the TWLF issued a leaflet summing up the major lessons from the 30 April 1968 high school orientation. This was precipitated by mischaracterizations of the event in several news articles. Excerpts from the leaflet read:

> Members of TWLF, beware. What resulted after the April 30 event is exactly what emasculates any effort, actions or programs within an organization when the constituents blame one another for what the outside sources of media . . . take to slander and falsify charges against whatever an organization, like TWLF, stands for or does.[69]

Disunity emerged during the May sit-in. According to one account, the BSU was granted some concessions preceding the sit-in. Several members were still on probation from an earlier confrontation between BSU members and the *Gator* campus newspaper staff. BSU decided not to join the sit-in, and their refusal caused mistrust among some in the TWLF. Also, MASC and PACE were reported to have set up the SDS-TWLF joint action without formal approval of the TWLF coordinators. This upset the Latin American Students Association (LASO), which reportedly pulled out of the action a few days before the sit-in.[70]

Conflicts with the white left on campus also shaped the functioning of the TWLF. Self-determination was applied to the movement itself; white students were expected to respect the right of Third World organizations to lead their respective movements. Nationalism, which deemed one nationality's struggle as important above all other causes, influenced some Third World activists. However, this viewpoint was distinct from sentiments for national pride, identity, and self-determination which were held by the majority of activists. Some sectors of the white left failed to distinguish between narrow nationalism and national self-determination. Additionally, members of the Progressive Labor Party considered all nationalism to be reactionary.

Nationalism was a point of conflict within the TWLF. While most activists were committed to improving the conditions of their people, there was a growing suspicion that some were looking out only for themselves. As the movement faced setbacks, the administration encouraged divisions by offering settlements to each group individually.

To counteract divisions and to insure internal accountability, the BSU developed an organizational structure which was to have great impact on the TWLF. BSU Central Committee member Terry Collins described this structure in a *Black Fire* article:

> In the spring of 1968 the Black Students Union saw that there was a need for democratic centralism. Before that time the Black Students Union had no formal structure. Dominant personalities of two or three people tyrannically reigned over the other students. Factionalism was rampant, potential revolutionary brothers were disillusioned, sisters were used and abused in the name of "blackness." It was the era of the bourgeois cultural nationalism, a stage of evolution that all black students involved in the move-

ment move through, but must shake quickly. Bourgeois cultural nationalism is destructive to the individual and the organization because one uses "blackness" as a criterion and uses this rationale as an excuse not to fight the real enemy when the struggle becomes more intense. That is why we presented a new structure to the people in the spring of 1968 and called for the election of a central committee.[71]

In the TWLF structure, each of the six organizations[72] had two representatives to a Central Committee whose decisions were to be implemented by all groups. Chairpersons would be alternated every four months to provide training and to share responsibilities. No one was authorized to speak for the coalition, negotiate with the administration, or make statements to the media without the sanction of the TWLF.[73] Democracy was to be promoted by input through the respective organizations around three principles : fight against racism, fight for self-determination for Third World peoples, and support the TWLF demands.[74]

Strategy and Tactics

The BSU's approach towards strategy also influenced the TWLF. BSU members popularized the concept of "heightening contradictions" in order to educate people. Black Studies professor Nathan Hare explained:

> For by heightening the contradictions, you prepare people for the confrontation which must come when they are fully sensitized to their condition. Rushing into confrontations without having heightened contradictions contrarily cripples the confrontation.[75]

Hare saw "heightening the contradictions" as a *strategy* to prepare people for confrontational *tactics*. The strategy was to educate the general student population about TWLF problems with the aim of involving them in confrontations to win demands. Violence was seen as a confrontational tactic rather than an organizing principle.

In contrast, P. N. of AAPA recalled a different interpretation:

> I guess the main reasons for using violent tactics . . . was . . . [to] heighten the contradictions, increase the level of confrontation. Because . . . the greater the amount of pressure, the more incentive there is to resolve it. So by heightening the contradictions, or by heightening the level of tensions . . . there may be a faster resolution than if things stayed at a lower level of activity.[76]

This interpretation defined "heightening the contradictions" as a tactic. P. N. also observed that "there was a certain amount of macho that was also involved, as distinguished from looking at violence in a more analytical perspective as a tactical movement."[77] The "macho" attitude may have reflected a larger difference; some students may have viewed violence as a *strategy* to win their demands.

The idea of exposing contradictions between students and the administration was based on the assumption that underlying the conflict was a fundamental difference in values, beliefs, and most of all, interests. Many students came to believe that racism, class, and political interests belied all rhetoric about the university as a neutral and objective entity.

1968–1969: "By Any Means Necessary"

The trustees are worried about a Black Studies department having an all-black faculty. They didn't mention that there are departments with all-white faculties. These people are scared of giving black people control over their own destinies. Does the college plan to do something about institutional racism or is it just going to fire Black Power advocates? I haven't seen anybody fired for being a racist.[78]

—Elmer Cooper, Dean of Student Activities

Students were angered by the refusal of the administration to act on their demands despite prior commitments. This period also saw police violence and political repression against mass movements, including the assassinations of Martin Luther King, Jr., and Robert Kennedy. Protesters at the Democratic National Convention were severely beaten. Many believed that substantive change would not be willingly given: it had to be won through force. Thus, they echoed the slogan of Malcolm X—"by any means necessary."

Many engaged in confrontational tactics after they had exhausted other channels. Some students had been seeking the expansion and institutionalization of ethnic studies and special admissions programs for four years. Promises had been made by Summerskill and others but were never implemented. Now, the administrators were using police to suppress student actions. Due to this repression, students began to understand that their demands represented a more fundamental challenge to the system. Although this understanding varied among students, it was widely shared and provided the basis for mobilizing hundreds in the confrontations with the administration. PACE's B. I. stated that even "the silence on the part of the administration [told me] that our demands were not relevant, told me that our contributions were not anything. So that's what led me to get more involved."[79]

Firing of George Murray Heightens Confrontation

BSU central committee member George Murray was fired from the English department for his political beliefs and activism in November. He had been hired in May to teach Educational Opportunity Program (EOP) courses. The Board of Trustees opposed his hiring due to his public statements challenging the racism of the university. Murray was also Minister of Education of the Black Panther Party. The alternative campus newspaper, *Open Process,* summarized the reason for his termination:

Institutionalized racism is embedded in the status quo of American society; to challenge it with that in mind is to challenge the very foundations of society. George Murray was suspended not because he is black, but because as a member of the Black Panther Party he has challenged the institutions which have always enslaved black people including the educational system.[80]

The controversy over Murray's case reflected a polarization within the administration and faculty. Smith, like other liberals, argued that "if we are to continue as a nation ruled by law, we must give all citizens the benefit of due process and the protection of the law."[81] Chancellor Dumke was less concerned with due process than with the problem of "certain tiny groups of students . . . who have lost faith in our system, and are simply interested in overthrowing the establishment." He expressed his determination to suppress any disruption with whatever force necessary.[82]

One month after the publication of Dumke's statements, George Murray gave a speech at a rally at a trustees board meeting in Fresno. In his speech, he spoke about the betrayal of America by politicians.

> So you get people deceiving college students, deceiving the general populace in the United States . . . to manipulate you to the extent that you'll die for some nonfreedom in Viet Nam, that you'll die for some nonfreedom throughout Asia, Africa, and Latin America fighting people of color who have never victimized any American persons.[83]

He discussed the demands of African Americans, including the right of self-determination and exemption from the draft. Murray pointed to the examples of revolutionary struggles to win demands.

> We understand that the only way that we're going to get them [is] the same way which folks got theirs in 1776, the same way black people in Cuba got theirs in the 1950s . . . that is with guns and force. We maintain that political power comes through the barrel of a gun.[84]

After the *San Francisco Chronicle* reported Murray advocating "guns on campus," trustee opposition to his appointment increased. On 1 November the administration announced his suspension. Murray was later arrested during the first week of Hayakawa's administration, suspended again, and jailed without parole.

War of the Flea

On 28 October, only days before Murray's suspension, the BSU called a rally to announce the strike and their demands.[85] In the following week, meetings were held by the BSU and TWLF, and the strike date was set as 6 November. On the day before the strike, the TWLF held a general meeting attended by nearly 700 Third World students and community supporters. SNCC representative Stokely Carmichael delivered a speech which raised the level of analysis of many students. He warned against trying to solve institutional racism simply by replacing white administrators with Blacks. He said, "Now the way to insure that you get somebody . . . who has the same political ideology that you have is to make sure that you can choose or you have control over that person." He also urged them to take the struggle seriously, stating "do not start off with something you cannot maintain because in the long run you not only hurt your-self but movements to come." He concluded, "It is easier to die for one's people than it is to work and live for them, to kill for them, and to continue to live and kill for them."[86]

Following Carmichael, Benny Stewart presented the strategy of the "war of the flea." This strategy was adapted from the guerrilla war conditions facing many anti-colonial movements in which the strength was based on mass support, familiarity with the terrain, and the advantage of elusivity. He pointed to the failure of other campus movements after leaders had been arrested and argued for a new strategy for a prolonged struggle:

> We call it the war of the flea. . . . What does the flea do? He bites, sucks blood from the dog, the dog bites. What happens when there are enough fleas on a dog? What will he do? He moves. He moves away. . . . We are the people. We are the majority and the pigs cannot be everywhere. . . . And where they are not, we are.[87]

One influential writer during this period was Frantz Fanon with his widely read book, *Wretched of the Earth.* He emphasized the role of revolutionary struggle by the oppressed to achieve liberation. Fanon and other Third World thinkers had great in-fluence on student activists. At the same time, these ideas were integrated with the stu-dents' own experiences, both on campus and in American society. This period was marked by a rash of police incidents, including violence against the Panthers, assaults on Chicano youth in the Mission district, and the shooting of a Chinese woman in the eye by a drunk officer. Students also rallied at UC Santa Barbara, San Jose State, Col-lege of San Mateo, and throughout the nation. Student activity in Czechoslovakia, France, Italy, Spain, Japan, and China also received publicity. All of these events pro-foundly affected San Francisco State activists.

On 6 November, mobile teams of Third World students entered buildings, dis-missed classes, set trash cans on fire, and otherwise disrupted campus operations. Meanwhile, 400 white students marched to President Smith's office in support of the TWLF demands. In contrast to characterizations of strikers as irrational youth, there was in fact a clear reasoning for actions based on a redefinition of violence.

Soon after the strike began, Smith called in the police and closed the campus. The next day, 600 persons marched on the administration building during a noon rally. By the third day, the *Gator* reported a 50 percent drop in classroom attendance. By that time, students altered tactics and sent "educational teams" into classrooms to explain the strike issues.[88]

On 13 November, the San Francisco police Tactical Squad beat several TWLF mem-bers. A rally was called and 1,000 students gathered, ending in more police violence. By the end of the day, seven students had been arrested and eleven taken to the hospi-tal for injuries.[89] Smith announced, "We'll keep classes closed until such time as we can reopen them on a rational basis."[90] The trustees gave Smith until 20 November to reopen the college. The faculty refused to resume classes and held "convocations" to try to resolve the problems. The BSU stated they would refuse to participate unless classes were canceled. When classes were not canceled on 21 November, 2,000 students rallied, and police again beat and arrested students. In the first two weeks of the strike, the police arrested 148 participants.[91] Though many Asian student activists participated in militant tactics, some were reluctant. AAPA member M. O. did not oppose the basic strategy because she believed that in order to gain ethnic studies, "the only answer at that time seemed to be: force them [administration]." However, she selectively chose not to participate in violent actions. "When I got in the palm of throwing, I could pick it up, but I couldn't throw it. I thought, 'no, my involvement will have to be in other ways.'"[92] Another student opposed these tactics as he saw that the debris was cleaned up by Third World workers, including his father, who worked as a custodian on campus.

Winter–Spring 1968: Repression and Continued Community Commitment

On 26 November, President Smith resigned, explaining his failure "to get from the chancellor and the trustees the resources and kinds of decisions I felt we needed. . . . Further, we could not get them to look past serious provocative acts to basic problems."[93] However, underneath the "problems" were basic differences, which the trustees and California Governor Ronald Reagan clearly understood.

The silencing of liberals matched the rise of conservative national and state political figures. Following the election of Reagan as governor in 1966, Nixon became President in 1968. Republicans won the majority in both houses of the California state legislature. Through appointments, Reagan gained control of the state college Board of Trustees.[94] The naming of faculty member S. I. Hayakawa as president of the college was part of this political realignment. Hayakawa and colleagues in the Faculty Renaissance organization had courted Chancellor Dumke. They proposed to deliver ultimatums, restrict due process, suspend students, and fire disobeying faculty.[95] Hayakawa was a perfect choice, being of Japanese descent. He took a hard line against the student movement and served as a public spectacle for media consumption.

On 2 December, 1,500 gathered after Hayakawa's ban on campus rallies. Hayakawa personally jumped onto the sound truck and ripped off the speaker cords. As the crowd was attempting to leave, several hundred police sealed off a section of campus and beat and arrested students, reporters, medics, and community supporters.[96] Hayakawa stated at a press conference, "This has been the most exciting day of my life since my tenth birthday, when I rode on a roller coaster for the first time!"[97]

On the evening of 2 December, the American Federation of Teachers (AFT) held an emergency meeting and voted to request strike sanction from the San Francisco Central Labor Council. Their main concerns were faculty issues, including a nine-unit teaching requirement. On 4 December, 6,000 persons rallied on campus, and on 6 December a large rally was marked by police violence and arrests.[98] On 11 December, the AFT set up an informal picket line in front of the administration building. And on 13 December, Hayakawa announced an early Christmas recess.

TWLF leaders noted the tentativeness of their alliance with the AFT, whose strike began 6 January. "We view it as positive that the AFT has finally gone on strike. It must be clear, however, that the AFT is, by their own admission, striking primarily for their own demands and only secondarily, under pressure, for the fifteen demands of TWLF."[99]

As students, faculty, and community supporters gained strength, the university prepared to take more repressive measures. On 23 January, over 500 persons demonstrated on campus. Within five minutes, the police encircled the crowd and arrested 453 people.[100] Many spokespersons were incarcerated, leaving a void in the organized leadership. P. Y. of AAPA summarized this period:

> We just didn't have the money or the time to deal with 400 arrests at one time. At that point a lot of energy went into preparing for trials. . . . From that point on, the strike went downhill. A lot of EOP students and people who weren't directly involved in the day to day organization just stopped showing up. . . . A large part of the white student population that had supported the strike stopped going to school. . . . And everybody's court dates were starting to come up. . . . Some people were being pulled in for probation violation, for previous arrests. That's what happened to me, all of February. I don't know what happened during the last part of the strike because I was in jail.[101]

For the following months, much time was consumed in legal support efforts. Most trials took between four and six weeks, and by the year's end, 109 persons were convicted, and many served jail sentences.[102] Statewide, over 900 students and faculty were arrested on the state college campuses between November 1968 and March 1969.[103] This repression severely crippled the movement.

State repression impacted Asian students' understanding of the police in several ways. For AAPA member P. Y., this experience reinforced his developing understanding of society:

> I think most kids have a real negative attitude [towards police]. What became clearer was that the political context they operated in . . . the role of the police [as] an internal army . . . against the working class and Third World people.[104]

P. Y. was indicted and served a jail sentence. In jail, he saw that the treatment in prison epitomized the status of poor and Third World people in society. From his four-month internment, he learned that "jail is like almost any other segment of society . . . class is such a determining thing on people's lives. For me that put into perspective a lot of the issues of the strike."[105] Meanwhile, Reagan, the trustees, and Hayakawa were able to distort the strike through the media and sway public support for their repressive measures. For example, Hayakawa described students as "a gang of goons, gangsters, con men, neo-Nazis, and common thieves."[106] Also, in a statement to the U.S. Congress on 3 February 1969, he boasted about the use of police repression:

> I believe that I have introduced something new to this business of preserving order on campuses. At most institutions the use of police is delayed as long as possible and when assistance is finally requested, the force is usually too small to handle the situation and new troubles develop. I went the other way. . . . The opposition has received my message. I think I have communicated successfully.[107]

B. L. stated his anger at the mischaracterization of the strike in the popular media:

Their main focus points were probably on Hayakawa and the so-called violence. Like maybe you break a window. But what about the inequity, the psychological damage inflicted on an individual and [the destruction] of their history. What about that kind of violence.[108]

Negotiation and Evaluation

The internal weaknesses of the student movement and the external repression of the state forced students into a position of negotiating the "nonnegotiable" demands. Their negotiating power was weakened when the AFT returned to work on 5 March after voting 112–104 to end the strike, despite an unsatisfactory compromise.[109] Meanwhile, to prevent public questioning of their repressive strategy, Hayakawa and Reagan felt pressure to reopen the campus.

After several attempts, Hayakawa recognized a "Select Committee" of faculty which "expected to act with the full authority of the president"[110] and negotiate with the TWLF. However, this committee was more liberal than Hayakawa, and it negotiated a compromise to his objection. On 14 March, the committee met with Hayakawa to formalize the settlement. Since Hayakawa was to leave at 9 A.M. for a meeting with President Nixon, their meeting was set for 7:30 A.M., at which time he was quoted as saying, "I'll give you a month. . . . If all is quiet by April 11, I'll consider your recommendations. Now, if you'll excuse me, I have to catch my plane for Washington. Good morning."[111] Hayakawa never signed the negotiated resolution. TWLF members and faculty proceeded to implement the resolution.

It is important to note the BSU's reasons for entering negotiations with the administration. BSU Central Committee member Leroy Goodwin outlined "major contradictions" in a May 1969 Black Fire article. A major reason to enter negotiations was "the determination and support of the people rapidly decreasing due to a low political level, communication gaps, and paranoia or fear of the Central Committee." Also, he pointed to five classifications of opportunism which plagued the movement. They included: those who fronted as spokespersons and collected honorariums for themselves; those who left the struggle after the BSU secured their grades; spokespersons motivated by their personal prestige over the plight of the people; "shit slingers" who mainly criticized; and disruptiveness of the Progressive Labor Party.[112] He concluded, saying sarcastically, "But we came to grips with the reality that the struggle of oppressed people was more important than fourteen individuals walking around with the myth of the revolution going on in their minds. Imagine a flea worried about losing face."[113]

The BSU summation reflects demoralization and an emphasis on internal problems. Although there were internal contradictions, they existed within a context. This context included the alliance of conservative forces, popular sanction of police repression, racism in society including chauvinism in the white left, and the youthfulness of the movement, which, among other things, lacked more experience and theoretical grounding to sustain itself in an organized form.

Community Commitment

The lives of Asian student activists were changed in many ways. A common theme, however, voiced by all participants focused on a deep-rooted commitment to social change for the benefit of their communities. Some students stated that the strike may not have drastically altered their life. E. I., for example, felt he "would have wound up here anyway,"[114] working as a housing advocate and social worker. Others, like G. C., reflected upon the strike as a pivotal time in their lives:

> I think it changed my life in terms of providing some focus to the extent that my career wasn't that important to me. . . . Take a look at the decisions people made back then. It was what the community needed first; and what you could contribute emanated from that.[115]

P. N. stated that her understanding of "what it means to be an Asian in American society"[16] shaped her view of legal work:

> I don't think I would have gone to law school if it hadn't been for the strike. . . . The reason why I did go to law school was to get some skills . . . to practice law, and look at law as a vehicle for social change. [117]

Others, including A. S., stated that student activism led them to utilize their skills in channeling resources to their communities "to build low-income housing, parks for the people."[118] A. W. stated that though most of the leadership went into the community, he "chose to stay [to teach] in the university."[119]

Many activists expressed a feeling of personal liberation. Speaking out and taking stands to the point of facing serious consequences instilled a boldness of character. P. N. added that she became "more adventurous, less looking for the safe way to do things," while at the same time "more cautious" in dealing with the complexities of human nature.[120]

M. W. discussed the political ramifications:

> What it did is, I think, make me more politically conscious . . . when a person in administration, who is supposed to have authority, a title, . . . [you find that those] people use that [power] to put the pressure on you. Then after getting involved with bureaucrats and politicians, [you realize] that they are people like anyone else. I think that is one of the things I learned: not to be intimidated.[121]

Some activists left the campus with the view of reforming society. B. I. remarked, "I saw myself as a reformist working within the system, to try and get those things that would benefit poor people, regardless of whether you are Black, White or Asian."[122] However, others like P. N. added: "I'd always felt since the strike that what was necessary to eliminate or alleviate racism was a major restructuring of our society, both economically and in eliminating barriers in terms of participation of Third World people in all walks of life."[123]

Conclusion: The Altered Terrain

Asian American students played a significant role in student movements of the sixties, as clearly demonstrated in the San Francisco State strike. The struggle was unique in that it was situated in an urban, multiethnic, liberal, working-class city. Perhaps that more closely tied the campus struggle to the respective national movements, while at the same time making bonds between them. In their challenge to the university, Asian students followed in the legacies of Pilipino farm labor organizers, International Hotel tenants, and concentration camp resisters. Their demand for a relevant and accessible education stemmed from the aspirations of peoples who had fought for justice and equality since their arrival in the United States. And, in many ways, it was this legacy which steeled the movement and today frames a context to understand the long-lasting significance of the strike.

The most obvious accomplishment was the establishment of the first School of Ethnic Studies in the nation. This school partially met the terms outlined in the TWLF demands, including the commitment of over twenty-two faculty positions, the establishment of a Black Studies department upon which the other ethnic studies departments were based, student participation in the committee to recommend the final plan for the school, and faculty power commensurate with that accorded other college departments. In addition, unused special admission slots were promised to be filled in spring 1969. Campus disciplinary action was recommended to be limited to suspension through fall semester 1969. Demands to retain or fire individual personnel were not met. Though negotiations fell short of meeting the demands in full, the school remains the largest national program in its faculty size and course offerings. The winning of these concessions set a precedent for other universities to follow. In fact, the organization and militancy shown by San Francisco State students led some administrators at other campuses to initiate minor concessions.

A less tangible, but equally significant, outcome of the strike was the emergence of a new generation of fighters who either remained on campus or entered their communities. Many took the concept of self-determination to establish self-help programs to continue political education and promote self-reliance. Many formed or joined organizations to define a collective approach to addressing problems. Some pursued advanced degrees to secure positions of influence within the system, while others concentrated on grassroots organizing to build progressive, community-based movements. Almost without exception, those interviewed affirmed a deep commitment to the basic values and beliefs forged during their days as students active in the strike; many traced their convictions to the period of the strike itself.

The legacy of the strike has also set the terrain for another generation of Asian students. Stemming from the post-1965 immigration, today's students have formed organizations based on the foundations set by an earlier generation. The institutionalization of ethnic studies and affirmative action programs has not only given students important support systems but has also led to greater political influence for Asians in higher education.

These gains, however, have been increasingly contested. Then-governor Reagan launched his political career to become President of the United States, marking the rise of the New Right. The U.S. economic decline has resulted in government cuts in education and social programs. Universities increasingly rely on private donations, defense-related contracts, and foundation grants, influencing the priorities of the university. Meanwhile, it is estimated that one-half of all ethnic studies programs have already been eliminated. Of those which remain, much of the emphasis has shifted away from the original intent for social change. Most programs have not enjoyed programmatic autonomy or student/community involvement in decision making, and many have lost relevance to community needs. Support for affirmative action has also waned. Since the landmark Bakke decision in 1978, minimum quotas for minority admissions have turned into invisible ceilings for Asians who are perceived as "over-represented." The attention called to these unfair practices is now being used to question affirmative action for Chicanos, African Americans, and Native Americans. And Asians have been effectively eliminated from virtually all such programs. Tenure cases, particularly for minority faculty, have become battlegrounds over the definition of legitimate and relevant research. In short, the essence of the conflict in the San Francisco State strike remains central today.

The strike offers no blueprint for movements today. Its history, however, begins to reveal the nature of clashes between students and administrators. It reminds us that the existence of ethnic studies and special programs for oppressed groups has only been the result of hard-fought struggle. Students of today's movements can study this history as a benchmark to assess their own conditions. And, with that, democratic empowerment movements may set a new terrain for the next generation.

NOTES

Originally published in *Amerasia Journal* 15.1 (1989): 3–41. © 1989 *Amerasia Journal,* reprinted by permission.

1. R. Q., Interview, 11 September 1985, San Francisco.
2. B. I., Interview, 5 September 1985, San Francisco.
3. See also, Kirkpatrick Sale, *SDS* (New York, 1974) and Harry Edwards, *Black Students* (New York, 1970).
4. I. C., Interview, 13 September 1985, San Francisco.
5. A. S., Interview, 12 September 1985, Fremont, California.
6. J. M., Interview, 11 September 1985, San Francisco.
7. B. I., Interview, 5 September 1985, San Francisco.
8. E. D. C., Interview, 3 September 1985, San Francisco.
9. William Barlow and Peter Shapiro, *An End to Silence: The San Francisco State College Student Movement of the 60s* (New York, 1971), 49.
10. Ibid., 68.
11. Robert Smith, Richard Axen, and DeVere Pentony, *By Any Means Necessary: The Revolutionary Struggle at San Francisco State* (San Francisco, 1970), 39.
12. Ibid., 8.
13. DeVere Pentony, Robert Smith, and Richard Axen, *Unfinished Rebellions* (San Francisco, 1971), 25.

14. Master Plan Survey Team, *A Master Plan for Higher Education in California, 1960–75* (Sacramento, 1960), 43.

15. Ibid., 73.

16. Ibid., 60.

17. Ibid., 74.

18. Staff Report to the National Commission on the Causes and Prevention of Violence, prepared by William H. Orrick, Jr. *Shut It Down! A College in Crisis: San Francisco State College* (Washington, D.C., 1969), 75. Figures not available for other ethnic groups.

19. E. Hornsby Wasson, "Business and Campus Unrest" (speech delivered 16 January 1969), *Vital Speeches* 35.11 (15 March 1969): 335.

20. B. I., Interview, 10 September 1985, San Francisco.

21. For a discussion on the influence of Malcolm X on the African American student movement, see Harry Edwards, *Black Students* (New York, 1970).

22. Compiled from William Barlow and Peter Shapiro, *An End to Silence*; Kuregiy Hekymara, "The Third World Movement and Its History in the San Francisco State College Strike of 1968–69" (Ph.D. diss., University of California, Berkeley, 1972).

23. A. W., Interview, September 1985, San Francisco.

24. Ibid.

25. I. C., Interview, 13 September 1985, San Francisco.

26. J. C., Interview, September 1985, San Francisco.

27. Ibid.

28. M. W., Interview, 13 September 1985, San Francisco.

29. See Sun Tzu, *The Art of War,* translated and with an introduction by Samuel Griffith (London, 1963).

30. M. W., Interview, 13 September 1985, San Francisco.

31. *East West,* 28 August 1968, 1, 4.

32. *East West,* 4 September 1968, 12.

33. A. W., Interview, September 1985.

34. ICSA Position Paper, mimeographed, Special Collections Library, San Francisco State University.

35. Ibid.

36. G. W., Interview, 21 March 1987, San Francisco.

37. Ibid.

38. Alex Hing, "'On Strike, Shut It Down!': Reminiscences of the S.F. State Strike," *East Wind* 2:2 (Fall/Winter 1983): 42.

39. G. W., Interview, 21 March 1987, San Francisco.

40. A. S., Interview, 12 September 1985.

41. "Statement of the Philippine-American Collegiate Endeavor (PACE) Philosophy and Goals" mimeograph.

42. P. S., Interviews, 14 May, 6 June 1986.

43. "PACE (Philippine-American Collegiate Endeavor) Program, S. F. State," mimeographed.

44. E. I., Interview, 13 September 1985, San Francisco.

45. Ibid.

46. Mimeographed roster of PACE members.

47. P. N., Interviews, 27 May 1984 and 11 September 1985.

48. Ibid.

49. "AAPA Is," *Asian American Political Alliance Newspaper* 1 (UC Berkeley, late 1968): 4.

50. "AAPA Perspectives," *Asian American Political Alliance Newspaper* 1:5 (UC Berkeley, fall 1969): 7.

51. P. N., Interviews, 27 May 1984 and 11 September 1985.

52. P. Y., Interviews, May 1984 and 9 September 1985.

53. M. O., Interview, 14 September 1985, San Francisco.

54. Y. W., Interview, 4 September 1985, San Francisco.

55. "Statement of the Third World Liberation Front Philosophy and Goals," undated mimeo.

56. Coordinating Council for Higher Education, *California Higher Education and the Disadvantaged: A Status Report* (Sacramento, March 1968), table v.

57. "Third World Liberation Front, School of Ethnic Area Studies," mimeographed packet, 2.

58. I. C., Interview, 13 September 1985.

59. R. Q., Interview, 11 September 1985.

60. M. W., Interview, 13 September 1985.

61. Smith et al., *By Any Means Necessary*, 332.

62. "School for Ethnic Area Studies."

63. Pentony et al., *Unfinished Rebellions*, 51.

64. Smith et al., *By Any Means Necessary*, 134.

65. Coordinating Council for Higher Education, *California Higher Education*, 53.

66. Barlow and Shapiro, *An End to Silence*, 167–170; "After the Strike: A Conference on Ethnic Studies Proceedings" (School of Ethnic Studies, San Francisco State University; Proceedings from 12, 13, 14 April 1984 Conference), 14; Smith et al., *By Any Means Necessary*, 58–59.

67. Smith et al., *By Any Means Necessary*, 50–51.

68. P. N., Interviews, 27 May 1984 and 11 September 1985.

69. *TWLF Newsletter,* n. d.

70. Barlow and Shapiro, *An End to Silence.*

71. Smith et al., *By Any Means Necessary*, 140–141.

72. The six organizations within the TWLF were the Mexican American Student Confederation (MASC), Intercollegiate Chinese for Social Action(ICSA), Philippine American College Endeavor (PACE), Asian American Political Alliance (AAPA), Latin American Student Organization (LASO), and Black Students Union (BSU).

73. "By the Direction of the Third World Liberation Front" (mimeographed TWLF leaflet, n.d.).

74. Ibid.

75. Nathan Hare, "Two Black Radicals Report on Their Campus Struggles," *Ramparts* 8 (July 1969):54.

76. P. N., Interviews, 27 May 1984 and 11 September 1985.

77. Ibid.

78. Staff report to the National Commission on the Causes and Prevention of Violence, prepared by William H. Orrick, 52.

79. B. I., Interview, 5 September 1985.

80. Quoted in Smith et al., *By Any Means Necessary*, 29.

81. Ibid., 113.

82. Campus Violence—Crackdown Coming: Interview with Glenn S. Dumke Leading College Official," *U.S. News and World Report* 65 (23 September 1968): 49.

83. Mimeographed copy of George Murray's speech, Fresno, California, n.d.

84. Ibid.

85. Barlow and Shapiro, *An End to Silence,* 213–217.

86. Dikran Karagueuzian, *Blow It Up! The Black Student Revolt at San Francisco State College and the Emergence of Dr. Hayakawa* (Boston, 1971), 100–102.

87. Quotes in Smith et al., *By Any Means Necessary,* 144–145.

88. Events compiled from Smith et al., *By Any Means Necessary*; Barlow and Shapiro, *An End to Silence*; Karagueuzian, *Blow It Up!*; and various chronologies.

89. Barlow and Shapiro, *An End to Silence.*

90. Smith et al., *By Any Means Necessary,* 166.

91. Ibid.

92. M. O., Interview, 14 September 1985.

93. Smith et al., *By Any Means Necessary,* 187.

94. Ibid., 90.

95. Ibid., 207–208.

96. Barlow and Shapiro, *An End to Silence,* 263–264.

97. Ibid., 264.

98. Ibid., 267–269 for a fuller account.

99. Quoted in Smith et al., 258–259.

100. Ibid.

101. P. Y., Interviews, May 1984 and 9 September 1985.

102. Smith et al., *By Any Means Necessary,* 282.

103. Glenn S. Dumke, "Controversy on Campus; Need for Peace and Order" (Speech delivered before the Town Hall of California, Los Angeles, 18 February 1969), *Vital Speeches* 35:11 (15 March 1969): 332–335.

104. P. Y., Interview, May 1984 and 9 September 1985.

105. Ibid.

106. S. I. Hayakawa, "Gangsters in Our Midst," in *Crisis at SF State,* edited by Howard Finberg (San Francisco, 1969), 11.

107. "Statement by President S. I. Hayakawa, of San Francisco State College: Order on Campuses," *Congressional Record* 115 (3 February 1969): 2462.

108. B. L., Interview, 10 September 1985.

109. Smith et al., 229.

110. Ibid., 311.

111. Ibid.

112. *Black Fire* [San Francisco] (May 1969).

113. Ibid.

114. E. I., Interview, 13 September 1985, San Francisco.

115. G. C., Interview, September 1985, San Francisco.

116. P. N., Interviews, 27 May 1984 and 11 September 1985, San Francisco.

117. Ibid.

118. A. S., Interview, 12 September 1985.

119. A. W., Interview, September 1985, San Francisco.

120. P. N., Interviews, 27 May 1984 and 11 September 1985, San Francisco.

121. M. W., Interview, 13 September 1985, San Francisco.

122. B. I., Interview, 5 September 1985, San Francisco.

123. P. N., Interviews, 27 May 1984 and 11 September 1985, San Francisco.

The "Four Prisons" and the
Movements of Liberation

*Asian American Activism from
the 1960s to the 1990s*

Glenn Omatsu

According to Ali Shariati, an Iranian philosopher, each of us exists within four prisons.[1] First is the prison imposed on us by history and geography; from this confinement, we can escape only by gaining a knowledge of science and technology. Second is the prison of history; our freedom comes when we understand how historical forces operate. The third prison is our society's social and class structure; from this prison, only a revolutionary ideology can provide the way to liberation. The final prison is the self. Each of us is composed of good and evil elements, and we must each choose between them.

The analysis of our four prisons provides a way of understanding the movements that swept across America in the 1960s and molded the consciousness of one generation of Asian Americans. The movements were struggles for liberation from many prisons. They were struggles that confronted the historical forces of racism, poverty, war, and exploitation. They were struggles that generated new ideologies, based mainly on the teachings and actions of Third World leaders. And they were struggles that redefined human values—the values that shape how people live their daily lives and interact with each other. Above all, they were struggles that transformed the lives of "ordinary" people as they confronted the prisons around them.

For Asian Americans, these struggles profoundly changed our communities. They spawned numerous grassroots organizations. They created an extensive network of student organizations and Asian American Studies classes. They recovered buried cultural traditions as well as produced a new generation of writers, poets, and artists. But most importantly, the struggles deeply affected Asian American consciousness. They redefined racial and ethnic identity, promoted new ways of thinking about communities, and challenged prevailing notions of power and authority.

Yet, in the two decades that have followed, scholars have reinterpreted the movements in narrower ways. I learned about this reinterpretation when I attended a class recently in Asian American Studies at UCLA. The professor described the period from the late 1950s to the early 1970s as a single epoch involving the persistent efforts of racial minorities and their white supporters to secure civil rights. Young Asian Americans, the professor stated, were swept into this campaign and by later antiwar protests to assert their own racial identity. The most important influence on Asian Americans during this period was Dr. Martin Luther King, Jr., who inspired them to demand access to policymakers and initiate advocacy programs for their own communities. Meanwhile, students and professors fought to legitimize Asian American Studies in college curricula and the representation of Asians in American society. The lecture was cogent, tightly organized, and well received by the audience of students—many of them new immigrants or the children of new immigrants. There was only one problem: the reinterpretation was wrong on every aspect.

Those who took part in the mass struggles of the 1960s and early 1970s will know that the birth of the Asian American movement coincided not with the initial campaign for civil rights but with the later demand for black liberation; that the leading influence was not Martin Luther King, Jr., but Malcolm X; that the focus of a generation of Asian American activists was not on asserting racial pride but reclaiming a tradition of militant struggle by earlier generations; that the movement was not centered on the aura of racial identity but embraced fundamental questions of oppression and power; that the movement consisted of not only college students but large numbers of community forces, including the elderly, workers, and high school youth; and that the main thrust was not one of seeking legitimacy and representation within American society but the larger goal of liberation.

It may be difficult for a new generation—raised on the Asian American codewords of the 1980s stressing "advocacy," "access," "legitimacy," "empowerment," and "assertiveness"—to understand the urgency of Malcolm X's demand for freedom "by any means necessary," Mao's challenge to "serve the people," the slogans of "power to the people" and "self-determination," the principles of "mass line" organizing and "united front" work, or the conviction that people—not elites—make history. But these ideas galvanized thousands of Asian Americans and reshaped our communities. And it is these concepts that we must grasp to understand the scope and intensity of our movement and what it created.

But are these concepts relevant to Asian Americans today? In our community—where new immigrants and refugees constitute the majority of Asian Americans—can we find a legacy from the struggles of two decades ago? Are the ideas of the movement alive today, or have they atrophied into relics—the curiosities of a bygone era of youthful and excessive idealism?

By asking these questions, we, as Asian Americans, participate in a larger national debate: the reevaluation of the impact of the 1960s on American society today. This debate is occurring all around us: in sharp exchanges over "family values" and the status of women and gays in American society; in clashes in schools over curricular reform and multiculturalism; in differences among policymakers over the urban crisis and approaches to rebuilding Los Angeles and other inner cities after the 1992 uprisings; and continuing reexaminations of U.S. involvement in Indochina more than two decades ago and the relevance of that war to U.S. military intervention in Iraq, Somalia, and Bosnia.

What happened in the 1960s that made such an impact on America? Why do discussions about that decade provoke so much emotion today? And do the movements of the 1960s serve as the same controversial reference point for Asian Americans?

The United States during the 1960s

In recent years, the movements of the 1960s have come under intense attack. One national bestseller, Allan Bloom's *Closing of the American Mind,* criticizes the movements for undermining the bedrock of Western thought.[2] According to Bloom, nothing positive resulted from the mass upheavals of the 1960s. He singles out black studies and affirmative-action programs and calls for eliminating them from universities.

Activists who have continued political work provide contrasting assessments. Their books include Todd Gitlin's *The Sixties: Years of Hope, Days of Rage*; James Miller's *"Democracy Is in the Streets": From Port Huron to the Siege of Chicago*; Ronald Fraser's *1968: A Student Generation in Revolt*; Tom Hayden's *Reunion: A Memoir*; Tariq Ali's *Street Fighting Years*; George Katsiaficas's *The Imagination of the New Left: A Global Analysis of 1968,* and special issues of various journals, including *Witness, Socialist Review,* and *Radical America.*

However, as Winifred Breines states in an interesting review essay titled "Whose New Left?," most of the retrospects have been written by white male activists from elite backgrounds and reproduce their relationship to these movements.[3] Their accounts tend to divide the period into two phases: the "good" phase of the early 1960s, characterized by participatory democracy, followed by the post-1968 phase, when movement politics "degenerated" into violence and sectarianism.

"Almost all books about the New Left note a turning point or an ending in 1968 when the leadership of the movement turned toward militancy and violence and SDS [Students for a Democratic Society] as an organization was collapsing," Breines observes. The retrospects commonly identify the key weaknesses of the movements as the absence of effective organization, the lack of discipline, and utopian thinking. Breines disagrees with these interpretations:

> The movement was not simply unruly and undisciplined; it was experimenting with antihierarchical organizational forms. . . . There were many centers of action in the movement, many actions, many interpretations, many visions, many experiences. There was no [organizational] unity because each group, region, campus, commune, collective, and demonstration developed differently, but all shared in a spontaneous opposition to racism and inequality, the war in Vietnam, and the repressiveness of American social norms and culture, including centralization and hierarchy.[4]

Breines believes that the most important contributions of activists were their moral urgency, their emphasis on direct action, their focus on community building, and their commitment to mass democracy.

Similarly, Sheila Collins in *The Rainbow Challenge,* a book focusing on the Jesse Jackson presidential campaign of 1984 and the formation of the National Rainbow Coalition, assesses the movements of the sixties very positively.[5] She contends that the

Jackson campaign was built on the grassroots organizing experience of activists who emerged from the struggles for civil rights, women's liberation, peace and social justice, and community building during the sixties. Moreover, activists' participation in these movements shaped their vision of America, which, in turn, became the basis for the platform of the Rainbow Coalition twenty years later.

According to Collins, the movements that occurred in the United States in the sixties were also part of a worldwide trend, a trend Latin American theologians call the era of the "eruption of the poor" into history. In America, the revolt of the "politically submerged" and "economically marginalized" posed a major ideological challenge to ruling elites:

> The civil rights and black power movement exploded several dominant assumptions about the nature of American society, thus challenging the cultural hegemony of the white ruling elite and causing everyone else in the society to redefine their relationship to centers of power, creating a groundswell of support for radical democratic participation in every aspect of institutional life.[6]

Collins contends that the mass movements created a "crisis of legitimation" for ruling circles. This crisis, she believes, was "far more serious than most historians—even those of the left—have credited it with being."

Ronald Fraser also emphasizes the ideological challenge raised by the movements due to their mass, democratic character and their "disrespect for arbitrary and exploitative authority." In *1968: A Student Generation in Revolt,* Fraser explains how these concepts influenced one generation of activists:

> [T]he anti-authoritarianism challenged almost every shibboleth of Western society. Parliamentary democracy, the authority of presidents . . . and [the policies of] governments to further racism, conduct imperialist wars or oppress sectors of the population at home, the rule of capital and the fiats of factory bosses, the dictates of university administrators, the sacredness of the family, sexuality, bourgeois culture—nothing was in principle sacrosanct. . . . Overall . . . [there was] a lack of deference towards institutions and values that demean[ed] people and a concomitant awareness of people's rights.[7]

The San Francisco State Strike's Legacy

The retrospects about the 1960s produced so far have ignored Asian Americans. Yet, the books cited above—plus the review essay by Winifred Breines—provide us with some interesting points to compare and contrast. For example, 1968 represented a turning point for Asian Americans and other sectors of American society. But while white male leaders saw the year as marking the decline of the movement, 1968 for Asian Americans was a year of birth. It marked the beginning of the San Francisco State strike and all that followed.

The strike, the longest student strike in U.S. history, was the first campus uprising involving Asian Americans as a collective force.[8] Under the Third World Liberation

Front—a coalition of African American, Latino, American Indian, and Asian American campus groups—students "seized the time" to demand ethnic studies, open admissions, and a redefinition of the education system. Although their five-month strike was brutally repressed and resulted in only partial victories, students won the nation's first School of Ethnic Studies.

Yet, we cannot measure the legacy of the strike for Asian Americans only in the tangible items it achieved, such as new classes and new faculty; the strike also critically transformed the consciousness of its participants who, in turn, profoundly altered their communities' political landscape. Through their participation, a generation of Asian American student activists reclaimed a heritage of struggle—linking their lives to the tradition of militancy of earlier generations of Pilipino farmworkers, Chinese immigrant garment and restaurant workers, and Japanese American concentration camp resisters. Moreover, these Asian American students—and their community supporters—liberated themselves from the prisons surrounding their lives and forged a new vision for their communities, creating numerous grassroots projects and empowering previously ignored and disenfranchised sectors of society. The statement of goals and principles of one campus organization, Philippine-American Collegiate Endeavor (PACE), during the strike captures this new vision:

> We seek . . . simply to function as human beings, to control our own lives. Initially, following the myth of the American Dream, we worked to attend predominantly white colleges, but we have learned through direct analysis that it is impossible for our people, so-called minorities, to function as human beings, in a racist society in which white always comes first. . . . So we have decided to fuse ourselves with the masses of Third World people, which are the majority of the world's peoples, to create, through struggle, a new humanity, a new humanism, a New World Consciousness, and within that context collectively control our own destinies.[9]

The San Francisco State strike is important not only as a beginning point for the Asian American movement but also because it crystallizes several themes that would characterize Asian American struggles in the following decade. First, the strike occurred at a working-class campus and involved a coalition of Third World students linked to their communities. Second, students rooted their strike in the tradition of resistance by past generations of minority peoples in America. Third, strike leaders drew inspiration—as well as new ideology—from international Third World leaders and revolutions occurring in Asia, Africa, Latin America, and the Middle East. Fourth, the strike in its demands for open admissions, community control of education, ethnic studies, and self-determination confronted basic questions of power and oppression in America. Finally, strike participants raised their demands through a strategy of mass mobilizations and militant, direct action.

In the decade following the strike, several themes would reverberate in the struggles in Asian American communities across the nation. These included housing and anti-eviction campaigns, efforts to defend education rights, union organizing drives, campaigns for jobs and social services, and demands for democratic rights, equality, and justice. Mo Nishida, an organizer in Los Angeles, recalls the broad scope of movement activities in his city:

> Our movement flowered. At one time, we had active student organizations on every campus around Los Angeles, fought for ethnic studies, equal opportunity programs, high potential programs at UCLA, and for students doing community work in "Serve the People" programs. In the community, we had, besides [Asian American] Hard Core, four area youth-oriented groups working against drugs (on the Westside, Eastside, Gardena, and the Virgil district). There were also parents' groups, which worked with parents of the youth and more.[10]

In Asian American communities in Los Angeles, San Francisco, Sacramento, Stockton, San Jose, Seattle, New York, and Honolulu, activists created "serve the people" organizations—mass networks built on the principles of "mass line" organizing. Youth initiated many of these organizations—some from college campuses and others from high schools and the streets—but other members of the community, including small-business people, workers, senior citizens, and new immigrants, soon joined.

The *mass* character of community struggles is the least appreciated aspect of our movement today. It is commonly believed that the movement involved only college students. In fact, a range of people, including high-school youth, tenants, small-business people, former prison inmates, former addicts, the elderly, and workers, embraced the struggles. But exactly who were these people, and what did their participation mean to the movement?

Historian George Lipsitz has studied similar, largely "anonymous" participants in civil rights campaigns in African American communities. He describes one such man, Ivory Perry of St. Louis:

> Ivory Perry led no important organizations, delivered no important speeches, and received no significant recognition or reward for his social activism. But for more than 30 years he had passed out leaflets, carried the picket signs, and planned the flamboyant confrontations that made the civil rights movements effective in St. Louis and across the nation. His continuous commitment at the local level had goaded others into action, kept alive hopes of eventual victory in the face of short-term defeats, and provided a relatively powerless community with an effective lever for social change. The anonymity of his activism suggests layers of social protest activity missing from most scholarly accounts, while the persistence of his involvement undermines prevailing academic judgments about mass protests as outbursts of immediate anger and spasmodic manifestations of hysteria.[11]

Those active in Asian American communities during the late 1960s and early 1970s know there were many Ivory Perrys. They were the people who demonstrated at eviction sites, packed City Hall hearing rooms, volunteered to staff health fairs, and helped with day-to-day operations of the first community drop-in centers, legal defense offices, and senior citizen projects. They were the women and men who took the concept of "serve the people" and turned it into a material force, transforming the political face of our communities.

The "Cultural Revolution" in Asian American Communities

But we would be wrong to describe this transformation of our communities as solely "political"—at least as our society narrowly defines the term today. The transformation also involved a cultural vitality that opened new ways of viewing the world. Unlike today—where Asian American communities categorize "culture" and "politics" into different spheres of professional activity—in the late 1960s they did not divide them so rigidly or hierarchically. Writers, artists, and musicians were "cultural workers" usually closely associated with communities, and saw their work as "serving the people." Like other community activists, cultural workers defined the period as a "decisive moment" for Asian Americans—a time for reclaiming the past and changing the future.

The "decisive moment" was also a time for questioning and transforming moral values. Through their political and cultural work, activists challenged systems of rank and privilege, structures of hierarchy and bureaucracy, forms of exploitation and inequality, and notions of selfishness and individualism. Through their activism in mass organizations, they promoted a new moral vision centered on democratic participation, cooperative work styles, and collective decision making. Pioneer poet Russell C. Leong describes the affinity between this new generation of cultural workers and their communities, focusing on the work of the Asian American Writers' Workshop, located in the basement of the International Hotel in San Francisco Chinatown/Manilatown:

> We were a post–World War II generation mostly in our twenties and thirties; in or out of local schools and colleges . . . [We] gravitated toward cities—San Francisco, Los Angeles, New York—where movements for ethnic studies and inner city blocks of Asian communities coincided. . . . We read as we wrote—not in isolation—but in the company of our neighbors in Manilatown pool halls, barrio parks, Chinatown basements. . . . Above all, we poets were a tribe of storytellers. . . . Storytellers live in communities where they write for family and friends. The relationship between the teller and listener is neighborly, because the teller of stories must also listen.[12]

But as storytellers, cultural workers did more than simply describe events around them. By witnessing and participating in the movement, they helped to shape community consciousness. San Francisco poet Al Robles focuses on this process of vision making:

> While living and working in our little, tiny communities, in the midst of towering highrises, we fought the oppressor, the landlord, the developer, the banks, City Hall. But most of all, we celebrated through our culture; music, dance, song and poetry—not only the best we knew but the best we had. The poets were and always have been

an integral part of the community. It was through poetry—through a poetical vision to live out the ritual in dignity as human beings.[13]

The transformation of poets, writers, and artists into cultural workers and vision makers reflected larger changes occurring in every sector of the Asian American community. In education, teachers and students redefined the learning process, discovering new ways of sharing knowledge different from traditional, authoritarian, top-down approaches. In the social service sector, social workers and other professionals became "community workers" and under the slogan of "serve the people" redefined the traditional counselor/client relationship by stressing interaction, dialogue, and community building. Within community organizations, members experimented with new organizational structures and collective leadership styles, discarding hierarchical and bureaucratic forms where a handful of commanders made all the decisions. Everywhere, activists and ordinary people grappled with change.

Overall, this "cultural revolution" in the Asian American community echoes themes we have encountered earlier: Third World consciousness, participatory democracy, community building, historical rooting, liberation, and transformation. Why were these concepts so important to a generation of activists? What did they mean? And do they still have relevance for Asian American communities today?

Political analyst Raymond Williams and historian Warren Susman have suggested the use of "keywords" to study historical periods, especially times of great social change.[14] Keywords are terms, concepts, and ideas that emerge as themes of a period, reflecting vital concerns and changing values. For Asian Americans in the 1980s and 1990s, the keywords are "advocacy," "access," "legitimacy," "empowerment," and "assertiveness." These keywords tell us much about the shape of our community today, especially the growing role of young professionals and their aspirations in U.S. society. In contrast, the keywords of the late 1960s and early 1970s—"consciousness," "theory," "ideology," "participatory democracy," "community," and "liberation"—point to different concerns and values.

The keywords of two decades ago point to an approach to political work that activists widely shared, especially those working in grassroots struggles in Asian American neighborhoods, such as the Chinatowns, Little Tokyos, Manilatowns, and International Districts around the nation. This political approach focused on the relationship between political consciousness and social change and can be best summarized in a popular slogan of the period: "Theory becomes a material force when it is grasped by the masses." Asian American activists believed that they could promote political change through direct action and mass education that raised political consciousness in the community, especially among the unorganized—low-income workers, tenants, small-business people, high school youth, etc. Thus, activists saw political consciousness as rising not from study groups but from involving people in the process of social change—through their confronting the institutions of power around them and creating new visions of community life based on these struggles.

Generally, academics studying the movements of the 1960s—including academics in Asian American Studies—have dismissed the political theory of that time as murky and eclectic, characterized by ultra-leftism, shallow class analysis, and simplistic notions of Marxism and capitalism.[15] To a large extent, the thinking was eclectic; Asian American activists drew from Marx, Lenin, Stalin, and Mao—and also from Frantz Fanon, Malcolm X, Che Guevara, Kim Il-sung, and Amilcar Cabral, as well as Korean revolutionary Kim San, W. E. B. DuBois, Frederick Douglass, Paulo Freire, the Black Panther Party, the Young Lords, the women's liberation movement, and many other resistance struggles. But in their obsessive search for theoretical clarity and consistency, these academics miss the bigger picture. What is significant is not the *content* of ideas activists adopted but what activists *did* with the ideas. What Asian American activists *did* was to use the ideas drawn from many different movements to redefine the Asian American experience.

Central to this redefinition was a slogan that appeared at nearly every Asian American rally during that period: "The people, and the people alone, are the motive force in the making of world history." Originating in the Chinese revolution, Asian American activists adapted the slogan to the tasks of community building, historical rooting, and creating new values. Thus, the slogan came to capture six new ways of thinking about Asian Americans.

- Asian Americans became active participants in the making of history, reversing standard accounts that had treated Asian Americans as marginal objects.
- Activists saw history as created by large numbers of people acting together, not by elites.
- This view of history provided a new way of looking at our communities. Activists believed that ordinary people could make their own history by learning how historical forces operated and by transforming this knowledge into a material force to change their lives.
- This realization defined a political strategy: political power came from grassroots organizing, from the bottom up.
- This strategy required activists to develop a broad analysis of the Asian American condition—to uncover the interconnections in seemingly separate events, such as the war in Indochina, corporate redevelopment of Asian American communities, and the exploitation of Asian immigrants in garment shops. In their political analyses, activists linked the day-to-day struggles of Asian Americans to larger events and issues. The anti-eviction campaign of tenants in Chinatown and the International District against powerful corporations became one with the resistance movements of peasants in Vietnam, the Philippines, and Latin America—or, as summarized in a popular slogan of the period, there was "one struggle, [but] many fronts."
- This new understanding challenged activists to build mass, democratic organizations, especially within unorganized sectors of the community. Through these new organizations, Asian Americans expanded democracy for all sectors of the community and gained the power to participate in the broader movement for political change taking place throughout the world.

The redefinition of the Asian American experience stands as the most important legacy from this period. As described above, this legacy represents far more than an ethnic awakening. The redefinition began with an analysis of power and domination in American society. It provided a way for understanding the historical forces surrounding us. And, most importantly, it presented a strategy and challenge for changing our future. This challenge, I believe, still confronts us today.

The Late 1970s: Reversing Direction

As we continue to delve into the vitality of the movements of the 1960s, one question becomes more and more persistent: Why did these movements, possessing so much vigor and urgency, seem to disintegrate in the late 1970s and early 1980s? Why did a society in motion toward progressive change seem to suddenly reverse direction?

As in the larger left movement, Asian American activists heatedly debate this question.[16] Some mention the strategy of repression—including assassinations—U.S. ruling circles launched in response to the mass rebellions. Others cite the accompanying programs of cooptation that elites designed to channel mass discontent into traditional political arenas. Some focus on the New Right's rise, culminating in the Reagan presidency. Still others emphasize the sectarianism among political forces within the movement or target the inability of the movement as a whole to base itself more broadly within communities.

Each of these analyses provides a partial answer. But missing in most analyses by Asian American activists is the most critical factor: the devastating corporate offensive of the mid-1970s. We will remember the 1970s as a time of economic crisis and staggering inflation. Eventually, historians may more accurately describe it as the years of "one-sided class war." Transnational corporations based in the United States launched a broad attack on the American people, especially African American communities. Several books provide an excellent analysis of the corporate offensive. One of the best, most accessible accounts is *What's Wrong with the U.S. Economy?*, written in 1982 by the Institute for Labor Education and Research.[17] My analysis draws from that.

Corporate executives based their offensive on two conclusions: First, the economic crisis in the early 1970s—marked by declining corporate profits—occurred because American working people were earning too much; and second, the mass struggles of the previous decades had created "too much democracy" in America. The Trilateral Commission—headed by David Rockefeller and composed of corporate executives and politicians from the United States, Europe, and Japan—posed the problem starkly: Either people would have to accept less, or corporations would have to accept less. An article in *Business Week* identified the solution: "Some people will obviously have to do with less. . . . Yet it will be a hard pill for many Americans to swallow—the idea of doing with less so that big business can have more."

But in order for corporations to "have more," U.S. ruling circles had to deal with the widespread discontent that had erupted throughout America. We sometimes forget today that in the mid-1970s a large number of Americans had grown cynical about U.S. business and political leaders. People routinely called politicians—including President Nixon and Vice President Agnew—crooks, liars, and criminals. Increasingly, they began to blame the largest corporations for their economic problems. One poll showed that half the population believed that "big business is the source of most of what's wrong in this country today." A series of Harris polls found that those expressing "a great deal of confidence" in the heads of corporations had fallen from 55 percent in 1966 to only 15 percent in 1975. By the fall of 1975, public opinion analysts testifying before a congressional committee reported, according to the *New York Times,* "that public confidence in the government and in the country's economic future is probably lower than it has ever been since they began to measure such things scientifically." These developments stunned many corporate leaders. "How did we let the educational system fail the free enterprise system?" one executive asked.

U.S. ruling elites realized that restoring faith in free enterprise could only be achieved through an intensive ideological assault on those challenging the system. The ideological campaign was combined with a political offensive, aimed at the broad gains in democratic rights that Americans, especially African Americans, had achieved through the mass struggles of previous decades. According to corporate leaders, there was "too much democracy" in America, which meant too little "governability." In a 1975 Trilateral Commission report, Harvard political scientist Samuel Huntington analyzed the problem caused by "previously passive or unorganized groups in the population [which were] now engaged in concerted efforts to establish their claims to opportunities, positions, rewards, and privileges which they had not considered themselves entitled to before." According to Huntington, this upsurge in "democratic fervor" coincided with "markedly higher levels of self-consciousness on the part of blacks, Indians, Chicanos, white ethnic groups, students, and women, all of whom became mobilized and organized in new ways." Huntington saw these developments as creating a crisis for those in power:

> The essence of the democratic surge of the 1960s was a general challenge to existing systems of authority, public and private. In one form or another, the challenge manifested itself in the family, the university, business, public and private associations, politics, the government bureaucracy, and the military service. People no longer felt the same obligation to obey those whom they had previously considered superior to themselves in age, rank, status, expertise, character, or talents.[18]

The mass pressures, Huntington contended, had "produced problems for the governability of democracy in the 1970s." The government, he concluded, must find a way to exercise more control. And that meant curtailing the rights of "major economic groups."

The ensuing corporate campaign was a "one-sided class war": plant closures in U.S. industries and transfer of production overseas, massive layoffs in remaining industries, shifts of capital investment from one region of the country to other regions and other parts of the globe, and demands by corporations for concessions in wages and benefits from workers in nearly every sector of the economy.

The Reagan presidency culminated and institutionalized this offensive. The Reagan platform called for restoring "traditional" American values, especially faith in the system of free enterprise. Reaganomics promoted economic recovery by getting government "off the backs" of business people, reducing taxation of the rich, and cutting social programs for the poor. Meanwhile, racism and exploitation became respectable under the new mantle of patriotism and economic recovery.

The Winter of Civil Rights

The corporate assault ravaged many American neighborhoods, but African American communities absorbed its harshest impact. A study by the Center on Budget and Policy Priorities measures the national impact:

- Between 1970 and 1980, the number of poor African Americans rose by 24 percent, from 1.4 million to 1.8 million.
- In the 1980s, the overall African American median income was 57 percent that of whites, a decline of nearly four percentage points from the early 1970s.
- In 1986, females headed 42 percent of all African American families, the majority of which lived below the poverty line.
- In 1978, 8.4 percent of African American families had incomes under $5,000 a year. By 1987, that figure had grown to 13.5 percent. In that year, a third of all African Americans were poor.[19]
- By 1990, nearly half of all African American children grew up in poverty.[20]

Manning Marable provides a stark assessment of this devastation in *How Capitalism Underdeveloped Black America*:

What is qualitatively *new* about the current period is that the racist/capitalist state under Reagan has proceeded down a public policy road which could inevitably involve the complete obliteration of the entire Black reserve army of labor and sections of the Black working class. The decision to save capitalism at all costs, to provide adequate capital for restructuring of the private sector, fundamentally conflicts with the survival of millions of people who are now permanently outside the workplace. Reaganomics must, if it intends to succeed, place the onerous burden of unemployment on the shoulders of the poor (Blacks, Latinos and even whites) so securely that middle to upper income Americans will not protest in the vicious suppression of this stratum.[21]

The corporate offensive, combined with widespread government repression, brutally destroyed grassroots groups in the African American community. This war against the poor ripped apart the social fabric of neighborhoods across America, leaving them vulnerable to drugs and gang violence. The inner cities became the home of the "underclass" and a new politics of inner-directed violence and despair.

Historian Vincent Harding, in *The Other American Revolution*, summarizes the 1970s as the "winter" of civil rights, a period in which there was "a dangerous loss of hope among black people, hope in ourselves, hope in the possibility of any real change, hope in any moral, creative force beyond the flatness of our lives."[22]

In summary, the corporate offensive—especially its devastation of the African American community—provides the necessary backdrop for understanding why the mass movements of the 1960s seemed to disintegrate. Liberation movements, especially in the African American community, did not disappear, but a major focus of their activity shifted to issues of day-to-day survival.

The 1980s: An Ambiguous Period for Asian American Empowerment

For African Americans and many other people of color, the period from the mid-1970s through the Reagan and Bush presidencies became a winter of civil rights, a time of corporate assault on their livelihoods and an erosion of hard-won rights. But for Asian Americans, the meaning of this period is much more ambiguous. On the one hand, great suffering marked the period: growing poverty for increasing numbers of Asian Americans—especially refugees from Southeast Asia; a rising trend of racist hate crimes directed toward Asian Americans of all ethnicities and income levels; and sharpening class polarization within our communities—with a widening gap between the very rich and the very poor. But advances also characterized the period. With the reform of U.S. immigration laws in 1965, the Asian American population grew dramatically, creating new enclaves—including suburban settlements—and revitalizing more established communities, such as Chinatowns, around the nation. Some recent immigrant businesspeople, with small capital holdings, found economic opportunities in inner-city neighborhoods. Meanwhile, Asian American youth enrolled in record numbers in colleges and universities across the United States. Asian American families moved into suburbs, crashing previously lily-white neighborhoods. And a small but significant group of Asian American politicians, such as Mike Woo and Warren Furutani, scored important electoral victories in the mainstream political arena, taking the concept of political empowerment to a new level of achievement.

During the winter of civil rights, Asian American activists also launched several impressive political campaigns at the grassroots level. Japanese Americans joined together to win redress and reparations. Pilipino Americans rallied in solidarity with the "People's Power" movement in the Philippines to topple the powerful Marcos dictatorship. Chinese Americans created new political alignments and mobilized community support for the pro-democracy struggle in China. Korean Americans responded to the massacre of civilians by the South Korean dictatorship in Kwangju with massive demonstrations and relief efforts and established an important network of organizations in America, including Young Koreans United. Samoan Americans rose up against police abuse in Los Angeles; Pacific Islanders demanded removal of nuclear weapons and wastes from their homelands; and Hawaiians fought for the right of self-determination and recovery of their lands. And large numbers of Asian Americans and Pacific Islanders worked actively in the 1984 and 1988 presidential campaigns of Jesse Jackson, helping to build the Rainbow Coalition.

Significantly, these accomplishments occurred in the midst of the Reagan presidency and U.S. politics' turn to the right. How did certain sectors of the Asian American community achieve these gains amidst conservatism?

There is no simple answer. Mainstream analysts and some Asian Americans have stressed the "model minority" concept. According to this analysis, Asian Americans—

in contrast to other people of color in America—have survived adversity and advanced because of their emphasis on education and family values, their community cohesion, and other aspects of their cultural heritage. Other scholars have severely criticized this viewpoint, stressing instead structural changes in the global economy and shifts in U.S. government policy since the 1960s. According to their analysis, the reform of U.S. immigration laws and sweeping economic changes in advanced capitalist nations, such as deindustrialization and the development of new technologies, brought an influx of highly educated new Asian immigrants to America. The characteristics of these new immigrants stand in sharp contrast to those of past generations and provide a broader social and economic base for developing our communities. Still other political thinkers have emphasized the key role played by political expatriates— both right-wing and left-wing—in various communities, but most especially in the Vietnamese, Pilipino, and Korean communities. These expatriates brought political resources from their homelands—e.g., political networks, organizing experience, and, in a few cases, access to large amounts of funds—and have used these resources to change the political landscape of ethnic enclaves. Still other analysts have examined the growing economic and political power of nations of the Asia Pacific and its impact on Asians in America. According to these analysts, we can link the advances of Asian Americans during this period to the rising influence of their former homelands and the dawning of what some call "the Pacific Century." Finally, some academics have focused on the significance of small-business activities of new Asian immigrants, arguing that this sector is most responsible for the changing status of Asian Americans in the 1980s. According to their analysis, Asian immigrant entrepreneurs secured an economic niche in inner-city neighborhoods because they had access to start-up capital (through rotating credit associations or from family members) and they filled a vacuum created when white businesses fled.[23]

Thus, we have multiple interpretations for why some sectors of the Asian American community advanced economically and politically during the winter of civil rights. But two critical factors are missing from the analyses that can help us better understand the peculiar shape of our community in the 1980s and its ambiguous character when compared to other communities of color. First is the legacy of grassroots organizing from the Asian American movement, and second is the dramatic rise of young professionals as a significant force in the community.

A stereotype about the movements of the 1960s is that they produced nothing enduring—they flared brightly for an instant and then quickly died. However, evidence from the Asian American movement contradicts this commonly held belief. Through meticulous organizing campaigns, Asian American activists created an extensive network of grassroots formations. Unlike similar groups in African American communities—which government repression targeted and brutally destroyed—a significant number of Asian American groups survived the 1980s. Thus far, no researcher has analyzed the impact of the corporate offensive and government repression on grassroots organizations in different communities of color during the late 1970s. When this research is done, I think it will show that U.S. ruling elites viewed the movement in the African American community as a major threat due to its power and influence over other communities. In contrast, the movement in the Asian American community received much less attention due to its much smaller size and influence. As a result, Asian American grassroots formations during the 1970s escaped decimation and gained the time and space to survive, grow, and adapt to changing politics.

The survival of grassroots organizations is significant because it helped to cushion the impact of the war against the poor in Asian American communities. More important, the grassroots formations provided the foundation for many of the successful empowerment campaigns occurring in the 1980s. For example, Japanese Americans built their national effort to win reparations for their internment during World War II on the experiences of grassroots neighborhood organizations' housing and anti-eviction struggles of the early 1970s. Movement activists learned from their confrontations with systems of power and applied these lessons to the more difficult political fights of the 1980s. Thus, a direct link exists between the mass struggles of activists in the late 1960s and the "empowerment" approach of Asian Americans in the 1980s and 1990s.

But while similarities exist in political organizing of the late 1960s and the 1980s, there is one crucial difference: Who is being empowered? In the late 1960s and 1970s, activists focused on bringing "power to the people"—the most disenfranchised of the community, such as low-income workers, youth, former prisoners and addicts, senior citizens, tenants, and small-business people. In contrast, the "empowerment" of young professionals in Asian American communities marks the decade of the 1980s. The professionals—children of the civil rights struggles of the 1950s and 1960s—directly benefited from the campaigns for desegregation, especially in the suburbs; the removal of quotas in colleges and professional schools; and the expansion of job opportunities for middle-class people of color in fields such as law, medicine, and education.

During the 1980s, young professionals altered the political terrain in our communities.[24] They created countless new groups in nearly every profession: law, medicine, social work, psychology, education, journalism, business, and arts and culture. They initiated new political advocacy groups, leadership training projects, and various national coalitions and consortiums. They organized political caucuses in the Democratic and Republican parties. And they joined the governing boards of many community agencies. Thus, young professionals—through their sheer numbers, their penchant for self-organization, and their high level of activity—defined the Asian American community of the 1980s, shaping it in ways very different from other communities of color.

The emergence of young professionals as community leaders also aided mass political mobilizations. By combining with grassroots forces from the Asian American movement, young professionals advanced struggles against racism and discrimination. In fact, many of the successful Asian American battles of the past decade resulted from this strategic alignment.

The growing power of young professionals has also brought a diversification of political viewpoints to our communities. While many professionals embrace concerns originally raised by movement activists, a surprisingly large number have moved toward neoconservatism. The emergence of neoconservatism in our community is a fascinating phenomenon, one we should analyze and appreciate. Perhaps more than any other phenomenon, it helps to explain the political ambiguity of Asian American empowerment in the decade of the 1980s.

Strange and New Political Animals: Asian American Neoconservatives

Item: At many universities in recent years, some of the harshest opponents of affirmative action have been Chinese Americans and Korean Americans who define themselves as political conservatives. This, in and of itself, is not new or significant. We have always had Asian American conservatives who have spoken out against affirmative action. But what is new is their affiliation. Many participate actively in Asian American student organizations traditionally associated with campus activism.

Item: In the San Francisco newspaper *Asian Week*, one of the most interesting columnists is Arthur Hu, who writes about anti-Asian quotas in universities, political empowerment, and other issues relating to our communities. He also regularly chastises those he terms "liberals, progressives, Marxists, and activists." In a recent column, he wrote: "The left today has the nerve to blame AIDS, drugs, the dissolution of the family, welfare dependency, gang violence, and educational failure on Ronald Reagan's conservatism." Hu, in turn, criticizes the left for "tearing down religion, family, structure, and authority; promoting drugs, promiscuity, and abdication of personal responsibility."[25]

Item: During the militant, three-year campaign to win tenure for UCLA Professor Don Nakanishi, one of the key student leaders was a Japanese American Republican, Matthew J. Endo. Aside from joining the campus-community steering committee, he also mobilized support from fraternities, something that progressive activists could not do. Matt prides himself on being a Republican and a life member of the National Rifle Association. He aspires to become a CEO in a corporation but worries about the upsurge in racism against Asian Pacific peoples and the failure of both Republicans and Democrats to address this issue.

The Asian American neoconservatives are a new and interesting political phenomenon. They are new because they are creatures born from the Reagan-Bush era of supply-side economics, class and racial polarization, and the emphasis on elitism and individual advancement. And they are interesting because they also represent a legacy from the civil rights struggles, especially the Asian American movement. The neoconservatives embody these seemingly contradictory origins.

- They are proud to be Asian American. But they denounce the Asian American movement of the late 1960s and early 1970s as destructive.
- They speak out against racism against Asian Americans. But they believe that only by ending affirmative-action programs and breaking with prevailing civil rights thinking of the past four decades can we end racism.
- They express concern for Asian American community issues. But they contend that the agenda set by the "liberal Asian American establishment" ignores community needs.
- They vehemently oppose quotas blocking admissions of Asian Americans at colleges and universities. But they link anti-Asian quotas to affirmative-actions programs for "less qualified" African Americans, Latinos, and American Indians.
- They acknowledge the continuing discrimination against African Americans,

Latinos, and American Indians in U.S. society. But they believe that the main barrier blocking advancement for other people of color is "cultural"—that, unlike Asians, these groups supposedly come from cultures that do not sufficiently emphasize education, family cohesion, and traditional values.

Where did these neoconservatives come from? What do they represent? And why is it important for progressive peoples to understand their presence?

Progressives cannot dismiss Asian American neoconservatives as simple-minded Republicans. Although they hold views similar at times to Patrick Buchanan and William Buckley, they are not clones of white conservatives. Nor are they racists, fellow travelers of the Ku Klux Klan, or ideologues attached to Reagan and Bush. Perhaps the group that they most resemble are the African American neoconservatives: the Shelby Steeles, Clarence Thomases, and Tony Browns of this period. Like these men, they are professionals and feel little kinship for people of lower classes. Like these men, they oppose prevailing civil rights thinking, emphasizing reliance on government intervention and social programs. And, like these men, they have gained from affirmative action, but they now believe that America has somehow become a society where other people of color can advance through their own "qualifications."

Neoconservative people of color have embraced thinkers such as the late Martin Luther King, Jr., but have appropriated his message to fit their own ideology. In his speeches and writings, King dreamed of the day when racism would be eliminated—when African Americans would be recognized in U.S. society for the "content of our character, not the color of our skin." He called upon all in America to wage militant struggle to achieve this dream. Today, neoconservatives have subverted his message. They believe that racism in U.S. society has declined in significance and that people of color can now abandon mass militancy and advance individually by cultivating the content of their character through self-help programs and educational attainment and retrieving traditional family values. They criticize prevailing "civil rights thinking" as overemphasizing the barriers of racism and relying on "external forces" (i.e., government intervention through social programs) to address the problem.

Asian American neoconservatives closely resemble their African American counterparts in their criticism of government "entitlement" programs and their defense of traditional culture and family values. But Asian American neoconservatives are not exactly the same as their African American counterparts. The growth of neoconservative thinking among Asian Americans during the past twenty-five years reflects the peculiar conditions in our community, notably the emerging power of young professionals. Thus, to truly understand Asian American neoconservatives, we need to look at their evolution through the prism of Asian American politics from the late 1960s to the early 1990s.

Twenty-five years ago, Asian American neoconservatives did not exist. Our community then had only traditional conservatives—those who opposed ethnic studies, the antiwar movement, and other militant grassroots struggles. The traditional conservatives denounced Asian American concerns as "special interest politics" and labeled the assertion of Asian American ethnic identity as "separatist" thinking. For the traditional conservative, a basic contradiction existed in identifying oneself as Asian American and conservative.

Ironically, the liberation struggles of the 1960s—and the accompanying Asian American movement—spawned a new conservative thinker. The movement partially transformed the educational curriculum through ethnic studies, enabling all Asian Americans to assert pride in their ethnic heritage. The movement accelerated the desegregation of suburbs, enabling middle class Asian Americans to move into all-white neighborhoods. Today, the neoconservatives are mostly young, middle class professionals who grew up in white suburbs apart from the poor and people of color. As students, they attended the elite universities. Their only experience with racism is name-calling or "glass ceilings" blocking personal career advancement—and not poverty and violence.

It is due to their professional status and their roots in the Asian American movement that the neoconservatives exist in uneasy alliance with traditional conservatives in our community. Neoconservatives are appalled by the violence and rabid anticommunism of reactionary sectors of the Vietnamese community, Chinese from Taiwan tied to the oppressive ruling Kuomintang party, and Korean expatriates attached to the Korean Central Intelligence Agency. They are also uncomfortable with older conservatives, those coming from small-business backgrounds who warily eye the neoconservatives, considering them as political opportunists.

Neoconservatives differ from traditional conservatives not only because of their youth and their professional status but, most important of all, their political coming of age in the Reagan era. Like their African American counterparts, they are children of the corporate offensive against workers, the massive transfer of resources from the poor to the rich, and the rebirth of so-called traditional values.

It is their schooling in Reaganomics and their willingness to defend the current structure of power and privilege in America that gives neoconservative people of color value in today's political landscape. Thus, Manning Marable describes the key role played by African American neoconservatives:

> The singular service that [they] . . . provide is a new and more accurate understanding of what exactly constitutes conservatism within the Black experience . . . Black conservatives are traditionally hostile to Black participation in trade unions, and urge a close cooperation with white business leaders. Hostile to the welfare state, they call for increased "self-help" programs run by Blacks at local and community levels. Conservatives often accept the institutionalized forms of patriarchy, acknowledging a secondary role for Black women within economics, political life, and intellectual work. They usually have a pronounced bias towards organizational authoritarianism and theoretical rigidity.[26]

Marable's analysis points to the basic contradiction for African American neoconservatives. They are unable to address fundamental problems facing their community: racist violence, grinding poverty, and the unwillingness of corporate and government policymakers to deal with these issues.

Asian American neoconservatives face similar difficulties when confronted by the stark realities of the post-Reagan period:

- The neoconservatives acknowledge continuing discrimination in U.S. society but deny the existence of institutional racism and structural inequality. For them, racism lies in the realm of attitudes and "culture" and not institutions of power. Thus, they emphasize individual advancement as the way to overcome racism. They believe that people of color can rise through merit, which they contend can be measured objectively through tests, grades, and educational attainment.
- The neoconservatives ignore questions of wealth and privilege in American society. In their obsession with "merit," "qualifications," and "objective" criteria, they lose sight of power and oppression in America. Their focus is on dismantling affirmative-action programs and "government entitlements" from the civil rights era. But poverty and racism existed long before the civil rights movement. They are embedded in the system of inequality that has long characterized U.S. society.
- The neoconservatives are essentially elitists who fear expansion of democracy at the grassroots level. They speak a language of individual advancement, not mass empowerment. They propose a strategy of alignment with existing centers of power and not the creation of new power bases among the disenfranchised sectors of society. Their message is directed to professionals much like themselves. They have nothing to offer to immigrant workers in sweatshops, the homeless, Cambodian youth in street gangs, or community college youth.
- As relative newcomers to Asian American issues, the neoconservatives lack understanding of history, especially how concerns in the community have developed over time. Although they aggressively speak out about issues, they lack experience in organizing around these issues. The neoconservatives function best in the realm of ideas; they have difficulty dealing with concrete situations.

However, by stimulating discussion over how Asian American define community problems, the neoconservatives bring a vibrancy to community issues by contributing a different viewpoint. Thus, the debate between Asian American neoconservatives and progressives is positive because it clarifies issues and enables both groups to reach constituencies that each could not otherwise reach.

Unfortunately, this debate is also occurring in a larger and more dangerous context: the campaign by mainstream conservatives to redefine civil rights in America. As part of their strategy, conservatives in the national political arena have targeted our communities. There are high stakes here, and conservatives regard the Asian American neoconservatives as small players to be sacrificed.

The high stakes are evident in an article by William McGurn entitled "The Silent Minority," appearing in the conservative digest *National Review*.[27] In his essay, he urges Republicans to actively recruit and incorporate Asian Americans into party activities. According to McGurn, a basic affinity exists between Republican values and Asian American values: Many Asian immigrants own small businesses; they oppose

communism; they are fiercely pro-defense; they boast strong families; they value freedom; and in their approach to civil rights, they stress opportunities, not government
"set-asides." McGurn then chastises fellow Republicans for their "crushing indiffer-
ence" to Asian American issues. He laments how Republicans have lost opportunities
by not speaking out on key issues such as the conflict between Korean immigrant
merchants and African Americans, the controversy over anti-Asian quotas in universities, and the upsurge in anti-Asian violence.

McGurn sees Republican intervention on these issues strategically—as a way of redefining the race question in American society and shifting the debate on civil rights
away from reliance on "an increasingly narrow band of black and liberal interest
groups." According to McGurn:

> Precisely because Asian Americans are making it in their adoptive land, they hold the
> potential not only to add to Republican rolls but to define a bona-fide American lan-
> guage of civil rights. Today we have only one language of civil rights, and it is inextri-
> cably linked to government intervention, from racial quotas to setaside government
> contracts. It is also an exclusively black-establishment language, where America's myr-
> iad other minorities are relegated to second-class citizenship.[28]

McGurn's article presages a period of intense and unprecedented conservative interest in Asian American issues. We can expect conservative commentaries to intensify
black-Asian conflicts in inner cities, the controversy over affirmative action, and the
internal community debate over designating Asian Americans as a "model minority."

Thus, in the coming period, Asian American communities are likely to become
crowded places. Unlike the late 1960s, issues affecting our communities will no longer
be the domain of progressive forces only. Increasingly, we will hear viewpoints from
Asian American neoconservatives as well as mainstream conservatives. How well will
activists meet this new challenge?

Grassroots Organizing in the 1990s: The Challenge of Expanding Democracy

> Time would pass, old empires would fall and new ones take their place, the relations of
> countries and the relations of classes had to change, before I discovered that it is not
> quality of goods and utility which matter, but movement; not where you are or what
> you have but where you have come from, where you are going and the rate at which
> you are getting there.[29]
>
> —C. L. R. James

On the eve of the twenty-first century, the Asian American community is vastly different from that of the late 1960s. The community has grown dramatically. In 1970, there
were only 1.5 million Asian Americans, almost entirely concentrated in Hawaii and
California. By 1980, there were 3.7 million, and in 1990, 7.9 million—with major Asian
communities in New York, Minnesota, Pennsylvania, and Texas. According to census

projections, the Asian American population should exceed 10 million by the year 2000 and will reach 20 million by the year 2020.[30]

Moreover, in contrast to the late 1960s—when Chinese and Japanese Americans composed the majority of Asian Americans—today's community is ethnically diverse —consisting of nearly thirty major ethnic groups, each with a distinct culture. Today's community is also economically different from the 1960s. Compared to other sectors of the U.S. population, there are higher proportions of Asian Americans who are very rich and very poor. This gap between wealth and poverty has created a sharp class polarization in our community, a phenomenon yet to be studied.

But the changes for Asian Americans during the past twenty-five years have not been simply demographic. The political landscape has also changed due to new immigrants and refugees, the polarization between rich and poor, and the emergence of young professionals as a vital new force. Following the approach of C. L. R. James, we have traced the origins of these changes. We now need to analyze where these changes will take us in the decade ahead.

Ideologically and politically, activists confront a new and interesting paradox in the Asian American community of the 1990s. On the one hand, there is a great upsurge of interest in the community and all things Asian American. Almost daily, we hear about new groups forming across the country. In contrast to twenty-five years ago, when interest in the community was minimal and when only progressive activists joined Asian American organizations, we now find a situation where many different groups—including conservatives and neoconservatives, bankers and business executives, and young professionals in all fields—have taken up the banner of Asian American identity.

On the other hand, we have not seen a corresponding growth in consciousness—of what it means to be Asian American as we approach the twenty-first century. Unlike African Americans, most Asian Americans today have yet to articulate the "particularities" of issues affecting our community, whether these be the debate over affirmative action, the controversy regarding multiculturalism, or the very definition of empowerment. We have an ideological vacuum, and activists will compete with neoconservatives, mainstream conservatives, and others to fill it.

We have a political vacuum as well. In recent years, growing numbers of Asian Americans have become involved in community issues. But almost all have come from middle-class and professional backgrounds. Meanwhile, vast segments of our community are not coming forward. In fact, during the past decade the fundamental weakness for activists has been the lack of grassroots organizing among the disenfranchised sectors of our community: youth outside of colleges and universities, the poor, and new immigrant workers. Twenty-five years ago, the greatest strength of the Asian American movement was the ability of activists to organize the unorganized and to bring new political players into community politics. Activists targeted high-school youth, tenants, small-business people, former prison inmates, gang members, the elderly, and workers. Activists helped them build new grassroots organizations, expanding power and democracy in our communities. Can a new generation of activists do the same?

To respond to this challenge, activists will need both a political strategy and a new ideological vision. Politically, activists must find ways to expand democracy by creating new grassroots formations, activating new political players, and building new coalitions. Ideologically, activists must forge a new moral vision, reclaiming the militancy and moral urgency of past generations and reaffirming the commitment to participatory democracy, community building, and collective styles of leadership.

Where will this political strategy and new consciousness come from? More than fifty years ago, revolutionary leader Mao Zedong, asked a similar question.

> Where do correct ideas come from? Do they drop from the skies? No. Are they innate in the mind? No. They come from social practice, and from it alone. . . . In their social practice, people engage in various kinds of struggle and gain rich experience, both from their successes and their failures.[31]

In the current "social practice" of Asian American activists across the nation, several grassroots organizing projects can serve as the basis for a political strategy and new moral vision for the 1990s. I will focus on three projects that are concentrating on the growing numbers of poor and working poor in our community. Through their grassroots efforts, these three groups are demonstrating how collective power can expand democracy, and how, in the process, activists can forge a new moral vision.

The three groups—the Chinese Progressive Association (CPA) Workers Center in Boston, Asian Immigrant Women Advocates (AIWA) in Oakland, and Korean Immigrant Worker Advocates (KIWA) in Los Angeles—address local needs. Although each organization works with different ethnic groups, their history of organizing has remarkable similarities. Each organization is composed of low-income immigrant workers. Each has taken up more than "labor" issues. And each group has fashioned very effective "united front" campaigns involving other sectors of the community. Thus, although each project is relatively small, collectively their accomplishments illustrate the power of grassroots organizing, the creativity and talents of "ordinary" people in taking up difficult issues, and the ability of grassroots forces to alter the political landscape of their community. Significantly, the focus of each group is working people in the Asian American community—a sector that is numerically large and growing larger. However, despite their numbers, workers in the Asian American community during the past decade have become voiceless and silent. Today, in discussions about community issues, no one places garment workers, nurses' aides, waiters, and secretaries at the forefront of the debate to define priorities. And no one thinks about the working class as the cutting edge of the Asian American experience. Yet, if we begin to list the basic questions now confronting Asian Americans—racism and sexism, economic justice and human rights, coalition building, and community empowerment—we would find that it is the working class, of all sectors in our community, that is making the most interesting breakthroughs on these questions. They are doing this through groups such as KIWA, AIWA, and the CPA Workers Center. Why, then, are the voices of workers submerged in our community? Why has the working class become silent?

Three trends have pushed labor issues in our community into the background during the past two decades: the rising power of young professionals in our community; the influx of new immigrants and refugees and the fascination of social scientists and policy institutes with the phenomenon of immigrant entrepreneurship; and the lack of grassroots organizing by activists among new immigrant workers.

Thus, although the majority of Asian Americans work for a living, we have relatively little understanding about the central place of work in the lives of Asian Americans, especially in low-income industries such as garment work, restaurant work, clerical and office work, and other service occupations. Moreover, we are ignorant about the role that labor struggles have played in shaping our history.[32] This labor history is part of the legacy that activists must reclaim.

In contrast to the lack of knowledge about Asian American workers, we have a much greater understanding about the role of young professionals, students, and, most of all, small-business people. In fact, immigrant entrepreneurs, especially Korean immigrants, are perhaps the most studied people of our community. However, as sociologist Edna Bonacich notes, the profile of most Asian immigrant entrepreneurs closely resembles that of workers, due to their low earning power, their long work hours, and their lack of job-related benefits. Thus, Bonacich suggests that while the world outlook of Asian immigrant entrepreneurs may be petit bourgeoisie, their life conditions are those of the working class and might better be studied as a "labor" question. Asian immigrant small businesses, she contends, play the role of "cheap labor in American capitalism."[33]

Other researchers have only begun to investigate the extent of poverty among Asian Americans and the meaning of poverty for our community. In California, the rate of poverty for Asian Americans rose from about 10 percent in 1980 to 18 percent in 1990. But, more important, researchers found that there are higher numbers of "working poor" (as opposed to "jobless poor") in the Asian American community than for other ethnic groups. Thus, in contrast to other Americans, Asian Americans are poor not because they lack jobs but because the jobs they have pay very low wages. According to researchers Dean Toji and James Johnson, Jr., "Perhaps contrary to common belief, about half of the poor work—including about a quarter of poor adults who work full-time and year-round. Poverty, then, is a labor question."[34]

Activists in groups such as KIWA, AIWA, and the CPA Workers Center are strategically focusing on the "working poor" in the Asian American community. KIWA—which was founded in 1992—is working with low-income Korean immigrants in Los Angeles Koreatown, including garment workers and employees in small businesses. AIWA—founded in 1983—organizes Chinese garment workers, Vietnamese garment and electronics workers, and Korean hotel maids and electronics assemblers. And the CPA Workers Center—which traces its roots to the landmark struggle of Chinese garment workers in Boston in 1985—is composed primarily of Chinese immigrant women. Although their main focus is on workers, each group has also mobilized students and social service providers to support their campaigns. Through these alliances, each group has carried out successful community organizing strategies.

The focus of the three groups on community-based organizing distinguishes them from traditional unions. Miriam Ching Louie of AIWA explains this distinction:

AIWA's base is simultaneously worker, female, Asian, and immigrant, and the organization has developed by blending together several different organizing techniques. As
compared to the traditional union organizing strategy, AIWA's approach focuses on
the needs of its constituency. *Popular literacy/conscientization/transformation* [based
on the teachings of Paulo Freire] is a learning and teaching method which taps into
people's life experiences as part of a broader reality, source of knowledge, and guide to
action. *Community based organizing* takes a holistic view of racial/ethnic people and
organizes for social change, not only so that the people can win immediate improvements in their lives, but so that they can also develop their own power in the course of
waging the fight.[35]

AIWA's focus on grassroots organizing is illustrated by its "Garment Workers' Justice Campaign," launched in late 1992 to assist Chinese immigrant women who were
denied pay by a garment contractor. AIWA organizers shaped the campaign to respond to the peculiar features of the garment industry. The industry in the San Francisco Bay Area is the nation's third largest—following New York and Los Angeles—
and employs some twenty thousand seamstresses, 85 percent of them Asian immigrant
women. The structure of the industry is a pyramid with retailers and manufacturers at
the top, contractors in the middle, and immigrant women working at the bottom.
Manufacturers make the main share of profits in the industry; they set the price for
contractors. Meanwhile, immigrant women work under sweatshop conditions.

In their campaign, AIWA and the workers initially confronted the contractor for
the workers' back pay. When they discovered that the contractor owed a number of
creditors, they took the unusual step of holding the garment manufacturer, Jessica
McClintock, accountable for the unpaid wages. McClintock operates ten boutiques
and sells dresses through department stores. The dresses—which garment workers are
paid $5 to make—retail in stores for $175. AIWA and the workers conducted their
campaign through a series of high-profile demonstrations at McClintock boutiques,
including picket lines and rallies in ten cities by supporters. AIWA designed these
demonstrations not only to put pressure on McClintock and educate others in the
community about inequities in the structure of the garment industry but also to serve
as vehicles for empowerment for the immigrant women participating the campaign.
Through this campaign, the women workers learned how to confront institutional
power, how to forge alliances with other groups in the community, and how to carry
out effective tactics based on their collective power.[36]

Thus, through its activities promoting immigrant women's rights, AIWA is expanding democracy in the community. It is bringing labor issues to the forefront of community discussions. It is creating new grassroots caucuses among previously unorganized sectors of the community and forming new political alignments with supporters, such as students, young professionals, labor unions, and social service providers.
Finally, AIWA is developing a cadre of politically sophisticated immigrant women and
promoting a new leadership style based on popular literacy, community building, and
collective power.

Similarly, in Boston, the CPA Workers Center is expanding democracy through
its grassroots efforts around worker rights. The Center emerged out of the Chinese

immigrant women's campaign to deal with the closing of a large garment factory in Boston in 1985.[37] The shutdown displaced 350 workers and severely impacted the local Chinese community due to the community's high concentration of jobs in the garment industry. However, with the assistance of the Chinese Progressive Alliance, the workers formed a labor-community-student coalition and waged an eighteen-month campaign to win job retraining and job replacement. Lydia Lowe, director of the CPA Workers Center, describes how the victory of Chinese immigrant women led to creation of the Workers Center, which, in turn, has helped other work place campaigns in the Chinese community:

> This core of women activated through the campaign joined with community supporters from the CPA to found a community-based workers' mutual aid and resource center, based at CPA. . . . Through the Workers Center, immigrant workers share their experience, collectively sum up lessons learned, find out about their rights, and develop mutual support and organizing strategies. Today, the Workers Center involves immigrant workers from each of its successive organizing efforts, and is a unique place in the community where ordinary workers can walk in and participate as activists and decision-makers.[38]

Moreover, forming the Workers Center reshaped politics in the local Chinese community, turning garment workers and other immigrant laborers into active political players. "Previously the silent majority, immigrant workers are gaining increasing respect as a force to be reckoned with in the local Chinese community," states Lowe.

In Los Angeles, the formation of KIWA in March 1992—only a month before the uprisings—has had a similar impact. Through its programs, KIWA is bringing labor issues to the forefront of the Asian American community, educating labor unions about the needs of Asian American workers, and forming coalitions with other grassroots forces in the city to deal with interethnic tensions. KIWA is uniquely positioned to take up these tasks. Out of the multitude of Asian American organizations in Los Angeles, KIWA distinguishes itself as the only organization governed by a board of directors of mainly workers.

KIWA's key role in the labor movement and community politics is evident in the recent controversy involving the Koreana Wilshire Hotel.[39] The controversy began in late 1991 when Koreana Hotel Co. Ltd., a South Korean corporation, bought the Wilshire Hyatt in Los Angeles. The change in ownership meant that 175 unionized members, predominantly Latino immigrants, were out of jobs. Meanwhile, the new hotel management hired a new work force, paying them an average of $1.50 per hour less than the former unionized work force. The former workers, represented by Hotel Employees and Restaurant Employees (HERE) Local 11, called upon labor unions and groups from the Asian American, African American, and Latino communities to protest Koreana's union-busting efforts. Local 11 defined the dispute as not only a labor issue but a civil rights issue. With the help of groups such as KIWA and the Asian Pacific American Labor Alliance, Local 11 initiated a letter-writing campaign against Koreana, began a community boycott of the hotel, and organized militant actions outside the hotel, including rallies, marches, and a picket line, as well as civil disobedience at the nearby Korean consulate. In each of these actions, Local 11 worked closely with KIWA and members of the Asian American community. Due to the mass pressure, in late 1992 the Koreana management agreed to negotiate with Local 11 to end the controversy and rehire the union members.

Throughout the campaign, KIWA played a pivotal role by helping Local 11 build alliances with the Asian American community. In addition, KIWA members promoted labor consciousness in the Korean community by urging the community to boycott the hotel. KIWA members also spoke at Local 11 rallies, mobilized for picket lines, and worked with the union in its efforts to put pressure on the South Korean government. By taking these steps, KIWA prevented the controversy from pitting the Korean community against Latinos and further enflaming interethnic tensions in Los Angeles.

Also, through campaigns such as this one, KIWA is educating Asian immigrants about unions; training workers around the tasks of political leadership; and creating new centers of power in the community by combining the resources of workers, young professionals, and social service providers.

Thus, through grassroots organizing, KIWA—like AIWA and the CPA Workers Center—is expanding democracy in the Asian American community. Moreover, the three groups collectively are reshaping community consciousness. They are sharpening debate and dialogue around issues and redefining such important concepts as empowerment. What is their vision of empowerment, and how does it differ from prevailing definitions?

The Twenty-first Century: Building an Asian American Movement

[A] movement is an idea, a philosophy. . . . Leadership, I feel, is only incidental to the movement. The movement should be the most important thing. The movement must go beyond its leaders. It must be something that is continuous, with goals and ideas that the leadership can then build on.[40]

—Philip Vera Cruz

In the late 1960s, Asian American activists sought to forge a new approach to leadership that would not replicate traditional Eurocentric models—i.e., rigid hierarchies with a single executive at the top, invariably a white male, who commanded an endless chain of assistants. In their search for alternatives, activists experimented with various ideas borrowed from other movements, but most of all, activists benefited from the advice and guidance of "elders" within the Asian American community—women and men with years of grassroots organizing experience in the community, the work place, and the progressive political movement. One such "elder" was Pilipino immigrant labor leader Philip Vera Cruz, then in his sixties. Vera Cruz represented the *manong* generation—the first wave of Pilipinos who came to the United States in the early twentieth century and worked in agricultural fields, canneries, hotels, and restaurants.

Now eighty-eight years old, Vera Cruz continues to educate a new generation of activists. His lifetime of experience in grassroots organizing embodies the historic themes of Asian American activism: devotion to the rights of working people, commitment to democracy and liberation, steadfast solidarity with all who face oppression throughout the world, and the courage to challenge existing institutions of power and to create new institutions as the need arises. These themes have defined his life and shaped his approach to the question of empowerment—an approach that is different from standard definitions in our community today.

Vera Cruz is best known for his role in building the United Farm Workers (UFW), a culmination of his many years of organizing in agricultural fields. In 1965, he was working with the Agricultural Workers Organizing Committee, AFL-CIO, when Pilipino farmworkers sat-down in the Coachella vineyards of central California. This sit-down launched the famous grape strike and boycott, eventually leading to the formation of the UFW. Many books and articles have told the story of the UFW and its leader Cesar Chavez. But, until recently, no one has focused on the historic role of Pilipinos in building this movement. Craig Scharlin and Lilia Villanueva have filled that vacuum with their new publication about Vera Cruz's life.

Following the successful grape boycott, Vera Cruz became a UFW vice president and remained with the union until 1977, when he left due to political differences with the leadership. He was critical of the lack of rank-and-file democracy in the union and the leadership's embrace of the Marcos dictatorship in the Philippines. Since 1979, Vera Cruz has lived in Bakersfield, California, and has continued to devote his life to unionism and social justice and to the education of a new generation of Asian American youth.

Vera Cruz's life experiences have shaped a broad view of empowerment. For Vera Cruz, empowerment is grassroots power: the expansion of democracy for the many. Becoming empowered means gaining the capacity to advocate not only for one's own concerns but for the liberation of all oppressed peoples. Becoming empowered means being able to fundamentally change the relationship of power and oppression in society. Thus, Vera Cruz's vision is very different from that of today's young professionals. For them, empowerment is leadership development for an elite. Becoming empowered means gaining the skills to advocate for the community by gaining access to decision makers. Thus, for young professionals, the key leadership quality to develop is assertiveness. Through assertiveness, leaders gain access to policymakers as well as the power to mobilize their followers. In contrast, Vera Cruz stresses the leadership trait of humility. For him, leaders are "only incidental to the movement"—the movement is "the most important thing." For Vera Cruz, empowerment is a process where people join to develop goals and ideas to create a larger movement—a movement "that the leadership can then build on."

Vera Cruz's understanding of empowerment has evolved from his own social practice. Through his experiences in the UFW and the AFL-CIO, Vera Cruz learned about the empty democracy of bureaucratic unions and the limitations of the charismatic leadership style of Cesar Chavez. Through his years of toil as a farmworker, he recognized the importance of worker solidarity and militancy and the capacity of common people to create alternative institutions of grassroots power. Through his work with Pilipino and Mexican immigrants, he saw the necessity of coalition building and worker unity that crossed ethnic and racial boundaries. He has shared these lessons with several generations of Asian American activists.

But aside from sharing a concept of empowerment, Vera Cruz has also promoted a larger moral vision, placing his lifetime of political struggle in the framework of the movement for liberation. Three keywords distinguish his moral vision: "compassion," "solidarity," and "commitment." Vera Cruz's lifetime of action represents compassion for all victims of oppression, solidarity with all fighting for liberation, and commitment to the ideals of democracy and social justice.

Activists today need to learn from Vera Cruz's compassion, solidarity, commitment, and humility to create a new moral vision for our community. In our grassroots organizing, we need a vision that can redefine empowerment—that can bring questions of power, domination, and liberation to the forefront of our work. We need a vision that can help us respond to the challenge of conservatives and neoconservatives, and sharpen dialogue with young professionals. We need a new moral vision that can help fill the ideological vacuum in today's community.

Nowhere is this ideological challenge greater than in the current debate over the model minority stereotype. The stereotype has become the dominant image of Asian Americans for mainstream society, and has generated intense debate among all sectors of our community. This debate provides an opportunity for activists to expand political awareness and, in the process, redefine the Asian American experience for the 1990s.

In the current controversy, however, activists criticize the model minority stereotype politically but not ideologically. Activists correctly target how the concept fails to deal with Asian American realities: the growing population of poor and working poor, the large numbers of youth who are not excelling in school, and the hardships and family problems of small-business people who are not "making it" in U.S. society. Activists also correctly point out the political ramifications of the model minority stereotype: the pitting of minority groups against each other and growing interethnic tensions in U.S. society. In contrast, conservative and neoconservative proponents of the model minority concept argue from the standpoint of both political realities and a larger moral vision. They highlight Asian American accomplishments: "whiz kids" in elementary schools; growing numbers of Asian Americans in business, politics, and the professions; and the record enrollment of youth in colleges and universities. Conservatives and neoconservatives attribute these accomplishments to Asian culture and tradition, respect for authority, family cohesion, sacrifice and toil, rugged individualism, and self-reliance—moral values that they root in conservative thinking. Conservatives and neoconservatives recognize that "facts" gain power from attachment to ideologies. As a result, they appropriate Asian culture and values to promote their arguments.

But is Asian culture inherently conservative—or does it also have a tradition of militancy and liberation? Do sacrifice, toil, and family values constitute a conservative moral vision only—or do these qualities also constitute the core of radical and revolutionary thinking? By asking these questions, activists can push the debate over the model minority concept to a new, ideological level. Moreover, by focusing on ideology, activists can delve into the stereotype's deeper meaning. They can help others understand the stereotype's origins and why it has become the dominant image for Asian Americans today.

Historically, the model minority stereotype first arose in the late 1950s—the creation of sociologists attempting to explain low levels of juvenile delinquency among Chinese and Japanese Americans.[41] The stereotype remained a social-science construct until the 1960s, when a few conservative political commentators began to use it to contrast Asian Americans' "respect for law and order" to African Americans' involvement in civil rights marches, rallies, and sit-ins. By the late 1970s, the stereotype moved into the political mainstream, coinciding with the influx of new Asian immigrants into all parts of the United States. But the widespread acceptance of the stereotype was not simply due to the increase in the Asian American population or the new attention focused on our community from mainstream institutions. More importantly, it coincided with the rise of the New Right and the corporate offensive against the poor. As discussed earlier, this offensive economically devastated poor communities and stripped away hard-won political gains. This offensive also included an ideological campaign designed to restore trust in capitalism and values associated with free enterprise. Meanwhile, conservatives and neoconservatives fought to redefine the language of civil rights by attacking federal government "entitlement" programs while criticizing the African American "liberal establishment."

In this political climate, the model minority stereotype flourished. It symbolized the moral vision of capitalism in the 1980s: a celebration of traditional values, an emphasis on hard work and self-reliance, a respect for authority, and an attack on prevailing civil rights thinking associated with the African American community. Thus, the stereotype took on an ideological importance above and beyond the Asian American community. The hard-working immigrant merchant and the refugee student winning the local spelling bee have become the symbols for the resurrection of capitalist values in the last part of the twentieth century.

Yet, we know a gap exists between symbol and reality. Today, capitalism in America is not about small-business activities; it is about powerful transnational corporations and their intricate links to nation-states and the world capitalist system. Capitalist values no longer revolve around hard work and self-reliance; they deal with wealth and assets and the capacity of the rich to invest, speculate, and obtain government contracts. And the fruits of capitalism in the last part of the twentieth century are not immigrant entrepreneurship and the revival of urban areas; they are more likely to be low-paying jobs, unemployment, bankruptcies, and homelessness.

However, as corporations, banks, and other institutions abandon the inner city, the immigrant merchant—especially the Korean small-businessperson—emerges as the main symbol of capitalism in these neighborhoods. For inner-city residents, the Asian immigrant becomes the target for their wrath against corporate devastation of their neighborhoods. Moreover, as this symbol merges with other historical stereotypes of Asians, the result is highly charged imagery, which perhaps underlies the ferocity of anti-Asian violence in this period, such as the destruction of Korean small businesses during the Los Angeles uprisings. The Asian immigrant becomes a symbol of wealth—and also greed; a symbol of hard work—and also materialism; a symbol of intelligence—and also arrogance; a symbol of self-reliance—and also selfishness and lack of community concern. Thus, today the model minority stereotype has become a complex symbol through the confluence of many images imposed on us by social scientists, the New Right, and the urban policies of corporate and political elites.

Pioneer Korean immigrant journalist K. W. Lee—another of our Asian American "elders"—worries about how the melding of symbols, images, and stereotypes is shaping the perception of our community, especially among other people of color. "We are not seen as a compassionate people," states Lee. "Others see us as smart, hard working, and good at making money—but not as sharing with others. We are not seen as a people who march at the forefront of the struggle for civil rights or the campaign to end poverty."[42] Like Philip Vera Cruz, Lee believes that Asian Americans must retrieve a heritage of compassion and solidarity from our past and use these values to construct a new moral vision for our future. Asian Americans must cast off the images imposed on us by others.

Thus, as we approach the end of the twentieth century, activists are confronted with a task similar to that confronting activists in the late 1960s: the need to redefine the Asian American experience. And, as an earlier generation discovered, redefining means more than ethnic awakening. It means confronting the fundamental questions of power and domination in U.S. society. It means expanding democracy and community consciousness. It means liberating ourselves from the prisons still surrounding our lives.

In our efforts to redefine the Asian American experience, activists will have the guidance and help of elders like K. W. Lee and Philip Vera Cruz. And we can also draw from the rich legacy of struggle of other liberation movements.

Thus, in closing this chapter, I want to quote from two great teachers from the 1960s: Malcolm X and Martin Luther King, Jr. Their words and actions galvanized the consciousness of one generation of youth, and their message of compassion continues to speak to a new generations in the 1990s.

Since their assassinations in the mid-1960s, however, mainstream commentators have stereotyped the two men and often pitted one against the other. They portray Malcolm X as the angry black separatist who advocated violence and hatred against white people. Meanwhile, they make Martin Luther King, Jr., the messenger of love and nonviolence. In the minds of most Americans, both men—in the words of historian Manning Marable—are "frozen in time."[43]

But, as Marable and other African American historians note, both King and Malcolm evolved and became very different men in the years before their assassinations. Both men came to see the African American struggle in the United States in a worldwide context, as part of the revolutionary stirrings and mass uprisings happening across the globe. Both men became internationalists, strongly condemning U.S. exploitation of Third World nations and urging solidarity among all oppressed peoples. Finally, both men called for a redefinition of human values; they believed that people in the United States, especially, needed to move away from materialism and embrace a more compassionate worldview.

If we, too, as Asian Americans, are to evolve in our political and ideological understanding, we need to learn from the wisdom of both men. As we work for our own empowerment, we must ask ourselves a series of questions. Will we fight only for ourselves, or will we embrace the concerns of all oppressed peoples? Will we overcome our own oppression and help to create a new society, or will we become a new exploiter group in the present American hierarchy of inequality? Will we define our goal of empowerment solely in terms of individual advancement for a few, or as the collective liberation for all peoples?

> These are revolutionary times. All over the globe men are revolting against old systems of exploitation and oppression, and, out of the wombs of a frail world, new systems of justice and equality are being born. The shirtless and barefoot people of the land are rising up as never before. "The people who sat in the darkness have seen a great light." We in the West must support these revolutions. It is a sad fact that, because of comfort, complacency, a morbid fear of communism, and our proneness to adjust to injustice, the Western nations that initiated so much of the revolutionary spirit of the modern world have now become the arch antirevolutionaries. . . . Our only hope today lies in our ability to recapture the revolutionary spirit and go out into a sometimes hostile world declaring eternal hostility to poverty, racism, and militarism.[44]
>
> —Martin Luther King, Jr.

> I believe that there will ultimately be a clash between the oppressed and those who do the oppressing. I believe that there will be a clash between those who want freedom, justice, and equality for everyone and those who want to continue the system of exploitation. I believe that there will be that kind of clash, but I don't think it will be based on the color of the skin.[45]
>
> —Malcolm X

NOTES

Originally published in *Amerasia Journal* 15.1 (1989): xv–xxx. © 1989 *Amerasia Journal,* reprinted by permission.

1. Iranian philosopher Ali Shariati's four-prisons analysis was shared with me by a member of the Iranian Students Union, Confederation of Iranian Students, San Francisco, 1977.

2. Allan Bloom, *The Closing of the American Mind,* New York: Simon and Schuster, 1987.

3. Winifred Breines, "Whose New Left?" *Journal of American History,* vol. 75, no. 2, September 1988.

4. Ibid., p. 543.

5. Sheila D. Collins, *The Rainbow Challenge: The Jackson Campaign and the Future of U.S. Politics,* New York: Monthly Review Press, 1986.

6. Ibid., p. 16.

7. Ronald Fraser, *1968: A Student Generation in Revolt,* New York: Pantheon Books, pp. 354–355.

8. Karen Umemoto, "'On Strike!' San Francisco State College Strike, 1968–69: The Role of Asian American Students," *Amerasia Journal,* vol. 15, no. 1, 1989.

9. "Statement of the Philippine-American Collegiate Endeavor (PACE) Philosophy and Goals," mimeograph: quoted in Umemoto, p. 15.

10. Mo Nishida, "A Revolutionary Nationalist Perspective of the San Francisco State Strike," *Amerasia Journal,* vol. 15, no. 1, 1989, p. 75.

11. George Lipsitz, "Grassroots Activists and Social Change: The Story of Ivory Perry," *CAAS Newsletter,* UCLA Center for Afro-American Studies, 1986. See also George Lipsitz, *A Life in the Struggle: Ivory Perry and the Culture of Opposition,* Philadelphia: Temple University Press, 1988.

12. Russell C. Leong, "Poetry within Earshot: Notes of an Asian American Generation, 1968–1978," *Amerasia Journal,* vol. 15, no. 1, 1989, pp. 166–167.

13. Al Robles, "Hanging on to the Carabao's Tail," *Amerasia Journal,* vol. 15, no. 1, 1989, p. 205.

14. Warren J. Susman, *Culture as History: The Transformation of American Society in the Twentieth Century,* New York: Pantheon Books, 1973; and Raymond Williams, *Keywords: A Vocabulary of Culture and Society,* revised edition, New York: Oxford University Press, 1976.

15. John M. Liu and Lucie Cheng, "A Dialogue on Race and Class: Asian American Studies and Marxism," *The Left Academy,* vol. 3, eds. Bertell Ollman and Edward Vernoff, Westport, CT: Praeger, 1986.

16. See Mary Kao, compiler, "Public Record, 1989: What Have We Learned from the 60s and 70s?" *Amerasia Journal,* vol. 15, no. 1, 1989, pp. 95–158.

17. Institute for Labor Education and Research, *What's Wrong with the U.S. Economy? A Popular Guide for the Rest of Us,* Boston: South End Press, 1982. See especially chapters 1 and 19.

18. Samuel Huntington, "The United States," *The Crisis of Democracy: Report on the Governability of Democracies to the Trilateral Commission,* ed. Michel Crozier, New York: New York University Press, 1975.

19. Center on Budget and Policy Priorities, *Still Far from the Dream: Recent Developments in Black Income, Employment and Poverty,* Washington, D.C., 1988.

20. Center for the Study of Social Policy, *Kids Count: State Profiles of Child Well-Being,* Washington, D.C., 1992.

21. Manning Marable, *How Capitalism Underdeveloped Black America,* Boston: South End Press, 1983, pp. 252–253.

22. Vincent Harding, *The Other American Revolution,* Los Angeles: UCLA Center for Afro-American Studies, and Atlanta: Institute of the Black World, 1980, p. 224.

23. For analyses of the changing status of Asian Americans, see Lucie Cheng and Edna Bonacich, eds., *Labor Immigration under Capitalism: Asian Workers in the United States before World War II,* Berkeley: University of California Press, 1984; Paul Ong, Edna Bonacich, and Lucie Cheng, *Struggles for a Place: The New Asian Immigrants in the Restructuring Political Economy,* Philadelphia: Temple University Press, 1993; and Sucheng Chan, *Asian Americans: An Interpretive History,* Boston: Twayne, 1991.

24. For an analysis of the growing power of Asian American young professionals, see Yen Espiritu and Paul Ong, "Class Constraints on Racial Solidarity among Asian Americans," *Struggles for a Place,* Philadelphia: Temple University Press, 1993.

25. Arthur Hu, "AIDS and Race," *Asian Week,* December 13, 1991.

26. Marable, *How Capitalism Underdeveloped Black America,* p. 182.

27. William McGurn, "The Silent Minority," *National Review,* June 24, 1991.

28. Ibid., p. 19.

29. C. L. R. James, *Beyond a Boundary,* New York: Pantheon Books, 1983, pp. 116–117.

30. LEAP Asian Pacific American Public Policy Institute and UCLA Asian American Studies Center, *The State of Asian Pacific America: Policy Issues to the Year 2020,* Los Angeles: LEAP and UCLA Asian American Studies Center, 1993.

31. Mao Zedong, "Where Do Correct Ideas Come From?" *Four Essays on Philosophy*, Beijing: Foreign Languages Press, 1966, p. 134.

32. See "Asian Pacific American Workers: Contemporary Issues in the Labor Movement," eds. Glenn Omatsu and Edna Bonacich, *Amerasia Journal*, vol. 18. no.1, 1992.

33. Edna Bonacich, "The Social Costs of Immigrant Entrepreneurship," *Amerasia Journal*, vol. 14, no. 1, 1988.

34. Dean S. Toji and James H. Johnson, Jr., "Asian and Pacific Islander American Poverty: The Working Poor and the Jobless Poor," *Amerasia Journal*, vol. 18, no. 1, 1992, p. 85.

35. Miriam Ching Louie, "Immigrant Asian Women in Bay Area Garment Sweatshops: 'After Sewing, Laundry, Cleaning and Cooking, I Have No Breath Left to Sing,'" *Amerasia Journal*, vol. 18, no. 1, p. 12.

36. Miriam Ching Louie, "Asian and Latina Women Take on the Garment Giants," *Cross-Roads*, March 1993.

37. Peter N. Kiang and Man Chak Ng, "Through Strength and Struggle: Boston's Asian American Student/Community/Labor Solidarity," *Amerasia Journal*, vol. 15, no. 1, 1989.

38. Lydia Lowe, "Paving the Way: Chinese Immigrant Workers and Community-based Labor Organizing in Boston," *Amerasia Journal*, vol. 18, no. 1, 1992, p. 41.

39. Namju Cho, "Check Out, Not In: Koreana Wilshire/Hyatt Take-over and the Los Angeles Korean Community," *Amerasia Journal*, vol. 18, no. 1, 1992.

40. Craig Scharlin and Lilia V. Villanueva, *Philip Vera Cruz: A Personal History of Filipino Immigrants and the Farmworkers Movement*, Los Angeles: UCLA Labor Center and UCLA Asian American Studies Center, 1992, p. 104.

41. For an overview of the evolution of the "model minority" stereotype in the social sciences, see Shirley Hune, *Pacific Migration to the United States: Trends and Themes in Historical and Sociological Literature*, New York: Research Institute on Immigration and Ethnic Studies of the Smithsonian Institution, 1977 (reprinted in *Asian American Studies: An Annotated Bibliography and Research Guide*, ed. Hyung-chan Kim, Westport, CT: Greenwood Press, 1989). For comparisons of the "model minority" stereotype in two different decades, see "Success Story of One Minority Group in U.S.," *U.S. News and World Report*, December 26, 1966 (reprinted in *Roots: An Asian American Reader*, ed. Amy Tachiki et al., Los Angeles: UCLA Asian American Studies Center, 1971), and the essay by William McGurn, "The Silent Minority," *National Review*, June 24, 1991.

42. Author's interview with K. W. Lee, Los Angeles, California, October 1991.

43. Manning Marable, "On Malcolm X: His Message & Meaning," Westfield, NJ: Open Magazine Pamphlet Series, 1992.

44. Martin Luther King, Jr., "Beyond Vietnam" speech, Riverside Church, New York, April 1967.

45. Malcolm X, interview on Pierre Breton Show, January 19, 1965, in *Malcolm X Speaks*, ed. George Breitman, New York: Grove Press, 1966, p. 216.

Chapter 3

Black Panthers, Red Guards, and Chinamen
Constructing Asian American Identity through Performing Blackness, 1969–1972

Daryl J. Maeda

On March 22, 1969, in Portsmouth Square, a public gathering place in San Francisco's Chinatown, a group of young Chinese Americans calling themselves the Red Guard Party held a rally to unveil their "10 Point Program." Clad in berets and armbands, they announced a Free Breakfast program for children at the Commodore Stockton school, denounced the planned destruction of the Chinese Playground, and called for the "removal of colonialist police from Chinatown." The Red Guard Party's style, language, and politics clearly recalled those of the Black Panther Party, with whom they had significant contact and by whom they were profoundly influenced (*AAPA*, March 1969; Lyman 1971). At the rally, the Red Guards performed an Asian American version of black nationalism by adopting the Panthers' garb, confrontational manner, and emphasis on self-determination.

Many years later, the Asian American playwright and critic Frank Chin dismissed the Red Guards' rally as a "yellow minstrel show" (Terkel 1992). But while Chin rejected the Red Guards' performance as a vain attempt to imitate blackness, in 1971, just two years after the rally, he offered his own dramatic take on the interplay between Asian Americans and blacks in his play *The Chickencoop Chinaman*. Widely acknowledged as a seminal work of Asian American literature, Chin's play explores the relationship between Asian American identity and blackness by featuring Chinese American and Japanese American protagonists who associate with, claim sympathy for, and exhibit speech and dress patterns most commonly associated with African Americans. Set in the late 1960s, *The Chickencoop Chinaman* chronicles the adventures of Tam Lum, a fast-talking Chinese American, and his Japanese American sidekick, Kenji, as they attempt to produce a film about the career of their childhood hero, the African American boxer Ovaltine Jack Dancer and his putative father, Charley Popcorn. As a story about the search for heroes, fathers, and a usable past, *The Chickencoop Chinaman* provides a powerful meditation on the relationship among masculinity, race, and Asian American identity.

Both the Red Guard Party and Frank Chin were key players in the Asian American political and cultural mobilization of the late 1960s and early 1970s. The Red Guards were among the first radicals to arise from Asian American communities and in their later incarnation as I Wor Kuen (IWK) constituted one of the two preeminent Asian American leftist organizations (Wei 1994). They built community programs, organized Asian American workers, fought for better living conditions, protested against the Vietnam War, and became integrally entwined in the Marxist-Leninist-Maoist Left. Chin was highly influential in his own right as a writer, critic, and activist. His play *The Chickencoop Chinaman* marked his emergence as a major figure. It won the 1971 playwriting contest sponsored by the East West Players, the prominent Los Angeles–based Asian American theater company, and became the first Asian American play to be produced off-Broadway (Chin 1981). Chin published numerous works of searing criticism, fiction, and nonfiction, cofounded the Asian American Theater Workshop in San Francisco, one of the most important venues for Asian American dramatic productions, coedited *AIIIEEEEE!,* a foundational anthology of Asian American literature, and organized the first Day of Remembrance to commemorate the incarceration of Japanese Americans during World War II (Shimakawa 2002, 61–62; Chin et al. 1974).

Yet Chin is also a controversial figure who has leveled highly gendered criticism at authors—most notably Maxine Hong Kingston—who he believes peddle "fake" depictions of Asian American culture for white consumption (Chin 1991). Critics charge that his attempts to create a heroic Asian American tradition inevitably "reassert male authority over the cultural domain by subordinating feminism to nationalist terms" (Kim 1990). It is not my intent here to rehash these critiques, but instead to point out that critical perspectives on Chin have thus far failed to locate his rehearsals of Asian American masculinity in the historical context of the black power period. Reading *The Chickencoop Chinaman* through a racial lens reveals the play's linkages of Asian American identity to blackness.

The Red Guard Party and Frank Chin engaged in divergent modes of performance. While rallies on the street and drama on stage constitute different genres, both were scripted with intentionality and visually constructed and displayed the politics and identities of their participants. Furthermore, the Red Guards and Chin exemplify the two distinct ideologies most commonly understood to have motivated the construction of Asian American identity: Third-World internationalist radicalism and domestic U.S. cultural nationalism. Comparatively examining the performances of radicals and cultural workers thus provides a valuable register of competing visions of Asian America.

The Red Guards and Chin intervened in an Asian America that had not yet been constituted. Through the mid-twentieth century, despite scattered instances of interethnic solidarity, most organizing among Asians in the mainland United States proceeded along ethnic or national lines. Indeed, at times, Asian ethnic groups strategically distanced themselves from each other (Espiritu 1992). In the late 1960s, however, a loosely organized social movement known as the Asian American movement arose to protest anti-Asian racism and exploitation. While the Asian American movement consisted of a variety of organizations and individuals with competing ideologies, all agreed with two fundamental premises: first, that Asians of all ethnicities in the United States shared a common racial oppression, and, second, that building a multiethnic, racially based coalition would provide an effective basis for resisting racism.[1]

Performances of blackness catalyzed the formation of Asian American identity. Far from being mere mimics, however, Asian Americans who began to consider their own racial positioning through contemplations of blackness went on to forge a distinct identity of their own. The Red Guards adopted the Black Panthers' language and style —two key elements of the Panther mystique—as a political statement that underlined their espousal of the Panthers' racial politics. Thus, they inserted Asian Americans into a racial paradigm, arguing that Asian Americans constituted a racialized bloc subject to the same racism that afflicted blacks. Chin also scripted performances that pointed to blackness as a model of racial resistance and identity. But importantly for him, emulating blackness provided a way to recuperate Asian American masculinity.

Understanding the construction of Asian American identity through its performance of blackness has three major implications for scholars of race and the 1960s. First, the extent to which Asian American identity was enacted through performances of blackness indicates the thorough imbrication of multiple processes of racial formation. It is by now widely accepted that racial formations proceed in parallel fashion; for instance, much of the literature on the social construction of whiteness argues that whiteness came to be defined in opposition to nonwhiteness (most often, blackness) (Roediger 1991). But the construction of Asian American identity through performing blackness demonstrates the interdependence of racial formations strictly among people of color.

Second, understanding the rise of Asian American identity in response to blackness answers charges that in the late 1960s, the New Left betrayed the promise of the early 1960s by descending into narrowly divisive identity politics. Historian David Burner excoriates black power for engendering a "narcissistic absorption in the group content of self-identity" and "solipsistic examination" of the self, and former sixties activist Todd Gitlin mourns the Left's putative decline into parochialism (Burner 1996, 50, 81; Gitlin 1995). However, Asian American mobilization powerfully refutes this narrative of declension. Asian American adaptations of black power's emphasis on race and racial identity not only contributed to the construction of Asian American identity but also provided points of conjunction around which African Americans and Asian Americans could connect political and cultural movements.

Finally, highlighting the importance of performances of blackness to the construction of Asian American identity helps to broach divergent histories of the category itself. The Red Guards and Chin offered dramatically different prescriptions for what ailed Asian America, as demonstrated in one striking skirmish. Chin recalls teaching a class in which he directed Asian American students to act out some anti-Asian stereotypes, when a group of Red Guards took exception to the repetition of the offensive imagery. The Red Guard leader knocked Chin to the ground, yelling, "Identify with China!" Chin countered, "We're in America. This is where we are, where we live, and where we're going to die" (Terkel 1992, 311). The exchange highlights a fundamental cleavage in understandings of Asian American identity. During the late 1960s and early 1970s, groups such as the Red Guard Party (later I Wor Kuen), Wei Min She, Asian Americans for Action, and the Asian American Political Alliance adopted frameworks that connected anti-Asian racism in the United States to Western imperialism in Asia. Meanwhile, Chin and his cohorts argued that Asian Americans were bound by a common culture that was born and bred strictly within U.S. national borders (Chin et al. 1974).

Discrepant genealogies of the origin of Asian American identity reproduce this tension: social histories and documentary collections of Asian American activism in the 1960s and 1970s tend to locate Third World internationalism as its central ideology, while literary and cultural histories generally privilege domestic U.S. nationalism (Louie and Omatsu 2001; Ho et al. 2000; Tachiki et al. 1971; Eng 2001; Palumbo-Liu 1999; S. C. Wong 1995; Dirlik 1996; Lowe 1996).[2] That both the Red Guards and Chin turned to blackness suggests the power of mimesis to produce new subjectivities and identifications across ideological boundaries. It also suggests that these strange bedfellows were engaged in the shared project of racial formation, and that neither anti-imperialist internationalism nor domestic nationalism alone can adequately account for the multifarious beginnings of Asian American identity.

Asian Americans and Assimilation

Asian American radicals and cultural workers turned to blackness as a model for Asian American identity as a way to resist assimilation into whiteness. At the Red Guards' initial rally in Portsmouth Square, David Hilliard, chairman of the Black Panther Party, castigated the audience for its lack of militance and called Chinese Americans the "Uncle Toms of the non-white people of the U.S." He went on to assert, "If you can't relate to China then you can't relate to the Panthers" (*AAPA*, March 1969). Hilliard's appeal for the Red Guards to relate to China was in part a call for political radicalism and commitment to the ideology of Mao Tse-Tung, but paired with an accusation of Uncle Tom-ism, it was also an admonition against assimilation. Locating Chinese Americans as insufficiently Chinese, Hilliard charged that they needed to reinvigorate themselves by renewing their relationship to Asia.

Hilliard's claim that Chinese Americans were overassimilated could not have been made prior to the 1960s. From the beginning of large-scale migrations to the United States in the mid-1800s through the beginning of World War II, Asians faced legal barriers to assimilation in the form of immigration restrictions, bars to naturalization, and antimiscegenation laws. In addition, the Yellow Peril discourse positioned Asians as inherently unassimilable perpetual foreigners (Daniels 1962; Lee 1999; Okihiro 1994). In the postwar era, however, U.S. responses to Cold War imperatives opened the possibility of Asian American assimilation. Between 1952 and 1967, Asian Americans gained rights to naturalization, immigration, and interracial marriage. These legal changes accompanied a social shift that suggested the possibility of Asian American assimilation in the form of a discourse that has come to be known as the "model minority myth."

Discussions of Asian American integration in the postwar era inevitably credited their putative assimilation to their status as a model minority (Simpson 2001). In 1966, the *New York Times Magazine* claimed that Japanese Americans were following the steps of white ethnics who initially suffered discrimination but "climbed out of the slums" to enter the mainstream. It praised Japanese Americans for their dedication to education, low crime rates, and strong family values (Petersen 1966). *U.S. News and World Report* extended the claim of assimilability to Chinese Americans, who were "winning wealth and respect" through "hard work," lack of juvenile delinquency, focus on education, and eschewal of welfare. Both articles compared Asian Americans favorably to blacks, arguing that unlike "Negroes," Asian Americans had overcome racial discrimination and were on the verge of achieving assimilation (*U.S. News and World Report* 1966, Okihiro 1994).

At this moment when Asian American assimilation seemed possible for the first time, the Red Guard Party's performance of black radicalism constituted an emphatic rejection of it. While black power encompassed a variety of ideologies, its advocates generally adopted discourses emphasizing power and self-determination over integration and equal inclusion (Van Deburg 1992). Stokely Carmichael and Charles Hamilton explained in 1967 that blacks needed to "redefine themselves," "reclaim their history, their culture," and "create their own sense of community and togetherness." They deemed "assimilated" and "integrated" blacks to be coopted by whites and hence ineligible to participate in creating this new black community and identity (Carmichael and Hamilton 1967, 37, 11, 29–31).

For Asian Americans, adopting black power's antipathy toward assimilation marked a significant departure from previous modes of political mobilization. In contrast to prior assimilationists such as the Japanese American Citizens League, Asian American activists viewed racial oppression as a systemic, rather than aberrant, feature of American society (Kurashige 2002; Ichioka 1986–87). They believed that the racial oppression of Asian Americans stemmed from and served to justify their economic exploitation, and sought to build Asian American power and culture autonomous of white approval.

The Red Guard Party's programs generally sought to build and strengthen Chinatown's community institutions rather than to insert Chinese Americans into mainstream programs. To that end, they started the Free Breakfast program, put on cultural programs and movie nights, published the *Red Guard Community Newspaper,* and confronted the police. As Minister of Information Alex Hing expressed, "We're going to attain power, so we don't have to beg anymore" (Lyman 1971, 185).

Like the Red Guard Party, Frank Chin rejected assimilation as a palliative to racism. *The Chickencoop Chinaman* features an assimilationist Chinese American character, Tom, whose very name positions him as the Uncle Tom that Hilliard had posited. He provides an unambiguous expression of the model minority discourse when he says, "We used to be kicked around, but that's history, brother. Today we have good jobs, good pay, and we're lucky. Americans are proud to say we send more of our kids to college than any other race. We're accepted. We worked hard for it" (Chin 1981, 59).

In contrast to Tom's assimilationism, the protagonists, Tam and Kenji, struggle against whiteness. The Lone Ranger (described in the dramatis personae as "a legendary white racist") appears in a fantasy scene and proclaims Asian Americans to be "honorary whites" (3). When Tam and Kenji protest, he insists that this bestowal is not a blessing, but a curse that they cannot refuse. The curse of whiteness mandates that Asian Americans refrain from vocal protest and remain "legendary passive." They must acknowledge their place in the racial hierarchy, as the Lone Ranger orders them to "kiss" his "ass" and "know . . . that it be white." And they must abandon attempts to create an independent Asian American culture, symbolized by the Lone Ranger shooting the writer Tam through the hand (32, 37–38). Tam and Kenji understand the Lone Ranger's curse as an attempt to buy Asian American compliance with a white-dominated social order; their refusal indicates the play's explicit rejection of assimilation via playing the model minority. Elsewhere, Chin has stated that aside from being "a strategy for white acceptance," the model minority discourse is dangerous because it encourages Asian Americans to "denigrate" blacks and see them as deserving of their oppression (Terkel 1992, 313).

Asian Americans and Blacks in Common Struggle

Cross-identifications between Asians and blacks arose at various moments during the twentieth century. At times, African Americans drew inspiration from Asian resistance to Western imperialism. During the 1930s, tens of thousands of blacks flocked to the Pacific Movement of the Eastern World, which proclaimed Japan to be the "champion" of the "dark and colored races" (Allen 1995). During World War II, Malcolm X proclaimed his eagerness to join the Japanese army, mostly to avoid being drafted but also echoing a strand of black sentiment that admired Japan as a militarily powerful, nonwhite nation opposed to Euro-American imperialism (Lipsitz 1998; Deutsch 2001).

Asia also figured prominently in the black imagination during the 1960s and 1970s. After fleeing the United States, the militant Robert F. Williams spent three years exiled in China (Tyson 2001). Black Panther political education prominently included Mao's Red Book. Indeed, Mao's writings were central to the ideologies and practices of an entire generation of black revolutionaries, some of whom went so far as to adopt Chinese peasant-style dress and aesthetics to signal their radicalism (Elbaum 2002; Kelley and Esch 1999). When Muhammad Ali refused his induction in 1967, his declaration, "Man, I ain't got no quarrel with them Vietcong," reflected the antiwar stance of black nationalists ranging from the Nation of Islam (in Ali's case) to the Black Panther Party (Deutsch 2001, 193–94). Indeed, BPP chairman David Hilliard suggested the necessity for Asian/black solidarity when he declared to National Liberation Front representatives in Vietnam, "You're Yellow Panthers, we're Black Panthers" (Hilliard and Cole 1993, 247). As these examples show, black identifications with Asians focused primarily across the Pacific rather than with Asians in the United States.

While Asian American and African American identifications were mutual, it would be an overstatement to deem them reciprocal. The black power movement's "*rearticulation* of racial ideology" in the 1960s clearly opened spaces for new subjectivities to emerge (Omi and Winant 1994, 88–91). Within these spaces, Asian Americans performing blackness and African Americans admiring Asian radicalism shared in creating what Vijay Prashad has aptly called the "multicolored Left" (2001, 136), a hybridized multiracial social movement with both Asian and black inflections.

Asian Americans and blacks crossed paths daily, especially in West Coast cities such as Seattle, San Francisco, Oakland, and Los Angeles. During World War II, many African Americans migrating westward settled in areas vacated by the Japanese Americans who had been imprisoned in concentration camps (Taylor 1994; Taylor 1998). Upon returning, Japanese Americans found their former neighborhoods transformed. Maya Angelou sensed the changes in San Francisco's Nihonmachi in the air: "Where the odors of tempura, raw fish and *cha* had dominated, the aroma of chitlings, greens and ham hocks now prevailed" (Taylor 1998, 273). These wartime demographic shifts meant that urban Asian Americans and blacks increasingly rubbed elbows in the post-war period.

Frank Chin grew up in the mixed-race context of Oakland. He recalls, "In the six-ties, [black culture] became a force in Asian-America. It always had a large presence in Oakland. I grew up with rhythm-and-blues, jazz." However, it was not just proximity but also politics that inspired Asian American adoptions. Chin credits the "sixties and the civil-rights movement" with making Asian Americans "aware that we had no pres-ence, no image in American culture as men, as people. . . . So a bunch of us began to appropriate 'blackness.' We'd wear the clothes, we'd affect the walk and we began to talk black. We'd call our selves 'Bro' and began talking Southern: 'Hey, man'" (Terkel 1992, 310). Chin's recollection highlights masculine modes of bodily comportment—clothing, gait, and speech—as the means of racial identification.

Asian Americans also encountered blackness intellectually. Historian Gary Okihiro recalls that many Asian Americans "found our identity by reading Frantz Fanon and Malcolm X, Cheikh Anta Diop and W. E. B. Du Bois, Leopold Senghor and Langston Hughes" (Okihiro 1994, 60). Indeed, the debt that the field of Asian American Stud-ies owes to black intellectual figures cannot be overstated. Steve Louie, a veteran of the Asian American Movement, believes that it "owes a huge political debt to the black power movement." He points to Stokely Carmichael, Malcolm X, Huey Newton, Bobby Seale, and the Black Panthers as visionaries "who laid the groundwork that re-ally brought . . . the Asian American movement out" (Louie 1997).

Some Asian American individuals participated directly in black social movements. Prior to the heyday of black power, the Chinese American political activist Grace Lee Boggs enjoyed a long association with C. L. R. James and worked closely with her hus-band, James Boggs (Boggs 1998; Choi 1999). Yuri Kochiyama, a nisei (second-genera-tion Japanese American) woman living in Harlem, was a friend of Malcolm X and fa-mously cradled his head as he lay dying in the Audubon Ballroom; she was also associ-ated with the black radicals Kwame Toure (formerly Stokely Carmichael) and H. Rap Brown (Fujino 2005). A few Asian American individuals even joined the Black Pan-thers (M. Wong 1998a, 1998b).

When Huey Newton and Bobby Seale founded the Black Panther Party, they turned to an Asian American to obtain the first of the weapons that would eventually make them famous. As Seale recalls in his memoir, *Seize the Time,*

> Late in November 1966, we went to a Third World brother we knew, a Japanese radical cat. He had guns for a motherfucker: .357 Magnums, 22's, 9mm's, what have you. We told him that we wanted these guns to begin to institutionalize and let black people know that we have to defend ourselves as Malcolm X said we must. . . . So he gave us an M-1 and a 9mm. (Seale 1970, 72–73).

The "Japanese radical" was actually a Japanese American named Richard Aoki who had grown up in West Oakland with the families of Seale and Newton and "hooked up with Bobby and Huey at [Merritt] College." Aoki went on to become a field marshal in the Black Panther Party and in 1968 cofounded the Asian American Political Alliance (AAPA) in Berkeley (Seale 1970, 79; Pearson 1994, 113; M. Wong 1998c; Aoki 2000).

Steve Louie joined the black liberation movement in part because he could relate to discrimination in personal terms. In 1960, his Chinese American family had been unable to purchase a home in La Cañada, a wealthy suburb of Los Angeles. Convinced that he "had more in common with black people" than anyone else in the United States, Louie began volunteering in 1967 at a storefront operation in Watts, where he mimeographed materials, leafleted, passed out fliers, and did other odd jobs. Although he did not fully understand the politics of the group sponsoring the storefront (which he later found out was backed by Ron Karenga's U.S. organization), Louie felt it important to aid in organizing the black community because he had personally experienced racial discrimination (Louie 1997).

Political Theater on the Street

While Asian Americans encountered blackness socially and intellectually, and through direct participation in black struggles, it was the actual performance of blackness that was critical to articulations of multiethnic Asian American racial identity. The "political theater" of rallies, marches, proclamations, and social programs—along with literary and cultural productions—produced a novel form of Asian American subjectivity by highlighting parallels between the common racialization affecting African Americans and Asian Americans of various ethnicities.

AAPA's support for the Free Huey movement provides an excellent example of the power of performance to consolidate multiethnic ties. The movement sought Huey Newton's release from jail on charges of killing a police officer. At a large rally for Huey's birthday, AAPA members hoisted "posters with 'Free Huey' inscribed in Mandarin, Japanese, Tagalog, and English" (Pearson 1994, 167). Asian American support for Newton was not in itself surprising, as radicals of all races were influenced by the Black Panther Party as the premier vanguard organization of the late 1960s. Puerto Ricans in the Young Lords Party and Chicanos in the Brown Berets adopted the language and style of black power, the American Indian Movement was initially inspired by Panthers, and progressive whites supported and praised them (Young Lords Party 1971; Melendez 2003; Chavez 2002; Smith and Warrior 1996). Even white socialites sought the "radical chic" of associating with Black Panthers (Wolfe 1970). However, adopting and adapting the ideology of black power had a particular effect for Asian Americans: it enabled them to construct Asian American identity as a new subjectivity that rejected assimilation and consolidated multiple Asian ethnicities under the rubric of race.

The significance of AAPA's participation in the Free Huey movement can thus be found in the manner in which the organization displayed its presence. Carrying posters written in Asian languages was an important statement for a group composed chiefly of native-born Asian Americans whose primary language was almost assuredly English. The posters suggested that Asian Americans' support for Newton derived from their own identities as racialized people. Furthermore, pointing to the racialization of Asian Americans drew an implicit parallel between the travails of blacks and those of Asian Americans. Finally, AAPA's posters visually represented the linguistic and ethnic diversity of the organization and of the San Francisco Bay area's Asian communities. Seeking justice for Huey in this forum thus brought together Chinese, Japanese, and Filipinos as Asian Americans.

Many other Asian Americans drew inspiration from the Black Panther Party's vision of militant blackness. Steve Louie recalls that he reveled in watching the televised spectacle of the Panthers marching into the California Statehouse armed with shotguns:

> I thought that was so great! Not because I thought that they needed to go and shoot somebody, but just the attitude. They're basically saying, "Fuck you!" up in your face. We're not taking this crap anymore, we're going to defend ourselves and we're going to do it by any means necessary . . . I just thought that kind of militance was just fantastic. (Louie 1997)

Louie found inspiration not only in the Panthers' self-reliance but also in their theatrically staged performance of militance; in short, he admired their political style.

The Red Guard Party was the Asian American group most directly and heavily influenced by the Black Panthers. It consisted primarily of disaffected American-born Chinatown youth who had been the subject of "some not too secret proselytization by Panther leaders" (Lyman 1971, 31). The Red Guards drew their membership from the crowd surrounding a nonprofit community agency called Legitimate Ways (Leway). Leway was founded in 1967 to provide the youth of Chinatown—who faced substandard housing, poor schools, overcrowding, and endemic poverty—with alternatives to street life and petty crime. It provided job placement assistance and recreational activities, the most popular of which was a pool hall. The Leway pool hall became a gathering place for young people, often attracting crowds of up to two hundred. However, it also became a focus of police harassment (A History of the Red Guard Party 1975).

Alex Hing, minister of information for the Red Guard Party, attributes the initial connection between the Leway youth and the Panthers to Chinese American women who were dating Panther men. When a core of about ten Leway members discussed forming an organization similar to the Black Panther Party, these "sisters," who were already "really politicized," invited the Panthers to visit Leway. Bobby Seale and David Hilliard did so in late 1967 or early 1968 and found a surprising scene: "When they went into Leway, it was like a Black thing that they saw pretty much. The music that was played out of Leway was jazz, soul music, that was the kind [of] ambience it had. People wore dark clothes, field jackets, sunglasses in the middle of the night, shooting pool, smoking cigarettes" (Hing 2000, 284). The music at Leway echoed the preference of most Asian American urban youth of the time, who primarily grooved to rhythm and blues and soul music, rather than rock and roll, which tended to be associated with whites, hippies, and college students.

The Panthers urged the radical core of Leway to build a revolutionary organization and invited them to weekly study sessions on revolutionary theory held at the Panthers' San Francisco headquarters on Fillmore Street, at their national headquarters in Oakland, and at Eldridge Cleaver's house. This core group returned to Leway armed with an ideological framework derived from reading Mao Tse-Tung, Frantz Fanon, Che Guevara, and Fidel Castro and began recruiting members. While forming, the new group stayed underground for several months and "took pretty much our directions from the Panthers" (Hing 2000, 285). Bobby Seale even named the new organization. While the Leway group wanted to call themselves the Red Dragons, in the manner of a street gang, Seale appreciated the value of the "Red Guard Party"—after Mao's youth brigade—as a "more political" and provocative name (Hing 2000, 296).

The influence of the Panthers on the Red Guard Party was unmistakable. The Red Guards adopted the militant rhetoric and style of their mentors across the bay. They wore berets and armbands at rallies, called police "pigs" and whites "honkies," used slogans like "All Power to the People" and "Fuck the Pigs," and appointed "ministers" of defense and information à la the Panthers ("History of the Red Guard Party" 1975, 81; Lyman 1971, 32; M. Wong 1998d; *Red Guard Community Newspaper,* 25 June 1969, 4 April 1969, 25 June 1969). The *Red Guard Community Newspaper* publicized numerous incidents of the "brutal harassment" of Chinatown residents by "the racist pig structure" (12 March 1969). The Red Guards' attention to police harassment belied the idyllic image of a quaint Chinatown, and instead cast Chinatown as a ghetto under siege from "pigs." In focusing on police brutality, the Red Guards reproduced one of the Panthers' most successful strategies. At the Panthers' behest the Red Guards also instituted a Free Breakfast program for Chinatown kids (Hing 2000, 288).

The Red Guard Party adopted its 10 Point Program explicitly from the Panthers' program, even borrowing its "What We Want, What We Believe" format (*Red Guard Community Newspaper,* 25 June 1969). Indeed, many of the Red Guard points echo verbatim points from the Black Panther program, simply substituting the word "yellow" for "black" throughout. The main points of the Red Guard program that follow the Black Panther program include demands for "freedom" for "Yellow people," decent housing, education, exemption from military service, an end to police brutality, release of all "Yellow men" from prisons and jails, trial by jury of peers from the "Yellow communities" for every "Yellow defendant," and full employment (*Red Guard Community Newspaper,* 12 March 1969; Foner 1995, 2–6).

The translation of "black" to "yellow" in the program was highly significant for two reasons. First, it suggested a racial parallel between Asian Americans and African Americans by locating Asian Americans within a paradigm focusing on power and self-determination. It argued that racial oppression was a constitutive feature of American society and that Asians, like blacks, were racialized subjects. Second, it signaled that Asians of all ethnicities shared this relationship of subordination. Instead of demanding freedom only for Chinese or Chinese Americans, the program demanded freedom for Asians of all ethnicities under the rubric of "yellow people." Re-rendering the Panthers' program in yellow thus not only emphasized the racial nature of being Asian American but also the multiethnic nature of that category as well.

Asian Americans also performed their racial radicalism by displaying "the symbols of Asian resistance to imperialism, particularly those of the Cultural Revolution—the Mao jackets, the Red Book, the slogans" (Prashad 2001, 139–40). Red Guard rallies melded stylistic elements borrowed from the Panthers with Asian elements alluding to Red China. While they wore berets and armbands in Panther fashion, they also donned Mao jackets and waved Chinese flags as ways to highlight their racial linkage to the Asian leader.

In retrospect, Alex Hing describes the Red Guards' rallies as "political theater." His description of an event on May 1, 1969, shows the aptness of that label: "We came in blasting the 'East Is Red,' marching in. We had these hand-made Chinese flags and these handmade Red Guard armbands. We all wore field jackets. . . . We marched in and it looked like we took over the rally but it was actually agreed upon" (Hing 2000, 286–87). The Red Guards had planned the rally in conjunction with Chinese foreign students who wanted to commemorate the fiftieth anniversary of the May 4th movement, but the American-born Red Guards instead wanted to emphasize the current-day problems of poverty and racism in Chinatown. The spectacle of the Red Guards in military attire, marching to martial music and appearing to seize control of the rally, visually displayed the militance they sought to convey.

Though obviously influenced by and indebted to the Panthers, the Red Guard Party was not a mindless replication of the Black Panther Party. Instead, the Red Guards sought to apply the lessons of black power to the specific needs of Asian Americans. When they found that few children were participating in their Free Breakfast program, the Red Guards turned their attention to aiding Chinatown elders, instituting a Free Sunday Brunch program. Every Sunday at 1:00 P.M., the Red Guards would provide free food to the seniors who congregated in the public gathering space of Portsmouth Square. At its peak, the program fed more than three hundred people per week. The Red Guards' shift in focus from schoolchildren to seniors demonstrated the application of the principle of black power to the specific needs of Chinatown, in which many elderly men lacked familial support networks because of decades of gendered immigration restrictions. Like the rallies, the brunch program can be read as a kind of performance, as it enacted the "true spirit of practicing socialism" by providing, in especially public and visible ways, free food to those who needed it (*Red Guard Community Newspaper,* 8 September 1969, 2). In addition to the Free Sunday Brunch program, the Red Guards developed an array of community service programs that included a legal clinic, a child-care center, and a women's health clinic (Hing 2000, 292).

The Red Guards also performed their radicalism by holding community events such as movie nights. They screened the film *East Is Red,* which extolled the virtues of the People's Republic of China. Although the Red Guards had planned only a single showing, the community demand was so great that they "showed it three nights in a row to a packed house" (Hing 2000, 287). The screening of this pro-Chinese movie positioned the Red Guards on the Left and highlighted their presence as a political force in Chinatown. The high-profile manner in which they conducted their political, social, and cultural programs was deliberately performative and intended to draw attention to their organization.

The tenth plank of the Red Guard Party's 10 Point Program stands out as distinct from any appearing on the Black Panthers Party's program: it demands that "the

United States government recognize the People's Republic of China" and asserts that "Mao Tse-Tung is the true leader of the Chinese people: not Chiang Kai Shek" (*Red Guard Community Newspaper,* 12 March 1969, 7). Locating Mao as their ideological leader, the Red Guards "openly advocate[d] patriotism to the People's Republic of China" and studied his writings assiduously. To demonstrate their avowed communism, the Red Guards unfurled the five-starred Chinese flag at their rallies in Portsmouth Square ("History of the Red Guard Party" 1975, 84). While radicals of all races studied and admired Mao, the Red Guards related to him specifically as an Asian proponent of the worldwide movement against Western imperialism.

Declaring allegiance to the People's Republic of China and support for the Black Panther Party were courageous acts in a Chinatown dominated by the Consolidated Chinese Benevolent Associations (CCBA), an organization of conservative business elites with close ties to the nationalist Kuomintang Party (KMT) (Lai 1991). The Chinese American Left had nearly disappeared during the 1950s, hounded by violence, harassment, and black-listing from the CCBA, as well as McCarthyism (Nee and Nee 1976; Yu 1994). Thus, it was audacious for the Red Guards to unfurl the five-starred Chinese flag in 1969, as such an act invited serious and possibly violent repercussions. By openly performing their radicalism, the Red Guards (who advocated armed self-defense) presented a countervailing force to the KMT and its allies. In fact, the foreign students who cosponsored the May 4, 1969, rally invited the Red Guards to participate because they could provide a security force to prevent a feared KMT attempt to shut down the event (Hing 2000). According to Alex Hing and Harvey Dong, the major impact of these performances of Asian American radicalism was that they "opened up Chinatown to politics" by loosening the "KMT's grip" (Hing 2000, 289; Dong 2001, 202).

While the Panthers clearly provided inspiration and guidance to the Red Guards, they did not create Asian American radicalism de novo. Before joining the Black Panthers, Richard Aoki had developed an oppositional stance to the war in Vietnam during his service in the army and after his discharge had participated in the Vietnam Day Committee (Aoki 2000). Similarly, Alex Hing was no political naïf. By the time he arrived at the Leway pool hall he had already racked up significant encounters with the New Left, including participating in Stop the Draft Week and demonstrating for free speech at San Francisco City College. Eventually he returned "back to Chinatown" to "hang out with my old gang, my old crowd and to try to politicize them." At Leway, however, he discovered that some of the people there (particularly the "sisters" who had been associating with Panthers) were already "miles ahead" of him politically (Hing 2000, 282–84). Hence, while the Panthers' influence on the Leway youth is undeniable, a core of Asian Americans had already begun to radicalize and merely needed a framework within which to articulate their discontent with society.

"A Yellow Minstrel Show"?

Asian Americans performing blackness raises the fascinating possibility of yellow minstrelsy. Like the Irish of the nineteenth century, whom David Roediger argues sought to resolve their ambivalent relationship to whiteness in part through practicing blackface minstrelsy, Asian Americans in the 1960s suffered from discrimination expressed in racial terms, yet occupied a higher socioeconomic position than did blacks (Roediger 1991). Furthermore, the Red Guards and Chin clearly explored Asian American identity by "playing in the dark" (Morrison 1992). Finally, they invested black male bodies with divergent types of potency: political, for the Red Guards, versus sexual, for Chin.

Frank Chin charged that the Red Guard Party's performances of blackness constituted "a yellow minstrel show." To him, it was the inauthenticity of the Red Guard Party's Panther-inspired rap of "brothers and sisters," "power to the people," and "fight the pig" that marked the Red Guards as minstrels. While acknowledging that blackness provided a lens through which to perceive the racial positioning of "yellows," Chin distinguished between the experiences of Asian Americans and African Americans: "We started talking about the sisters in the street and the brothers in the joint. I'd been in the joint and I didn't see any yellows there. I didn't see so many of our sisters walking the streets. That wasn't our thing" (Terkel 1992, 310). Chin's comment reflects a suspicion of Asian American radicals who overly romanticized the revolutionary potential of the lumpen, a hallmark of Panther ideology.

While charging the Red Guards with inauthentic performances of blackness, Chin specifically denies that his characters in *The Chickencoop Chinaman* practice minstrelsy. Lee, the main woman in the play, accuses Tam and Kenji of deriding blacks by the way they walk and talk (Chin 1981, 13). Kenji had earned the nickname "Blackjap Kenji" during high school in postwar Oakland because of his full-fledged adoption of black style, fashion, and language. As an adult, he continues to identify with blacks, saying, "I live with 'em, I talk like 'em, I dress . . . maybe even eat what they eat." Although he is a dentist, he lives in the Oakland section of Pittsburgh, "right in the heart of the black ghetto," because it feels "just like home" (Chin 1981, 3, 20, 21, 9). Like Kenji, Tam adopts black speech patterns to the extent that when Charley Popcorn first meets Tam, he cannot believe that the black-sounding voice he had heard on the telephone belongs to the Chinese American standing before him (Chin 1981, 40). Tam and Kenji deny being minstrels, because their performances express an identity that feels genuine and appropriate to them. "Maybe we act black," Kenji insists, "but it's not fake" (Chin 1981, 19). This emphasis on verisimilitude takes on additional significance, given Chin's later distinction between the real and the fake as an analytical tool for Asian American cultural criticism.

Chin thus distinguished between a generative adoption of blackness—which highlighted Asian Americans as a racialized group, spoke directly to conditions in Asian American communities, and emerged from organic relations between Asian Americans and blacks—and a nongenerative, vulgar, and overly romantic imitation of blackness. The critical distinction for Chin was *political*. The Red Guard Party's rap constituted yellow minstrelsy to Chin because he rejected its emphasis on the Panther's version of revolutionary nationalism as a way to "organize" and "get together" (Terkel 1992, 310).

Asian American 1960s performances of blackness can be seen in contrast to the earlier minstrel performances of probationary whites in the mid-nineteenth to early twentieth centuries, when blackface provided a means by which the Irish could earn the "wages of whiteness" and Jews established a "conjunction between blackface and Americanization" in motion pictures (Roediger 1991; Rogin 1993, 13). If the essence of minstrelsy was whites and soon-to-be whites performing blackness in order to partake in, while simultaneously disavowing, the pleasures thought to reside in unrestrained blackness, then one could argue that Asian American performances of blackness did not constitute minstrelsy. Asian Americans fit only half of Eric Lott's definition of blackface minstrelsy as ambivalent—both desirous and anxious (Lott 1993, 50–52). Covetous of black radicalism and masculinity, but not fearful of being stained by blackness, they sought to connect Asian Americans to African Americans. The Red Guards sought political unity with blacks through radicalism, and in *The Chickencoop Chinaman* Chin covets the supposed (indeed, stereotypical) virility of black men, but neither distanced Asian Americans from blacks. Rather than pursuing whiteness, these performances were intended to locate Asian Americans as a racialized group along-side blacks. The Red Guards and Chin argued that Asian Americans should share an affinity with African Americans based on their common subjugated racial position, and that Asian Americans should consider the problems and possibilities—first explored by blacks—involved in mobilizing around a racial identity. Their performances of blackness thus signaled an explicit rejection of rather than an assimilation into whiteness.

Asian American mimesis was neither minstrelsy nor parody. Instead, following Homi Bhabha's suggestion that mimicry is always ambivalent, I argue that these performances of blackness produced a "subject of difference" that was "almost the same, but not quite" (Bhabha 1994, 86). Instead of reproducing blackness, they constructed a new form of Asian American subjectivity, one organized around racial commonality among Asians.

Blackness and Asian American Masculinity

Both the Red Guard Party and Frank Chin enacted performances that articulated a black-inspired vision of Asian American masculinity as a form of resistance to racism. But whereas the Red Guards admired the radical politics enacted by black men, Chin sought the sexual potency that they embodied.

As Tracye Matthews has argued, the Panthers' early actions and statements created a "self-consciously masculine, 'lumpen' public identity for the Party" that equated resisting racism with black men regaining their masculinity" (Matthews 1998, 278–82). Over time, however, women in the Black Panther Party became increasingly visible, not only in the rank and file but also in leadership positions. Eldridge Cleaver's 1969 repudiation of "male chauvinism" in his statement of support for Erica Huggins reflected a new official ideology that sought the "liberation of women" (Cleaver 1969). Of course, this shift was hardly seamless, as women in the party continued to struggle with sexism and barriers to leadership (Matthews 1998, 285–92).

The Red Guard's initial adoption of the Panthers' style and strategies reflected the Black Panthers' first phase of hypermasculinity in several ways. Donning berets and armbands, and marching into rallies in formation, cast the Guards as a paramilitary organization. Using confrontational language and terminology—such as "pigs" and "honkies"—also demonstrated a certain swaggering machismo. Finally, calling attention to police brutality as a main concern not only replicated a key Panther strategy but also framed the problems of Chinatown in primarily male-centered ways.

Although performances of masculinity were key to the Red Guard Party's initial phase, some evidence points to an uneven evolution in the gender ideologies and practices of its members. When the Red Guard Party disbanded in 1971, one faction merged with I Wor Kuen, a radical group based in New York City, to form National I Wor Kuen (IWK) (Wei 1994; "History of the Red Guard Party" 1975). IWK explicitly advocated equality for women: its "12 Point Program and Platform" included a plank that demanded "an end to male chauvinism and sexual exploitation" and declared unequivocally, "Sisters and brothers are equals fighting for our people" (I Wor Kuen 2000). Women such as Carmen Chow played prominent, perhaps even preeminent, roles as leaders (Wei 1994). Furthermore, IWK (along with other Asian American organizations, including Wei Min She) struggled for higher wages, better working conditions, and unionization for female garment workers and stressed the necessity of women's liberation as integral to national liberation ("Political Summation of the Jung Sai Strike" 1975). Finally, IWK repudiated the Red Guards' prior "ultra-military line"—which advocated "armed struggle" and "violence"—as being "narrow and incorrect" to the extent that it neglected building class consciousness among workers ("History of the Red Guard Party" 1976, 81, 86–87; League of Revolutionary Struggle 1978, 42).

This shift in rhetorical focus from militarism to community organization indicates a reordering of the archetypal roles within RGP/IWK's imaginary. The role of badass Chinatown cat, which could be played only by a man, was eclipsed by the dedicated community worker, which a woman could play just as well as a man. Thus, the transformation from the Red Guard Party (hypermasculine, militarist, male-led) to IWK (egalitarian in principle, vanguardist, female-led) suggests that ideologies and practices of gender among Asian American revolutionaries were contested and dynamic.

While the Red Guards initially performed masculinist blackness to express their political radicalism, Frank Chin turned to black masculinity to recover the lost virility of Asian American men. *The Chickencoop Chinaman* has been the subject of extensive literary criticism. But remarkably little attention has been paid to its racial dynamics, and literary critics have generally failed to properly historicize the play as a product of the black power period. Reading the play within this context opens it to interpretations of its delicate intertwining of race, gender, and sexuality.

Finding Asian American masculinity lacking, Tam and Kenji turn toward black men as role models. In particular, they idolize a boxing champion named Ovaltine Jack Dancer. Chin links Asian American men to black men specifically through their penises. At one point, Tam and Kenji fondly remember how they had once been driving with Ovaltine, when all three of them had stepped outside the car and begun "pissing in the bushes." Amid this reflection, Kenji recalls the previous time he had urinated with a black man. While visiting New Orleans, he couldn't decide whether to use the segregated white or black facilities. A "black dishwasher," seeing his "plight," guided him to the black restroom and they had stood together pissing into adjacent urinals (Chin 1981, 20). The dishwasher resolved Asian American racial indeterminacy by directing Kenji away from whiteness and toward blackness.

Later, when Lee, the only Asian American woman in the play, insists that she's "just one of the boys," Kenji facetiously suggests that she "go out by the car and piss in the bushes" (Chin 1981, 25). Lee's inability to do so further emphasizes the phallic link between Tam and Kenji and the various African American men. Furthermore, Lee, who is only part Chinese and can pass for white, is thus granted only partial status as an Asian American.

Tam initially travels to Pittsburgh to track down Charley Popcorn, whom the boxer Ovaltine claims as his father, in order to make a movie exploring how this "mighty Daddy" made his son into a great fighter (Chin 1981, 14). Ovaltine maintains that he was inspired to be a fighter when he saw his father's "mighty back ripplin [sic] with muscles" and covered with "whiplash scars." According to this genealogy, Ovaltine derived his own masculinity from his father's manliness, which was stymied by racial oppression, as even Popcorn's rippling muscles had not exempted him from the Jim Crow humiliation of whipping. Ovaltine goes on to assert that as an adolescent, he had physically beaten a white boy, an act that symbolically redressed his father's degradation. Fearing the consequences, Ovaltine and Popcorn had fled in their automobile. When clear of danger, they had stopped, stepped out of the car, and stood "pissin [sic] by the roadside" (Chin 1981, 48). By partaking in the ceremonial urination, Popcorn had bestowed upon Ovaltine his masculinity—signified by his phallus and redeemed by his son's transgressive resistance—and Ovaltine does likewise with Tam and Kenji. Popcorn begets Ovaltine. Ovaltine begets Tam and Kenji. Masculinity and racial pride flow from the Adamic black father to his figurative Asian American sons.

This tidy story of masculine descent disintegrates almost immediately. Upon hearing Tam relate Ovaltine's story, Popcorn first denies that he is Ovaltine's father, then pulls up his shirt to reveal a smooth, scarless back (Chin 1981, 48–49). Charley Popcorn, bearing no whiplash marks and being "nobody's father," fails to be the virile progenitor Tam seeks (Chin 1981, 63). The revelation that Ovaltine's past is fictitious suggests Chin's ambivalence toward Asian American romanticization of blackness. Though acknowledging that performances of blackness played an instrumental role in galvanizing Asian American considerations of their racial positioning, Chin indicates that blind imitation will ultimately prove insufficient. Tam and Kenji begin by performing blackness to recuperate their masculinity, but ultimately find blackness to be an unsatisfactory model for Asian American identity.

His dreams of masculine descent from blackness crushed, Tam turns to Asian American history as a source of manly endeavors. Earlier, Lee had expressed disapproval of people trying to "make it on the backs of blacks," a metaphor that Chin enacts literally (Chin 1981, 20). In a soliloquy between scenes, Tam sits astride Popcorn's back as he recalls the day his white wife left him, a story emphasizing his emasculation at the hands of a white woman. He concludes with the Chickencoop Chinaman's lament, "Buck Buck Bagaw," the phrase recalling Chinese American male impotence (Chin 1981, 51–52). At his lowest point, weak and humiliated by a white woman, Tam relies on a black man to hold him up. However, in the next scene the men reverse positions: Tam hoists Popcorn onto his back. As he carries Popcorn upstairs, Tam shouts, "We built the fuckin [sic] railroad. Moved a whole Sierra Nevada over" (Chin 1981, 53). This reversal signals Chin's departure from the model of black masculinity and a turn —expressed more fully in later works—toward excavating Asian American heroism in historical acts like building the railroad (Chin 1988; Chin 1991).

In the play's final scene, Kenji announces that he and Lee are expecting a baby (Chin 1981, 64). Impending fatherhood marks the end of his inmaturess, which is achieved only through establishing a phallic connection to black men, first in New Orleans with the dishwasher and later on the roadside beside Ovaltine. In *The Chickencoop Chinaman*, Asian American men regain their masculinity by taking hold of their phalluses, alongside black men doing the same.

Conclusion

Despite their divergent politics, in the late 1960s and early 1970s, both the Red Guard Party and Frank Chin performed blackness as a way to conceptualize Asian American identity, resist assimilation, and build multiethnic solidarity. However, both the Red Guards and Chin founded their versions of racial solidarity on problematic notions of masculinity.

Performances of black masculinity by the Red Guard Party and Frank Chin did not exhaust the range of possibilities for Asian American subjectivities. Instead, their late-1960s versions of Asian American power, which tended to marginalize women and homosexuals, required substantial revisions. Women in the Asian American movement commonly confronted sexism, within both organizations and personal relationships. Like others in the New Left, some Asian American women were relegated to performing menial tasks, struggled to be heard on matters of ideology and strategy, and faced opposition when they sought leadership positions (Wei 1994; "Asian Women as Leaders" 1971). Asian American women also confronted men who sought control over the sexuality of "their" women and saw them simply as "legit lay[s] for the revolutionary" men (Wei 1994, 76–77; Tanaka 1971). But the Asian American women's movement was not separatist, and instead sought to make women's liberation central to the larger Asian American movement (Ling 1989). Indeed, the Asian American women's and antiwar movements opened new spaces for Asian American women to develop "sisterhood" with each other and develop leadership skills (Geron and Lee 2003). Women like Pat Sumi, Evelyn Yoshimura, and Carmen Chow performed key, visible leadership roles within the Asian American Movement.

During the early 1970s, the gender ideologies and practices of the Asian American Left underwent dramatic contestation. *Gidra*, the premier movement periodical, published a special issue on women and men in 1972. IWK and its chief rival, Wei Min She, organized female sweatshop workers in 1974 and 1975 ("Political Summation of the Jung Sai Strike" 1975; "Who Dares to Make Waves?" 1974, 5; Wei 1994). By 1975, declarations linking women's oppression to U.S. imperialism and capitalism were obligatory. However, these changes in the Asian American Left were not mirrored by Frank Chin, whose convictions about gender and sexuality remained steadfast.

As the Asian American women's movement demonstrates, the Red Guards and Chin were by no means solely responsible for shaping the category "Asian American." Activism by Filipino, Korean, and Japanese Americans, which I have not discussed here, contributed vitally to its formation. Since 1965, new migrants have radically altered its ethnic composition and immigrant status, and technological innovations have made its national boundaries more porous. Yet the challenge to twenty-first-century Asian American identity remains the same as it was in 1969: how to make sense of a landscape marked by fissures of ethnicity, class, gender, and sexuality, and how to build political solidarities that bridge these rifts (Lowe 1996). At the birth of Asian America, the Red Guard Party and Frank Chin demonstrated through their performances of blackness both the power and limitations of organizing around racial identity.

NOTES

Originally published in *American Quarterly* 57.4 (2005): 1079–1103. © 2005 The Johns Hopkins University Press, reprint by permission. I would like to thank Kate Masur, Wendy Kozol, Pablo Mitchell, Laura Pulido, Josephine Lee, and the editors and anonymous readers at *American Quarterly* for helpful comments on this essay and previous versions.

1. Espiritu labels this solidarity "Asian American panethnicity." I propose instead the admittedly somewhat unwieldy term "multiethnic Asian American racial identity," because it underlines the process of racialization that binds Asian ethnic groups together.

2. Although Wong, Dirlik, and Lowe allow for complexities in the origins of Asian American identity, they tend to argue that American nationalism formed its basis.

REFERENCES

A History of the Red Guard Party. 1975. *IWK Journal* 2.

Asian American Political Alliance Newspaper (AAPA). 1969. 1.4 (March).

Allen, Ernest, Jr. 1995. Waiting for Tojo: The Pro-Japan Vigil of Black Missourians, 1932–1943. *Gateway Heritage* 16(2): 38–55.

Aoki, Richard. 2000. Interview by Dolly Veale. In *Legacy to Liberation: Politics and Culture of Revolutionary Asian/Pacific America,* eds. Fred Ho et al. Boston: AK Press.

Asian Women as Leaders. 1971. In *Roots: An Asian American Reader,* eds. Amy Tachiki et al. Los Angeles: UCLA Asian American Studies Center Press, 297–98.

Bhabha, Homi K. 1994. *The Location of Culture.* New York: Routledge.

Boggs, Grace Lee. 1998. *Living for Change: An Autobiography.* Minneapolis: University of Minnesota Press.

Burner, David. 1996. *Making Peace with the 60s.* Princeton, NJ: Princeton University Press.

Carmichael, Stokely and Charles V. Hamilton. 1967. *Black Power: The Politics of Liberation in America.* New York: Vintage Books.

Chavez, Ernesto. 2002. *Mi Raza Primero! Nationalism, Identity, and Insurgency in the Chicano Movement in Los Angeles, 1966–1978.* Berkeley: University of California Press.

Chin, Frank. 1981. *The Chickencoop Chinaman and Year of the Dragon: Two Plays by Frank Chin.* Seattle: University of Washington Press.

Chin, Frank. 1988. *Chinaman Pacific and Frisco R.R. Co.* Minneapolis, MN: Coffee House Press.

Chin, Frank. 1991. Come All Ye Asian American Writers of the Real and the Fake. In *The Big AIIIEEEEE! An Anthology of Chinese American and Japanese American Literature*, ed. Jeffery Paul Chan et al. New York: Meridian, 1–92..

Chin, Frank. 1991. *Donald Duk: A Novel.* Minneapolis, MN: Coffee House Press.

Chin, Frank, et al. (eds.). 1974. *Aiiieeeee! An Anthology of Asian-American Writers.* Washington, DC: Howard University Press.

Choi, Jennifer Jung Hee. 1999. At the Margin of Asian American Political Experience: The Life of Grace Lee Boggs. *Amerasia Journal* 25(2): 18–40.

Cleaver, Eldridge. 1969. Message to Sister Erica Huggins of the Black Panther Party. *The Black Panther,* 5 July.

Daniels, Roger. 1962. *The Politics of Prejudice: The Anti-Japanese Movement in California and the Struggle for Japanese Exclusion.* Berkeley: University of California Press.

Deutsch, Nathaniel. 2001. "The Asiatic Black Man": An African American Orientalism? *Journal of Asian American Studies* 4(3): 193–208.

Dirlik, Arif. 1996. Asians on the Rim: Transnational Capital and Local Community in the Making of Contemporary Asian America. *Amerasia Journal* 22(3): 1–24.

Dong, Harvey. 2001. Transforming Student Elites to Community Activists. In *Asian Americans: The Movement and the Moment,* ed. Steve Louie and Glenn Omatsu. Los Angeles: UCLA Asian American Studies Center Press, 186–205.

Elbaum, Max. 2002. *Revolution in the Air: Sixties Radicals Turn to Lenin, Mao, and Che.* London: Verso.

Eng, David. 2001. *Racial Castration: Managing Masculinity in Asian America.* Durham, NC: Duke University Press.

Espiritu, Yen Le. 1992. *Asian American Panethnicity: Bridging Institutions and Identities.* Philadelphia: Temple University Press.

Foner, Philip S. (ed.). 1995. *The Black Panthers Speak* (2nd ed.). New York: Da Capo Press.

Fujino, Diane C. 2005. *Heartbeat of Struggle: The Revolutionary Life of Yuri Kochiyama.* Minneapolis: University of Minnesota Press.

Geron, Kim and Pam Tau Lee. 2003. Unpublished interview with Daryl Maeda, January 31.

Gitlin, Todd. 1995. *Twilight of Common Dreams: Why America Is Wracked by Culture Wars.* New York: Metropolitan Books.

Hilliard, David and Lewis Cole. 1993. *This Side of Glory.* Boston: Little, Brown.

Hing, Alex. 2000. Former Minister of Information for the Red Guard Party and Founding Member of I Wor Kuen: Interviewed by Fred Ho and Steve Yip. In *Legacy to Liberation: Politics and Culture of Revolutionary Asian/Pacific America,* eds. Fred Ho et al. Boston: AK Press, 279–96.

Ho, Fred, et al. (eds.). 2000. *Legacy to Liberation: Politics and Culture of Revolutionary Asian/Pacific America.* Boston: AK Press.

I Wor Kuen. 2000. Twelve-Point Platform and Program. In *Legacy to Liberation: Politics and Culture of Revolutionary Asian/Pacific America,* eds. Fred Ho et al. Boston: AK Press, 406.

Ichioka, Yuji. 1986–87. A Study in Dualism: James Yoshinori Sakamoto and the Japanese American Courier, 1928–42. *Amerasia Journal* 13: 49–81.

Kelley, Robin D. G. and Betsy Esch. 1999. Black Like Mao: Red China and Black Revolution. *Souls* 1(4): 6–41.

Kim, Elaine. 1990. "Such Opposite Creatures": Men and Women in Asian American Literature. *Michigan Quarterly Review* 39(1): 68–93.

Kurashige, Lon. 2002. *Japanese American Celebration and Conflict: A History of Ethnic Identity and Festival in Los Angeles, 1934–1990.* Berkeley: University of California Press, 2002.

Lai, Him Mark. 1991. The Kuomintang in Chinese American Communities before World War II. In *Entry Denied: Exclusion and the Chinese Community in America, 1882–1943*, ed. Sucheng Chan. Philadelphia: Temple University Press, 170–212.

League of Revolutionary Struggle (LRS). 1978. Statements on the Founding of the League of Revolutionary Struggle (Marxist-Leninist). New York: Getting Together Publications.

Lee, Robert G. 1999. *Orientals: Asian Americans in Popular Culture*. Philadelphia: Temple University Press.

Ling, Susie. 1989. The Mountain Movers: Asian American Women's Movement in Los Angeles. *Amerasia Journal* 15(1): 51–67.

Lipsitz, George. 1998. *The Possessive Investment in Whiteness: How White People Profit from Identity Politics*. Philadelphia: Temple University Press.

Lott, Eric. 1993. *Love and Theft: Blackface Minstrelsy and the American Working Class*. New York: Oxford University Press.

Louie, Steve. 1997. Unpublished interview with Daryl J. Maeda.

Louie, Steve and Glenn Omatsu (eds.). 2001. *Asian Americans: The Movement and the Moment*. Los Angeles: UCLA Asian American Studies Center Press.

Lowe, Lisa. 1996. *Immigrant Acts: On Asian American Cultural Politics*. Durham, NC: Duke University Press.

Lyman, Stanford M. 1971. Red Guard on Grant Avenue. In *Culture and Civility in San Francisco*, ed. Howard S. Becker. Chicago: Transaction Books, 20–52.

Matthews, Tracye. 1998. "No One Ever Asks, What a Man's Place in the Revolution Is": Gender and the Politics of the Black Panther Party, 1966–1971. In *The Black Panther Party Reconsidered*, ed. Charles E. Jones. Baltimore: Black Classics Press.

Melendez, Miguel. 2003. *We Took the Streets: Fighting for Latino Rights with the Young Lords*. New York: St. Martin's Press.

Morrison, Toni. 1992. *Playing in the Dark: Whiteness and the Literary Imagination*. Cambridge, MA: Harvard University Press.

Nee, Brett de Bary and Victor Nee. 1976. The Kuomintang in Chinatown. In *Counterpoint*, eds. Emma Gee et al. Los Angeles: UCLA Asian American Studies Center Press, 146–51.

Okihiro, Gary Y. 1994. *Margins and Mainstreams: Asians in American History and Culture*. Seattle: University of Washington Press.

Omi, Michael and Howard Winant. 1994. *Racial Formation in the United States: From the 1960s to the 1990s*. New York: Routledge.

Palumbo-Liu, David. 1999. *Asian/American: Historical Crossings of a Racial Frontier*. Stanford, CA: Stanford University Press.

Pearson, Hugh. 1994. *Shadow of the Panther: Huey Newton and the Price of Black Power in America*. Reading, MA: Addison-Wesley.

Petersen, William. 1966. Success Story, Japanese-American Style. *New York Times Magazine*, January 9.

Political Summation of the Jung Sai Strike. 1975. *IWK Journal* 2: 49–72.

Prashad, Vijay. 2001. *Everybody Was Kung Fu Fighting: Afro-Asian Connections and the Myth of Cultural Purity*. Boston: Beacon Press.

Roediger, David. 1991. *The Wages of Whiteness: Race and the Making of the American Working Class*. New York: Verso.

Rogin, Michael. 1993. *Blackface, White Noise: Jewish Immigrants in the Hollywood Melting Pot*. Berkeley: University of California Press.

Seale, Bobby. 1970. *Seize the Time: The Story of the Black Panther Party and Huey P. Newton*. Reprint, Baltimore: Black Classics Press, 1991.

Shimakawa, Karen. 2002. *National Abjection: The Asian American Body Onstage.* Durham, NC: Duke University Press.

Simpson, Caroline Chung. 2001. *An Absent Presence: Japanese Americans in Postwar American Culture, 1945–1960.* Durham, NC: Duke University Press.

Smith, Paul Chaat and Robert Allen Warrior. 1996. *Like a Hurricane: The Indian Movement from Alcatraz to Wounded Knee.* New York: Norton.

Tachiki, Amy, et al. (eds.). 1971. *Roots: An Asian American Reader.* Los Angeles: UCLA Asian American Studies Center Press.

Tanaka, Tomi. from a lotus blossom cunt. In *Roots: An Asian American Reader,* eds. Amy Tachiki et al. Los Angeles: UCLA Asian American Studies Center Press, 109.

Taylor, Quintard. 1994. *The Forging of a Black Community: Seattle's Central District from 1870 through the Civil Rights Era.* Seattle: University of Washington Press.

Taylor, Quintard. 1998. *In Search of the Racial Frontier: African Americans in the American West.* New York: Norton.

Terkel, Studs. 1992. *Race: How Blacks and Whites Think and Feel about the American Obsession.* New York: New Press.

Tyson, Timothy. 2001. *Radio Free Dixie: Robert F. Williams and the Roots of Black Power.* Chapel Hill: University of North Carolina Press.

U.S. News and World Report. 1966. Success Story of One Minority Group in the U.S. December 26.

Van Deburg, William. 1992. *New Day in Babylon: The Black Power Movement and American Culture, 1965–1975.* Chicago: University of Chicago Press.

Wei, William. 1994. *The Asian American Movement.* Philadelphia: Temple University Press.

Who Dares to Make Waves? 1974. *Wei Min Newspaper,* October–November.

Wolfe, Tom. 1970. *Radical Chic and Mau-Mauing the Flak-Catcher.* New York: Farrar, Straus, and Giroux.

Wong, Martin. 1998a. Yellow Panther. *Giant Robot* 10: 66–69.

Wong, Martin. 1998b. Panther Brotherhood. *Giant Robot* 10: 76–77.

Wong, Martin. 1998c. Berkeley and Beyond. *Giant Robot* 10: 70–71.

Wong, Martin. 1998d. Red Star in America. *Giant Robot* 10: 80

Wong, Sau-ling C. 1995. Denationalization Reconsidered: Asian American Cultural Criticism at a Theoretical Crossroads. *Amerasia Journal* 21(1): 1–27.

Young Lords Party. 1971. *Palante: Young Lords Party.* New York: McGraw-Hill.

Yu, Renqiu. 1994. *To Save China, to Save Ourselves: The Chinese Hand Laundry Alliance of New York.* Philadelphia: Temple University Press.

1. Trace the evolution of the San Francisco State College strike as outlined by Ume-moto: What motivated the strike? Who was involved? In what ways did the strike transform the consciousness of its participants? What other struggles evolved out of the Strike? What were the significant effects of the strike and what legacy did it leave behind for Asian Americans?

2. Omatsu contends that the 1970s signaled the ultimate disintegration of the social movements founded in the 1960s, specifically those movements centered on the lib-eration for racial/ethnic minorities. How did this process of disintegration contrib-ute to what Omatsu calls "the winter of civil rights"? What implications were there for Asian American Studies?

3. How has the political landscape changed for Asian Americans in the 1980s? Why were the 1980s an ambiguous period for Asian American empowerment? How does this period compare with the 1960s and with the 1990s? Are the concepts developed during the Asian American Movement—self-determination, liberation, militant struggle—meaningful and relevant to Asian Americans today? Are the ideas of the movement alive today, or have they atrophied into relics—the curiosities of a by-gone era of youthful and excessive idealism?

4. Maeda points out that both the Red Guard Party and Frank Chin "performed" blackness as a way to conceptualize Asian American identity, resist assimilation, and build multiethnic solidarity. However, both the Red Guards and Chin founded their versions of racial solidarity on problematic notions of masculinity. Moreover, the late-1960s versions of Asian American power tended to marginalize women and homosexuals. Provide examples from the reading that demonstrate both the possibilities and limitations of blackness as a model for Asian American identity formation.

SUGGESTED READINGS

Deutsch, Nathaniel. 2001. "The Asiatic Black Man": An African American Orientalism? *Journal of Asian American Studies* 4(3): 193–208.

Dirlik, Arif. 1996. Asians on the Rim: Transnational Capital and Local Community in the Mak-ing of Contemporary Asian America. *Amerasia Journal* 22(3): 1–24.

Gee, Emma, et al. (eds.). 1976. *Counterpoint: Perspectives on Asian America.* Los Angeles: UCLA Asian American Studies Center.

Ho, Fred. 2000. *Legacy to Liberation: Politics & Culture of Revolutionary Asian/Pacific America.* New York: AK Press.

Hune, Shirley. 1989. Opening the American Mind and Body: The Role of Asian American Stud-ies. *Change,* November/December.

Kibria, Nazli. 1998. The Racial Gap: South Asian American Racial Identity and the Asian Amer-ican Movement. Pp. 69–78 in Lavina Dhingra Shankar and Rajini Srikanth (eds.), *A Part Yet Apart: South Asians in Asian America.* Philadelphia: Temple University Press.

Lien, Pei-Te. 2001. *The Making of Asian America through Political Participation.* Philadelphia, PA: Temple University Press.

Ling, Susie. 1989. The Mountain Movers: Asian American Women's Movement in Los Angeles. *Amerasia Journal* 15(1): 51–67.

Louie, Steve Louie and Glenn Omatsu (eds.). 2001. *Asian Americans: The Movement and the Moment.* Los Angeles: UCLA Asian American Studies Center Press.

Nakanishi, Don. 1995/96. Linkages and Boundaries: Twenty-Five Years of Asian American Studies. *Amerasia Journal* 21(3): xvii–xxv.

Narasaki, Karen and June Han. 2004. Asian American Civil Rights Advocacy and Research Agenda after 9/11. *AAPI Nexus* 2(1). 1–17.

Ongiri, Amy Abugo. 2002. "He Wanted to Be Just Like Bruce Lee": African American, Kung Fu Theater and Cultural Exchange at the Margins. *Journal of Asian American Studies* 5(1): 31–40.

Ono, Kent A. 2004. *Asian American Studies after Critical Mass.* New York: Blackwell Publishing.

Ono, Kent A. 2005. Asian American Studies after 9/11. Pp. 439–51 in Cameron McCarthy, Warren C. Richlow, Greg Dimitriadis, and Nadine Dolby (eds.), *Race, Identity, and Representation in Education* (2nd ed.). New York: Routledge.

Prashad, Vijay. 2000. *The Karma of Brown Folk.* Minneapolis: University of Minnesota Press.

Prashad, Vijay. 2001. *Everybody Is Kung Fu Fighting: Afro-American Connections and the Myth of Cultural Purity.* Boston: Beacon Press.

Saito, Leland T. , K. Geron, E. De La Cruz, and J. Singh. 2001. Asian Pacific Americans Social Movements and Interest Groups. *PS: Political Science and Politics* 34(3).

Shimakawa, Karen. 2002. *National Abjection: The Asian American Body Onstage.* Durham, NC: Duke University Press.

Tachiki, Amy, Eddie Wong, Franklin Odo, with Buck Wong (eds.). 1971. *Roots: An Asian American Reader.* Los Angeles: UCLA Asian American Studies Center.

Wang, L. Ling-Chi. 1996. Asian Americans and Debates about Affirmative Action. *Asian American Policy Review* 6: 49–57.

Wei, William. 1993. *The Asian American Movement.* Philadelphia: Temple University Press.

Zia, Helen. 2001. *Asian American Dreams: The Emergence of an American People.* New York: Farrar, Strauss, Giroux.

FILMS

Choy, Curtis (producer/director). 1993. *The Fall of the I-Hotel* (58-minute documentary).

Ding, Loni (producer/director). 1991. *Claiming a Voice: The Visual Communications Story* (60-minute documentary).

Shiekh, Irum (director/producer). *On Strike! Ethnic Studies, 1969–1999.* (30-minute documentary).

Tajima-Peña, Rene (director, coproducer). *My America (Or Honk If You Love Buddha)* (87-minute documentary).

Tajiri, Rea and Pat Saunders (directors/producers). 1993. *Yuri Kochiyama: Passion for Justice* (57-minute documentary).

Winn, Robert (director). 2005. *Grassroots Rising* (60-minute documentary).

Part II

Traversing Borders

*Contemporary Asian Immigration
to the United States*

Transforming Asian America
Globalization and Contemporary Immigration to the United States

Min Zhou and J. V. Gatewood

Anyone who rides the subway in New York, drives on the freeway in California, or walks into any urban classroom will immediately feel the impact of contemporary immigration. Large-scale, non-European immigration to the United States began in the late 1960s and has accelerated at rapid speeds since the early 1990s after a long hiatus due to restricted immigration. Between 1971 and 1995, approximately 17.1 million immigrants came to the United States, almost matching the total number of immigrants who arrived during the first quarter of the century (17.2 million admissions between 1901 and 1925) when immigration was at its peak.[1] Since 1995, another 8.8 million have immigrated legally to the United States as permanent residents. Unlike turn-of-the-century immigrants, today's newcomers have come predominantly from non-European countries. Since the 1980s, 88 percent of the immigrants admitted to the United States have come from the Americas (excluding Canada) and Asia, and only 10 percent have come from Europe compared to more than 90 percent at the earlier peak. The share of immigrants from Asia as a proportion of the total admissions grew from a tiny 5 percent in the 1950s to 11 percent in the 1960s and 33 percent in the 1970s, and has remained at around 35 percent since 1980.[2] The Philippines, China/Taiwan, Korea, India, and Vietnam have been on the list of top-ten sending countries since 1980. What caused this massive human movement in recent years, particularly from Asia? Who are these newcomers? How does the host society receive them? How do they affect U.S.-born peoples of Asian descent who share their cultural heritage and their communities, and how are they affected by the natives and their new homeland? These questions are of central importance, as they will certainly determine the future of Asian America.

The Driving Forces behind Contemporary Immigration from Asia

U.S. immigration legislation has always appeared humanitarian in principle and democratic in ideology. However, beginning with the Chinese Exclusion Act of 1882, Congress passed various laws to restrict immigration from the "barred zone" (known as the Asia-Pacific triangle) and to single out Asian immigrants for exclusion. Asian immigrants not only were barred from reentering the country but also were deemed "aliens ineligible to citizenship" and consequently prevented from owning land, attaining professional occupations, sending for their family members, marrying white Americans, and becoming equal participants in American society. World War II marked a watershed for Asian Americans since their homelands, Japan excepted, were allies of the United States. Congress repealed the Chinese Exclusion Act in 1943 and other Asian exclusion acts at the end of the war and passed the War Brides Act in 1945 to allow American GIs to reunite with their Asian wives in the United States. The public began to shift its perception of Asian Americans from "yellow peril" to "model minorities." This change in perception included Japanese Americans, whose population —some 120,000 at its peak—languished in American-style concentration camps for the duration of World War II. Two-thirds of these prisoners were American citizens. In 1952, Congress passed the McCarran-Walter Act, making all national-origin groups eligible for naturalization. While this act eliminated race as a barrier to immigration, it still maintained the national-origins quota system in immigration policy that limited migrants from specific regions to token numbers up until the late 1960s.

During the 1960s, at the time when the United States was entangled in an unpopular war against Vietnam while also in the throes of the civil rights movement, both international and domestic crises pushed Congress to clean up the remaining discriminatory immigration legislation. Meanwhile, labor-market projections showed that an acute shortage of engineering and medical personnel would soon materialize unless the United States opened its door to foreign labor. In response, Congress passed the Hart-Cellar Act in 1965. This landmark piece of legislation abolished the national-origins quota system and strove toward two goals: reuniting families and meeting the labor market demand for skilled labor. Since the law went into effect in 1968, immigration from Asia and the Americas has accelerated rapidly, with little sign of slowing down. Between 1971 and 2005, a total of 8.7 million Asians were admitted into the United States as legal immigrants (not counting the thousands of refugees who began to arrive in the mid-1970s).[3] The majority of contemporary Asian immigrants were either family-sponsored migrants (more than two-thirds) or employer-sponsored skilled workers (about one-fifth). The Hart-Cellar Act of 1965 has impacted Asian immigration, but the main driving forces are beyond the scope of U.S. immigration policy. Recent changes worldwide—global economic restructuring, rapid economic development in Asia, and increasing U.S. political, economic, and military involvement in Asia—have all combined to perpetuate Asian immigration to the United States.

The globalization of the U.S. economy in the postindustrial era, particularly since World War II, has forged an extensive link of economic, cultural, and ideological ties between the United States and many developing countries in the Pacific Rim. Globalization at this stage has perpetuated emigration from developing countries in two significant ways. First, direct U.S. capital investments into developing countries transform the economic and occupational structures in these countries by disproportionately targeting production for export while taking advantage of raw material and cheap labor. Such twisted development, characterized by the robust growth of low-skilled jobs in export manufacturing, draws a large number of rural, and particularly female, workers into the urban labor markets. Increased rural-urban migration, in turn, causes underemployment and displacement of the urban work force, creating an enormous pool of potential emigrants (Sassen 1989). Second, economic development following the American model in many developing countries stimulates consumerism and consumption and raises expectations regarding the standard of living. The widening gap between consumption expectations and the available standards of living within the structural constraints of the developing countries, combined with easy access to information and migration networks, in turn creates tremendous pressure for emigration (Portes and Rumbaut 1996). Consequently, U.S. foreign capital investments in developing countries have resulted in the paradox of rapid economic growth and high emigration from these countries to the United States.

On the U.S. side, unprecedented growth in capital-intensive, high-tech industries and services forecasts a severe shortage of skilled workers. American businesses and policy makers believed that importing skilled labor was the quickest solution. Since the 1980s, about one-third of the engineers and medical personnel in the U.S. labor market have come from abroad—mostly from India, China, Taiwan, and the Philippines. However, the shortage of skilled labor is not a sufficient explanation for the trends in highly skilled migration, since skilled immigration disproportionately originates from selected countries in Asia (almost 60 percent of the total skilled immigration in 1995). It is the global integration of higher education and advanced training in the United States in interaction with the opportunity structure in the homelands that has set in motion the highly skilled immigration. The infusion of the educational systems with globalization in many developing countries—notably India, Korea, the Philippines, and Taiwan—has given rise to a sizable professional class within these countries. Many members of this emerging middle class are frustrated by the uneven economic development and lack of mobility opportunities at home that devalue their education and skills, and in some cases they also feel powerless to make changes because of repressive political systems in their homelands. They therefore actively seek emigration as a preferred alternative, and the change in U.S. immigration policy facilitates this move (Liu and Cheng 1994). Also, the emergence of the United States as the premier training ground for international students has been instrumental in supplying the U.S. economy with needed skilled labor (Ong et al. 1992). Many foreign students have found permanent employment in the United States after completing their studies or practical training. For example, in fiscal year 1995, close to 40 percent of the immigrants from mainland China were admitted under employment-based preferences. Almost all of them had received higher education or training in the United States.

In addition, Southeast Asian refugees constitute a significant share of contemporary Asian immigration. Since 1975, more than one million refugees have arrived from Vietnam, Laos, and Cambodia as a direct result of the failed U.S. intervention in Southeast Asia. The United States originally had little economic interest in Southeast Asia but was drawn in because of the threat of Communist takeovers in the region. The development of the Communist bloc dominated by the former Soviet Union, the Communist takeover in China in the late 1940s, and the direct confrontation with Communist troops in the Korean War prompted a U.S. foreign policy aimed at "containing" communism, which ultimately dragged Americans into Indochina. The Vietnam War, its expansion into Southeast Asia, and political turmoil in the region left millions of people living in poverty, starvation, and constant fear, while forcing many others to flee from their homelands. One ironic consequence of the U.S. involvement in Indochina is that sizable parts of the populations of Vietnam, Laos, and Cambodia are now in America (Rumbaut 1995). As of 1996, more than 700,000 refugees from Vietnam, 210,000 from Laos, and 135,000 from Cambodia had been admitted to the United States. Since then, Southeast Asian refugee inflows have declined, but such decline has been accompanied by a rapid increase of family-sponsored migrants from the region.

Southeast Asian refugees fled their countries in different waves. Although Saigon, Vientiane, and Phnom Penh fell to the Communist forces roughly at the same time in 1975, only the Vietnamese and a small number of the Hmong resistance force had the privilege of being "paroled" (being allowed under special provision of the law) into the United States immediately after the war. Approximately 130,000 Vietnamese refugees and only 3,500 Hmong refugees landed on U.S. soil in 1975 (Chan 1994), while the majority of Hmong resistance forces, Laotian royalists, and Cambodians sought refuge in Thailand. During what is known as the second wave, a large refugee exodus occurred at the end of the 1970s when thousands fled Vietnam. About a quarter of a million Vietnamese refugees went to China while some half a million floated in the open sea to be rescued by the national guards of whichever country they happened to be near. Almost half of the "boat people" were reported to have perished at sea, and the remaining half to have ended up in camps in Thailand, Indonesia, Malaysia, Singapore, the Philippines, and Hong Kong. Thousands of refugees also fled Laos and Kampuchea (formerly Cambodia) on land to seek refuge in crowded camps along the Thai border. Despite harsh repatriation efforts by the Thai government, about 600,000 Cambodians (15 percent of the country's population) and some 100,000 Hmong and 200,000 lowland Laotians (10 percent of the country's population) fled on land to Thailand, awaiting resettlement in a third country (Chan 1991). The refugee exodus continued in large numbers in the early 1980s. Although the newly established governments in Southeast Asia did not plunge the three countries into a bloodbath as so many had once feared, continuing political and religious repression, economic hardship, incessant warfare, and contacts with the outside world led many Southeast Asians to escape in search of a better life (Zhou and Bankston 1998).

Once set in motion, international migration is perpetuated by extensive and institutionalized migration networks. Networks are formed by family, kinship, and friendship ties, facilitating and perpetuating international migration because they lower the costs and risks of movement and increase the expected net returns to such movement (Massey et al. 1987). U.S. immigration policy has been instrumental in sustaining and expanding family migration networks. The Hart-Cellar Act of 1965 and its subsequent amendments give preference to family reunification, providing immediate relatives of U.S. citizens with unlimited visa numbers and other relatives with the majority of visa allocations subject to the numerical cap. More than two-thirds of the legal immigrants admitted to the United States since the 1970s have been family-sponsored immigrants. Even among employer-sponsored migrants and refugees, the role of networking is crucial. Family, kin, and friendship networks also tend to expand exponentially, serving as a conduit to additional and thus potentially self-perpetuating migration. In the next decade or so, immigration from Asia is expected to continue at its high volume because many recent immigrants and refugees will have established citizenship status and will become eligible sponsors who can send for family members to reunite in the United States.

Overall, contemporary immigration has been influenced and perpetuated not simply as a result of the Hart-Cellar Act but also by the interplay of a complex set of macro- and micro-structural forces. Understanding its dynamics requires a reconceptualized framework that takes into account the effects of globalization, uneven political and economic developments in developing and developed countries, the social processes of international migration, and the role of the United States in world affairs. One significant implication arising from these processes is that high levels of immigration will continue to remain an inseparable part of Asian American life for years to come.

The New Face of Asian America

Immigration is transforming Asian America in ways unanticipated by long-time Asian immigrants and their U.S.-born children. Although Asian Americans as a group are relatively few in number, making up less than 4 percent of the U.S. population, they have aggressively asserted their presence in the American milieu, fighting their way, with varied success, into mainstream economic, social, and political institutions. Before the immigration surge in the late 1960s, the Asian American population was a tiny fraction of the total U.S. population—about a third of 1 percent in 1900 and 0.7 percent in 1970—and was composed mainly of three national-origin groups: Japanese, Chinese, and Filipinos. Figure 4.1 shows the percentage distribution of the Asian American population from 1900 to 1970 (Barringer et al. 1993). Prior to 1930, Asians

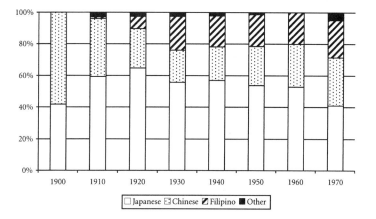

Fig. 4.1. Percentage Distribution of Asian American Population: 1900–1970. *Source*: Barringer et al. 1993, p. 42.

in America were mainly either Chinese or Japanese, mostly immigrants. Between 1930 and 1970 the number of Filipinos increased significantly. Filipinos were mostly brought into the United States to fill the labor shortage caused by anti-Asian legislation and the restrictive National Origins Act of 1924. By 1970, Japanese Americans were the largest national-origin group, making up 41 percent of the Asian American population, followed by Chinese Americans (30 percent) and Filipino Americans (24 percent). Members of other national-origin groups (mostly Koreans) represented less than 5 percent of the total.

Pre–World War II immigrants from Asia represented less than 5 percent of the total new arrivals admitted to the United States, a direct result of anti-Asian prejudice and various restrictive immigration laws. Most of the earlier Asian immigrants came from China and Japan, with a smaller number from the Philippines, India, and Korea. These earlier immigrants, like "the tired, huddled masses" from Europe, were typically poor and uneducated peasants, and many of them intended to make a quick fortune to bring back to their homelands. Because of the drastic differences in migration histories among the earlier Asian-origin groups, only Japanese immigrants were able to develop family-based communities with a significant U.S.-born population in the pre-WWII period. Chinatowns, the rather dispersed Filipino enclaves, and other Asian immigrant communities were primarily bachelor societies with single adult males overrepresented and with few women, children, and families (Chan 1991; Takaki 1989; Zhou 1992).

The distorted population growth in Asian American communities is living evidence of decades of legal exclusion and discrimination. From the time of their arrival, Asian immigrants were subject to laws that served to exclude them from the social and economic opportunities available to most white immigrants. Despite the eventual repeal of the laws that excluded Asian immigrants and barred them from the rights of naturalization, the Asian American population grew very slowly, making up barely half a percent of the total U.S. population by 1950. The number of people in some Asian-origin groups was so minuscule, in fact, that the U.S. Census did not even categorize them until 1980 (Nash 1997).[4] Nonetheless, the relaxation of immigration legislation during the early 1940s and 1950s, combined with a postwar baby boom, did give rise to a notable native-born youth cohort, most of whom lived on the West Coast. This group, comprising mostly Japanese and Chinese Americans, came of age in the late 1960s to form the core force of the Asian American Movement at college campuses on the West Coast and in the Northeast.

The diversity of the Asian American population started to take shape during the 1970s. The dramatic increase in Asian immigration marked the beginning of contemporary Asian America. In sheer numbers, the U.S. Asian and Pacific Islander population grew from a total of 1.4 million in 1970 to 7.3 million in 1990 and to nearly 12 million in 2000 (in contrast to 205,000 in 1900), an impressive ninefold increase in just three decades. Much of this growth is attributed to immigration, which has accounted for more than two-thirds of the total population growth. The population of most of the new national-origin groups—Indians, Koreans, Vietnamese, Cambodians, Laotians, and the Hmong—grew at spectacular rates, almost entirely because of immigration. It is estimated that, if the current levels of net immigration, intermarriage, and

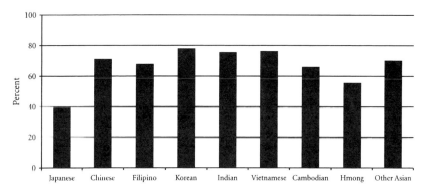

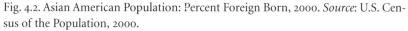

Fig. 4.2. Asian American Population: Percent Foreign Born, 2000. *Source*: U.S. Census of the Population, 2000.

ethnic affiliation hold, the size of the Asian population will increase from 12 million in 2000 to 34 million in 2050, growing from 4 to 8 percent of the total U.S. population (Smith and Edmonston 1997).

The recency of Asian immigration highlights two distinct demographic characteristics of the Asian American population: a disproportionately large foreign-born component and a disproportionately young native-born component. As indicated in figure 4.2, the foreign-born component dominates all Asian American groups, except for Japanese Americans; more than three-quarters of Koreans, Indians, and Vietnamese, and more than two-thirds of Chinese, Filipinos, Cambodians, and other Asians are foreign born. While many immigrant children move with their parents, the great majority of the immigrant generation is of working age. By contrast, the native-born Asian American population is an extremely young group. More than half of native-born Asian Americans are under eighteen years of age. One implication about this emerging new second generation is that it will grow up in an era of continuously high immigration, joined by a sizable foreign-born cohort—the 1.5 generation—whose members are far more diverse in ethnic background, timing of immigration, degree of acculturation, orientation, and outlook. This is a situation quite distinct from that which faced the second generation of immigrants in the 1950s and 1960s, because of restrictive immigration.

Diverse National Origins

The dramatic growth in absolute numbers of Asian immigrants has been accompanied by increasing ethnic diversity within the Asian American population itself. As of 2000, the U.S. Census recorded eleven national-origin or ethnic groups with populations exceeding 150,000, as revealed in table 4.1. Since 1980, no single group has accounted for more than one-third of the Asian American population. While major national-origin groups—Japanese, Chinese, Filipino, Korean, Indian, and Vietnamese—were proportionally represented in 2000, other national-origin or ethnic groups—Cambodian, Laotian, the Hmong, Pakistani, and Thai—marked their presence in Asian America only very recently, since the late 1970s. Because of the unique migration

TABLE 4.1
Asian American Population: 1980–2000 (1,000s)

	1980	% Total	1990	% Total	2000	% Total
Chinese	812	23.1	1,545	22.8	2,858	24.1
Filipino	782	22.3	1,407	20.8	2,385	20.1
Japanese	716	20.4	848	12.5	1,152	9.7
Indian	387	11.0	815	12.0	1,856	15.7
Korean	357	10.2	799	11.8	1,227	10.3
Vietnamese	245	7.0	615	9.1	1,212	10.2
Cambodian	16	0.5	149	2.2	213	1.8
Pakistani	—	—	—	—	209	1.8
Laotian	5	0.1	147	2.2	197	1.7
Hmong	48	1.4	94	1.4	185	1.6
Thai	45	1.3	91	1.3	150	1.3
Other Asian	98	2.8	265	3.9	215	1.8
Total	3,511	100.0	6,775	100.0	11,859	100.0

SOURCE: U.S. Census of the Population, 1980, 1990, 2000.

patterns in each of the originating countries, national origins are strongly associated with the type of legal admission (family-sponsored, employer-sponsored, or refugees) and with the skill levels of immigrants. For example, many Filipino immigrants to the United States are college graduates with transferable job skills; many are physicians and nurses sponsored by U.S. employers in the health care industry. Indian immigrants are mostly employed as physicians and computer programmers, as well as small entrepreneurs. Koreans are predominantly middle-class professionals but tend to be disproportionately self-employed in small-scale retail trade. Chinese immigrants are more mixed, including fairly even proportions of rural peasants, urban workers, and the highly skilled. Southeast Asian refugees, in contrast, were pushed out of their homelands by force and suffer tremendous postwar trauma and social displacement, compounded by a lack of education and professional skills, which negatively affects their resettlement.

Diverse Socioeconomic Backgrounds

Another distinguishing characteristic of contemporary Asian America is the tremendous heterogeneity in socioeconomic status. The 2000 U.S. Census attests to the vast differences in Asian Americans' levels of education, occupation, and income by national origins. For example, 64 percent of Indian American adults (aged twenty-five years or older) reported having attained bachelor's degrees or more, and more than 40 percent of Chinese, Korean, and Japanese Americans reported so, but only 19 percent of Vietnamese Americans and fewer than 10 percent of Cambodian, Laotian, and Hmong Americans reported so (compared to 24 percent of average American adults). Among employed workers (age sixteen years or older), about 60 percent of Indian Americans and more than half of Chinese and Japanese Americans held managerial or professional occupations, but about a quarter of Vietnamese and fewer than 20 percent reported so (compared to 34 percent of average American workers). Further, Indian and Japanese Americans reported a median family income of more than $70,000, and Chinese and Filipino Americans, more than $60,000, but Korean and Southeast

Asian families reported a median family income significantly below the national average of $50,000. Poverty rates for Asian Americans ranged from a low of 6 percent for Filipinos and 10 percent for Indians and Japanese to a high of more than 38 percent for the Hmong and 29 percent for Cambodians (compared to about 12 percent for average American families) (Reeves and Bennett 2004).

Diverse Settlement Patterns

A third salient feature of contemporary Asian America is the diverse geographic settlement patterns of immigrants and their offspring. Historically, most Asian immigrants in the United States have been concentrated in Hawaii and in states along the Pacific coast, with a small number of Chinese moving east to settle in New York. Within each area of settlement, they have been highly segregated in ethnic enclaves, such as Chinatowns, Little Tokyos, and Little Manilas. Today, geographic concentration continues to be significant as newcomers follow the footsteps of their predecessors to settle on the West Coast in disproportionate numbers. California has become the preferred destination for immigrants from Asian countries and has 40 percent of the nation's Asian American population. Tables 4.2 and 4.3 show the geographic distribution of Asian Americans by metropolitan areas (PMSAs or MSAs),[5] further confirming historical and contemporary patterns of ethnic concentration.

Nonetheless, the Asian American population has begun to disperse throughout the Northeast, the Midwest, and the South. For example, sizable ethnic communities are found in New Orleans (Vietnamese), Houston (Vietnamese and Chinese), and Minneapolis (the Hmong), cities that traditionally received few Asian immigrants. Although there is still evidence of clustering along national or ethnic lines at the local level, there are very few examples of the large and distinctly mono-ethnic enclaves that were common in the past. In San Francisco, Los Angeles, and New York, there are no new Chinatowns where more than half of the residents are coethnics; Koreatowns in New York and Los Angeles, and Little Saigon in Orange County are no exception. Filipino Americans and Indian Americans are comparatively more spread out across the urban landscape, with few identifiable ethnic enclaves. For example, as of 2000, only 2

TABLE 4.2
Top Ten Metro Areas with Largest Asian American Population, 2000

	Asians (1,000)	% Asians
New York, NY PMSA	892	11.1
Los Angeles–Long Beach, CA PMSA	505	11.5
San Jose, CA PMSA	356	29.0
San Francisco, CA PMSA	259	33.3
Honolulu, HI, MSA	279	75.0
San Diego, CA MSA	203	14.7
Chicago, IL PMSA	163	4.8
Houston, TX PMSA	118	5.7
Seattle-Bellevue-Everett, WA PMSA	116	15.2
Oakland, CA PMSA	109	19.0
Total	11,895	3.9

SOURCE: U.S. Census of the Population, 2000. Data was downloaded from http://mumford.albany.edu/census/AsianPop/AsianDownload.html on September 2006.

TABLE 4.3
Top Three Metropolitan Areas of Concentration by National Origin or Ethnic Groups (1,000s)

	Largest Concentration	2nd Largest Concentration	3rd Largest Concentration	All U.S.	Top Three as a Percent of Total
Chinese	New York, NY 375	San Francisco, CA 160	LA–Long Beach, CA 80	2,858	21.52%
Filipino	LA–Long Beach, CA 141	San Diego, CA 90	San Jose, CA 70	2,385	12.62%
Japanese	Honolulu, HI 113	LA–Long Beach, CA 52	New York, NY 27	1,152	16.67%
Indian	New York, NY 207	San Jose, CA 52	LA–Long Beach, CA 33	1,856	15.73%
Korean	LA–Long Beach, CA 99	New York, NY 90	Honolulu, HI 22	1,227	17.20%
Vietnamese	San Jose, CA 92	Orange County, CA 35	LA–Long Beach, CA 29	1,212	12.87%

SOURCE: U.S. Census of the Population, 2000. Data was downloaded from http://mumford.albany.edu/census/AsianPop/Asian Download.html on September 2006.

percent of Los Angeles County's Chinese Americans lived in Chinatown (decreased from 12 percent in 1990), 7.4 percent of Los Angeles County's Korean Americans lived in Koreatown (decreased from 22 percent in 1990), and a tiny number of Japanese Americans (less than 700) lived in Little Tokyo. Overall, trends of spatial integration (moving into white, middle-class neighborhoods) and suburbanization among Asian Americans have been particularly strong in recent years, resulting in decreasing levels of residential segregation even in areas of high concentration.

Identity, Emerging Ethnicity, and the Assimilation Problem

"Who Am I?"

> We ABC [American-born Chinese] were ridiculed by the old immigrants as "Bamboo Stick" for not being able to speak Chinese and not being accepted as "white people." We are not here. We are not there. . . . We are different. Most of us are proud of the Chinese cultural heritage, but due to the pressure to assimilate and the lack of opportunity, we don't know much about the Chinese way.[6]

The issue of identity has always occupied a central place in the minds of Asian Americans. Changing demographics and residential mobility in contemporary Asian America make it more salient than ever before. However, this issue has concerned native-born generations more than the first generation, because native-born generations are caught in the insider/outsider divide: they suffer from the paradoxical experience of being in America but not fully a part of it. Both immigrants and their native-born children encounter this paradoxical experience, yet their feelings about it are different.

Mainstream American society pressures all immigrants to "fit in" and "not rock the boat." The society also expects immigrants, however diverse or initially disadvantaged they may be, to assimilate into the mainstream as quickly as possible. Behind this ideology of assimilationism, however, there is an invisible force for inclusion and exclusion. Writing in 1872, J. Hector St. John de Crevecoeur described an American as "either an European or the descendant of an European." More than a century later, Israel Zangwill characterized an American as an "immaculate, well-dressed, accent-free Anglo" (1914). These kinds of definitions of "American," widely if often unconsciously held, make it hard, if not impossible, for people to feel fully American if they happen to be nonwhite, including those whose ancestors settled on this land long before the first Europeans reached American shores. The 1790 National Origin Act prohibited all but free white persons from becoming U.S. citizens. Thus, not all outsider groups were afforded the privilege of becoming American. A second-generation Chinese American in her sixties explained her isolation from mainstream American society and her socially imposed otherness in these words:

> The truth is, no matter how American you think you are or try to be, you do not look "American." If you have almond-shaped eyes, straight black hair, and a yellow complexion, you are a foreigner by default. People will ask where you come from but won't be satisfied until they hear you name a foreign country. And they will naturally compliment your perfect English.[7]

Immigrants are deemed "outsiders," and they tend to cope with their alienation from the immigrant perspective. Historically, people of Asian descent were considered members of "inferior races" and were negatively portrayed as the "indispensable enemy" and as the "yellow peril." No matter how hard they tried to accommodate to American ways, Asian immigrants and Americans of Asian ancestry were considered undesirable and unassimilable aliens (Chan 1991). The Chinese Exclusion Act of 1882, the first immigration act in U.S. history to exclude an entire category of immigrants purely on the basis of national origin, is a prime example. The forced removal and incarceration of Japanese Americans during World War II is another case in point. The federal government, under provision of President Franklin D. Roosevelt's Executive Order 9066, justified these actions as a "military necessity" vital to the national defense of the United States (despite the fact of evidence confirming the loyalty of Japanese Americans). In contrast, no such categorical treatments were imposed on German Americans and Italian Americans.

As a reactive strategy to resist subjugation and discrimination, Asian immigrants retreated into their own ethnic communities, rebuilding ethnic institutions that resembled those found in the homeland and relying on one another for moral and practical supports. Extreme adversity allowed them to develop a clear sense of their position in the host society as "foreigners" and to maintain tangible ties to their ethnic community and their homeland, which became internalized as part of their shared experience. Since most Asian immigrants chose to come to the United States to seek better opportunities either for themselves or for their children, their shared experience of marginalization reinforced their determination to push their children into the mainstream by choosing a path of least resistance (Kitano 1969). For example, prewar issei (first generation) drew on extensive ethnic resources in developing trade and business associations to negotiate favorable arrangements with the larger economy and to support their children's education (Matsumoto 1993; Nishi 1995). War-trauma-tized Japanese American parents or grandparents were reluctant to share wartime memories with their children and grandchildren for fear of hurting their children's chances of social integration (Takezawa 2000). Post-1965 Korean immigrants pushed their children toward prestigious universities because they looked to their children to regain the social status the parents had lost in the host society (Zhou and Kim 2006).

Unlike most members of the first generation, who tend to avoid arousing antago-nism by subscribing to the dominant society's mode of behavior—hard work, educa-tion, delayed gratification, nonconfrontational attitudes in the face of injustice—their offspring, American citizens by birth, are likely to fully embrace the principles of free-dom, equality, and civil liberties on which citizenship is based. They are unlikely to think of their parents' home country as a place to which they might return, nor do they use it as a point of reference by which to assess their progress in the new land. Rather, their expectations are governed by the same standards to which other Ameri-cans aspire, and it is by those standards that native-born Asian Americans assess themselves and are assessed by others. However, American society is not color blind, and the phenotypes of the second generation subject them to the same types of dis-crimination and injustice faced by the first generation regardless of how long they have been in the United States. A third-generation Japanese American from Monterey Park, California, expressed frustration at being objectified as a "foreigner":

> Asian Americans fought for decades against discrimination and racial prejudice. We want to be treated just like everybody else, like Americans. You see, I get real angry when people come up to me and tell me how good my English is. They say: "Oh, you have no accent. Where did you learn English?" Where did I learn English? Right here in America. I was born here like they were. We really hated it when people assumed that just because Asian Americans looked different we were foreigners. It took us a long time to get people to see this point, to be sensitized to it. Now the new immigrants are setting us back. People see me now and they automatically treat me as an immigrant. I really hate that. The worst thing is that these immigrants don't understand why I am angry. (Cheng and Yang 2000)

An examination of today's Asian American populations highlights the demarcation between the different generations. Because of the recency of immigration, this group still remains primarily an immigrant group, in which the first generation makes up more than two-thirds of the total Asian American population.[8] It is only among Japa-nese Americans and Chinese Americans that we notice a sizable third or fourth gener-ation. Among Asian American children under eighteen years of age, more than 90 per-cent are either foreign born or children of foreign-born parents. Growing up in the context of an immigrant family is extremely difficult for Asian American children. Parents often place multiple pressures on their children to "do and say the right things" or to "act white" as a means of moving into the mainstream and accessing re-sources typically reserved for "insiders." In the process of growing up, the children of-ten find themselves vacillating between the outsider's world from which they came and an insider's world into which they were born; they are increasingly ambivalent about their conflicting identities.

Many second-generation Asian Americans of the 1960s and 1970s went through a period of profound confusion, feeling trapped by the ironies of being in America but not a part of it. In the wake of the Asian American Movement, young Asian Americans who entered American institutions of higher education began to confront these identity issues. The Movement forged a space in which these young people not only shared their own personal experiences of racism and suffering in American society but also began to articulate an Asian American consciousness and to refashion their own identities in ways that were meaningful to their experiences—an Asian American identity. At a time when Asian Americans began to empower themselves across panethnic lines and to raise an ethnic consciousness to a new level for future generations, it is ironic that much of the shame and frustration that previously engulfed the second generation has resurfaced among the children of contemporary immigrants from Asia. Some of the children, especially those who live in suburban, white, middle-class neighborhoods, internalize the negative stereotypes that society imposes upon their parents' generation and have undergone traumatic, even suicidal, identity crises, in which they feel ashamed of who they are, try to become who they are not, and end up being neither, as so vividly described in "A Letter to My Sister" (Park, this volume). A Chinese-American college student, born in the early 1980s, reveals her confusion as a teenager:

> As a child, I had a very difficult time coping with my ethnic identity. I was hesitant to call myself American because as I perceived it, American meant all the beautiful Anglo children in my classes. Yet I was also hesitant to call myself Chinese for two reasons. First, I had no clear concept of what Chinese was besides the fact that my parents were from China. [Second,] I did not feel Chinese. I did not want to be Chinese. I wanted to be White. . . . I tried to hide my identity. I buried it deep within my subconscious, became oblivious to it. Yet every so often, it would be invoked. . . . Perhaps the most notorious manifestation of my shame was my inability to answer the simple question, "What are you?" . . . When I was confronted with questions concerning my racial background, I found myself unable to answer. . . . Unable to utter the simple words, "I am Chinese." I just could not do it. It was too painful for some reason. The words seemed too dissonant and distasteful. So many times I simply shrugged and said: "I don't know."[9]

The pressure to assimilate and the conditional acceptance by mainstream society takes a heavier toll on the second generation growing up in suburban, white, middle-class neighborhoods than on those who live in inner-city ethnic enclaves (Sung 1987). Within the enclave, the homeland is transplanted, ancestral culture and values are honored and practiced as a way of life, and ethnic pride is invigorated. Outside the enclave, ethnicity is subject to the rank order of the racial stratification system, which operates on the assumption that ethnic traits should be abandoned in order to become "American." In the midst of an identity crisis, native-born children who are seemingly assimilated structurally may find that they lack a homeland on which they can fall back and an ethnic space in which they can express their fear and anxieties. This explains in part why so many Asian American college students demand ethnic studies classes. These classes do not merely serve to disseminate information or transport knowledge but provide a space in which Asian Americans address the issue of identity, allowing them to release negative feelings about themselves as well as inner tensions and anxieties. These classes let them rebuild a sense of self-worth and a group identity as a means of ethnic empowerment.

The Salience of Ethnicity

Identity crises are not uncommon among adolescents as they grow into adulthood, but they are not necessarily defining experiences for all members of native-born generations. Since the birth of the Asian American Movement, a vibrant and multifaceted ethnic culture has emerged and been reconstructed among native-born Asian Americans in their attempt to reclaim their identity. This culture is neither mainstream American nor clearly associated with the immigrant generation. It is a hybrid form that has come to assume tremendous significance among Asian Americans as a viable means of resistance and compromise within the existing power structure. This phenomenon indicates the fluid nature of ethnicity.

The sociologist William Yancey and his colleagues argue that the emergence of an ethnic culture has relatively little to do with the country of origin but more to do with the structure of opportunity in America. Instead of viewing the transplanted cultural heritage as the principal defining characteristic of an ethnic group, these scholars suggest that the development and persistence of ethnicity is a paradoxical process. On the one hand, it is defined in the context of frequent association and interaction with others of common origins and cultural heritage. On the other hand, it is dependent on structural conditions that characterize the positions of groups in American society and create common experiences and interests, thereby setting the potential for collective mobilization around shared goals. Ultimately, it is "a manifestation of the way populations are organized in terms of interaction patterns, institutions, personal values, attitudes, lifestyle, and presumed consciousness of kind"—the result of a process that continues to unfold (Yancey et al. 1976, 400). Drawing on this reasoning, we see that Asian Americans develop different patterns of ethnic identification according to the length of time in the United States, internal group dynamics, and structural situations that the particular immigrant group and its descendants have encountered.

As we have discussed, identity formation varies across generations and national-origin groups. The immigrant generation generally reaffirms its ethnic identity on the basis of homeland cultures and life experiences not only through ethnic practices but also through memories of its lived experiences in the homeland or during the process of movement. For example, Southeast Asian refugees share the common experience of having lived through internal power struggles in their home countries, the horrors of war, and the ordeal of exile and death. These life-threatening experiences become the basis for ethnic solidarity. Drastic cultural changes and adverse societal treatments or disadvantages associated with immigrant status in the host society can reinforce ethnic identity, as in the case of ethnic enclaves where transnational ties and kinship networks remain strong and homeland cultures are often frozen in time as the result of a collective, concerted effort to preserve them.

Native-born Asian Americans and those who arrived in the United States as infants or as school-age children, in contrast, usually do not seize on traditional cultural symbols as a mode of defining their ethnicity. Rather, they tend to build their identities largely on the basis of mediating *interpretive memories* of homeland cultures in which they have never personally lived, and their own diverse life experiences in the United States. Living in immigrant families and in (or close to) ethnic communities has made life in the homeland a continuing reality because parents often communicate to children with a strong sense of determination and instill in them a sense of origin. Close proximity to kinship networks and ethnic enclaves certainly exerts an important effect on the native born, providing an infrastructure that keeps alive the memories of homeland cultures. The collective memory of Chinese exclusion, the U.S. colonization of the Philippines, and the incarceration of Japanese Americans serve as pivotal organizational principles for ethnic identity among native-born Chinese Americans, Filipino Americans, and Japanese Americans, respectively. The support of Asian American donors to the Museum of the Chinese in the Americas in New York and the Japanese American National Museum in Los Angeles are living proofs that even the most "assimilated" of Asian Americans clearly retain vital links to their ethnic culture and to the community that sustains it.

Often, however, actual experiences in American society outweigh memories. Transplanted cultural heritage is no longer the requirement or the defining characteristic of ethnicity for the native born. Rather, the emergence and persistence of ethnicity depends on the structural conditions of the host society and the position that the immigrant groups occupy in that social structure. The treatment of Asian Americans as foreigners, the glass ceiling, and racially motivated hate crimes all serve to reaffirm ethnic identity. However, this ethnic identity, even when it is affiliated with a national origin, differs for the first generation and its native-born offspring in that the ethnicity of the first generation has a taken-for-granted nature, whereas that of native-born generations is derived in a more self-conscious, reflexive way both from the collective memory of the historical experience and from the native-born generations' actual experience.

This vibrant emergent ethnic culture transcends the spatial boundaries of ethnic enclaves as well as the symbolic meaning of ethnicity. It is a culture characterized by structures that promote cooperation among coethnics while adopting activities and organizations (e.g., ethnic churches, sports clubs, trade guilds, political organizations) as a means of resistance (Espiritu 1992; Tuan 1999). Yet, what ethnicity means, stands for, or symbolizes differs from region to region, city to city, and town to town in the vast expanse of the United States. Being Japanese American in Hawaii or Chinese American in Monterey Park or Vietnamese American in Little Saigon is not the same as having those identities in New York, Houston, or New Orleans.

Is this emergent ethnicity symbolic? The sociologist Herbert Gans asserts that "as the functions of ethnic cultures and groups diminish and identity becomes the primary way of being ethnic, ethnicity takes on an expressive rather than instrumental function in people's lives, becoming more of a leisure-time activity" (Gans 1979, 9).

Among the features of symbolic ethnicity is that it does not carry with it material consequences and does not serve to enhance group solidarity. Indeed, ethnic identity associated with a homeland has become blurred among the second or third generations, who have lost their ancestral languages, have intermarried at rates far exceeding the national average, and no longer involve themselves with their ethnic communities on a daily basis, making their ethnicity "symbolic." Our argument about interpretive memories of homeland culture points to the importance of symbolic ethnicity. Clearly, ethnicity is not an either/or matter but rather a variable outcome that varies in its intensity. As we have noted earlier, Asian Americans, both foreign born and native born, experience high levels of educational attainment, occupational mobility, and residential integration, have high rates of intermarriage, and rapidly lose facility in the native language; hence, much of Asian ethnicity may be optional. As they climb up the socioeconomic ladder in American society, many established Asian Americans may have more choices as to whether they want to be Asian and how Asian they should be when they want to.

At the societal level, however, we argue that the notion of symbolic ethnicity does not always apply well to Asian Americans or to other racial minority groups, since being nonethnic American is still not an option for them, as it is for most European immigrants and their offspring (Takezawa 2000; Waters 1990). The outcry that "America does not include me, only a part of me," is heard from many native-born, "well assimilated" Asian Americans. This suggests that unless the whole racial perception of Americans changes and includes other groups as Americans, emergent ethnicity, often in the form of panethnicity, will continue to remain instrumental for the excluded social groups. Such emergent panethnicity serves as both a defense mechanism against racism and an empowering mechanism for unity and solidarity.

Ethnicity is situational and structurally conditioned. Under certain circumstances, it can evolve into panethnicity, a form of ethnic aggregation typically oriented toward achieving certain material ends and empowerment. In thinking about panethnicity, we draw on the work of the sociologists David Lopez and Yen Espiritu, who link it to a set of cultural and structural preconditions: shared cultural values and life experiences in American society, imposed societal perception and treatment as one phenotypical group, and the internal need for political mobilization to fight for minority rights and to protect group interests (Lopez and Espiritu 1990). We add to these rapid language switch to English and increasing interethnic and interracial marriages, which also contribute to the formation of panethnicity. Today, Asian Americans intermarry extensively with members of other racial or ethnic groups. In Los Angeles County, for example, about one-third of Asian Americans, and about half of all second-generation Asian Americans, marry outside their ethnic groups. Ambiguous phenotype may ease social constraints imposed by the existing racial stratification system while fostering a strong sense of panethnicity among multiracial or multiethnic Americans.

However, lumping together all peoples of Asian ancestry complicates the notion of ethnicity and its subsequent application to a particular ethnic group, because panethnicity accounts neither for regional or national differences nor for the historical legacies of intergroup conflicts. At this juncture, the term "Asian American," in and of itself, assumes a political agenda for those who subscribe to it, and panethnicity remains a political identity for instrumental purposes. The Asian American community today is, and continues to be, marked by tremendous diversity in the era of high immigration. Diverse languages and religions and differing historical legacies of domination and colonization in Asia make it unlikely that a panethnic coalition will develop in the near future. Differences in class background among the immigrant generation and divergent modes of incorporation of that generation can also deter the formation of panethnicity. The success of Asian Americans' integration into American society as individuals can both enhance and weaken their ability to act collectively. Also, while it is true that discrimination and violence against one Asian group serve to unite Asian Americans, it can also create intragroup conflict. During World War II, the U.S. government singled out Japanese Americans as enemies and targets for incarceration. Fearing similar treatment, some Chinese Americans found themselves constantly invoking their Chinese ethnicity and even wore buttons with derogatory anti-Japanese words to distinguish themselves. The negative stereotypes about welfare dependency and gang violence among Southeast Asians also cause some Asian American groups to distance themselves from them and even blame them for their plight.

The Assimilation Problem

The issue of assimilation has been the core of a classic scholarly debate on immigration, and racial and ethnic relations. Classical assimilation theory predicts a linear trajectory toward structural integration into the mainstream of society. In this view, the children and the grandchildren of the immigrants move beyond the status of the first generation and progressively become less distinct from other Americans. This particular perspective shares a series of assumptions: outsider groups, however diverse and initially disadvantaged, all absorb a common culture and gain equal access to the opportunity structure; they do so in a more or less natural way, gradually deserting old cultural and behavioral patterns in favor of new ones; and the whole process, once set in motion, moves inevitably and irreversibly toward the dissolution of the original group. Consequently, observable ethnic differences are largely a function of time and generational status in the United States. In some cases, the time span for assimilation may be prolonged, but, in the end, distinctive ethnic characteristics eventually fade, retaining only some symbolic importance (Alba and Nee 2003; Gans 1979; Gordon 1964; Warner and Srole 1945).

Assimilation theories arose as an abstraction from the experience of earlier European immigration. The theoretical reflections developed largely while the process of immigrant adaptation was underway. Now that it is over, one can safely conclude that the descendants of the 1880–1920 wave have overcome earlier disadvantages, achieving parity with, if not outdistancing, "white" Americans of English ancestry, or what Milton Gordon calls the "core cultural group" (Gordon 1964). Unfortunately, assimilation theories provide no account of why this outcome should have transpired—unless one subscribes to that variant of the modernization theory that most earlier writers embraced but many contemporary social scientists have now challenged. Most important, past success may be due to the specific circumstances encountered by earlier immigrants and their offspring—the fact that between the 1920s and the 1950s, America experienced a long period of restricted immigration, which almost certainly weakened immigrants' attachment to their culture and patterns of group affiliation. Should this be the case, the past is unlikely to prove a useful guide to the future, since we appear to be headed for more, not less, immigration in the years to come.

Assimilationism—the ideology that imposes the dominant core culture on all immigrants to American society—is highly exclusive. The "melting pot" does not wholeheartedly embrace non-European immigrants. The experiences of African Americans are a case in point. Nathan Glazer (1993) shows how racism serves to exclude African Americans from assimilating or sharing in the opportunities of economic and social mobility. Racism and prejudice have also affected the situation of Asian Americans, although to a different degree. Examples are ample, but we point out three of the most obvious.

First, the perception of Asian Americans as "foreigners" has imposed and perpetuated the "otherness" on the group. As we have discussed in detail in the previous section, it is the socially imposed category based on phenotype, rather than acculturation and social mobility, that governs the way group members are received and treated in American society. Speaking perfect English, effortlessly practicing mainstream cultural values, and even marrying members of the dominant group may help reduce this "otherness" at the individual level but have little effect on the group as a whole, given the relatively small size of the third or later generations of the Asian American population (only 10 percent of the total) and the high levels of recent immigration.

Second, the image of "the yellow peril," although largely repudiated in the post–World War II period, has repeatedly resurfaced throughout American history, especially in situations when the United States is at odds with immigrants' ancestral homelands in Asia. The bombing of Pearl Harbor during World War II turned Japanese immigrants and Americans of Japanese ancestry into enemies who were forcibly exiled from their homes and put into internment camps. The Communist takeover of China in the late 1940s and the subsequent Cold War made Chinese Americans of the 1950s prime suspects of treason and espionage. The perceived economic threat from Japan in the 1980s led to the murder of Vincent Chin, a Chinese American, mistaken for a Japanese, who was beaten to death by disgruntled unemployed auto workers in Detroit. The renewed spy stereotype is currently manifested in the case of a Taiwan-born scientist, Wen Ho Lee, who was convicted of stealing nuclear secrets for China in the court of public opinion before even appearing in a court of law. The litany of examples is endless.

Third, the "model minority" stereotype has reinforced the "otherness" of Asian Americans. It is important to note that this stereotype derives from a larger political agenda, serving the ideological function of delegitimizing African American (in particular) claims for equalization of outcomes as opposed to equalization of opportunities. Although Asian Americans as a group are above average on just about any socioeconomic indicator that counts, the "model minority" stereotype obscures the very real problems that many highly "successful" Asians encounter. In particular, highly skilled professionals, who are most definitely part of the middle, if not the upper middle, class, are not doing quite as well as their non-Hispanic white counterparts; they experience disproportionate underemployment because of overqualification and overwork (Zhou and Kamo 1994). Furthermore, the stereotype paints a one-sided picture of the Asian American population, obscuring the plight of those who are not doing well and thus further absolving the broader society of any responsibility for redress. There are immigrant workers who are doing poorly, some subjected to severe exploitation. Some groups—Laotians, Hmong, and Cambodians—are still struggling at the very bottom of the social ladder, facing the risk of being trapped in the urban underclass, and others—perhaps the Filipinos—may be stuck in the lower middle class, showing trends of downward mobility (Oropesa and Landale 1997).

In sum, the notion of assimilation, whether it is manifested in a straight or bumpy line, seems to clearly imply a *single* line—an idea that is very difficult to reconcile with the historical record of large and significant differences in the rate at which various groups move ahead in American society. Because of the complexity of the reality with its multifaceted and dynamic nature, it is difficult to comprehend the experiences of today's racial minorities, Asian Americans included, within the assimilationist framework that makes explicit or implicit Anglo-conformist assumptions. Assimilationism may still be a social or moral imperative imposed on immigrants by the dominant culture, but it may not necessarily be the imperative toward which all immigrant groups and their succeeding generations are striving.

Discussion and Conclusions

Diversity is the hallmark of contemporary Asian America. The influx of Asian immigrants in response to the 1965 Hart-Cellar Act and broader economic, social, and geopolitical factors has brought new challenges for the adaptation of new immigrants and their children into society. As the community continues to grow in number, so too will its representation in the broad cultural, social, and economic milieu that we typify as "mainstream American society."

The implications of the dramatic changes in contemporary Asian America that we have just described are particularly relevant for the development of a coherent vision for future Asian America. First and foremost, diversity in national origins produces stark disparities within the Asian American community. National origins evoke drastic differences in homeland cultures, such as languages, religions, foodways, and customs; histories of international relations; contexts of emigration; reception in the host society; and adaptation patterns. Such differences persist most significantly in the private domain, affecting not only the immigrant generation but also the native-born generations. For some national-origin groups, such as the Chinese and Indians, internal differences in languages or dialects and religions are quite substantial. While ethnic diversity among the second and third generation may be blurred because of a rapid switch to English and high rates of out-marriages, it is extremely difficult to group everybody under a pan-Asian umbrella at the individual level. Increasing differences within an emerging Asian America will create obstacles for panethnic coalitions.

Second, socioeconomic diversity gives rise to diverse mobility patterns. New immigrants may continue to follow the traditional bottom-up route to social mobility, starting their American life in isolated urban enclaves, but some segment of this urban population may be permanently trapped in poverty with dim prospects for the future. Those with sufficient social and economic resources may simply bypass the bottom starting line, moving directly into mainstream labor markets and settling directly into suburban, middle-class communities (Portes and Zhou 1993). These trajectories to social mobility not only affect the life chances of the first generation but also have profound social implications for the new second generation, since the current state and future prospects of immigrant offspring are related to the advantages or disadvantages that accrue through parental socioeconomic status.

Socioeconomic diversity leads to divergent destinies, creating a bifurcated distribution of the Asian American population along class lines. Some national-origin groups, such as the Chinese, Filipinos, Japanese, Koreans, and Asian Indians, have converged with the general U.S. population, with the rich and the poor on the ends and an ever growing affluent class in the middle. But, many others, especially the most recent refugee groups, are struggling in the most underprivileged segment of U.S. society. Consequently, class bifurcation toward two ends of society's class spectrum will probably lead to fragmentation of the larger Asian American community, creating new obstacles for political mobilization and ethnic solidarity. Bifurcation also affects the new second generation. Unlike the second generation of the 1960 and 1970s, most of whom grew up in segregated urban enclaves, a visible proportion of today's second generation is growing up in affluent Euro-American neighborhoods in suburbia. Members of the suburban middle class maintain little contact with their working-class coethnics in urban enclaves and show limited interest in working-class issues.

Third, diverse settlement patterns also have long-term implications for the development of a cohesive Asian American community. Those who are currently segregated in the inner city are confronted with a reality more daunting than the one faced by their earlier counterparts. Today, the United States has an emerging "hourglass" economy in which movement from bottom to top has gotten progressively more difficult. Those newcomers who are poorly educated and lack marketable skills may find themselves stalled or, even worse, stumbling beneath the ranks of the lower working class, either because they are unable to obtain employment or because the jobs they do obtain do not pay a decent family wage. Consequently, they and their children may become trapped in poverty and isolated from mainstream American society. While successful structural integration may not automatically lead to social acceptance, those who have achieved residential mobility are undoubtedly more privileged, enjoying comfortable homes, safe neighborhoods, quality schools, and more channels to mobility.

Last but not least, immigration complicates intergenerational relations and ethnic solidarity. Native-born Asian Americans, especially those assumed to be "assimilated," have been rudely reawakened with renewed images of being "foreigners." Stereotyped images of "American" create both psychological and practical problems for native-born Americans who phenotypically resemble the new arrivals. One frequently hears of the harassment of native-born Mexican Americans suspected of being undocumented immigrants and of comments about third-generation Japanese Americans' "good English." The children, U.S.-born and similar to other American children, suffer from persistent disadvantages merely because they look "foreign" (U.S. Commission

on Civil Rights 1988, 1992). While they are infuriated by their unfair treatment as foreigners, native-born Asian Americans are also caught between including immigrants
in their struggle for racial equality and excluding them. Similar to other Americans in
speech, thought, and behavior, native-born Asian Americans often hold values about
labor rights, individualism, civil liberty, and, ultimately, the ideology of assimilationism that are different from those of their foreign-born counterparts. These differences, intertwined with the acculturation gap between immigrant and native born
generations, have impeded ethnic coalition, ideological consensus, and collective action (Zhou 2001).

Negotiating differences and coalition building within this very heterogeneous eth
nic community will continue to remain the foremost priority in the twenty-first century. Policies reflecting the interests and needs of Asian Americans must develop a
flexible framework to incorporate the diversity that characterizes the contemporary
community. New generations of Asian Americans will have to vie for their own place
within their respective communities and challenge stereotypes that serve to denigrate
their agency in mainstream American society. Although Asian Americans will continue to rally (as they have historically) around issues that unite them on the basis of a
shared sense of racial identity—ethnic stereotyping, hate crimes, economic and political scapegoating, and the glass ceiling—specific national and cultural interests es-
poused by Asian American ethnic groups will demand innovative approaches to promoting the continued development of pan-Asian coalitions while reflecting interethnic
nic differences.

NOTES

1. The number includes 1.6 million formerly unauthorized aliens and 1.1 million Special
Agricultural Workers who were granted permanent-resident status under the provisions of the
Immigration Reform and Control Act of 1986 (Zhou 2001).

2. The number of Asian immigrants excludes those from Iran, Israel, and Turkey. The exception to the statement in the text is 1991, when the Asian share dropped to 18 percent due to
the sudden increase in the legalizees under the Immigration Reform and Control Act of 1986,
most of whom were Mexicans or Central Americans.

3. *Yearbook of Immigration Statistics: 2005,* retrieved on August 31, 2006, from http://www
.uscis.gov/graphics/shared/statistics/yearbook/LPR05.htm.

4. A small number of Asian Indians were present at the time. They were, however, classified
as "Hindu" in the 1900, 1920, and 1940 Censuses, as "white" in 1950 and 1960, and as "Asian or
Pacific Islander" since 1970 (Nash 1997).

5. As defined by the U.S. Bureau of the Census, PMSA stands for Primary Metropolitan Statistical Area and MSA for Metropolitan Statistical Area. These terms generally refer to central
cites.

6. Originally quoted in Bernard Wong 1982, p. 33. Also cited in Morrison G. Wong 1995, p. 86.

7. Personal communication with a retired Chinatown activist in New York.

8. The detailed generation breakdown among Asian Americans is as follows: 65 percent belong to the first generation (foreign born), 25 percent to the second generation (U.S.-born with
foreign-born parentage), and 10 percent to the third or later generations (U.S.-born with U.S.-
born parentage), compared to 9 percent, 11 percent, and 80 percent, respectively, in the general

U.S. population. Figures are from the 2000–02 Current Population Survey of the U.S. Census Bureau.

9. Class discussion on ethnic identity, UCLA, March 1999.

REFERENCES

Alba, Richard and Victor Nee. 2003. *Remaking the American Mainstream: Assimilation and Contemporary Immigration.* Cambridge, MA: Harvard University Press.

Barringer, Herbert, Robert B. Gardner, and Michael J. Levin. 1993. *Asians and Pacific Islanders in the United States,* p. 42, table 2.5. New York: Russell Sage Foundation.

Chan, Sucheng. 1994. *Hmong Means Free: Life in Laos and America.* Philadelphia: Temple University Press.

———. 1991. *Asian Americans: An Interpretive History.* New York: Twayne.

Cheng, Lucie and Philip Q. Yang. 2000. The "Model Minority" Deconstructed. Pp. 459–482 in Min Zhou and J. V. Gatewood (eds.), *Contemporary Asian American: A Multidisciplinary Reader* (1st ed.). New York: New York University Press.

De Crevecoeur, J. Hector St. John. 1904 [1782]. *Letters from an American Farmer.* New York: Fox, Duffield, and Company.

Espiritu, Yen Le. 1992. *Asian American Panethnicity: Bridging Institutions and Identities.* Philadelphia: Temple University Press.

Gans, Herbert J. 1979. Symbolic Ethnicity: The Future of Ethnic Groups and Cultures in America. *Ethnic and Racial Studies* 2: 1–20.

Glazer, Nathan. 1993. Is Assimilation Dead? *Annals of the American Academy of Political and Social Sciences* 530: 122–36.

Gordon, Milton M. 1964. *Assimilation in American Life: The Role of Race, Religion, and National Origins.* New York: Oxford University Press.

Kitano, Harry. 1969. *Japanese Americans: The Evolution of a Subculture.* Englewood Cliffs, NJ: Prentice-Hall.

Liu, John M. and Lucie Cheng. 1994. Pacific Rim Development and the Duality of Post-1965 Asian Immigration to the United States. Pp. 74–99 in Paul M. Ong, Edna Bonacich, and Lucie Cheng (eds.), *The New Asian Immigration in Los Angeles and Global Restructuring.* Philadelphia: Temple University Press.

Lopez, David and Yen Espiritu. 1990. Panethnicity in the United States: A Theoretical Framework. *Ethnic and Racial Studies* 13: 198–224.

Massey, Douglas S., Rafael Alarcon, Jorge Durand, and Humberto Gonzalez. 1987. *Return to Aztlan: The Social Process of International Migration from Western Mexico.* Berkeley: University of California Press.

Matsumoto, Valerie. 1993. *Farming the Homeplace.* Ithaca, NY: Cornell University Press.

Nash, Philip Tajitsu. 1997. Will the Census Go Multiracial? *Amerasia Journal* 23(1): 17–27.

Nishi, Setsuko Matsunaga. 1995. Japanese Americans. Pp. 95–133 in Pyong Gap Min (ed.), *Asian Americans: Contemporary Trends and Issue.* Thousand Oaks, CA: Sage.

Ong, Paul M., Lucie Cheng, and Leslie Evans. 1992. Migration of Highly Educated Asians and Global Dynamics. *Asian and Pacific Migration Journal* 1(3–4): 543–67.

Oropesa, R. S. and N. S. Landale. 1997. Immigrant Legacies: Ethnicity, Generation, and Children's Family and Economic Lives. *Social Science Quarterly* 78(2): 399–416.

Portes, Alejandro and Rubén G. Rumbaut. 1996. *Immigrant America: A Portrait* (2nd ed.). Berkeley: University of California Press.

Portes, Alejandro and Min Zhou. 1993. The New Second Generation: Segmented Assimilation and Its Variants among Post-1965 Immigrant Youth. *Annals of the American Academy of Political and Social Science* 530: 74–98.

Reeves, Terrance J. and Claudette E. Bennett. 2004. *We the People: Asians in the United States* (2000 Census Special Report, censr-17). Washington, DC: U.S. Census Bureau.

Rumbaut, Rubén G. 1995. Vietnamese, Laotian, and Cambodian Americans. Pp. 232–70 in Pyong Gap Min (ed.), *Asian Americans: Contemporary Trends and Issues.* Thousand Oaks, CA: Sage.

Sassen, Saskia. 1989. America's Immigration Problems. *World Policy Journal* 6(4).

Smith, James P. and Barry Edmonston (eds.). 1997. *The New Americans: Economic, Demographic, and Fiscal Effects of Immigration.* Washington, DC: National Academy Press.

Sung, Betty Lee. 1987. *The Adjustment Experience of Chinese Immigrant Children in New York City.* Staten Island, NY: Center for Migration Studies.

Takaki, Ronald. 1989. *Strangers from a Different Shore: A History of Asian Americans.* New York: Penguin.

Takezawa, Yasuko I. 2000. Children of Inmates: The Effects of the Redress Movement among Third-Generation Japanese Americans. Pp. 299–314 in Min Zhou and J. V. Gatewood (eds.), *Contemporary Asian American: A Multidisciplinary Reader* (1st ed.). New York: New York University Press.

Tuan, Mia. 1999. *Forever Foreign or Honorary White? The Asian Ethnic Experience Today.* New Brunswick, NJ: Rutgers University Press.

U.S. Commission on Civil Rights. 1992. *Civil Rights Issues Facing Asian Americans in the 1990s: A Report.* Washington, DC: U.S. Government Printing Office.

———. 1988. *The Economic Status of Americans of Asian Descent: An Exploratory Investigation.* Washington DC: Clearing House Publications.

Warner, W. Lloyd and Leo Srole. 1945. *The Social Systems of American Ethnic Groups.* New Haven, CT: Yale University Press.

Waters, Mary C. 1990. *Ethnic Options: Choosing Identities in America.* Berkeley: University of California Press.

Wong, Bernard. 1982. *Chinatown: Economic Adaptation and Ethnic Identity of the Chinese.* New York: Holt, Rinehart, and Winston.

Wong, Morrison G. 1995. Chinese Americans. Pp. 58–94 in Pyong Gap Min (ed.), *Asian Americans: Contemporary Trends and Issues.* Thousand Oaks, CA: Sage.

Xie, Y. and K. A. Goyette. 2004. *The American People, Census 2000: A Demographic Portrait of Asian Americans.* New York: Russell Sage Foundation Press; Washington, DC: Population Reference Bureau.

Yanagisako, Sylvia. 1995. Transforming Orientalism: Gender, Nationality, and Class in Asian American Studies. Pp. 275–98 in Sylvia Yanagisako and Carol Delaney (eds.), *Naturalizing Power: Essays in Feminist Cultural Analysis.* New York: Routledge.

Yancey, William, Richard Juliani, and Eugene Erikson. 1976. Emergent Ethnicity: A Review and Reformulation. *American Sociological Review* 41(3): 391–403.

Yu, Henry. 1998. The "Oriental Problem" in America, 1920–1960: Linking the Identities of Chinese American and Japanese American Intellectuals. Pp. 191–214 in K. Scott Wong and Sucheng Chan (eds.), *Claiming America: Constructing Chinese American Identities during the Exclusion Era.* Philadelphia: Temple University Press.

Zangwill, Israel. 1914. *The Melting Pot: Drama in Four Acts.* New York: Macmillan.

Zhou, Min. 2001. Contemporary Immigration and the Dynamics of Race and Ethnicity. Pp. 200–242 in Neil Smelser, William Julius Wilson, and Faith Mitchell (eds.), *America Becoming: Racial Trends and Their Consequences.* Washington DC: National Academy Press.

Zhou, Min. 1992. *Chinatown: The Socioeconomic Potential of an Urban Enclave.* Philadelphia: Temple University Press.

Zhou, Min and Carl L. Bankston. 1998. *Growing up American: How Vietnamese Children Adapt to Life in the United States.* New York: Russell Sage Foundation.

Zhou, Min and Yoshinori Kamo. 1994. An Analysis of Earnings Patterns for Chinese, Japanese, and Non-Hispanic Whites in the United States. *The Sociological Quarterly* 35(4): 581–602.

Zhou, Min and Susan S. Kim. 2006. Community Forces, Social Capital, and Educational Achievement: The Case of Supplementary Education in the Chinese and Korean Immigrant Communities. *Harvard Educational Review* 76(1): 1–29.

The Waves of War
Immigrants, Refugees, and New Americans from Southeast Asia

Carl L. Bankston III and Danielle Antoinette Hidalgo

Southeast Asia stretches from the northern borders of Laos and Vietnam through the southern islands of Indonesia. It includes Myanmar (Burma), Thailand, and Cambodia, as well as Malaysia and the Philippines. The overwhelming majority of Southeast Asian Americans, who made up about one-third of the total Asian American population at the beginning of the twenty-first century, came from the Philippines, Vietnam, Laos, Cambodia, and Thailand. There is a great deal of diversity among these nations. The people of the Philippines, for example, speak mostly nontonal, grammatically complex languages related to the Malay and Indonesians. Most Filipinos are Catholic, although a substantial minority is Muslim, and their culture was deeply influenced by a Spanish colonial history. The Vietnamese speak a tonal language and have received cultural influences from China, including Confucianism and the Mahayana Buddhism common in other parts of East Asia. Vietnam also has a large number of Catholics, as a result of French colonial domination. Thailand, Laos, and Cambodia have had close historical and cultural ties with each other. Most people in all three practice the Theravada Buddhism of southern Asia and the three nations have had long cultural ties to India, the source of their writing systems. The Thai and the Lao speak closely related tonal languages, while the Cambodians (also known as the Khmer) speak an unrelated nontonal language. All of these nations also have significant internal variation, with large minority groups, such as the Hmong from the mountains of Laos.

While there is diversity among the ancestral homelands of America's Southeast Asian population, there is also similarity. All have maintained traditional societies based on wet-rice farming. More important for their immigration history, all of them came into contact with the United States as a result of the American military interventions from the end of the nineteenth through the end of the twentieth centuries. War created the paths of migration between North America and Southeast Asia. The timing of the wars, and the parts played by the Southeast Asians in these wars, shaped many of the conditions of migration and the processes of adaptation to the new homeland. Filipinos, the first to be affected by America's rise to global dominance, developed a deep but complicated familiarity with American society. The war in Indochina brought new nationalities to the United States as refugees, but it also affected nonrefugee migration from both the Philippines and Thailand, where the United States had military bases during the second half of the twentieth century.

American foreign policy in the form of military activities created connections between the United States and the nations of origin of major Southeast Asian American groups. American immigration and refugee policies then played a great part in determining who would arrive in the United States from this distant part of the world and what opportunities and barriers they would find.

War, Occupation, and Migration from the Philippines

The Philippines was a Spanish colony from the second half of the sixteenth century until the end of the nineteenth, when Filipino independence forces rose against the colonial power. The United States was an expanding industrial force and some American leaders believed the United States needed a strong navy and overseas stations for it, as well as new resources. At the beginning of the Spanish-American War in 1898, as a strategic move against Spain and as a tactic for expanding the international role of the United States, Assistant Secretary of the Navy Theodore Roosevelt secretly ordered a U.S. fleet to attack Spanish forces at Manila, the chief city of the Philippines. The Spanish were ill prepared for the American attack and were quickly defeated. Instead of turning the island colony over to the Filipino rebel forces, the United States made arrangements with Spain and placed the Philippines under American rule (Bankston 2006).

For several years Filipino forces struggled with the new occupying power. Scholars have estimated that 200,000 to 500,000 Filipinos died in the fight against American colonization (San Juan 1998). After putting down the Filipino independence fighters, the United States began to attempt to remake the Philippines according to American concepts. The Americans created an extensive public school system and founded the University of the Philippines on the model of U.S. research universities. The new colonists constructed roads and public buildings. The Americans created a U.S.-style government and encouraged the growth of political parties.

The American occupation of the Philippines marked the first movement of the United States into Southeast Asia. As the English language and familiarity with North American ways began to spread through the Philippines, the contact established by war also promoted migration from the Philippines to the United States and its territories. From 1903 to 1938, the Pensionado Act passed by the U.S. Congress provided funds for Filipino students to study in the United States. Following the example of these Pensionados, or sponsored students, other nonsponsored Filipinos entered American schools and universities, creating the movement of people and ideas between the two nations.

From 1910 to 1920, the Filipino American population increased from under 3,000 to over 26,000 (Bankston 2006). During the 1920s, this population grew even more rapidly as a result of the demand for agricultural workers in Hawaii and California. Canneries in Alaska and other locations also began to draw Filipino workers. Filipinos

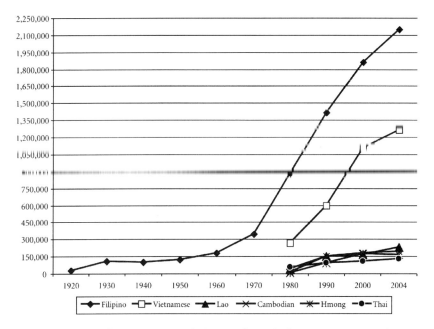

Fig. 5.1. Major Southeast Asian Populations in the United States, 1920–2004. *Source*: U.S. Bureau of the Census, 1970 Census of Population (for numbers through 1970), 1980 & 1990 Census of Population, Summary File 4, American Community Survey, 2005.

found work at sea, as well, working in the American merchant marine until 1936 and in the U.S. navy, where they were typically assigned to be mess stewards.

As figure 5.1 shows, the American occupation and control of the Philippines, together with American demand for Filipino labor, caused the number of Filipinos in the United States to grow from under 27,000 in 1920 to over 100,000 ten years later. After the United States established the Philippine Commonwealth and placed the Philippines on the track to independence in 1934, migration went down and the Philippine American population even decreased slightly by 1940. The Tydings-McDuffie Act, which created the Commonwealth, redefined Filipinos as aliens, rather than U.S. nationals, and gave Filipinos an admission quota of only fifty individuals per year (Bankston 2006). However, another war changed relations between the two nations once again.

Following the attack on Pearl Harbor, the Japanese invaded and occupied the Philippines in 1942. Some Filipinos at first saw the Japanese as liberators from the Americans. Others joined with the Americans against the new invaders. Opposition to the Japanese soon intensified pro-American feelings among many Filipinos (Bankston 2003).

The United States recognized Philippine independence in 1946, but the Americans kept large military bases in the Philippines. These major centers of the U.S. armed forces in Southeast Asia became one of the most important sources of migration. By one estimate, about half of all the immigrants who came to the United States between 1946 and 1965 arrived as wives of U.S. military personnel (Reimers 1985). Postwar immigration policies also helped foster an expanding Filipino American population. The Luce-Cellar Bill of 1948 increased the quota of Filipino migrants to the United States to one hundred per year, and spouses of U.S. citizens were entirely outside the quota. The Education Exchange Act of 1946 began what would later become one of the most important sources of Filipino migration to the United States: nurses. This act enabled foreign nurses to spend two years in the United States for study and professional experience. The difference between living standards in the two countries encouraged many nurses to stay after the two years, and the demand for nurses in the United States made it relatively easy for them to find work. Once again, national relations shaped by war were followed by immigration policies to direct flows of migrants. During the post–Word War II period, though, the bases in the Philippines became staging points for the next great involvement of the United States in Southeast Asia, the Vietnam War. Migrant flows were to become waves.

New Filipino Migrants

Although Filipino Americans are the oldest Southeast Asian group in the United States, their population grew most rapidly during the same period of time when other Southeast Asians began to arrive. The growth of the Filipino American population, though, began a few years earlier than that of other Southeast Asian American groups. In 1965, the United States greatly amended its immigration policy. The new immigration law replaced a national-origins quota system that allotted places mainly to Europeans with caps for each hemisphere and a system of preferences to be used in allocating places in overall quotas. Spouses, unmarried children under eighteen, and parents of U.S. citizens could enter the United States without numerical restriction. Adult family members of U.S. citizens had first preference, and spouses and unmarried adult children of resident aliens had second preference. Professionals and people with special abilities had third preference. In the descending system of preferences, family connections became the primary basis for acceptance, and professional and job skills became a secondary basis. Because the U.S. occupation of the Philippines had created complex, long-standing ties between the two nations, Filipinos were poised to take advantage of the 1965 change in immigration laws. Largely educated in English and familiar with North American culture, Filipinos had skills that were in demand in the United States. Highly skilled professionals made up a large segment of the post-1965 migrants from the Philippines. Before 1960, fewer than 2 percent of the people of Filipino ancestry residing in the United States had professional occupations, compared to 6 percent of all Americans. By 1980, though, about a quarter of Filipinos in the United States were professionals, and twenty years later this had gone up to nearly a third (Bankston 2006). The American demand for medical workers, and the fact that the American occupation had established American training and standards for Filipino medical professionals, accounted for the overrepresentation of nurses, physicians, and medical technicians who immigrated from the Philippines. Nurses, who had already begun moving from the Philippines to the United States following the 1948 Education

Exchange Act, emigrated in even greater numbers following the passage of the Health Professions Assistance Act in 1976. This piece of legislation required professional immigrants to have job offers from American employers, and it was followed by active cooperation of immigration officials with American hospitals in recruiting nurses. Again, the connections between the United States and the Philippines created by the invasion and long occupation meant that the Philippines was training nurses ready for work in the United States and it was therefore an ideal setting for recruitment (Bankston 2006).

Spouses of American service personnel who had served in the Philippines continued to make up a substantial portion of the post 1965 immigration, with much of this due to the American buildup in Southeast Asia during the Vietnam War. In 1980, one out of every four married Filipino American women had husbands who had served in the U.S. military during the Vietnam War period. The popular identification of the Philippines as a source of wives also expanded into civilian American society, so that marriages arranged by mail between women in the Philippines and men in the United States had become fairly common by the 1970s. By the early 1990s, an estimated 19,000 "mail-order brides" were leaving the Philippines each year to join husbands and fiancés abroad, with the United States as the primary destination (Bankston 1999; Bankston 2006).

As the Filipino American population grew, there were more people in the United States with immediate relatives in the Philippines. Because the 1965 change in immigration law had made family reunification the category that allowed the most immigrants, this meant that each immigrant opened the way for others, resulting in an exponential growth in the Filipino American population throughout the end of the twentieth century (Bankston 2006).

While the post-1965 Filipino immigrants were fairly widely dispersed around the nation, they did have some centers of settlement, promoted by the family reunification emphasis of U.S. immigration law. In 2000, just under half of all Filipinos in the United States lived in California. The Los Angeles–San Diego region of southern California was home to 480,000 Filipino Americans, or more than one out of every four in the United States, in that census year (Ruggles et al. 2003).

The Vietnam War and New Sources of Migration

Following World War II, the Cold War between the United States and the Communist nations of the Soviet Union and China led the United States to extend its involvement in Southeast Asia beyond the Philippines. Communists, headed by former Soviet Comintern agent Ho Chi Minh, led the struggle for the independence of the French colony of Vietnam. Unable to reestablish control over Vietnam, France accepted a peace agreement in 1954 that divided Vietnam into a Communist-dominated northern portion and a southern portion, where the French at first hoped to maintain some influence. Anti-Communist, disproportionately Catholic groups established themselves in South Vietnam. North Vietnam, together with dissidents in the South, sought to reunify the country. With this Cold War setting as the backdrop, the United States saw the conflict in Vietnam as critical to prevent the spread of communism. By 1965, the U.S. effort to maintain the South Vietnamese government led the United States to send huge numbers of their own troops.

The Vietnam War brought the United States into closer contact with other nations in the region of Vietnam. As early as 1950, the United States forged ties with Thailand as a response to the Korean War (Randolph 1986). Thailand began to receive substantial foreign aid and military assistance from the United States. With direct American intervention in Vietnam, these ties grew even closer and stronger. Following the American lead, Thailand sent troops into Vietnam. Even more important for the future Thai American population, by the height of the Vietnam War in the early 1970s, "Thailand harbored more than 750 U.S. aircraft actively involved in operations over Indochina and served as temporary home to some 50,000 American servicemen" (Randolph 1986, preface). As part of the Vietnam War activities, the United States established seven major U.S. air bases in Thailand (Bishop and Robinson 1998), which have been described as "highly sexualized" zones promoting interaction between American men and local Thai women (Enloe 2000, 231). Even more American servicemen passed temporarily through Thailand from Vietnam and other parts of the region for "R & R" (rest and recreation). Aside from purely military activities during this period, the United States also provided Thailand with a wide array of programs from the Agency for International Development (AID), the U.S. Information Service (USIS), and other acronymic organizations (Randolph 1986).

American war efforts from Thailand moved into Laos, as well as Vietnam. In Laos, the guerilla forces known as the Pathet Lao ("Lao Nation") were allies of the North Vietnamese, and the "Ho Chi Minh Trail," North Vietnam's main supply route to its troops in the south, ran the length of eastern Laos. The United States began massive bombing in Laos, conducted from Thailand, and recruited a secret army among the Laotian minority group known as the Hmong.

The war also spread into Cambodia, which had been part of French Indochina along with Vietnam and Laos. Cambodia had its own Communist-led insurgents known as the Khmer Rouge. It was also used by Communist Vietnamese forces as a sanctuary and a base for launching attacks into South Vietnam. In the late 1960s, Cambodia's leader, Prince Norodom Sihanouk, allowed the Americans to engage in bombing the Cambodian countryside in order to drive the Vietnamese forces out. The prince's cooperation was limited, though, and the Americans acquiesced when the Cambodian military, under General Lon Nol, staged a coup, establishing the Khmer Republic. The coup caused Sihanouk to flee to the Khmer Rouge and to urge his supporters to take up arms against the new Cambodian government.

With Lon Nol in power, there were no limits on American bombing. Eager to force the North Vietnamese to come to an agreement that would enable American troops to withdraw from a highly unpopular war, the Americans dropped an estimated 539,129 tons of bombs on the small country. This was about three and a half times the bombs dropped on Japan during all of World War II. Social disruption, together with the political appeal of Sihanouk, greatly increased the power of the radical Khmer Rouge. After the Khmer Rouge took power in 1975, they forced the populace out of the cities and into concentration camps, where millions of Cambodians died from sickness, starvation, and executions.

Although the Philippines was separated from the events in Thailand, Cambodia, Laos, and Vietnam by the South China Sea, relations between this former U.S. colony and the United States were also affected by the Vietnam War. Under pressure from the Americans, the Philippines sent a modest number of troops to fight in Vietnam. More importantly, though, "the United States was vastly increasing its use of Philippine and Thai facilities in its war" (Thompson 1975, 87). As in Thailand, this expansion of military facilities brought an increase in the military personnel stationed in Philippine bases.

In 1973, with growing unwillingness among the American people for continuing the war in Vietnam, the United States withdrew nearly all of its forces from Vietnam, Cambodia, and Laos. In the spring of 1975, South Vietnam fell to the forces of the North and Cambodia fell to the Khmer Rouge. The Royal Government of Laos allowed the Pathet Lao into a coalition government, and the Pathet Lao rapidly took over the country.

The United States continued to have dwindling numbers of troops in Thailand until the summer of 1976, after negotiations with the Thai government failed to renew agreements for a U.S. military presence (Randolph 1986). By that time, though, well over 30,000 Thai people had left for the United States. Thailand had become a familiar place to many Americans, and a clear migration route had been established. The bases in the Philippines, product of the first American military intervention in Southeast Asia and central locations for the intervention in Vietnam, closed in 1991.

Refugees from Vietnam, Cambodia, and Laos

In 1965, the same year the United States began sending significant numbers of troops to Vietnam, the United States changed its immigration laws, removing discriminatory national-origins quotas and thereby opening the gates to immigrants from Asia. As figure 5.1 shows, the Filipino American population grew rapidly in the years following 1970, and other Southeast Asian groups became significant parts of the nation during this time. The change in immigration laws also set the stage for the growth of the Southeast Asian population, in particular, by formalizing refugee policy and creating a special type of visa for refugees, known as the "seventh preference" visa category.

This new visa category for refugees should be understood in terms of the global foreign policies that led to American involvement in the Vietnam War. The Refugee Relief Act of 1953, one of the earliest pieces of refugee legislation in the United States, resulted from President Harry Truman's appeal to Congress to authorize visas for escapees from the Communist-dominated nations of Eastern Europe. The Hungarian Refugee Adjustment Act of 1958 was designed to help Hungarian refugees remain in the United States as permanent residents following the Hungarian uprising against Soviet control. The most energetic U.S. governmental efforts on behalf of refugees prior to the mid-1970s were products of the Cuban Refugee Program, established in the early 1960s to help those fleeing from Fidel Castro's Cuba. Many of the voluntary agencies and even individuals who would later become active in resettling Southeast Asian refugees had earlier been involved with resettling Cuban refugees. American refugee policy, like American defense policy, was almost entirely concerned with communism during the second half of the twentieth century.

Ten years after the new immigration policy in 1965, U.S. involvement in the war in Vietnam led to a refugee program that entirely overshadowed Cuban resettlement. In the spring of 1975, the U.S.-supported governments of South Vietnam, Laos, and Cambodia fell to Communist forces. As North Vietnamese forces took control of what had been South Vietnam, hundreds of thousands of South Vietnamese, many formerly associated with the American war effort, fled by boat into the China Sea. The United States rapidly created a program known as Operation New Life, which moved refugees to American military bases to prepare them for temporary resettlement in the United States. In this way, 126,000 Vietnamese, most of whom were well educated and fairly familiar with the American way of life, became the first wave of Southeast Asian refugees to settle in the United States.

During the late 1970s, Vietnamese continued to leave their country by boat, or on foot across Cambodia to Thailand. Cambodians and Laotians also continued to flee, most of them into Thailand. In 1977, Attorney General Griffin Bell used his parole authority, his power to admit emergency cases into the country temporarily, to allow thousands of people from the three Indochinese countries of Cambodia, Laos, and Vietnam to resettle in the United States. That same year, President Carter signed legislation that permitted the Indochinese to become permanent residents, establishing a path to eventual citizenship.

When tensions between Vietnam and Cambodia led to the Vietnamese invasion of Cambodia in December 1978, Vietnam was attacked by Cambodia's ally, China. These events resulted in an outpouring of refugees from both Cambodia and Vietnam, including many ethnic Chinese living in Vietnam. In response to the refugee crisis, Congress passed the most comprehensive piece of refugee legislation in American history, the Refugee Act of 1980. In place of the "seventh preference category" established in 1965, which admitted refugees as part of the total number of immigrants allowed into the United States, the Refugee Act provided for an annual number of admissions for refugees. This number was to be independent of the number of immigrants permitted, and it was to be established each year by the president in consultation with Congress.

Refugees began entering the United States in unprecedented numbers. The Orderly Departure Program (ODP) was created in 1980 by an agreement between the American and Vietnamese governments. This program enabled Vietnamese political prisoners and Amerasians (half-Vietnamese children of American soldiers) to leave Vietnam legally for resettlement in the United States (Zhou and Bankston 1998).

The vast majority of those allowed into the United States by Operation New Life in 1975 were Vietnamese. In the spring of that year, the United States brought in 4,600 Cambodians and 800 people from Laos, as well as the 126,000 from Vietnam. At the end of 1975, though, the U.S. Congress agreed to accept more of the people from Laos who were languishing in refugee camps in Thailand. During the following year, the United States brought in 10,200 refugees from Laos who had been living in the Thai border camps. Most of those admitted at that time were members of families headed by people who had been employed by the United States Agency for International Development, the U.S. Information Service, or the U.S. embassy in the Laotian capital of Vientiane.

In the late 1970s, the numbers of those arriving from Laos went down again, to 400 in 1977, and then rose to 8,000 in 1978. At the end of the 1970s, war between Vietnam and Cambodia created new, highly publicized waves of refugees to Southeast Asia, bringing increased public attention to the region and creating a favorable environment for the admission of new Southeast Asian refugees. Refugee resettlement in the United States of people from Laos grew to 30,200 in 1979, 55,500 in 1980, and 19,300 in 1981, or about 105,000 individuals during this three-year period. Admissions from Laos reached the high point in 1980 and then gradually slowed to a trickle over the course of the twentieth century. These admissions included both ethnic Lao, frequently families of soldiers associated with the former Kingdom of Laos, and members of the Hmong secret army that had been recruited by American intelligence. Seen as enemies by the new government of the Lao People's Democratic Republic, people in these two groups fled across the border into Thailand. The Thai government responded by pressuring the Americans to accept more refugees.

Large-scale refugee movement from Cambodia to the United States began in the year of the 1980 Refugee Act. In 1981, over 38,000 Cambodian refugees reached the United States. By the end of the 1980s, the numbers of Cambodian refugees began to decline. With the withdrawal of Vietnam from Cambodia in the late 1980s, the flow of refugees came to an end. After 1995, the movement of 1,000 to 2,000 legal immigrants per year replaced the refugee movement from Cambodia (Bankston and Hidalgo 2006).

None of the Southeast Asian groups except Filipinos appears before 1980 in figure 5.1 because there were no significant numbers of any of these other groups. However, in 1980, the first year the other Southeast Asians appeared, there were already over a quarter of a million Vietnamese and close to 68,000 people from Cambodia and Laos in the United States. These new arrivals had come onto the American scene so suddenly because the U.S. government was coordinating their resettlement because they were connected to the United States through the American military engagement in their nations. The government coordination of resettlement also had important implications for the ways in which the members of the new groups would fit into American society.

Concerned about the social and political impact of its refugee policy, the U.S. government at first attempted to scatter people from Vietnam, Laos, and Cambodia around the nation. The government pursued its resettlement efforts by working through voluntary agencies, such as religiously based charities and social service groups. Refugees settled in locations where voluntary agencies were available to find housing and organize support. Both the initial attempt to scatter refugees and the use of voluntary agencies tended to create relatively small Southeast Asian communities throughout the country, so that members of the Southeast Asian refugee groups were neither dispersed as individuals nor concentrated entirely into single large ethnic enclaves (Zhou and Bankston 1998).

By the end of the twentieth century, the large concentrations of Southeast Asian refugee groups that did exist were primarily in southern California. However, other communities of Vietnamese, Cambodians, Lao, and Hmong were widespread. The ethnic Lao were the least concentrated of the groups, often forming small communities around the United States. Texas was home to a number of these, with populations of 500 to roughly 1,000 Laotians in each of the following places: Amarillo, Dallas, Euless, Houston, and Irving. An estimated three to four thousand Lao Americans lived in St. Paul and Minneapolis, Minnesota, drawn by the support programs that also served the Hmong (Bankston and Hidalgo 2006).

In 2000, Los Angeles was home to over 30,000 Cambodians, and nearly 5,000 lived in neighboring Orange County. Within Los Angeles, Long Beach had the greatest concentration of Cambodians, containing about 20,000 people of this ethnicity. By the mid-1980s, the area along Tenth Street in Long Beach had become known among Cambodian Americans as the "New Phnom Penh," after the capital of Cambodia. Outside of California, Lowell, Massachusetts, was home to the greatest concentration of Cambodians in the eastern United States, with a Cambodian American population of about 11,000. In the Northwest, approximately 15,000 Cambodians lived in the Seattle area, mostly in Seattle itself (Bankston and Hidalgo 2006).

Many Hmong were initially resettled by voluntary agencies in Minnesota. As a result, the city of St. Paul became a magnet, and by the end of the twentieth century Hmong was the single largest non-English language in St. Paul's public schools. By 2000, the cities of Minneapolis and St. Paul together were home to an estimated 40,000 Hmong. Other Hmong sought to concentrate in the warmer climate of California, seeking relatively rural areas. By the mid-1980s, an estimated 20,000 Hmong had resettled in the three California Central Valley Counties of Merced, San Joaquin, and Fresno. U.S. Census data in 2000 indicated that approximately over 24,000 Hmong lived in Fresno, with another 6,000 in San Joaquin, and 6,600 in Merced. Another 17,000 to 18,000 Hmong had settled in Sacramento County, bordering San Joaquin County on the north, by 2000 (Bankston and Hidalgo 2006).

The Vietnamese, largest of the refugee groups, began to establish their most notable ethnic community in southern California during the 1980s. By 1990 California's Orange County had become home to "Little Saigon" in the city of Westminster. With its Vietnamese-style shop fronts and Vietnamese language signs, Little Saigon could easily be confused with an upscale neighborhood in its Asian namesake. One-fourth of the Vietnamese people in the United States had settled in the Los Angeles–Orange County–San Diego metropolitan area by 2000 (Rumbaut 2006). Still, the original government policy of scattering refugees around the nation, together with sponsorship by geographically dispersed voluntary agencies, continued to have consequences for the settlement of the Vietnamese. Montana, North Dakota, and Wyoming were the only states in the United States to hold fewer than one hundred Vietnamese in the U.S. Census, and identifiable Vietnamese communities could be found around the country.

Migration from Thailand

Until the late 1960s, Thailand was a distant and unfamiliar land for most Americans, and very few Thai people reached American shores. The new post-1965 immigrants from Thailand to the United States generally fell into two categories: professional jobseekers and Thai spouses of American service personnel (Cadge and Sangdhanoo 2002; Footrakoon 1999). The path to migration for the professionals had been opened both by the change in immigration law and by the American military presence in Thailand that facilitated contact and movement between the two countries. The migration path of the spouses was, of course, even more directly linked to U.S. military intervention in Southeast Asia, and it was a path taken by many new arrivals from Thailand. The 1980 U.S. Census showed that nearly 30 percent of all Thai immigrants and 40 percent of all female Thai immigrants were married to veterans of the U.S. military. By that census year, a majority of married Thai American women (57 percent) had husbands who had been Vietnam-era veterans. Migration through marriage led to a predominance of women among the Thai in America. According to U.S. Census data, women made up 62 percent of the Thai American population in 1980, 63 percent in 1990, and just over 60 percent in 2000 (Hidalgo and Bankston 2005). In their overview of the development of Thai Buddhism in America, Cadge and Sangdhanoo (2002, n.p.), remark that "largely as a result of marriages between Thai women and American men who served in Viet Nam, more women than men born in Thailand have and continue to live in the United States."

As figure 5.1 shows, the Thai American population established during the Vietnam War years continued to grow throughout the twentieth century, so that the U.S. Census counted 111,000 immigrants in 2000. This figure may fail to account for substantial numbers of undocumented immigrants from Thailand, smuggled into the country as workers by coethnics or arriving on tourist and student visas and remaining after visa expiration. Since so many of the legal immigrants were professionals or spouses of U.S. citizens, Thai Americans had settled in various locations throughout the country. Nevertheless, they had established some notable ethnic concentrations by the end of the century. The Los Angeles area was also home to nearly one out of every four Thai Americans in 2000, with 20,000 residing in Los Angeles County itself by census estimates and over 3,000 in neighboring Orange County. At the beginning of the year 2000, the section of Hollywood Boulevard between Western and Normandie Avenues was officially designated as Thai Town. Other fairly large Thai concentrations were located in New York City, which was home to over 4,500 Thai Americans in 2000, and in Chicago, where about 2,700 Thai Americans lived in that year (Bankston and Hidalgo 2006).

Variations in Patterns of Immigrant Adaptation

The Vietnamese, Lao, Hmong, and Cambodians have generally differed somewhat from the Thai and Filipinos in their processes of adaptation to life in the United

States. The first four groups arrived in America in mass waves of refugees, resettled by agencies and available for assistance on arrival. Although some members of these groups, particularly in the first wave of Vietnamese refugees, had high levels of education and professional experience in their own countries, they generally had little familiarity with life in the United States. By contrast, the Filipinos and the Thai came as individual immigrants, frequently with professional qualifications that could be fairly readily put to use or with marital or family connections that could ease their entry into U.S. society.

The five Southeast Asian groups also differ in a number of other respects, aside from their connections to refugee status. Cambodians and Hmong often arrived in the United States with serious disadvantages. Cambodian society had been torn apart during the Khmer Rouge years, and Cambodian Americans often had to recover from horrific personal tragedies while they sought to adapt to life in the United States. The Hmong had lived in a largely nonliterate, rural culture in the mountains of Laos, and North America was an utterly strange world to many of them. Although Filipinos and Thai shared many characteristics as immigrant groups, the long familiarity of the Filipinos with American ways distinguished them from the Thai, as well as from the other Southeast Asians. Below, we look briefly at the patterns and processes of adaptation of each of the Southeast Asian national groups.

Filipino Americans

In general, people of Filipino ancestry in the United States are well educated, tend to work at white-collar jobs, and move fairly easily through American society. As shown in table 5.1, at the close of the twentieth century, Filipino Americans were more likely than others in the United States to work at management and professional jobs, showed rates of English proficiency similar to the rest of the American population, and had higher percentages of high school graduates and college graduates than other Americans did. While only 43 percent of traditionally college-aged young adults in the United States were enrolled in institutions of higher education, a majority of Filipinos in this age group were attending such institutions.

Filipinos were no more likely to be unemployed or receive public assistance than the rest of the U.S. population, and they were less likely than others to be poor. Their median per capita income was approximately the same as that of the nation at large, but they enjoyed substantially larger household incomes. The most probable explanation of this discrepancy is that Filipino American households tended to contain more workers than other households, an explanation that is consistent with the somewhat larger family sizes of Filipinos. Filipino Americans had rates of home ownership only slightly below those of other Americans and their homes were generally worth more than those of other Americans. Their relatively highly valued homes were probably only partly a result of their professional jobs and high household incomes. As with many other Asian groups, highly valued homes also reflect the high housing prices on the West Coast.

Despite their relatively advantageous socioeconomic settings, Filipino Americans showed a higher probability than other Americans of living in single-parent families.

TABLE 5.1
*Socioeconomic and Family Characteristics of the U.S. Population and of
Major Southeast Asian Groups in the United States, 2000*

	All U.S.	Filipinos	Thai	Vietnamese	Cambodians	Lao	Hmong
% in management, professional jobs	33.6	38.2	33.4	26.9	17.8	13.4	17.1
% Speak English Well or Very Well	96.0	94.5	85.8	69.3	73.1	75.0	73.5
% High School Grads (over 25)	80.4	87.3	78.4	53.1	50.5	48.3	40.5
% College Grads (over 25)	24.4	43.8	41.4	19.4	10.2	7.6	10.0
% 19–22 in higher education	42.5	51.6	61.8	60.3	52.5	34.2	32.1
Unemployment Rate	3.7	3.4	2.5	3.5	3.6	5.0	7.1
Poverty Rate	9.1	6.3	14.4	16.0	29.3	18.5	37.8
% w Public Assistance Income	3.4	3.5	2.0	10.3	22.4	14.2	30.3
Median HH Income ($)	41,994	60,570	40,329	45,085	36,155	42,978	32,076
Median Per capita income	21,587	21,267	19,966	15,655	10,366	11,830	6,600
Home Ownership (%)	66.2	60.0	64.2	53.2	46.0	56.9	41.2
Median home value ($)	119,600	188,100	160,900	151,400	120,800	100,500	92,600
Average Family Size	3.17	3.77	3.04	4.00	4.85	5.05	7.41
% Single mother households	10.9	16.9	7.3	14.2	17.0	10.1	13.6
% Single father households	3.5	6.0	4.1	9.6	3.9	5.4	2.0

SOURCE: Ruggles, Sobek, et al. (2000 5% IPUMS), U.S. Census Summary File 4 (2000).

To some extent, this may reflect the strains of a high degree of assimilation in largely urban environments. It may also reflect the complications of extensive intermarriage. By 2000, 16 percent of Filipino American men and over 36 percent of Filipino American women were married to members of other ethnic groups (not shown in table 5.1).

The high degree of out-marriage among Filipino Americans naturally meant that to outward appearance many of them were completely absorbed in mainstream American society. It also meant that the ethnic identification of the children of Filipino Americans was often unclear. There were an estimated 521,000 people of mixed Filipino ancestry in the United States in 2000, or about 22 percent of all Americans with a Filipino background. Despite this apparent absorption, though, even Filipinos married to non-Filipinos have often formed networks of Filipino friends. Filipino American clubs have sponsored events such as beauty pageants and celebrations of Philippine national holidays to maintain the sense of connection to the ancestral land.

Vietnamese Americans

The Vietnamese, largest of the refugee groups and second largest Southeast Asian nationality in the United States, were less well represented in management and professional jobs than the Filipinos or Thai; over 30 percent of Vietnamese Americans spoke English less than well by 2000, as seen in table 5.1. However, while Vietnamese Americans had proportionately fewer adult high school and college graduates than other Americans or nonrefugee Southeast Asian groups, a high percentage of traditionally college-aged Vietnamese was enrolled in higher education.

The participation of young Vietnamese in college-level institutions reflects their striking educational success in the United States. Some scholars have attributed this success to cultural values brought from Vietnam (Caplan, Choy, and Whitmore 1991). Zhou and Bankston (1998) have argued that the Vietnamese communities dispersed around the nation have been the source of much of this success. Their studies indicate that the Vietnamese developed high levels of ethnic solidarity in response to resettlement, often in low-income neighborhoods, in an alien society. The ethnic solidarity, frequently centered on Vietnamese Catholic churches or Vietnamese Buddhist temples, provided social controls and encouragement for young people to concentrate on education as a means of bypassing disadvantaged environments to jump into the American middle class. This ethnic solidarity, together with a generation gap between young people growing up in America and their elders, also produced alienation from Vietnamese adult society on the part of a substantial portion of Vietnamese youth. The two trends of educational success and alienation, according to Zhou and Bankston (1998), have been the sources of the competing stereotypes of Vietnamese young people as "delinquents" or "valedictorians."

Vietnamese Americans had relatively high poverty rates and high rates of participation in public assistance, but unemployment rates about equal to those in the general population. Although a majority of Vietnamese Americans were homeowners by 2000, their rates of home ownership still lagged behind those of the rest of the country. Again, the high valuation of homes owned by Vietnamese Americans probably reflects their large numbers on the West Coast. With somewhat larger families than other Americans, the native-born part of the Vietnamese American population was likely to grow rapidly over the first part of the twenty-first century.

One of the consequences of the planting of Vietnamese communities around the United States is that Vietnamese Americans have frequently maintained close ties among widely distributed ethnic concentrations. On the negative side, this has meant that members of Vietnamese youth gangs have been able to move relatively easily from one location to another. On the positive side, it has meant that Vietnamese in one place can often seek help from those in another. When Hurricane Katrina devastated New Orleans at the end of August 2005, for example, residents of the Vietnamese neighborhoods of that city were able to seek refuge in the Vietnamese community of Houston.

Cambodian Americans

Cambodians in the United States continued to be haunted by events in their homeland. Their stress had psychological and physical consequences. Settled in low-income, urban neighborhoods in the United States, Cambodians often suffer from violence and hostility. During the 1980s and 1990s, Cambodian youth gangs developed in several of these neighborhoods. Adults often had trouble finding work, since most of them had been farmers in their native land and had few skills that were relevant to life in the United States.

As seen in table 5.1, Cambodians were underrepresented in professional and management jobs and had very high unemployment rates and rates of participation in public assistance at the close of the twentieth century. They also had a median per capita income only about half that of other Americans and less home ownership than all of the other groups except the Hmong.

Despite the disadvantages of the Cambodians in adapting to American society, they have made substantial progress. A majority (53 percent) of those aged nineteen to twenty-two were enrolled in higher education, even though those twenty-five and over tended to have only limited educational backgrounds. Cambodian cultural organizations have been active in the United States and by the early 1990s at least fifty Cambodian Buddhist temples had been established around the nation.

Lao Americans

Like most of the other refugee nationalities, the ethnic Lao in the United States live mostly in cities, although they come from mainly rural locations in Laos. The Lao, as seen in table 5.1, have been the least likely of all the Southeast Asian nationalities to work at professional or management occupations. This is more a reflection of the tendency of the Lao to work at blue-collar trades than an indication of lack of adaptation to American society. While the unemployment rate of the Lao was double that of other Americans, it was lower than the rates of the Cambodians and Hmong and only slightly higher than that of the Vietnamese. As a consequence of the apparent orientation of the Lao toward jobs that involve working with their hands, in 2000 they were the second least likely among Southeast Asians to be enrolled in higher education during the first years of early adulthood.

Families tend to be close in Laos, where all family members need to work together to produce rice harvests and care for the elderly. In the United States, the Lao retain this emphasis on family life, although many adults worry about their Americanized children drifting away from their families. Partly as a result of the importance of family, Lao Americans have had much larger families than other Americans and larger families than any Southeast Asian nationality except the Hmong.

Although the Lao have generally experienced less difficulty in adapting to American society than the Cambodians or the Hmong, they have faced their share of challenges. Often living in relatively low-income neighborhoods, they face all the difficulties presented by these environments, particularly those of rearing children in strange and sometimes dangerous settings. Lao youth gangs have formed in a number of ethnic communities, and the generation gaps between parents and children are often great.

Hmong Americans

As table 5.1 suggests, the Hmong have faced great challenges in adapting to life in the United States. Six out of every ten Hmong over the age of twenty-five had completed less than high school, they had an unemployment rate nearly double that of other Americans, over one-third lived below the poverty level, and nearly one-third received public assistance income in 2000. Influenced by the traditions of their homeland, the Hmong had much larger families than other Americans in general or other Southeast Asian nationalities. Nevertheless, considering the great cultural differences between the mountains of Laos and American cities, the Hmong have dealt with their transition with strength and resilience. They have developed self-help organizations and many have achieved rapid upward mobility.

Of all the Southeast Asian groups, the Hmong have experienced some of the most serious problems in adapting to American society and have had to deal with some of the most negative reactions from other Americans. A number of localities have objected to the arrival of the Hmong. Concerned about the influx of Hmong to Minnesota, in 1986 Republican Senator Dave Durenberger asked the U.S. State Department to restrict the number of Hmong sent to that state. Senator Durenberger said he believed the Hmong had few prospects for employment and were difficult to assimilate. High rates of reliance on public assistance rendered the Hmong vulnerable to changes in American domestic policies. The welfare reform bill that the U.S. Congress passed in 1996 denied several forms of public assistance to Hmong families and in 1997 the Department of Agriculture began cutting off food stamps to some of the Hmong.

The controversial Hmong practice of "bride capture" has placed a number of Hmong in conflict with American authorities. This practice involves the ritual seizure of a bride by a prospective husband. In the 1985 *People v. Moua* case, bride capture became a legal issue when a Hmong bride with an American upbringing and perspective charged a suitor with kidnapping and rape.

Thai Americans

Since many contemporary Thai arrive in the United States as professionals or as students, as of 2000 Thai Americans showed about the same representation as other Americans in professional and managerial jobs, and they had very high rates of college completion and current enrollment in higher education (see table 5.1). They also had median per capita and household incomes only slightly lower than those of the general American population. However, these indicators of socioeconomic position may be a bit misleading with regard to Thai immigrants, who tend to be either relatively prosperous or disadvantaged in American society (Cadge and Sangdhanoo 2002; Bankston and Hidalgo 2006). This is why the Thai also showed a substantially higher percentage of people below the poverty level than Filipinos or most other Americans, although the Thai were less likely to be poor than any of the immigrant groups.

Despite Thailand's rapid economic rise in the late twentieth century, it still has many desperately poor people, and this has led to a largely unrecognized problem of low-income Thai being smuggled into the United States. This problem came to national attention in August 1995, when United States Immigration officials staged a raid on a garment factory in El Monte, California. Surrounded by barbed wire, the factory held seventy-two workers from Thailand, kept in virtual slavery by coethnic employers. In a number of other cases, immigration officials in the United States have found Thai women brought illegally to the United States and forced to work as prostitutes (Bankston and Hidalgo 2006).

The fact that so many Thai Americans who are legally in the United States are married to non-Thai means that they tend to be highly assimilated in many respects. Although English is not widely spoken in Thailand, 86 percent of Thai Americans spoke

English well in 2000. As in the case of Filipinos, out-group marriage by the Thai has also meant a heavily mixed-race native-born population. In 2000, over 26 percent of all those in the United States with a Thai ethnic heritage were of mixed ancestry (not shown in table 5.1). Thai American mixed marriages moved away from their mainly military origins as the Vietnam War receded into history. Still, by 2000, about one out of every five married Thai American women had a husband who had served in the U.S. military during the war in Vietnam (Ruggles et al. 2003).

Despite the apparent assimilation of many Thai Americans, they often retain strong ethnic identities. As the Thai American population has grown, these identities have frequently been expressed through Thai Buddhist temples. According to Wendy Cadge, a scholar specializing in Thai American Buddhism, about eighty-seven Thai temples have been established in twenty-nine states across the United States. These temples help to maintain transnational connections, since the monks have generally been trained in Thailand and the temples sometimes receive financial assistance from the Thai government. Further, Thai American children's participation in cultural events at the *wat* (temple) serves as an important link to networks in Thailand and their cultural heritage (Cadge 2004). Thai temples also frequently serve as ways of connecting non-Thai spouses to Thai culture (Perreira 2004).

Conclusion

As the United States rose to global power at the end of the nineteenth century, North America came into close contact with different parts of the world. Southeast Asia played an important part in this American rise to power. The Philippines became the site of the earliest American military activities outside of the western hemisphere and it was conquered and occupied by the United States. American involvement in mainland Southeast Asia during the 1960s later became one of the central episodes of the Cold War.

The American military movement into Southeast Asia resulted in waves of migration. The time and nature of this movement in turn shaped the time and nature of the migration. The Philippines, with its long connection to the United States, became the source of one of the largest Asian American populations. Spouses of soldiers were one of the big categories of immigrants from the Philippines. Often English-speaking, educated in American-style institutions, and familiar with American culture, other immigrants from these islands flowed into the United States after the liberalization of American immigration laws. The Vietnam War stimulated more immigration from the Philippines, location of American bases, and it put American service personnel into Thailand. The increased contact with Thailand resulted in more migration from that nation, disproportionately in the form of spouses of American citizens, but also in the form of new professional migration. The end of the Vietnam War led to the massive relocation of refugees from Vietnam, Cambodia, and Laos.

U.S. immigration and resettlement policies, often shaped by the same global concerns that produced U.S. military intervention in Southeast Asia, followed the international connections produced by war. These policies helped to select who in the Philippines, Thailand, Vietnam, Cambodia, and Laos would move to the United States, and they helped to direct patterns of settlement and adaptation around the nation.

REFERENCES

Bankston, Carl L. III. 1999. "Mail-Order Brides." Pp. 866–69 in *Encyclopedia of Family Life,* edited by Carl L. Bankston III and R. Kent Rasmussen. Pasadena, CA: Salem Press.

Bankston, Carl L. III. 2003. "The Philippines." Pp. 441–59 in *World Conflicts: Asia and the Middle East,* edited by Carl L. Bankston III. Pasadena, CA: Salem Press.

Bankston, Carl L. III. 2006. "Filipino Americans." Pp. 180–205 in *Asian Americans: Contemporary Trends and Issues* (2nd ed.), edited by Pyong Gap Min. Thousand Oaks, CA: Pine Forge Press.

Bankston, Carl L. III and Danielle Antoinette Hidalgo. 2006. "Southeast Asia: Laos, Cambodia and Thailand." In *The New Americans: A Guide to Immigration since 1965,* edited by Mary Waters and Reed Ueda. Cambridge, MA: Harvard University Press.

Bishop, Ryan and Lillian S. Robinson. 1998. *Night Market: Sexual Cultures and the Thai Economic Miracle.* New York: Routledge

Cadge, Wendy. 2004. *Heartwood: The First Generation of Theravada Buddhism in America.* Chicago: University of Chicago Press.

Cadge, Wendy and Sidhorn Sangdhanoo. 2002. "Thai Buddhism in America: A Historical and Contemporary Overview." Paper presented at the October annual meeting of the Society for the Scientific Study of Religion, Salt Lake City, Utah.

Caplan, N. H., M. H. Choy, and J. K. Whitmore. 1991. *Children of the Boat People: A Study of Educational Success.* Ann Arbor: University of Michigan Press.

Enloe, Cynthia. 2000. *Maneuvers: The International Politics of Militarizing Women's Lives.* Berkeley: University of California Press.

Footrakoon, Orapan. 1999. "Lived Experiences of Thai War Brides in Mixed Thai-American Families in the United States." Unpublished Dissertation: University of Minnesota.

Hidalgo, Danielle Antoinette and Carl L. Bankston III. 2005. "The Demilitarization of the Thai Wives: Thai American Exogamy, 1980–2000." Paper presented at the August meeting of the American Sociological Association, Philadelphia, Pennsylvania.

Perreira, Todd. 2004. "Sasana Sakon and the New Asian American: Intermarriage and Identity at a Thai Buddhist Temple in Silicon Valley." Pp. 313–37 in *Asian American Religions,* edited by Tony Carnes and Fenggang Yang. New York: New York University Press.

Randolph, R. Sean. 1986. *The United States and Thailand: Alliance Dynamics, 1950–1985.* Berkeley: University of California Press.

Reimers, David M. 1985. *Still the Golden Door: The Third World Comes to America.* New York: Columbia University Press.

Ruggles, Steven, Matthew Sobek, Trent Alexander, Catherine A. Fitch, Ronald Goeken, Patricia Kelly Hall, Miriam King, and Chad Romander. 2003. *Integrated Public Use Microdata Series: Version 3.0* (5% PUMS Samples). Minneapolis: Historical Census Projects, University of Minnesota.

Rumbaut, Ruben. 2006. "Vietnamese, Laotian, and Cambodian Americans." Pp. 262–89 in *Asian Americans: Contemporary Trends and Issues* (2nd ed.), edited by Pyong Gap Min. Thousand Oaks, CA: Pine Forge Press.

San Juan, Epifanio. 1998. "One Hundred Years of Producing and Reproducing the 'Filipino.'" *Amerasia Journal* 24(2): 1–33.

Thompson, W. Scott. 1975. *Unequal Partners: Philippine and Thai Relations with the United States, 1965–75.* Lexington, MA: D.C. Heath.

Zhou, Min and Carl L. Bankston III. 1998. *Growing Up American: How Vietnamese Children Adapt to Life in the United States.* New York: Russell Sage Foundation.

Chapter 6

Indians in North Carolina
Race, Class, and Culture in the Making of Immigrant Identity

Ajantha Subramanian

Over the past thirty years, North Carolina has refashioned itself as a center of transnational, "high-tech" industry. The changing landscape of the state has been witnessed in the in-migration of new, white-collar populations attracted by employment opportunities in the state's Research Triangle Park (RTP), the proliferation of gated communities for these "knowledge workers," and the further marginalization of poor black and white residents. My work documents the insertion of professional immigrants from India—the beneficiaries of the Indian state's investment in science and technology education—into the race and class dynamics of North Carolina and examines their role in integrating the state into transnational circuits of culture and capital. This multi-sited ethnography covers the institutional contexts in India where the transnational class of professionals is produced, and the community and professional spaces inhabited by Indian Americans in North Carolina. How has the goal of technological modernity shaped the political economy of development in India and the United States? How has North Carolina's transformation into a center of "high-tech" industry been reflected spatially and demographically? What role have Indian professionals played in this transformation? And how have North Carolina's Indians situated themselves in the changing race and class dynamics of a region increasingly more tightly integrated into transnational circuits of labor and capital?

In her book *Flexible Citizenship*, Aihwa Ong (1999) urges us to pursue an ethnographic approach to understanding "how nation-states articulate with capitalism in late modernity." She suggests that we go beyond a zero-sum account of the battle between nation-state and capital and attend to "the transnational practices and imaginings of the nomadic subject and the social conditions that enable his flexibility" (3). Only by weaving the analysis of political economy and of cultural politics, she maintains, "can we hope to provide a nuanced delineation of the complex relations between transnational phenomena, national regimes, and cultural practices in late modernity" (16). Following her lead, I have begun to explore both the social conditions (state developmental priorities, corporate demand for labor, and geopolitics) that have enabled the mobility of Indian professionals and the way Indian migrants have constituted themselves socially, culturally, and politically in a new, First World home.

The lives and narratives of Indian transnationals help me juxtapose the developmental strategies of the Indian and U.S. states over the latter half of the twentieth century, and the operations of social hierarchy and status in both national contexts in ways that will hopefully illuminate some of the nuances of globalization.

Rethinking Diaspora

One of the theoretical goals of this project is to rethink the relevance of diaspora as an analytical tool for documenting the lives of transnational subjects. Are we better off thinking of Indian Americans, for instance, as diasporic Indians or as people moving from one context of unequal power to another? One reason for questioning the use of "diaspora" is the term's assumption of an original or organic cultural identity that, through movement, is then "hybridized" with other cultural elements. In evoking a place from which movement originates, diaspora creates a singular homeland that then becomes the site of an originary cultural identity. Land and culture are thus conflated, and the movement "away" from the land necessarily becomes a displacement from a pure or authentic cultural identity. By extension, diasporic consciousness is characterized by a yearning for a lost center and an anxiety over loss of cultural purity. Diaspora thus maintains the notion of cultural wholes, indeed even of national cultures, that have been soundly and rightly critiqued by anthropology (cf. Fox 1990). For me, to move beyond diaspora (so to speak) is to give up using "Indianness" as a referent for assessing cultural change and to turn instead to a more contextualized approach to cultural identity. It is to understand subjectivity in terms of the situated practices of people in specific locales. For the purposes of this study, then, I document the imaginings and practices of North Carolina's Indian Americans not in terms of continuity or change from an original, premigration cultural identity but as an expression of an American immigrant, and even more specifically, of a southern immigrant consciousness. Similarly, I understand their premigration subjectivities not in terms of an organic "Indianness" but as an expression of their participation in caste, class, and gender hierarchies, and of their relationship to the Indian state. In effect, then, I am approaching this as a study of a population operating within a global political economy that structures relationships between states and classes, and between migrants and locals.

How does this affect my attitude to culture? I deal with "culture" as a political and historical construct and not as an objective fact. "Culture" has emerged as a key political trope of globalization and has been put to multiple uses by states, corporations, and transnational subjects. Its ubiquitous presence in immigrant Indian discourses of self and community forces an examination of the implications of culture's elevation to global prominence for the politics of transnationality, and for the politics of race and class in the United States. My research suggests that the key to the puzzle of "culture's" ubiquity lies in the very nature of the term. Unlike "race" and "class," which point to structural hierarchies, "culture" appears to be atomistic and power neutral. Cultures can be pluralized without suggesting inequity and accommodated without contradictions within a single global or national framework. As I hope to show through my ethnography, in the case of the United States, culture has emerged as a form of collectivity that fits neatly into the logic of corporate capitalism. And Indian professionals have been extremely adept at navigating the terrain of this "corporate multiculturalism."

State Intervention and Class Formation

What are the attributes of Indian American "culture"? A key attribute, one that has buttressed Indian Americans' claim to first-class citizenship, is professional class status. How did Indian professionals come to wield the scientific and technological skills that have made them a coveted immigrant population? This question concerns the political economy of technological development in India and the United States. The goal of technological modernity prompted specific forms of state developmental and legal intervention in the two national contexts that produced this class of highly skilled, and subsequently highly mobile, professionals. This section outlines the intimate link between the state and this global professional class, a link that is crucial to understanding both their transnational mobility and their subjectivity. It is also offered as a political intervention. In this era of market triumphalism, when the Indian state has supposedly been disciplined by the free flow of capital and expatriate Indians celebrate the end of Indian "underdevelopment," it is politically necessary to recognize the extent to which these transnational subjects have benefited from the very state whose development role they now decry.

Some may think that Indians are naturally gifted in science and technology—that they are born with an aspiration to build engines and program computers. But it is no accident that the percentage of high-tech professionals in the Indian American community is higher than in all other immigrant groups. For independent India's leading statesmen, most significantly Jawaharlal Nehru, scientific progress anchored the goal of an independent, self-sufficient nation. The India of Nehru's dreams was closely linked to the world of science, not only because science encapsulated the secular principles he held so dear but also because it promised advances that would alleviate the misery of the Indian poor. On the eve of independence, Nehru expressed his faith in science and in independent India's potential to the Indian Science Congress. "If we could tap, say, even five percent of the latent talent in India for scientific purposes," he proposed, "we could have a host of scientists in India" (Nehru 1984). Toward the goals of economic self-sufficiency and poverty alleviation, the postcolonial Indian state invested massively in science and technology education. The All India Council of Technical Education and the Scientific Manpower Committee worked together to expand the number of technical institutions and foster a culture of science in the country. In 1947, 38 scientific and technical institutions trained 2,940 students; by 1961, 102 institutions trained 13,820 students, and this rate of growth continues to this day (Prashad 2000).

Through the good graces of the socialistic Indian state, then, a class of high-tech professionals championed as the architects of the developing nation was produced. Interestingly, most of these beneficiaries of the state are drawn from the uppermost echelons of Indian society. Just as the high numbers of technically trained Indians is a direct outcome of state developmental planning, this too is no accident. Take, for instance, the cream of the technical institutions—the Indian Institutes of Technology (IITs). In the name of an unqualified standard of excellence, the IITs have maintained their selective character by exemption from the affirmative action policies that sought to correct the caste-based inequalities standing as barriers to democratic possibility. As a result, these institutions have remained bastions of caste privilege, and the breeding ground for a transnational class of "high tech" professionals. Of the migrants who came to the United States from India after 1965, an overwhelming majority were upper castes trained in the IITs and other centers of Indian state-funded professional education. Caste status and educational capital have served them as vehicles of transnational mobility.

While Indians have migrated to the United States for a variety of personal reasons since the late nineteenth century, changes in U.S. immigration policy in 1965 created the social conditions for a more rapid influx of professionals. These legal changes were in large part due to Cold War hostilities. In 1957, the USSR launched Sputnik I and II into orbit and began a panic in the United States over the technological prowess of its Cold War rival. In response, the U.S. government began a concerted effort to promote the study of science and technology, most directly through an enhanced National Science Foundation. Rather than training Americans, however, U.S. science came to rely for its development upon immigrants. The Soviet cosmonaut Yuri Gagarin's successful orbit of the earth in 1961 was a key catalyst in the decision to import technical labor. President Kennedy spearheaded the move to overhaul the immigration system so that professional migrants could enter without securing employment beforehand. As early as 1958, Kennedy registered his protest against the "indefensible racial preference" in immigration law by caricaturing the poem inscribed on the pedestal of the Statue of Liberty. He wrote, "as long as they come from Northern Europe, are not too tired or poor or slightly ill, never stole a loaf of bread, never joined any questionable organization, and can document their activities for the past two years, let them enter" (Kennedy 1964, quoted in Prashad 2000). A change towards a more egalitarian legal framework, he felt, would attract "talented people who would be helpful to our economy and our culture." An additional political reason to amend immigration policy was to offset the image of a racist nation publicized by the civil rights movement, an image that some feared would provide a basis for Communist propaganda. Finally, in 1965, on the heels of civil rights legislation, President Johnson approved new statutes that aimed specifically at increasing professional immigration—most importantly of scientists and engineers—to bolster the U.S. position in the space and nuclear races (Ungar 1990). The 1965 Immigration and Nationality Act sought to reunite families, allow those with some disabilities such as epilepsy, barred earlier, to immigrate, and encourage skilled labor to enter the United States to fulfill the need for more technical manpower.

The U.S. concern for global dominance in the arenas of science and technology precipitated a transnational wave of Western migration that, in India, came to be called "the brain drain." Between 1966 and 1977, 83 percent of the Indian Americans who migrated to the United States entered under the occupational category of professional and technical workers. Roughly, there were twenty thousand scientists, forty thousand engineers, and twenty-five thousand doctors (Leonard-Spark and Saran 1980; Liu 1992). By 1976, however, the U.S. government had tightened its immigration laws. The Immigration and Nationality Act Amendments of 1976 required that migrants have firm job offers. While this restriction slowed down the entry of technical and professional migrants from India, it did not stop the entry of family members, who entered through the family reunification program. Since the 1980s, the percentage of technical workers among Indian migrants has steadily decreased, and the percentage of family members has grown. While in 1969, 45 percent of Indians came in the occupational category, by 1985 this number had decreased to 12.6 percent. By contrast, the percentage of Indians who came under the family reunification scheme increased from 27 to 85.9 between 1969 and 1985 (Hing 1993). By 1994, employer preference for Indian technical and professional workers became almost negligible largely because of the stringent demands placed on employers by the labor certification process in the Immigration Act of 1990. The late 1990s witnessed another shift prompted once again by technical needs. Even in the midst of immense pressure to slow down immigration, the U.S. legislature created loopholes to accommodate the needs of corporate America. The special rights afforded to corporations were highlighted in the controversy over the H1B visa used by transnational corporations to import highly skilled technicians on a temporary basis. Even while Congress increased the power of the INS to beat down doors and incarcerate long-term residents in detention centers for minor misdemeanors, the flow of labor into the information technology industry increased. This industry has been the primary beneficiary of the H1B program, which has helped to concentrate IT activity in places like Silicon Valley. Unlike the early professionals however, the Indian "migrant programmers" who come over on H1B visas wield neither economic nor social capital and are subject to the contracts between their home companies and the U.S. firms to whom they outsource their labor (Prashad 1994; Haniffa 1998a, 1998b).

The profile of Indian America has thus shifted from the 1980s, from a predominantly professional to a more varied one. However, the early influx of professional immigrants and their economic and social capital has consolidated their power within Indian America and significantly shaped its politics. One of the results is a reconstitution of community in cultural terms that appears simply to be derivative of the "homeland" but that, I argue, is as much an expression of status and rights concerns in a new social context.

America—Multicultural or Racial?

Indians are currently one of the most affluent U.S. minority populations.[1] They have emerged as a "model minority" whose public profile fits neatly into the logic of American multiculturalism. They are "hard-working," they have their community institutions and practices, and they subscribe to a political conservatism that supports their material interests. Most importantly, they have attempted to define themselves in cultural terms that avoid any obvious racial referent. The coincidence of Indian professional migration to the United States and civil rights legislation that instituted a formal equality has permitted the ascendance of a politics of culture. The discrediting of racial ideology after World War II and the civil rights movement (cf. Steinberg 1995) has further contributed to this formulation of Indian identity. Now, "culture," with its constituent elements of region, language, and religion, has superseded race as the definitive characteristic of Indian immigrant identity.

North Carolina's Indian Americans too appear to have recognized and embraced this model of multicultural America. Lalit Patel, an executive body member of the Indian American Forum for Political Education and a twenty-year resident of North Carolina, encapsulated the logic of American cultural politics:

> In this country you protect your interests, your visibility, your long-term survival only by showing your involvement *as a cultural community*. If you isolate yourself, nobody will recognize your interests. Jewish people are the shining example of solidarity and success: they have a strong community, they have a lobby. Chinese Americans are also becoming stronger because of community influence. If they included the rest of us, their strength would become diluted. . . . And this is happening everywhere. Nowadays, the global environment . . . it used to be more a melting pot, and nowadays the situation has changed. Your identity as a community has to be cultivated. You have to show that your community is involved in mainstream America. Nowadays, people are looking at what the Indian community is doing locally, statewide, or nationally . . . and without that community-based unity, you can't speak to the American political leadership. Each community has a different interest, different expectations. The Indian community has different interests than the Chinese, Germans, Irish, or Mexican.

Patel presents a picture of the American political system as a balancing act of different cultural groupings, each with their own interests and demands. He equates "community" with interest group and represents American society as the sum of its constituent "cultures." Patel's view of "culture" is biological—it is an expression of ethnicity—and national—it is derived from an original homeland. Significantly, class and gender differences within "the Indian community" are completely erased in this model of American society and politics, and unsurprisingly, it is the professional class to which Patel belongs that emerges as representative of the singular collective interest.

However, this model of a multicultural America was not the only one that he worked with. Patel also pointed to an America with degrees of citizenship where "ethnics" were permanent foreigners. "After twenty-six years," he said with regret and not a little anger, "many people still ask me when I came here. I've been a citizen for twenty years but that's the perception, the stereotype." When I asked who was assumed to be American, he stated strongly, "In America, whites are American. Even Irish and Germans who have just arrived here, the first instinct is that they're American." When I followed with, "What about blacks?" he hesitated, then replied, "Well . . . yes, they are considered to be American . . . up to a point." Although Patel did eventually include African Americans in his characterization of who is "automatically" American, the total absence of black America in his initial consideration of U.S. society, and his subsequent hesitation over the status of African Americans speaks volumes. For him, I believe, U.S. national identity is structured by a racial hierarchy in which "whiteness" is the mark of privilege and first-class citizenship, and "blackness" is the "internal Other." Black America represents the negative side of belonging, a racialized citizenship that is a permanent disadvantage. The politics of "community" that Patel referred to in his explanation of the American political system serves as leverage to gain the "right" kind of citizenship while avoiding the "wrong" kind. In other words, "community" or "culture" has served Indian Americans, among others, as a means to claim white privilege and disown blackness.

Indian Immigrants and U.S. Racial Hierarchies

Indian professionals in America did not always stake claims to citizenship in terms of "culture." In the past, elite Indians responded to American racial hierarchies by adopting strategies such as claiming white identity (Mazumdar 1991). The migration of Indians to the United States began as early as the late nineteenth century. By 1900, U.S. Census reports placed the "East Indian" or "Hindu" population—mostly urban, upper caste Hindu students, businessmen, and professionals—at 2,050 (Melendy 1977).[2] After 1904, a new category of Indian arrived: immigrants from rural peasant backgrounds, predominantly from the Punjab province of northwestern India. Between 1907 and 1910, approximately one thousand immigrants entered each year, and by 1910 there were up to ten thousand Indians in the United States (Mazumdar 1991). Following as they did in the footsteps of Chinese and Japanese immigration, these "pioneers" were subject to the "Yellow Peril" racism sweeping the country. Dubbed the "Turbaned Tide," they were targeted by newly formed groups such as the Asian Exclusion League, which demanded the termination of Indian immigration (Mazumdar 1991). Legislation followed social hostilities: the California Alien Land Act of 1913 excluded Indians from land ownership; the "barred zone" Immigration Act of 1917 stopped all Asian immigration except from Japan; the Thind case of 1923 declared "Hindus" ineligible for citizenship on the basis that they were not "white persons" (Singh 1998, 5–7).

In spite of the racial targeting of Indians as a whole, class proved an important factor in determining what form of discrimination they faced. While the immigrants who came to work the land, in lumber yards, or on the railroads bore the brunt of physical attacks, educated professionals who did not confront such direct hostility began crafting a racial politics that would distinguish them from poorer compatriots, from other nonwhite immigrants, and from black Americans. The lack of solidarity across class and race lines framed the Indian elite struggle for citizenship as an individual fight for justice rather than a collective battle against a white establishment. Drawing on the Aryan theory of race elaborated in the work of nineteenth-century British ethnologists and German Romantics, educated Indians engaged in court battles to prove that they, unlike those of African, Chinese, and Japanese origin, were "members of the Aryan race . . . entitled to naturalization as a white person" (Melendy 1977, quoted in Mazumdar 1991, 50). Between 1907 and 1923, seventy educated professionals gained citizenship on the grounds that they were members of the "Aryan race," and as such of white, or Caucasian, origin. These "advances" were reversed in the verdict of the Thind case, in which the Supreme Court ruled that "while ['Caucasian'] and the words 'white persons' are treated as synonymous . . . they are not of identical meaning." As a result, more than half of the seventy had their citizenship annulled by 1926 (Mazumdar 1991, 50).

In the early twentieth century, then, laying claim to whiteness was a necessary step to claiming equal citizenship. Today, in the aftermath of the civil rights movement and the celebration of multiculturalism, this early Indian claim to white identity might sound both unnecessary and absurd. But we must ask to what extent the racial hierar chics of the early twentieth century—in particular, the equation of whiteness with privilege—have been dismantled or whether they continue to structure American society and politics.

Stephen Steinberg (1995), for instance, questions the retreat from racial thinking that has marked post-civil-rights cultural politics. He maintains that, rather than marking an end to white privilege, liberal discourses of formal equality have served to mask its continued operations. Steinberg argues that the early split between civil rights leaders such as Martin Luther King, who demanded substantive equality, and white liberals, who felt that preferences to compensate for historical injustice would subvert formal equality, set the stage for the retreat from racial justice in American thought and policy. Echoing Steinberg's argument, Cheryl Harris (1993) points to the landmark judgment in *Brown vs. Board of Education* as a turning point for American racial politics, not only because it marked the end of legal segregation but also because it permitted the reemergence of white privilege in a more subtle form. "White privilege accorded as a legal right was rejected," she argues,

> but de facto white privilege not mandated by law remained unaddressed. In failing to clearly expose the real inequities produced by segregation, the status quo of substantive disadvantage was ratified as an accepted and acceptable base line—a neutral state operating to the disadvantage of Blacks long after de jure segregation had ceased to do so.

Finally, George Lipsitz (1988) provides an exhaustive account of the various institutional forms that whiteness as a form of property takes, from preferential lending to potential white homeowners to scaling back affirmative action in order to ensure whites their entitled right to education and jobs.

North Carolina's Indians: Class Privilege and Racial Difference

How does the liberal base line apply to professional Indians? And how in particular does it apply to them in the U.S. South? North Carolina has had its own share of Indian immigration. South Asians, who numbered 10,540 in 1990, are currently the fourth largest group after whites, African Americans, and Latinos.[3] The number of South Asians who entered North Carolina increased rapidly in the 1970s, taking the total from 604 in 1969 to 2,502 by 1979.[4] The largest wave, however, came in the 1980s, when 8,038 South Asians arrived in the state.[5] This group, especially the Indian majority within it, has consisted overwhelmingly of educated professionals, namely, doctors, engineers, academics, and scientists. Over the last fifteen years, in addition to more professionals, a group of entrepreneurs has arrived and opened groceries, video stores, and restaurants to serve the growing community. Aside from the permanent residents, the late 1990s also witnessed a steady inflow of highly mobile computer programmers whose time spent in the state is determined by the nature of their contracts with employer firms.

While most Indians arrived in North Carolina after the 1964 Civil Rights Act, a few were here previously. Their experiences of a segregated South provide an early instance of the role Indians play in its race dynamics. John Cherian, a professor of nuclear engineering at North Carolina State University (NCSU), was one of those who arrived in the state in 1963 at the height of the civil rights movement. Born into an upper-middle-class, south Indian Christian family, he was the youngest of five children. "Education was very important in my family," Cherian explained and as additional emphasis he stated, "My three eldest siblings were all girls and they all had college degrees." He and his brother took up engineering in Kerala University and then Cherian went on to an advanced degree at one of the IITs in North India. While he had no immediate plans to continue his education in the United States, when the opportunity presented itself, he took it. His brother-in-law, then a Ph.D. student at the University of Iowa, urged Cherian to apply to its up-and-coming nuclear engineering program. It didn't take much persuasion, and in 1959, Cherian found himself a doctoral candidate in Ames, Iowa. He arrived in North Carolina to take up his first job after completing his Ph.D. in nuclear engineering at the University of Iowa.

While there were already quite a few Indians in Iowa, Cherian found that, at the time, there were hardly any in North Carolina where he took up his first job at NCSU. In the university itself, he was one of two Indians, the other a professor of statistics who had arrived two years previously. The year was 1963, and police crackdowns on civil rights demonstrators were rampant. Cherian found himself in a racially polarized society where he was a noncategory. "My professor in Iowa warned me about the South," he recalled, "and I knew what he meant. He said North Carolina was the most progressive [state] but nevertheless the South." His first moments as a visitor in the state seemed to confirm that North Carolina was definitely southern, and in the South, Indians were definitely "black":

> When I came in April 1963 for an interview, the university folks reserved a room for me at the Velvet Cloak, a new hotel. When I got there at 11:30 P.M., lady behind the counter said, "Would you mind waiting until the manager comes?" I think she had no clue what it was that had shown up! I could hear her making telephone calls, and I didn't want to be humiliated when the manager showed up. I probably would have had a room because the university made the reservation but I decided to leave anyway. I had seen a YMCA so I went there instead.

When he arrived in North Carolina to stay, however, he encountered a different situation. Initially, he said, it was more of the same. "I had to find an apartment. I would call up and they would say, 'Yes, come and look,' and the lady would open the door and say 'I'm sorry, it's rented.' Then I decided to first say, 'I'm faculty at NCSU' and then there was no problem at all." When I asked him if he thought his profession was the key to this change in attitude that he experienced, he hesitated, then replied, "Yes and no. Telling people I was Indian seemed to have the same effect. As soon as they figured out that I was a nonwhite foreigner, they treated me very well."

In fact, Cherian stated strongly, it was as if white southerners were trying to prove a point:

> I got the impression that the South was embarrassed to be mistreating foreign visitors. They had no problem discriminating against U.S. blacks, but they went to lengths to ensure that we were fine. I think southerners knew they weren't doing the right thing. Hudson Belk, for instance, had segregated bathrooms. I would go into the "Whites Only," maybe as protest, and never encountered any problem. There was a public swimming pool right outside the university. Of course, there were no blacks swimming. It had water fountains marked "White" and "Colored." It was all very explicit but they didn't want someone from another country to think they did this with everybody.

To drive his point home, Cherian told me about the experience of a friend of his, a fellow Indian graduate student, who had a similar experience when he moved from Iowa to Mississippi. "I had an Indian classmate in Iowa who moved to Mississippi which was supposed to be far worse than North Carolina and there too he encountered the same situation. They were treated fine, especially if his wife was wearing a sari because that was a clear sign that they weren't from here."

Once the flow of Indian professionals into North Carolina increased, their identity as the exception that proved the rule of racism was further crystallized. As Indians have populated the state's universities, corporations, and research institutions, their image as a "model minority" has strengthened. Their place as a nonwhite population that approximates white privilege within a racially polarized society has been manifest both economically and spatially: class privilege has taken them into white neighborhoods, both older ones that were desegregated after the Civil Rights Act and the increasing number of new subdivisions peppered across Durham, Raleigh, and Cary. Cherian remembered how much and how rapidly his neighborhood of Cary changed and how the change dovetailed with the Indian influx.

> In our subdivision there were three or four others who worked at NCSU, people who worked at IBM, public school teachers, insurance salesmen. It was not an elite community. But when the RTP started to grow, it started to change. Houses went from being modest 1–2,000-square-foot homes to much bigger ones. And at the same time that it became more prosperous, it also became more diverse. Soon we had an incredible number of Indian neighbors!

Spatially and economically, then, Indians have separated themselves from the state's black, and now also its Latino, population. With the end of legal segregation, they have benefited from the less explicit, or at least less articulated, code for segregation: class. Several of the local Indians I spoke with applauded the transformation of the Raleigh-Durham area into a cosmopolitan center where the racism of the old South was no longer apparent. Sita Sharma, a past president of the Hindu Society who has lived in Cary since the late 1960s, pointed to the RTP as the salvation of the state. She told me,

> The image of the South when I moved here wasn't good, and the biggest thing that happened in North Carolina to change the image and reality of the South was opening the RTP. Now, the South is so nice to live in, it's so cosmopolitan. It used to be so difficult to get Indian spices and videos, and now there are so many groceries and restaurants to choose from!

Like Sharma, others also attributed North Carolina's acceptance of foreigners to the economic boom. Ravi Srinivas, a south Indian and former professor of psychiatry at Duke who arrived in the state in 1986, echoed her sentiments:

> We moved into a predominantly white neighborhood but felt no racism at all. I thought the South would have been more hostile to foreigners but it was not so. There was already a big Indian community here so it was very easy for us to adjust. . . . We would go to the Hindu temple on Sundays. I also started a Telugu Association so I could speak in my mother tongue. Now with the computer industry boom, there are so many more south Indians programmers here and they all come to the association.

A number of local Indians spoke of the ease of living in the South without speaking of the growing disparities of wealth or class segregation that also follows racial lines. Rather, many referred to their comfortable relationships with white colleagues and neighbors as a sign of the spread of "liberal values" in the South, and an end to racism. Significantly, there was almost no one who addressed Indians' relationship to black southerners as a way of situating themselves in North Carolina. Sanjay Wadhwani, the CEO of an internet technology firm in Cary, was one exception. Wadhwani characterized the position and attitude of local Indians bluntly:

> Indians have enjoyed economic independence here. We are not even considered minorities, because we're not economic minorities. By extension, we don't think of ourselves as minorities. Let me be frank: most Indians here cross the street when they see a black person. We're all biased. With our economic prosperity, we tend to associate more with successful people than with those without privilege.

While Wadhwani's stark portrayal of local Indian privilege and the prejudice it generates may be an overgeneralization, his sense of how Indians identify along class lines is very relevant. That Indian professionals prefer to associate with their "own people," namely, other Indian professionals, and only infrequently widen this circle to include others of their class is more than apparent.

Publicly, North Carolina's Indians have expressed their differences from other minorities in the language of culture. In the 1980s, they began building a variety of institutions. As in most Indian diasporic contexts, religion, as a ritualized performance of collective identity and a link to a perceived cultural "essence," was pivotal to this process. North Carolina currently has four Hindu temples, two Sikh *gurudwaras,* and four

Muslim mosques. With growth in numbers, other markers of identity, such as nation and language, have also emerged as focal points of institution building. The India Heritage Society and the Indian American Forum for Political Education express solidarity along national lines. A growing number of regional language associations—there are twelve to date—reflect the power of language as a unifying force. Second-generation Indians too have been active cultural producers. Duke, UNC–Chapel Hill, and NCSU all house South Asian student associations that promote ties to and knowledge of the subcontinent through music, religious festivals, and films. At Duke, Hindu students have also formed a unit of the national Hindu Students Council, an organization begun by the Vishwa Hindu Parishad of America to foster Hindu nationalist "values" in Indian American youth. Most recently, and in keeping with their parents' class aspirations, a group has founded the South Asian Young Professionals Association in Chapel Hill.

As they have across the United States since 1965, North Carolina's Indians have combined strategic involvement in domestic politics with engagement in the cultural politics of the "homeland." In their application transnationally, the cultural markers of religion, language, and nation have assumed an overt political charge. The significance of particular political events, and the social ruptures they have produced in South Asia, have been mirrored within the local population. The massacre of Sikhs by Hindus in Delhi that followed the assassination of Prime Minister Indira Gandhi by her Sikh bodyguards in 1984 fractured relations between Hindus and Sikhs in North Carolina. In the years that followed, this polarization was reinforced by the steady immigration to the United States and to North Carolina of Sikh refugees escaping state terrorism in India. The radical politics of a sizable section of the state's Sikhs is seen in their choice of Bhindranwale, a Sikh separatist leader and Mrs. Gandhi's nemesis, as the patron saint of one of the local *gurudwaras*. They have even exchanged Republican and Democratic campaign contributions for the labeling of India as a terrorist state.[6] Hostilities between North Carolina's Hindus and Muslims too have increased in recent years. The demolition of the Babri Masjid mosque by Hindu extremists in 1992, and the silent approval of the Hindu Society in Raleigh, further strained already fragile ties between Indian Muslims and Hindus. And finally, local Hindus' tacit support for the recent spate of violence against Indian Christians, whom they see orchestrating a conversion drive to reduce the number of Hindus in India, has also injured relations between North Carolina's Indian Hindus and Christians.

These dynamics are partly in continuity with the caste and class origins of Indian Americans and ongoing political dynamics in the homeland, and partly reflect their experiences as an American minority. The anxiety over minority status in the United States has produced a vehement opposition to cultural loss seen in the policing of the U.S.-born generation's social activities, and in the proliferation of the abovementioned institutions where children can absorb "cultural values." This is especially apparent among immigrant Hindus for whom Hindu nationalist politics in India resonates even more strongly as a result of their minority experience in the United States. The threat of a Muslim or Christian "takeover" through reproduction and conversion appears far more likely from a distance and as a minority in a majority Christian country. The anti-Muslim sentiment that has swept the United States since the Gulf

War has also exacerbated local Hindu perceptions of a global Muslim terrorist conspiracy.

Class and culture have thus served as vehicles of community identity and politics and as wedges separating Indian professionals from black Americans and poorer immigrants like the large number of local Latinos. Cherian's account of his early experiences in North Carolina and Sharma, Wadhwani, and Srinivas's accounts of later experiences speak to a shift in the structural position of Indians in U.S. racial hierarchies from the first to the second half of the twentieth century. According to these accounts, Indians seem to have secured a safe place by virtue of their economic status.

Other experiences, however, betray this narrative of an accommodative society, and show by contrast that Indian appropriation of privilege based on class and culture has not exempted them from U.S. racial hierarchies and experiences of discrimination. Even those Indians who lauded the transformation of North Carolina into a place without prejudice expressed their frustration over a permanent sense of "not belonging." Srikanth, a mechanical engineer and resident of Cary, recollected a particularly jarring incident that made him feel unsafe for the first time.

> We do have experiences. There was an Indian cultural program in NC State that we went to with friends. After the program, all of us Indians came out and were walking to our cars. Suddenly, there were two carloads of white students who drove by and started yelling, "You Indians, why don't you go home?" They were just kids, but they were drunk and seemed violent.

Being from upper-caste or affluent backgrounds, most Indians who come to North Carolina are incensed when they do experience discrimination, especially when it blurs the boundaries between their own community and other, less prosperous or "respectable" minorities. Speaking resentfully of white North Carolinians' confusion between Latinos and Indians, another long-term resident of the state and a staff person at Duke University confessed his outrage at being mistreated at a local bank.

> It has never happened to me before. I went into the bank and tried to cash my check and they asked me for two forms of I.D. Two! So I challenged them and said, "I've never shown more than one so why are you asking for this?" When the clerk said it was bank policy, I said, "I have been coming here for the last thirty years and it has never been policy before!" She saw that I was getting angry so she called the manager who came out, saw who I was, and apologized. He said the clerk had mistaken me for a Mexican.

This sense of permanent foreignness, and the experiences of discrimination that foster it, undercuts the hope that class privilege will win uncontested acceptance into multicultural America.

However, the majority of professionals I spoke with concluded from their experiences of discrimination that they needed even more aggressively to wield class power to force acceptance and respect. In words almost identical to those of Lalit Patel, Ravi Srinivas asserted,

If you're white, you're automatically identified as American. Easily assimilated into culture without being recognized as immigrants. I don't resent it. It's human nature. But we don't use our economic clout to fight anti-immigrant sentiment. After all, we're less than a hundredth of 1 percent but control 5 percent of wealth. We need to educate politicians and industry leaders about how we're contributing to this society. After all, Indians own 30 percent of hotels in America, we're giving ten thousand jobs to Americans. Same way with stores. And in the construction businesses. We also need community solidarity and philanthropy in business. Nobody is going to give you a loan for your idea because we're ethnic. We have to give ourselves loans.

The importance of wealth for the consolidation and protection of immigrant culture is a theme that cut across lines of age, gender, and religion. Gautam, a student at Duke who grew up in Durham, commented on the rules of acceptance in his high school:

If you have money, you can buy your kids acceptance. But if your kid wears K-Mart rather than Abercrombie, *and* he's doing cultural stuff, he'll definitely be ridiculed.

Rather than identifying with other nonwhites against white privilege, then, these local Indians seem to have opted to pit the positive associations of class privilege against the negative associations of racial difference.

Cultural Diversity versus Social Justice

To the extent that Indian professionals *do* identify with other nonwhites, it is through an interesting kind of *mis*identification. Let me briefly explain what I mean through two examples. The Indian American Forum for Political Education is the key political vehicle for "Indian American interests" operating both nationally and locally. IAFPE members constituted the delegation that accompanied Bill Clinton to India on his diplomatic visit (five of the twenty delegates were IAFPE members from North Carolina). The IAFPE president was recently awarded a Padma Bhushan by the Indian government in recognition of his work in nurturing and facilitating nonresident Indian investment in India.

The IAFPE supports affirmative action. However, it appears to have interpreted affirmative action as a means to greater diversity. Consider the following two quotes from an executive board member of the IAFPE. The first argues for affirmative action as a corrective to historical discrimination:

It's a big issue for minority communities. Now with the Bush administration, what's going to happen is that it'll be removed legally from the policy. They think it's reverse discrimination but they're forgetting that discrimination was there for last two hundred years and reverse is only for five years.

However, the second, which follows from the first, shifts the meaning of affirmative action from preferences to diversity:

> There is a hidden quota system in the universities that benefits whites. There are a lot of highly qualified Indian students that apply for Ivy Leagues and other universities. What's happening is that though we're qualified, our students are denied on the basis that too many Indian students are applying and if we give them all admission, they'll exceed their percentage ratio. . . . Biggest help is in state and federal employment. When you hit the glass ceiling, you can use affirmative action to argue against the denial of promotion.

Here, Patel defines affirmative action not as a corrective for historical injustice but as a vehicle for ethnic diversity. For him, it is a means to battle the limits to Indian progress into elite academic institutions and into the managerial class. In effect, then, for him as for the IAFPE, affirmative action guarantees equal access to the top echelons of society and has little to do with social justice. What we see here is a blanket classification of all nonwhites as "minority communities" and the extension of this into the argument that all minorities should benefit from affirmative action as a means to enhance diversity. Minority is thus substituted for race, and diversity for social justice.

Another instance of misidentification is in local Indians' relationship with Latinos. The IAFPE had this to say about Latino activism as a local "model" to emulate:

> Two years back, NC State Assembly leaders recognized that the Mexican community is the fastest growing ethnic community in North Carolina. They are influential economically, socially, politically: North Carolina economy cannot flourish without their help. Every development is built with Mexicans, fast food restaurants, they work at the back of high-class restaurants, on roads . . . politicians realize that they are driving the economy. If they leave, whole thing will collapse. Also they have growing social and political influence. They are influencing the interaction between other groups . . . there's a growing rift between Mexicans and blacks. Siler City is 80 percent Mexican. They are influencing festivals and everything. And politically, Mexican kids are growing up here, they're Americans. In ten to fifteen years, they'll be voters and these politicians are smart and recognize that. They are opening an office in the governor's house to address their concerns. One hundred and seventy-five thousand Mexicans together have done this. Now, Mexicans working in North Carolina can live, work, interact more safely, more comfortably. They used to work like slaves in agricultural fields. That situation is changing and I know because I've talked to them.

This, again, is a kind of misidentification on the basis of minority community status. The IAFPE plans to use "the Mexican model" to organize themselves politically, not for living wages and safe working conditions but to enhance their economic and political role as intermediaries in U.S.–India bilateral trade relations. As one IAFPE member said to me, "We understand both cultures and, although we don't have a large number of votes, we have the money power to help shape the course of U.S. relations with India. But for this, we need to be recognized as a valuable ethnic community, just as the Mexicans have been." Again, the identification with Latinos is not based on a shared structural position in national class hierarchies but on a shared minority status that obscures a dramatic difference in class status. The IAFPE seeks to emulate the

"Mexican model" in order to secure a place within the governor's house and make it a more "culturally diverse" outfit.

"Trickle Back" and Global "Comparative Advantage"

This emphasis on "culture" and "community" has also grounded ongoing efforts by the IAFPE and The Indus Entrepreneurs (TIE), a national organization begun by some of the first Indian Information Technology successes in Silicon Valley, to reinvest in India. A TIE member explained to me that this was a process of "trickle back" through which the Indian government's investment in producing a transnational class of science and technology professionals was now being repaid.

> India is now at an advantage because of Non-Resident Indian [NRI] investment. Politicians both here and there are recognizing how important we are! In this global society, competitiveness comes down to talent. That is the only survival mechanism. But high-tech manufacturers are still not going [to India] that easily because local labor, infrastructure, government policy is still not supportive enough. But IT industry loves and wants to invest in India. . . . You can't find that concentration of technical capability anywhere, and that's what we need to compete globally. And the best way to do this is through the NRIs who are the cultural offspring of India. We're going from brain drain to reinvestment. I guess you could call it "trickle back"!

Here we see the extension of the logic of corporate multiculturalism to global scale. The nonresident Indian, armed with his cultural links to the "homeland" and his business acumen, is to be the vehicle for enhancing India's competitive edge in the global economy. And he is to do this by tapping India's comparative advantage in technical capability. This special role identified for the NRI rests upon notions of the power of cultural origins, and the irresistible pull of a cultural "homeland" for a diasporic population. This process, by which Indian Americans will join the ranks of a global capitalist class, is thus folded into a cultural narrative of the reunion of distant offspring with their mother.

Conclusion

What do the experiences of North Carolina's Indian professionals tell us about the dynamics of late capitalism, the politics of multiculturalism, and the U.S. immigrant experience? First, that the universalizing logic of capitalist expansion does not mean an erasure of particularity. Indeed, what we see instead with economic globalization is the increasing tendency for non-European societies and minority populations within the West to make their own claims on the history of capitalism by finding capitalist ethics within their own "cultural traditions." Indian Americans are only one group among others that has come to articulate its own brand of "vernacular capitalism" based on community solidarity and cultural identity as a response to Anglo American hegemony. Far from claiming "sameness," they wield cultural difference as a necessary vehicle of social mobility and capitalist success.

Second, national citizenship is yet another arena defined by the tension between universalism and particularism. Ironically, the civil rights movement both ushered in equality of a civic variety—civic universalism—and set the stage for a rapidly proliferating politics of cultural difference, or ethnic particularism. In the case of Indian American professionals in the U.S. South, the claim to cultural difference has obscured the persistence of substantive inequality structured by race and class beneath the liberal base line of a multicultural democracy.

Finally, my essay argues that, far from class-neutral, multiculturalism is a new hegemonic discourse that has allowed Indian professionals to distance themselves from more plebeian solidarities that may cut across ethnic and class lines. The post-civil-rights shift from a racial to a cultural model of citizenship has allowed for a rearticulation of minority identity in cultural terms that secures class privilege. When we consider that this adopted professional politics dovetails with the state's own efforts at managing diversity, it appears that multiculturalism is a new kind of class politics, although one that is fragmented by multiple histories of migration and that is peculiarly blind to its own elitism.

NOTES

Originally published in *Comparative Studies of South Asia, Africa and the Middle East* 20.1–2 (2000): 105–14. © 2000 Duke University Press, reprint with permission.

1. According to Mazumdar (1991), the 1990 U.S. Census placed the per capita income of Asian Indians at $17,777, second only to the Japanese at $19,373 and above the national average of $14,143.

2. Mazumdar (1991) notes that many of the immigrants were Muslim and Sikh so the term "Hindu" was mistakenly used as an ethnic catch-all category.

3. 1990 Census of the State of North Carolina.

4. 1980 Census of the State of North Carolina.

5. 1990 Census of the State of North Carolina.

6. Interviews with members of the Sikh Societies of New York and North Carolina.

REFERENCES

Fox, Richard G. (ed.). 1990. *Nationalist Ideologies and the Production of National Cultures.* Washington, DC: American Anthropological Association.

Haniffa, Aziz. 1998a. "Key Republican Reopens Debate on Legal Immigration." *India Abroad*, May 1, p. 38.

———. 1998b. "Bills Aim to Boost Visas for Computer Professionals." *India Abroad*, March 13, p. 40.

Harris, Cheryl I. 1993. "Whiteness as Property." *Harvard Law Review* 106: 1707.

Hing, Bill Ong. 1993. *Making and Remaking Asian America through Immigration Policy, 1850–1990.* Stanford, CA: Stanford University Press.

Kennedy, John F. 1964. *A Nation of Immigrants.* New York: Harper and Row.

Leonard-Spark, Philip and Paramatma Saran. 1980. "The Indian Immigrant in America: A Demographic Profile." In P. Saran and E. Eames (eds.), *The New Ethnics: Asian Indians in the United States.* New York: Praeger.

Lipsitz, George. 1988. *The Possessive Investment in Whiteness: How White People Profit from Identity Politics.* Philadelphia: Temple University Press.

Liu, John M. 1992. "The Contours of Asian Professional, Technical, and Kindred Work Immigration, 1965–1988." *Sociological Perspectives* 35: 4.

Mazumdar, Sucheta. 1991. "Racist Responses to Racism: The Aryan Myth and South Asians in the United States." *South Asia Bulletin* 9: 1.

Melendy, Brett H. 1977. *Asians in America: Filipinos, Koreans, and East Indians.* Boston: Twayne.

Nehru, Jawaharlal. 1984. "Science in the Service of the Community" (1947). In S. Gopal (ed.), *Selected Works of Jawaharlal Nehru.* New Delhi: Oxford University Press.

Ong, Aihwa. 1999. *Flexible Citizenship: The Cultural Logics of Transnationality.* Durham, NC: Duke University Press.

Prashad, Vijay. 2000. *The Karma of Brown Folk.* Minneapolis: University of Minnesota Press.

———. 1994. "Contract Labor: The Latest Stage of Illiberal Capitalism." *Monthly Review* 46: 5.

Singh, Jane. 1998. *South Asians in North America: An Annotated and Selected Bibliography.* Berkeley: University of California Press.

Steinberg, Stephen. 1995. *Turning Back: The Retreat from Racial Justice in American Thought and Policy.* Boston: Beacon.

Ungar, Sheldon. 1990. "Moral Panics, the Military-Industrial Complex, and the Arms Race." *Sociological Quarterly* 31: 2.

1. In what ways did the passage of the 1965 Immigration Act (Hart-Cellar Act) remedy the litany of anti-Asian immigration legislation passed in the years leading up to World War II? How did the 1965 Immigration Act alter the preference system? Why have so many well-educated Asians immigrated into the United States after the passage of this act? What impact does Asian immigration have upon the ethnic composition of the U.S. labor force? To what extent will Asian immigrants continue to enter the United States in the twenty-first century? Drawing upon evidence presented by the authors, make a case that Asian immigrants will continue to come in a steady pace to the United States, slow down significantly, or halt altogether. What factors might promote immigration among this group and what factors might stem its tide?

2. Bankston and Hidalgo note that diversity is one of the defining characteristics of Southeast Asians who come to the United States. How is each of the subgroups similar or different? What factors have shaped the patterns of settlement and secondary migration that later emerged? What occupational and economic progress has been made by immigrant/refugee populations? To what extent have members of the refugee groups made use of public assistance programs? Why have some groups—Filipino and Thai—adapted to life in the United States more successfully than their counterparts from the same general region?

3. One of the defining features of Southeast Asia as a region is its longstanding history of war. What role has American foreign policy—including the U.S. legacy of colonialism—played in the migration histories of Southeast Asians? In what ways have armed struggles in the region shaped international migration? How does the legacy of war continue to shape the fortunes of Southeast Asians once resettled in the United States? How do Southeast Asian refugees differ from other refugees from Cuba and the former Soviet Union and from other Asian immigrants?

4. One of the issues raised by Subramanian in her article is that transnational identities are common among contemporary Asian immigrants to the United States (specifically, those individuals who came to the United States after 1965). Immigrants maintain a number of cultural and economic ties to their homelands while living and working in the United States. Is this term applicable to the experiences of the South Asian immigrants studied by Subramanian? If so, why? What other terms might one use to describe their experiences? How are individual immigrant identities in North Carolina mediated by race, class, and gender?

5. Subramanian notes that Indian immigrants possess more high-tech professionals per capita than any other group entering the United States. What historical changes within India gave rise to this professional class? What conditions in the United States encouraged their migration beginning in the 1960s? From what specific class do these professionals originate in India? What impact has the brain drain had upon the Indian subcontinent? How has the composition of the Indian American community changed over time? Who continues to wield power within the community? Why?

6. What do the experiences of North Carolina's Indian professionals tell us about the dynamics of late capitalism, the politics of multiculturalism, racism, and the U.S. immigrant experience? How has the goal of technological modernity shaped the political economy of development in India and the United States? How has North Carolina's transformation into a center of "high-tech" industry been reflected spatially and demographically? What role have Indian professionals played in this transformation? And how have North Carolina's Indians situated themselves in the changing race and class dynamics of a region increasingly more tightly integrated into transnational circuits of labor and capital?

SUGGESTED READINGS

Chan, Sucheng. 1990. European and Asian Immigration into the United States in Comparative Perspective, 1820s–1920s. Pp. 37–75 in Virginia Yans-Mclaughlin (ed.), *Immigration Reconsidered: History, Sociology, and Politics.* New York: Oxford University Press.

Chan, Sucheng. 1991. *Asian Americans: An Interpretive History.* Boston: Twayne.

Choy, Catherine Ceniza. 2003. *Empire of Care: Nursing and Migration in Filipino American History.* Durham, NC: Duke University Press.

Daniels, Roger. 1997. United States Policy towards Asian Immigrants: Comparative Developments in Historical Perspective. Pp. 73–89 in Darrell Y. Hamamoto and Rudolfo D. Torres (eds.), *New American Destinies: A Reader in Contemporary Asian and Latino Immigration.* New York: Routledge.

Dirlik, Arif. 1996. Asians on the Rim: Transnational Capital and Local Community in the Making of Contemporary Asian America. *Amerasia Journal* 22(3): 1–24.

Gosha, Joseph D. 1993. Perilous Journey: 1979. Pp. 320–35 in James Freeman (ed.), *Hearts of Sorrow: Vietnamese American Lives.* Stanford, CA: Stanford University Press.

Hing, Bill Ong. 2004. *Defining America through Immigration Policy.* Philadelphia: Temple University Press.

Kung, Cleo. 2000. Supporting the Snakeheads: Human Smuggling from China and the 1996 Amendment to the U.S. Statutory Definition of "Refugee." *Journal of Criminal Law & Criminology* 90: 1271.

Liu, J., P. Ong, and C. Rosenstein. 1991. Filipino Immigration to the United States. *International Migration Review* 25: 487–513.

Maira, Sunaina. 2002. *Desis in the House: Indian American Youth Culture in New York City.* Philadelphia: Temple University Press.

Ngai, Mae. 1999. The Architecture of Race in American Immigration Law: A Reexamination of the Immigration Act of 1924. *Journal of American History* 86.

Ngai, Mae. 2005. *Impossible Subjects: Illegal Aliens and the Making of Modern America.* Princeton, NJ: Princeton University Press.

Ong, Paul and Tania Azores. 1994. The Migration and Incorporation of Filipino Nurses. Pp. 164–98 in Paul Ong, Edna Bonacich, and Lucie Cheng (ed.), *The New Asian Immigration in Los Angeles and Global Restructuring.* Philadelphia: Temple University Press.

Park, Jung-Sun. 2004. Korean American Youth and Transnational Flows of Popular Culture across the Pacific. *Amerasia Journal* 30(1): 147–69.

Parreñas, Rhacel S. 2003. Asian Immigrant Women and Global Restructuring, 1970s and 1990s. Pp. 271–85 in Shirley Hune and Gail Nomura (eds.), *Asian/Pacific Women.* New York: New York University Press.

San Juan, E. 1998. *From Exile to Diaspora: Veterans of the Filipino Experience in the United States.* Boulder, CO: Westview Press.

Shukla, Sandhya. 2000. New Immigrants, New Formations of Transnational Community: Post-1965 Indian Migrations. *Amerasia Journal* 25(3): 19–36.

Shukla, Sandhya. 2003. *India Abroad: Diasporic Cultures of Postwar America and England.* Princeton, NJ: Princeton University Press.

Singh, Jane. 1998. *South Asians in North America: An Annotated and Selected Bibliography.* Berkeley: University of California Press.

Takaki, Ronald. 1989. *Strangers from a Different Shore.* Boston: Little, Brown.

Tyner, James A. 1994. The Social Construction of Gendered Migration from the Philippines. *Asian and Pacific Migration Journal* 3(4): 589–617.

Verghese, Abraham. 1997. The Cowpath to America. *New Yorker,* June 23 and 30, 70–88.

Zhou, Min. 2006. The Chinese Diaspora and International Migration. *Social Transformations in Chinese Societies* 1(1): 161–90.

FILMS

Coffman, Tom (producer/director). 2000. *Arirang: The Korean American Journey/The Korean American Dream* (55/56-minute documentary).

De Castro, Naomi (director). 1988. *In No One's Shadow: Filipinos in America* (28-minute documentary).

Ding, Loni (producer/director). 1998. *Chinese in the Frontier West: An American Story* (60-minute documentary).

Lowe, Felicia (producer/director). 1988. *Carved in Silence.* (45 minutes docu-drama).

Meerman, Marije (director). 2001. *The Chain of Love* (50-minute documentary).

Ohama, Corey (producer/director). 1997. *Double Solitaire* (20-minute documentary).

Wehman, John (producer/director). 1994. *Filipino Americans: Discovering Their Past for the Future* (54-minute documentary).

Razvi, Raeshma and G.A.P. (producers). 2002. *One Family* (10-minute documentary).

Part III

Ties That Bind

*The Immigrant Family and the
Ethnic Community*

Chapter 7

Southeast Asian Women in Lowell
Family Relations, Gender Roles, and Community Concerns

Tuyet-Lan Pho and Anne Mulvey

> The three most important values for me and my husband, that we have tried to teach our children, are the value of education, to be loyal to members of their family, and to have respect for older people. . . . I like the equal opportunity at work where men and women are treated the same. This is not the way we live at home.
> —Interview with Lien Tran

> Our culture has always placed a high value on families, even during the terrible Pol Pot regimes. . . . Unfortunately, some families cannot seem to find harmony. Instead, there is violence in the home . . . usually directed at a woman by a man.
> —Narrator, *Domestic Violence in the Cambodian Community*

Between 1975 and 1995 more than one million Southeast Asian refugees from Cambodia, Laos, and Vietnam settled in the United States. They are an ethnically diverse group with a wide range of socioeconomic, cultural, linguistic, and educational backgrounds. Some are tribal mountain dwellers and farmers with limited literacy, and others are urban professionals holding advanced degrees. They suffered directly or indirectly the effects of the Vietnam War and the turmoil of forced resettlement on another continent. The populations that are most vulnerable to the effects of the war and refugee relocation are women and children. However, the postwar effects of resettlement on women and children in the United States have not been adequately studied or documented. Many of the existing studies overlook the interpersonal relationships between wives and husbands or between parents and children and the way their integration into American society has reinforced or weakened these relationships.[1]

Based on our collaborative work with Southeast Asian women in Lowell, Massachusetts, we argue that resettlement in the United States poses new problems but also offers greater opportunities for these women and their families. Our work suggests that there are a number of factors affecting the ways many Southeast Asian women cope with and integrate themselves into a new society. These factors include the methods by which they maintain their traditional values while adapting to American culture; the changing gender roles they play in marriage and raising children and in paid work; the level of control and related expectations they have over their lives in the United States; and their strategies for understanding and challenging dysfunctional situations, including teen pregnancy and domestic violence.[2]

Two Southeast Asian perspectives that emerged from our collaborative work center around family relationships, especially between mothers and daughters and between women and men of the Lowell community. The first perspective presents the voices of Vietnamese, Lao, and Cambodian women who reflect on their lives in a new city, the changing roles and relationships they experienced, and the level of control they have over their lives. These voices were documented in the evaluation reports of the Lowell public schools' desegregation programs in Tuyet-Lan Pho's dissertation research, conducted between 1991 and 1994, and in the introduction to *Fractured Identities: Cambodian Children of War* by James Higgins and Joan Ross.[3] In addition, Pho recorded personal contacts she made with numerous women receiving social and educational services provided by the Indochinese Refugees Foundation, of which she was a founding member and president, between 1978 and 1990. The Indochinese Refugees Foundation was a community-based organization funded by federal and state grants to provide language training, employment orientation, and other social services to Cambodian, Lao, and Vietnamese refugees resettled in Lowell.

The second perspective is based on participant observation work conducted by Anne Mulvey during a five-year period with a community group that mobilized against domestic violence. In the latter section of the paper, Mulvey reflects on her experiences as a participant in a multicultural coalition project designed to plan, produce, and distribute a film against domestic violence in the Cambodian community of Lowell. She discusses the process of creating culturally appropriate educational material and issues of representation. Her discussions focus on the gender and racial-ethnic politics involved with community-based coalition work against domestic violence.

Both perspectives are woven together to highlight three particularly important themes in Southeast Asian refugee/immigrant communities: (1) the restructuring of family relationships and expectations between wives and husbands and between parents and children in a new community and cultural context; (2) the conflicting demands and related personal dilemmas associated with the maintenance of traditional values and changing gender roles; and (3) the different approaches among community members to addressing and resolving social problems such as domestic violence.

The Politics of Resettlement of Southeast Asian Refugees in Lowell

The United States has resettled the largest number of Southeast Asian refugees as a result of its involvement in the Vietnam War. According to the Office of Refugee Resettlement, the total number of Southeast Asian refugee arrivals in the United States from 1975 through September 30, 1994, was 1,180,538. Massachusetts ranks number ten among states that have resettled a large number of Southeast Asian refugees. Many Southeast Asians came to Lowell as refugees who left their homeland involuntarily and are unable to return to their country of origin for fear of persecution by their government. The traumatic experiences of escape and time spent in temporary refugee camps before their arrival in the United States pose additional problems for refugees.

Lowell is a midsize city located approximately thirty miles northwest of Boston. According to the School Department records, the Lowell population is composed of 113,000 people from more than fifty different ethnic backgrounds. Southeast Asian refugees who have resettled in Lowell since the mid-1980s represent approximately 20 percent of the city's population. The Southeast Asian population residing in Lowell comprises about twenty thousand Cambodians, five thousand Lao, and two thousand Vietnamese.[4] These figures make Lowell the city with the second largest Cambodian population in the United States after Long Beach, California. The refugees started to resettle in Massachusetts in very small numbers in 1975. The influx did not really begin until 1985 and lasted through 1990. Many refugees first entered the United States in one city or state but later moved to another city or state because of job opportunities or to be close to other family members. A substantial proportion of this population growth is thus the result of secondary migration.

The concentration of Southeast Asian refugees in Lowell has led to dramatic changes in the city. Southeast Asians have had an impact on the city's housing patterns, schools, and businesses in the area. More than one hundred shops and stores are owned and operated by Southeast Asians. Numerous service-providing agencies cater to the needs of this new population, and cultural centers, such as Buddhist temples, have also been established. These ethnicity concentrations and centers have encouraged the preservation of cultural heritage. At the same time, this level of ethnic retention and cohesiveness has fostered a greater level of resentment toward the settlement of Cambodians, Lao, and Vietnamese in the city.[5]

The influx of Southeast Asian students to Lowell public schools was one of the major reasons for the school desegregation movement in 1986 and one of the principal causes for well-established residents to pass a referendum to support English as the official language of the city in 1988.[6] At the peak of the influx of Southeast Asian refugees to Lowell, some schools in the district enrolled up to 85 percent minority students while others had less than 5 percent. The school desegregation movement was led by Latino parents and later joined by a number of Southeast Asian community leaders. Together they developed a 33-point program of demands for educational reform and filed a Title VI lawsuit against the City of Lowell for unconstitutional segregation and denial of educational opportunities to students with limited English proficiency.[7] Busing was part of the desegregation plan to achieve racial balance in the public schools. In the fall of 1987, Pho and Mulvey were among a small group of faculty and administrators who helped Hispanic and Southeast Asian parents get their children on the right buses for their new schools across town.

However, many Cambodian, Lao, and Vietnamese parents had mixed feelings about the movement, partially because they were too busy with the mundane tasks of resettlement and partially because they were not familiar with the political and social ramifications associated with school choice, busing, and the English-only movement. For example, some Southeast Asian parents were confused about why their children were taken out of the neighborhood schools and sent to a school farther away. Most Southeast Asian parents felt grateful to the city for providing their children with an education. As a result, they failed to see the discrepancy between well-equipped and better-instructed schools in the affluent neighborhoods and schools that used hallways, closets, and storage space as makeshift classrooms. Parents who did not speak English relied on their school-age children to act as their interpreters, and they were eager to have their children learn to speak English as soon as possible. The parents Pho spoke to at the Parents Information Center were eager to sign waivers of bilingual classes for their children because they did not understand the benefits of bilingual education or the costs of losing one's cultural heritage.[8]

The politics of resettlement will probably continue to impact the Southeast Asian community in Lowell for many years to come. Statements made by public officials and local politicians concerning the way Southeast Asian children have allegedly drained the limited budget of the Lowell School Department have drawn more public attention than the struggles parents have experienced in establishing a new life in the city. As these refugees felt they had overcome the external hurdles of securing adequate housing, employment, and schooling for their children, they also began to contend with the internal problems facing their families. Not only did they have to deal with achieving economic self-sufficiency in a new and sometimes hostile environment, but they also had to adjust to changing family relations, expectations, and gender roles.

Restructuring Family Relations: The Balance between Southeast Asian and American Family Expectations and Gender Roles

Pho conducted a case study with two Cambodian (the Soths and the Oums), two Lao (the Yangs and the Souriyas), and two Vietnamese families (the Trans and the Vus) from 1991 to 1994 as part of an ethnographic study of family values and academic performance among Southeast Asian students in order to provide an analysis of how family relations are being restructured. Two parents and two children, a daughter and a son, from each family participated in this ethnographic study. Data were collected from various sources, including audiotaped interviews and discussions with the parents, children, teachers, counselors, and other informants in the community; observations of family's events; and reviews of school records.[9]

Traditional Values and Family Structure

Traditional values and family structure continue to play an important role in the acculturation of many Southeast Asian women. In 1987, Nathan Caplan, Marcella H. Choy, and John K. Whitmore conducted a survey study of two hundred nuclear families, including 536 school-age children, of Vietnamese, Lao, and Chinese-Vietnamese refugees from five urban areas in the United States. They identified twenty-six traditional and Westernized values that affect the ways Southeast Asian Americans relate to each other or raise their children. These values include respect for authority, perpetuation of ancestral lineage, seeking salvation, hard work, restraint and discipline, family loyalty, valuing education, respect for elders, cooperative and harmonious family relations, the family's status in the community, the family's belief that the past is more important than the future, seeking out new experiences, and securing a comfortable life.[10]

When the above values were used in the interview questions with women and their daughters in six families in Lowell, it was evident that the maintenance of traditional values, including family loyalty, valuing education, respect for elders, and cooperative and harmonious family relations had strengthened the family relationship for some women. However, the practice of perpetuation of ancestral lineage, seeking salvation, and maintaining family status in the community, coupled with the adaptation of more Westernized values such as seeking out new experiences and securing a comfortable life, had posed challenges as these women pursued their lives in a new society.

The Southeast Asian family is highly structured, with traditional roles that shape the relationships between wife and husband, parents and children, and older and younger siblings. The backbone of this structure is a paternal hierarchy that may not be clearly articulated but that permeates the home environment and is projected in filial piety behaviors, including the respect, obedience, and loyalty that members of the family are expected to demonstrate toward each other. Inherent in these values is an underlying contradiction related to the practice of a paternal hierarchical structure and the maintenance of a cooperative and harmonious family.

The paternal hierarchy is more prominent in families who practice Confucian teachings and ancestor worship.[11] Among the six families interviewed, two are of the Buddhist faith, two are Protestant, and two practice ancestor worship. In a conversation about parental roles and responsibilities, Lien Tran and her daughter Kim admitted that in their household, Mr. Tran, Lien's husband, is a devout follower of Confucius who made all important decisions and whose words were always the final. On the other hand, the Soths, one of the two Cambodian families in the case study, had converted from Buddhism to Christianity and enjoyed a close family relationship. Chenda Soth recalled,

> My Dad was Buddhist, but he doesn't go to the temple all that much; just on holidays. Before she was in Thailand, my Mom wasn't really sure what she believed in. In the Thai refugee camp, she started becoming a Christian. My Dad was against that; he told her not to go to church. He's not against it now. Now, we all go to church, except my Dad. But he listens to my Mom more and shows more affection to my younger brothers. I see God is working in his heart.[12]

Regardless of their religious faith, all six families are familiar with and follow some Confucian teachings.

Gender Roles

When parents in the case study were asked to describe their roles in the upbringing of their children, their responses indicated a clear distinction between the ways fathers and mothers influence their offspring. The children look to their fathers to tell them how to plan their education and careers. The mother is expected to be supportive; to nurture the children with values and virtues concerning acceptable norms of behavior, such as hard work, honesty and integrity; and to enhance those virtues through maintaining a trusting relationship with her daughters and sons. While the father deals with issues concerning life outside the family, the mother tends to set the moral tone for the upbringing of her children. This nurturing role also brings the mother closer to her daughters. Naly Yang, a daughter of a Lao family, and Chenda Soth, a daughter of a Cambodian family, were asked about the relationship with their parents. Naly Yang said,

> Both of my parents talk with me a lot about education in general, and sometimes I go to my father and talk with him about school exams and where to go to college. I usually go to my mother to ask about money for clothes because she's more generous. When I'm wearing something my mother doesn't think is appropriate, she'll tell me about it. But then we'll discuss it, and sometimes she'll decide that what I'm wearing is okay after all. For my father, if he does not like what I wear, I'll not wear it anymore.[13]

Chenda Soth replied,

> My father doesn't show affection too much with us girls, but he always says kind words to me, so I know he cares. He tells me that he's proud of me; that I do a good job when I get good grades. And he pats me and tells me I'm a good girl. The little boys, he hugs them and he loves them a lot. I can hug my Mom. In my family, the girls are closer to my mom, and the boys are closer to my dad.

The preferential treatment of sons over daughters is also prominent. When the mothers in all six families were asked who they would select if there were only enough money to send one child to college, the answers were unanimous: The oldest son would go to college so that he might take care of his brothers and sisters. This finding reflects the maintenance of traditional values among Southeast Asian families. Traditionally, the daughter is prepared for the next phase of her life: to be the wife of another man and the daughter-in-law of another family. In order to help her cope with this future, her family prepares her at a very young age to be self-sufficient and to help others, so that she will be worthy of her husband and his family. How many daughters truly internalize this teaching and act out such a role is not always clear, but the pattern is persistent. In contrast, sons are encouraged to get an education and to pursue a career because they are expected to become the breadwinners, to support their families, and to carry on the family name. As Sam Oum, a male student attending Lowell High School, said,

> My father is happy for me to buy books and school materials. But sometimes, when my sister asks him, he is sort of reluctant to help her out. He says, "Again?" I guess he sometimes feels like my sister's schooling isn't as important, because a boy's got to be

able to support his family. I guess I agree with him, because for a girl to take care of you, if you're a man, it's not right.[14]

Daughters are aware of this preferential treatment and in some cases accept it, as Mai Vu said:

There are many problems that come from the differences between parents and children. This becomes more of a problem for the girls than the boys, since girls have to obey their parents, being subjected to more restrictions than boys, because most Asian parents are afraid that their daughters may get into trouble with boyfriends, dating, etc. I have no problem following my parents' orders. I only wish I could speak my mind.[15]

When Mai Vu was asked to give examples of some restrictions, she eagerly named three "Nos"—no hanging out with friends after school, no dating, and no attending evening or overnight school functions.

On the subject of teen pregnancy, Naly Yang, a Lao high school student, half-jokingly cited her grandmother's remark when she was on a diet: "You did not eat much and you are so pale. Are you pregnant or something?" Teen pregnancy is a constant source of worry among Southeast Asian mothers with teenage daughters. Some mothers even arrange to marry their daughters off at the age of twelve or thirteen to avoid a teen pregnancy that would bring shame to the family.[16] The possible relationship between early marriage and domestic violence will be discussed in a later section of this article.

Although many Southeast Asian households in the United States have tried to maintain the traditional family structure, the relationships between members of the family have been altered by economic necessity. The war claimed many Cambodian and Vietnamese men's lives and left the women as heads of their families. According to the U.S. Department of Commerce, 21 percent of Cambodian families with children under age eighteen are headed by women, 9 percent among the Lao, and 10 percent among the Vietnamese.[17] For economic reasons, numerous Southeast Asian women have joined the paid workforce.

Even women with male partners preferred to work to contribute to the family income. Three of the six mothers interviewed are working in factories on a regular basis, and the other three are doing piecework at home. Their annual incomes range from ten thousand dollars to fifteen thousand dollars, and such outside work helps bring the family total income above the poverty level.[18] They are also faced with competing demands of time for their jobs and the tasks of raising children and household chores. When the husbands in the case study were asked if they would pitch in with the household chores, four out of six said that housework is a woman's job and that it should be shared between their wives and their daughters. This male view, coupled with the paternal hierarchy that is found in many Southeast Asian families, may have influenced the way women readily accepted household chores as part of their responsibilities. When a Vietnamese husband tried to help his wife with the house chores, his wife, Cuc Vu, declined the assistance: "My husband is very helpful. Sometime he washed the dishes. But I don't think it's right for men to wash dishes. Beside, what would my relatives say when they see my husband in the kitchen."[19] Cuc Vu's feeling about her husband's help and her concern over her relatives' perception of men doing housework reflect the family tensions that changing gender roles have created and signal the need for family members to recognize that their roles have changed since they moved to Lowell.

Younger Vietnamese women also internalize the traditional gender role and share similar views, as indicated by Kim Tran, who was brought up by her grandmother in Vietnam before she moved to Lowell with her parents in 1992: "My mother does all of the cooking for us, whether she is working or staying home. I don't mind helping her when my brother is doing his homework."

Because gender differences and the preferential treatment of sons over daughters are common in many Southeast Asian families, some women are willing to take a secondary role for the sake of keeping harmony in the family, as Nazli Kibria describes in her book *Family Tightrope: The Changing Life of Vietnamese-Americans.*[20] However, other women want to change this traditional structure by changing their roles and becoming more assertive in family affairs. As a result, they were considered by their partners as being "too Americanized" or were subjected to domestic violence, which is discussed in another section of this paper.

The feelings of being culturally oppressed and the lack of support from other family members were found in many interviews with Southeast Asian women across generations. In their isolation, many women found ways to be self-empowered.

Self-Empowerment

The religious beliefs and the cultural values of many Southeast Asians tend to make them fatalistic regarding the control they have over their own lives and the welfare of their families.[21] This fatalism can also be explained by the traumas they experienced or witnessed during their escape from their countries and the cultural shock they experienced in the United States. These factors contribute to the feeling that they have no control over their lives. The struggle experienced by Southeast Asians in Lowell may not be too different from that of other immigrants who came to the city before them. However, Southeast Asians probably have to overcome more hurdles than their predecessors due to the vast difference between their cultures and that of mainstream society. A historical analysis of Irish and Cambodian struggles for community development and educational empowerment argues that languages as well as visible physical differences pose extra hurdles for Asian immigrants.[22] Other literature about Southeast Asians also supports this point of view. However, the literature does not address the specific needs or concerns of Southeast Asian women.

The process of resettlement among immigrants and newcomers to the United States could be generalized as putting one's life together and exercising some control over it. As immigrants succeeded in their resettlement, they gained more confidence and felt less fatalistic. Many Southeast Asian women in the case studies equate economic self-sufficiency with self-empowerment. They seized the opportunity to work outside the home even if it meant additional responsibility. These mothers and daughters said that with their earned income or their education, they were able to make more decisions that affect their home life, which they equate with having more control or more power. Economic self-sufficiency and educational attainment seemed to improve their power and their level of control over family matters. They considered independence from their husbands or parents to be a major aspect of their lives since moving to the United States. Some women recognize that being economically self-sufficient has benefits and costs that they have to pay for at home. Kongkeo Yang, for example, who is in her forties and had graduated from a technical school in Vientiane before she worked full time in Lowell, knew well the costs and benefits of working. She admitted, "I do not make a lot of money working in the electronic firm, but I like it. I can help pay rent and send gifts to my relatives in Laos. I don't have to ask my husband for money anymore, but I have to work harder at the company and at home." The earned income also enables women to have more control over the family budget and have more money for their personal needs. However, five of six husbands interviewed considered their wives' influence on major family decisions a "win-lose" situation, and saw themselves on the losing side. The friction between husband and wife usually stems from the husband's perception that his wife cannot attend to her responsibilities as a wife, a mother, and a working woman. Some husbands tried to help out with the house chores; others were resigned to the fact that "dinner is not always ready when they come home from work." As La Yang, Kongkeo's husband, lamented, "My wife works long hours at MA/COM; nothing gets done at home. I told her that she cannot do both."

The price of economic self-sufficiency or self-empowerment has been high for some women. One Vietnamese woman who worked at a local textile company found herself often in distress and late for work because of her husband's threats to beat her for spending too much money on cosmetics and dresses. She confided to her supervisor that her children need money for shoes to wear to school more than she needs new dresses, but that she did not want to look different from her American coworkers.[23]

Intergenerational Differences and Related Conflicts

Many middle-aged Southeast Asian women are still bound by the Confucian code of behavior, the traditional teachings of "three obediences" and "four virtues." When a woman is young, she should obey her father; when she gets married, she should obey her husband; and when her husband dies, she should obey her oldest son. Throughout her life, she is expected to do housework, to project a dignified personal appearance, to speak properly, and to behave in a ladylike manner. The six mothers in the case study recognize that their daughters are growing up in a different culture and are resigned to the fact that they may not observe these codes of behavior. However, they do expect their daughters to help with the household chores, respect their elders, and be in harmony with other family members. This expectation has amplified the friction between mothers and daughters. Younger Southeast Asian women, like Kim Tran, are more critical of these codes and teachings:

I believe that the "Four Virtues" and the "Three Moral Codes" that are the expectation of a good woman in the Vietnamese traditional value system are too strict and too narrow. They are only concerned about the woman's behavior and life within the family. They do not encourage the woman to have an education or a professional life, and they demand that a woman has to always obey and be dependent upon somebody else. I do believe that a woman should be allowed to express her ideas and opinions, to go to school, and to plan for her future life.

A 58-year-old mother from Laos who attended an ESL class for homebound women expressed deep concern over the relationship between her son and his wife. She complained that her daughter-in-law was too busy working, shopping, and going places. She stated that her daughter-in-law was not respectful to her husband and did not take good care of her children. The young woman was fighting with her husband all the time over money matters. Sometimes they were so loud that they woke up the whole household and frightened their five- and seven-year-old children. The children often missed the school bus, and they did not dress properly. When Nelly Souriya, the daughter-in-law who was in her twenties and worked full time as a teller at a local bank, was asked how she felt about living in the same house with her parents-in-law, she said, "It's difficult to have too many relatives living together. When I do not agree with my mother-in-law, I can only talk to my husband. But he gets mad at me for criticizing his mother. Then I just keep it to myself and wait for the day we can have our own apartment." This story highlights a common family discord experienced by many young Southeast Asian women. It also resonates with the differences in values and lifestyle between older and younger generations. Many parents complained that their daughters were too Americanized and have abandoned their traditional roles. Naly Yang explained, "My father feels that the discipline in American schools is too light and not effective; it shows in children's behavior, such as not obeying parents and talking back to parents. He also said I'm too Americanized, always talk about friends and sports."

All six fathers in the case study accepted the fact that their children are growing up in a different world and are embracing a different culture. However, their expectations concerning husband-wife roles and responsibilities remain quite traditional. These expectations create more friction and pose additional threats to family harmony.

Strategies for Coping with Changes

The traditional family structure, although familiar, has its shortcomings. The hierarchy hinders meaningful communication and equitable relationships between wife and husband and parents and children. In Cambodia, Laos, and Vietnam, communication skills are rarely taught or practiced in the family or in school. "Children should be seen, but not heard" seems to be a common practice in many families. As a result, many Southeast Asian women have not had the opportunity to learn and to develop the skills needed to articulate their ideas and to negotiate for their position. In the United States these women found that equal opportunity in education and in employment empowers and enables them to play a more assertive role in family matters, including managing the family budget and raising children. Schooling and working outside the home have also opened a window to different role models and different lifestyles that Southeast Asian women have not experienced before. However, at home, their partners have not accepted this changing role, and parents are not ready to relinquish the paternal hierarchy of authority. The lack of communication skills, coupled with the changing roles and the pressure to be assertive in school or at work, has widened the gap between wives and husbands and parents and children. Coping with changes has become a very complex task for these women. Each individual has to develop her own strategy.

Four women in the six families created avoidance mechanisms to deal with difficulties or friction. Nelly Souriya, a young Lao mother with two school-age children, chose to keep it to herself when she had conflict with her family members. "When I cannot talk to my mother-in-law because she always wanted to do things the old ways, I went to my room and closed the door," she said.

Sophy Soth, Chenda's mother, married her soldier husband when she was sixteen in Cambodia. In her forties, she still preferred to find something else to do when there were conflicts with him:

> My husband used to be a violent man. He used to drink all the time, and smoke, and that's bad. Now, he still smokes—he tries very hard to stop, but he's addicted to it. But he doesn't drink anymore, and his attitude has changed. He is a loving man now. Sometimes we do not agree. If I cannot talk to him, I find something else to do.

Daughters had more resources to draw on in dealing with conflicts than mothers did. The skills they learned in mediation sessions in school help them resolve differences at home in a more peaceful way. One Vietnamese daughter used her friends as an example when she wanted to break new ground with her parents on issues that might create tension; another daughter resorted to a third-party negotiator to express her wish or deliver a message to her relatives. Mai Vu even tried to resolve her differences through a friendly discussion with her parents:

> For girls who try to explain or speak their mind, they would be perceived as being disobedient, since parents do not like to have their children talk back to them. And this is something that my older sister and I have been experiencing. My older cousin, before moving to Hawaii, sometimes helped us by acting as an intermediary between us and our parents. She explained to our parents what we meant or what we wanted, and our parents listened to her.

Each family in the study developed its own way of coping with tensions, but some were more successful than others. Some women were deeply ambivalent about changes in their family life, and they struggled to reconcile the new American values and their traditional relationships. Kibria found many Vietnamese American women "walked an ideological tightrope, struggling to use their new resources to their advantage but not in ways that significantly altered or threatened the traditional family system."[24]

Changes in the family structure, adaptation to Western values, coping with new roles, and exercising individual rights and independence all provide challenges and opportunities for Southeast Asian women. Each person experiences the acculturation process differently and finds her own ways to make adjustments to her new life in Lowell. The adaptations to this new life range from a simple matter of wearing Western clothes to the more difficult task of juggling between two different sets of values and lifestyles. For many women, the dilemmas between individual freedom and family obligation, and between new opportunities and the maintenance of traditional customs, are a part of their new life. Some women have successfully taken advantage of the educational opportunities and the socioeconomic advancements they found in Lowell; others have experienced major setbacks, including emotional distress, depression, or domestic violence.

Domestic Violence: Challenging Cultural and Community Resistance

It's very preventable. My mother came across the ocean on her own. Wife abusers shouldn't have this power.
> —Linh, daughter of Cuc Nguyen, who was murdered by her husband[25]

For many Southeast Asian women in Lowell, domestic violence is the most serious and devastating of challenges. It poses threat of injury and possibly death, as it does for so many other women.[26] Southeast Asian women who are battered, however, face cultural and linguistic barriers to services that other women do not face. Police, the criminal justice system, and social service agencies have neither linguistically nor culturally trained staff to cope with the problem. When available, services are usually not culturally appropriate. In many cases, children are expected to serve as cultural and linguistic translators for their parents. Christine Cole, a victim witness advocate in Lowell, noted, "It's not fair to say to a child, 'Get your parents into court so Mom can prosecute Dad.'"[27] Even perpetrators sometimes translate for their victims, reinforcing inequity, dependence, and fear.[28] Traditional roles and prohibitions against speaking of private matters publicly add to the devastation of domestic violence. Many Southeast Asian women fear that reporting abuse to authorities will result in the imprisonment or deportation of their partners or that government intervention will be worse than the abuse itself.

Domestic violence is recognized as a serious problem in Lowell's Southeast Asian community. This is partially a reaction to particularly gruesome crimes that received much media coverage. In 1995, for example, three brothers of the Men family were murdered by their mother's ex-boyfriend, and their sister was seriously injured.[29] While the city was holding a fundraiser for the Men family, another angry boyfriend killed the friend of a woman who had ended a relationship with him and attempted to kill other members of her family.[30] Even before these murders, however, a committee had been formed to address domestic violence in the Southeast Asian community. Perhaps partially due to increased awareness leading to increased reporting of the crime, domestic violence is the only crime that has increased in Lowell since 1993.[31]

As noted earlier, Southeast Asians make up about 20 percent of the city's population. Reports of domestic violence, however, are considerably higher.[32] Unreported cases of domestic violence among Southeast Asians are also higher than in other groups for many reasons, including adherence to traditional values and roles, fear of government and legal authorities related to political histories, fear of deportation, language barriers, and immigrant status. High domestic violence levels are attributed to war-related violence, post-traumatic stress disorder, and urban violence in the United States generally.

Building a Multicultural Coalition: Making a Film against Domestic Violence

For about ten years, multicultural coalitions of Southeast Asian groups and others have been working against domestic violence.[33] A film project developed out of the work of the Southeast Asian Task Force, a city-wide group of grassroots and mutual-assistance associations and human-service, health-care, government, and educational organizations. The task force was formed in the mid-1980s to address pressing economic, linguistic, and political needs of the newly arrived communities.[34] In 1991, a subcommittee was formed to address the increasingly visible devastation of domestic violence. The subcommittee was composed of between fifteen and twenty active members, about half of whom were Southeast Asian, mostly Cambodian, and about half of whom were of other backgrounds, mostly European Americans.

The group had decided to make a film before Mulvey became a member. Film was considered a good medium for community education because it could be done in multiple languages, shown in various settings, and used to encourage group discussion. The diversity of experiences within and between Southeast Asian groups—and long-term effects of trauma and relocation—were considered throughout the planning process. The committee also realized that the experience of living in Lowell could be frightening and sometimes dangerous for newcomers. Concern with cultural appropriateness and respect were ongoing priorities.

From 1991 through 1994, the film subcommittee discussed several critical issues at length, including which groups to reach, what content was most important given limited resources, and who would speak. Input was solicited from several city groups, state agencies, and organizations as far away as California. Programs that were contacted include local Cambodian and Lao mutual-assistance associations; the local battered women's shelter and the rape crisis program; a local Southeast Asian women's health project; the District Attorney's Office; state departments of health; and Asian women's projects and shelters in Boston and San Francisco.

Committee members conducted interviews with several Southeast Asian leaders and agency representatives concerning the reasons for domestic violence, ways to educate about domestic violence, and obstacles to services. Not surprisingly, individuals and groups had different views and priorities. Representatives of European descent from the battered women's shelter were especially interested in having a staff training film about Southeast Asian culture; staff from the Cambodian Mutual Assistance Association (CMAA) were more concerned about focusing on intragroup differences and about highlighting interventions that would reach women who were extremely isolated. Most interviews were conducted jointly by two committee members; summaries were usually similar. Sometimes, however, they diverged: For example, one interviewer (Anglo) felt that the person being interviewed (Cambodian) was inappropriately blaming women for being abused, while the other interviewer (Cambodian) felt the interviewee's intended message was simply to understand why abuse was happening and not to blame anyone. The resolution of differences like these provided an ongoing challenge for the committee.

Recognizing Intergroup and Intragroup Differences among Southeast Asians

Though often categorized as homogenous by the larger Lowell community, intergroup and intragroup differences among Southeast Asians were important and recurrent concerns. As noted earlier, there is immense diversity within and between groups in terms of nationality, age, education, class, politics, and conditions associated with relocation and degree of acculturation. At the same time, Cambodians, Lao, and Vietnamese each had two groups of women at especially high risk of domestic violence: women who were older, homebound, did not speak English, and were very isolated; and women who were younger, spoke English, and were more immersed in American culture. These groups parallel the age groups interviewed in the case study, and similar intergenerational concerns emerged in committee discussion.

Effective outreach to older Southeast Asian women is very difficult due to high incidences of trauma-related mental and physical health problems, including post-traumatic stress disorder, memory and cognitive losses, and psychosomatic blindness.[35] Language barriers and lack of participation in community groups exacerbate these difficulties. There was serious concern that the proposed film might increase violence or backlash against older women who did not speak English. Ways to avoid negative unintended consequences were developed: show the film to informal groups in homes; educate broader networks through mutual-assistance associations, temples, or churches; and recast domestic violence as a community concern and responsibility rather than as primarily a private family matter. While the group avoided simplistic generalizations, social isolation remained a central concern for Southeast Asian women who were older.

In contrast, social involvement was considered a risk factor for younger women, especially teens. Some of the same intergenerational and marital values, dynamics, and stresses discussed in the case study were perceived as contributing to domestic violence: younger women working outside the home; loss of men's status that was often attributed to women's public roles and to American culture; gender-based norms for dating, family, and parenting roles; and power inequities associated with hierarchical family structures.

The marriage of very young women—sometimes as young as twelve or thirteen—was perceived as a risk factor for domestic violence. Dating is forbidden by many parents because it is considered culturally inappropriate and brings shame to the family. Soruep Im, who works in Lowell, notes, "So many traditional parents here don't want their teenage girls dating in the American fashion for fear it will tarnish the family reputation . . . [while] it is very unusual for a family at home [Cambodia] to marry off their daughters before they are eighteen."[36] Socializing in heterosexual groups is often seen as dating and as being sexual or promiscuous, while marriage provides an acceptable context for social and sexual involvement. Arranged marriages are traditional and sometimes still expected, though often not desired or accepted by younger people. Though it is not legal to marry without parental permission until age eighteen, and a license is required at any age, religious marriage ceremonies are often performed with parental permission (or even insistence) and without adhering to legal requirements. Thus, there are multilayered cultural clashes between older and younger generations and between Southeast Asian and American cultural mores and laws. Rhea Gordon, who runs an early marriage group for Cambodian girls in Lowell, makes an explicit connection between early marriage and domestic violence: "The system is totally breaking down for these girls and it is fueling the overall problem of abusive domestic relationships in the Cambodian community." Vesna Nuon, a victim witness advocate who participated in the film project, says, "Some would call me a traitor to my community, but unless we address this phenomenon of early marriage as a problem it will affect the ability of the community to sustain itself in the future." While it is impossible to assess how common these marriages are, Nuon notes, "There are at least two or three Cambodian weddings a weekend in Lowell and many, many of those involve younger brides."[37]

Described as "Lowell's quiet crisis" in a series of newspaper articles, teen pregnancy is also considered a risk factor for domestic violence. A Lowell High School program for pregnant and parenting teens has grown so much over the years that young men are no longer accepted due to lack of space. Of ninety-eight teen participants, twenty-nine were Southeast Asian, and twenty-one of the ninety-eight were first-year students. While acknowledging that teen pregnancy occurs across social, economic, and cultural categories, the series author, Deborah Straszheim, notes, "Some [of these teens] are from immigrant families, coming from cultures where sex is not discussed, marriages are arranged, or pregnancies among youth are considered acceptable."[38] Statistics for 1993 showed that "68 of every 1,000 [Lowell] girls aged 15 to 19 gave birth [which was] 116 percent higher than the state average." Teen pregnancy prevention information published in 1999 by the Lowell Teen Coalition states that while the city's teen pregnancy rate has dropped recently, Lowell has the seventh highest teen birth rate in Massachusetts.[39]

After consideration of many intergroup and intragroup differences, including age, the subcommittee made preliminary decisions as to film content and format. The committee agreed that a great need existed for sensitivity training and educating European American providers about Southeast Asian cultures, but that the priority would be to reach out to Southeast Asians. The priority would be to address concerns of older and younger Southeast Asian women by connecting high levels of domestic violence with social isolation for older women and with social or sexual relationships for younger women. While there was concern for all Southeast Asian cultural groups, the committee decided to focus on Cambodians because they were a much larger group than Vietnamese and Lao combined. Limited funds prohibited producing the film in more than two languages, Khmer and English. Three perspectives were to be combined: "story telling," with survivors speaking about their abuse and how they managed to leave; "consciousness-raising" focused on educating about multiple inter-related forms of abuse; and "information providing" that described community, legal, and social service resources and how to access them. Once agreement was reached re-garding an overall framework, differences of opinion surfaced about what informa-tion to convey, and about how to present information in culturally appropriate ways. In the sections that follow, some of these issues are discussed.

Conflicts over Cultural Values

While there was agreement that domestic violence was caused by multiple factors, disagreement emerged about which factors were most important. Committee mem-bers also held differing views regarding cultural appropriateness. Factors seen as en-couraging domestic violence included traditional cultural and religious values, and horrendous trauma and loss associated with the Pol Pot regime, cultural clashes with American values, and American values themselves.[40] Factors perceived as discouraging domestic violence included all of these factors, too; that is, the same factor was seen by some as contributing to domestic violence and by others as working against it. Some people felt, for example, that extended families in pre–Khmer Rouge Cambodia served as buffers against domestic violence and that parents-in-law intervened to dis-courage violence. Others felt that extended families in traditional Khmer culture ig-nored or even condoned domestic violence.

There were discussions of how American culture reshaped traditions. As discussed above, young women were told, or forced, to marry so that norms against social and sexual heterosexual contact would not be violated. There was agreement that young women in this situation were at increased risk of violence, but disagreement as to which cultural values were associated with it. Some saw domestic violence as a mani-festation of the violence and narcissism of American culture, while others felt that freedom and democracy—especially women's paid job opportunities and legal rights —discouraged domestic violence. Some viewed cultures as inherently fluid and open to varied interpretations and shifts. Others thought that traditional Cambodian and Buddhist values and roles were static and should be protected and preserved, not questioned.

Many of the same issues and stresses raised by the case study participants emerged in film committee discussions. Material from the case study suggests that extended families play a powerful, often controlling, role in the lives of Southeast Asian women, especially younger women. Although the committee agreed that family and children were highly valued in Cambodian culture, initially there was not agreement about how to use cultural values to discourage domestic violence.

Linda Silka and Jahnvibol Tip have found that culturally valued reasons to chal-lenge domestic violence exist and are likely to be effective, noting,

> Southeast Asian women who receive little cultural support for leaving an abusive rela-tionship for their own sakes report experiencing less difficulty when the emphasis is reformed as one of protecting the opportunities for future generations. . . . Support for

enlarged roles for women is not culturally destabilizing . . . [and] flows out of cultural assumptions about women's responsibilities for next generations.[41]

While the case study interviews suggest that women are blamed for marital problems by husbands and extended family, and that negative control is exerted, families sometimes do support women. In a class taught by Mulvey, for example, a young Lao woman talked about her family's experience of domestic violence. Her mother had managed to leave the abuser and to set up a safe situation for herself and her children through the ongoing encouragement and assistance of relatives. This family could not have left without substantial ongoing material and emotional help. Since most Southeast Asian women facing domestic violence do not receive support from extended family, there is great need for a broad range of culturally appropriate community-based services, including resources associated with temples and churches, shelters, hotlines, and schools, to name just a few. The film was seen as a way to encourage the development and the use of a broad range of services like these.

Focus on Families and Children

Committee members voiced divergent beliefs about families, children, and men. Many of the family conflicts mentioned by case study participants were seen as factors related to high levels of domestic violence: women wearing makeup, going out too much, earning money, and being too independent. Reasons for staying in abusive situations were related to the importance of the family unit, especially children, and to women's responsibility for family and children. Sympathy and concern for male family members were important to some but not to all committee members. Opinions differed as to how much emphasis should be placed on children's safety or future success as compared with the well-being and rights of women. There were debates about whether to highlight the impact of domestic violence on boys rather than girls and whether to use only male narrators. Views on these issues did not break down neatly into gender or cultural categories. Some Southeast Asian men (for example, Vesna Nuon) were outspoken against using any reason—traditional roles, affairs, alcohol, stress, or dress—to justify violence against women. Some European American women preferred the term "family violence" to "men's violence against women" and "domestic violence" because they felt the latter terms were antimale. Police officers and victim witness advocates sometimes agreed and sometimes disagreed about priorities. Ultimately, opposing viewpoints were incorporated into the film in ways that were approved by the whole group.

After considerable debate, it was decided that the devastating effects of domestic violence on children (both girls and boys) would be emphasized in the film; that women and men would narrate; and that cultural values meant to discourage victim blaming would be highlighted (that is, family unity and children's welfare). The introduction to the *Domestic Violence in the Cambodian Community* film sets this tone:

Our culture has always placed a high value on families, even during the terrible Pol Pot times, in the refugee camps, and here in the United States. We have treasured our families and sought to keep them safe and together as best we could. Unfortunately, some families cannot seem to find harmony. Instead, there is violence in the home . . . usually directed at a woman by a man.

Note that the high value Southeast Asian cultures place on families is being used to challenge men's violence against women though this value is often used to support male dominance. Inclusion of the last phrase, "violence . . . usually directed at a woman by a man," was debated. Some committee members did not want to call men "perpetrators" or women "victims," while others felt that it was accurate to note these gender patterns. In one of the most compelling moments of the film, an older woman speaks of her struggles to survive, drawing parallels between personal and political violence: "Do not let your husband abuse you. Cambodian women have received their share of violence and abuse during the Pol Pot regime. I had one reason [for coming to the United States] . . . to keep my children safe." Weaving together varied perspectives was a constructive way to work with differences that ultimately strengthened the film.

There was consensus that the difficulties likely to be faced when leaving or seeking services—physical, cultural, linguistic, and economic—must be presented honestly.[42] Longstanding cultural barriers against seeking help outside the family and deep fear of authority associated with the Khmer Rouge would be acknowledged as powerful deterrents. There were times when these obstacles seemed insurmountable, even in the planning process. At the same time, the subcommittee knew that it was as important to offer hope as it was to provide tangible resources. After difficult deliberations, the subcommittee achieved consensus on the following priorities: (1) give clear information; (2) realistically describe limited local and regional resources; (3) discourage victim blaming; (4) avoid blaming the culture and men as a group; and (5) support and encourage women.

From Committee Dissension to Consensus

The film subcommittee met once a month for over two years and worked independently between meetings. Shared concern for Southeast Asian women and families was the common ground that supported the group through this long process. Despite and because of diverse viewpoints, the group worked successfully to challenge domestic violence. Rooted in Khmer cultural traditions and in the Lowell community, the film we created provides important information about formal and informal resources. It takes a clear stand against domestic violence, describing it as a tragedy devastating to many women and families *and* as a community problem that must be confronted collectively. The film is visually rich with footage in a local temple, at cultural festivals, and at a traditional wedding. The breadth of information and the "braiding" of cultural perspectives are impressive. For example, there are scenes of neighborhoods with brightly colored signs in Khmer and English and local Southeast Asian businesses. Cambodian, Buddhist, and American traditions, values, and laws are used to educate and to advocate against domestic violence.

Personal and Political Reflections

As a middle-class woman of Irish ancestry and a longtime feminist activist, I (Mulvey) found the planning process ideologically challenging.[43] I sometimes felt that male privilege was being condoned in the name of culture; that past traumas and present hardships were being used to rationalize men's violence against women, or that women's right to safety was not being advocated. I heard comments that suggested that women were to blame for being battered because they had affairs, went out too much, or earned more money than their partners. I experienced internal tension between my desire to learn about and to respect Southeast Asian cultures and my conviction that domestic violence—though normative in most cultures—is a human rights violation. I worried that voicing my views might discourage Southeast Asians, particularly women, from voicing theirs. Occupying positions of race and class privilege, and realizing that teachers are held in high esteem in Southeast Asian cultures, added to these dilemmas, especially because some committee members had been my students. I tried to listen (not easy for me) and to speak from convictions and from the heart, while acknowledging and respecting deeply held convictions and commitments that were different from mine.

I conducted an interview with a Southeast Asian woman who thought that education should be the film's priority. She felt that women sometimes betray men or hurt their families by seeking help and expressed concern that men might be offended by the film. This woman had been a student of mine and had expressed frustration about restrictions placed on her that were not placed on her brother (early curfews and not being allowed to go away to college). She disliked these restrictions, but she also loved and respected her parents and valued her culture. She seemed to be grappling with very complicated, painful dilemmas. Many Southeast Asian women I have taught have described similar dilemmas. Working on the film helped me to see that interpreting information out of context could lead to cross-cultural misunderstandings. Apparent inconsistencies expressed in relation to gender inequalities represent a delicate, stressful balancing of traditional and new values and struggles to sustain positive relationships with parents, family, and community. Material from the multigenerational study presented earlier also supports this interpretation, as does other literature.[44]

"Unbreaks the Stone Walls": Southeast Asian Coalitions against Domestic Violence in Lowell

Since the film was completed and distributed, other projects have been developing. In 1996, a city-wide task force against domestic violence was formed (Mulvey is a member). Representatives from Southeast Asian groups and many other organizations participate. A new group, Southeast Asian Families Against Domestic Violence, is updating the film. The Boston-based Asian Task Force against Domestic Violence has opened a satellite office in Lowell. Local and state networks are expanding, interacting, and growing stronger.

Challenges to addressing the particular needs of Southeast Asian women continue.

There are strong cultural prohibitions against women speaking in public, and shame is still associated with public talk about family problems. The assumption that women are responsible for all that happens in the family, including even their own abuse, complicates these pressures.[45] Genocide and relocation traumas add unspeakable terror to deeply rooted cultural prohibitions. As Theanvy Kuoch, Richard A. Miller, and Mary Scully have documented, "Telling your story was part of the Khmer Rouge process for controlling the population. . . . The questioning process was repeated many times to catch people in lies."[46] It will take much time, sensitivity, and hard work to build effective multicultural coalitions against domestic violence. Nonimmigrant service providers and community members who have been immersed in local and regional systems are often in better structural positions to implement changes and to advocate for services. Coalitions with Southeast Asian groups (and others) offer rich opportunities to see and address cultural "blind spots." Working in coalitions to develop culturally appropriate interventions against domestic violence has the potential to strengthen other formal and informal networks, providing additional benefits to Southeast Asian women and others in the process. At the end of the film, a woman who works in a battered women's program says, "It is important for me to be in this field and to help Cambodian women and children because it unbreaks the stone walls. We need help, so tell her to get the message around our community. We should leave and not be beaten."

Young women in Lowell—Southeast Asian, Hispanic, and Anglo—have been literally spreading the message. Working with Lowell's battered women's shelter, they posted tear-off hotline numbers and referral information in the stalls of women's bathrooms. Sophy Suon, their organizer, said working on the project facilitated more open conversation about relationships that group members were in, particularly abusive ones.[47] This is a great example of community action and education fostering growth across personal and political levels. Southeast Asian women who are victims of domestic violence will continue to face "stone walls" unless domestic violence is addressed as a community problem within each cultural community. Unless others working in community with Southeast Asian peoples challenge the xenophobic notion that domestic violence is ever only a particular marginalized group's problem or the product of their culture, the larger community will be contributing to the problem and diminishing the community as a whole. It is encouraging that people from diverse Southeast Asian groups are working with others in Lowell to "unbreak the stone walls," building multicultural communities through their work against domestic violence.

As our work presented here suggests, the lives of Lowell women from Cambodia, Laos, and Vietnam are characterized by complex and interwoven losses and gains. Women's own descriptions of their lives and descriptions of community-wide initiatives against domestic violence argue against simplistic categories or analyses. Many experiences simultaneously represent adaptations, transformations, and continuities: foods, language, and cultural customs have been changed, not lost. Domestic violence —evidenced by intergroup and intragroup work—has been named and exposed. It is becoming less acceptable publicly, if not privately. Some women worry that cultural values are being lost or that the authority of elders is eroding, though these same women appreciate the greater individual autonomy that is possible in America.

Women want education for their daughters as well as their sons, though they continue to place greater family demands and more restrictions on girls than boys. Most of the women interviewed are combining paid work with primary responsibility for children and home. They struggle to balance multiple roles as women of other backgrounds do, but economic barriers, linguistic and cultural conflicts, and experiences of war and resettlement are distinctive.

In stories of intergeneration, in tensions about women's educational and relational choices, and in planning ways to challenge domestic violence, diversity within and between Southeast Asian cultures is evident. Age, education, financial circumstances, and social norms are factors that influence adaptation, either enhancing or discouraging coping and resources for conflict resolution. Differences like these must be taken into account to guide effective personal and political change.

Due to successful adaptation of Southeast Asian traditions and to innovative multicultural coalitions that have reduced domestic and youth violence, in 1999 Lowell was named an "All-America City" by the National Civic League.[48] An article in the local paper about the competition, "Asians a Strong Thread in Lowell's Fabric," described the Southeast Asian Water Festival and the Angkor Dance Troupe: "The popularity of the two Southeast Asian aspects of the program—as well as their inclusion in the program—struck a resonating chord in the community."[49] The director of the Angkor Dance Troupe noted that other Lowell delegates thought the dance troupe represented the Cambodian community, while the troupe saw themselves as representing Lowell. Highlighting contested values and views, the "All America" designation was earned not long after a new wing of the only public high school was named after the member of the School Committee who led Lowell's successful English-only movement.

Serious problems have been discussed: the devastation of domestic violence, the impact of xenophobic community initiatives, and difficult personal, interpersonal, and intergenerational experiences. Too often, simply surviving is a challenge. Much more conversation is needed about how to retain cultural traditions while developing supports and opportunities for Southeast Asian women of all ages. A major challenge is finding a way to do these things without perpetuating hierarchical values and structures. This challenge sits right next to the need to work against xenophobia in the broader community. At the same time, creative problem solving, healing, and community building are occurring individually, with family and friends, and in monocultural and multicultural networks. New businesses have opened and traditions are being preserved. Southeast Asian women are going to school, are employed outside the home, and are appreciating their new roles and opportunities. They are working with others to stop violence and to foster safety for women. Through strength and resilience, Southeast Asian women are making Lowell their home and, in so doing, are enriching the community socially, economically, and culturally.

NOTES

Reprint from *Frontier: A Journal of Women Studies* 24.1, by permission of the University of Nebraska Press. Copyright © 2004 by Frontier Editorial Collective.

1. U.S. Department of Health and Human Services, Office of Refugee Resettlement, *Refugee Resettlement Program, Report to the Congress* (Washington, DC: GPO, January 31, 1995); David W. Haines, ed., "Introduction," *Refugees as Immigrants: Cambodians, Laotians, and Vietnamese in America* (Totowa, NJ: Rowman & Littlefield, 1989), 1–23; Thanh Van Tran, "The Vietnamese American Family," in *Ethnic Families in America: Patterns and Variations,* ed. Charles H. Mindel, Robert W. Habenstein, and Roosevelt Wright (New York: Elsevier, 1997), 254–83; Ellen Cole, Oliva M. Espin, and Esther D. Rothblum, eds., *Refugee Women and Their Mental Health: Shattered Societies, Shattered Lives* (New York: Haworth Press, 1992); and Nira Yuval-Davis, *Gender and Nation* (London: Sage Publications, 1997). Much of the published literature on Southeast Asian refugees focuses on general issues as they relate to refugee resettlement programs and language acquisition by children (bilingual education or English as a second language) or the mechanics of camp maintenance and the psychological aspects of resettlement. See William T. Liu, Maryanne Lamana, and Alice Murata, *Transition to Nowhere: Vietnamese Refugees in America* (Nashville, TN: Charter House, 1979); Haines, "Introduction"; and Tuyet-Lan Pho, "Family Education and Academic Performance among Southeast Asian Students" (Ph.D. diss., University of Massachusetts, Lowell, 1994).

2. Tuyet-Lan Pho, of Vietnamese ethnic background, and Anne Mulvey, of Irish descent, have been executive members of the Council on Diversity and Pluralism at the University of Massachusetts, Lowell, since 1995. One of the council's major goals is to provide, through research and community work, awareness and understanding to faculty and students about the acculturation processes experienced by different immigrant groups living in the greater Lowell area. Pho and Mulvey have coordinated several community projects and conducted separate studies about the Southeast Asian refugees.

3. Tuyet-Lan Pho, *Promoting Integration and School Improvement in the Lowell Public Schools: Chapter 636 Evaluation Report, Academic Year 1987–88* (Lowell: College of Education, University of Massachusetts); Pho, "Family Education and Academic Performance among Southeast Asian Students," and Pho, "Introduction," *Fractured Identities: Cambodia's Children of War,* ed. James Higgins and Joan Ross (Lowell, MA: Loom Press, 1997), 9–16.

4. The estimate was compiled by multiplying the number of students enrolled in the public schools by a factor of 5.2 (Massachusetts Office for Refugees and Immigrants, 1997, *Demographic Update: Refugees and Immigrants in Massachusetts*).

5. Numerous antirefugee incidents occurred between 1975 and 1990 in cities and states with large concentrations of Southeast Asian refugees. These conflicts included protests aimed at new arrivals, property destruction, job and social service disputes, harassment and altercations, assaults, arson to homes, and incidents that resulted in death for either refugees or natives (Jeremy Hein, *From Vietnam, Laos, and Cambodia: A Refugee Experience in the United States* [New York: Twayne Publishers, 1995], 50–68).

6. Peter Kiang, "When Know-nothings Speak English Only: Analyzing Irish and Cambodian Struggles for Community Development and Educational Empowerment," in *The State of Asian America: Activism and Resistance in the 1990s,* ed. Karin Aguilar-San Juan (Boston: South End Press, 1994), 125–45.

7. James Crawford, *Hold Your Tongue: Bilingualism and the Politics of "English Only"* (Reading, MA: Addison-Wesley, 1992).

8. Pho, "Family Education and Academic Performance among Southeast Asian Students"; and Pho, *Promoting Integration and School Improvement in the Lowell Public Schools.*

9. All names of individuals used in this paper are pseudonyms to protect the privacy of the subjects. Lien is a Vietnamese member of one of the six families who were interviewed by Tuyet-Lan Pho in a followup study of her dissertation research about family education among

Southeast Asians in Lowell. The other families are the Soths and the Oums, who came from Cambodia, the Yangs and the Souriyas, from Laos, and the Vus, from Vietnam.

10. Nathan Caplan, Marcella H. Choy, and John K. Whitmore, *Children of the Boat People* (Ann Arbor: University of Michigan Press, 1991).

11. Pho, "Family Education and Academic Performance among Southeast Asian Students."

12. Many Southeast Asians became Christian when they encountered religious organizations that provided health and educational services in refugee camps. Chenda Soth was born in 1975 in Cambodia. Her parents and their four children were resettled in the United States in 1981. They lived in Texas and California before moving to Lowell in 1992.

13. Naly Yang was born in 1975 in Vientiane, the second child in a family of four children. Her parents, of Hmong ethnic background, migrated to Laos, attending school and working there prior to their departure to the United States in 1985. The family moved to Lowell in 1986.

14. Sam Oum was born in Cambodia in 1975, the third child in a family of six children. His family moved to the United States in 1984 and to Lowell in 1986.

15. Mai Vu was born in Saigon in 1972, the fourth child in a family of seven children. Her family moved to Lowell in 1990.

16. Caroline Louise Cole, "Cambodian Youths Forced into Marriage: Cultural Crisis Seen in Community," *Boston Globe,* June 2, 1996, 1, 9.

17. U.S. Department of Commerce, *1990 Census of Population: Asians and Pacific Islanders in the United States* (Washington, DC: GPO, 1993).

18. The U.S. poverty level is set at $18,000 as annual income for a family of five (Massachusetts Department of Employment and Training, Field Service Research Department, "Northeast Region Employment Fact Sheet," September 1993).

19. Cuc Vu is Mai's mother. She was in her late forties at the time of this study. She had some education in Vietnam and was working at home as a stitcher to supplement the family income.

20. Nazli Kibria, *Family Tightrope: The Changing Life of Vietnamese Americans* (Princeton, NJ: Princeton University Press, 1993).

21. Dang T. T. Wei, *Vietnamese Refugee Students: A Handbook for School Personnel* (Cambridge, MA: Lesley College, 1984); Center for Applied Linguistics, *The Peoples and Cultures of Cambodia, Laos, and Vietnam* (Washington, DC: Center for Applied Linguistics, 1981); and Sun-Him Chhim, Khamchong Luangpraseut, and Dinh Te Huynh, *Introduction to Cambodian, Lao, and Vietnamese Cultures,* 2nd ed. (San Diego, CA: Multifunctional Service Center, San Diego State University, 1989).

22. Kiang, "When Know-nothings Speak English Only"; and Linda Silka and Jahn-vibol Tip, "Empowering the Silent Ranks: The Southeast Asian Experience," *American Journal of Community Psychology* 22.4: 497–529.

23. Tuyet-Lan Pho, "Issues and Challenges in Educational Programs for Vietnamese Women," paper presented at Women of Color: The American Road to Empowerment, University of Rhode Island Chautauqua, Kingston, Rhode Island, April 1990.

24. Kibria, *Family Tightrope,* 9; and Daniel Golden, "Battered Lives," *Boston Globe Magazine,* December 29, 1991, 10–11, 17–20, 23–24.

25. Golden, "Battered Lives," 24.

26. Raymond D. Fowler, ed., "International Perspectives on Domestic Violence," *American Psychologist* 54.1: 1–76; and Golden, "Battered Lives."

27. Golden, "Battered Lives," 23.

28. Golden, "Battered Lives"; and Governor's Commission on Domestic Violence, *Statewide Hearings on Domestic Violence: Findings and Recommendations,* unpublished manuscript

available from Governor's Commission on Domestic Violence, Boston; and Silka and Tip, "Empowering the Silent Ranks."

29. William Sinagra and Marcia Cassidy, "Four Children Shot; Mother's Boyfriend Charged," *Lowell Sun,* November 13, 1995, 1, 4.

30. Brian MacQuarrie, "Lowell Cambodians Feel Urgency to Find Solutions to Violence," *Boston Globe,* January 31, 1996, 15, 22.

31. Brian Martin, "Annual Report to the Lowell City Manager's Domestic Violence Task Force" (Lowell, MA: City Manager's Office, Lowell City Hall); and Anne Mulvey, "Gender, Economic Context, Perceptions of Safety, and Quality of Life: A Case Study of Lowell, Massachusetts," *American Journal of Community Psychology* 30.5 (2002): 655–79.

32. MacQuarrie, "Lowell Cambodians Feel Urgency"; Southeast Asian Task Force, *Domestic Violence in the Cambodian Community,* Mitch Shuldman, prod. (Media Center, University of Massachusetts, Wilder Street, Lowell, MA 01854); and Silka and Tip, "Empowering the Silent Ranks."

33. This discussion is based on committee minutes, reports, and notes taken by one of the authors, Mulvey, who was a member of the planning committee. Scholarly and popular sources are used to interpret issues raised in the film project and to link it to other initiatives.

34. Hai Pho, "The Politics of Refugee Resettlement in Massachusetts," *Immigration World* 19.4: 4–10; and Silka and Tip, "Empowering the Silent Ranks."

35. Richard F. Mollica, Grace Wyshak, and James Lavelle, "The Psychosocial Impact of War Trauma and Torture on Southeast Asian Refugees," *American Journal of Psychiatry* 144.12 (1987): 1567–72; and Gretchen B. Van Boemel and Patricia D. Rozee, "Treatment for Psychosomatic Blindness among Cambodian Refugee Women," in Cole, Espin, and Rothblum, *Refugee Women and Their Mental Health,* 239–65.

36. Soruep Im, as cited in Cole, "Cambodian Youths Forced into Marriage," 10.

37. Rhea Gorden and Vesna Nuon, as cited in Cole, "Cambodian Youths Forced into Marriage," 1.

38. Deborah Straszheim, "Teenage Pregnancy: Lowell's Quiet Crisis," *Lowell Sun,* February 12, 1995, 1, 4–5, and "Why? Teen-age Pregnancy: Lowell's Quiet Crisis," *Lowell Sun,* February 13, 1995, 1, 4.

39. *Teens Reaching Out,* Teen Pregnancy Prevention Materials (Lowell, MA: Lowell Teen Coalition, 585 Merrimack Street, 1999).

40. Estimates of the number of people murdered during Pol Pot's "reign of terror" (1975–79) range from one million to more than two million people. Most survivors lost many family members or did not know if they were alive. See Patricia K. Robin Herbst, "From Helpless Victim to Empowered Survivor: Oral History as a Treatment for Survivors of Torture," in Cole, Espin, and Rothblum, *Refugee Women and Their Mental Health,* 141–54. Herbst found that when women talked about these experiences they felt great shame that "Khmer killed Khmer"(152). Escape and relocation involved life-threatening danger. Rape was common, but is rarely acknowledged because blame and shame are placed on survivors and their families. Protection of children and families was often the strongest reason to keep going. See Theanvy Kuoch, Richard A. Miller, and Mary F. Scully, "Healing the Wounds of the Mahantdori," in Cole, Espin, and Rothblum, *Refugee Women and Their Mental Health,* 191–207.

41. Silka and Tip, "Empowering the Silent Ranks," 518.

42. For example, there is evidence that leaving an abuser is associated with increased violence and greater risk. See Ronet Bachman and Linda. E. Saltzman, *Violence against Women: Estimates from the Redesigned Survey* (Washington, DC: Bureau of Justice Statistics, U.S. Department of Justice, 1995).

43. Because this section consists mostly of personal reflections by Mulvey about her participation in the film project, it is written in the first person singular.

44. Kibria, *The Family Tightrope*; and Silka and Tip, "Empowering the Silent Ranks."

45. Kuoch, Miller, and Scully, "Healing the Wounds of the Mahantdori"; and Silka and Tip, "Empowering the Silent Ranks."

46. Kuoch, Miller, and Scully, "Healing the Wounds of the Mahantdori," 204

47. Sophy Suon, personal communication with Mulvey, Lowell, October 1998.

48. Christine McConville, "It's Official: Lowell an All-America City," *Lowell Sun,* June 27, 1999, 1, 7.

49. Matt Wickenheiser, "Asians a Strong Thread in Lowell's Fabric," *Lowell Sun,* June 29, 1999, 1, 4.

New Household Forms, Old Family Values

The Formation and Reproduction of the Filipino Transnational Family in Los Angeles

Rhacel Salazar Parreñas

Much like other immigrant groups in the United States, Filipino migrants turn to the family for support against the social and economic pressures that they encounter upon settlement. They use the family in myriad ways. For example, Filipino migrants are known to have preserved various cultural practices to secure the use of the family as a source of support in settlement. They create fictive kinship, enforce a keen sense of obligation among kin, and use an extended as opposed to a nuclear base for the family (Almirol 1982; Agbayani-Siewart and Revilla 1995). In general, Filipino migrants preserve various cultural practices so as to secure from the community mutual support for the economic mobility of the family and assistance in difficult periods of adjustment in settlement.

In my own observations, Filipinos use the family in other ways. The family is a social institution that adapts strategies variably in response to structural, cultural, and ideological forces in society. Concomitantly, Filipinos have taken advantage of this flexibility by incorporating various strategies of household maintenance. For example, multiple nuclear families may reside in one household so as to decrease expenses and in some cases may go as far as to purchase a house collectively. They also share tasks such as child care across households. These examples show that Filipino families are neither monolithic nor static but instead consist of diverse household forms.

This chapter presents one strategy of household maintenance utilized by Filipino migrants for easing their settlement into the United States. In particular, I document the formation and reproduction of the Filipino transnational household. By "transnational" family or household, I refer to a family whose core members are located in at least two or more nation-states. In such a family, a migrant settles in the host society, while his or her family—spouse, children, and/or parents—stays in the Philippines. The purpose is to explain how and why transnational households form and reproduce among contemporary Filipino migrants in Los Angeles. Thus, I elaborate on the *structural factors* propelling Filipinos into transnational households as well as the *cultural factors* to which Filipinos turn in order to form such households.

Background

The data are derived from a comparative study of migrant Filipina domestic workers in Rome and Los Angeles. I rely primarily on interviews conducted with twenty-six Filipina domestic workers in Los Angeles. I supplement this data with interviews that I had gathered with fifty-six domestic workers in Rome and ten children who had grown up in transnational households. Transnational households are in fact the dominant strategy of household maintenance for migrant Filipina domestic workers. Of the twenty-six women interviewed in Los Angeles, twenty maintain transnational households. Of these twenty women, fourteen have dependent children living in the Philippines, one lives apart from her husband in the Philippines, and five are single women whose monthly remittances sustain the day-to-day living expenses of their families.

Before I proceed with my discussion of the transnational household, I need to first acknowledge the limitation in my data. The sample of domestic workers does not represent the wide range of occupations held by Filipino migrants in the United States and correspondingly does not reflect the varying demands imposed on the family by different work routines. Because live-in work arrangements are still common among Filipina domestic workers, they can more or less be expected to turn to transnational household structures. Responsibilities for the families of employers prevent them from meeting the demands of child care and other reproductive labor in their own families. As a result, they send their children to the Philippines or leave them there, where a wide kin network inclusive of blood and affinal relations may provide care for dependents.

However, professional Filipino women such as nurses are also known to maintain transnational households in the community. They do so to balance their work inside and outside the home. Immigrant Filipinas have one of the highest rate of labor force participation, reaching 83 percent in 1980 among married immigrant women (Espiritu 1997). In 1990, immigrant Filipino women also held the highest employment ratio among women in Los Angeles, with 83 percent of the working-age population gainfully employed (Ong and Azores 1994a). Confronted with a wage gap, Filipina immigrants often maximize their earnings by working extended hours (Yamanaka and McClelland 1994; Espiritu 1997). For example, it is common for Filipina nurses in Los Angeles to hold two full-time jobs (Ong and Azores 1994b). Despite their high rate of labor force participation, Filipina women are still expected to do most of the housework and child care in their families. Consequently, long hours at work coupled with their continued responsibility for domestic chores may lead even professional women to send their children back to the Philippines. They usually do so only for a short period of time, during infancy, when child care demands are greatest. They also usually do so because of their preference for child care to be provided by kin instead of strangers in child care facilities in the United States.

Notably, the formation of transnational households is not exclusive to Filipino labor migrants. Various studies document its formation among contemporary migrants from the traditional sending countries of Haiti and Mexico.[1] Transnational families are also not particular to present-day migrants. They have historically been a common form of household maintenance for temporary labor migrants in various regions of the world. The earliest Chinese migrant workers in the United States, "guest workers" in Western Europe, and Mexican *braceros* in the southwestern United States, to name a few examples, adapted "split households" because of the disparate levels of economic development in the sending and the receiving countries and the legal barriers to the integration of migrants in the United States (Glenn 1983); these conditions continue today.

We can also speculate that it was not uncommon for Filipino migrants in the pre–World War II period to adopt such households. Prior to World War II, the Filipino community was composed mostly of single men. The cost of bringing women to the United States, coupled with the uncertainty of life for migrant farm workers, discouraged the migration of women. In 1930, women composed only 16.6 percent of the population (Espiritu 1995). Yet, this skewed gender composition does not reflect the distribution of marital status in the community. In 1930, the number of married Filipino men (7,409) far exceeded the number of Filipino women (1,640) on the U.S. mainland (Parreñas 1998b). This strongly suggests that Filipino migrants, as they were subject to antimiscegenation laws, adapted transnational households when wives could not join them because of either economic uncertainties or legal restrictions barring the entry of Filipinos into the United States.[2]

Yet, while split households in earlier migrant communities were homogeneous and composed primarily of a male income producer living apart from female and young dependents in the sending country, contemporary split households, for example, those from the Philippines and the Caribbean (Basch et al. 1994), include income-producing female migrants. Unlike in the past, with the split households of male migrants, traditional gender roles are contested in today's transnational families of female migrants, with women acting as the breadwinners of families.

How and why do transnational households form among contemporary Filipino migrants? This is the question I answer in this chapter. My discussion of the transnational household is divided into three sections. In the first section, I describe the structural forces propelling the formation of transnational households. Then, in the second section, I enumerate the cultural practices enabling the formation of such households. The third and final section proceeds to describe the Filipino transnational family. In this section, I present two vignettes that illustrate the difficulties and sacrifices entailed in the reproduction of the transnational family.

Global Capitalism: Structural Factors of Transnational Household Formation

Global capitalism and its resulting processes within sending and receiving communities of migration propel the formation of transnational households. Migrants form transnational households to mediate the following structural forces: the unequal level of economic development in sending and receiving nations; legal barriers that restrict their full incorporation into the host society and polity; and the rise of anti-immigrant sentiments. Transnational households result from a conglomeration of contemporary social realities. However, these constitutive features are not particular to global capitalism. Instead, they are old practices—longstanding realities—that are merely being redeployed with greater speed and force with the advent of globalization.

As structural forces in society spur the formation of transnational households, they are not uncommon strategies of household maintenance for low-wage migrant workers, such as Filipina domestic workers. While affording their families a comfortable, middle-class lifestyle in the sending country, the meager wages of low-paid migrant workers do not provide a comparable lifestyle in receiving countries. The lesser costs of reproduction in sending countries such as the Philippines enable migrant laborers to provide greater material benefits for their children, including comfortable housing, as opposed to the cramped living quarters imposed on migrants by high rents in "global cities," burgeoning economic centers that rely on the "routine" services of low-wage immigrant laborers (Sassen 1988, 1994). Finally, the family can expedite the achievement of its goals of accumulating savings and property by forming transnational households. Thus, migrants create transnational households as a strategy to maximize resources and opportunities in the global economy. The migrant family transcends borders and the spatial boundaries of nation-states to take advantage of the lower costs of reproducing—feeding, housing, clothing, and educating—the family in the "Third World." Its spatial organization is in direct response to the forces of global capitalism as the geographical split of the family coincides with the uneven development of regions and the unequal relations between states in the global economy.

Restrictions against the integration of immigrants in postindustrial nations today also fuel the formation of transnational families. The displacement of workers and loss of stable employment for middle-income "native" workers have led to the scapegoating of immigrants, particularly Latinos in the United States (Perea 1997; Feagin 1997). The resulting enforcement of barriers against the integration of migrant laborers and especially their families promotes the maintenance of transnational households. In the United States, lawmakers are entertaining the promotion of temporary labor migration and the elimination of certain preference categories for family reunification, including the preference categories for adult children and parents of U.S. citizens and permanent residents—the trend being to preserve the labor provided by migrants but to discontinue support for their reproduction (Chavez 1997). Moreover, nativist grassroots organizations (e.g., Americans for Immigration Control, Stop the Out-of-Control Problems of Immigration Today) aimed at the further restriction and exclusion of immigration have sprouted throughout the United States.[3] With anti-immigrant sentiments brewing in the United States, migrant parents may not want to expose their children to the racial tensions and anti-immigrant sentiments fostered by the social and cultural construction of low-wage migrants as undesirable citizens (Basch et al. 1994; Ong 1996). Yet, among my interviewees, many had been caught in the legal bind of being either undocumented or obtaining their legal status only after their children had reached adult age, when children are no longer eligible for immediate family reunification. Hence, while they may have wanted to sponsor the migration of their children to the United States, they have legally been unable to do so.

"Receiving" societies such as the United States most likely support the formation of transnational households. This is the case because such households guarantee them the low-wage labor of migrants without forcing them to accept responsibility for their reproduction. By containing the costs of reproduction in sending countries, receiving countries can keep to a minimum the wages of immigrant workers. Thus, while receiving countries need the low-wage labor of migrants, they want neither the responsibilities nor the costs of the reproduction of these workers. This is particularly shown by the passage of Proposition 187, the 1995 California state referendum that bars undocumented immigrants from receiving any tax-supported benefits, including education, health, and social services (Martin 1995). Thus, the formation of transnational households, though a strategy of resistance in globalization, maintains the inequalities of globalization. Receiving countries benefit from the minimized wage demands of a substantial proportion of their workforce. Such economic benefits translate to increased production activities, leading to growth and profits for the higher-tier workers of receiving countries.

The formation of transnational households further enforces the limited integration of low-wage migrant workers. The separation of the migrant family stunts the incorporation of the migrant into the host society, since it is often the children whose greater ability to acculturate paves the way of integration in settlement (Portes and Rumbaut 1996). The consideration of the workings of border politics in transnational households also illustrates the enforcement of limited integration in this process of household formation. On the one hand, the operation of transnational households transcends territorial borders, with the family acting as a conduit between localized communities in separate nation-states. Transcendence, however, does not signify elimination of barriers (i.e., borders). Transnational households should not be praised as a small-scale symbol of the migrant's agency against the larger forces of globalization, because the formation of transnational households marks an enforcement of "border control" on migrant workers. If transnational households can be seen as representing transcendence, they also signify segregation. Transnational households form from the segregation of the families of immigrant workers in sending countries. Thus, they form from the successful implementation of border control, which makes families unable to reunite. Border control further aggravates the experience of transnational families by making return migration difficult for undocumented workers. In turn, family separation is often prolonged and may even extend to a span of a life cycle. Among my interviewees, for example, the length of separation between mothers and their now-adult children in transnational families is as long as sixteen years.

The Persistence of Familism: Cultural Factors of Transnational Household Formation

Transnational households emerge in response to the global labor market but also form because of strong kinship ties (Basch et al. 1994). However, in the Philippines, transnational households have come to signify the decline and disintegration of family values and consequently "the destruction of the moral fabric" of society (Tadiar 1997, 171). Because they fail to fulfill the ideological notion of a traditional Filipino family, transnational households are considered "broken homes."

Filipino families are traditionally nuclear in structure. Members carry a strong sense of solidarity and obligation to members of their nuclear family and, to a lesser extent, to their larger kin group inclusive of consanguineal (i.e., parent and sibling), affinal, and fictive kin (Medina 1991). The kinship base on which Filipinos may rely is extended by the multilineal and bilateral descent system in the Philippines. Filipinos maintain an equal sense of allegiance to maternal and paternal kin. Moreover, they extend their kinship network by including in their families fictive kin, kin obtained spiritually (e.g., *compadrazgo* system), and cross-generational and cousin ties.

Transnational households are considered "broken" for a number of reasons. First, the maintenance of this household form diverges from traditional expectations of cohabitation among spouses and children. Second, transnational households do not meet the traditional division of labor in the family, as transnational mothers do not maintain the social expectation that women perform domestic chores. Notably, this expectation still stands despite the high labor-force participation of women in the Philippines (Medina 1991). Third, they diverge from traditional practices of socialization in the family. While the socialization of children is expected to come from direct supervision and interaction with parents as well as other adults, the geographic distance in transnational households inhibits the ability of mothers to provide direct supervision to their children.

Yet, the formation of these households depends on the persisting cultural value of *pakikisama,* meaning mutual cooperation or familism, that is, sentiments of collectivism and mutual obligation among kin. Transnational households would not be able to form and reproduce without the cultural value of *pakikisama,* and the mechanisms strengthening such an allegiance, including (1) mutual assistance, (2) consanguineal responsibility, (3) "generalized family exchange networks" (Peterson 1993), and (4) fosterage. Transnational households have come to show the resilience of the Filipino family in the advent of globalization.

The operation of transnational households rests on the strength of mutual assistance among extended kin in the Philippines. In transnational households, the migrant shoulders the responsibility of providing for primary and extended kin by remitting funds regularly. In fact, not one of my interviewees has failed to provide consistent financial assistance to her family. Notably, most single migrants send remittances to elderly parents on a monthly basis. Only those with relatives (e.g., brothers and sisters) working outside the Philippines do not send money regularly since they are able to share the responsibility of financial support.

Another mechanism on which transnational families rely is consanguineal responsibility, that is, the extension of responsibility to parents, siblings, and even nieces and nephews for those without children. The high level of interdependency in extended families of Filipina domestic workers is first illustrated by the tremendous responsibility women have for their extended kin in the Philippines. Many single domestic workers shoulder the financial costs of reproduction of the extended family by investing in the education of younger generations. While married domestic workers with children usually cover the schooling only of their own children, those who migrated as single women support extended kin prior to marriage. Besides sending remittances to cover the day-to-day living expenses of their parents and other relatives, Pacita Areza and

Letty Xavier, for example, covered the costs of the college education of at least four nieces and nephews before getting married in the United States.

> I sent my sisters to school. . . . One finished a degree in education and the other one in commerce. One only finished high school. . . . Until now, I still help my nieces and nephews. I am sending them to school. With one of my brothers, I am helping him send his two children to college. One just graduated last March and one has two more years to go. With one of my sisters, she has two children and she does not have a job and she is separated from her husband. I help her out—I am helping by paying for their schooling. Once all my nieces and nephews are done with their schooling, I can go back to the Philippines. (Pacita Domingo Areza, married with no children, domestic worker in Los Angeles)

> From the start, when I started working in the Philippines, I have helped my family significantly. My nieces and nephews, I sent them to school. . . . One of the first nephews I sent to school is a civil engineer. . . . The second one is a midwife, and the third one is a teacher. The next two sisters are also in education, and they are all board passers. My dreams have come true through them. Right now, one is in nautical school, and he is going overseas soon. Right now, I have stopped supporting them. Those I sent to school, I want them to be the ones supporting their younger brothers and sisters. They are their responsibilities already. I think I have done my part. (Letty Xavier, married, domestic worker in Los Angeles)

Of thirteen migrant workers who at one point had been single women in Los Angeles, five women sent at least three or more nieces and nephews to college. Others provided valuable financial support to their families. Besides subsidizing the everyday living expenses of elderly parents, some purchased the house where their parents and siblings, including those with children, now live and sent at least one younger relative to college. As Gloria Diaz, a domestic worker in Rome with a sister in the United States, explains, they would feel guilty if they did not provide for their relatives in need: "When I don't send money, I feel guilty because my mother is alone, and it is my obligation to help."

Often, the primary contribution of migrant domestic workers to the "kin work" of the extended family is the education of younger generations. In acknowledgment of their extensive support, younger members of their extended family often consider the migrants second mothers. Nieces and nephews refer to them as "Mama" or "Nanay" (Mom) as opposed to just the customary reference of "Tita" (Aunt). For domestic workers, their financial assistance to the family provides them the most tangible reward for their labor. Because of a cultural system based on an economy of gratitude, the immense generosity of migrant workers, especially adult single migrants, guarantees them a well-established kinship base if they choose to return to the Philippines. This economy of gratitude is premised on the value of *utang na loob,* literally, debt of the soul, in which favors are returned with lifelong debt.

The cooperation of sending younger members of the extended family to college also operates on the system of generalized family exchange among kin (Peterson 1993).

In such a system, the success of one member of the family represents the success of the family as a collective unit. Peterson defines this family exchange system as entailing an open reciprocal exchange: "Generalized exchanges are those in which A gives to B, B gives to C, C gives to a D, and D gives to an A" (1993, 572). By sending one or more persons to college, domestic workers assume that those whom they send to school will reciprocate by later supporting their younger siblings and relatives through school. These younger relatives are then culturally expected to provide care and support for the domestic worker once she chooses to return and retire in the Philippines.

The high level of interdependency among extended families is also reflected in the reliance of migrant parents on grandparents, aunts, and other relatives for the care of dependents left in the Philippines. In the Philippines, it is not uncommon for families to take in extended family members whose own immediate families may not be able to provide as much material or emotional security. Fosterage of children is in fact a common practice among extended kin in the Philippines (Peterson 1993). For example, Cecilia Impelido, a street vendor in Rome, was raised by her grandmother for fourteen years. The arrangement, she claims, strengthened kinship ties to her maternal grandmother in the province even as it eased the financial costs of reproduction for her parents in Manila. Transnational families are embedded in the cultural practice of fosterage. Parents outside the Philippines rely on other relatives to act as "guardians" of their children. In exchange, the remittances sent by parents to dependents in the Philippines benefit the "guardians." The reciprocal bond of dependency between migrant parents and guardians keeps the family intact: migrant parents usually rely on female kin—grandmothers, aunts, and other relatives—to care for the children they have left behind in the Philippines, while caregiving relatives are more than likely ensured a secure flow of monthly remittances.

Inasmuch as their maintenance is aided by relations with extended kin, transnational households strengthen extended family kinship, with children (and also elderly parents) acting as the enduring embodiment of the bond of interdependency. Migrants rely on extended kin to care for their dependents, while extended kin raise their standard of living with the financial support provided by migrant workers. The extended family bolsters the option of migration for individuals otherwise bound by duties and responsibilities to dependents in the Philippines. Thus, transnational households depend on the resilience of extended family bonds in the Philippines. They form not solely from the limits imposed by the structures of globalization and the manipulation of these structures by migrants. The persisting cultural value of familism assists with the formation of transnational households as much as the structural forces of globalization.

A Description of the Filipino Transnational Family

In this section, I describe the Filipino transnational family by presenting vignettes of the two most common forms of transnational households in the Filipino diaspora. Transnational households can be divided into three subcategories: one-parent-abroad transnational households, two-parent-abroad transnational households, and adult-child(ren)-abroad transnational households. One-parent-abroad transnational households are families with one parent—a mother or a father—producing income abroad as other members carry out the functions of reproduction, socialization, and the rest of consumption in the Philippines. In two-parent-abroad transnational households, both the mother and the father are migrant laborers, while the children usually reside together in the Philippines under the care of other relatives. Finally, adult-children-abroad transnational households are families in which the earnings of adult children as migrant laborers provide necessary or additional financial support to relatives (e.g., parents, brothers, and sisters) in the Philippines.

The two most common forms of transnational households are one-parent-abroad and adult-children-abroad households. Among my interviewees in Los Angeles, twelve of twenty married domestic workers maintain one-parent-abroad transnational households. Only three married women maintain two-parent-abroad transnational households, which suggests that parents are hard pressed to leave children behind without any direct parental supervision. Finally, five of six single women maintain adult-children-abroad transnational households.[4]

The two vignettes that follow place a microscope on the migrant family to interrogate its transformations, household dynamics, and the meanings and consequences of migration to family relations. Recognizing and examining the various ways and means by which migrants maintain their families illustrate the social process of transnational household formation. Hence, analyzing migrant households reveals the structures that mold and influence the family life of migrants and the resources that families in turn utilize to perform essential tasks in household maintenance.

Vicky Diaz: An Example of a One-Parent-Abroad Transnational Family

In 1988, Vicky Diaz, a 34-year-old mother of five children between the ages of ten and two years old, left the Philippines for Taiwan. Lured by the financial rewards of employment outside the Philippines, Vicky Diaz had not been content with her salary as a public school teacher in the Philippines, nor had she been comfortable with the insecurities of running a travel agency in Manila. Although made more lucrative by the greater demand for employment outside the Philippines in the preceding ten years, the business of travel agencies had not been as profitable in the late 1980s. And so Vicky decided to move to Taiwan, because there the wages of a domestic worker would give her a more secure income.

In Taiwan, Vicky worked as a housekeeper and a factory worker but mostly as a janitor, for which she earned a salary of approximately $1,000 a month. Vicky, who speaks English very well, also subsidized her earnings by teaching English part-time at nights:

> In Taiwan, darling, what I mopped everyday would be five floors. If you put them all together, it would be around five miles. I surely learned how to use the floor polisher and mop the whole day. I would have to clean thirty bathrooms and thirty toilets, that much. I was able to work part-time in the evenings. At night, I got my chance to teach. I taught English grammar. I made good money doing that because per head it is ten

dollars an hour. And I had five students who would pay me and so that is $50 an hour. That is how I made good money. Every other day, I would teach them English. That was my additional income.

Although satisfied with her earnings in Taiwan, Vicky found that the situation of illegal workers like herself became more tenuous with the greater enforcement of restrictive polices against migrants in the early 1990s. She decided to leave Taiwan and return to the Philippines in 1992.

Yet, her return to the Philippines after five years in Taiwan turned out to be just a "stopover" on her way to the United States:

> From Taiwan, I only stayed in the Philippines for three months. I used this time to fix my papers to come here. After Taiwan, my real target was the United States. It was because I knew that America is the land of promises and the land of opportunities. I had several friends who went to America and never went back to the Philippines. I figured it was because life was wonderful in the United States. . . . So, why not give myself the same opportunity?

Although geographically distanced from her children for at least five years, Vicky did not seem at all concerned about or interested in spending "quality" time with them. The prolonged distance from her family seemed to have fostered feelings of emotional distance in Vicky. Only a few months after her return to the Philippines, Vicky used her savings from Taiwan to pay a travel agency 160,000 pesos (approximately $8,000) for the use of another woman's passport to enter the United States. As Vicky herself states, "You know, in the Philippines, nothing is impossible if you have the money."

Considering her middle-class status after running a travel agency in the Philippines and her ability to raise such a huge sum of money for her trip to the United States, one can easily wonder why Vicky risked such a prolonged separation from her family. Over a span of nine years, Vicky spent only three months with her husband and children in the Philippines. Clearly an absentee mother for most of her children's adolescence, Vicky explained that it was for her family's benefit that she came in the United States:

> They were saddened by my departure. Even until now my children are trying to convince me to go home. . . . The children were not angry when I left because they were still very young when I left them. My husband could not get angry either because he knew that was the only way I could seriously help him raise our children, so that our children could be sent to school.

When assessing the effects of separation to her family, Vicky downplayed the emotional strains engendered by separation by highlighting its material rewards. Neither her marriage nor her relations with her children were of great concern to her. Clearly, her family's desire for her to return to the Philippines was not given much consideration. Instead, Vicky insisted that her family needed her higher earnings outside the

Philippines. Although aware of her children's persistent requests for her return to the Philippines, Vicky was not convinced that her family could sustain its middle-class status without her earnings outside the country.

In the United States, Vicky initially worked as a domestic worker, primarily caring for a two-year-old boy for a wealthy family in Beverly Hills. As the mother "would just be sitting around, smoking and making a mess," Vicky cleaned, cooked, and cared for the boy for $400 a week, clearly a sharp contrast to the $40 she pays her own family's live-in domestic worker in the Philippines. Vicky did not like being a housekeeper for two main reasons: the physically demanding load and the excruciating loneliness, heightened by the contradiction of caring for someone else's children while not caring for her own.

> Even though it paid well, you are sinking in the amount of your work. Even while you are ironing the clothes, they can still call you to the kitchen to wash the plates. It was also very depressing. The only thing you can do is give all your love to the child. In my absence from my children, the most I could do with my situation is give all my love to that child.

Not completely indifferent about the separation her family has endured for almost ten years, Vicky did entertain feelings of regret over missing the formative years of her children's adolescence:

> What saddens me the most about my situation is that during the formative years of their childhood, I was not there for them. That is the time when children really need their mother, and I was not there for them.

Yet for Vicky, the economic rewards of separation softened its emotional costs:

> In my one year in the U.S., I was able to invest on a jitney. I wanted to do that so that no matter what happens with me, my husband does not have a hard time financially. . . . *Of course, I have neglected them and the least I could do to make up for this is to make their lives a little bit easier. I could ease their lives for them materially.* That's how I console myself. . . . Besides the jitney, there's the washing machine and TV. In the Philippines, it is hard to get to buy these things, right? At least they are not desolate and are at least provided for well.

To overcome the emotional gaps in her family, Vicky relied on "commodifying her love" and compensated for her absence with material goods. Yet while Vicky claimed that she works outside the Philippines so that her family would not "starve," it is actually more accurate to say that Vicky worked in the United States to sustain a comfortable middle-class life for her family in the Philippines.

Vicky hoped that her family would eventually reunite in the United States, because she was convinced that there are few opportunities available for her family in the Philippines. Yet without legal documents, she was unable to sponsor the migration of her family. Obtaining legal status continues to be the biggest challenge for Vicky and has been the main obstacle blocking the reunification of her family. Yet, while Vicky hopes for the relocation of her entire family to the United States, her children ironically prefer to witness the reunification of their family much sooner and would rather have Vicky return to the Philippines.

Maria Batung: An Example of a Children-Abroad Transnational Household in Los Angeles

A single domestic worker in Los Angeles, Maria Batung has been working for a Filipino family for more than twelve years and supports her family in the Philippines with her earnings in the United States.

In the Philippines, Maria also worked as a domestic worker—a nanny—because without a college degree or appropriate networks she did not have access to other types of employment in Manila. Maria had been attending college prior to entering domestic work, but she had to give up her aspirations for a college degree because her parents, whose sole income had been her father's sporadic earnings as a carpenter, could not afford to send her or any of her five brothers and sisters to school.

In Manila, she usually worked for foreigners, mostly diplomats and businessmen. In 1980, ten years after she started working as a domestic helper, Maria accepted the offer of a former employer to move to London with them. Although she could have continued working for the English family, Maria decided, after four years in London, to take up the offer of another former employer, a Filipino family, but this time for a job in the United States. These employers were migrating to the United States to establish an import-export rattan furniture business in southern California and, by investing capital in the United States, qualified to bring a small number of employees with them, including their former domestic worker, Maria. They covered all of her travel expenses and the costs of obtaining legal papers to work in the United States. With their sponsorship, Maria was able to obtain a green card to stay in the United States permanently.

Maria has been very satisfied with her work, earning far more than she ever did in London ($150 per month), always having a manageable workload, and not having to deal with demanding or strict employers.

> I earn enough so that I could help my family in the Philippines. I get more than $1,000 a month, and everything is free. They pay for my Social Security, and they handled my papers. They pay for my ticket home every year. When I go, they also give me vacation pay for two months. That is why I don't have a problem here. Everything is free and they also cover my insurance. . . . It is OK. Anytime I want to leave I can. . . . That is why I lasted long with this family. If that were not the case, I would have probably returned to the Philippines a long time ago.

Of all the employment benefits she receives, the one Maria appreciates the most is her annual vacation—a two-month paid vacation and a round-trip ticket to the Philippines—for it affords her time to spend with her father. Very satisfied with her job, Maria plans to keep it until she is old herself.

Without personal expenses to cover, Maria invests all of her earnings in her family in the Philippines. She has sent numerous relatives to college, wanting to ensure that no one else in her family has to abandon his or her studies and settle for domestic work as she was forced to do almost thirty years ago. When asked whether she had sent her relatives money, she replied,

> I send my father money and my nieces and nephews I equally sent to school. For every single sibling of mine, I sent one of their children to school. So there is no jealousy. The rest they could send to school on their own, but each one of them I sent at least one of their children to school. It was equal so there were no bad feelings. . . .
>
> So, I am very happy. Although I was not able to finish school, these are the ones that I was able to ensure finished their education. It is hard when you don't finish. I told them that they would have a hard time if they did not have a degree and that it was necessary that they finish school. Thank God they were able to finish school.

Because Maria sends most of her earnings to the Philippines, she has not been able to accumulate any savings after many years of domestic work, a fact that is not of concern for Maria. With her legal status in the United States, she is secure that she will qualify to receive government aid such as Social Security once she retires.

Maria's earnings not only cover the college education of younger relatives but also assist her family with day-to-day living expenses.

> The last time I sent money it was for $500. That is the lowest. It is mostly $1,000 or $600 or $700. So I have no savings. My bank is with all those that I sent to school. I also had a house built in the Philippines where my father lives right now. I had that house remodeled and everything. My father was telling me that maybe when I get older I would regret what I did because they would no longer recognize me. But I told him that they can do what they want to do, but I am happy that I was able to help them.

The generosity of Maria is voluntary, and for it her most satisfying rewards have been the love of her family and their appreciation for her tremendous financial support. While very appreciative of the money and material goods Maria provides them, Maria's relatives also hope that she will soon return and settle down in the Philippines so that they may have the opportunity to transform their relationship to one that is more intimate than the monthly remittances she sends them. A single adult migrant in a transnational family, Maria Batung works in Los Angeles to sustain her family in the Philippines.

Conclusion

The formation of transnational families is a creative response to and an adaptive strategy against the economic challenges and legal barriers faced by migrant workers. It has been adapted as a household form by members of numerous migrant groups in the United States, including those from the Philippines. By structurally reconstituting their family form from a nuclear to a transnational household, Filipino migrants, like other migrants, increase the material benefits afforded by their wages; maintain a family despite the legal restrictions constraining the migration of dependents; and, in many cases, reconstitute the traditional gender roles in the family. However, the formation of transnational households does more than reveal the creativity, agency, and resistance of migrants facing structural barriers in society. To some extent, it unavoidably causes emotional distance and strains among members of transnational families.

The challenge for members of transnational families is to confront and negotiate the emotional costs imposed by geographic distance. They do so in various ways. Like the Latina transnational mothers interviewed by Hondagneu-Sotelo and Avila (1997) in Los Angeles, Filipina transnational mothers and daughters rationalize distance by taking advantage of the communication technology in this age of late capitalism. They increase their familiarity with members of their families located thousands of miles away by using the telephone frequently and by writing letters at least once a week.

The familiarity allowed by the rationalization of distance is, however, limited and cannot replace fully the intimacy of daily interactions. Mothers such as Vicky Diaz and daughters such as Maria Batung are aware of this fact, but they reason that the financial gains afforded by the maintenance of transnational families is worth its emotional costs. Thus, adult children such as Maria generally do not see an end to their separation from their families in the near future as they plan to maximize their earnings and work until they are no longer able bodied. Similarly, mothers such as Vicky Diaz extend the duration of separation in their families so as to maximize the financial gains of migration. Lured by the greater income available in the United States, most of them plan to stay indefinitely. In the process, they have to put emotional tensions in their families aside for the sake of financial security.

The priority given to material rewards in the family results in the temporal extension of transnational households. Parents in Los Angeles do wish for their children to somehow join them in the United States so as to take advantage of the greater opportunities in this country (especially education, as is recognized universally). Yet, in Los Angeles, many transnational mothers, like Vicky, are undocumented. If not undocumented, they have been caught in the legal bind of obtaining their legal status only after their children reach adult age, when children are no longer eligible for immediate family reunification. Hence, family reunification for U.S. migrants may be possible only with their return to the Philippines. This may explain why the dependents of migrants such as Vicky and Maria strongly prefer to see their families reunify via return migration.

The emotional difficulties wrought in the maintenance of transnational households remain a continuous challenge for migrants and the relatives they have left behind in the Philippines. Interestingly, members of transnational households have varying opinions regarding this problem. Migrants tend to see the material gains of transnational households as being worth their emotional costs. This reasoning enables them to prolong the geographic separation of the family. In contrast, family members in the Philippines consider the material gains not worth the emotional costs. As a result, they prefer to see the immediate reunification of their families in the Philippines.

This cross-national difference in opinion shows that, just like other family forms, the reproduction of the transnational household entails varying and sometimes conflicting experiences, concerns, and priorities for different members of the family.

NOTES

This chapter is an abridged version of chapter 4 of my doctoral dissertation, *The Global Servants: (Im)Migrant Filipina Domestic Workers in Rome and Los Angeles,* University of California at Berkeley. I would like to thank Evelyn Nakano Glenn, Arlie Hochschild, Michael Omi, and Raka Ray for their helpful comments and suggestions. I would also like to thank Charlotte Chiu, Angela Gallegos, Mimi Motoyoshi, and Jennifer Lee for their support through the completion of this chapter.

1. See Basch et al. 1994; Chavez 1992; Curry 1988; Hondagneu-Sotelo 1994; Laguerre 1994; Massey et al. 1987; Paz-Cruz 1987.

2. In 1934, the Tydings-McDuffie Act limited the migration of Filipinos into the United States to an annual quota of fifty (Takaki 1989).

3. See the recent anthology by Perea, *Immigrants Out!* (1997).

4. Only one single woman does not send remittances to her family in the Philippines regularly, because her parents and all of her siblings also live in Los Angeles. She therefore falls under the category of single householder.

REFERENCES

Agbayani-Siewart, Pauline, and Linda Revilla. 1995. Filipino Americans. Pp. 134–68 in Pyong Gap Min (ed.), *Asian Americans: Contemporary Trends and Issues.* Thousand Oaks, CA: Sage.

Almirol, Edwin. 1982. Rights and Obligations in Filipino American Families. *Journal of Comparative Family Studies* 3(3): 291–306.

Basch, Linda, Nina Glick Schiller, and Cristina Szanton Blanc. 1994. *Nations Unbound: Transnational Projects, Postcolonial Predicaments, and Deterritorialized Nation States.* Langhorn, PA: Gordon and Breach Science Publishers.

Chavez, Leo. 1997. Immigration Reform and Nativism: The Nationalist Response to the Transnationalist Challenge. Pp. 61–77 in Juan F. Perea (ed.), *Immigrants Out! The New Nativism and the Anti-Immigrant Impulse in the United States.* New York: New York University Press.

———. 1992. *Shadowed Lives: Undocumented Immigrants in American Society.* Fort Worth, TX: Harcourt Brace.

Curry, Julia. 1988. Labor Migration and Familial Responsibilities: Experiences of Mexican Women. Pp. 47–63 in Margarita Melville (ed.), *Mexicanas at Work in the United States.* Houston: Mexican American Studies Program, University of Houston.

Espiritu, Yen Le. 1997. *Asian American Women and Men.* Thousand Oaks, CA: Sage.

———. 1995. *Filipino American Lives.* Philadelphia: Temple University Press.

Feagin, Joe. 1997. Old Poison in New Bottles: The Deep Roots of Modern Nativism. Pp. 13–43 in Juan F. Perea (ed.), *Immigrants Out! The New Nativism and the Anti-Immigrant Impulse in the United States.* New York: New York University Press.

Glenn, Evelyn Nakano. 1983. Split Household, Small Producer, and Dual Wage Earner: An Analysis of Chinese-American Family Strategies. *Journal of Marriage and the Family* 45 (February): 35–46.

Hondagneu-Sotelo, Pierrette. 1994. *Gendered Transitions: Mexican Experiences of Migration.* Berkeley: University of California Press.

Hondagneu-Sotelo, Pierrette, and Ernestine Avila. 1997. "I'm Here, but I'm There": The Meanings of Latina Transnational Motherhood. *Gender and Society* 11(5): 548–71.

Laguerre, Michel. 1994. Headquarters and Subsidiaries: Haitian Immigrant Family Households in New York City. Pp. 47–61 in Ronald Taylor (ed.), *Minority Families in the United States.* Englewood Cliffs, NJ: Prentice-Hall.

Martin, Philip. 1995. Proposition 187 in California. *International Migration Review* 29(1): 255–63.

Massey, Douglas et al. 1987. *Return to Aztlan: The Social Process of International Migration from Western Mexico.* Berkeley: University of California Press.

Medina, Belinda T. G. 1991. *The Filipino Family: A Text with Selected Readings.* Quezon City: University of the Philippines Press.

Ong, Aihwa. 1996. Cultural Citizenship as Subject-Making: Immigrants Negotiate Racial and Cultural Boundaries in the United States. *Contemporary Anthropology* 37(5): 737–62.

Ong, Paul, and Tania Azores. 1994a. Asian Immigrants in Los Angeles: Diversity and Divisions. Pp. 100–129 in Paul Ong et al. (eds.), *The New Asian Immigration in Los Angeles and Global Restructuring.* Philadelphia: Temple University Press.

———. 1994b. The Migration and Incorporation of Filipino Nurses. Pp. 164–95 in Paul Ong et al. (eds.), *The New Asian Immigration in Los Angeles and Global Restructuring.* Philadelphia: Temple University Press.

Parreñas, Rhacel Salazar. 1998a. "White Trash" Meets the "Little Brown Monkeys": The Taxi Dance Hall as a Site of Interracial and Gender Alliances between White Working-Class Women and Filipino Immigrant Men in the 1920s and '30s. *Amerasia Journal* 24(2): 115–34.

———. 1998b. *The Global Servants: (Im)Migrant Filipina Domestic Workers in Rome and Los Angeles.* Ph.D. dissertation, University of California, Berkeley.

Paz-Cruz, Victoria. 1987. *Seasonal Orphans and Solo Parents: The Impacts of Overseas Migration.* Quezon City, Philippines: Scalabrini Migration Center.

Perea, Juan, ed. 1997. *Immigrants Out! The New Nativism and the Anti-Immigrant Impulse in the United States.* New York: New York University Press.

Peterson, Jean Treloggen. 1993. Generalized Extended Family Exchange: A Case from the Philippines. *Journal of Marriage and the Family* 55 (August): 570–84.

Portes, Alejandro, and Rubén Rumbaut. 1996. *Immigrant America: A Portrait* (2d ed.). Berkeley: University of California Press.

Sassen, Saskia. 1994. *Cities in a World Economy.* Thousand Oaks, CA: Pine Forge Press.

———. 1988. *The Mobility of Labor and Capital: A Study in International Investment and Labor.* New York: Cambridge University Press.

Tadiar, Neferti Xina. 1997. Domestic Bodies of the Philippines. *Sojourn* 12(2): 153–91.

Takaki, Ronald. 1989. *Strangers in a Different Shore.* Boston: Little, Brown.

Yamanaka, Keiko, and Kent McClelland. 1994. Earning the Model-Minority Image: Diverse Strategies of Economic Adaptation by Asian American Women. *Ethnic and Racial Studies* 17(1): 79–114.

Chapter 9

Enclaves, Ethnoburbs, and New Patterns of Settlement among Asian Immigrants

Wei Li and Emily Skop

Since the late 1960s, the combination of global economic restructuring, changing geopolitical contexts, and shifting American immigration policies has set in motion significant flows of Asian immigrants and refugees to the United States. Even as refugee admissions wax and wane, family-sponsored immigration continues to grow, and record numbers of highly skilled, professional immigrants and wealthy investors have also joined the flow. At the same time, patterns of Asian immigrant settlement have changed. Traditional central city enclaves such as "Chinatown," "Little Tokyo," or "Manila Town" no longer absorb the majority of newcomers from various countries of origin and with diverse socioeconomic backgrounds. Instead, many Asian immigrants (especially upper- and middle-class newcomers) tend to avoid central city enclaves since they have the financial resources to settle directly in suburbs that offer decent housing, high-performing schools, and superior living conditions and public amenities. As a result, more and more suburban neighborhoods in the nation are becoming increasingly multiracial, multiethnic, multilingual, multicultural, and multinational. This new pattern of Asian American settlement challenges the widely accepted characterization of the suburbs as the citadel of non-Hispanic white, middle-class America.

This chapter discusses the issues surrounding the changing settlement patterns among Asian American groups in the United States. It will first provide a brief demographic overview of contemporary Asian America, followed by a description of shifting geographic distributions of the Asian American population at the state and metropolitan levels. The chapter then focuses on different settlement types among Asian American groups within metropolitan areas, from traditional central city enclaves to multiethnic suburbs (known as "ethnoburbs"), and demonstrates the similarities and differences between these settlement types. The chapter concludes with a discussion of the implications of divergent settlement forms for the economic, cultural, and political incorporation of contemporary Asian Americans as well as of the way these patterns reinforce transnational processes in a globalizing world.

Demographic Overview of Asian Americans

Since the mid-nineteenth century, Asian Americans have been present in the United States, traditionally working as laborers in agriculture, fishing, mining, manufacturing, and construction, and as service workers and small business owners. Historically, however, their numbers and growth rates have been low, primarily because of exclusionary national immigration and naturalization laws (like the 1882 Chinese Exclusion Act, the 1917 Asiatic Barred Zone, and the 1923 *U.S. v. Bhagat Singh Thind* Supreme Court case) and restrictive state legislation on marriage, landholding, and voting (including antimiscegenation laws and anti-alien land laws). These discriminatory regulations, along with other prohibitive social practices, resulted in declining Asian immigration, extreme sex ratio imbalances, limited occupation choices, and forced spatial segregation in isolated communities. Imbalanced natural growth rates among different Asian American groups and the lack of significant and self-sustaining communities of Asian Americans existed well into the twentieth century.

In the 1960s the situation began to change. Since then, the number of Asian Americans has dramatically increased, primarily because of shifting U.S. immigration policies, rapid economic development in Asia, as well as sometimes unstable geopolitical situations in home countries, as in Vietnam during and after the Vietnam War. Thus, the local, lived experiences of Asian Americans in the United States are set within the shifting landscape of globalization.

Because international economic restructuring promotes the flows of capital, information, services, and people across national borders, there has been a growing demand for a highly skilled workforce and capital investors to engage in an advanced economy. When such needs cannot be fulfilled domestically, the United States, along with other developed countries, looks overseas for an alternative source of labor and investors. Many immigrants from Asia are well prepared for, and fit into, the employment needs of the globalizing U.S. economy: this fact is partially the result of the economic take-off of the four Asian Little Dragons (Hong Kong, Singapore, South Korea, and Taiwan) beginning in the 1960s, followed by mainland China, India, and some ASEAN countries (e.g., Indonesia, Malaysia, and Thailand) in more recent decades. As these economies have become increasingly incorporated into the global economy, a highly educated and highly skilled middle- and upper-class population, some with entrepreneur experiences, has emerged. Many of these individuals are primed to immigrate to the United States because they have high levels of education, professional training, entrepreneurial skills, and/or financial resources needed in the burgeoning knowledge-based economy.

At the same time, a large number of lower-skilled and less-educated individuals, lured by family sponsorship and American job opportunities, join the immigrant waves from Asia. In fact, family reunification is the most important avenue through which many individuals qualify for admission and "lawful permanent residence" in the United States. Family reunification is particularly important for immigrants from places like the Philippines, Vietnam, and China. Moreover, the end of the Vietnam War in 1975 yielded large refugee flows from Southeast Asia. Many Vietnamese, Cambodian, Laotian, and Hmong refugees arrived penniless and mentally distressed after surviving war and trauma when their lives were constantly threatened. But as refugees, they were able to access a variety of social service programs that distinguishes their experiences from those of other types of newcomers to the United States.

The unprecedented growth of the Asian population in the United States since the 1960s could not have taken place without the key role of the state in initiating flows. The first of many U.S. immigration policies to prompt this growth was the 1965 Immigration Act, which opened the door to new flows of immigration from all parts of the world, including Asia, since the national-origin quota system was abolished and a preference system was introduced based on two general categories of admission: family sponsored and employment based. More recently, the 1980 Refugee Act facilitated the migration and settlement of many Southeast Asian refugees in the United States. Then, the Immigration and Nationality Act of 1990 prompted the growth of highly skilled immigration from Asia, especially from India and China, to the United States. The 1990 legislation tripled the ceiling on employment-based visas and created the H-1B nonimmigrant visa program to allow for the admission of temporary workers employed in "specialty occupations" that require highly specialized knowledge and at least a bachelor's degree or its equivalent; INS data reveals that Asia is the leading contributor of both employment-based immigrants and H-1B temporary workers. At the same time, the legislation allowed H-1B visa holders to bring their immediate families with them (under the H-4 visa program) and also made H-1B visa holders eligible to adjust their legal status to that of permanent residence during their six-year maximum visa period, thus allowing Asian immigrants further opportunities for settling in the United States. Additionally, more recent immigration legislation created L-1 visas (which allow companies operating both in the United States and abroad to transfer certain classes of employee from its foreign operations to the U.S. operations for up to seven years) and EB-5 visas (for investor immigrants who bring $1 million and create at least ten jobs).

The result of all of these shifting immigration policies is the rapid and continued growth of the Asian immigrant population in the United States. Even though Asian Americans remain a relatively small part of the total population—currently less than 5 percent—they are among the fastest growing minority groups in the United States today (with a growth rate of 18.1 percent in the first four years into the twenty-first century alone). According to the U.S. Census, from 1990 to 2004, the increase in the Asian American population was upwards of 80 percent, from 6.9 million in 1990 to 12.1 million in 2004.[1] In comparison, the total U.S. population grew by 21 percent, from 248.7 million in 1990 to 285 million in 2004.[2]

Contemporary Asian America is not only growing but also more diverse than it has ever been. As figure 9.1 illustrates, the population includes first-generation immigrants as well as increasing percentages of second- and third-generation American-born natives. At the same time, among all subgroups, the Chinese remain the largest subgroup with a total of 2.9 million in 2004, a 76 percent increase from 1990. Other Asian American subgroups include the rapidly increasing Asian Indian population, which reached 2.2 million in 2004 (a 175 percent increase from 1990), the fast-growing Vietnamese population, which grew to almost 1.3 million in 2004 (a 106 percent increase from 1990), the more moderately growing Filipino (2.1 million) and Korean (1.3 million)

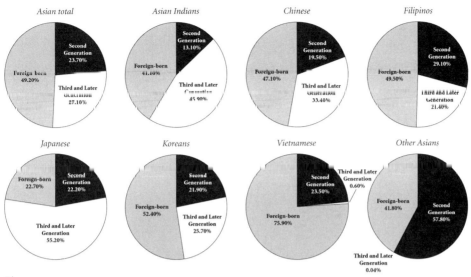

Fig. 9.1

populations, whose populations grew approximately 50 percent since 1990, and the slowly declining Japanese population, which numbered 847,562 in 1990 and 832,039 in 2004. The majority of this increase in contemporary Asian America stems from immigration, but clearly, natural increase has begun to stimulate the growth of a burgeoning, native-born Asian American population.

Geographic Distribution of Asian Americans

The geographic distribution of Asian Americans in the United States has always been uneven, but fairly stable, with the same ten states appearing on the list year in and year out. California, New York, and Hawaii, as historical destination states, have traditionally had the largest numbers of Asian Americans. These three states remained as the top three concentrations for the Asian population until 1990, when new patterns began to emerge. Most importantly, Hawaii was surpassed by Texas in 2000 and by both Texas and New Jersey in 2004; by 2004, it was ranked number five among the top ten states for Asian Americans. At the same time, Illinois, Washington, Florida, Virginia, and Massachusetts have been on the list of top ten states for the Asian American population since 1990, with little change between years.

These top ten states still dominate Asian Americans' presence in the United States, with more than three-quarters of the national total. However there is a slight trend towards deconcentration, largely due to the rapid increase of some nontraditional destination states for Asian Americans. As shown in table 9.1, the share of top ten states combined has slightly decreased in recent years, from 79 percent in 1990 to less than 76 percent in 2004. California shows the most marked (though minor) decline among these states; only 35 percent of Asian Americans, compared with nearly 40 percent in 1990, call this traditional destination "home" in 2004.

TABLE 9.1
Asian Americans in the U.S. and Top Ten States, 1990–2004

	1990—% national total	2000—% national total	2004—% national total
National total	*6,908,638*	*10,242,998*	*12,097,281*
1	California - 39.6	California - 36.1	California - 35.2
2	New York - 10.0	New York - 10.2	New York - 10.0
3	Hawaii - 7.6	Texas 5.5	Texas - 5.8
4	Texas - 4.5	Hawaii - 4.9	New Jersey - 5.0
5	Illinois - 4.1	New Jersey - 4.7	Hawaii - 4.3
6	New Jersey - 3.9	Illinois - 4.1	Illinois - 4.2
7	Washington - 2.8	Washington - 3.1	Washington - 3.2
8	Virginia - 2.3	Florida - 2.6	Florida - 2.9
9	Florida - 2.2	Virginia - 2.5	Virginia - 2.7
10	Massachusetts - 2.1	Massachusetts - 2.3	Massachusetts - 2.3
% top ten total	*79.0%*	*76.2%*	*75.6%*

SOURCE: Calculations based on U.S. Census—1990 STF1; 2000 SF2; 2004 ACS.

The most dramatic changes in the geographic distributions of Asian Americans have occurred among states that historically have had very limited numbers of Asian Americans. These new destination states include Nevada and Georgia; both states ranked highest in terms of the overall growth of Asian Americans; Nevada experienced a 271 percent increase from 1990 to 2004 (45 percent of which occurred in the 2000–2004 period alone), and Georgia's Asian American population grew by 223 percent between 1990 and 2004 (38 percent of which occurred in the 2000–2004 period alone). In fact, by 2004, the number of Asian Americans in Georgia reached 238,281, which means that this state is now ranked thirteenth in terms of its Asian American population, whereas in 1990 it ranked much lower. Arizona, Delaware, and New Hampshire also experienced at least 100 percent growth between 1990 and 2000, and more than 30 percent increase from 2000 to 2004.

Asian Americans are largely urban bound, and this population continues to cluster in traditional immigrant gateways, which have built upon a rich history of immigration from Asia (and elsewhere), and which have been continually reshaped as a result. In fact, the ten metropolitan areas with the largest Asian populations are the same in 2004 as in 1990, as table 9.2 illustrates. Los Angeles, New York, and San Francisco continue to be the highest-ranking metropolitan areas. Silicon Valley now ranks as the fourth largest Asian American population concentration and has become increasingly important as a destination since 1990. Meanwhile, Honolulu, which used to have one of the largest Asian populations, continues to sustain population losses, primarily because (1) fewer and fewer Asian Americans are moving to this metropolitan area; and (2) the Asian Americans already living there are rapidly aging, so natural increase no longer plays as important a role in the growth of the population.[3]

Interestingly, even though traditional immigrant gateways are still the most significant centers for Asian Americans, these metropolitan areas' share of recent Asian population gains dropped noticeably in recent years. From 2000 to 2004, fewer than half (47 percent) of Asian American population increase occurred in these metropolitan areas, compared to the majority (53 percent) in the 1990s. As a result, some important emerging and expanding metropolitan areas that may not commonly be thought of as Asian American population centers have become important destinations, especially since 1990. Table 9.3 outlines the metropolitan areas exhibiting the highest growth rates for Asian Americans, and provides a measure of where the newest gains in population are taking place. Most of this increase occurs because of significant in-migration, as Asian Americans move to newly emerging immigrant gateways. These metropolitan areas may not commonly be thought of as Asian American destinations, nor do they have significant concentrations of the group; in other words, less than 3 percent of the total population is Asian American, and most have fewer than sixty thousand Asian American residents. Even so, ten years ago, Las Vegas, Riverside, Orlando, Atlanta, Stockton, Tampa, Austin, and Phoenix were not metropolitan areas known in terms of their Asian American populations. But today, each of these newly emerging immigrant gateways is experiencing tremendous population change, sometimes as much as a 200 percent increase in their Asian American population from 1990 to 2004.

TABLE 9.2
Metropolitan Areas with Largest Asian American populations, 2004

Rank 2004	Rank 2000	Rank 1990	Metro area	Population 2004	Share of metro area population (%)
1	1	1	Los Angeles–Long Beach–Santa Ana, CA	1,712,127	13.2
2	2	2	New York–Northern New Jersey–Long Island, NY NJ PA	1,616,189	8.6
3	3	3	San Francisco–Oakland–Fremont, CA	879,495	21.2
4	4	5	San Jose–Sunnyvale–Santa Clara, CA	491,876	28.2
5	6	6	Chicago–Naperville–Joliet, IL-IN-WI	454,300	4.8
6	5	4	Honolulu, HI	413,015	45.9
7	7	7	Washington–Arlington–Alexandria, DC-VA-MD-WV	405,859	7.9
8	8	9	Seattle–Tacoma–Bellevue, WA	308,600	9.7
9	9	8	San Diego–Carlsbad–San Marcos, CA	283,037	9.7
10	10	10	Houston–Baytown–Sugarland, TX	281,894	5.4

SOURCE: Calculations based on Frey's (2006) analysis of U.S. Census—1990 STF1; 2000 SF2; 2004 ACS.

TABLE 9.3
Metropolitan Areas with the Highest Asian American Growth Rates, 2000–2004 and 1990–2000

Rank 2004	Metro area	Population Change 2000–2004 (%)	Rank 2000	Metro Area	Population Change 1990–2000 (%)
1	Las Vegas–Paradise, NV	38.5	1	Las Vegas–Paradise, NV	191.2
2	Riverside–San Bernardino–Ontario, CA	31.1	2	Atlanta–Sandy Springs–Marietta, GA	169.4
3	Orlando, FL	30.2	3	Austin–Round Rock, TX	140.8
4	Atlanta–Sandy Springs–Marietta, GA	28.5	4	Orlando, FL	125.3
5	Stockton, CA	28.4	5	Dallas–Fort Worth–Arlington, TX	108.7
6	Tampa–St. Petersburg–Clearwater, FL	28.4	6	Tampa–St. Petersburg–Clearwater, FL	103.2
7	Austin–Round Rock, TX	28.2	7	Phoenix–Mesa–Scottsdale, AZ	93.4
8	Phoenix–Mesa–Scottsdale, AZ	27.0	8	Minneapolis–St. Paul–Bloomington, MN-WI	92.3
9	Sacramento–Arden–Arcade–Roseville, CA	25.6	9	Detroit–Warren–Livonia, MI	87.3
10	Dallas–Fort Worth–Arlington, TX	24.8	10	Houston–Baytown–Sugar Land, TX	81.9

SOURCE: Calculations based on Frey's (2006) analysis of U.S. Census—1990 STF1; 2000 SF2; 2004 ACS.

Of course, the geographic distributions of Asian Americans vary by subgroup. The traditional immigrant gateway states and metropolitan areas account for the lion's share of most individual Asian American groups. Even so, nearly half of all U.S. states (twenty-four) witnessed a 100 percent or more increase in their Chinese population, topped by Georgia (233 percent) and Kentucky (208 percent). Similarly twenty-nine states witnessed at least a 100 percent increase in their Vietnamese population growth, led by Alabama (476 percent), whereas sixteen states saw their Filipino population more than double, led by Nevada (387 percent). The growth rates of Asian Indians are likewise remarkable during the same period, with many of the highest growth states known for their high-tech economic development, e.g., Utah (538 percent), Arizona (480 percent), Washington (401 percent), Colorado (290 percent), and North Carolina (266 percent). On the other hand, while the population of Japanese grew steadily in some states, about two dozen states experienced absolute decrease among this group.

In terms of metropolitan-level distributions, the New York metropolitan area has the largest number of Chinese and Asian Indians, and the second largest share of Koreans. The greatest percentages of Koreans, as well as Filipinos, live in the Los Angeles metropolitan area. This metropolitan area is the second most important concentration for Chinese and Japanese, while adjacent suburban Orange County has the most Vietnamese. Honolulu has the most Japanese and second most Filipinos. Washington, DC, is the third most important center of Asian Indian and Korean settlement, while Chicago and San Diego act as the second-most and third-most concentrations for Asian Indians and Filipinos, respectively. Finally, Houston and Dallas, both locations that are not typically thought of as Asian American population centers, are home to more than 6 percent of the nation's Vietnamese and nearly 8 percent of its Asian Indians. So, there is considerable regional variation among Asian American subgroups. Though there are clearly some significant concentrations of each group in particular states and particular metropolitan areas, the overall trend is towards deconcentration, and the expansion of the Asian American population to new destinations.

Changing Asian American Settlement Forms

Metropolitan areas in the United States have traditionally been magnets for Asian American immigration, but in the modern metropolis, more complex residential geographies materialize. This is the case primarily because metropolitan areas have undergone major restructuring since the earliest immigrants arrived in U.S. cities. Indeed, the central city has lost its former preeminence as the staging ground for the integration of immigrant newcomers. This shift away from the central city takes place as economic activity moves to exurbia, diverse housing types and housing qualities appear throughout metropolitan areas, and automobiles transform the urban landscape. The changing geography of immigrant settlement is also directly related to a shifting global political and social context, and the diversifying socioeconomic and ethnic origins of immigrants as a result of amended U.S. immigration policy.

Urban ecology describes the process of immigrant spatial succession and assimilation, and its role in the development of the metropolis. The enduring Chicago School model suggests that, upon entry, new arrivals settle in central city ethnic enclaves to save transportation costs, locate near employment opportunities, access the cheapest housing, and gain support from coethnic networks. When the immigrants (and/or their children) move up the economic ladder, they move away from ethnic-specific, central city enclaves to suburbs where they are spatially dispersed among, and racially mixed with, the majority white community. Inherent in the model is the idea that the residential location of immigrants (and subsequent generations) reflects (and affects) the degree of sociocultural and economic incorporation of that ethnic group.

This scenario traditionally fits many Asian immigrants' settlement patterns. For instance, San Francisco's "Chinatown" (known among Chinese immigrants as "the fist big city") has been a historical gateway for Chinese immigrants since the nineteenth century. The 1882 Chinese Exclusion Act further solidified this process, as large numbers of Chinese Americans, immigrants as well as native born, sought refuge and sanctuary in the central city ethnic enclave. Filipinos, also hoping to take advantage of coethnic social networks and to avoid discrimination and violence, settled in "Manila Town," which was adjacent to San Francisco's "Chinatown." Other Chinese enclaves existed in Sacramento (known among Chinese immigrants as "the second city") and Stockton (known among Chinese immigrants as "the third city"). Similarly, the Japanese established "Japan Town" in San Francisco and "Little Tokyo" in Los Angeles. During the late-nineteenth and early-twentieth centuries, "Chinatowns" and other Asian central city enclaves were established across the country in many major metropolitan areas, almost exclusively in inner-city neighborhoods where low rents and run-down conditions predominated.

Some better-off Asian Americans moved out of Asian American–specific enclaves once they achieved socioeconomic success, but others were stuck in these central city neighborhoods regardless of their socioeconomic status as the result of restrictive covenants or discriminatory practices by realtors, lenders, or neighbors. In fact, large-scale suburbanization of Asian Americans did not begin until World War II and after, when mainstream jobs were finally opened up to Asian Americans, racial discrimination in the housing market became outlawed, and the American urban landscape became a predominantly suburban landscape. Even then, however, the suburbanization trend included mostly well-to-do Asian Americans. This process became known as the "uptown vs. downtown" phenomenon: assimilated immigrants or native-born Asian Americans with the economic means moved to suburbs and left the elderly, recently arrived, and poorer immigrants behind in downtown "Chinatowns" or other Asian central city enclaves.

Today, some central city Asian enclaves have survived and endured, as figure 9.2 illustrates. Indeed, some of these communities continue to serve as immigrant gateways, especially the "Chinatowns" of New York City and San Francisco, as well as the smaller ethnic enclaves in other major cities like Chicago and Los Angeles. New immigrants land in these traditional ethnic neighborhoods with job opportunities and housing options, kinship ties and/or social support networks, regardless of their immigration status and English proficiency or lack thereof.

Whether these central city enclaves will persist is a topic that is constantly subject to debate. While "Chinatowns" may remain significant areas of concentration, given

Fig. 9.2

the fact that emigration from China continues at unprecedented rates and the fact that this subgroup is already the largest and longest established of all Asian American subgroups, other predominant Asian American subgroups, like Japanese and Filipinos, face different situations. The former subgroup does not have large new immigrant inflows to sustain central city enclaves, while the latter groups do not have long-lasting ethnic enclaves in most cities to which to turn. Moreover, contemporary globalization trends include a variety of divergent and competing processes that make these central city enclaves a nexus for change. Foreign investment, in the form of financial inflows crossing the Pacific Ocean, as well as the emergence of gentrification in most major downtowns, means that these sites are ripe for urban restructuring. The situation becomes even more complex as these ethnic enclaves become increasingly heterogeneous due to the influx of a variety of newcomers from a multiplicity of sending communities, with heterogeneous legal, demographic, and socioeconomic profiles ranging from undocumented migrants to prominent politicians; from poor immigrants to wealthy second- and later-generation Americans who made their fortunes either in the United States or overseas.

So, the traditional notion of spatial assimilation that the Chicago School characterizes no longer encompasses the spectrum of sociospatial experiences of Asian Americans. While some Asian Americans disproportionately stay in centralized ethnic enclaves, other newcomers are more diverse in their residential behavior. The changing social geography of cities, combined with the recent influx of heterogeneous immigrants, as well as the fact that second-generation (and later) offspring are reaching adulthood, results in both dispersed and concentrated forms.

Perhaps the most intriguing pattern exhibited by Asian Americans is their rapid rate of suburbanization in the United States. Indeed, empirical studies have documented the remarkable suburban-bound trend of contemporary Asian Americans. Data from the 2004 American Community Survey indicates that Asian Americans are more likely to reside in the suburbs than in the central cities of the 102 largest metropolitan areas in the United States. Indeed, over half (54.6 percent) of Asian Americans in these metropolitan areas live in the suburbs. A majority or near majority of every Asian American group lives in suburbia—nearly 60 percent of Asian Indians and Koreans, and about 50 percent of Chinese and Vietnamese.

These results illustrate that newly arrived immigrants do not consider the often crowded and run-down neighborhoods in central cities as their ideal places to live. Most tend to have the financial resources to afford the newer houses, nicer neighborhoods, and better schools that suburbs typically offer. But poorer Asian Americans are also making their way to the suburbs; many are locating in predominantly renter-occupied and/or older inner-ring housing in less affluent suburbs. Consequently, increasing numbers of Asian Americans settle directly in the suburbs without ever having experienced living in a central city ethnic enclave.

Many Asian Americans live in scattered suburbs across metropolitan areas in what are known as dispersed, "heterolocal" communities. In these suburban communities, recent immigrants arrive in a metropolitan area and quickly adopt a dispersed pattern of residential location, all the while managing to maintain and re-create a cohesive community through a variety of means, at a variety of scales, from the local to the transnational. At the same time, immigrants in these suburban communities remain largely invisible because there are few significant, conspicuous concentrations in any particular neighborhoods. The sprinkling of job opportunities near major employers (particularly among highly skilled immigrants working in knowledge-based industries) and the location of well-ranked school districts are oftentimes the only clues to more dense clusters in particular suburban neighborhoods. Though some immigrant institutions and businesses also tend to be located near knowledge-based companies, they are not spatially concentrated either. The newcomers typically occupy what have been habitually thought of as "white" suburban neighborhoods, schools, workplaces, strip malls, movie theaters, and parks. Consequently, the quintessential ethnic enclave (i.e., "Little India" or "Manila Town") does not develop. As a result of living, working, and socializing in the spaces and places associated with "whiteness," the immigrants reinforce their invisible status within the larger sociopolitical community, though many newcomers preserve their ethnic identities through social and religious gatherings. Interestingly, the inconspicuousness of these "heterolocal" cultural landscapes means that immigrants and natives alike interact within both public and private spaces of the community. The scattered patterns of Asian Americans in particular suburban communities is quite common, as in the case of the "saffron suburbs" in metropolitan Phoenix, or the "melting pot suburbs" of the Dallas–Ft. Worth and Washington, DC, metropolitan areas.

With the mushrooming of the Asian American population, particularly in the past decade, it is likely that previously dispersed groups will become increasingly more concentrated in the suburbs. In some places, chain migration has already begun to play an important role in the further agglomeration of Asian Americans. In some cases, Asian American realtors, along with overseas developers who are promoting particular neighborhoods, also direct customers to certain communities. Thus, size-able concentrations emerge where once there were just a few families. Research on the Chinese in San Gabriel Valley in Los Angeles demonstrates this process. When the Asian American population reached a critical mass here in the mid-1990s, and as immigrants became increasingly heterogeneous, suburban residential concentrations materialized. In time, a wider range of ethnic-specific businesses and professional services proliferated, including travel agencies and language schools, realtors, ethnic supermarkets, and immigration, financial, and legal services. A more complete ethnic institutional structure emerged, as did a more collective political voice. The outcome was an "ethnoburb" (i.e., an ethnic suburb), where visible, nonwhite ethnic clusters of residential areas and business districts materialize in the suburbs; and where both established and newer immigrants increasingly seek political representation. Unlike traditionally segregated ethnic enclaves, "ethnoburbs" are open communities where daily interactions occur among multiethnic and multilingual neighbors.

The San Gabriel Valley case is not unique. Filipinos have created their own "ethnoburb" in Daly City, California, as a result of suburbanization and immigration; and Vietnamese congregate in suburban Orange County, California, as result of refugee secondary migration. Koreans have become increasingly concentrated both residentially and commercially in places like Bergen County, in northern New Jersey. Similarly, Asian Indians have a large presence in Edison, New Jersey, which, along with the surrounding communities of Middlesex County, is commonly known throughout the state and the New York metropolitan area as being a main center of Asian American cultural diversity. Moreover, comparable dynamics at the global, national, and local levels have made the transformation of predominantly white suburbs to multiethnic suburbs possible in other large metropolitan areas across the Pacific Rim.

In some cases, Asian Americans have established suburban enclaves in places where a particular group has a large concentration in a smaller geographic area. For instance, Vietnamese Americans, including first-generation refugees and their offspring, have lived in the easternmost suburbs of New Orleans since the late 1970s, making the area probably the densest Vietnamese settlement in the nation. In an area known as "Village d l'est and Versailles" Vietnamese Americans counted for 41.7 percent of total population in 2000. Sadly, as a victim of Hurricane Katrina in 2005, this suburban ethnic enclave's future was unclear. But a few months later, many have already returned and rebuilt their houses and businesses. And a community redevelopment plan carved by local Vietnamese Americans and architects from Vietnam envisions this neighborhood becoming a future "Asian Quarter" of New Orleans, a parallel to the famous French Quarter in downtown.

Most suburban communities are multiethnic communities; newcomers establish a significant concentration within particular neighborhoods but do not necessarily constitute a majority of the population. The ever-increasing heterogeneity within the immigrant community (stemming from a diversity of primary languages, provincialisms, religious affiliations, class statuses, and family types) results in more complex community structures. And with continued growth of the knowledge economy and flexible U.S. immigration policy, spatially clustered and socioeconomically heterogeneous multiethnic communities are likely to continually develop and increase. Unfortunately, this pattern could potentially lead to inter- and intragroup tensions. With increasing concentration and a large influx of immigrants with various backgrounds in American suburbs, there is an imperative need to examine the dynamics under which these communities evolve. The worry is that tensions among newcomers and longtime residents of various backgrounds may arise due to rapid changes of local demographic composition, residential and business landscapes, and community and political dynamics.

Suburban Communities: Implications for Economic, Cultural, and Political Incorporation

Immigrants are often perceived as those who arrive poor and uneducated, who achieve the "American dream" after many years of hard work as manual laborers or through the success of their American-born children. In contrast, many Asian immigrants arrive armed with academic degrees, proficiency in English, professional training, and/or financial resources. They have the advantages and the means to integrate into U.S. society at a much faster pace.[4] Asian Americans also possess the capabilities and know-how to rapidly transform local residential, business, and community landscapes in the suburbs that they call "home."

The new suburban Asian American communities have important implications in terms of Asian American cultural, economic, and political incorporation. Asian Americans have integrated into various aspects of the local fabric by owning/operating businesses, presenting their cultural heritage, and participating in both grassroots and electoral politics. And, as more immigrants become American citizens, many actively participate in local economic, cultural, and political affairs.

Cupertino, California, offers a rich case of transformation from a predominantly non-Hispanic white American suburb to a multiethnic community. Known as the "high-tech heart of Silicon Valley," Cupertino's residential landscapes have been altered with the influx of Asian Americans. Commercial infrastructures display prominent Asian signatures, and multicultural activities abound in community centers. Asian Americans have become an integrated part of daily life, and participate in community affairs and electoral politics. But the transformation has not been without controversies, and sometimes has involved racially connoted incidents. Both Cupertino's city government and its residents are aware of these potential forces dividing their community, and have carried out both top-town and bottom-up initiatives to address such concerns. They are committed to becoming a "model multicultural community in the twenty-first century." How this process happens in other rapidly changing suburban communities remains to be seen, though there is evidence that the metamorphosis of traditionally "white" suburban neighborhoods prompts a variety of reactions, including collectivity, cooperation, and/or conflict.

As Asian Americans settle in the suburbs, suburban Asian American businesses flourish, including those serving the mainstream market's increasing taste for Asian food, fashion, or other culture, as well as those primarily serving coethnics. The latter is especially true in "ethnoburbs." Moreover, contemporary Asian American businesses range from traditional mom-and-pop small retail stores, gift shops, and restaurants to professional services, such as those provided by health, finance, insurance, real estate, and high-tech firms. At the same time, many of these businesses are no longer solely family owned and operated: often firms take on paid employees. Given that central city Asian American enclaves occupy smaller geographic areas with limited capability for further spatial expansion, the suburban Asian American ethnic economy will become an increasingly important and integrated part of the general U.S. economy. As this process unfolds, and to ensure the overall success of Asian American–owned businesses, many hope that new immigrants will be provided more opportunities not only to learn about American business practices and government regulations but also to receive small business loans, in order to assist in their economic incorporation.

At the same time, with the increasing and rapid exchange of immigrants from all parts of Asia to the United States, the influence of Asian arts and culture has great consequences in this new setting. Asian immigrants and American-born natives blend both contemporary and traditional elements of Asian culture with American culture to create a hybridized Asian American culture, which includes literature, music, and the visual arts. In celebration of this transnational culture, Asian American festivals proliferate in both central city enclaves as well as in suburban settings. These festivals are popular in both traditional Asian American immigrant gateways such as New York City and San Francisco and in smaller Asian American communities such as in Phoenix, Arizona, or Austin, Texas. Chinese Lunar New Year celebrations, the Japanese American Masturi festival, the Vietnamese Tet, and more pan-Asian festivals aim at incorporating both historical and contemporary cultural traditions as well as educating other Americans about their cultures. Asian-language schools are also flourishing, often with the hopes of providing native-born Asian Americans with new cultural encounters and language skills beyond those experienced as a consequence of growing up in the United States. Concomitantly, Asian-language media, including print and audiovisual, has rapidly expanded across the country. These activities and institutions not only serve to preserve Asian American culture but also facilitate the overall integration process. Asian languages and cultures have increasingly become part of the "mainstream," evident in Mandarin, Cantonese, Korean, and other Asian-language immersion programs in public schools and the "Asian-inspired fashion" in designing world.

Cultural activities and festivals contribute to the appreciation and mutual understanding of different groups in various communities, but political participation, both in grassroots and electoral politics, is more complicated. Still it is a key step for the overall incorporation of Asian Americans. Many new immigrants, due to their lack of understanding of American politics and/or their noncitizen status, typically stay away from overt forms of political activism. They often use their participation in community organizations as a way to become involved in local politics. For instance, because these neighborhoods are usually located in superior school districts, they guarantee a better-quality education for the immigrant second generation. Many immigrant parents become involved in local school activities and some run for offices of local school boards.

In addition, sometime business organizations, trade unions, and professional organizations also serve political functions. Thus active participation in community-centered activities and political activism are not necessarily mutually exclusive. Indeed, active participation in community organizations and volunteering in local events probably serves as a pre-step for further political integration and activism. Still, it is important to note, especially for many Asian immigrants, particularly those of voting age, that it will take time to acquire English proficiency, to become naturalized, to get used to the American political system, and, for those interested in serving as political candidates, to build up their political resumes.

Among those areas with a strong Asian American presence, especially among later-generation Asian Americans, participating in grassroots and/or electoral politics is more common, as well as more imperative. Oftentimes, participation is a direct response to outlandish cries from some long-time, native-born, non-Hispanic white suburban residents that immigrants are either "unassimilated" or "taking over our city." Thus, in ethnoburbs, where there are more educated and middle-class Asian American residents and voters, the potential political impacts on local, state, and eventually national political scenes are increasingly becoming more apparent and more important. Many actively participate in the political process as fundraisers, campaigners, and/or volunteers. Meanwhile, increasing numbers of Asian Americans are being elected or appointed to political positions.

Summary

By outlining the changing demographics and geographic distributions of Asian Americans, along with the differences among various contemporary community forms within metropolitan areas, from traditional central city enclaves to multiethnic suburbs (known as "ethnoburbs"), this chapter begins the process of understanding the varied characteristics, outlooks, and concerns of Asian American communities in the United States. This kind of analysis is critical in creating a successful future, since Asian Americans are rapidly transforming what were previously known as the citadels of non-Hispanic white America to increasingly multiracial, multiethnic, multicultural, and multilingual communities.

NOTES

We are grateful for the invaluable research assistance of Yun Zhou at Arizona State University. All possible errors that remain, however, are entirely ours. Inquiries can be sent to us at wei.li@asu.edu or eskop@prc.utexas.edu.

1. All 2000 and 2004 data used here includes only Asian Americans who chose the "Asian alone" racial category.

2. The Census 2004 data should be viewed with caution. It is based on sample data from the American Community Survey, which was not fully implemented across the nation until July 2005. This means that the data is subject to sampling error, especially among minority populations.

3. Another possible contributing factor is the way that changing self-identification racial categories provided by the U.S. Census skew the results. Some individuals are selecting the multiple-race category, rather than the "alone" racial category. We only analyze Asian Americans who chose the "Asian alone" racial category in 2000 and 2004 (see note 1).

4. This is not to say that there isn't any disparity in the integration experiences of Asian Americans. There are a growing number of Asian Americans with less education and lower occupational status, and the "glass ceiling" effect is often encountered by higher-status individuals. We in no way want to add to the myth of the "model minority" that already circles around this minority group by suggesting that all Asian Americans are successful.

BIBLIOGRAPHY

Asian American Justice Center and Asian American Legal Center. 2006 *A Community of Contrasts: Asian Americans and Pacific Islanders in the United States.* Washington, DC: Asian American Justice Center.

Frey, William H. 2006. *Diversity Spreads Out: Metropolitan Shifts in Hispanic, Asian, and Black Populations since 2000.* Washington, DC: Brookings Institute.

Lai, Eric and Dennis Arguelles, eds. 2003. *The New Face of Asian Pacific America: Numbers, Diversity, and Changes in the Twenty-First Century.* San Francisco, CA: Asian Week.

Li, Wei, ed. 2006. *From Urban Enclave to Ethnic Suburb: New Asian Communities in Pacific Rim Countries.* Honolulu: University of Hawaii Press.

Logan, John R. 2001. *From Many Shores: Asians in Census 2000.* Albany, NY: Lewis Mumford Center for Comparative Urban and Regional Research.

Skop, Emily. Forthcoming. *Saffron Suburbs: The Social and Spatial Construction of an Asian Indian Community.* Chicago: University of Chicago Press.

Zelinsky, Wilbur and Barrett A. Lee. 1998. Heterolocalism: An Alternative Model of the Sociospatial Behaviour of Immigrant Ethnic Communities. *International Journal of Population Geography* 4: 1–18.

1. In the article "Southeast Asian Women in Lowell," Pho and Mulvey describe the experiences of Lowell's Southeast Asian women as a series of "losses and gains" that are complex in their origins and even more complex in their solutions. How has economic necessity changed the structure of the traditional patriarchy? How have expanded opportunities for women in these families changed the transmission of traditional values within these families? What unique economic, social, and cultural challenges do these women face from the communities in which they live and from their own families? How do these challenges differ by generation (mothers vs. daughters)? How have women empowered themselves in the face of these challenges? What kinds of coping mechanisms do these women employ?

2. One of the consequences of changing gender roles within Southeast Asian families in Lowell has been an upsurge of domestic violence directed toward women. What are some of the risk factors that expose these women to domestic violence? Which risk factors were identified as the most important? How do these factors figure into counseling and education programs?

3. How does transnationalism truly affect what we consider to be an Asian American identity? To what extent would a transnational household promote or retard adaptation to an American or Asian American cultural identity? Will Asian Americans whose families have been in the United States for several generations distance themselves from these newcomers, from individuals with stronger ties to the homeland countries? How different may contemporary transnational households shared by Filipino, Chinese, Koreans, Japanese, and Asian Indians differ from those sustained by the first wave of pre–World War II immigrants from these countries?

4. To which regions of the country have Asian immigrants historically settled and why? Why have Asian immigrants historically settled in urban locales? What advantages did they derive from these enclaves?

5. At what point, according to the authors, did Asian immigrants begin to settle in "ethnoburbs"? How do the authors define this term? How do "ethnoburbs" differ from ethnic enclaves? What are some of the cultural, economic, and political implications of living in the suburbs?

SUGGESTED READINGS

Abraham, Margaret. 2002. Addressing Domestic Violence and the South Asian Community in the United States. Pp. 191–202 in Linda Vo and Rick Bonus (eds.), *Contemporary Asian American Communities: Intersections and Divergences*. Philadelphia: Temple University Press.

Bao, Jiemen. 2005. Merit-Making Capitalism: Reterritorializing Thai Buddhism in Silicon Valley, California. *Journal of Asian American Studies* 8(2): 115–42.

Cimmarusti, R. A. 1996. Exploring Aspects of Filipino-American Families. *Journal of Marital and Family Therapy* 22(2):205–17.

Espiritu, Yen. 1995. *Filipino American Lives*. Philadelphia: Temple University Press.

Espiritu, Yen Le. 2003. *Home Bound: Filipino American Lives across Cultures, Communities, and Countries.* Berkeley: University of California Press.

Fong, Timothy. 1994. *The First Suburban Chinatown: The Remaking of Monterey Park, California.* Philadelphia: Temple University Press.

Gill, Dhara S. and Bennett Matthews. 1995. Changes in the Breadwinner Role: Punjabi Families in Transition. *Journal of Comparative Family Studies* 26(2): 255–64.

Glenn, Evelyn Nakano and Rhacel Salazar Parrenas. 1996. The Other Issei: Japanese Immigrant Women in the Pre–World War II Period. Pp. 124–40 in Silvia Pedraza and Rubén G. Rumbaut (eds.), *Origins and Destinies: Immigration, Race, and Ethnicity in America.* Belmont, CA: Wadsworth.

Kang, K. Connie. 1995. *Home Was the Land of the Morning Calm.* New York: Addison-Wesley.

Kibria, Nazli. 1993. *Family Tightrope: The Changing Lives of Vietnamese Americans.* Princeton, NJ: Princeton University Press.

Kallivayalil, Diya. 2004. Gender and Cultural Socialization in Indian Immigrant Families in the United States. *Feminism & Psychology* 14(4): 535–59.

Lessinger, Johanna. 1995. *From the Ganges to the Hudson: Indian Immigrants in New York City.* Boston: Allyn and Bacon.

Li, Wei. 1999. Building Ethnoburbia: The Emergence and Manifestation of the Chinese Ethnoburb in Los Angeles' San Gabriel Valley. *Journal of Asian American Studies* 2(1): 1–28.

Liu, Haiming. 2005. *The Transnational History of a Chinese Family: Immigrant Letters, Family Business, and Reverse Migration.* New Brunswick, NJ: Rutgers University Press.

Matsumoto, Valerie. 1993. *Farming the Homeplace: A Japanese American Community in California, 1919–1982.* Ithaca, NY: Cornell University Press.

Pyke, Karen. 2000. "The Normal American Family" as an Interpretive Structure of Family Life among Grown Children of Korean and Vietnamese Immigrants. *Journal of Marriage and the Family* 62(1): 240–55.

Smith-Hefner, Nancy J. 1998. *Khmer American: Identity and Moral Education in a Diasporic Community.* Berkeley: University of California Press.

Toji, Dean S. and Karen Umemoto. 2003. The Paradox of Dispersal: Ethnic Continuity and Community Development among Japanese Americans in Little Tokyo. *AAPI Nexus* 1(1): 21–46.

Vo, Linda and Mary Y. Danico. 2004. The Formation of Post-Suburban Communities: Koreatown and Little Saigon, Orange County. *International Journal of Sociology and Social Policy* 24(7/8): 15–45.

Ying, Yu-Wen and Chua Chiem Chao. 1996. Intergenerational Relationship in Iu Mien American Families. *Amerasia Journal* 22(3): 47–64.

Yoshioka, M. R., J. DiNoia, and K. Ullah. 2001. Attitudes toward Marital Violence: An Examination of Four Asian Communities. *Violence against Women* 7(8): 900–926.

Zhao, Xiaojian. 2002. *Remaking Chinese America: Immigration, Family, and Community, 1940–1965.* New Brunswick, NJ: Rutgers University Press.

Zhou, Min and Carl L. Bankston III. 1998. *Growing Up American: How Vietnamese Children Adapt to Life in the United States.* New York: Russell Sage Foundation.

Zhou, Min and Susan S. Kim. 2006. Community Forces, Social Capital, and Educational Achievement: The Case of Supplementary Education in the Chinese and Korean Immigrant Communities. *Harvard Educational Review* 76(1): 1–29.

FILMS

Flanary, Lisette Marie and Evann Siebens (codirectors/coproducers). 2003. *American Aloha: Hula beyond Hawai'i* (documentary).

Friedman, Daniel and Sharon Grimberg (directors/producers). 1997. *Miss India Georgia* (56-minute documentary).

Ishizuka, Karen L. (producer). 1993. *Moving Memories* (31-minute documentary)

Koster, Henry (director). 1961. *Flower Drum Song* (comedy).

Krishnan, Indu (director). 1990. *Knowing Her Place* (40-minute documentary).

Mallozzi, Julie (director). 2004. *Monkey Dance* (65-minute documentary)

Mishran, Ahrin and Nick Rothenberg (coproducers). 1994. *Bui Doi: Life Like Dust* (29-minute documentary).

Moyers, Bill (producer). 2003. *Becoming American: The Chinese Experience* (87-minute documentary).

Nakasako, Spencer (producer/director). 1998. *Kelly Loves Tony* (57-minute documentary).

Uno, Michael T. (producer/director). 1988. *The Wash* (94-minute drama).

Yasui, Lise (producer/director/writer). 1988. *A Family Gathering* (60- or 30-minute documentary).

Part IV

Struggling to Get Ahead
Economy and Work

Striving for the American Dream
Struggle, Success, and Intergroup Conflict among Korean Immigrant Entrepreneurs

Jennifer Lee

It takes intellectual sophistication to resist blaming the economic ills of the ghetto on the immediate agents of exploitation, whether Jewish or not, and to see these ills as products of impersonal social and economic forces that transcend the responsibility of particular individuals.[1]

Introduction

The highest self-employed immigrant ethnic group in the United States, Koreans have changed the commercial landscape of today's cities. Fresh fruit and vegetable markets, nail salons, dry cleaners, and fresh fish stores have become ubiquitous symbols of Korean immigrant entrepreneurship. Koreans offer their services not only to fellow ethnics but also to the white and minority populations alike. Studies estimate that approximately one-third of Korean immigrant families are engaged in small business, figures that parallel the staggering self-employment rate of Jewish immigrants in the early twentieth century. Following in the footsteps of Jewish immigrants, Korean immigrants are experiencing rapid economic mobility through self-employment. Second- and third-generation Jewish Americans have largely moved into the primary labor market (with substantial portions in professional and white-collar occupations), and today's second-generation Koreans are quickly following suit.

Korean immigrant entrepreneurs seem to have "made it" in their new host country. Touted as "model minorities," Koreans have become symbols that the American dream is alive—if an individual works hard enough, delays gratification, makes sacrifices, and most of all perseveres, he or she can make it too. The opportunity structure is equal, and the path open to anyone who wants to follow it.

However, their relatively rapid economic success has come with social costs. Black nationalists have charged Korean merchants with disrespectful treatment toward their customers, prejudice, and exploitation of the black community. They have also accused Korean merchants of buying all of the stores in their neighborhoods, draining the communities of their resources, and failing to "give back" by hiring local residents (Lee 1993; Min 1996). Labeled as "absentee owners," Korean storeowners are accused of owning businesses in poor black neighborhoods yet not living in these neighborhoods, thereby removing the profits from the communities in which they serve (Min 1996).

The tension between Korean merchants and black customers crystallized in 1990 with an eighteen-month-long boycott of a fruit and vegetable market in the Flatbush section of Brooklyn, New York (Lee 1993).[2] Much of the media coverage focused on individual-level differences between Korean merchants and black customers, pointing to the cultural and linguistic misunderstandings between two minority groups while ignoring the structural conditions under which intergroup conflict can emerge. The friction mounted on March 16, 1991, when Korean storeowner Soon Ja Du shot and killed African American teenager Latasha Harlins in South Central Los Angeles. Finally, the tension climaxed on April 29, 1992, after four white police officers were acquitted of beating 25-year-old African American motorist Rodney King. The nation remained paralyzed as it watched buildings in South Central and Koreatown burning while inner-city residents looted stores, taking everything from televisions and VCRs to food and diapers. The worst domestic uprising in the twentieth century ended with a toll count of 16,291 arrested, 2,383 injured, 500 fires, and 52 dead (Njeri 1996). Korean merchants suffered almost half of the property damage, amounting to more than $400 million, affecting more than 2,300 Korean-owned businesses in Los Angeles (Ong and Hee 1993). The nation was left stunned.

I address four main research questions in this article. First, I investigate why Korean immigrants enter self-employment at such high rates, especially compared to native-born Americans. Second, I examine the resources that these immigrants utilize in starting and maintaining their businesses. Third, I explore the "retail niches" that Korean immigrants dominate, and also study the reasons why they choose to locate in inner-city neighborhoods. Finally, I investigate the interactions between Koreans and blacks and examine the structural conditions under which tension between merchants and customers becomes racially coded and turns into conflict.

The study is based on thirty face-to-face, in-depth interviews of Korean merchants in five predominantly black neighborhoods in New York City and Philadelphia.[3] Each of these neighborhoods has bustling commercial strips lined with small businesses that offer a variety of merchandise, some of which is geared specifically for a black clientele, including wigs, ethnic beauty supplies, inner-city sportswear, and beauty salons and barber shops that service black customers. The data also includes seventy-five in-depth interviews of black customers from each of these research sites. African American research assistants conducted face-to-face, open-ended interviews of local residents from these communities who were asked about their shopping experiences in Korean-owned stores and about their opinions of Korean merchants more generally.[4] Unlike previous studies of black-Korean relations that include interviews of only the Korean merchants, my study, by including interviews of black customers, enables me to examine these relations from both perspectives.

Choosing Self-Employment as a Means to
Upward Mobility

Post-1965 Korean immigrants come to the United States with relatively high levels of "human capital," measured by educational attainment and occupational skills. Thirty percent of Korean immigrants ages twenty-five and over have completed four years of college—about twice the rate for the U.S. native-born population—and a large proportion hold white collar and professional jobs in Korea (Yoon 1997). Yet because the supply of college graduates in South Korea exceeds the demand for such a highly educated workforce, the average rate of unemployment in Korea for male college graduates is 30 percent. Hence, Koreans view immigration to the United States as a more viable route to mobility, not only for themselves but also for their children. Yet after their arrival to the United States, Korean immigrants often find that they are unable to transfer their "human capital" into commensurate professional occupations, and consequently, turn to self-employment.

Social scientists note that certain ethnic groups, particularly when they are immigrants, enter self-employment to overcome disadvantages in the American labor market (Light 1972; Light and Bonacich 1988; Min 1984; Yoon 1997). A language barrier, unfamiliarity with American customs and culture, and the inability to transfer educational and occupational capital leave immigrants severely disadvantaged to compete with the native-born in the primary labor market. For example, U.S. companies often have little understanding of educational and work credentials obtained outside of the country. Whereas a degree from Seoul National, Yonsei, or Ewha Universities immediately connotes academic rigor and high status in Korea, companies in the United States have difficulty translating and measuring these credentials. Furthermore, like many first-generation immigrants, Koreans have difficulty mastering a new language, thereby making their transition into an English-speaking workforce extremely difficult.

Compared to the native-born, immigrants have fewer "high-priced salable skills" (Light 1972) and therefore turn to self-employment as an alternative to entering the secondary labor market where they would receive relatively low wages in unskilled or low-skilled occupations. Hence, Korean immigrants opt to open small businesses not because self-employment is their primary occupational choice but instead because their alternatives in the U.S. labor market are less promising and less lucrative. In short, self-employment becomes a means of achieving upward mobility in the face of severe handicaps in the primary labor market.

However, disadvantages in the labor market alone cannot explain why Korean immigrants enter self-employment at such high rates since ethnic groups who find themselves similarly disadvantaged in the labor market such as Laotians and Malaysians have self-employment rates of less than 3 percent (Yoon 1997). To explain the variance in the rates of self-employment, social scientists have focused on the importance of class and ethnic resources and social capital in the development and success of small business among immigrant groups such as Cubans, Israelis, and Koreans.

Resources Used in Business

Class and Ethnic Resources

Class resources are characterized as human capital, economic capital, and wealth, and ethnic resources are defined as "forms of aid preferentially available from one's own ethnic group."[5] Social capital, in the form of rotating credit associations, has also contributed to the survival of Korean-owned businesses. These resources are invaluable to business success and are used not only at the initial stages of capitalization but also throughout business ownership. Access to class and ethnic resources and the utilization of social capital are crucial to understanding how Korean immigrants are able to open small businesses at such high rates.

Korean business owners use a variety of class and ethnic resources such as personal savings, loans from family and coethnic friends, and advertising in Korean-language newspapers to purchase their businesses. But unlike previous literature that stresses the significance of rotating credit associations (*gae*) in the formation of businesses (Light 1972; Light and Bonacich 1988), I find that the majority of Korean immigrant merchants do not use this resource at the start-up phase. Table 10.1 indicates that only 7 percent acquired capital to open their business through funds from a rotating credit association. By contrast, 76 percent bought their businesses using a combination of other resources: personal savings, loans from family and coethnic friends, and credit from the previous coethnic storeowner. The remaining 17 percent bought their business from a family owner—usually a brother, sister, or in-laws who immigrated several years before they did.

When coethnics purchase businesses from one another, rather than going through a third financial party like a bank, the new Korean owner will normally pay the previous owner one-third of the business's value as a down payment and the remaining two-thirds in monthly installments over a period of a few years. Bates (1994) notes that Koreans use this debt source more frequently than other groups since Korean are more likely to purchase retail firms that are already in business.

Social Capital—The Rotating Credit Association

Although the use of rotating credit associations may not be as prevalent at the start-up phase, this resource is highly utilized at the later stages of business. Rotating credit associations range in both membership size and value, with participation extending from only a few people to over thirty, and the value ranging anywhere from $100 to over $100,000. Korean merchants report that the average *gae* ranges from ten to twenty people, with each member contributing between $1,000 and $2,000 into a pot totaling $10,000 to $40,000. Each member contributes to the fund, and every member takes turns in receiving the lump sum of money. For example, a Korean merchant explained that she belonged to a rotating credit association with twenty members. Each member contributed $2,700 per month, and the first member who received the pot received $51,300 ($2,700 x 19). The pot rotated according to a predetermined schedule until each member received his or her share. After receiving the pool of

TABLE 10.1
Resources Korean Merchants Used in Starting Their Business

Means of Establishing Business Ownership	Number of Businesses	Percent
Savings + loans from family/friends + credit from previous coethnic storeowner	23	76
Bought from a family member	5	17
Rotating credit association (*gae*)	2	7
TOTAL	30	100

money, each individual must contribute $3,100 until the rotation is complete. Therefore, the member who received the money first got only $51,300 while the one who received the pot last was rewarded with $58,900—the surplus accounting for interest and appreciation for those at the tail end of the rotation. Implicit in such a system is a high degree of mutual trust, obligation, and expectation among its members.

Rotating credit associations are less important when Korean merchants purchase their first business but become very significant after they have already established their businesses for various purposes such as buying new merchandise or equipment, remodeling, or purchasing their second business. *Gae* also serve as a crucial economic resource when merchants have little cash flow or in case of unforeseen emergencies, such as break-ins or fires, that are not uncommon in low-income neighborhoods. Even though the use of *gae* varies among Korean merchants, all have admitted that the rotating credit association is a resource they *could* draw upon if they needed to quickly accumulate capital. The facility with which Korean immigrants can draw upon such ethnic resources attests to their easy access to social and economic capital.

Sociologist James Coleman explains (1988, 98),

> Social capital is defined by its function. It is not a single entity but a variety of different entities, with two elements in common: they all consist of some aspect of social structures, and they facilitate certain actions of actors—whether persons or corporate actors—within the structure. Like other forms of capital, social capital is productive, making possible the achievement of certain ends that in its absence would not be possible. Like physical and human capital, social capital is not completely fungible but may be specific to certain activities. A given form of social capital that is valuable in facilitating certain actions may be useless or even harmful to others.

Central to Coleman's concept of social capital is the role of closure in the social structure; closure facilitates the trust needed to allow actions such as exchange, lending, and borrowing from members within the social structure. Also essential is the degree to which these relations are indispensable, or the extent to which members within the social structure depend on one another. Coleman offers the rotating credit association as a prime example by which social capital is manifested among its members as a form of obligation, trust, and expectation, the absence of which would prevent such a system from functioning.

Social capital differs from economic or human capital in that it is not a tangible resource but is instead the capacity of individuals to command and mobilize resources by virtue of membership in networks (Portes 1995). But without a group's economic capital, a high degree of social capital is not nearly as beneficial. For example, Stack (1974) and Liebow (1967) illustrate that informal networks of exchange exist among poor African Americans in urban communities, but they "swap" resources that are significantly smaller in scale such as food stamps, a few dollars, food, or child care. The high degree of social capital among Korean immigrant entrepreneurs, coupled with their wealth of economic resources, gives them a distinct advantage in business over other ethnic groups.

Koreans are not the only ethnic group to benefit from social capital. In fact, first-generation immigrants of many ethnic backgrounds draw upon their versions of rotating credit associations. However, as these groups acculturate into the American social structure, they utilize this resource far less frequently. For example, whereas first-generation Jewish immigrant entrepreneurs used mutual loan associations, later generations have long abandoned this tradition. Second-generation Koreans, like the sons and daughters of Jewish immigrants, have also abandoned this practice.

As instrumental as *gae* may be, some Korean merchants have become wary of using rotating credit associations since they realize the inordinate amount of trust involved for such a system to operate. Many have heard of *gae* failures where one person will take the lump sum of money and leave the country. For instance, a Korean merchant who has used *gae* a few times illustrates the risks involved and the difficulty in holding someone legally responsible for defaulting:

> Some people, they don't do *gae* because no matter what they don't trust because it could happen too. When a guy gets $40,000, after a couple of months, you don't see him anymore. Then where are you going to go get him? You cannot tell anybody what happened. It's no protection. . . . So let's say you owe a big company, you don't pay enough on your credit card. They're going to send you a thousand letters. They going to send you [to a] collection [agency], but those big companies can afford it, but a lot of people, you want to get $10,000 from that guy who run away. You want to hire a lawyer, you want to go to court, this and that, time and money, headache. Forget about it. They know what is the risk, so they don't even want to involved.

Although Korean merchants explain that there are no legal ramifications to defaulting since none of these agreements is written, the social sanctions—such as loss of standing in the immigrant community and exclusion from it—are strong enough to prevent losses on a regular basis.

Korean merchants not only complain of the risks; they also mention the costly interest payments, which can be as high as 30 percent, surpassing the legal limit in New York state, for instance, which must be less than 25 percent. Although rotating credit associations may be helpful to those who need cash very quickly, they also function as financial investments for more affluent coethnics who benefit from accruing high interest payments.

Although not all Korean merchants have participated in *gae,* all have admitted to borrowing funds from their family or coethnic friends at one point, either at the start-up phase or while in business. Koreans often borrow tens of thousands of dollars from other family members or coethnic friends. The high degree of social and economic capital remains the most valuable resource for these immigrant entrepreneurs that should be underscored, since the availability of cash resources can determine whether small businesses will be able to withstand emergencies such as break-ins or slow periods when cash flow is extremely tight (Lee 2002).

Ethnic Succession and Vacant Niches

By the last quarter of the twentieth century, the once ubiquitous Jewish shopkeeper had faded from the scene: the storekeepers' sons and daughters had better things to do than mind a shop; and their parents, old, tired, and scared of crime, were eager to sell out to new groups of immigrant entrepreneurs . . . the Jewish withdrawal from New York's traditional small business sectors provided a chance for a legion of immigrants, and not just Koreans. (Waldinger 1996, 100–101)

The Jewish exodus from the inner cities left a vacant niche for Korean immigrants to ethnically succeed them in small business.

Entering the Inner City

Immigrant entrepreneurs such as Koreans open businesses in black neighborhoods largely because there is little competition from larger, chain corporations that predominate in white, middle-class neighborhoods and suburban malls. Considered high-risk and high-crime neighborhoods, poor black communities are largely ignored by larger corporations, consequently leaving a vacant niche for Koreans to set up shop. And because the market is less saturated in low-income neighborhoods, rent is relatively cheaper. Korean immigrants also claim that running a business in a middle-class, white neighborhood is more difficult because they do not have the language fluency and middle-class mannerisms to deal with a more educated and sophisticated clientele. For example, when asked why she opened a business in a low-income, black neighborhood as opposed to a middle-income, white neighborhood, a Korean store-owner in Harlem replies,

Because easier. First of all, you don't have to have that much money to open up the store. And second of all, easier because you don't need to that much complicate. White people is very classy and choosy, and especially white people location is not like this, mostly they go to mall. Here they don't have many car, so easier, cheaper rent. When you go to white location, Second Avenue, Third Avenue, rent is already cost $20,000, you know, and they don't have any room for us. But black people area, other people hesitate to come in because they worry about crime and something like that, so they got a lot of room for Koreans.

After gathering experience and accumulating capital running businesses in low-income neighborhoods, some Korean storeowners often leave the inner city and open stores in safer, middle-income white neighborhoods.

Immigrant entrepreneurs also cluster in particular "retail niches" (Lee 1999). The newest immigrant storeowners find themselves in the most physically exhausting, labor-intensive businesses that require relatively little capital and have low profit margins, such as green groceries, take-out restaurants, and fresh fish stores (Light and Bonacich 1988). The extremely long hours and physically demanding labor often insures that first-generation immigrants will be the ones to occupy these lines of business. Accordingly, Korean immigrants presently dominate these niches, but they are merely the successors in a line of immigrant ethnic groups who occupied these business lines before them. Immigrant entrepreneurs will continue to succeed one another and flourish in low-income black neighborhoods because they bring products and services to an underserviced population by taking advantage of previously unfilled niches. As long the second and third generation find better opportunities in the mainstream labor market, retail businesses (particularly those catering to a low-income clientele) will remain a protected niche among immigrant groups who will continue to ethnically succeed one another.

"Mass Marketing" a Once-Exclusive Product

Immigrant entrepreneurs concentrate mostly in retail trade and manufacturing, and their success often depends on their ability to "mass market" a once-exclusive product. In other words, they take a luxury product and make it cheaper, thereby making it more accessible for a wider population. For instance, before Korean-owned manicure salons opened on virtually every block in New York City, manicures used to be only available in full-service beauty salons. In upscale salons, manicures would cost about $20, making them accessible to an elite group of people, namely, upper- and upper-middle-class white women. Koreans took this luxury service out of the beauty salon and mass marketed the manicure. They made it cheaper by charging women only $7, consequently making manicures more widely available to a greater population (Kang 1997). Koreans have used the same strategy in selling fresh flowers, once only available at florist shops, now readily available at corner delis.

These business owners have successfully adapted to the changing demands of the service economy by bringing small, full-service retail shops close to both high- and low-income consumers (Sassen 1991). Korean-owned manicures and delis have become a ubiquitous symbol of New York City, as evidenced by a recent article in the *New York Times* by a woman who moved out of the city and complains, "There are no Koreans. Which explains why you can never find flowers and why manicures cost $15."[6] This strategy of "mass marketing" transcends industries and also explains immigrants' success in marketing ethnic beauty supplies (including both hair and skin care for an ethnic clientele) and ethnic urban sportswear. Since low-income blacks cannot afford to purchase designer clothing, Korean-owned businesses that sell designer knock-offs for the urban teenage market prosper in this market.

Interethnic Conflict: Korean Merchants and Black Customers

The relationship between black customers and Korean merchants has been popularized and exploited by the media with splashy newspaper headings that read, "Will Black Merchants Drive Koreans from Harlem?" (Noel 1981), "Blacks, Koreans Struggle to Grasp Thread of Unity" (Jones 1986), "Cultural Conflict" (Njeri 1996), and "Scapegoating New York's Koreans."[7] "Black-Korean conflict"—as it quickly became framed and labeled by both journalists and scholars—was featured in mainstream and ethnic presses alike, spilling over into other forms of popular culture. Spike Lee's poignant film *Do the Right Thing* and Ice Cube's controversial lyrics in the rap song "Black Korea" brought black-Korean tension and conflict to the fore in both communities. The shooting of African American teenager Latasha Harlins by Korean storeowner Soon Ja Du on March 16, 1991, in South Central Los Angeles intensified tensions between these minority communities. And finally, the "not guilty" verdict rendered by a Simi Valley jury in the Rodney King case on April 29, 1992, sparked the Los Angeles riots—the first multiethnic riot in U.S. history. Although many ethnic groups were involved, the riots were framed as the culmination of black-Korean conflict—an oversimplified and misleading framework that failed to capture the depth and complexity of the issues at hand. In this section of the article, I describe the daily interactions between Korean merchants and black customers and also shed light on the larger structural processes under which simple economic arguments transform into racialized anger.

Dispelling the Myths: The Intersection of Race, Class, and Experience

To be a Korean merchant in an inner-city neighborhood such as New York's Harlem or South Central Los Angeles is a mixture of prosaic routine and explosive tension, of affectionate customers and racial anger. Yet despite the violent media image of Korean merchants armed with 9-millimeter handguns and black customers looting stores during the Los Angeles riots, most striking is the sheer ordinariness of most merchant-customer relationships. In fact, for most merchants and customers, their everyday shopping experiences boil down to a simple formula: "business as usual" (Lee 1996). However, there is a considerable amount of variation within the merchant-customer relationship, and there are two important factors that shape the daily interactions between Korean business owners and their black clientele: (1) the merchants' experience and (2) the class composition of the customer population.

Korean merchants who are veterans on the street have far better relations with their black customers than newer merchants who have little experience dealing with a minority clientele. With time, merchants come to realize that contrary to the dominant stereotypes, inner-city residents are not all welfare queens, drug addicts, or criminals; experience teaches Korean storeowners that even the poorest neighborhoods are economically and culturally diverse. For example, merchants who have been in business for ten or fifteen years know and recognize their customers, speak with them more frequently than newer merchants, and generally feel more comfortable doing business in low-income black neighborhoods. They see their customers as a diverse population, recognizing differences in ethnicity, class, and character. Years of experience have taught veteran business owners that negative experiences—no matter how traumatic —come few and far between.

Class differences also matter. Running a small business in a low-income, urban neighborhood is not easy, especially for new immigrants who come from an ethnically homogeneous country, and therefore have little understanding of the nuances of America's pluralistic society. Without prior business experience and with only a loose command of the English language, they set up shop in inner cities where they are exposed to persistent poverty and its resultant consequences—welfare dependency, teenage pregnancy, single motherhood, unemployment, and drugs (Wilson 1987). From the black customers' perspective, Korean merchants not only appear successful, but they also seem to take away business opportunities for blacks. While immigrant merchants may not directly compete with black merchants or black residents for jobs, low-income residents are more likely to *perceive* immigrant newcomers as outside competitors who take away opportunities from them.

Frustrated by the infusion of immigrant newcomers who barely speak English, yet seem to easily set up shop in their communities, black customers often direct their resentment toward immigrant merchants (Rieder 1990). Poor black customers often question what U.S. government agency helped them out and also wonder why aid has not come their way. It is a common misperception among low-income black customers that immigrants, especially Korean immigrants, receive special loans from the government to help them open businesses. Although this is untrue, low-income residents are quick to embrace the misconception because they cannot otherwise explain how these "foreigners" are able to accumulate the mass amounts of capital and "take over" the businesses in their communities.

However, the scenario is far different in middle-class black communities. When Korean merchants serve middle-class black customers, the tension between these groups virtually disappears. Middle-class customers do not perceive Korean merchants in their communities as economic competitors who take away opportunities from them since most middle-class blacks have jobs, are economically stable, and therefore do not express feelings of economic and ethnic antagonism. Instead, they view merchants as businessmen and women who provide services for the community and have the right to open a business wherever they choose. Economic security affords this opinion. The stark differences in low- and middle-income black neighborhoods reveals that class—rather than race or ethnicity—is more salient in determining the level of tension or conflict between blacks and Koreans.

Racially Coding Economic Arguments

Writing about the black-Jewish relationship of the 1960s, Herbert Gans (1969, 10) noted, "When Negroes express their anger in anti-Semitic terms, it is only because many of the whites who affect their lives are Jewish; if the ghetto storeowners, landlords and teachers were Chinese, Negro hostility would surely be anti-Chinese." Although most merchant-customer encounters in black neighborhoods may be quite ordinary, when tensions arise, both merchants and customers can lose cognitive control, and even those who do not normally engage in stereotypes may do so under strained conditions. Seemingly trivial economic arguments between black customers and out-group merchants such as Koreans can quickly become racially coded. In this tricky area of merchant-customer conflict, Robert K. Merton's concept of "in-group virtues" and "out-group vices" is particularly useful. Merton (1968) demonstrates that similar patterns of behavior by in-group and out-group members are differently perceived and evaluated. Yet because the most apparent distinction between Korean merchants and their black customers is race, the economic relationship is often overlooked by customers as a source of tension in favor of racial or ethnic explanations.

All of the Korean merchants have admitted that at some point while they have been doing business, particularly at the beginning, economic arguments have become racially or ethnically coded. For example, a furniture storeowner in West Philadelphia explains when customers become very angry over economic disputes, "the argument always comes down to race." Accusations such as, "You damn Orientals are coming into our neighborhoods taking over every fucking store!" are not uncommon when merchants and customers come to a halt over exchanges or refunds.

For instance, when the Korean storeowner refused to take back the floor display furniture model that he recently sold to a female customer at a discount, she immediately uttered to her mother, "He's just a chink and a gook." Incensed by the racial insult, the Korean merchant retorted, "Now wait a minute, what would happen if I called you a nigger? What would happen then? You're sitting here calling me these names, what if I did that to you?" Infuriated by the hint of a racial epithet, the woman threatened to start picketing outside of his store. Quickly realizing the potential problems that could ensue from this incident, the Korean merchant immediately called the Philadelphia Commission on Human Relations to intervene, which later proved to be unnecessary since the woman did not follow through on her threat. The Korean furniture storeowner comments about the situation:

> I called up City Hall because I thought it was going to be a problem, but it wasn't. The next day they were gone, but it just shows that it's totally backwards. It's reverse racism is what it is. And anytime there's an argument about anything, it always comes down to, "You damn Orientals are taking over all the businesses in the neighborhood!" or "You Koreans are doing it!"
>
> This isn't all the time, but every once in a while you get a customer who's totally unreasonable, and if things don't go their way, they pull that old card out of their pocket, the race card, and throw it down. And it's a shame that they got to stoop to that level just to get what they want. I mean if they were to talk to me reasonable, without yelling and ranting and raving, we probably would have got things worked out more to their liking. But you can't come in here and yell at somebody and expect to get what you want.

Even Korean merchants who are veterans of the black communities they serve—who know most of their customers—fully recognize that their nonblack status can easily make them targets for hostile customers and boycotters. For example, a Korean carry-out restaurant owner who has been in the Harlem community for thirteen years explains that racial tension is a fact of life in Harlem. As a mainstay in West Harlem's community, she has many customers who frequent her eating establishment on a daily basis. Yet even she understands that as a nonblack merchant on 125th Street in New York's Harlem, she is always at risk of potential conflict such as a boycott, regardless of how many people in the community support her,

> We always feel like a boycott could happen no matter how you famous on 125th Street, no matter how much they like you, no matter how you good to this community. Always one bum or one knucklehead hates you. He can bring you a ton of problem. So far, people support me but some people against me too.

When asked whether this insecurity stems from the simple fact that she is not black, she immediately confirms,

> That's right. And they can put me as Korean merchant coming here to make money out of this community. So I got a thousand of them full of respect, it don't mean anything. Something happen, a thousand people I don't know them, they can against me, coming here for protesting, hollering, shut down business. It could happen, you know. Some person get mad at me, so I argue, and he could start picket outside. Maybe some other people say, "You crazy, why you do that to this store?" But few people going to do that.
>
> And a lot of those protesters, they don't know me, they could stay there shouting and give me a lot of trouble because it always could happen no matter how much you are good to this community or something like that. And that kind of crazy thing can happen, and nobody can stop it. . . . Nobody can move those protesters out in front of my door. They got a right to stand there and shouting. And the ones who shouting, I don't know them, and they don't know me. They just want to be here. They angry because I'm Korean. But they not get mad at me, they get mad some place else.

When customers engage in stereotypes, they may not necessarily react to the objective features of the situation, but rather to the symbolism that the situation represents. For instance, when merchants refuse a customer's request for a refund or an exchange, their refusal becomes symbolic of stingy, cheap commercial outsiders who exploit the community in which they serve. And similarly, when black customers become angry and yell at merchants, storeowners may quickly engage in stereotypes about blacks— that they are ignorant, uneducated, and irresponsible. In each scenario, merchants and customers alike may interpret and racially code what are essentially economic arguments. Race can polarize the simplest interactions and become mobilized in conflict-ridden ways.

In order to defuse tensions in poor black communities, Korean merchants hire black employees and managers to act as "cultural brokers" between them and their predominantly black clientele (Lee 1998). Black employees serve as bridges who link the linguistic and cultural differences; they also serve as visible symbols that merchants are "giving back" to the low-income communities in which they serve. Most critically, black employees act as conflict-resolvers who can quickly deracialize rising tensions between merchants and customers.

Placing Black-Korean Conflict in the Context of Urban Poverty

In the context of urban poverty, small arguments can explode into racial conflict. This heightened tension can result from the daily strains and frustrations of inner-city life—joblessness, crime, and persistent poverty—leading customers to racially code economic arguments. An African American customer in Philadelphia explains the complexities of the merchant-customer relationship and offers insights about the tension and frustration resulting from life in the inner city:

> Well there is a certain amount of sensitivity here because black folks, living the way we do, we have a certain amount of cynicism, so when we go into these stores, we're like angry, cursing them out and everything, and they're like, "You come in my store and you're cursing at me! You get out my store!" And a lot of people around here, they're stealing, they're strung out on something, don't know no better, trying to be cool. It's a whole myriad of things. That's why when I walk into a store, they're watching me. I haven't stole a thing in my life, too scared. I'm not going to say I never had a thought, but I'm just too scared, and I'm not going to do it. And there's a certain amount of despair, which is why they don't care if they get caught.

The media often depicts merchant-customer interactions in poor, inner-city neighborhoods as the principle sources of black-Korean tensions. However, the source of this tension lies in the nature of the economics of poverty and its resultant pattern of dominant-subordinate contact between merchants and customers. These tensions are symptoms of larger circumstances in which both the merchants and the customers are victims. As David Caplovitz (1967, 192) stated in his classic work, *The Poor Pay More,* "the consumer problems of low-income families cannot be divorced from the other problems facing them. Until society can find ways of raising their educational level, improving their occupational opportunities, increasing their income, and reducing the discrimination against them—only limited solutions to their problems as consumers can be found." This was true in the 1960s when Jewish merchants predominated in poor black neighborhoods and still holds true today as a new legion of immigrants has entered these communities.

Conclusion

Immigrant entrepreneurs have made distinct inroads in many large U.S. cities. Approximately one-third of Korean families are engaged in small business, representing the highest rate of self-employment among all U.S. ethnic groups. Their access to class and ethnic resources, coupled with their utilization of social capital, contributes to the extraordinary rate of entrepreneurship. And once a nucleus of entrepreneurs becomes established, ethnic networks have a "fateful effect," paving the path for other family members and coethnic friends to follow suit.

Running a small business in an inner-city neighborhood is not what Korean immigrants had in mind when they came to the United States. Because they have been educated and trained as white-collar professionals, self-employment is a symbol of downward mobility for many Korean immigrants who find themselves extremely underemployed. Korean immigrant entrepreneurs work twelve to sixteen hours a day, six to seven days a week in physically demanding and routine work. To succeed in a competitive market, they exploit themselves, their family members, and fellow ethnics. However, given the obstacles they face in the primary labor market and their inability to transfer their education and pre-immigrant skills, Koreans turn to self-employment as an alternative to working in relatively low-wage salaried jobs. Entrepreneurship becomes the ladder to reaching the American dream of upward mobility.

This dream was shattered on April 29, 1992—the first day of the Los Angeles riots —when they suffered devastating losses totaling $400 million in property damage. Koreans now refer to this unforgettable turning point as *Sai-I-Gu* (April 29 in Korean). The worst domestic uprising of the century placed black-Korean conflict in the fore. However, this dyadic relationship fails to capture the depth and complexities facing the nation's inner-city communities. Placing black-Korean conflict at the core of the Los Angeles riots also distorts the nature of most merchant-customer interactions. Most day-to-day encounters are not fraught with racial animosity but rather are characterized by civility (Lee 2002).

Against the backdrop of inner-city poverty, heightened tension can transform small economic arguments into racialized conflict. A Korean merchant's refusal to give a cash refund for a defective beeper or an already-worn dress may become symbolic of cheap, exploitative "out-group" business owners who make money from the community and drain it of its resources. The irate customer who is not given the refund may not necessarily react to the objective features of the situation but rather to the symbolism that the situation represents, leading the customer to racially code economic arguments. Even though civility may characterize the daily lives for both merchants and customers, the normalcy of everyday encounters does not preclude the possibility of interethnic conflict such as boycotts or urban riots.

In speaking of black-Jewish relations, Gans (1969, 3) explains that

> it is more useful to look at the Negro-Jewish relationship from a longer sociological perspective. From that perspective, the recent incidents are only more visible instances in a long series of primarily economic conflicts between blacks, Jews, [and other ethnic groups] which are endemic to New York and to several other large American cities, and which can only be dealt with through economic solutions.

Korean merchants are not the first group to experience conflict with the black customers in poor neighborhoods and they will undoubtedly not be the last until we address the structural problems that plague inner-city communities.

NOTES

The author wishes to thank Herbert Gans, Kathryn Neckerman, Katherine Newman, John Skrentny, Rob Smith, Roger Waldinger, and Rhacel Parreñas for helpful comments on an earlier version of this paper. The author gratefully thanks the International Migration Program of the Social Science Research Council, the Andrew W. Mellon Foundation, and the National Science Foundation SBR-9633345 for research support on which this paper is based. The University of California President's Office provided research support during the writing of this paper. This article is based on the author's book, *Civility in the City: Blacks, Jews, and Koreans in Urban America* (Cambridge, MA: Harvard University Press, 2002).

1. Quoted from Selznick and Steinberg 1969, 130.

2. "Black" refers to a generic category that includes African Americans, West Indians, and Africans.

3. The research sites include three low-income and two middle-income black communities. The three low-income neighborhoods are West Harlem, NY, East Harlem, NY, and West Philadelphia, and the two middle-income communities include Jamaica, Queens, and East Mount Airy, Philadelphia.

4. The customers were paid $10 to thank them for taking their time to participate in the study. The funds were provided by a Dissertation Improvement Grant from the National Science Foundation, SBR-9633345.

5. Pyong Gap Min and Charles Jaret, "Ethnic Business Success: The Case of Korean Small Business in Atlanta," *Sociology and Social Research* 69 (1984): 432.

6. Laura Zigman, "Living Off-Center on Purpose," *New York Times,* December 12, 1996, C6.

7. "Scapegoating New York's Koreans," *New York Post,* January 25, 1990.

REFERENCES

Abelmann, Nancy and John Lie. 1995. *Blue Dreams.* Cambridge, MA: Harvard University Press.
Bates, Timothy. 1994. An Analysis of Korean-Immigrant-Owned Small-Business Start-Ups with Comparisons to African-American and Non-Minority-Owned Firms. *Urban Affairs Quarterly* 30: 227–48.
Bonacich, Edna. 1987. "Making It" in America: A Sociological Evaluation of the Ethics of Immigrant Entrepreneurship. *Sociological Perspectives* 30: 446–66.
Caplovitz, David. 1967. *The Poor Pay More.* New York: Free Press.
Coleman, James S. 1988. Social Capital in the Creation of Human Capital. *American Journal of Sociology* 94: S95–S121.
Gans, Herbert J. 1969. Negro-Jewish Conflict in New York City. *Midstream* 15: 3–15.
Jo, Moon H. 1992. Korean Merchants in the Black Community. *Ethnic and Racial Studies.* 15: 395–410.
Jones, Jon. 1986. Black, Koreans Struggle to Grasp Thread of Unity. *Los Angeles Times,* May 1.
Kang, Miliann. 1997. Manicuring Race, Gender, and Class. *Race, Gender, and Class* 4: 143–64.
Kim, Illsoo. 1981. *The New Urban Immigrants.* Princeton, NJ: Princeton University Press.
Lee, Heon Cheol. 1993. *Black-Korean Conflict in New York City.* Ph.D. Dissertation, Columbia University.
Lee, Jennifer. 1996. Business as Usual. *Common Quest: The Magazine of Black-Jewish Relations* 1: 35–38.
Lee, Jennifer. 1998. Cultural Brokers. *American Behavioral Scientist* 41: 927–37.

Lee, Jennifer. 1999. Retail Niche Domination among African American, Jewish, and Korean Entrepreneurs. *American Behavioral Scientist* 42: 1398–1416.

Lee, Jennifer. 2002. *Civility in the City.* Cambridge, MA: Harvard University Press.

Liebow, Elliot. 1967. *Tally's Corner.* Boston: Little, Brown.

Light, Ivan H. 1972. *Ethnic Enterprise in America.* Berkeley: University of California Press.

Light, Ivan and Edna Bonacich. 1988. *Immigrant Entrepreneurs.* Berkeley: University of California Press.

Light, Ivan and Angel A. Sanchez. 1987. Immigrant Entrepreneurs in 272 SMSA's. *Sociological Perspectives* 30: 373–99.

Merton, Robert K. 1968. Self-fulfilling Prophecy. *Social Theory and Social Structure.* New York: Free Press.

Min, Pyong Gap. 1984. From White-Collar Occupations to Small Business. *Sociological Quarterly* 25: 333–52.

Min, Pyong Gap. 1996. *Caught in the Middle.* Berkeley: University of California Press.

Njeri, Itabari. 1996. Kimchee and Grits. *CommonQuest: The Magazine for Black-Jewish Relations* 1: 39–45.

Noel, Peter. 1981. Koreans Vie for Harlem Dollars. *NY Amsterdam News,* July 4.

Ong, Paul and Suzanne Hee. 1993. *Losses in Los Angeles Civil Unrest April 29–May 1, 1992.* Los Angeles: Center for Pacific Rim Studies, University of California.

Park, Kyeyoung. 1997. *The Korean American Dream.* Ithaca, NY: Cornell University Press.

Portes, Alejandro. 1995. *The Economic Sociology of Immigration: Essays on Networks, Ethnicity, and Entrepreneurship.* New York: Russell Sage Foundation.

Rieder, Jonathan. 1990. Trouble in Store. *New Republic* 203: 16–22.

Sassen, Saskia. 1991. The Informed Economy. In John Mollenkopf and Manuel Castells (eds.), *Dual City: Restructuring New York.* New York: Russell Sage Foundation, pp. 79–101.

Selznick Gertrude J. and Stephen Steinberg. 1969. *The Tenacity of Prejudice.* New York: Harper & Row.

Stack, Carol B. 1974. *All Our Kin.* New York: Harper & Row.

Waldinger, Roger. 1996. *Still the Promised City?* Cambridge, MA: Harvard University Press.

Wilson, William Julius. 1987. *The Truly Disadvantaged.* Chicago: University of Chicago Press.

Yoon, In-Jin. 1997. *On My Own.* Chicago: University of Chicago Press.

Chapter 11

Gender, Migration, and Work
Filipina Health Care Professionals
in the United States

Yen Le Espiritu

The ferocity of U.S. (neo)colonial exploitation, the mismanagement of the Philippines by the country's *coamprador* elite, and the violence of globalized capitalism have flung Filipinos "to the ends of the earth" as contract workers, sojourners, expatriates, refugees, exiles, and immigrants (San Juan Jr. 1998, 190).[1] Although Filipinos could be found in more than 130 countries and territories by the early 1990s, with most earning a living as short-term contract workers, the vast majority of the Filipinos who migrated to the United States have resettled there as "permanent" immigrants (Tyner 1999). According to the 2000 U.S. Census, Filipinos totaled 1.8 million, constituting the second largest immigrant group as well as the second largest Asian American group in the United States.[2] Filipino migration to the United States differs in many respects from that to other labor-importing states. The history of U.S. colonialism in the Philippines, combined with a relatively liberal U.S. immigration policy and the proximity to alternative "cheapened" labor supplies, particularly from Central America and the Caribbean, means that a larger proportion of Filipino immigrants in the United States than elsewhere find employment in higher-status and higher-skilled occupations (Tyner 1999).

Since 1960, women have dominated Philippine labor flows to the United States. In 2000, of the roughly forty-three thousand Filipinos who immigrated to the United States that year, 61 percent were women (U.S. Immigration and Naturalization Service 2001). Unlike their counterparts in Europe, the Middle East, and East Asia, the majority of whom are contract domestic workers, Filipina immigrants in the United States are decidedly more concentrated within professional sectors, a phenomenon that can be largely accounted for by the migration of Filipina health care professionals, especially nurses (Tyner 1999). Since the 1970s, the Philippines has been the largest supplier of health care professionals to the United States, sending nearly twenty-five thousand nurses to this country between 1966 and 1985 and another ten thousand between 1989 and 1991. In 1989, Filipino nurses constituted close to 75 percent of the United States's total foreign nurses; in 2003, this figure had climbed to 85 percent (Advincula 2004; Ong and Azores 1994). In fact, many women (and increasingly men) in the Philippines studied nursing in the hope of securing employment abroad, and many of the nursing programs in the Philippines accordingly oriented themselves toward supplying the overseas markets (Ong and Azores 1994).[3]

There is a widespread assumption—in the scholarly literature as well as in the popular imagination—that immigrants, especially those from developing countries, come to the United States primarily for economic reasons such as obtaining a higher income and standard of living. These economic explanations are well documented in the "push-pull" approaches to the study of migration. The neoclassical economic theory casts the individual migrant as a calculating economic agent, weighing the benefits and costs of migrating from low-wage to high-wage economies (Thomas 1973; Borjas 1990); and the updated "new economics of labor migration" (Stark 1991) approach claims that migration decisions are made not just by individuals but by the whole family to maximize the household income and survival chances (Massey et al. 1993; Taylor 1999). But migrants do not act in a vacuum devoid of historical and political context. Linking U.S. imperialism and migration to the United States, I argue that the overrepresentation of health care professionals among contemporary Filipino immigrants is the result of intertwined influences of U.S. (neo)colonialism in the Philippines, deliberate recruitment from U.S. health institutions, transnationalism, and gender ideologies and practices in both the Philippines and the United States. As a much-sought-after group among U.S. immigrants, Filipina health care nurses can enter the United States as principal immigrants. A female-first migration, especially when the women are married, has enormous ramifications for both gender roles and family relations. Therefore, in the second half of the article, I examine the way migration processes, labor recruitment practices, and employment conditions have reconfigured gender and family relations for Filipina health care professionals.

A Critical Transnational Perspective on Migration Studies

Transnational migration studies form a highly fragmented field; there continues to be much disagreement about the scope of the field and the outcome of the transnational processes under observation (Portes, Guarzino, and Landolt 1999; Glick Schiller 1997). From an epistemological stance, I find transnationalism to be a valuable *conceptual* tool, one that disrupts the narrow emphasis on "modes of incorporation" characteristic of much of the field of U.S. immigration studies and highlights instead the range and depth of migrants' lived experience in multinational social fields (Levitt 2001; Glick Schiller and Fouron 2001; Perez 2004). In this paper, I employ a critical transnational perspective to call attention to yet another way of thinking beyond the limits of the nation-state: one that stresses the global relations that set the context for immigration and immigrant life. That is, today's global world is not just some glorious hybrid, complex mixity; it is systematically divided and historically produced (Guarnizo and Smith 1998; Massey 1999).

In the United States, public discussions about immigration fundamentally centers on people who cross borders. However, the media, elected officials, and the general public often represent border crossers to be desperate individuals migrating in search of the "land of opportunity." From the perspective of immigration restrictionists, immigrants unfairly "invade" the United States, drain its scarce resources, and threaten its cultural unity (Perea 1997). Besides fueling nativist hysteria, this anti-immigrant rhetoric makes invisible other important border crossers: U.S. colonizers, the military, and corporations that invade and forcefully deplete the economic and cultural resources of less powerful countries (Lipsitz 1998, 54). Given these multiple forms of border crossing, a critical approach to immigration studies must begin with the unequal links between First and Third World nations forged by colonization, decolonization, and the globalization of late capitalism. A critical transnational perspective that stresses the global structures of inequality is critical for understanding Asian immigration and Asian American lives in the United States. Linking global economic development with global histories of colonialism, Edna Bonacich and Lucie Cheng (1984) argue that the pre–World War II immigration of Asians to the United States has to be understood within the context of the development of capitalism in Europe and the United States and the emergence of imperialism, especially in relation to Asia. From World War II onward, as the world economy has become much more globally integrated, Asia has been a site of U.S. expansion. As a result, contemporary immigrants from the Philippines, South Vietnam, South Korea, Cambodia, and Laos come from countries that have been deeply disrupted by U.S. colonialism, war, and neocolonial capitalism (Lowe 1996; Campomanes 1997).

In the case of the Philippines, the prior flow of population, armies, goods, capital, and culture—moving primarily from the United States to the Philippines—profoundly dislocated many Filipinos from their home and subsequently spurred their migration to the United States and elsewhere. In 1802, in the aftermath of the Spanish American War, the United States brutally took possession of the Philippines over native opposition and uprising, thereby extending its "manifest destiny" to Pacific Asia. U.S. colonialism (1898–1946) stunted the Philippine national economy, imposed English as the lingua franca, installed a U.S.-style educational system, and Americanized many Filipino values and aspirations (Espiritu 2003). Even long after the Philippines regained its independence in 1946, the United States continued to exert significant influence on the archipelago—through trade, foreign assistance, and military bases. Infected with U.S. colonial culture and images of U.S. abundance, and saddled by the grave economic and political conditions in the Philippines, many Filipinos migrated to the United States to claim for themselves the promises of the "land of opportunity" (Espiritu 2003).

U.S. Colonialism, Labor Recruitment, and the Production of Filipina Nurse Migrants

Although many scholars have conceptualized the contemporary Filipina nurse migration to the United States as a post-1965 phenomenon,[4] Catherine Choy (2003)[5] argues that we need to trace the origins of this international migrant labor force back to early-twentieth-century U.S. colonialism in the Philippines. According to her, the introduction of nursing in the Philippines was part of a larger U.S. colonial attempt to "civilize" and "sanitize" the medically defective Filipino bodies under the guise of benevolent rule. In a nuanced analysis of the role of colonial medicine in the formation of colonial hegemony, Warwick Anderson (1995) delineates the ways by which the language of American medical science in the Philippines fabricated and rationalized images of the bodies of the American colonizers and the Filipinos—and in so doing, biologized the social and historical context of U.S. imperialism. The scientific papers produced by the colonial laboratory during the early 1990s racialized Filipino bodies as dangerous carriers of foreign antibodies and germs that threatened white bodies; and American bodies as vulnerable but resilient, capable of guarding against the invisible foreign parasites lodged in native bodies.[6] The fears of the "innately unhygienic" Filipinos led to and justified house-to-house sanitary inspections and the quarantining of the "sick" from the communities. As such, the American medical discourse, as a privileged site for producing the "truth" about the "tropics," served to consolidate racial hierarchies, naturalizing the power and legitimacy of American foreign bodies to appropriate, command, and contain the Philippines and its people.

Like previous American medical interventions, the introduction of nursing in the Philippines reinforced many of the racialist functions and beliefs of Western medicine—all in the name of a humane imperialism. The opening of the first government school of nursing in the Philippines in 1907 was part of the larger U.S. colonial project of transforming Filipino bodies into a strong and healthy people capable of self-rule. In other words, the racialist construction of the Philippines as always already diseased justified the need for more American medical intervention in the form of nursing. Viewing the teaching of nursing to Filipinos as a "moral obligation," American nursing educators often derided their young Filipina charges for their perceived temporal backwardness, "primitive" health practices, and lack of "rudimentary knowledge" about sanitation (Choy 2003, 23–25). For their part, despite their initial rebuff of the idea of women nursing, Filipinas who attended American-founded nursing schools gradually learned American nursing work culture, gained English fluency, and came to associate the United States with glamour, opportunity, and upward mobility. Professional nursing provided them with newfound opportunities to interact with colonial government officials, to attend government functions, to enter a prestigious profession, to serve their country—and, most of all, to travel (Choy 2003).

In the early twentieth century, as part of their effort to acculturate elite Filipinos and to augment their devotion to the United States, the U.S. colonial government sent several hundred individuals, including those in nursing, to study in U.S. colleges and universities. Highly selected, these *pensionados* often were the children of prominent Filipino families whose loyalty the colonial regime hoped to win (Lawcock 1975; Posadas and Guyotte 1990). As anticipated, these early exchange programs, which brought Filipinos to the United States for "advanced training," reconstructed a global, cultural, and intellectual hierarchy in which U.S. institutions—educational, political, medical—were superior to those of the Philippines. As exchange visitors, Filipina nurses became Philippine cultural ambassadors in the United States, and U.S. nursing ambassadors upon their return to the Philippines. The possibilities of going to America as exchange students and nurses dramatically increased nursing's popularity. Eventually, studying and working abroad in the United States became a de facto prerequisite for occupational mobility in the nursing profession in the Philippines.

During the post–World War II period, the establishment of the Exchange Visitor Program (EVP) in 1948, which allowed visitors to stay in the United States for two years for training, made the dream of going abroad to the United States a possibility not only for elite women but for the majority of nurses in the Philippines. The prestige associated with study and work abroad propelled Filipino nurses to transform the EVP into an avenue for the first wave of mass migration of nurses to the United States, even despite troubling reports of exploitation by U.S. hospitals, which largely regarded the exchange nurses as a "cheapened" workforce. By the late 1960s, 80 percent of exchange visitors in the United States were from the Philippines, with nurses composing the majority of the participants (Asperilla 1976). The long-established presence of an Americanized professional nursing training system in the Philippines, coupled with the existence of a transnational community of Filipino nurses created by the EVP, laid the professional, social, and cultural groundwork for a "feminized, highly-educated and exportable labor force" (Choy 2003, 13). Goaded by grave economic and political conditions in the Philippines, this available labor force took full advantage of the relaxation of U.S. immigration rules and preference for health care professionals in 1965 to migrate en masse to the United States. Like other immigrants, Filipina migrant nurses have had to accept inequitable pay and work arrangements in exchange for the comparatively higher salaries and immigration opportunities available in the United States (Ong and Azores 1994).

The overrepresentation of health care professionals among contemporary Filipino immigrants is also the result of deliberate and aggressive recruitment from U.S. hospitals, nursing homes, and health organizations seeking a "cheapened" workforce ostensibly in response to domestic shortages in trained nurses (Ong and Azores 1994; Chang 2000). Since the passage of the 1965 Immigration Act, U.S. health organizations, in collaboration with Philippine travel agencies, actively recruited Filipino nurses, especially former exchange nurses, to migrate to the United States for permanent employment in their institutions. Many hospitals and nursing homes recruited workers via the H-1 nursing visa program, which enabled them to sponsor nurses from abroad on temporary work visas to fill permanent positions.[7] Recruitment advertisements, conspicuously placed in the major local newspapers and in the *Philippine Journal of Nursing,* promised potential migrants interest-free loans for travel expenses as well as such bonuses as continuing education, tuition assistance at U.S. universities, a higher salary, health plans, pension plans, paid vacation, and sick leave (Ong and Azores 1994; Choy 2003, 99–101, 107). However, in their aggressive hunt for nurses, nurse recruiters have often misinformed recruited nurses about U.S. licensing requirements, educational credentials, work conditions, and pay and benefits. Some recruiters demanded a "fee" averaging $7,000 to $9,000 from the recruitees, ostensibly to pay for the recruiter's fee and to arrange the nurse's visa. Since few women could afford this fee, most agreed to have it deducted from their meager monthly wages, a condition that left many H-1 immigrants in "debt peonage for at least two years" (Chang 2000; also Choy 2003, 173; Ong and Azores 1994).

Gender and Migration: The Formation of a Gendered Labor Force

The field of gender and immigration research has moved from the "immigrant women only" approach that emphasizes sex differences in migration systems to one that examines how gender as a social system contextualizes migration processes for both women and men (Hondagneu-Sotelo 1999; Tyner 1999). In particular, this scholarship has interrogated the ways in which constructions of masculinities and femininities organize migration and migration outcomes (Hondagneu-Sotelo 1994). Although the concept of gender is invaluable for the understanding of migration experiences, women of color have argued that the gender process cannot be understood independently of class and race and other structures of oppression (Espiritu 1997; Glenn 2002). Accordingly, contemporary approaches to migration have increasingly questioned the premise of a universal, shared experience of womanhood and have developed theories and designed research that capture the multiple and mutually constitutive relations of race, class, nationality, and legal status (Pessar 1999).

Gender beliefs, often working in tandem with and through racial beliefs, affected the content and scope of U.S. colonialist policies and practices in the Philippines. As feminist theorists have reminded us, the construction of "otherness" is achieved not only through racial but also through sexual and gendered modes of differentiation (Mohanty 1991; Stoler 1991; Yegenoglu 1998). Attentive to the mutually constitutive aspects of race and gender, historian Kristin Hoganson (1998) has shown how the racialization of Filipinos as biologically unfit for independence drew on ideas about gender. Through a careful reading of a range of official and cultural discourses of the time, she convincingly demonstrates that the prominent stereotypes of the Filipinos—as uncivilized, savages, rapists, or children—all presented the Filipinos as lacking the *manly* character seen as necessary for self-government. She adds to this list the stereotype of the *feminized* Filipino: the depiction of the Philippines as woman, Filipino men as effeminate, and Filipino women as highly feminine and sexualized (Hoganson 1998, 137). The hyperfeminization of Filipino men and women misrepresented and distorted gender relations in the Philippines, pitting the two sexes against each other. They also bolstered the racialized conviction that Filipino men lacked the manly character for self-government and justified the need for U.S. interventions to rectify the Philippine "unnatural" gender order (Espiritu 2003). The extensive U.S. military presence in the Philippines (1898–1992) has also produced stereotypes of Filipinas as desirable but dangerous "prostitutes" and/or submissive "mail-order" brides (Halualani 1995; Egan 1996). Many Filipino nationalists have charged that the "prostitution problem" in the Philippines stemmed from U.S. and Philippine government policies that promoted a sex industry—brothels, bars, and massage parlors—for U.S. servicemen stationed or on leave in the Philippines. During the Vietnam War, the Philippines was known as the "rest and recreation" center of Asia, housing approximately ten thousand U.S. servicemen daily (Coronel and Rosca 1993; Warren 1993). In this context, *all* Filipinas were racialized as sexual commodities, usable and expendable. These established images often "travel" with Filipinas overseas and prescribe their racialization there. For example, Christine Chin (1998, 144–46) reports that many middle-class Malaysian employers regard their Filipina domestic workers as sexually promiscuous and thus in need of intense methods of surveillance and control.

U.S. colonial nursing in the Philippines highlights the complex intersections of gender ideologies with those of race and class in shaping U.S. colonial agendas and practices. U.S. colonial training of Filipino nurses, recruited primarily from "respectable" families, involved the imposition of Americans' gendered (and also racialized and classed) assumptions about labor, which, as feminist scholar Louise Newman (1999, 34) points out, posited that "the more civilized the race, the more the men and women of that race had to differ from one another." Since American women colonialists linked differentiated gender roles with racial progress, they viewed the construction of a separate sphere of Filipino women nurses to be foundational to the uplift of the Filipino race. Thus the gendered notions of nursing as *women's* work—widely accepted in early-twentieth-century white middle-class America—was an idea that American nursing educators "actively had to reproduce" in the Philippines (Choy 2003, 26). The U.S. colonial government deliberately separated and excluded Filipino men from the labor of nursing; it also attempted to legislate the creation of a female nursing labor force through a 1909 act that appropriated funds for women-only nursing classes (Choy 2003, 44). The construction of this gendered labor force—and gendered form of mobility—would lay the foundation for the significant women-dominated migrations of Filipino nurses beginning in the second half of the twentieth century.

The women-dominated migrations of Filipino nurses also reflect women's segmentation into nursing professions in the United States (Tyner 1999). The endemic and recurring shortage of nurses in the Untied States constitutes the primary underlying factor for the recruitment of Filipino nurses to the United States. Although fueled by the rapid growth in the demand for health care and the changing character of U.S. medical care, the shortage of nurses is also the result of sex-based discrimination in the profession (Ong and Azores 1994; Tyner 1999). Since nursing was consistently women's work in the United States, wage levels in the field have been kept comparatively low. Even in a competitive market, where demand for nurses has consistently outstripped the supply of labor, wages for nurses have not risen to the levels needed to entice U.S.-born women to enter the field (Ong and Azores 1994, 166). In response to this glaring wage disparity, nurses in the United States have unionized and filed comparable-worth suits to demand higher pay (Blum 1991, 104–8; Hunter 1986, ch. 7). The lack of decent wages—coupled with poor working conditions and a lack of professional prestige—have induced many American nurses to leave the profession and others to shun these jobs (Ong and Azores 1994; Tyner 1999).

The U.S. chronic labor shortage of nurses, most acute in inner-city and rural facilities, had led to the active recruitment and continued preferential treatment of foreign-trained nurses in U.S. immigration laws. In response, since the 1970s, the Philippine government has actively promoted the export of its nurses in exchange for their remittance dollars, which are critically needed to alleviate the nation's mounting external debt and trade deficits.[8] Once denigrated for abandoning the health needs of their own people for the mighty dollar, Filipino nurses working abroad became the Philippines' new national heroes whose earnings would help to revitalize the nation's economy (Choy 2003, 116). In a 1973 address to Filipino migrant nurses, Philippine Secretary of Health Clemente S. Gatmaitan proclaimed, "we are proud of you. Another benefit that accrues from your work is the precious dollar you earn and send back to your folks at home. In this manner, you help indirectly in the improvement of our economic conditions" (cited in Choy 2003, 117). Gatmaitan's declaration does not apply to nurses only, but reflects the Philippine nation-state's economic strategy since 1974: to "export" its workers worldwide in exchange for their remittances (Rafael 2000, 205–6).

Philippine government officials and recruitment agencies exploit gendered depictions of Filipinas to market the Filipino nurses. As expected, these officials and agencies extol the nurses' English-speaking skills and American professional training, both a legacy of U.S. colonialism. However, in their aggressive promotion of the migration of nurses, they also praise Filipino nurses for their purported "tenderness" and natural knack for care giving, thereby relying on and perpetuating stereotypical depictions of the "Oriental woman" as inherently feminine and servile. In a 2001 speech commemorating the 103rd founding anniversary of the Philippine Department of Foreign Affairs, Philippine Vice President and Foreign Affairs Secretary Teofisto T. Guingona, Jr. (2001), praised the Filipino migrant nurses' predisposition for the gendered work of nursing:

> In Canada, in America, in Europe, and in other places Filipina nurses are in demand. Why? Because they do their job with a smile, with charm, with grace, with the real purpose of helping to ease the patients' pain, without looking at the clock, without minding the overtime, really trying to cure the patient and comforting him in his time of crisis. And that is why Filipino nurses are in demand.

In addition to gendering the patient as male and the nurses as female, Guingona depicted the Filipina nurses as cheerful about and even welcoming of their harsh working conditions, such as long hours and hard physical labor. In the same way, Annabelle Reyes Borromeo, founding president and CEO of STI-Universal Worker Inc., an international consulting firm based in the Philippines that specializes in training, educating, and preparing qualified nurses for careers abroad, imbued Filipina nurses with feminine virtues: "Our nurses need not necessarily be taught to care—they're natural at this—from the way we talk and touch, it's like second nature to us already and it's what they like about Filipino nurses" (*Manila Times* 2004).

Female-First Migration and Changing Gender Relations

Through the process of migration and settlement, patriarchal relations undergo continual negotiation as women and men rebuild their lives in the new country. An important task in the study of migration has been to examine this reconfiguration of gender relations. Central to the reconfiguration of gender hierarchies is the change in immigrant women's and men's relative positions of power and status in the country of settlement. Theoretically, migration may improve women's empowerment and social position if it leads to increased participation in wage employment, more control over earnings, and greater participation in family decision making (Pessar 1984). Alternatively, migration may leave gender asymmetries largely unchanged even though certain dimensions of gender inequalities are modified (Espiritu 1997).

As a result of the recurring shortage of nurses in the United States, Filipina health care workers are a much sought after group among U.S. immigrants, and thus can enter the United States as principal immigrants. This means that unmarried women can immigrate on their own accord and that married women can enter as the primary immigrants, with their husbands and children following as dependents. Drawing from in-depth interviews of Filipino Americans in San Diego,[9] California, the rest of this paper explores the impact of the female-first migration of health-care professionals on gender and family relations. San Diego has long been a favorite site of settlement for Filipinos and is today the third largest U.S. destination of contemporary Filipino immigrants. In 2000, there were approximately 120,000 Filipinos in San Diego County. Although these immigrants constituted only 4 percent of the country's general population, they constituted more than 50 percent of the Asian American population (Espiritu 2003, 17). A 1992 survey of approximately eight hundred Filipino high school students in San Diego found that close to a quarter of the respondents' mothers worked in the field of health care, about half of them as registered nurses (Espiritu and Wolf 2001).

"We Were Young and We Wanted to See the World": Migration of Single Women

Rose Ocampo grew up in Cavite among four sisters and three brothers as the fourth of eight children. She decided to become a nurse because "it was a trend": "All my friends were going into nursing so I went ahead and went into nursing too." Rose came to the United States in 1961 under the auspices of the U.S. Exchange Visitor Program (EVP). She explained that she and a friend wanted to visit the United States "to see the country." "It wasn't for the money," she said quickly. "The stipend was only a hundred dollars a month and they worked you forty-eight hours a week." What the two young women wanted was "a new environment, for adventure. We were young and we wanted to see the world." Rose was sent to a small town in Minnesota, where she befriended other EVP Filipino nurses who helped her to integrate into her new community. When her exchange visa expired at the end of two years, Rose wanted to extend her stay because "my friends and I still wanted to go around the world." Instead of returning to the Philippines, she exited the United States by going to Canada, where she worked for a year. However, just before she left for Canada, she befriended a Filipino American man who followed her to Canada. The two married a year later, which allowed Rose to officially immigrate to the United States.

Rose's experience illustrates the power of gender in shaping migration. First, it shows that gender-based transnational social networks circumscribe migration opportunities. Women nurses migrated to and settled in the United States with the help of other women. Through letters, phone calls, and return visits, Filipino nurses who had gone abroad created new expectations, goals, and desires among young Filipino women still in the Philippines. According to Luz Latus, her nursing friends' and colleagues' decisions to apply for U.S. visas influenced her own decision to emigrate:

> After I graduated, I decided to come here. I thought, "Well, it seems like everybody wants to go there." So I thought I'd try. Why not, you know? There is always a farewell party for so-and-so. She's leaving for the U.S., to do this and that. Well, somehow, a whole bunch of us, we decided, let's go ahead and apply. You know how when you were young, I mean . . . you know, you're really, just want to experience this. What is this thing they're talking about? America.

In the process of relocating and settling in the United States, Filipino health care migrants also create new transnational networks of support, helping each other to adjust to their new occupational, social, economic, and cultural settings (Choy 2003).

Second, Rose's experiences reveal that men and women often give different reasons for migrating. When asked about their motivations for migrating to the United States, the Filipino men in my study tended to give the following reason: to better represent themselves as able economic providers and desirable sexual partners. In contrast, while Filipina nurses also mentioned economic motives, many more cited desire to be liberated from gendered constraints: to see the world and experience untried ways of living (see also Parreñas 2001, 62–69). The Exchange Visitor Program, and the new occupational preference categories of the 1965 Immigration Act, created opportunities for the Filipina women health professionals to enter the United States on their own accord. Indeed, the majority of the nurses that I interviewed came to the United States initially as single women, a fact corroborated by other studies of Filipina nurses (Choy 2003). In the interviews, many of these nurses represented their decision to come to the United States as an effort to expand gender roles, especially to unshackle themselves from family discipline that hindered their individual development. For example, Cecilia Bonus indicated that she applied to study in the United States because "my family was just so protective. I just kind of wanted to get away and be independent." Being away from home enabled many young women to free themselves temporarily from strict parental control on their activities and movements. In the United States, many traveled freely, socialized widely, lived in their own apartments, and stayed out late at night.

Perhaps most important, Filipina health care professionals reveled in their newfound freedom to befriend and date men. Carmen Reynila described how she and her fellow exchange nurses enjoyed company of Filipino sailors[10] in town:

> There used to be a lot of Filipino gatherings around. So you got to meet each other, and then the sailors, you know, they would come to our apartments, and then, you know, we would go out with them, but then always in a group [laughter]. Because I would say there is a safety in numbers [laughter].

Many Filipino women seized their newfound freedom to make more independent choices about marriage. Some elected to marry in the United States, partly to mute any possible objections from their parents. In an example, Rosie Roxas, who met her

Filipino Navy husband while in San Diego, explained why she did not return to the Philippines to marry: "My parents would not have approved of him. Their background . . . it would have been very difficult. . . . They wanted me to marry a professional. . . . He would not have passed." In her study of Filipino nurses, Choy (2003) reports that Philippine government health officials and nursing leaders used a rhetoric of spirituality and morality to create the new lifestyles of Filipino exchange nurses abroad. These critics charged that some Filipino exchange nurses had become morally corrupt and associated the nurses' new lifestyles in the United States with licentiousness. Choy accurately interprets these charges as efforts to persuade Filipino nurses to return to work in the Philippines. However, in light of the women's newfound independence, I believe these charges must also be viewed as retaliating moves to reassert patriarchal control over the bodies of these women.

Negotiating Changing Gender Roles: The Migration of Married Women

When the women are married, a female-first migration stream can have enormous ramifications for both family relations and domestic roles. In a reversal of historical patterns of migration, many married women health professionals enter the United States as primary immigrants, with their husbands and children following as dependents. Take Cecile Garcia's story, for example. Cecile had always dreamed of "America" and going abroad figured prominently in her decision to select a nursing career. In 1973, married with two young children, she left for the United States under the auspices of the Exchange Visitor Program. Although both she and her mechanic husband shared a desire to move the family to the United States, it was her profession that allowed them to do so. As an exchange nurse, she came alone; her husband stayed behind to care for their two young daughters. Eighteen months later, when she had successfully adjusted her status from exchange visitor to permanent resident, she petitioned for her family to join her. But the temporary separation from the children had its costs:

> My daughter who was two when I left didn't even know me when I went back to get them. She would not come to me. I stayed there for three weeks when I picked them up . . . still she would not come to me. I was very hurt by that. I was like a stranger . . . and that really struck me. I don't want to not be known by my children.

These separations, even when temporary, can leave lifelong scars. At the age of twenty-one, Melanie Villa still harbored unresolved grief over her mother's decision to leave for the United States during her first two years of life: "Sometimes, I still think about it . . . like the fact that I was never breast-fed like my sister, who was born here. . . . It doesn't seem fair, you know. . . . And I wonder if it had affected my relationship with my mother." These experiences of transnational motherhood, albeit temporary, continue a long historical legacy of people of color being incorporated into the United States through restrictive systems of labor that do not recognize the workers' family needs and rights (Dill 1988; Glenn 1986; Hondagneu-Sotelo and Avila 1997; Parreñas 2001).

A female-first migration stream also affects traditional gender roles. In many instances, men who immigrate as their wives' dependents experience downward occupational mobility in the United States, while their wives maintain their professional status. Pyong Gap Min (1998, 52) reports that among Korean immigrant families in New York, while Korean nurses hold stable jobs, many of their educated husbands are unemployed or underemployed. Gender role reversals—wives' increased economic role and husbands' reduced economic role—challenge men's sense of well-being and place undue stress on the family. For example, Elizabeth Mayor, a Filipina medical technologist, entered the United States in 1965 through the Exchange Visitor Program, leaving behind her husband and two sons. One year later, Elizabeth changed her status to permanent resident and petitioned for her family. Elizabeth's husband, who had a degree in criminology, could not find work comparable to his education and training in the United States. Elizabeth described their differential access to suitable employment:

> For me, since I had the training in Illinois, and had my license as a med tech, I was able to work in the medical profession in the laboratory. I had no problems finding a job. But for him, it was difficult. He had to work odd jobs, anything that was available there. That was a minus for him. . . . My husband was more dependent on me because I had a stable job.

Her husband was "bitter" about this role reversal: "He had a big problem. His self-esteem was really low. When he first came, he worked as a janitor, then as a dishwasher. He was working all the time but in blue-collar jobs. It took a lot out of his self-esteem, as far as that goes." Because of this loss of status, Elizabeth's husband repeatedly expressed his desire to return to the Philippines—for the entire duration of their thirteen-year stay in Illinois. In 1989, Elizabeth's sister urged them to leave Chicago and join the family business in San Diego. Although Elizabeth had a "good job" in Chicago, she decided to accept her sister's invitation, in part because it included a job offer for her husband. At the time of our interview in 1994, Elizabeth reported that her husband's self-esteem has been restored: "My husband is happy now. That was the first steady job he'd held since he came to the United States." In contrast, Elizabeth had difficulty finding a stable job and instead worked part-time for a local company. But Elizabeth expressed that she was content with her new life: "So it is just the opposite here. He has a steady job and now I work part time. Which I like too. . . . As an Oriental, my upbringing is . . . usually the husband is the bread earner back home. So that worked perfect for me. It's a lot better for him here than back East. So I am happy."

Elizabeth's account of her family experiences calls attention to the dissimilar structure of opportunities that many immigrant men and women encounter in the contemporary United States (Hondagneu-Sotelo 1994; Espiritu 1997; Menjivar 1999). The dynamics of the U.S. economy, in this case the shortage of medical personnel, places many women in a relatively favorable position with respect to access to paid work, whereas their male peers do not fare as well. At the same time, Elizabeth's experience challenges the relative resource models that predict that as women's earnings rise relative to their husbands', their authority and status in the family will correspondingly rise. Elizabeth's story suggests that the labor market advantage does not automatically or uniformly lead to more egalitarian relations in the family. Instead, perceived cultural ideals about gender and spousal relations that were held in the Philippine, some of which were imported through U.S. colonialism, such as the belief that the men should be the primary economic providers and heads of households, continue to influence the outcomes of the changing balance of resources in the new country.

Working at Family Life

One of primary themes in gender and immigration research concerns the impact of immigrant women's employment on gender equality in the family. Like other case studies on gender relations among salaried professionals, my research on women health professionals indicates that women's employment has led to the greater involvement of men in household labor (Chen 1992; Min 1998; Pesquera 1993). However, this more equitable household division of labor is not attributable to women's earning power, but rather to the women's demanding job schedules and to the couple's recognition that at least two incomes are needed to "make it" in this country. Like other immigrants, the health care professionals' success requires the work of the whole family, with husbands and children at times having to assume tasks not usually expected of them.

A survey of Filipino nurses in Los Angeles County reveals that these women, to increase their incomes, tend to work double shifts or the higher-paying evening shifts and night shifts (Ong and Azores 1994, 183–84).[11] Given the long hours and the graveyard shifts that typify a nurse's work schedule, many husbands have had to assume more child-care and other household responsibilities in their wives' absences. Some nurses have elected to work the night shift, not only because of the higher pay but also because they can leave the children with their husbands instead of with paid child-care providers. According to Cecilia Bonus, "I work mostly at night. So my husband takes care of the kids. . . . He's pretty good at helping when I have to work. . . . He's pretty understanding as far as that goes." Maricela Rebay's mother took pride in the fact that she never left her children with baby-sitters:

> We never had baby sitters. Oh, my mom is the toughest person in the world. She just managed. When she was in nursing, she would work at night. And my dad would take care of us when she was at work. So, like, in the morning, when she gets home, she makes breakfast for the kids, and then my dad drives us to school, and then she would go to sleep.

In her research on shift work and dual-earner spouses with children, Harriet Pressner (1988) finds that the husbands of night-shift workers do a significant part of child care; in most cases, it was the husbands who supervised the often-rushed routines of getting their children up and off to school or to child care.

When wives and/or husbands are unable to manage around-the-clock care for their children, they sometimes rely on the eldest child to shoulder the responsibility. When Maria Galang turned fifteen, both of her parents worked the night shift, her mother as a nurse at the local hospital and her father as a janitor at the local mall. Maria was forced to take care of her younger sister during her parents' absence:

> Because mom and dad worked so much, I had to assume the role of mother hen. And it was a strain especially at that point when I hit high school. They figured that I was old enough now. I remember frequent nights when my sister would cry and she wanted mom. What could I do? While mom and dad provided that financial support, we needed emotional support as well, which was often lacking.

This arrangement can take a toll on family relations: A child who has grown up without the mother's presence may no longer respond to her authority (Hondagneu-Sotelo and Avila 1997, 562). As an example, for five years, Rose Dumlao "mothered" her younger brother while her navy father was away at sea and her nurse mother was working long hours at the hospital. As a result, Rose's brother channeled his affection and respect to Rose, his "other mother," instead of to his mother:

> I think the reason why my brother doesn't really respect my mom the way he should is because he never really saw my mom as the caretaker because she was never around. So even now, whenever my parents want my brother to do something, like if they have to talk to him, I have to be either in the room or I have to be the one that's talking to him because he's not going to listen to them. Because I spent more time with him.

Even when there are no younger siblings to care for, the parents' absence still pains their children. Gabriela Garcia, whose parents divorced when she was nine years old, recounted how she managed when her mother worked the graveyard shift:

> After my parents divorced, my mother was working two shifts. She would work basically from three in the afternoon till seven in the morning. She would be gone by the time I had come home from school. And then I was by myself. . . . So I slept by myself. I had to have the radio, the TV, and the light on because I was so scared sometimes.

Research on gender relations among salaried professionals indicates that gains in gender equality have been uneven. Even when there is greater male involvement in child care in these families, women continue to perform more of the household labor than their husbands (Chen 1992; Min 1998; Pesquera 1993). Moreover, Pesquera (1993, 185) reports that, for the most part, the only way women have altered the distribution of household labor has been through conflict and confrontation, suggesting that ideologically most men continue to view housework as women's work. These findings remind us that professional women, like most other working women, have to juggle full-time work outside the home with the responsibilities of child care and housework. Cecilia Bonus, a nurse mother of three young children, confided that she felt overwhelmed by the never-ending chores: "Here you have to work so hard. You have to do everything. You have to wash the dishes, you have to do laundry, you have to clean the house, you have to take care of the kids. It's just endless." Although Cecilia's husband took care of the children when she worked the night shifts, she wished that he would do more:

> The husbands should help out more, I think . . . as far as the children go, and the housework. . . . That's one thing I like about Western culture. They have more liberty as a female and the rights that men have. It's not just a one-way thing where women have to do everything. Men should do things like chores at home, too, you know.

Cecilia, who came from a middle-class family in the Philippines, confided that she missed the "helpers" that she had in the Philippines. "Over there, you have maids to help you," she said. "You don't have to do the chores. You have one maid for each child. Life is so much easier there. Every little thing is offered to you, even a glass of water. I just wished I had a helper here." Like Cecilia, the majority of the women in my study longed for the "helpers" they once had or expected to have had they stayed in the Philippines. In the United States, instead of enlisting their husbands' help with the housework, these women often chose to "solve" their "double-day syndrome" by hoping to displace it on less privileged women. As Parreñas (2001, 79) correctly observes, "As women transfer their reproductive labor to less and less privileged women, the traditional division of labor in the patriarchal nuclear household has been significantly renegotiated in various countries in the world." At the same time, in the context of migration in which many Filipina nurses are working in higher-paid jobs but leading lower-status lives, the nurses' desire for "helpers" must also be understood as a longing for the social class status that many once had in the Philippines—one that entails the hiring of less privileged women to carry out reproductive chores.

Conclusion

Since 1960, women have dominated the Filipino immigrant population, the majority of whom are nurses. The development of this international mobile labor force is inextricably linked to the history of early-twentieth-century U.S. colonialization of the Philippines, the preference for foreign-trained nurses by Philippine and U.S. agencies, and the pervasive cultural Americanization of the Philippines, which exhorted Filipinos to regard the U.S. culture, political system, and way of life as the model par excellence for Philippine society. In other words, the development of the quintessential Filipina nursing care provider and the origins of Filipino nurse migration are not solely the results of contemporary global restructuring, the "liberalization" of U.S. immigration rules, or individual economic desires but rather are historical outcomes of early-twentieth-century U.S. colonial rule in the Philippines.

NOTES

Reprinted with permission of REMI from *Revue Europeenne des Migrations Internationales* 21: 55–75.

1. International migration is so prevalent in the Philippines that in 1997, the Philippine Secretary of Foreign Affairs called for "international migration" to be made a subject for elementary and high school students to prepare them for what he termed the "reality of immigration" (Okamura 1998, 5).

2. Filipinos constituted the second largest immigrant group, behind Mexicans. According to the 2000 Census, Chinese Americans, at more than 2.4 million, constituted the largest Asian American group in the United States. In California, Chinese Americans, who neared the one million mark, also pushed past Filipinos (918,678) to become the state's largest Asian group. Though the Filipino population rose by 31.5 percent nationwide and 25.6 percent statewide, it fell well short of predictions that the 2000 Census would crown Filipinos as the largest Asian group in the nation and in California.

3. Beginning in the early 1960s, as the demand for nursing education exceeded the enrollment slots available in Philippine colleges and schools of nursing, Filipino businessmen and health educators opened new schools of nursing in the provinces as well as in urban areas. Between 1950 and 1970, the number of nursing schools in the Philippines increased from just seventeen to 140 (Choy 2003).

4. The 1965 Immigration Act, which abolished the national-origins quotas and permitted entry based primarily on family reunification or occupational characteristics, dramatically increased the number of Asian immigrants to the United States.

5. Catherine Choy's *Empire of Care* is the first and only study on the introduction of nursing in the Philippines during U.S. colonial rule and on the impact of the U.S. Exchange Visitor Program of the 1950s and 1960s on Filipino migration to the United States. Therefore, this section of my paper necessarily relies on Choy's pioneering research.

6. In his 1936 extraordinarily popular autobiography, Victor Heiser, the commissioner of health in the Philippines, described Filipinos in the following terms: "grown-up children, dirty, unsanitary, diseased, ignorant, unscrupulous, superstitious, born actors, resigned to death, untrustworthy, cowards, a nation of invalids, incubators of leprosy, unhygienic" (cited in Anderson 1995, 100).

7. In 1970, a U.S. immigration amendment introduced the H-1 temporary work visa program, which enables a hospital or nursing home to sponsor or bring a nurse with a professional license from abroad to work in the United States for two years. However, under this program applicants must pass the U.S. nurses' licensing exam. If she passes, she can gain permanent residency after two years. If she fails the exam, she loses her temporary work visa status and faces the threat of deportation (Chang 2000). The majority of foreign-trained nurses (between 75 and 90 percent) who took the exam failed (Ong and Azores 1994). In 1989, the Filipino Nurses Organization fought for passage of the Immigration Nursing Relief Act, which enabled H-1 visa nurses who were present in the United States on September 1, 1989, and had worked for three years as a registered nurse in the United States, to adjust their status to permanent resident (Ong and Azores 1994).

8. According to the Philippine Overseas Employment Administration, between 1989 and 1993, Filipino Americans remitted approximately $5 billion, averaging well over $1 billion each year (Okamura 1998, 126). By 1989, consumer goods sent via *balikbayan* (returnee or homecomer) boxes contributed 4.2 billion pesos (or $190 million) annually to the Philippine economy (Basch, Glick Schiller, and Szanton Blanc 1994, 257–58). These numbers are rising. In the first half of 1994, overseas Filipinos remitted almost $800 million through official bank transfers —a likely underestimate (Okamura 1998, 44, 126). In 2001, over seven million overseas Filipino workers sent over $6 billion in remittances to the Philippines (U.S. Treasury Department 2003).

9. Over the course of eight years (1992–2000), I interviewed just over one hundred Filipinos

in San Diego County. The majority of the interviewees were Filipino navy men, Filipino nurses, and their families.

10. During the ninety-four years of U.S. military presence in the Philippines, U.S. bases served as recruiting stations for the U.S. navy; Filipinos were the only foreign nationals who were allowed to enlist in the U.S. armed forces; and the navy was the only military branch they could join. As a result, Filipino sailors have always formed a significant segment of the Filipino community in the United States, especially in San Diego, the home of the largest U.S. naval base and the navy's primary west coast training facility until 1998.

11. Data from the 1984 National Sample Survey of Registered Nurses indicate that Filipinas had the highest earnings among all groups, averaging almost $5,000 more annually than white nurses (Moses 1984). Ong and Azores (1994) report that Filipina nurses use various strategies to increase their earnings: working double shifts or in the higher-paying evenings and night shifts, and in inner-city hospitals, which offer higher salaries than the national average. In other words, they earn more because they are more likely to work under the least desirable conditions.

REFERENCES

Advincula, Anthony D. 2004. Filipino nurses get government support for NCLEX Initiative. *Filipino Express Online*, October, 11–17.

Anderson, Warwick. 1995. "Where every prospect pleases and only man is vile": laboratory medicine as colonial discourse. Pp. 83–112 in Vicente Rafael (ed.), *Discrepant histories: translocal essays on Filipino cultures.* Philadelphia: Temple University Press.

Asperilla, Purita Falgui. 1976. Problems of foreign educated nurses and job satisfaction of Filipino nurses. *Academy of Nursing of the Philippine Papers,* July-September, 2–13.

Basch, Linda, Nina Glick Schiller, and Cristina Szanton Blanc. 1994. *Nations unbound: transnational projects, postcolonial predicaments, and deterritorialized nation-states.* Langhorn, PA: Gordon and Breach.

Blum, Linda. 1991. *Between feminism and labor: the significance of the comparable worth movement.* Berkeley: University of California Press.

Bonacich, Edna and Lucie Cheng. 1984. Introduction: a theoretical orientation to international labor migration. Pp. 1–56 in Lucie Cheng and Edna Bonacich (eds.), *Labor immigration under capitalism: Asian workers in the United States before World War II.* Berkeley: University of California Press.

Borjas, George. 1990. *Friends or strangers: the impact of immigrants on the U.S. economy.* New York: Basic Books.

Campomanes, Oscar. 1997. New formations of Asian American studies and the question of U.S. imperialism. *Positions* 5(2): 523–50.

Chang, Grace. 2000. Importing nurses: a moneymaking venture. *Dollars & Sense,* September.

Chen, Hsiang Shui. 1992. *Chinatown no more: Taiwan immigrants in contemporary New York.* Ithaca, NY: Cornell University Press.

Chin, Christine B. N. 1998. *In service and servitude: foreign female domestic workers and the Malaysian "Modernity" project.* New York: Columbia University Press.

Choy, Catherine Ceniza. 2003. *Empire of care: nursing and migration in Filipino American history.* Durham, NC: Duke University Press.

Coronel, Sheila and Ninotchka Rosca. 1993. For the boys: Filipinas expose years of sexual slavery by the U.S. and Japan. *Ms.,* November/December, 11.

Dill, Bonnie Thornton. 1988. Our mother's grief: racial-ethnic women and the maintenance of families. *Journal of Family History* 13: 415–31.

Egan, Timothy. 1996. "Mail-order marriage, immigrant dreams, and death." *New York Times,* May 26.

Espiritu, Yen Le. 1997. *Asian American women and men: labor, laws, and love.* Thousand Oaks, CA: Sage.

Espiritu, Yen Le. 2003. *Home bound: Filipino American lives across cultures, communities, and countries.* Berkeley: University of California Press.

Espiritu, Yen Le and Diane L. Wolf. 2001. The paradox of assimilation: children of Filipino immigrants in San Diego. Pp. 188–228 in Ruben Rumbaut and Alejandro Portes (eds.), *Ethnicities: children of immigrants in America.* Berkeley: University of California Press and Russell Sage Foundation.

Glenn, Evelyn Nakano. 1986. *Issei, Nisei, war bride: three generations of Japanese American women at domestic services.* Philadelphia: Temple University Press.

Glenn, Evelyn Nakano. 2002. *Unequal freedom: how race and gender shaped American citizenship and labor.* Cambridge, MA: Harvard University Press.

Glick Schiller, Nina. 1997. The situation of transnational studies. *Identities* 4(2): 155–66.

Glick Schiller, Nina and Georges Eugene Fouron. 2001. *Georges woke up laughing: long-distance nationalism and the search for home.* Durham, NC: Duke University Press.

Guarnizo, Luis Eduardo and Michael Peter Smith. 1998. The location of transnationalism. Pp. 3–34 in Michael Peter Smith and Luis Eduardo Guarnizo (eds.), *Transnationalism from below.* New Brunswick, NJ: Transaction Publishers.

Guingona, Teofisto T. Jr. 2001. Transcript of the speech of Vice President and Foreign Affairs Secretary His Excellency Teofisto T. Guingona, Jr., during the 103rd founding anniversary of the Department of Foreign Affairs, Department of Foreign Affairs Auditorium, Philippines, July 11.

Halualani, Rona Tamiko. 1995. The intersecting hegemonic discourses of an Asian mail-order bride catalog: Pilipina oriental butterfly dolls for sale. *Women's Studies in Communication* 18(1): 45–64.

Hoganson, Kristin L. 1998. *Fighting for American manhood: how gender politics provoked the Spanish-American and Philippine-American wars.* New Haven, CT: Yale University Press.

Hondagneu-Sotelo, Pierrette. 1994. *Gendered transitions: Mexican experiences of immigration.* Berkeley: University of California Press.

Hondagneu-Sotelo, Pierrette. 1999. Introduction: gender and contemporary U.S. immigration. *American Behavioral Scientist* 42(4): 565–76.

Hondagneu-Sotelo, Pierrette and Ernestine Avila. 1997. "I'm here, but I'm here": the meanings of Latina transnational motherhood. *Gender & Society* 11(5): 548–71.

Hunter, Frances. 1986. *Equal pay for comparable worth.* New York: Praeger.

Lawcock, Larry Arden. 1975. *Filipino students in the United States and the Philippine independence movement: 1900–1935.* Ph.D. dissertation, University of California, Berkeley.

Levitt, Peggy. 2001. *The transnational villagers.* Berkeley: University of California Press.

Lipsitz, George. 1998. *The possessive investment in whiteness: how white people profit from identity politics.* Philadelphia: Temple University Press.

Lowe, Lisa. 1996. *Immigrant acts: on Asian American cultural politics.* Durham, NC: Duke University Press.

Manila Times Internet Edition. 2004. Annabel Borromeo: an IT-enabled healthcare. May 21.

Massey, Doreen. 1999. Imagining globalization: power-geometries of time-space. In Avtar Brah,

Mary J. Hickman, and Mairtin Mac an Ghaill (eds.), *Global futures: migration, environment, and globalization.* New York: St. Martin's Press.

Massey, Douglas, Joaquin Arango, Graeme Hugo, Ali Kouaouci, Adela Pellegrino, and J. Edward Taylor. 1993. Theories of international migration: a review and appraisal. *Population and Development Review* 19(3): 431–66.

Menjivar, Cecilia. 1999. The intersection of work and gender: Central American women and employment in California. *American Behavioral Scientist* 42(2): 601–27.

Min, Pyong Gap. 1998. *Changes and conflicts: Korean immigrant families in New York.* Needham Heights, MA: Allyn & Bacon.

Mohanty, Chandra. 1991. Cartographies of struggle: Third World women and the politics of feminism. Pp. 1–47 in Chandra Mohanty, Ann Russo, and Lourdes Torres (eds.), *Third world women and the politics of feminism.* Bloomington: University of Indiana Press.

Moses, Evelyn B. 1984. National sample survey of registered nurses, November 1984 [computer file]. Rockville, MD, Bureau of Health Professionals.

Newman, Louise Michele. 1999. *White women's rights: the racial origins of feminism in the United States.* New York: Oxford University Press.

Okamura, Jonathan Y. 1998. *Imagining the Filipino American diaspora: transnational relations, identities, and communities.* New York and London: Garland.

Ong, Paul and Tania Azores. 1994. The migration and incorporation of Filipino nurses. Pp 164–95 in Paul Ong, Edna Bonacich, and Lucie Cheng (eds.), *The new Asian immigration in Los Angeles and global restructuring.* Philadelphia: Temple University Press.

Parreñas, Rhacel Salazar. 2001. *Servants of globalization: women, migration, domestic work.* Stanford, CA: Stanford University Press.

Perea, Juan F., ed. 1997. *Immigrants out! The new nativism and the anti-immigrant impulse in the United States.* New York: New York University Press.

Perez, Gina M. 2004. *The new Northwest side story: migration, displacement, and Puerto Rican families.* Berkeley: University of California Press.

Pesquera, Beatriz M. 1993. "In the beginning he wouldn't lift a spoon": The division of household labor. Pp. 181–95 in Adela de la Torre and Beatriz M. Pesquera (eds.), *Building with our hands: new directions in Chicana studies.* Berkeley: University of California Press.

Pessar, Patricia R. 1984. The linkage between the household and workplace in the experience of Dominican immigrant women in the United States. *International Migration Review* 18(4): 1188–211.

Pessar, Patricia R. 1999. Engendering migration studies: the case of new immigrants in the United States. *American Behavioral Scientist* 42(4): 577–600.

Portes, Alejandro, Luis E. Guarzino, and Patricia Landolt. 1999. The study of transnationalism: pitfalls and promises of an emergent research field. *Ethnic and Racial Studies* 22(2): 217–37.

Posadas, Barbara M. and Roland L. Guyotte. 1990. Unintentional immigrants: Chicago's Filipino foreign students become settlers, 1900–1941. *Journal of American Ethnic History* (Spring): 26–48.

Pressner, Harriet. 1988. Shift work and childcare among young dual-earner American parents. *Journal of Marriage and the Family* 50: 133–48.

Rafael, Vicente L. 2000. *White love and other events in Filipino history.* Durham, NC: Duke University Press.

San Juan, E. Jr. 1998. *Beyond postcolonial Theory.* New York: St. Martin's Press.

Stark, Oded. 1991. *The migration of labour.* Cambridge: Basil Blackwell.

Stoler, Ann Laura. 1991. Carnal knowledge and imperial power: gender, race, and morality in colonial Asia. Pp. 51–101 in Micaela di Leonardo (ed.), *Gender at the crossroads of knowledge: feminist anthropology in the postmodern era.* Berkeley: University of California Press.

Taylor, Edward J. 1999. The new economics of labor migration and the role of remittances in the migration process. *International Migration* 37: 63–88.

Thomas, Brinley. 1973. *Migration and economic growth: A study of Great Britain and the Atlantic economy.* Cambridge: Cambridge University Press.

Tyner, James A. 1999. The global context of gendered labor: migration from the Philippines into the United States. *American Behavioral Scientist* 42(4): 671–89.

U.S. Immigration and Naturalization Service (INS). 2001. *2000 Statistics Yearbook.* Washington, DC: U.S. Government Printing Office.

U.S. Treasury Department. 2003. U.S.-Philippine agrees to improve remittance service. News release, May 20.

Warren, Jennifer. 1993. Suit asks Navy to aid children left in Philippines. *Los Angeles Times,* March 5.

Yegenoglu, Meyda 1998. *Colonial fantasies: towards a feminist reading of orientalism.* Cambridge: Cambridge University Press.

Zolberg, Aristide. 1986. International factors in the formation of refugee movements. *International Migration Review* 20 (Summer): 151–69.

Chapter 12

Mothers without Citizenship
Asian Immigrants and Refugees Negotiate Poverty and Hunger after Welfare Reform

Lynn H. Fujiwara

Ling Chen, a 32-year-old immigrant woman from China, has two children ages two and five. Ms. Chen and her husband are currently unemployed, and both remain ineligible for naturalization for another two years. They used to receive $200 in food stamps until September 1, 1997, when that amount was cut in half. Standing in line for free bags of groceries at the food bank distribution center at Cameron House in Chinatown, San Francisco, Ms. Chen states, "My husband and I don't mind, but what can you say to your children when they ask for food?"

On September 1, 1997, most legal immigrants were terminated from the federal food stamp benefits program as mandated through the Personal Responsibility Work Opportunity Reconciliation Act (PRWORA) of 1996. The General Accounting Office (GAO) reported that an estimated 935,000 of the 1.4 million legal permanent residents receiving food stamps lost their benefits (Cook 1998). Although some individual states continued to provide state-funded food stamps, they primarily served children, the elderly, and the disabled. Thus, by December 1997, 685,000 (73 percent) legal permanent residents who had previously received food stamps were no longer receiving the food stamps they once relied upon to help nourish their families (Cook 1998). Since food stamps were cut for most noncitizens, several major research groups have found a significant increase in levels of food insecurity and food insecurity with hunger within affected immigrant households.

Less understood and underexamined are the complexities and experiences of Asian immigrant families facing poverty. Contrary to popular narratives of "Asian success," between 1990 and 1994 poverty among Asian Pacific American families rose from 11.9 to 13.5 percent (Shinagawa 1996). Because Asian American income patterns are characterized as having a bimodal income distribution, popular understandings of those patterns do not usually recognize that particular Asian groups within the United

States possess higher poverty and welfare utilization rates than any other group. According to the 2000 Census, while 12.6 percent of Asian Americans lived below the poverty level in 1999, 29.3 percent of Cambodians, 37.6 percent of Hmong, and 19.1 percent of Laotians lived below the poverty level (Niedzwiecki and Duong 2004). Consequently, the percentage of households utilizing public assistance in 1999 measured accordingly, with 22.2 percent, 30.2 percent, and 14.2 percent, respectively, for Cambodian, Hmong, and Laotian families (Niedzwiecki and Duong 2004).

When PRWORA passed in August 1996, a myriad of specific provisions directly worked to reduce the eligibility and access of public assistance to noncitizens. The immigrant provisions of the welfare law created new qualifications for eligibility based on citizenship status, according to which documented "legal" immigrants were generally excluded from numerous benefit programs, except for specifically defined exceptions that did not include the majority of existing recipients. In this chapter I examine the complexities of poverty and welfare reform among Asian immigrants by focusing on the implications of food stamp cuts. Drawing from field work conducted from 1996 to 1998 in the bay area of northern California that consisted of participant observation in community-based organizations in Asian immigrant communities, I focus on the immediate consequences of welfare reform and the subsequent response from community advocates and organizations. I argue that the targeting of noncitizens as undeserving of public benefits not only jeopardized human rights to immigrants facing poverty; it also reflects the existing and pervasive devaluation of immigrant families who as a result experience higher levels of hunger and food insecurity due to the loss of their benefits. In addition, given that 80 percent of children with immigrant parents are U.S. citizens, I further argue that anti-immigrant social policy aimed at immigrant mothers threatens the citizenship of their citizen children who are prevented from accessing benefits to which they are legally entitled. I present food stamp legislation as a particular case of the convergence of welfare and immigrant social policy that systematically reduces the health and well-being of immigrant families. A focused analysis of the loss of food stamps for immigrant families highlights the intersecting forces of race, gender, class, and citizenship formed through social policy that reinforces the persistence of poverty within immigrant communities.

In this chapter, I pay special attention to Southeast Asians who came as refugees due to the U.S. war in Vietnam. This research reveals even greater concerns given this country's obligation to Southeast Asian veterans, and those who fled and resettled in the United States and remain unable to integrate into a postindustrial economy. I argue that the increasing significance of citizenship in social policy perpetuates a persistent devaluation of immigrant families, and a specific analysis of Asian immigrants and refugees demonstrates the complexities of citizenship that need greater consideration within social policy for immigrants in general.

Race, Gender, Citizenship, and the Politics of Welfare Reform

The decade of the 1990s revealed a notable moment in contemporary politics, with the convergence of welfare and immigration reform directed strategically at immigrant women. The construction of immigrants as undeservingly taking resources from hard-working Americans targeted poor and laboring-class noncitizens as primary culprits for the downward economic turn felt through the 1980s and 1990s. The "new nativism" of that decade resulted in a unique juncture of social policy and public opinion in which the targeting of poor immigrant women and their children through a popularly recognized discourse of citizenship worked to redefine their basic rights to social, economic, and political entitlement in the United States (Chavez 1997). The convergence of welfare and immigration reform more definitively established legal citizenship status as a targeted axis by which to exclude needy immigrants and their families from public assistance.

When President Clinton signed PRWORA, the extent of the law was broad sweeping in that it altered public assistance in multiple realms, including aid for the elderly and disabled, as well as food stamps, and completely dissolved the program we have known as Aid to Families with Dependent Children (AFDC), a guaranteed family assistance program meant to prevent families from falling into complete destitution. However, less recognized within poverty studies were the ways in which immigrants were central to the policy changes mandated through alterations in eligibility based on citizenship status. Under the welfare law, noncitizen immigrants and legal permanent residents were no longer eligible for Supplemental Security Income (SSI: a federal assistance program for the poor elderly, blind, and disabled) and food stamps unless they became naturalized citizens, or could show documented proof of formal employment for at least forty quarters (ten years). This proved impossible for many who have worked in the United States in the informal economy or invisible labor sector. Noncitizens could also continue their SSI and food stamp benefits if they were U.S. military veterans or the wives or children of veterans (this became a problem for most Southeast Asian and Filipino veterans who were not initially granted veteran status). For Asian immigrants and refugees the exceptions for eligibility must be understood in relation to their gendered impact. There are more foreign-born Asian Pacific American women than men (71.8 percent of women compared to 69.7 percent of men are over age sixty-five), and among foreign born, 26 percent of the women rely on public assistance, compared to 18.5 percent of the men. Approximately 72 percent of the immigrants scheduled to lose their SSI benefits were women. Hence citizenship as a filter through welfare reform particularly affects women, leading to a disproportionate harm to women and their children.

The use of legal citizenship status as a form of demarcation for entitlement to life-sustaining benefits further delineates immigrants as "outside" the social, political, and economic policy of the nation. An examination of food stamp legislation that established different criteria for noncitizens provides an opportune moment to consider the increasing significance of citizenship in racial and gendered contemporary politics. According to Nira Yuval-Davis (1999), citizenship is a multilayered construct that is at constant play on the local, national, and international political terrain. On the most fundamental level, citizenship signifies the rights and responsibilities of membership within the nation state. Significant critical feminist work has cogently examined the ways in which the welfare state creates structures of unequal citizenship for poor mothers (Mink 1998; Roberts 1997). Invasive screening practices and punitive sanctioning have resulted in the loss of privacy and reproductive autonomy for women subject to increased discretion and power within welfare agencies to adjudicate women's eligibility to maintain their benefits.

While immigrant mothers experience these same forms of differential rights as welfare recipients, their noncitizenship status sets them apart even beyond the existing systems of race, gender, and class inequality within the welfare system. For immigrant women the differential system of rights in PRWORA is based on a dichotomous and absolute coding of citizenship as a conditional element that demarcates them as unentitled. An examination of the convergence of welfare and immigration reform demonstrates the ways that citizenship status as "formal belonging" has become a clearer means to deem specific groups as not entitled to public support. Given that the two primary immigrant groups impacted by welfare cuts were Latino and Asian, their level of "outsiderness" underscored the racialized campaign that blamed immigrants for larger economic problems. Stuart Hall and David Held (1990) refer to this nativist process as the "politics of closure," in which differential citizenship is accessed to exclude citizen members from full participation in the social polity, as well as the more general demarcation that delineates who can belong and acquire inclusion at all. Through her examination of unequal citizenship, Evelyn Nakano Glenn's (2002) work suggests that race, class, and gender shape the way particular immigrant groups are further excised from social provisions already infused with systems of inequality, such as the welfare state.

In an ethnographic exploration of Cambodian refugees negotiating the welfare system, Aihwa Ong (2003) demonstrates the way social service agency workers perceived and treated their Cambodian clients as particularly unworthy of welfare benefits and in need of more direct disciplining to move towards self-reliance and accountability. Ong argues that Southeast Asian refugees who fail to "fit into" a perceived model minority image are racialized not only as racial others but also as deviant in their foreignness, which requires a limit on their entitlement. Immigrants and refugees dealing with welfare agencies must engage in this process with minimal English, fewer marketable labor-force skills, as well as with traumatic historical backgrounds of war and displacement.

PRWORA operated off the assumption that those residing within the United States without citizenship status occupy an "alien" position as outsiders to American membership. Although their integration into the labor force, consumer economy, and system of taxation remains unimpeded by their citizenship status, these contributions remain assumed expectations, as is the expectation that they never rely on the U.S. government for assistance. Reports by Congress argued that welfare had become the primary magnet attracting immigrants to the United States. Little thought was given to the preponderance of immigrants who were here to work or be with their families, to those who have resided in this country for decades but have been unable to fulfill the requirements for citizenship, or to those who had until this point no compelling reason to naturalize. Nor did Congress take account of the fact that a large proportion of noncitizens utilizing public assistance came to this country as refugees. Rather, Congress argued that it possessed a "compelling government interest to enact new rules for eligibility and sponsorship agreements in order to assure that aliens be self-reliant in accordance with national immigration policy" (P.L. 104-193, Title IV, Sec. 400). The immigrant provisions clearly tied eligibility for basic public benefits to citizenship status. Through this chapter, I demonstrate how citizenship has become increasingly important for economic, social, and political well-being.

Asian Immigrants and Refugees and Welfare: A Brief Background

To understand the significance of the current welfare reform movement for these Asian immigrant communities, it is important to understand the complex history of public assistance and high levels of poverty that have persisted within many Asian immigrant groups. In the Great Society and War on Poverty social transformations of the 1960s, for the first time since its inception welfare became more accessible to communities of color. Initially, Asian immigrants underutilized publicly funded programs due to fear, language inaccessibility, and lack of information. Not until the 1980s did the public take notice of the increased use of public assistance by Asian immigrants. It was not until the refugee resettlement policies that followed the end of U.S. involvement in the war in Vietnam that elevated levels of welfare use became characterized as a "social problem."

In the immediate aftermath of the war in Vietnam, policymakers stressed that public assistance was a necessary entitlement in the resettlement process. Under the 1980 Refugee Act, refugees were given thirty-six months of stipends, including special refugee cash assistance, medical assistance, and other support services (Hing 1993). However, with the entry of the poorer, less educated, and more devastated second wave of refugees in 1982, the 1980 Refugee Act was amended to reduce refugee cash assistance to eighteen months to pressure refugees to become economically independent more quickly (Hing 1993). Refugees entering in the late 1970s through the 1980s had by then spent many years in refugee camps awaiting approval and entry into the United States. More diverse, the majority of these refugees were Cambodian, Laotian, Mien, and Hmong. With refugee assistance limited to eighteen months, the minimal English instruction, employment counseling, and mental health services provided were not enough to move refugees from war-torn Southeast Asia into self-sufficient employment. Once assistance based upon refugee status ceased, Southeast Asian refugees continued to receive benefits as legal permanent residents.

According to the 1980 Census, the percentage of Laotian and Hmong families with incomes below the poverty level was over 65 percent, over 46 percent for Cambodian families, and over 33 percent for Vietnamese families (U.S. Commission on Civil Rights 1992). By the 1990s the proportion of Southeast Asians utilizing public assistance had remained significantly high. Of those whose first year in the United States was fiscal year 1991, about 45 percent of Vietnamese, 44 percent of Laotians, and almost 100 percent of Cambodians depended on welfare (Le 1993). Soon to emerge was a public commentary that Asian refugees were becoming dependent on welfare. Aiwha Ong argues that these new immigrants who struggled to gain a foothold within the service economy found that remaining a part of the welfare system proved to be essential for the economic survival of their families (Ong 2003). Although Southeast Asians continue to struggle to survive within the U.S. postmodern economy, their high poverty rates have faced a "compassion fatigue" (Ong 2003) in the form of direct cuts to welfare based upon their citizenship status.

Thus, when PRWORA ruled that all noncitizen aliens would no longer be eligible for federal food stamps, the devastation to Asian immigrant and refugee communities was disproportionately high and deeply felt. In San Francisco County alone, nearly 75 percent of the immigrants to lose food stamps were from Asia. According to the Food Research and Action Center, at the time of the cuts, the average food stamp benefit for a permanent legal resident household unit was $196 per month. This amount is significant when we consider that over 70 percent of all immigrant food stamp households had gross incomes below 75 percent of the poverty line. At the time of the cuts, the average food stamp recipient in California received approximately $71 per month in coupons to supplement the food budget. If two adults lost their food stamps, that meant a loss of $142 per month. The food purchasing power lost when food stamps were cut was substantial and placed immigrant-headed households at risk for increased food insecurity and hunger. In the following section, I lay out my methodology for studying Asian immigrants and the impact of welfare reform.

The Research Project

In order to gain a better understanding of the implications and consequences of PRWORA for Asian immigrant and refugees, I spent two years working with community-based organizations that were dealing directly with immigrants and welfare reform. From 1996 to 1998 I conducted fieldwork that included interviews and participant observation. My primary region of research was three counties of the northern California bay area: San Francisco, Alameda, and Santa Clara. I visited and interviewed directors, staff, and volunteers at organizations and agencies that worked with immigrant communities. I conducted twenty-one formal interviews with legal advocates, directors of resource centers, staff from immigrant programs, and service providers. I also volunteered and participated in service programs (such as conducting citizenship drives and teaching citizenship classes), information forums about welfare reform, and community-based organizing of demonstrations and protests. Scheduled interviews were tape recorded and later transcribed, and field notes were recorded and analyzed thematically. To track the proliferation of media constructions of immigrants facing welfare cutoffs, I compiled and examined local and national newspapers (i.e., local bay area publications, the *San Francisco Chronicle*, the *Los Angeles Times*, the *New York Times*) that focused on immigrants and welfare reform from 1996 to 1998. Following media reports proved essential, as the primary goal of community mobilization efforts was to make the hardships caused by welfare reform visible to the public in order to pressure legislators to restore benefits.

I had not initially entered the field with the intention of examining community mobilization and grass-roots organizing. Rather, this process emerged as I was attempting to understand the circumstances of Asian immigrant women. After several months of engagement with the community organizations, I became immersed in community mobilizing efforts. My project emerged into a more definitive "participatory research," where my roles as researcher and as advocate often merged (Hondagneu-Sotelo 1993). Participatory research is characterized by the concern to implement social change not from the top down but rather by following the course of action determined by the community participants (Hondagneu-Sotelo 1993; Cancian 1996).

I found myself in meetings with city officials, county task-force groups, and state representatives, representing grass-roots organizations and presenting information and data that I had acquired through my research. Through my participatory methods, I was able to conduct an ethnographic examination of the processes and development of the mobilization efforts that shaped this immigrant-rights movement. While embedded in the community mobilization processes in the bay area, the immigrant-rights movement was occurring in cities across the country. Thus, different cities may have different demographic immigrant representations; my examination demonstrated the mobilization process with a large Asian immigrant and refugee concentration. What unfolded was a major community-based campaign to restore food stamps. Through this campaign emerged narratives of citizenship that challenged assumptions of nonbelonging, entitlement, and obligation. The struggle to challenge the cuts to food stamps because of their citizenship status revealed a greater challenge given the pervasive assumption that noncitizens should no longer receive public assistance.

Hunger and Hardship in Asian Immigrant Families

A Noted Increase of Food Insecurity and Hunger since PRWORA

Since the passing of PRWORA, numerous research groups have conducted studies to monitor the effects of welfare reform on preexisting benefit recipients. Several reports have become invaluable for scholarly work by providing important descriptive data that details the effects and demographics of the implementation of particular welfare reform restrictions for immigrants. The California Food Security Monitoring Project of the California Food Policy Advocates was one of the most immediate studies to examine the impact of food stamp cuts among immigrants residing in Los Angeles and San Francisco. California is home to at least 40 percent of the nation's legal immigrant population. According to the food security report, as of June 1996 an estimated 460,000 legal immigrants were receiving federal food stamp benefits in California. With the implementation of new noncitizen eligibility requirements, 241,000 of those recipients were cut from federal food stamp benefits. Although the California legislature partially restored state-funded food stamps to noncitizens under the age of eighteen or over sixty-five, these restorations only benefited about one-fourth of those impacted by the cutoffs.

One month after the cut-offs, 40 percent of the impacted group experienced moderate or severe hunger compared to 33 percent of the control group. By March, 50 percent of the impacted households experienced moderate or severe hunger compared to 38 percent of the unimpacted group. In San Francisco, one-third (33 percent) of the impacted households with children were experiencing moderate or severe hunger and were 35 percent more likely to experience this level of hunger than those living in non-impacted households. Immigrant households in San Francisco whose benefits had been cut were almost three times as likely (173 percent) to experience the most serious food problems—food insecurity with severe hunger—than those who did not lose food stamps. The study concluded that the cuts mandated through welfare reform were actually generating hunger and harming children and adult immigrants alike.

Like the California Policy Advocates, Physicians for Human Rights funded a study to track the level of food insecurity and hunger among Latino and Asian immigrants in California, Texas, and Illinois. The findings from this study revealed high levels of food insecurity and hunger among immigrant families. Of the 672 study participants, only 20 percent of the households were classified as food secure, 40 percent were food insecure without hunger, and 41 percent were food insecure with hunger. Thirty-three percent of the respondents reported that they or other adults in the household skipped meals; 10 percent said that they or other adults in the household had not eaten for a whole day at least once during the past six months; and 25 percent reported that they cut the size of their children's meals. Sixteen percent reported that their children had to skip meals, and 8 percent reported that their children had not eaten for a whole day because of insufficient money for food. These findings reveal a persistently high prevalence of hunger among low-income immigrants, which these medical researchers argue is unacceptably high.

To date, perhaps the broadest research on immigrants since welfare reform has come from the Urban Institute. In March of 2001 the report "Hardship among Children of Immigrants," based on a nationally representative sample from the 1999 National Survey of America's Families, documented the greater hardship among children of immigrant parents. Nationwide, 37 percent of all children of immigrants lived in families that worried about or encountered difficulties affording food, compared with 27 percent of children of natives. This study found that the extent of food concerns and difficulties varied considerably by state. Immigrants in states without state food stamp replacement programs experienced higher rates of food insecurity than legal immigrants who had access to some state-funded food stamps.

These major reports provide evidence of substantial food insecurity and hunger among immigrant families. Hunger levels varied by region, family structure (single parent/two-parent), language proficiency, and the presence of naturalized or citizen-born family members. Regardless, the general condition for low-income immigrant families with less access to food assistance revealed a serious problem of food insecurity and hunger. The medical researchers from the Physicians for Human Rights project state, "a relation has been shown between hunger and susceptibility to disease; adverse medical outcomes for people with chronic illness; abnormal growth patterns, anxiety and aggression, poor academic performance, and need for special educational services among children" (Kasper et al. 2000). The implications of this data underscore the role of social policy in determining the well-being of all children living in the United States.

The detriment to immigrant families that corresponds with these documented conditions of hunger and food insecurity is also evident through qualitative examinations. By focusing on the ways in which community organizations and social services responded to the distress and needs of immigrants who were facing welfare cut-offs, I was able to examine the implications of the loss of food stamps for immigrant communities. One immediate response was the fortification of food banks and food distribution centers that raised unique challenges for immigrants. Second was the controversial status of Hmong and Laotian refugees, who challenged their cuts to food stamps on the basis of their veteran status and refugee experience. These situations illustrate the dire circumstances immigrants experienced with the loss of much needed resources to keep their families from hunger.

Immediate Consequences of Food Stamp Cuts: Confusion and Food Insecurity

Fairly soon after the passing of PRWORA, the Social Service Administration sent letters to noncitizen food stamp recipients explaining that their food stamps were going to be cut. With all the shifts and changes in public assistance eligibility, the level of confusion was astounding. Community organizations were flooded with calls from panicked immigrants regarding the benefits they were losing. To offset this heightened level of anxiety, community organizations held "welfare information workshops" in immigrant communities. At a local community forum in the Korean Resource Center in Japan Town, San Jose, the director of the Northern California Coalition for Immigrant Rights (NCCIR) spoke passionately to the mainly Asian immigrant and refugee audience of the ways the impending cuts in food stamps were going to impact immigrant communities.

> The federal government will no longer provide food stamps to legal residents anymore, unless the person naturalizes, or unless they've worked in this country for about ten years. We were hopeful that our state government would supply the food stamps that our families lost from the federal government, but the only thing that they did here in the state, is provide state-funded food stamp coupons to kids under eighteen and seniors over sixty-five. That leaves thousands and thousands of families in between who will no longer qualify for food stamps if they are hungry. So here in San Jose we have a little bit over eight thousand legal immigrant adults who fall between the ages of eighteen and sixty-four who will be losing their food stamps any day now. (Field Notes, 9/12/97)

The immediate concern over food security and the impending rise in hunger among immigrant families was initially dealt with through the fortification of food banks and the proliferation of food distribution sites, making them more accessible to immigrant communities. In San Francisco the immediate response by the Department of Human Services was to allocate $250,000 for a food-distribution program in partnership with the San Francisco Food Bank and local nonprofit agencies. According to John Young, the department's coordinator for citizenship services, "in order to meet the needs of the 75 percent Asian immigrants and their children, food distribution sites were based on organizations that have provided services over the years and are respected within their respective communities" (Field Notes, 10/15/97). In hopes of providing culturally appropriate food and compatible languages, the sites in San Francisco were strategically located at the Cameron House in Chinatown, the Southeast Asian Community Center in the Tenderloin, and the Richmond Area Multi-Services Center.

In Santa Clara County, Asian immigrants constituted a little over 70 percent of the noncitizens cut from food stamps. Likewise, 75 percent of the immigrants who lost food stamps had children under the age of eighteen, with an average of three children per household. Like San Francisco, the county of Santa Clara built upon the existing infrastructure of their food bank system, Second Harvest, to meet the needs of families discontinued from food stamps. In attempts to make the food bank system more accessible, funds were designated for bilingual Vietnamese, Spanish, Cambodian, and Russian interpreters. Likewise, funds were allocated to hire three full-time community organizers to prepare a food accessibility plan that would address barriers to meeting the food needs of their Vietnamese-, Spanish-, and Cambodian-speaking communities. As a result, three community organizations were designated to fulfill the outreach process: Asian Americans for Community Involvement, the Indochinese Resettlement and Cultural Center, and the Sacred Heart Community Service.

While food banks are often considered the very last resort to prevent starvation, in this instance they appeared to be the only governmental effort to prevent hunger among the immigrants and their families who had just been cut from food stamps. Along with the documented rise in hunger and food insecurity among immigrants came the observation that the food banks were underutilized. County social service offices and community organizations became aware that acquiring free food from food banks was not that simple a task for immigrants in need of food. Complex and culturally sensitive barriers emerged that revealed complicated issues that Asian immigrants faced in negotiating the food bank system, while also attempting to work as much as possible for their families' survival.

A volunteer from Bread, Jobs, and Justice at a food distribution site in San Jose expressed the complicated, confusing, and intimidating matrix a person must go through in order to receive free food.

> People have to show residency and may be at the wrong food bank location. The location requirements need to be made more clear. Some people can't show their residency, or have to experience more humiliating procedures when they come to pick up food. Ethnic food needs to be made available. There is an underutilization by Asian immigrants at the food banks, possibly because the food is incompatible, or the food bank is not close enough to their homes. Also transportation is a big problem for many who have a hard time getting around. (Field Notes, 2/27/98)

These observations were documented and examined through the Santa Clara County Social Services Food Safety Net Project, which included a telephone survey with 376 randomly selected immigrants recently cut off from food stamps. The survey found that the main barriers to access to food banks was lack of information and knowledge about the existence of the food banks, the location, language, and the hours of the day in which the food banks were open. More than half of the targeted immigrant families did not have their own vehicle and relied on other means of transportation; thus proximity to the distribution sites was critical. Almost half of the participants in the study indicated that they did not have enough food. The study reported that the primary ways that families have made up for their food stamp loss is to work more hours, purchase less food, or rely on relatives. The most common types of food needed by the immigrant respondents included meat, rice, milk, vegetables, and fish, which are all foods unavailable through the food banks. Likewise, as immigrants have had to increase their work hours, or take on more part-time employment, they are unable to get to the food distribution sites during the hours of operation. And finally, even with the understood need for language and culturally appropriate outreach and information, the hiring of several interpreters was not sufficient for the language needs of the vastly diverse group of immigrants with varying levels of literacy.

Thus, even with all of the attempts to make food banks accessible, culturally appropriate, and language compatible, the food banks could not adequately replace the loss of food caused by the cut from food stamps. While the logistics of food-distribution sites tended to occupy the primary attention of county officials in their attempts to make the food banks more accessible to immigrants, the deeper issues of dignity, respect, and degradation were often overlooked. It became quite clear within immigrant communities that the manifestations of stigma, depression, and anxiety would be the consequences of the lost benefits. Already a vulnerable group, refugees and immigrants from Southeast Asia share a unique history of war, dislocation, trauma, and resettlement. In order to understand the specific circumstances Southeast Asian refugees faced as they lost their food stamps, it is necessary to see their resettlement in the context of trauma and displacement due to U.S. involvement in the war in Southeast Asia.

Obligation and Betrayal: Southeast Asian Refugees and the Loss of Food Stamps

U.S. involvement in the Vietnam War entangled peoples from Vietnam, Laos, and Cambodia. In exchange for the support and collusion of political allies within Southeast Asian ethnic groups, the United States promised the spoils of victory, or refuge if defeated. In the immediate aftermath of the fall of Saigon and the withdrawal of American troops, policymakers stressed remorse and support of Southeast Asian groups who would need to flee to avoid persecution. Less known among Americans was the political and military incorporation of Laotian, Cambodian, Hmong, and Mien groups to assist the United States in their more clandestine campaigns across Southeast Asia. Enlisted by U.S. operations, thousands of men and young boys from these various groups fought for American forces in their campaign against communism. From 1966 to 1974, the Central Intelligence Agency, carrying out the foreign policy of the United States, enlisted the mountain tribes of Laos as guerrillas in the Vietnam War. Some thirty-six thousand Laotians battled the North Vietnamese troops, rescued downed American pilots, and guarded the radars that guided Air Force bombers (Weiner 1997, A1). Thousands of these recruits lost their lives, while their widows and surviving children were denied any form of compensation. When the United States pulled out of Southeast Asia, refuge for these groups was not immediate.

Thousands trekked by foot across hostile territory in fear of persecution to reach refugee camps in peripheral countries like Thailand. Many waited for years in these camps for permanent resettlement in the United States and other receiving countries.

The challenges for the less educated, "underskilled," or agrarian immigrants proved monumental. Welfare utilization was essential, as many found obtaining employment impossible. Before PRWORA, once refugees no longer qualified under refugee status, they were able to continue assistance as legal permanent residents. At this time, eligibility requirements were the same for legal permanent residents as for citizens. However, with PRWORA, legal permanent residents, regardless of their previous refugee status, fall within "alien" status and are subject to all provisions directed at all noncitizens. The cut of benefits like food stamps, as well as other much needed forms of assistance, including Supplemental Security Income, and the difficulties of maintaining Temporary Assistance to Needy Families pushed some immigrants into despair. In the most extreme situations, the cut from benefits drove already vulnerable and anxious immigrants to suicide.

Perhaps the most tragic of circumstances can be documented through the level of anxiety and despair that led several Hmong women to take their own lives as they faced welfare cutoffs. Ethnically referred to as the Hmong, they came from agrarian societies of highland Laos. Tribes and clans were enlisted and utilized by the United States through CIA covert operations in Laos from 1961 to 1975. The CIA utilized men and boys without discretion, and thousands lost their lives fighting for the United States. In exchange for their military participation, the United States promised Hmong leaders that when the United States won the war in Vietnam, the Hmong would be awarded their own territory. However, when the United States pulled out of Southeast Asia, the United States promised the Hmong refuge, as they would face political persecution in their homeland for their U.S. allegiance. Once resettled in the United States the Hmong found it most difficult to obtain self-sufficient employment and thus maintained higher levels of poverty and welfare use.

A year after the Personal Responsibility Act, Congress adopted language in the Balance Budget Act of 1997 that set forth its "intent" that those refugees who served with U.S. forces in Laos should be considered veterans. According to the Balanced Budget Act "It is the sense of the Congress that Hmong . . . who fought on behalf of the armed forces of the United States during the Vietnam conflict . . . should be considered veterans for the purpose of continuing certain welfare benefits" (P.L. 105-33 Sec. 5561). However, the U.S. Department of Agriculture insisted that since Congress did not provide a budget to implement its "intent," the benefit could not be extended to the Hmong and other refugees from Laos. The Clinton administration also agreed that the statement did not amend the Personal Responsibility Act and thus lacked the force of law, and therefore approximately sixteen thousand Laotian veterans and their family members lost food stamps and other benefits (Weiner 1997). On September 1, 1997, approximately twenty thousand Hmong in California lost their food stamp benefits (Eljera 1997). Given that the poverty rate for the Hmong in the United States was 60 percent, the loss of food stamps was not only nutritionally detrimental to entire families, but the emotional and physical stress for parents proved to be devastating. Two Hmong women committed suicide in California, and another in Wisconsin.

With the intensity of the tragic suicides along with the flood of panicked and terrified immigrants, the media began to cover the impact of welfare reform particularly in relation to Southeast Asian refugees. Most publicized and widely covered was the suicide of Chia Yang from Sacramento because she left behind an audiotape specifically blaming the U.S. government for her unbearable despair. Already vulnerable and in poor health, Chia Yang's story reflected the collective betrayal the Hmong felt over the loss of their benefits. At fifty-four and illiterate, Mrs. Yang received a notice stating that she was going to lose her Supplemental Security Income because she had not become a naturalized citizen. Although she tried several times, Mrs. Yang could not pass the citizenship exam. Before she actually lost her SSI, the benefits were restored through the Balanced Budget Act of 1997. She suffered from a stroke in April of 1997, and at that same time she received another letter stating that her food stamps were going to be cut in half because noncitizens between the ages of eighteen and sixty-four were no longer eligible. Her family stated that their mother slipped into a depression and became inconsolable. She hung herself late one night after her family had gone to sleep. On an audiotape she stated,

> What if I lose my SSI? What if my husband and children lose their AFDC grant? If they stop my grant I'm going to die anyway. . . . I am very sorry I had to bring you to this country and leave you behind. It feels like I'm sitting in a pot of boiling water every day. . . . It's not because you didn't support me, my sadness over the American system and my health problems drove me over the edge. (Maganini 1997, A1).

Like the thousands of other Hmong refugees, Mrs. Yang's husband and brothers served for the United States during the Vietnam War. Once here, she believed the government was going to ensure their well-being, as they had been promised.

The suicides and fear that resulted with the loss of benefits such as food stamps led community organizers to advocate for restorations to Hmong and Lao noncitizens based on veteran status. With heightened visibility and exposure of the unique situation faced by Hmong veteran refugees resettled in the United States, the media elevated public awareness over the contradictory nature of welfare reform and its harsh impact on legal immigrants. Articles in major newspapers written within months after immigrants were cut from food stamp benefits focused on the sense of betrayal, abandonment, and injustice experienced by Hmong refugees. Revisiting the bloodiest years of the Vietnam War, the "secret war" in Laos, and the devastation, trauma, and genocide faced by entire families and communities who were left behind when America pulled out in 1975, news articles exposed the hypocrisy of the U.S. government in denying these veterans and their families the food stamps they needed for basic survival in their deeply impoverished communities.

In a front-page article of the *New York Times* in December 1997, three months after immigrants began losing food stamp benefits, journalist Tim Weiner explained how the Hmong people were a casualty of U.S. involvement in the Vietnam War.

> Some 36,000 Laotians battled North Vietnamese troops, rescued downed American pilots and guarded the radars that guided Air Force bombers. Thousands of tribesmen

died. In return, the United States gave the tribespeople rice and promised them refuge if things went badly. . . . They [the Hmong] were left behind when the United States left their country in 1974. Thousands of them, many physically or mentally wounded by war and exile, trekked through jungles to refugee camps in Thailand in the late 1970s. They settled in California, Minnesota, Wisconsin and a handful of other states, and have tried to overcome high barriers of skill, education, language and culture in a land far from their roots. (Weiner 1997, A1).

Because of the insurmountable barriers to employment, 60 percent of the Hmong population relied on public assistance for their survival. According to Khao Insixiengmay, a veteran of the CIA war in Laos, "with the cutbacks, people are under the poverty line and they have a problem to survive in this new society. They do not know who to turn to" (Weiner 1997).

In a news conference held on the one-year anniversary of President Clinton's signing of the welfare bill, 65-year-old Sarouen Meas spoke of the dire situation his family faced with the loss of his food stamp benefits. His story, printed in the Associated Press, stated,

Disabled from torture and malnutrition, Meas and his wife now struggle to raise their five teenage children. Worried by the loss of $350 in food stamps a month, Meas said through an interpreter, "I now fear my children will suffer starvation as well." (Mittlestadt 1997, 1)

In public hearings before administrative law officials across California counties, Hmong veterans and their families testified about the aggressive enlistment of Hmong men and boys by the CIA, and the difficulties they had encountered in their attempts to secure self-sustaining employment in the United States. According to Ernest Velasquez, the former welfare director in Fresno County, "we [the United States] recruited them [the Hmong]. We made them our secret army and now all of a sudden we aren't even going to give them food stamps" (Ellis 1997).

By spring of 1998 the Clinton-supported Agriculture Research Bill, which proposed to grant veteran status to those enlisted by the United States in Southeast Asia, was under deliberation. Senator Phil Gramm, one of the Agriculture Research Bill's main opponents, argued that by offering immigrants food stamps, the bill "puts a big neon sign at the border of the United States of America, 'Come and get welfare.' I want people to come to America to work . . . not for welfare as a way of life" (Dewar 1998). Sharing Senator Gramm's sentiment was also Senator Lauch Faircloth, who stated, "The Statue of Liberty holds a torch of freedom, not a book of food stamps and a lifetime right not to have to work" (Dewar 1998). Since the provisions of the Agriculture Research bill only restored food stamps for those eighteen or younger and sixty-four and older who have been in the country on or before August 22, 1996, and Hmong and Laotian veterans, the senator's logic that the restoration of food stamps would attract immigrants does not logically coincide with the terms of the provisions.

To support the immigrant provisions of the Agriculture Research bill, the Northern California Coalition for Immigrant and Refugee Rights and the Asian Pacific American Legal Center, among other organizations, waged a national "paper plate campaign" calling for everyone to send messages to legislators on paper plates that stated, "Cutting Food Stamps Is Not Reform! It Is a Recipe for Hunger! RESTORE FOOD STAMPS FOR IMMIGRANTS! In addition, National Call-In Day was designated for Monday, April 20, 1998, before the bill was to hit the Senate floor. Consistent letter writing, faxes, media outreach, and local elected official statements and resolutions were all tactics that mobilized a national awareness of the ongoing plight of immigrants facing food stamp cutoffs (Field Notes 3/27/98).

Simultaneous campaigns consisted of class action lawsuits brought in the name of veterans' rights. Victor Hwang of the Asian Law Caucus of San Francisco and other civil rights attorneys filed at least thirty-five hundred appeals on behalf of Hmong immigrants throughout the state of California. Legal arguments held that the U.S. Department of Agriculture and the California Department of Social Services were unjustly denying food stamps to Hmong veterans based on the language set forth by Congress in the budget bill. A tearful Hmong mother threatened to kill herself and her five children if her food stamps were not restored. She tearfully stated in a hearing before a county judge, "you might as well send a soldier to just kill us because that's what you're doing" (Maganini 1997).

On June 23, 1998, President Clinton signed the Agriculture Research, Extension, and Education Reform Act of 1998 (Public Law 105-185). This act restored eligibility for noncitizens under eighteen and over sixty-five, as well as Hmong and other Laotian veterans. Even though these benefits were partially restored, the levels of hunger and food insecurity among immigrants continued to rise. This rise was largely due to the fact that these piecemeal restorations were not enough. They still failed to provide enough purchasing power for immigrants to adequately feed their families. The struggle to retain food stamps for Hmong and Laotian veterans reflects the harsh levels of indignity the U.S. government was willing to impose on people on the basis of citizenship status. Having to "prove" their U.S. veteran status is a historical denial that negates an entire set of obligations and promises. In this particular instance legislators attempted to supersede citizenship status over veteran status as a means to demarcate entitlement. In the following section I consider the implications for immigrants when "legal" citizenship becomes the differentiating principle by which to define entitlement through social policy.

Immigrants and Entitlement: The Increasing Significance of Citizenship

The federal policies of the 1990s, the welfare and immigration reform laws, clearly established citizenship as a demarcating axis by which to deem certain individuals as not entitled to programs that could help prevent their families from experiencing food insecurity and hunger. The logic behind the cut in food stamps as well as other benefits rested on the idea that immigrants should rely on themselves or other means besides the U.S. government. Regardless of the fact that immigrants contribute to the U.S. economy just like citizens, by virtue of their citizenship status the logic of "outsider" pervaded their positions within this country as undeserving of government support. The anti-immigrant reasoning behind the restrictions to eligibility based on citizenship status has had far-reaching consequences. Immigrants who remained eligible for benefits did not utilize them. Data from the USDA show that participation in the Food Stamp Program by noncitizens declined 64 percent between 1996 and 2000, from about 1.7 million to 600,000 (Leighton et al. 2003). Even though a significant proportion of noncitizens and their citizen children remained eligible for food stamps, the resultant climate of fear prevented immigrants from seeking the assistance to which they were entitled.

The Tufts University Center on Hunger and Poverty, in a 1995 study, showed that poor children in families receiving food stamps are significantly better nourished than poor children in families that do not receive food stamps. For families that are unable to provide the adequate nutrition for developing children, they have greater health problems, lower academic performance, and heightened anxiety and stress (Cook 1998). Because 80 percent of children in immigrant families are citizens, any social policy directed at immigrant heads of households will ultimately impact American citizen children. The move to utilize citizenship status as a means to reduce people deemed not entitled to government support reflects a devaluation of the lives of immigrant families and children. The heightened awareness of the dilemmas that emerged since the implementation of food stamp cuts pressured Congress to restore benefits to legal permanent residents.

On May 13, 2002, President Bush signed the Farm Security and Rural Investment Act of 2002 (P.L. 107-171), commonly known as the Farm Bill. This bill fundamentally altered the continued exclusion of all noncitizens between eighteen and sixty-four that was established in PRWORA. As of April 2003, food stamps were restored to legal immigrants who have lived in the country for at least five years, and to both legal immigrant children and individuals receiving disability benefits, regardless of the number of years they have been in the country. An estimated 363,000 immigrants who continued to be barred from food stamp assistance became eligible. On the one hand legislation that moves noncitizens towards equal footing as citizens is institutional progress towards alleviating state-sanctioned discrimination. However, one most prominent finding that continues to weigh heavily since the passing of welfare reform is the drastic decline in food stamp participation that continued among eligible immigrants and citizen children of immigrants. Many speculate that too few will return to food stamps even though eligibility for many has been restored. The harm has been done, and it will take more than piecemeal restorations to address the hunger and food insecurity that persists within immigrant households. As with all households facing hunger in the United States, policymakers need to look at all factors impacting low-income families. Perhaps policymakers need to address the factors that caused hunger and food insecurity in the first place, rather than delineating who should be eligible and have access to this one primary means to alleviate their family's hunger. Citizenship status as a clear demarcating axis by which to determine eligibility not only relies on inaccurate understandings of immigrant contributions to the economy but also presents ethical and moral issues that remain shrouded in assumptions of American identity and national belonging.

NOTES

Originally published in *Race, Gender & Class* 12.2 (2005): 120–40. © 2005 *Race, Gender & Class*, reprint by permission.

REFERENCES

Cancian, F. M. (1996). Participatory research and alternative strategies for activist sociology. In H. Gottfried (ed.), *Feminism and social change: Bridging theory and practice,* pp. 107–205. Chicago: University of Illinois Press.

Chavez, L. (1997). Immigration reform and nativism: The nationalist response to the transnational challenge. In Perea J. (ed.), *Immigrants out: The new nativism and the anti-immigrant impulse in the United States,* pp. 61–77. New York: New York University Press.

Cook, J. T. (1998). The food stamp program and low-income legal immigrants. *Nutrition Reviews* 56(7): 218–21.

Dewar, H. (1998). Senate action would restore benefits to 250,000 thrown off rolls in welfare bill. *Washington Post,* May 13.

Eljera, B. (1997). Hmong desperate on welfare reform. *Asian Week,* December, 4–10.

Ellis, V. (1997). Hmong seek exemption from food stamp cuts. *Los Angeles Times,* Nov. 2.

Glenn, E. N. (2002). *Unequal freedom.* Cambridge, MA: Harvard University Press.

Hall S. and D. Held. (1990). Citizens and citizenship. In S. Hall and M. Jacques (eds.), *New times: The changing face of politics in the 1990s,* p. 175. London: Verso Press.

Hing, B. O. (1993). *Making and remaking Asian America through immigration policy.* Stanford, CA: Stanford University Press.

Hondagneu-Sotelo, P. (1993). Why advocacy research?: Reflections on research and activism with immigrant women. *American Sociologist* 24: 56–68.

Kasper, S., S. K. Gupta, J. T. Cook, and A. F. Meyers. (2000). Hunger in legal immigrants in California, Texas, and Illinois. *American Journal of Public Health* 90(10): 1629–33.

Le, N. (1993). The case of Southeast Asian refugees: Policy for a community at risk. *Policy Issues to the Year 2020.* Los Angeles: LEAP Asian Pacific American Public Policy Institute and UCLA Asian American Studies Center.

Leighton K., F. Fremstad, and M. Broaddus. (2003). Noncitizens' use of public benefits has declined since 1996: Recent report paints misleading picture of impact of eligibility restrictions on immigrant families. Center on Budget and Policy Priorities.

Maganini, S. (1997). Suicide illustrates welfare reform's toll among Hmong. *Sacramento Bee,* Nov. 9.

Mink, G. (1998). *Welfare's end.* Ithaca, NY: Cornell University Press.

Mittlestadt, M. (1997). Nearly one million noncitizens lopped off food stamp rolls. *Associated Press,* Aug. 24.

Niedzwiecki, M. and T. C. Duong. (2004). Southeast Asian Americans: Population, immigration, and naturalization. Southeast Asian American Statistical Profile. Washington, DC: Southeast Asia Resource Action Center (SEARAC).

Ong, A. (2003). *Buddha is hiding: Refugees, citizenship, the New America.* Berkeley: University of California Press.

Personal Responsibility Work Opportunity Reconciliation Act. P.L. 104-193, 104th Congress, August 22, 1996.

Report to the Ranking Minority Member, Subcommittee on Children and Families, Committee on Labor and Human Resources, U.S. Senate. (1998). Welfare Reform: Many States Continue Some Federal or State Benefits for Immigrants.

Roberts D. (1997). *Killing the Black body: Race, reproduction and the meaning of liberty.* New York: Pantheon.

Shinagawa, L. H. (1996). The Impact of immigration on the demography of Asian Pacific Americans. In B. Ong Hing (ed.), *Reframing the immigration debate.* LEAP Asian Pacific American Public Policy Institute and UCLA Asian American Studies Center.

U.S. Commission on Civil Rights. (1992). *Civil rights issues facing Asian Americans in the 1990s.* Washington, DC: U.S. Commission on Civil Rights.

Yuval-Davis, N. (1999). The "multi-layered citizen": Citizenship in the age of "Globalization." *International Feminist Journal of Politics* 1(1): 122.

Weiner T. (1997). To many Laotians, U.S. is land of false promises. *New York Times,* Dec. 27, 1.

STUDY QUESTIONS

1. Lee argues that Korean immigrants possess certain resources that give them a distinct advantage when entering into self-employment. What are these resources? Give examples for each. How do Korean immigrants mobilize these resources when beginning a business? When sustaining their business? What role do *gaes* (rotating credit associations) play in supporting these business ventures? Why, according to Lee, have some Korean immigrants become wary of relying upon such capital?

2. Lee suggests that the presence of Asian American businesses in inner-city neighborhoods as entrepreneurs, occupying a position as "middleman minorities," has often sparked intergroup tensions. Why do Korean immigrants in the United States open businesses, especially in inner-city neighborhoods, at such high rates? What are the sources of these antagonisms? Can you think of any additional factors that might weigh upon interethnic tensions between Korean merchants and African American customers? How might these factors shift when one considers relationships between Korean American merchants and Latino American customers? When tensions develop between Korean American merchants and their African American customers, what mechanisms are employed by both groups to diffuse tensions? How do interethnic conflicts become racially coded? Why is this significant to the nature of African American and Korean American relations? To what extent are these animosities displaced on the Asian American entrepreneurs?

3. According to Espiritu's article, what accounts for the overrepresentation of health professional in contemporary immigration from the Philippines? Why is migration from the Philippines gendered in ways different from other migration flows (such as migration from India or from Mexico)? How have work and working conditions of Filipino nurses changed gender roles in their families? What impact has this massive influx of nurses to the United States from the Philippines had upon the Filipino medical system?

4. Fujiwara's analysis of Asian immigrants and refugees demonstrates the complexities of citizenship. She argues that the increasing significance of citizenship in social policy, as in the Personal Responsibility Work Opportunity Reconciliation Act (PRWORA), perpetuates a persistent devaluation of immigrant families and particularly refugee families. To what extent has PRWORA altered public assistance and how has it affected families in poverty? How does the use of legal citizenship status as a form of demarcation for entitlement to life-sustaining benefits exclude immigrants/refugees as outsiders from the social, political, and economic policies of the nation?

SUGGESTED READINGS

Bonacich, Edna and John Modell. 1980. *The Economic Basis of Ethnic Solidarity: Small Business in the Japanese American Community.* Berkeley: University of California Press.
Chan, Sucheng. 2004. *Survivors: Cambodian Refugees in the United States.* Champaign: University of Illinois Press.

Chin, Margaret. 2005. *Sewing Women: Immigrants and the New York City Garment Industry.* New York: Columbia University Press.

Donnelly, Nancy D. 1997. *Changing Lives of Refugee Hmong Women.* Seattle: University of Washington Press.

Faderman, Lillian with Ghia Xiong. 1998. *I Begin My Life All Over: The Hmong and the American Immigrant Experience.* Boston: Beacon Press.

Friday, Chris. 1994. *Organizing Asian American Labor: The Pacific Coast Canned Salmon Industry.* Philadelphia: Temple University Press.

Glenn, Evelyn Nakano. 1986. *Issei, Nisei, Warbride: Three Generations of Japanese American Women in Domestic Service.* Philadelphia: Temple University Press.

Glenn, Evelyn Nakano. 2004. *Unequal Freedom: How Race and Gender Shaped American Citizenship and Labor.* Cambridge, MA: Harvard University.

Ha, Daisy. 2001. An Analysis and Critique of KIWA's Reform Efforts in the Los Angeles Korean American Restaurant Industry. *Asian Law Journal* 8.

Kalita, S. Mitra. 2003. *Suburban Sahibs: Three Immigrant Families and Their Passage from India to America.* New Brunswick, NJ: Rutgers University Press.

Lee, Gen Leigh. 1996. Chinese Cambodian Donut Makers in Orange County: Case Studies of Family Labor and Socioeconomic Adaptations. In *The State of Asian Pacific America: Reframing the Immigration Debate: A Public Policy Report.* (Los Angeles: LEAP Asian Pacific American Public Policy Report and UCLA Asian American Studies Center), 208–19.

Leonard, Karen and Chandra S. Tibrewal. 1993. Asian Indians in Southern California: Occupations and Ethnicity. In Ivan Light and Parminder Bhachu (eds.), *Immigration and Entrepreneurship: Culture, Capital, and Ethnic Networks.* New Brunswick, NJ: Transaction.

Leong, Andrew. 1997. The Asian Exclusion Act of 1996: Welfare Reform and Asian Pacific America. *Asian American Policy Review* 7: 88–101.

Leong, Frederick T. L. and Mark C. Johnson. 1994. Mothers of Vietnamese Amerasians: Psychological Distress and High-Risk Factors. *Asian American and Pacific Islander Journal of Health* 2.1 (Winter): 31–48.

Min, Pyong Gap. 1996. *Caught in the Middle: Korean Merchants in America's Multiethnic Cities.* Berkeley: University of California Press.

Nagasawa, R., Z. Qian, and P. Wong. 2001. Theory of Segmented Assimilation and the Adoption of Marijuana Use and Delinquent Behavior by Asian Pacific Youth. *The Sociological Quarterly* 42(3): 351–72.

Ong, Paul and Tania Azores. 1994. The Migration and Incorporation of Filipino Nurses. Pp. 164–98 in Paul Ong, Edna Bonacich, and Lucie Cheng (eds.), *The New Asian Immigration in Los Angeles and Global Restructuring.* Philadelphia: Temple University Press.

Park, Kyeyoung. 1997. *The Korean American Dream: Immigrants and Small Business in New York City.* Ithaca, NY: Cornell University Press.

Park, Kyeyoung. 2004. Confronting the Liquor Industry in Los Angeles. *IJSSP* 24(7/8): 103–36.

Park, Lisa Sun-Hee. 2005. *Consuming Citizenship: Children of Asian Immigrant Entrepreneurs.* Stanford, CA: Stanford University Press.

Park, Yungsuhn. 2005. The Immigrant Workers Union: Challenges Facing Low-Wage Immigrant Workers in Los Angeles. *Asian Law Journal* 12.

Parreñas, Rhacel S. 2001. *Servants of Globalization: Women, Migration, and Domestic Work.* Stanford, CA: Stanford University Press.

Shibusawa, T. and A. Mui. 2001. Stress, Coping, and Depression among Japanese American Elders. *Journal of Gerontological Social Work* 36(1/2): 63–81.

Uba, L. 1994. *Asian Americans: Personality Patterns, Identity, and Mental Health.* New York: Guilford Press.

Welaratna, Usha. 1993. *Beyond the Killing Fields.* Stanford, CA: Stanford University Press.

Wu, Diana Ting Liu. 1997. *Asian Pacific Americans in the Workplace.* Lanham, MD: AltaMira Press.

Zhou, Min. 1992. *Chinatown: The Socioeconomic Potential of an Urban Enclave.* Philadelphia: Temple University Press.

Zhou, Min. 2004. Revisiting Ethnic Entrepreneurship: Convergences, Controversies, and Conceptual Advancements. *International Migration Review* 38(3): 1040–74.

FILMS

Boti, Marie (director). 1997. *Modern Heroes, Modern Slaves* (45-minute documentary).

Choy, Christine and Elaine Kim (coproducers). 1993. *Sa-I-Gu: From Korean Women's Perspectives* (36-minute documentary).

Ding, Loni (producer/director). 1982. *Four Women* (30-minute documentary).

Ding, Loni (producer/director). 1982. *Frankly Speaking* (30-minute documentary).

Dunn, Geoffrey and Mark Schwartz (codirectors). 1984. *Dollar a Day, Ten Cents a Dance* (29-minute documentary).

Nakasako, Spencer and Sokly Ny (codirectors). 1995. *a.k.a. Don Bonus* (55-minute documentary).

Sakya, Sapana, Donald Young, Kyung Yu (codirectors). 2003. *Searching for Asian America* (90-minute documentary).

Tajima-Peña, Renee (director). 2002. *Labor Women* (35-minute documentary).

Tang, Eric (director). 2001. *Eating Welfare* (57-minute documentary).

Tsumo, Keiko (director). 1990. *The Story of Vinh* (60-minute documentary).

Wang, Wayne (director). 1989. *Eat a Bowl of Tea* (102-minute drama).

Young, Donald (director). 1994. *Chrysanthemums and Salt* (25-minute documentary).

Part V

Sexuality in Asian America

Chapter 13

Stories from the Homefront

Perspectives of Asian American Parents with Lesbian Daughters and Gay Sons

Alice Y. Hom

> Having been a classroom teacher since 1963, I have new
> knowledge that ten percent of all the students who came
> through my classroom have grown up and are gay and
> lesbian. . . . Because I cannot undo the past, I want to
> teach people the truth about homosexuality so people
> will not abandon these children.[1]

These are stories from the homefront: the emotions, responses, and attitudes of Asian American parents about their lesbian daughters or gay sons. The stories attempt to shed some light on parents' attitudes and inform lesbians and gay men of various ways parents may react and respond to their coming out.

I focus on four themes that illustrate important concepts around understanding Asian American parents and their views on homosexuality. These themes emerged from the interviews: (1) the attitudes of parents before disclosure/discovery; (2) the attitudes and reactions of parents after disclosure/discovery; (3) disclosure to friends and their communities; and (4) advice for other parents.

Sexuality is an issue rarely or never discussed amongst Asian families, yet it remains a vital aspect of one's life. What are the implications of alternative sexualities in family situations? Coming out stories and experiences of Asian American lesbians and gay men have had some exposure and publication,[2] however the voices of the parents are rarely presented or known.

I found the majority of interviewees through personal contacts with individuals in organizations such as Asian Pacifica Sisters in San Francisco, Mahu Sisters and Brothers Alliance at UCLA and Gay Asian Pacific Alliance Community HIV Project in San Francisco. I met one set of parents through the Parents and Friends of Lesbians and Gays group in Los Angeles. Obviously, this select group of people, who were willing to talk about their child, might represent only certain perspectives. Nonetheless, I managed to pool a diverse set of parents despite the small size in terms of disclosing time and time lapse—some parents have known for years, and a few have recently found out. I did receive some "no" answers to my request. I also offered complete anonymity in the interviews; most preferred pseudonyms. Names with an asterisk sign denote pseudonyms.

I interviewed thirteen parents altogether, all mothers except for two fathers.[3] The interviewee pool consisted of four single mothers by divorce, a widower, two couples, and four married mothers. The ethnicities included four Chinese, four Japanese, three Pilipinas, one Vietnamese, and one Korean. Most live in California, with one in Portland and another in Hawaii. All of the interviews occurred in English with the exception of one interview conducted in Japanese with the lesbian daughter as translator. Ten out of the thirteen interviewees are first-generation immigrants. The other three are third-generation Japanese American. I interviewed four mothers of gay sons, including one mother with two gay sons. The rest had lesbian daughters, including one mother with two lesbian daughters. Six were told and seven inadvertently discovered about their children's sexual orientation.[4]

Most books on the topic of parents of lesbian and gay children report mainly on white middle-class families.[5] *Beyond Acceptance: Parents of Lesbians and Gays Talk about Their Experiences,* by Carolyn W. Griffin, Marian J. Wirth, and Arthur G. Wirth, discusses the experiences of twenty-three white middle-class parents from a Midwestern metropolitan city involved with Parents and Friends of Lesbians and Gays (PFLAG).[6] Another book, titled *Parents Matter: Parents' Relationships with Lesbian Daughters and Gay Sons,* by Ann Muller, relates the perspectives of lesbian and gay children with a few stories by the parents. Seventeen percent of the seventy-one people interviewed were black.[7] These examples present mainly an Anglo picture and fail to account for the diversity of lesbian and gay communities as well as different experiences of parents of color.

Attitudes of Parents toward Gays and Lesbians Predisclosure

The knowledge of lesbians and gay men in their native countries and in their communities in the United States serves as an important factor in dismantling the oft-used phrase that a son or daughter is gay or lesbian because of assimilation and acculturation in a Western context. The parents interviewed did not utter "it's a white disease," a phrase often heard and used when discussing coming out in an Asian American community and context. Connie S. Chan in her essay, "Issues of Identity Development among Asian American Lesbians and Gay Men," found in her study that nine out of ninety-five respondents were out to their parents. Chan suggested that this low number might be related to ". . . specific cultural values defining the traditional roles, which help to explain the reluctance of Asian-American lesbians and gay men to 'come out' to their parents and families."[8]

Nonetheless, the parents interviewed recounted incidents of being aware of lesbians and/or gays while they were growing up and did not blame assimilation and Anglo American culture for their children's sexual orientation. One quote by Lucy Nguyen, a fifty-three-year-old Vietnamese immigrant who has two gay sons, does, however, imply that the environment and attitudes of the United States allowed for her sons to express their gay identity. She stated:

> I think all the gay activities and if I live at this time, environment like this, I think I'm lesbian. You know, be honest. When I was young, the society in—Vietnam is so strict —I have a really close friend, I love her, but just a friendship nothing else. In my mind, I say, well in this country it's free. They have no restraint, so that's why I accept it, whatever they are.[9]

This revealing remark assumes that an open environment allows for freedom of sexual expression. Nevertheless, it does not necessarily suggest lesbians and gay men exist solely because of a nurturing environment. Rather, lesbians and gay men must live and survive in different ways and/or make choices depending on the climate of the society at the time.

Midori Asakura,* a sixty-three-year-old Japanese immigrant with a lesbian daughter, related an example of lesbianism in Japan. She remembered, while studying to be a nurse, talk in the dorm rooms about "S," which denotes women who had really close friendships with one another.[10] She recalled,

> One day you'd see one woman with a certain blouse and the next day, you'd see the other woman with the same blouse. They would always sit together, they went everywhere together. There was talk that they were having sex, but I didn't think they were. . . . People used to say they felt each other out. I thought, "Nah, they're not having sex, why would they?" Everyone thought it was strange but no one really got into it.[11]

When asked what she thought of the "S" women, Midori replied, "I didn't think much of it, although I thought one was man-like, Kato-san, and the other, Fukuchi-san, who was very beautiful and sharp-minded was the woman."[12]

Another parent, George Tanaka,* a fifty-three-year-old Japanese American who grew up in Hawaii and has a lesbian daughter, remembers a particular person known as *mahu*.[13] Toni Barraquiel, a fifty-four-year-old Pilipina single mother with a gay son, commented on gay men in Manila because of their effeminacy and admission of being gay. Toni asserted these men would be in certain careers such as manicurists and hairdressers. When asked of the people's attitudes toward them, she replied,

> that they look down on those gays and lesbians, they make fun of them. . . . It seems as if it is an abnormal thing. The lesbian is not as prominent as the gays. They call her a tomboy because she's very athletic and well built.[14]

Maria Santos,* a fifty-four-year-old Pilipina immigrant with two lesbian daughters, spoke of gays and lesbians in Luzon. She said, "There were negative attitudes about them. 'Bakla' and 'Tomboy'—it was gay-bashing in words not in physical terms. There was name-calling that I did not participate in."[15]

Lucy Nguyen* had lesbian classmates in her all-girls high school. She said, "They were looked down upon, because this isn't normal. They were called 'homo.'"[16] A common thread throughout the observations of the parents about gays and lesbians lies in stereotypical gender role associations. For example, Margaret Tsang,* a sixty-year-old Chinese single parent who has a gay son, recalled a family member who might possibly be gay, although there was not a name for it. She observed, "He was slanted toward nail polish and make-ups and all kinds of things. And he liked Chinese opera. He behaved in a very feminine fashion."[17]

Similarly, Liz Lee, a forty-two-year-old Korean single parent with a lesbian daughter, clearly remembered lesbians in Seoul. "My mother's friend was always dressed like man in suit. She always had mousse or grease on her hair and she dressed like a man. She had five or six girlfriends always come over."[18] Liz related that she did not think anything about it and said they were respected.[19] When asked of people's attitudes toward these women, Liz responded, "They say nature made a mistake. They didn't think it was anybody's choice or anybody's preference."[20]

For the most part, the interviewees, aware of gays and lesbians during their growing-up years, associated gender-role reversals with gays and lesbians. The men were feminine and the women looked male or tomboy, with the women couples in a butch-femme type relationship. The belief and experiences with lesbians and gay men who dress and act in opposite gender roles serve as the backdrop of what to compare their children with when faced with their coming out. Most of what these parents see is a part of homosexuality, the dress or behavior. They have not seen the whole range of affectional, emotional, intellectual, and sexual components of a person. Although I asked the interviewees if they had any thoughts or attitudes about lesbians or gay men, most said they did not think about them and did not participate in the name calling or bashing. This might not be necessarily true because they were able to relate quite a few incidents of homophobic opinions which might have been internalized. Moreover, once they know they have a lesbian or gay child, that distance or non-judgmental attitude radically changes. As one mother remarked, "the fire is on the other side of the river bank. The matter is taking place somewhere else, it's not your problem."[21]

Disclosure or Discovery

For the most part, parents experience a wide range of emotions, feelings, and attitudes when they find out they have a lesbian daughter or gay son. Parents find out through a variety of ways, ranging from a direct disclosure by the children themselves, discovering the fact from a journal, confronting the child because of suspicions, or by walking in on them.

For example, Liz Lee, who walked in on her daughter Sandy, said, "[it was] the end of the world. Still today I can't relate to anything that's going on with my daughter, but I'm accepting."[22] She found out in 1990 and said,

> I was hoping it was a stage she's going through and that she could change. I didn't accept for a long time. I didn't think she would come out in the open like this. I thought

she would just keep it and later on get married. That's what I thought but she's really out and open. . . . I said to myself I accept it because she is going to live that way.[23]

Because Sandy serves as the cochair of the Gay, Lesbian, and Bisexual Association at school, her mother sees Sandy as happy and politically fulfilled from this position, which assists her process in accepting Sandy's sexual orientation. However, like many of the parents interviewed, she initially thought she had done something wrong. "I didn't lead a normal life at the time either. But Sandy always accept me as I was and she was always happy when I was happy and I think that's love. As long as Sandy's happy."[24]

Toni Barraquiel responded differently when Joel told her at an early age of thirteen or fourteen that he was gay back in the mid-1980s. She plainly asked him if he felt happy, to which he replied affirmatively. Thus her response, "well, if you're happy I'll support you, I'll be happy for you."[25] Their relationship as a single mother and only child has always been one of closeness and open communication, so problems did not arise in terms of disclosing his sexual orientation. Toni Barraquiel experienced confusion because at the time he had girlfriends and she did not think of him as a typical feminine gay man, since he looked macho. She also wondered if her single-mother role had anything to do with Joel's gay orientation:

> Maybe because I raised him by myself, it was a matriarchal thing. I have read now that these gays, there is something in the anatomy of their bodies that affect the way they are. So it is not because I raised him alone, maybe it's in the anatomy of the body. Even if I think that because I raised him alone as a mother, even if he came out to be gay, he was raised as a good person. No matter what I would say I'm still lucky he came out to be like that.[26]

In the end she accepted Joel no matter what caused his sexual orientation.

Katherine Tanaka,* a fifty-three-year-old Japanese American from Hawaii, found out about Melissa's lesbianism through an indirect family conversation. George Tanaka* brought up the issue of sexuality and asked Melissa* if she was a lesbian. He suspected after reading her work on the computer. Katherine* remembered her response:

> I was in a state of shock. I didn't expect it, so I didn't know how to react. It was the thing of disbelief, horror and shame and the whole thing. I guess I felt the Asian values I was taught surface in the sense that something was wrong. That she didn't turn out the way we had raised her to be.[27]

George Tanaka* recalled, "After we hugged, she went off to her bedroom. As she was walking away from us, all of a sudden I felt like she was a stranger. I thought I knew [her]. Here was a very important part of her and I didn't know anything about it."[28] The idea of not knowing one's children anymore after discovering their sexual orientation remains a common initial response from the interviewees. Because of this one aspect, parents believe their child has changed and is no longer the person they thought they knew. For example, one parent said:

The grieving process took a long time. Especially the thing about not being a bride. Not having her be a bride was a very devastating change of plans for her life. I thought I was in her life and it made me feel when she said she was a lesbian that there was no place for me in her life. I didn't know how I could fit into her life because I didn't know how to be the mother of a lesbian.[29]

Upon finding out, the parents interviewed spoke of common responses and questions they had. What did I do wrong? Was I responsible for my child's lesbian or gay identity? What will others think? How do I relate to my child? What role do I have now that I know my child is a lesbian or gay man? The emotions a parent has ranged from the loss of a dream they had for their child to a fear of what is in store for them as a gay or lesbian person in this society.

Nancy Shigekawa,* a third-generation Japanese American born and residing in Hawaii, recalled her reaction:

I had come home one night and they were in the bedroom. Then I knew it wasn't just being in the room. My reaction was outrage, to say the least. I was so angry. I told them to come out . . . and I said [to her girlfriend], "I'm going to kill you if you ever come back." That's how I was feeling. I look back now and think I must have been like a crazy lady.[30]

Maria Santos* remembered her discovery.

I found out through a phone call from the parents of [her] best friend. They [Cecilia* and her friend] were trying to sneak out, and they had a relationship. I thought it would go away. Let her see a psychiatrist. But she fooled me. In her second year at college she told me she was a lesbian. It broke my heart. That was the first time I heard the word lesbian, but I knew what it meant. Like the tomboy.[31]

She also had a feeling about her youngest daughter, Paulette*:

At Cecilia's graduation I saw them talking secretly and I saw the pink triangle on her backpack. I can't explain it. It's a mother's instinct. I prayed that it would not be so [starts to cry]. Paulette told me in a letter that she was a lesbian and that Cecilia had nothing to do with it. I wanted it to change. I had the dream, that kids go to college, get married, and have kids.[32]

Maria Santos* did not talk to anyone about her daughters. She grew up having to face the world on her own without talking to others. However, she said, "But I read books, articles all about gays and lesbians as members of the community. They are normal people. I did not read negative things about them."[33]

In this sense, parents also have a coming-out process that they go through. They must deal with internalized homophobia and re-evaluate their beliefs and feelings about lesbians and gay men. One method in this process includes reading about and listening to gay men and lesbians talk about their lives. Having personal contact or at least information on lesbian and gay life takes the mystery out of the stereotypes and misconceptions that parents might have of lesbian and gay people. What helped some women was the personal interaction and reading about lesbian and gay men's lives. They had more information with which to contrast, contradict, and support their previous notions of lesbians and gay men.

Yet, sometimes some parents interviewed have not yet read or do not seek outside help or information. Some of the parents did not talk to others and have remained alone in their thinking. This does not necessarily have negative effects. Liz Lee said, "Still today I don't think I can discuss with her in this matter because I can't relate. . . . I can't handle it. I wouldn't know how to talk to her about this subject. I just let her be happy."[34]

MG Espiritu,* a sixty-year-old Pilipina immigrant, believes her daughter's lesbianism stems from environmental causes such as being with other lesbians. Nonetheless, less than a couple of years after finding out about her daughter Michelle, she went with her daughter to an Asian Pacific lesbian Lunar New Year banquet. MG* did so because her daughter wanted it and she wanted to please her. When asked how she felt at the event, MG* replied, "Oh, it's normal. It's just like my little girls' parties that they go to."[35] She speaks of little by little trying to accept Michelle's lesbianism.

Parents, Friends, and Their Ethnic Communities

For some parents, having a lesbian or gay child brings up the issue of their status and reputation in the community and family network. Questions such as: What is society going to think of me? Will the neighbors know and what will it reflect upon us? Did they raise a bad child?

> I told her we would have to move away from this house. I felt strongly neighbors and friends in the community would not want to associate with us if they knew we had a child who had chosen to be homosexual.[36]

The above quote reflected one parent's original reaction. Now she feels differently but is still not quite out to her family in Hawaii.

Some parents have told their siblings or friends. Others do not talk to relatives or friends at all because of fear they will not understand.

The following quote highlighted a typical anxiety of parents:

> I was ashamed. I felt I had a lot to do with it too. In my mind I'm not stupid, I'm telling myself, I know I didn't do it to her. I don't know if it's only because I'm Japanese . . . that's the way I saw it. I felt a sense of shame, that something was wrong with my family. I would look at Debbie* and just feel so guilty that I have these thoughts that something's wrong with her. But mostly I was selfish. I felt more for myself, what I am going to say? How am I going to react to people when they find out?[37]

Despite her apprehension in the beginning, she did disclose Debbie's lesbianism to a close friend:

> I have a dear friend who I finally told because she was telling me about these different friends who had gay children. I couldn't stand it, I said, "You know, Bea, I have to tell you my daughter is gay." She was dumbfounded. I'm starting to cheer her up and all that. That was a big step for me to come out.

Nancy Shigekawa's* quote emphasizes the complexity of feelings that parents have when adjusting to their children's sexual orientation.

If parents are not close to their immediate family, they might not have told them. Others have not spoken because they do not care whether or not their family knows. Some parents do not disclose the fact of their gay son or lesbian daughter to protect them from facing unnecessary problems.

When asked how their respective ethnic communities feel about lesbians and gay men, some parents responded with firm conviction. Liz Lee, who spoke about the Korean community, said, "As long as they're not in their house, not in their life, they accept it perfectly."[38] She mentioned her daughter's lesbianism to a nephew but not to others in her family. "I'm sure in the future I have to tell them, but right now nobody has asked me and I don't particularly like to volunteer."[39] Jack Chan,* a sixty-one-year-old Chinese immigrant, claimed, "Shame, that's a big factor. Shame brought upon the family. You have to remember the Chinese, the name, the face of the family is everything. I don't know how to overcome that."[40]

Lucy Nguyen* gave this answer about the Vietnamese community: "They won't accept it. Because for a long, long time they say they [gays and lesbians] are not good people, that's why."[41] Lucy felt that talking about it would help and teach the community to open their minds. The frankness and openness of speaking out about gays and lesbians will inform people of our existence and force the issue in the open. In this way having parents come out will make others understand their experiences and allow for their validation and affirmation as well.

Although most of these parents have negative views about the acceptance level of friends and particularly with ethnic communities, some have taken steps to confide in people. One must also realize their opinion reflects their current situation and opinion which might change over time. Three of the parents have participated in panels and discussions on Asian American parents with lesbian and gay kids.

Advice to Other Parents

In many ways the mere fact these parents agreed to the interview has much to say about their feelings or attitudes toward lesbian and gay sexuality and their kids. Although some parents might feel some unease and reservations, they had enough courage to speak to me and voice their opinions. Many of the parents did so out of love and concern for their children. A few thought that they did not have anything to say but agreed to talk to me. In the process of these interviews, some parents expressed appreciation and comfort in talking to someone about their experiences. Their struggle of coming to terms with their lesbian daughters and gay sons merits notice.

One of my last questions related to helping other parents. While some did not have an answer to the question, "What advice do you have for other parents with lesbian and gay kids?" a few responded with the following suggestions. For example,

> Love them like a normal individual. Give all the compassion and understanding. Don't treat your child differently because the person is gay, because this is an individual. . . . I cannot understand why it is so hard for these parents to accept their child is gay. What makes them so different, because they are gay? The more you should support your kid, because as it is in society, it has not been accepted one hundred percent.[42]

> I cannot throw them out. I love them so much. Even more now because they are more of a minority. They are American Asian, women and lesbian. Triple minority. I have to help fight for them. . . . Accept them as they are. Love them more. They will encounter problems. It will take years and years to overcome homophobia. Make them ambitious, well educated, better than others so they can succeed.[43]

Tina Chan,* a fifty-eight-year-old Chinese immigrant, offers similar advice. Other parents concurred:

> My advice is to accept them. They haven't changed at all. They're still the same person. The only thing different is their sexual orientation. They should really have the support from the family, so they would not have this battle like they're not even being accepted in the family. They should look at them like they have not changed. Parents can't do it. They think the whole person has changed, and I think that's terrible because they haven't. I mean it's so stupid.[44]

Jack Chan* also leaves us with advice to take to heart:

> Don't feel depressed that their parent[is] coming around so slow or not coming around at all. Remember when you come out to them, the parent generally go[es] into the closet themselves. However long it take you to come out, it'll probably take them longer to accept. It's a slow process. Don't give up.[45]

Concluding Remarks

George Tanaka* relates an incident where he and his wife told their coming out process in front of ten Asian American gay men and in the end found some of the men crying. "The tears surprised me. . . . We were representing the sadness that there could not be loving parents. Representing some hope their parents would likewise be able to become loving about it."[46] The belief that parents can change and go through a process of eventual acceptance and supportiveness appears to have a basis in reality, although a happy ending might not always be the case.

From these interviews one can sense some of the thoughts, actions, and experiences of Asian American parents. These stories are not the last word but signal the beginning of a more informed dialogue.

What would the stories of their daughters and sons look like against their parents' perceptions? It would be helpful to have the stories side by side to evaluate the differences. Moreover, gay and lesbian children might have perspectives that inform parents. Other issues such as socialization processes, religious, language, and cultural issues, and spouses' opinions need further exploration. I did not include a discussion on the origins of lesbian and gay sexual identity. I hope these stories from the homefront can serve as an initial mapping of a complex sexual territory that is part of Asian American family dynamics.

NOTES

Originally published in *Amerasia Journal* 20.1 (1994): 19–32. © 1994 *Amerasia Journal,* reprinted by permission. The desire to work on this project came after listening to two Japanese American parents, George and Katherine Tanaka, talk about their lesbian daughter. They revealed a painful process of going through their own coming out while grappling with their daughter's sexual identity and their own values and beliefs. As members of Parents and Friends of Lesbians and Gays (PFLAG), they mentioned they were the only Asian Americans, the only parents of color, for that matter, in this organization. Despite being the Asian American contact, Katherine has received less than ten calls during a two-year time span, and not one Asian American parent has ever come to PFLAG. She recounted her feelings and belief of being the only Asian parent with a gay child. That feeling of loneliness and alienation struck me deeply because as an Asian American lesbian I could identify with her feelings.

1. Interview with Katherine Tanaka. Los Angeles, California, February 21, 1993.
2. See Kitty Tsui, *the words of a woman who breathes fire* (San Francisco: Spinsters Ink, 1983). C. Chung, Alison Kim, and A. K. Lemshewsky, eds., *Between the Lines: An Anthology by Pacific/ Asian Lesbians* (Santa Cruz: Dancing Bird Press, 1987). Rakesh Ratti, ed., *A Lotus of Another Color: The Unfolding of the South Asian Gay and Lesbian Experience* (Boston: Alyson Press, 1993). Silvera Makeda, ed., *A Piece of My Heart: A Lesbian of Colour Anthology* (Toronto: Sister Vision Press, 1993).
3. Mothers constitute the majority of the parents interviewed. Perhaps mothers are more apt to talk about their feelings and emotions about having a gay son or lesbian daughter than the father. Mothers might be more understanding and willing to discuss their emotions and experiences than the fathers who also know.
4. I did not interview parents who had a bisexual child. I believe a son or daughter who comes out as bisexual might encounter a different set of questions and reactions. Especially since the parent might hope and persuade the daughter or son to "choose" heterosexuality instead of homosexuality.
5. See Carolyn W. Griffin, Marian J. Wirth, and Arthur G. Wirth, *Beyond Acceptance: Parents of Lesbians and Gays Talk about Their Experiences* (New York: St. Martin's Press, 1986).
6. Parents and Friends of Lesbians and Gays (PFLAG) has chapters all around the United States. One couple and a father interviewed are involved with PFLAG in their respective locales.
7. Ann Muller, *Parents Matter: Parents' Relationships with Lesbian Daughters and Gay Sons* (Tallahassee: Naiad Press, 1987), 197.

8. Connie S. Chan, "Issues of Identity Development Among Asian-American Lesbians and Gay Men." *Journal of Counseling and Development,* 68 (September/October, 1989), 19.

9. Interview with Lucy Nguyen. Los Angeles, California, February 20, 1993.

10. Interview with Midori Asakura. Los Angeles, California, April 18, 1993.

11. Midori Asakura.

12. Ibid.

13. *Mahu* does not necessarily mean gay but defines a man who dresses and acts feminine. However, its common usage does denote a gay man.

14. Interview with Toni Barraquiel. Los Angeles, California, April 18, 1993.

15. Telephone interview Maria Santos. Portland, Oregon, May 9, 1993.

16. Lucy Nguyen.

17. Interview with Margaret Tsang. San Francisco, California, February 5, 1993.

18. Interview with Liz Lee. Los Angeles, California, May 11, 1993.

19. Liz based this respect on this particular woman's election to something similar to a city council and her standing in the community.

20. Liz Lee.

21. Midori Asakura.

22. Liz Lee.

23. Ibid.

24. Ibid.

25. Toni Barraquiel.

26. Ibid.

27. Katherine Tanaka.

28. Interview with George Tanaka. Los Angeles, California, February 21, 1993.

29. Katherine Tanaka.

30. Telephone interview with Nancy Shigekawa. Kaneohe, Hawaii, March 20, 1993.

31. Maria Santos.

32. Ibid.

33. Ibid.

34. Liz Lee.

35. Interview with MG Espiritu. Northern California, July 20, 1993.

36. Katherine Tanaka.

37. Nancy Shigekawa.

38. Liz Lee.

39. Ibid.

40. Interview with Jack Chan. Northern California, July 18, 1993.

41. Lucy Nguyen.

42. Toni Barraquiel.

43. Maria Santos.

44. Interview with Tina Chan. Northern California, July 18, 1993.

45. Jack Chan.

46. George Tanaka.

Searching for Community
Filipino Gay Men in New York City

Martin F. Manalansan IV

Introduction

In 1987, a Filipino gay man named Exotica was crowned Miss Fire Island. The Miss Fire Island beauty contest is an annual drag event in Fire Island (located off the coast of Long Island) and is considered to be the premier gay summer mecca in America. It was interesting to note that a considerable number of the contestants who were not Caucasian were Filipinos. Furthermore, Exotica was not the first Filipino recipient of the crown; another Filipino was crowned earlier in the seventies. In 1992, a Filipino gay and lesbian group called *Kambal sa Lusog* marched in two parades in New York City, Gay Pride Day and Philippine Independence Day. These iconic events suggest the strong presence of Filipinos in the American gay scene, particularly in New York City.

This chapter delineates this presence by analyzing the issues of identity and community among fifty gay Filipino men in the city in their attempts to institutionalize or organize themselves. Through excerpts from life history interviews and field observations, I explore the ways in which being "gay" and being "Filipino" are continually being shaped by historical events.

I use the term "community" not as a static, closed, and unified system. Rather, I use the term strategically and conceptualize it as a fluid movement between subjectivity/identity and collective action.[1] Therefore, intrinsic to this use of the term "community" is a sense of dissent and contestation along with a sense of belonging to a group or cause. I also use Benedict Anderson's notion of community as "imagined,"[2] which means symbols, language, and other cultural practices and products, from songs to books, are sites where people articulate their sense of belonging. The concept of identity is not a series or stages of development or a given category but a dynamic package of meanings contingent upon practices that are both individually and collectively reconfigured.[3]

The first section briefly explores the cleavages that gave rise to a diversity of voices and outlines differences such as class, attitudes toward various homosexual practices, and ethnic/racial identity. In the next two sections, two pivotal moments, the *Miss Saigon* controversy and the AIDS pandemic, are discussed in terms of the patterns of cultural actions and counteractions. I focus on new or reconfigured collective discourses, specifically language and ritual. I also emphasize the organizing efforts of Filipinos to create a gay and lesbian group (*Kambal sa Lusog*) and an AIDS advocacy group. A specific activity called the *Santacruzan* by *Kambal sa Lusog* incorporates symbols from different national traditions and provides an example of the collective representation of community.

Divergent Voices

Ang sabi nila, iba't iba daw ang bakla, mayroon cheap, may pa-class, nandito yoong malandi at saka ang mayumi—kuno! [They say there are different kinds of *bakla*, those who are tacky, those who pretend they have class, then there are the whorish and the virginal—not!]

We are all gay. We are all Filipinos. We need to empower ourselves as a group.

Tigilan ako ng mga tsismosang bakla, wiz ko type maki-beso-beso sa mga baklang Pilipino—puro mga intrigera! [Get me away from those gossipy *bakla*, I don't want to socialize with those Filipino *bakla*, they are all gossip mongers!]

If we take these voices as indices of the opinions and stances of Filipino gay men, we will find a spectrum of similarities and divergences. Most Filipino gay men consider place of birth as an important gauge of the attitudes and ideas of a gay individual. The dichotomy between U.S.-born versus Philippine- or native-born Filipino gay men is actually used by many informants I have interviewed. This simplistic dichotomy is inadequate and erroneous. It does not begin to address the diversity among Filipino gay men.

Attitudes toward Homosexual Practices

In a group discussion I led with a group of Filipino gay men and lesbians, one gay man pointed out that the culture in which one was raised and, more importantly, where one was socialized into a particular homosexual tradition mattered more than place of birth. This is particularly true of many of my informants who immigrated as young children or in their early teens. Many of them explored their sexual identities under the symbols and practices of American culture. Many of them were not exposed to the *bakla* traditions[4] and more frequently followed the idioms and practices of American gay culture. These men were usually concerned with issues of coming out and identified more with a hypermasculine gay culture.

While almost all of my informants identified as gay, many of those who immigrated as adults and had some encounters in *bakla* practices and traditions were emphatic in delineating major differences between American gay and Philippine *bakla* culture. Most of these differences centered on the issue of cross-dressing and effeminacy.

However, there were some informants, including two American-born Filipinos, who through frequent visits to the Philippines as well as extended stays as students in Philippine schools were exposed to and involved in the *bakla* tradition. This group of men were more familiar with the cross-dressing traditions of homosexuality in the Philippines and usually spoke versions of Filipino swardspeak (a kind of gay argot).[5]

A case illustrates this point. One informant who was born and raised in California said that a turning point in his life was when he went to the Philippines at the age of sixteen and his uncle introduced him to cross-dressing and other practices among homosexuals. That brief (month and a half) visit was to become an important element in the way he now socialized in the gay community. He seeks cross-dressing opportunities not only with other transvestites but with other Filipinos. He said that Filipino gay men did not cross-dress for shock value but for realness. He further mentioned that he was unlike those gay men who were into queer androgyny, consciously looking midway between male and female. He and other gay men who cross-dressed attempted to look like real women. More important, despite the fact that he was raised speaking English at home, his friendships with other Philippine-born gay men has encouraged him to attempt to speak at least some smattering of the Filipino gay argot.

Some informants felt that Filipino cross-dressers had illusions (*ilusyonada*) and were internally homophobic or self-hating. These same informants were the ones who reported that they were part of the mainstream gay community. Some of them go to gyms and assume masculine ("straight-acting") mannerisms. They saw the cross-dressing practices of other Filipinos to be either low-class or archaic/anachronous (meaning cross-dressing belonged in the Philippines and not here in America).

On the other hand, the cross-dressers would call these guys *pamacho* (acting macho) or *pa-min* (acting like men). Filipino gay cross-dressers accused these "masculine" men of mimicking white Americans and of having illusions of being "real" men. Exotica,[6] one of my informants, said that cross-dressing for him was a way of getting men. He liked assuming more exotic identities and *nom de plumes* such as "Suzie Wong" or "Nancy Kwan." In the Philippines, he said he was able to get men for sex, but he had to pay them. In America, he said there was a "market" for his cross-dressing talent and exotic beauty. He said that he could not compete in the hypermasculine, gym-oriented world of mainstream gay life in New York. He said, "With my slight build, who would even give me a second look if I was wearing a T-shirt." However, he said that there were men, particularly those who were not gay-identified, who were attracted to "beautiful," "oriental" cross-dressers. He said that here in America, he did not have to pay the man to have sex with him, it was the other way around. He said, "Sometimes I feel so cheap because the man will insist on paying for everything including the pleasure of having sex with you. It is like everything goes on an opposite current here in America. I like it."

Conflicts between Filipino gay cross-dressers and non-cross-dressers are not dramatically played out in violent confrontations, but rather in avoidance. Furthermore, the differences are usually played down with a "live and let live" or *"yun ang type niya"* (that is his/her choice) attitude.

Social Class

Class is a more implicit boundary marker among gay Filipinos. Many of my infor-mants denied noting any difference between themselves and other gay Filipinos. How-ever, upon further probing, several of them (mostly those who were born and raised in the Philippines) will say, "Well, there are those who gossip a lot and just make bitchy remarks," or "Other Filipino gays are so tacky." Some Filipino gay men actu-ally used such terms as *baklang talipapa* (the *bakla* of the wet market), *baklang cheap* (tacky *bakla*), and *baklang kalye* (*bakla* of the streets), to designate gay Filipinos who they think are of a lower class standing or of lower "breeding." The indices of "low breeding" are myriad, but some informants agree that some important ones are flu-ency in the English language, styles of dress, schools attended, and "bearing" or how a gay Filipino carries himself.

Family roots are said to be another marker of class. *De buena familia* (from a good family) is a term used by gay men to portray how someone has class and social stand-ing. Another word used to describe somebody who has a lot of money is *datungera* (*datung* is swardspeak for money, and the noun is given the feminine form). In most conversations between Filipinos that I have heard and observed, the typical insult hurled at other gay men apart from physical traits were the idioms derived from class or the lack thereof.

Despite these occurrences, many still assert that America has leveled off some of these distinctions. An informant said, "There are some Filipinos I would normally not have contact with back home in the Philippines, but here in America we are thrown together in the bars, in the streets, some neighborhoods . . . you know."

The case of David, a gay Filipino in his forties, is particularly instructive. He was very proud of his aristocratic background in the Philippines. He said America was very funny because he was able to maintain relationships with people who were not of his class. Coming from a landed family in the Philippines, he said that he tried to cre-ate some distance from people who were not his equal. But this was not true in Amer-ica. For a long time, his lover was a telephone linesman with a high school degree. He said there were times when the class disparity showed. For example, conflicts occurred in situations when their tastes for particular leisure activities were divided into, in his mind, the classy and the tasteless, between a concert and bowling.

He further reported that his first ten years of living in America were spent as an illegal alien. Despite having money and a good education, he started as a janitor or a busboy due to lack of legal papers. He said, "I guess living during those years and do-ing those kinds of jobs were exciting in a way . . . a different way of experiencing America." Indeed, David's own class-conscious ways have been tempered to a large extent by the immigration experience. He now has contacts with several Filipino gay men, many of whom were of lower class origins.

Most of those who were born in America did not report any class distinctions among Filipinos. They were, however, more up front about their class origins. Two of my informants who were born and raised in California prefaced their stories about childhood by stating that they were from working-class families in the U.S. army.

Ethnic/Racial Identity

Most articles on Asian American gay men regard identity as a static given and construct ethnic identity as a polar opposite of gay identity.[7] Among the questions I asked my fifty Filipino informants was how they identified ethnically or racially. All but one said that they identified as Filipino or Filipino American. When I asked about the category Asian/Pacific Islander, most of them said that while they assumed this category in official papers and functions, they perceived Asia or Asian only in geographic terms. When I asked the Filipino gay men how they differed from Asian gay men, many Filipino informants said that they did not have the same kind of issues such as coming out and homophobia.

A majority of informants, mostly immigrants, felt that Philippine society was relatively tolerant of homosexuality. Some informants reported very good responses from families when they did "come out." Others felt that they didn't have to come out about being gay because they thought that their families knew about their identity without their having to verbally acknowledge it. Filipino informants felt that other Asian men, particularly those who had just immigrated to America, did not speak English as well as they did. Important cultural differences, such as religion, were cited by informants as significant. Many felt that they had a closer cultural affinity with Latinos.

Among those who were born in the Philippines, regional ethnolinguistic differences became apparent in relation to other Filipinos. Some of the informants did not speak Pilipino or Tagalog and instead spoke a regional language such as Bisaya or Ilongo. However, differences in languages and region were usually displaced by the use of English or Filipino swardspeak by many of the informants.

What I have presented above is a broad outline of the differences and similarities among Filipino gay men. This is to provide a kind of foundation upon which to situate the succeeding discussions of Filipino men coming together and acting in a more collective manner. This section has shown how there are pivotal points that act as markers of difference such as class, cultural traditions, and practices of homosexuality.

The Miss Saigon Interlude: Irony of a Different Kind

In the first full-length article on Asian gays and lesbians in the now-defunct magazine *Outweek*,[8] Nina Reyes (a Filipino American lesbian) wrote how the controversy surrounding the Broadway show *Miss Saigon* acted as a catalyst in bringing together many Asian gay and straight political activists to the forefront. According to Reyes, apart from the controversy around hiring (specifically, the use of a Caucasian, Jonathan Price, to play a Eurasian pimp) and the allegedly racist Madame Butterfly–inspired storyline, the opening night of *Miss Saigon* was the venue of protests by Asian gay and lesbian groups.

It is ironic that in the same article, Miss Reyes quoted a Filipino gay man who pointed out that not all Filipinos agreed with the protests since, after all, the star of the show, Lea Salonga, was a Filipina. Indeed, many of my informants have seen the show and have reported how relatives and Filipino friends (both gay and straight), particularly those from other states and the Philippines, would include seeing the show as the highlight of their visits to the Big Apple. The issue here was not just a matter of taste but had important political underpinnings. Many Filipinos felt that their sentiments and thoughts about the show were not represented in the mass media.

This was not to be the end of this controversy. The Gay Asian Pacific Islander Men of New York (GAPIMNY), one of the most vociferous groups in the *Miss Saigon* protest, celebrated its anniversary with a variety show and dance at the Lesbian and Gay Community Center in Manhattan in the summer of 1992. One of the drag performers, a Filipino gay man, decided to participate with a lipsync performance of one of Lea Salonga's songs in *Miss Saigon.* This caused a lot of ruckus. Before the performance, attempts were made by certain non-Filipinos to dissuade the drag performer from going though his intended repertoire even while the emcee was reading a disclaimer by GAPIMNY that stated that the group disavowed any connection with the Broadway show. Furthermore, the disclaimer also stated that the audience should enjoy the performance and at the same time remember the racist underpinnings of the show's storyline and production practices.

It is important to note not only the effects of the *Miss Saigon* controversy on Asian American gay politics but also how the representations and characters of this Broadway show have become icons of Filipino gay men. After each show, many Filipinos gathered backstage to talk to the actors and actresses (many of whom are Filipino or Filipino American). A good number of these fans are gay men.

Filipino gay men have appropriated many of the symbols and figures of this Broadway play. For Halloween in 1991, Leilani, a Filipino cross-dresser, bought a *cheongsam* in Chinatown, had a friend pull his hair back into a bun, and paraded around Greenwich Village with just a small woolen scarf to protect him from the blustery cold weather. He was extremely delighted to hear people scream "Miss Saigon" at him.

Several cross-dressing Filipinos I interviewed have admitted to using either Kim (the main character in *Miss Saigon*) or Lea Salonga as drag names. In fact, they said that when they talk about another gay Filipino who is either in a moody sad state or is extremely despondent, they say that he is doing a *Miss Saigon* or he is playing the role of Kim (*nagmi—Miss Saigon* or *Kim ang drama niya ngayon*).

The issues surrounding the controversy and the reaction of Filipinos, particularly gay men, have to do with several factors. The first is that of immigration and the American dream. For many of these gay Filipinos, Lea Salonga represented their own aspirations regarding America. She initially had to be certified by Actor's Equity to enable her to work on Broadway since she was neither an American citizen/resident nor a member of the group. Her success in winning the Tony Award and her receiving the green card (permanent resident status) was very much seen as a collective triumph. An informant pointed to Miss Salonga's Tony acceptance speech as particularly meaningful. After receiving the award, she said, "Your dreams can come true."

Indeed, for many Filipinos, gay or straight, these words seemed to be directed at them. Since a large number of my informants are immigrants, some of whom are illegal, the play provided an alternative narrative to the frustrations of daily life as foreigner trying to attain the American dream. As one informant said, "*Mahirap dito sa Amerika pero kaunting tiyaga . . . byuti ka na.*" [It is hard here in America, but with a little perseverance, you will succeed (beauty here is used as part of swardspeak, and connotes good luck or fate).]

Race and racism, which were the central issues of the controversy, were less significant for many of my informants. Those who saw the play talked about the singing abilities of the actors and the magnificent stage design. When queried about the themes of the show, they said that the bar scenes reminded them of Olongapo and Angeles cities in the Philippines. These cities were sites of the two biggest U.S. military installations outside America. In these places, bars, prostitutes and American servicemen were everyday scenes.

The discourse of race was not particularly meaningful for many of my informants, a majority of whom immigrated in their twenties. Out of the fifty informants, four reported an incident of racial discrimination. Most reported never encountering it. This was not entirely fortuitous. These men may have encountered some kind of discriminatory practices but interpreted it as part of the hardships of being an immigrant in America.

While many of them did not pick up on the Orientalist symbolisms of *Miss Saigon*, this should not be interpreted as a case of false consciousness, rather this kind of reaction is symptomatic in immigrant cultures. Immigrants constantly negotiate both dominant/hegemonic and subordinate (minority) cultural products and practices into meaningful arrangements that inform their lives.[9] In the case of *Miss Saigon,* the racial stereotypes are subsumed, and instead, the play is interpreted as a symbolic and literal vehicle for attaining success in America. Many of my informants felt that the crucial element of the play was that of getting to America and attaining the American dream.

In sum, with the *Miss Saigon* controversy, we have a historical moment which provided Filipinos in the U.S. a pool of collective symbols from which they could create discursive practices from cross-dressing to swardspeak. For many gay Filipino men in New York City, *Miss Saigon* was the impetus for the generation of camp symbols and discourses about some kind of national/ethnic and immigrant identities and aspirations.

AIDS: Or the Aunt That Pulled Us Together

I remember that around 1986, I began to hear about some Filipino *bakla* dying of AIDS in the West Coast. Then soon after that I heard about a Filipino who died in New York City. Then, I heard about this famous Filipino hairdresser who died. Afterwards the first of my friends came down with pneumonia. It was of course, Tita Aida. She struck again and again.

Tita Aida or Auntie/Aunt Aida is the name Filipino gay men have coined for AIDS. I have explored this unique construction of AIDS by this group of men in an earlier paper,[10] but it is necessary to note that this construction is not idiosyncratic. It emanates from Philippine concepts of illness, gender, and sexuality. The personification of the disease by gay Filipinos reflects the growing number of AIDS cases among Filipino gay men in America.[11] During the period from 1986 to 1988, the rise of AIDS cases among Asians in San Francisco was first documented.[12]

It was the same period of time when many of my informants started to become aware of the devastation of the disease. Most of them thought that the disease only affected white men. One informant said, "I thought that only white men, *yung mga byuti* (the beautiful ones) who were having sex constantly, were the only ones getting it." Before 1986, there were rumors as well as some published articles both in Filipino publications here and back in the Philippines which talked about the natural immunity of Filipinos against the disease. Some articles talked about the diet (such as eating *bagoong* or salted shrimp paste) as the reason why there were no Filipinos with AIDS.

This was soon dispelled by the sudden onslaught of Filipino cases during the late eighties. An informant remembered how he took care of about five friends. He said,

> *Ang hirap . . . manash* [it was hard, sister]. I had to massage, clean, shop, and do so many things. It was a horror watching them die slowly and painfully. And when they died . . . my friends and I realized that there was no money for a burial or to send the bodies back to the Philippines. That was when we had some fundraising dinners. We just had dinner, not the *siyam-siyam* [traditional Filipino prayer ritual held several days after a burial], but just a simple get-together at somebody's place and a hat is passed to get some money to defray some expenses.

Many of the informants who have had friends die of AIDS reported similar themes and situations. Many of their friends were alone and without family because they were the first in their families to settle here or because their families refused to have anything to do with them after the truth came out. Some families took these ailing gay Filipinos back and refused to acknowledge both these men's disease and sexual orientation. However, there were also a number of families who accepted them, their gay friends, and lovers. In cases where there was a lover (usually Caucasian), it was he who oftentimes took care of the ailing Filipino.

In cases when the Filipino was alone, going back home to the Philippines was not seen as a viable option. First, because there were no adequate medical facilities that could take care of a patient with AIDS. Second, there were horror stories going around about how some Filipinos with AIDS were deported from the Philippines. Third, coming down with the disease was seen by some as a failure on their part of attaining the American dream, particularly those who found out as part of their naturalization (citizenship) process. American immigration laws prohibit (despite high hopes for changes in the new Clinton administration) the immigration of people who either have AIDS or are HIV seropositive.

AIDS has created a common experience from which gay Filipinos in New York build and create new discourses and practices. *Abuloy* or alms for the dead have become institutionalized and have acquired a new dimension. Gay Filipinos put up fashion shows and drag parties to help defray the burial or medical expenses of friends who have died. These collective efforts have become a regular occurrence.

Other collective efforts (most of which are by gay and lesbian) include symposiums about AIDS in the Filipino community in New York. A group of gay Filipino men was formed to institutionalize efforts to help Filipinos with AIDS. This group, the Advocacy Group, got Filipinos with HIV/AIDS and formed to provide support services. There are still problems. Some Filipino gay men with AIDS are wary of other Filipino gay men helping them because of the interlocking network of gay Filipinos. There is a real possibility of coming into contact with other Filipinos whom one knows. Other problems include Filipinos' inadequate access to services due to fear and lack of information.

Notwithstanding these difficulties, AIDS has provided a way of pulling Filipinos into some kind of collective action. While there are still sporadic attempts at solving some of the issues and problems many Filipino gay men face in the pandemic, there is a growing systematization of efforts.

Coming Together: Some Voices and (Re)Visions

In March 1991, an organization of Filipino gay men and lesbians called *Kambal sa Lusog* (which literally means "twins in health" but is interpreted to be "comrades in the struggle") was formed. Some informants who were members of this organization said that one of the impetuses for the formation of this group was the *Miss Saigon* controversy. However, after talking to one of the founders of the group, he said that there has been talk about such a group even before the *Miss Saigon* controversy. A large factor was that many Filipinos do not relate to other Asians or to an Asian identity.

This statement had been confirmed by my interviews with Filipino gay men. Many perceived Asia only in terms of geography; significant differences existed between other Asians and themselves. Furthermore, there was also a perception that Asian meant East Asians such as Japanese and Chinese. Due to these views, many felt that their interests as gay men would not be served by a group like GAPIMNY.

Kambal sa Lusog is a unique group because it includes gay men, lesbians, and bisexuals. It has a newsletter that usually comes out monthly. The group meets almost every month at the Lesbian and Gay Community Center in Manhattan. They have had numerous fundraisers and other group activities.

Among such fundraising activities was the *Santacruzan*. It was not only successful in attracting other Filipino gay men who were not members but more importantly, this particular production of the traditional Filipino ritual is perhaps the most evocative example of the kind of community and identity formation that Filipino gay men in New York are struggling to achieve.

The *Santacruzan* is an important traditional Catholic celebration in the Philippines held every May. It is a street procession that begins and ends in the church. The procession is essentially a symbolic reenactment of the finding of the cross of Christ by Queen Helena or Reyna Elena, the mother of Emperor Constantine of the Holy Roman Empire. The procession usually includes female personages, both mythical and historical. Among the usual figures are: *Reyna Sentenciada* (Justice), the three Virtues (*Fe, Esperanza,* and *Caridad* or Faith, Hope, and Charity), *Reina Banderada* or Motherland (Queen of the Flag), Reina Elena, Rosa Mistica, Constantino (the young Emperor Constantine), and biblical characters such as Judith and Mary Magdalene.

In the Philippines, the important figures in the processions are usually portrayed by women with male escorts. Constantino is the only named male figure and is usually played by a child. However, in some areas, there have been cases when cross-dressing men have participated in these processions. In fact one of these kinds of *Santacruzans* in Pasay City (one of the cities in the metropolitan Manila area) is famous for its cross-dressing procession.

Kambal sa Lusog's Santacruzan is significant not only for its cross-dressing personages, but because of the reconfiguration of the whole structure of the ritual. By describing the procession staged at the Lesbian and Gay Community Center in Manhattan in August, 1992, I am presenting what can be interpreted as a collective representation of identity and community. It is in this ritual where idioms of American and Philippine social symbolisms are selectively fused to provide structure to an implicit and subtle narrative of a community as well as a common cache of meanings and sentiments. This specific event locates the efforts of the organization at establishing a sense of collectivity.

First of all, this *Santacruzan* was not presented as a procession but as a fashion show. The focal point of the show was the stage with a fashion runway. In the center of the stage, before the runway began, was a floral arch which is reminiscent of the mobile arches of flowers that are carried in the procession for each mythical or historical personage.

The personages or figures were a combination of traditional *Santacruzan* figures as well as configurations of traditional figures and personages together with the creation of new ones. For example, while *Reyna Sentenciada,* who is usually portrayed like the figure of Justice, carrying scales and in a blindfold, the "gay" *Reyna Sentenciada* is dressed in a leather (S&M) dominatrix garb. During the presentation, before he left the stage, *Reyna Sentenciada,* lifted his wig to show his bald pate. *Reyna Libertad* or Liberty was dressed also in a dominatrix garb complete with a whip. Liberty in this instance was construed to be sexual freedom. The three Virtues were the only figures who were portrayed by women (lesbians) dressed in denim shorts, combat boots, and *barong tagalog* (the traditional Filipino male formal attire). Constantino, who is usually portrayed by a child, was a muscular Filipino in brief swimming trunks.

Other bolder representations were *Reyna Banderada,* who usually carried the Philippine flag and incorporated the symbols of the flag, such as the stars and the red and blue stripes, in a slinky outfit. The three stars of the flag were strategically placed in each nipple and in the crotch area. A mask of the sun was carried by this new version of the motherland. Infanta Judith came out as a Greek goddess, and, instead of the head of Holofernes, the gay Judith revealed the head of George Bush. A new kind of queen was created for this presentation, *Reyna Chismosa* or Queen of Gossip. This queen came out in a tacky dressing gown, wearing hair curlers and screaming on a cordless phone.

However, the finale was a return to tradition as *Reyna Elena* and the Emperatriz were dressed in traditional gowns and tiaras. The *Reyna Elena* carried an antique cross and flowers as all *Reyna Elenas* have done in the past.

The combination of secular/profane and religious imagery as well as Filipino and American gay icons provided an arena where symbols from the two countries were contested, dismantled, and reassembled in a dazzling series of statements. This *Santacruzan* therefore was built on shared experiences that juxtaposed such practices such as S&M and cross-dressing with androgyny (the pulling off of the wig) with traditional Filipino ones like the *bakla* notion of drag.

Filipino gay men who participated in this presentation operated within the contours of the *Santacruzan* ritual while at the same time transgressing long-held beliefs and practices by injecting the culture and politics of the adopted country (i.e., George Bush's head). The *Santacruzan* can be seen as "a style of imagining" a community. In other words, the presentation can be seen as an attempt by Filipino gay men to negotiate and represent their collectivity to themselves and to others.

The Future of a Filipino Gay Community

The edges or borders of a Filipino gay community cannot be clearly demarcated as they traverse the edges of other communities of this diasporic world. However, despite the cleavages that run across individuals and group interests, Filipino gay men, as I have shown, respond to various historical instances, such as the AIDS pandemic, anchored to shared cultural traditions that are continually renewed and reassembled. This kind of anchoring is never complete or final. There will always be oscillations between attachments or allegiances to particular groups, be it the Filipino gay community, the Asian gay community, or even the so-called American gay community.

While many observers and theorists of Asian American political movements see both the political necessity and historical inevitability of pan-Asian ethnic groupings, I argue that the path of the political evolution of Filipino gay men in America will not be unilinear. Filipinos as a group will not "mature" into a monolithic pan-Asian stage of development. Rather, there will emerge a multiplicity of identities and groupings.[13] Sentiments and allegiances to cultural traditions are continually strengthened and reshaped by the circular pattern of diasporas and migrations. The Filipino diaspora is continually replenished and altered by the sentiments and allegiances of its migrants and exiles.

Such responses are reflected nationally in Filipino gay men's reactions to the *Miss Saigon* controversy and the AIDS pandemic. Especially with the *Santacruzan*, we find a vigorous and continued creation and reconstitution of cultural symbols and practices that go hand in hand with the revivification of a sense of belonging. These discourses will pave the way for a stronger future of a Filipino gay community in New York.

NOTES

Originally published in *Amerasia Journal* 20.1 (1994): 59–73. © 1994 *Amerasia Journal*, reprinted by permission.

1. Terralee Bensinger, "Lesbian Pornography: The Re/Making of (a) Community," *Discourse* 15:1 (1992): 69–93.

2. Benedict Anderson, *Imagined Communities: Reflections on the Origin and Spread of Nationalism* (London: Verso, 1983).

3. See Gillian Bottomley, *From Another Place: Migration and the Politics of Culture* (Melbourne: Cambridge University Press, 1992).

4. See William Whitam and Robin Mathy, *Homosexuality in Four Societies* (New York: Praeger, 1986), as well as my paper "Tolerance or Struggle: Male Homosexuality in the Philippines," which explored the tolerant and seemingly benign attitude of Filipinos as well as the cultural practices towards that *bakla.*

I do not use the term *bakla* as the equivalent of gay. Rather, I juxtapose the native term for homosexual/faggot as a way of portraying the different homosexual traditions, U.S. and Philippines. *Bakla* is socially constructed as a transvestic and/or effeminized being that occupies an interstitial position between men and women. In this paper, therefore, I use the term gay only as a provisional term and do not imply a totally "gay"-identified population. I also do not want to portray *bakla* traditions as static and unchanging but rather as specifically demarcated practices continually being shaped and reshaped by both local and global influences and processes.

5. See Donn Hart and Harriet Hart, "Visayan Swardspeak: The Language of a Gay Community in the Philippines." *Crossroads* 5:2 (1990): 27–49; and M. F. Manalansan, "Remapping Frontiers: The Lives of Filipino Gay Men in New York City" (Ph.D. diss., University of Rochester, 1995).

6. All names of informants and other identifying statements have been changed to protect their identities.

7. Examples include Connie S. Chan, "Issues of Identity Development Among Asian-American Lesbians and Gay Men," *Journal of Counseling & Development* 68 (1989): 16–20; and Terry Gock, "Asian Pacific Islander Identity Issues: Identity Integration and Pride," in Betty Berzon (ed.), *Positively Gay* (Los Angeles: Mediamix Association, 1984).

8. Nina Reyes, "Common Ground: Asians and Pacific Islanders Look for Unity in a Queer World," *Outweek* 99 (1990).

9. See Bottomley, chapter 6.

10. Manalansan, ibid.

11. While more than 85 percent of Filipino AIDS cases in America are gay and bisexual men, the opposite is true in the Philippines, where more than half of the cases are women.

12. Jean M. Woo, George W. Rutherford, Susan F. Payne, J. Lowell Barnhardt, and George F. Lemp, "The Epidemiology of AIDS in the Asian and Pacific Islander Population in San Francisco," *AIDS* 2 (1988): 473–475.

13. See Yen Le Espiritu, *Asian American Panethnicity* (Philadelphia: Temple University Press, 1992), ch. 7.

1. What are the general attitudes adopted by parents interviewed about gays and lesbians prior to their learning about their own children's sexual identities? How have these attitudes changed once they learn about their children's coming out?

2. The majority of the parents interviewed by Hom are immigrants and women. How may homeland cultures and cultural exposure in the host society affect the acceptance process of Asian American parents? How does gender affect this process? What are the common trends that these parents experienced in their own "coming out" process? Why are Asian American parents reluctant to confide in their friends and family within the ethnic community? To what degree do you think that ethnicity played a role in their hesitation to share their feelings with others?

3. One of the things that comes out of Manalansan's study is the number of obstacles that have prevented gay Filipino Americans from buttressing solidarity within their "community." Explain what these obstacles are and how they might be overcome. What obstacles have prevented gay and lesbian Filipinos from forging ties within pan-Asian gay and lesbian organizations? With other Filipino Americans?

SUGGESTED READINGS

Cheung, King-Kok. 1998. Of Men and Men: Reconstructing Chinese American Masculinity. Pp. 173–99 in Sandra Stanley (ed.), *Other Sisterhoods: Literary Theory and U.S. Women of Color.* Urbana: University of Illinois Press.

Cruz-Malavé, Arnaldo and Martin Manalansan (eds.). 2002. *Queer Globalizations.* New York: New York University Press.

Eng, David and Alice Hom (eds.). 1998. *Q&A: Queer in Asian America.* Philadelphia: Temple University Press.

Espiritu, Yen Le. 2001. "We Don't Sleep Around Like White Girls Do": Family, Culture, and Gender in Filipina American Lives. *Signs* 26 (2): 415–40.

Fung, Richard. 1998. Looking for My Penis: The Eroticized Asian in Gay Porn. Pp. 115–34 in David Eng and Alice Hom (eds.), *Q&A: Queer in Asian America.* Philadelphia: Temple University Press.

Fuss, Diana. 1991. Inside/Out. Pp. 1–10 in Diana Fuss (ed.), *inside/out.* New York: Routledge.

Green, Donald, Dara Strolovitch, Janelle Wong, and Robert Bailey. 2001. Measuring Gay Population Density and the Incidence of Anti-Gay Hate Crime. *Social Science Quarterly* 82(2): 281–97.

Jew, Victor. 2003. "Chinese Demons": The Violent Articulation of Chinese Otherness and Interracial Sexuality in the U.S. Midwest, 1885–1889. *Journal of Social History* 37(2): 389ff.

Kim, Daniel. 1998. *The Strange Love of Frank Chin.* Pp. 270–303 in David Eng and Alice Hom (eds.), *Q&A: Queer in Asian America.* Philadelphia: Temple University Press.

Kimmel, D. C. and H. Yi. 2004. Characteristics of Gay, Lesbian, and Bisexual Asians, Asian Americans, and Immigrants from Asia to the USA. *Journal of Homosexuality* 47(2): 143–72.

Kudaka, Geraldine (ed.). 1995. *On a Bed of Rice: An Asian American Erotic Feast.* New York: Doubleday/Anchor Books.

Lana, Mobydeen. 2004. Something Old, Something New, Something Borrowed, Something Mail Ordered? *Wayne Law Review* 49.

Leong, Russell (ed.). 1996. *Asian American Sexualities: Dimensions of the Gay and Lesbian Experience.* New York: Routledge.

Lim-Hing, Shirley (ed.). 1994. *The Very Inside: An Anthology of Writing by Asian and Pacific Island Lesbian and Bisexual Women.* Toronto: Sister Vision Press.

Maira, Sunaina Marr. 2001. B-Boys and Bass Girls: Sex, Style, and Mobility in Indian American Youth Culture. *Souls* 3(3): 65–86.

Manalansan, Martin. 2003. *Global Divas: Filipino Gay Men in the Diaspora.* Durham, NC: Duke University Press.

Mura, David. 1996. *Where the Body Meets Memory: An Odyssey of Race, Sexuality, and Identity.* New York: Anchor Books.

Ordona, Trinity. 2003. Asian Lesbians in San Francisco: Struggles to Create a Safe Space, 1970s–1980s. Pp. 319–34 in Shirley Hune and Gail M. Nomura (eds.), *Asian/Pacific Islander American Women: A Historical Anthology.* New York: New York University Press.

Pyke, Karen and Denise L. Johnson. 2003. Asian American Women and Racialized Feminists: "Doing" Gender across Cultural Worlds. *Gender & Society* 17(1): 33–53.

Roy, Sandip. 1998. The Call of Rice: (South) Asian American Queer Communities. Pp. 168–85 in Lavina Dhingra Shankar and Rajini Srikanth (eds.), *A Part Yet Apart: South Asians in Asian America.* Philadelphia: Temple University Press.

Shimizu, Celine. 2005. The Bind of Representation: Performing and Consuming Hypersexuality in *Miss Saigon. Theatre Journal* 57(2): 247–65.

Sueyoshi, Amy and Russell Leong (eds.). 2006. *Asian Americans in the Marriage Equality Debate.* A special issue of *Amerasia Journal* 32(1).

Tajima, Renee. 1996. Site-Seeing Through Asian America. Pp. 263–94 in Avery Gordon and Chris Newfield (eds.), *Mapping Multiculturalism.* Minneapolis: University of Minnesota Press.

Ting, Jennifer P. 1998. The Power of Sexuality. *Journal of Asian American Studies* 1(1): 65–82.

Wat, Eric C. 2002. *The Making of a Gay Community: An Oral History of Pre-AIDS Los Angeles.* Lanham, MD: Rowman & Littlefield.

Wilson, Patrick A. and Hirokazu Yoshikawa. 2004. Experiences of and Responses to Social Discrimination among Asian and Pacific Islander Gay Men: Their Relationship to HIV Risk. *AIDS Education and Prevention* 16(1): 68–83.

FILMS

Bautista, Pablo (producer). 1992. *Fated to Be Queer* (25-minute documentary).

Choy, Christine (producer/director). 1994. *Out in Silence: AIDS in the Pacific American Community* (37-minute documentary).

Fung, Richard (producer/director). 1984. *Orientations* (52-minute documentary).

Fung, Richard (producer/director). 1995. *Dirty Laundry* (30-minute documentary).

Ganatra, Nisha (producer/director). 1997. *Junky Punky Girlz* (12-minute experimental).

Hima, B. (director). 1996. *Coming Out/Coming Home: Asian & Pacific Islander Family Stories* (44-minute documentary).

Lee, Ang (producer/director). 1993. *The Wedding Banquet* (106-minute drama).

Lee, Quentin (producer/director). 1995. *Flow.* (80-minutes experimental).

Okazaki, Steven (producer/director). *American Sons* (28-minute documentary).

Part VI

Race and Asian American Identity

Chapter 15

Are Asians Black?

*The Asian American Civil Rights Agenda and
the Contemporary Significance of the
Black/White Paradigm*

Janine Young Kim

Introduction

The phrase "civil rights movement" evokes the powerful words and images of the mass movement by Black Americans in the United States during the 1950s and 1960s. In recent years, however, Asian Americans have increasingly laid claim to a place in the history of the struggle for civil rights. Just as Derrick A. Bell harkens back to *Dred Scott v. Sanford* as the first of the "leading cases" in civil rights (Bell 1980), Hyung-Chan Kim's anthology of Asian American civil rights cases and essays recalls cases such as *Yick Wo v. Hopkis* as proof of Asian Americans' longstanding participation in the development of civil rights law in the United States (Kim 1992).

When tensions within American multicultural, multiracial society exploded in Los Angeles in 1992, not only history but immediate reality itself seemed to insist on the inclusion of Asian Americans within the larger discourse on civil rights. Because what began as an arguably Black (Rodney King)–White (LAPD officers) conflict transformed into multiracial strife involving not only Black and White Americans but also Latinos and Asian Americans, the riots brought into sharp relief the complex racial interrelationships within Los Angeles. As a result, two race scholars announced that the riots "marked the beginning of a new period of U.S. racial politics," one that must "decisively break with the bipolar model of race" (Omi and Winant 1994, 154–55).[1] Since then, the black/white paradigm has been a subject of increasing academic debate; the controversy has probably entered the popular consciousness as well, due to the highly publicized conflict between Angela Oh and John Hope Franklin within President Clinton's race relations commission.[2]

Although existing legal scholarship on the paradigm generally assumes the paradigm to be a biracial model of racism that focuses exclusively on the relationship between Black and White Americans, an explicit definition is rare and difficult to find (Calmore 1997; Chang 1994; Omi and Winant 1994; Perea 1997; Ramirez 1995; Tamoyo 1995). The dearth of legal scholarship that endeavors to outline the contours of the black/white paradigm is problematic not only because the inadequacy of the para-

digm is an often unexplored and unchallenged assumption but also because the assumption may be incorrect or misleading.

This chapter focuses on the (uneasy) relationship between the black/white paradigm and the Asian American civil rights agenda. My primary project is to intervene
in the seemingly unproblematic discussion of the black/white paradigm in order to
caution that current race discourse oversimplifies the paradigm and fails to articulate
the full cost of its abandonment. One reason for my argument is that a paradigm once
so powerful should not, as a principle, be discarded without serious analysis. A second, more compelling reason is that the black/white paradigm retains contemporary
significance despite demographic changes in American society. It is, therefore, imperative that race scholars understand the paradigm's enduring resonance and potential
before concluding that it nevertheless ought to be abandoned. It is my belief, however,
that the paradigm is important to the Asian American civil rights agenda today and
that to eliminate it from race discourse would mean losing an important tool for living in and understanding our evolving, racially stratified society.

Part 2 of this chapter very briefly summarizes some scholarship on the black/
white paradigm and questions the boundaries and assumptions embedded within the
scholarship. Part 3 clarifies my own assumptions about race and race relationships—
namely, that they are constructed and therefore unstable—and identifies six dimensions of the black/white paradigm. These six dimensions, through which I attempt to
(re)define the black/white paradigm, are elaborated in part 4. Finally, part 5 is devoted
to addressing the objection that the black/white paradigm is inapplicable to the Asian
American civil rights agenda by analyzing immigrants' rights and affirmative action
through the lens of the paradigm as I envision it.

"Black/White": Scholarship on the Paradigm

Condemnation of the black/white paradigm is usually premised on the argument that
the nation is no longer Black and White but multiracial, such that the paradigm has
become obsolete. This critique of the black/white paradigm suggests that many scholars reduce the black/white paradigm to a purely descriptive function; the paradigm
was acceptable in 1960 when 96 percent of the minority population was Black, but
now that Black Americans constitute only 50 percent of the people of color, the paradigm can no longer stand (Ramirez 1995).

While the descriptive function is a significant aspect of the black/white paradigm,
it is not the paradigm's only, nor its most important, function. Thus, a rejection of the
paradigm based solely on its apparent failure to reflect racial demographics underesti-
mates its sophistication and fails to explain its longevity. Recent race scholarship by
Asian American and Latino/a scholars has relied on this oversimplified, descriptive
version of the black/white paradigm (Chang 1994; Omi and Winant 1994; Perea 1997).
The works of Robert Chang, a leading American race theorist, and Juan Perea, a Latino scholar who has grappled directly with the "dominant and pervasive character" of
the black/white paradigm, are particularly thoughtful. Still, neither Professor Chang
nor Professor Perea takes the discussion of the paradigm much further than Michael

Omi and Howard Winant's seminal work on the racial formation theory and their 1994 critique of the black/white bipolar model (Omi and Winant 1994). This part will summarize these scholars' representations of the black/white paradigm and question some of their assumptions and prescriptions.

Omi and Winant and the Los Angeles Riot

Michael Omi and Howard Winant's project on racial formation in the United States is to explore the construction of race (Omi and Winant 1994). They argue that race is not essential but social and political; the concept of race can be transformed through political struggle and sociohistorical processes generally. They call this continual process of constructing and reconstructing race "racial formation" (55). The theory of racial formation embraces the notion that race is not merely a classificatory system based on the distinctions among human bodies at any given moment, but that it also contains traces of past struggle over, and present understanding of, social and political relationships.

In the epilogue to the second edition of *Racial Formation in the United States,* written after the 1992 Los Angeles riots, Professors Omi and Winant seem to address the prevalence of the black/white paradigm.[3] They reject the project of dichotomizing race and identify five problems in the black/white conception. First, they argue that the complex nature of race relations must be analyzed in light of changing dynamics within and among racial groups. Second, they suggest that biracial theories ignore issues specific to non-Black, non-White racial groups. Third, in a related point, they argue that biracial theories also ignore the different consequences of policies such as affirmative action or welfare to different racial groups. Fourth, they assert that the black/white model overlooks "particularities of contemporary racial politics" such as nativism (154). Finally, they posit that the model marginalizes or eliminates other— non-Black, non-White—voices in race discourse.

These critiques provide important insights, but Professors Omi and Winant clearly indicate that their critiques are aimed at biracial theorizing because the privileging of the Black-White relationship ignores "widespread and multiracial discontent" (153). There is, however, a difference between a focus on the Black-White relationship and the black/white paradigm, and Professors Omi and Winant's discussion does not clarify to which it is that they object.

Juan Perea and Race Paradigms

Juan Perea's *Binary Paradigm of Race: The "Normal Science" of American Racial Thought* (1997) can be seen as an extension of the discussion Professors Omi and Winant began in *Racial Formation in the United States.* Professor Perea attempts to prove the existence of the black/white paradigm by applying Thomas Kuhn's study of paradigms to race discourse (Kuhn 1970). Professor Perea finds that even as paradigms help us to frame knowledge, they also exclude and distort by defining, and thus limiting, relevance. Accordingly, he defines the black/white paradigm as "the conception that race in America consists, either exclusively or primarily, of only two constituent racial groups, the Black and the White" (Perea 1997, 1219). Professor Perea then documents the ways in which the black/white binary paradigm has excluded the experiences and struggles of Latinos and other non-Black, non-White groups by examining textbooks and history books that purport to deal with the race problem in general but focus primarily on the struggles of the African American population.

Professor Perea focuses largely on the effect of the black/white paradigm on scholarship and "normal research" on race (Perea 1997, 1219). I emphatically agree with Professor Perea that the absence or marginalization in scholarship of other racialized groups such as Latinos, Asian Americans, and Native Americans is harmful not only to these groups but to the richness of race discourse in general. But I disagree with his suggestion that the black/white paradigm has an unimportant role in forming or understanding the racial identities and positions of non-White, non-Black groups and individuals because, as I attempt to demonstrate in part 4, the black/white paradigm is more sophisticated than Professor Perea's narrow, race-specific definition of it.

Moreover, the ultimate purpose of Professor Perea's discussion remains somewhat confusing. He states that he opposes the use of paradigms and instead advocates the development of an inclusive and particularized understanding of race. Although he denies that his "new understanding" of race is another paradigm, it is not clear how or why it manages not to be one (1254).[4]

Robert Chang and a Theory of Asian American Legal Scholarship

Within Asian American legal academia, Robert Chang has been one of the most vocal scholars in denouncing the paradigm as "inadequate" to address the concerns of the Asian American community. His article, "Toward an Asian American Legal Scholarship: Critical Race Theory, Structuralism, and Narrative Space," suggests themes and theories of Asian American legal scholarship, offering a generalized perspective on the direction that the scholarship should take (Chang 1994). One of the most noteworthy sections in his article is Professor Chang's critique of the current racial paradigm, which he identifies as the black/white paradigm. Professor Chang claims to analyze the paradigm on two levels. First, on the level of lived reality, he observes that the color of the American population has become variegated in the last four decades. He calls this conflict between the black/white paradigm and demographic transformations a "problem of coverage" (26). Second, Professor Chang argues (in a maneuver that conflates the black/white paradigm with the civil rights movement) that the theory and philosophy of the traditional civil rights movement—that is, its focus on individual rights—is antithetical to many Asian philosophies of no-self.[5]

Unfortunately, Professor Chang's short critique (about six paragraphs) of the current racial paradigm begs more questions about the author's assumptions than it answers. For example, he does not explain why the black/white paradigm should be identified with traditional civil rights work, and he fails to defend his assertion that traditional civil rights is indeed centrally concerned with individual rights as opposed to group rights or equal protection.[6] Moreover, he glosses over the unverified and essentializing notion that Asian Americans share a no-self worldview that is theoretically opposed to individual rights.

Although Professor Chang writes about Asian American civil rights on two levels, his main critique of the traditional civil rights movement and the contemporary dominance of the black/white paradigm is devoted to the problem of coverage. He forcefully argues that the black/white paradigm "misunderstands" the racial situation in the United States because race hierarchy has "more than just a top and a bottom" (Chang 1994, 27). By framing the argument in this way, Professor Chang implies that Asian Americans fall somewhere in the middle of the race hierarchy. On the other hand, such an understanding tends to confuse his own position on the "model-minority myth," which he claims is a "complimentary façade . . . [that] works a dual harm by (1) denying the existence of present-day discrimination against Asian Americans and the present-day effects of past discrimination, and (2) legitimizing the oppression of other racial minorities and poor whites" (20). If indeed the "model-minority" is a façade and race hierarchy is not bipolar, where or how are Asian Americans situated in the racial landscape? Although he denies the black/white paradigm a place in Asian American legal scholarship, Professor Chang does not offer an answer to this question.

"Black/White": The Meaning and Impact of the Paradigm

The Judge: But now, why do you refer to you people as blacks? Why not brown people? I mean you people are more brown than black.
Biko: In the same way as I think white people are more pink than white.[7]

A shared assumption among Professors Omi, Winant, Perea, and Chang is that the black/white paradigm is a race-specific, descriptive model of race in the United States. The new conventional wisdom seems to be that (at least) "yellow," "brown," and "red" need to be included in order for race discourse to be inclusive and effective towards the eradication of discrimination. In other words, these critics of the black/white paradigm emphatically declare that yellow, brown, and red are neither black nor white.

One problem with this view of the black/white paradigm is that it considers only one of the paradigm's many dimensions. As Gary Okihiro (1994) has noted (in the context of speaking about Asian Americans), the simple question of whether yellow is black or white or neither encompasses many other, more complex questions: questions of American identity, Asian American identity, Third World identity, the relationships among people of color, and the nature of American racial formation. I would add that the question of black or white is also explicitly a question of the accumulation and concatenation of social and cultural symbols and meanings about race, at any given moment, recognizing that such symbols and meanings continually change. This view reflects the "constructedness" of racialized individuals and groups in society.

Race scholars in the United States have explored extensively the social and legal construction of race. Professors Omi and Winant's racial formation theory is one prominent example of an anti-essentialist perspective on the "social nature of race" (Omi and Winant 1994, 4). Ian Haney López (1996) has taken the racial formations theory further and examined the legal construction of race by analyzing citizenship and naturalization cases that attempted to define "white" with confusing and contradictory results, especially as whiteness related to Asians and Latinos. With this project, Professor Haney López destabilizes whiteness by exploring some of the biological and anthropological alternatives that American law and society considered in its attempt to circumscribe racial privilege. He writes that "race is highly contingent, specific to times, places, and situations. . . . [H]owever powerful and however deeply a part of our society race may be, races are still only human inventions" (Haney López 1996, xiii–xiv). Hence, to recognize the "constructedness" of race is also to understand that "black" and "white" may signify more than our immediate understanding of specific racial categories. Professor Haney López's examination of the racial prerequisite cases of the late nineteenth and first half of the twentieth centuries reveals that "white" does not simply stand for members of the White race, but for a set of concepts and privileges associated with that race. Accordingly, "black" is defined by the denial of those same privileges (Haney López, 1996).[8]

Thus, the black/white paradigm is rife with complexities that reach beyond the races for which the words "black" and "white" stand. There are at least six significant dimensions to the paradigm: (1) descriptive; (2) theoretical; (3) political; (4) historical; (5) linguistic/poetic; and (6) subversive. The descriptive dimension is the most limiting because of its association with specific races, although, as I argue in part 4, there is more even to the descriptive dimension than critics of the paradigm acknowledge. But it is the theoretical dimension of the black/white paradigm that reveals the paradigm's full scope as well as its possibilities. Recognition of these various dimensions is important for the American civil rights agenda and legal scholarship because they reveal where and how Asian Americans are situated within American racial structure and suggest openings for collective, counterhegemonic discourse.

Although the six dimensions are presented more or less discretely below, they are, in fact, interdependent aspects of the paradigm. Each must be fleshed out and examined before rejection of the paradigm can be justified. On the other hand, such an investigation may lead to a revitalization of the paradigm for the Asian American civil rights agenda.

The Six Dimensions of the Black/White Paradigm

The Descriptive Dimension

There are two ways in which the black/white paradigm could occupy a descriptive role in race discourse. The first and more facile would be to view the black/white paradigm as descriptive of the relationship between two specific races: "black" signifying African Americans and possibly West Indians, and "white" signifying European Americans. This descriptive definition is of central importance in Professors Chang's and Perea's articles, as well as in Professors Omi and Winant's book. If the black/white paradigm's sole purpose is to reflect racial demographics, it would be truly false and underinclusive, rendering invisible in race discourse Asians, Latinos, Native Americans, and other groups. In that case, the paradigm would indeed suffer from a problem of "coverage" by failing to understand and incorporate the experiences of other groups that also contend with racism and discrimination. Another harmful effect of a race-specific paradigm would be its ratification of the notion that only the relationship between Blacks and Whites matters. This is the starting point for Professor Perea's critique of the black/white paradigm as expressed in textbooks and history books that do not document the struggle of Asian Americans, Latinos, or Native Americans while purporting to write about race and civil rights history in general. In this way, both Professor Chang and Professor Perea are attempting to discuss what they perceive to be certain groups' fundamentally existential crisis in race discourse in the United States.

This definition is, however, too limited and superficial. A more complex aspect of the descriptive dimension of the paradigm is its reflection of racial stratification and conceptualization in the United States (Calmore 1997).[9] This more complex descriptive dimension is implicit in both Professors Chang's and Perea's discussions of the black/white paradigm's persistence in race discourse. Racial conceptualization and stratification in the United States are dominated by the notion that "black" and "white" are positioned at opposite extremes that denote race oppression and privilege.

The black/white structure may exist in the form that it does because of the priority in time of racial discrimination against Blacks or because of the sheer virulence of racism targeting Blacks, thereby rendering the Black American experience most salient. Regardless of how the paradigm came about, it is undeniably one of the chief mechanisms by which individuals and groups become racialized, and even self-identify, on both legal and social/cultural planes. One example of the way Asian Americans have been racialized according to the black/white paradigm can be found in *People v. Hall*,[10] a case that nullified a Chinese witness's testimony under a law that prohibited Blacks, mulattos, and Indians from testifying in trials involving White defendants. In that decision, the court determined that "black" included all non-White. An event of self-identification within the black/white paradigm occurred in *Hudgins v. Wrights*,[11] a case that illustrates how slavery laws constructed "black" to be almost synonymous with "enslavement" in 1806, prompting three Native American women to declare themselves not Black (Davis 1996a, 703). Finally, Professor Haney López's analysis of the racial-prerequisite cases demonstrates that both dynamics can occur simultaneously through legal and social pressures (Haney López 1996). "White" in the late nineteenth and early twentieth centuries meant citizenship, and individuals of Asian ancestry attempted to define themselves as "white" in order to naturalize and acquire the rights attendant to citizenship.[12] But because Blacks were also granted citizenship by the U.S. government, the prerequisite cases reveal that Asians attempting to define themselves as "white" may have wanted more than citizenship: By casting themselves as "white" rather than "black," they rejected the negative attributes and stereotypes associated with blackness.

Racialization by association with blackness and whiteness endures. Frank Wu has been most eloquent in discussing the ways in which Asian Americans have interacted with the paradigm. In an article on affirmative action, Professor Wu writes that "[r]acial groups are conceived of as white, black, honorary whites, or constructive blacks" (Wu 1995, 249). Professor Wu's choice of the words "honorary" and "constructive" expresses the poles of privilege and oppression. Asian Americans have stood on unstable ground between "black" and "white," falling under the honorary white category in anti-affirmative action arguments, but considered constructive blacks for the purposes of school segregation or antimiscegenation laws (249–50). To say that Asian Americans have been perceived as honorary whites or constructive blacks is, however, slightly misleading in that it tends to convey a notion of race specificity. It is important to keep in mind that although the status of honorary white does affect identity, recognition, and appellation, its more insidious function is cooptation. For example, within the economy of affirmative action policy, "whiteness" encompasses victimization through "reverse racism" and race-based disadvantage in certain educational or occupational opportunities. Insofar as a conservative like Newt Gingrich treats Asian Americans as honorary whites,[13] he refers to common experience under affirmative action, not racial similarity.

In exploring the descriptive dimension of the black/white paradigm, I do not mean to ascribe a naturalness to the current race hierarchy. It is true that the black/white paradigm has played a leading role in shaping race discourse and ideology in the United States, and as such, it is not merely descriptive of a thing already in existence. As Professor Davis (1996b, 615) remarked, "[T]he black-white paradigm is an intriguing piece of white supremacy." The black/white paradigm is derived from a racism that has created this particular hierarchy and method of race conceptualization. To that extent, the black/white paradigm not only posits that the Black American race experience is the paradigmatic race experience in the United States, but it also describes the manifestations and systematic organization of racism as well.

The Theoretical Dimension

Breaking down the notion that the "black" and the "white" of the black/white paradigm are race-specific clears space for a refreshed understanding about racial stratification in the United States and the role of the paradigm. It should be clear from the discussion so far that the paradigm is not simply race-specific. To be nonwhite is to be the other, and that other is constructed as black, regardless of where a particular individual or group comes from or what it looks like.[14] The theoretical dimension of the black/white binary paradigm is perhaps most significant because of its clarity on the issue of domination and subordination. In the binary system, Whites "fashioned themselves as the superior opposite to those constructed as others" (Haney López 1996, 167). Those "others" have included various White races, but the fluidity or ambiguity of their positions within the black/white paradigm has sometimes served to cloud the bases upon which dominance and subordination are conditioned.

The othered status of Asians was plainer in the last century and first half of this century. It was manifested in race-based exclusion laws, naturalization laws, and miscegenation laws. Asians' racially subordinated status was also socially and culturally evident: It has been said that the status that the White American preferred Asians to occupy was that of "biped domestic animals in the white man's service" (Haney López 1996, 167). The association between Asian and black was also more explicit in the last century: There has been important scholarship on the "negotiation" of the Chinese and the attribution to the Chinese of characteristics formerly ascribed to Blacks, Black slaves in particular (Haney López 1996; Okihiro 1994).

In the latter half of the twentieth century, the subordinated status of Asian Americans has become obfuscated. The most obvious example of this obfuscation at work is the model-minority myth, which has been embraced not only by White Americans in order to allege reverse discrimination, but to some degree by Asian Americans content to claim their superiority over Blacks and Latinos (Wu 1995).[15] Placing Asian Americans in the middle, however, does not necessarily mean that they are beyond or outside of the black/white paradigm. Asian Americans are now defined by their proximity to White conservative values and economic success as much as they were formerly compared to Blacks. The process of racialization and correlated valuation of individuals and groups occurs regardless of whether Asian Americans actually possess White or Black traits, whatever such traits may be. Professor Okihiro (1994) expresses this instability (and arbitrariness) in the following way:

> Asian Americans have served the master class, whether as "blacks" in the past or as "near-whites" in the present or as "marginal men" in both the past and the present. Yellow is emphatically neither white nor black; but insofar as Asians and Africans share a subordinate position to the master class, yellow is a shade of black, and black, a shade of yellow. (34)

In light of the indeterminacy of "black" and "white," it is unclear what it means to go beyond the black/white paradigm. For Professor Perea, going beyond the black/white paradigm would mean the rejection of any type of race paradigm in favor of "the development of particularized understanding of the histories of each and every racial group" (Perea 1997, 1256). But we have seen through the scholarship of Professors Haney López, Davis, and Okihiro that close examination of these groups' histories magnifies the ways in which the black/white paradigm organizes groups' social, legal, and racial identities and relationships in the United States. Although critics of the paradigm may condemn this method of organization, it is important to account for the fact that the paradigm may be a part of many people's understanding and experiences.

The Political Dimension

The black/white paradigm offers a robust, unequivocal understanding of the relationship between race-based domination and subordination. Its political dimension is closely related to its theoretical one in that a claim to blackness by Asian Americans can lead to coalition building among people of color against white supremacy.

The notion of a coalition against white supremacy is forcefully articulated by Charles Lawrence, although, curiously, he rejects the black/white paradigm as "dysfunctional in a multiracial society" because it is "not first about the eradication of white supremacy" (Lawrence 1995, 819, 826). Professor Lawrence writes of the need for a theory that seeks societal transformation, a theory that "sees [racism's] injury as done to the collective, as suffered by us all" (825). He unfortunately fails to explain why the black/white paradigm does not capture the spirit of the nonwhite collective "whom white supremacy . . . relegates to varying degrees of inferiority" (826).

Chris Iijima, on the other hand, identifies the potential of the black/white paradigm to accomplish the goals articulated by Professor Lawrence. According to Professor Iijima, "deconstructing the old black/white paradigm carries with it new dangers. . . . The original paradigm, while constructing and reaffirming white dominance, also permitted a useful counter-focus on the effect and operation of white supremacy (Iijima 1997, 69). In other words, to recognize the operation of white supremacy, we are forced to rely on the black/white paradigm. Professor Iijima illustrates this proposition by analyzing the racialization of Blacks and Koreans during the 1992 Los Angeles riots:

> It is significant to note that in the construction of the conflict, nativist arguments that Koreans were foreigners and less American positioned African Americans as "white" relative to Asians. On the other hand, Korean Americans were also placed within the entrepreneurial American Dream and positioned as white. This kind of positioning becomes coherent only if the assumptions of the old paradigm and the placement of whiteness within it are accepted as the operating framework. (70)[16]

Professor Iijima makes a subtle point here about the black/white paradigm. He argues that even as the paradigm forces us to speak about race experiences according to its vocabulary and not one of our own choosing, it also permits us to understand (and potentially counter) the deployment of white supremacy and privilege.

Professor Iijima (1997) adds another important insight about the critique of the black/white paradigm. He argues that the current focus on "categories of difference" may have overtaken the "search for political commonality" among those raced as non-White (55). For Professor Iijima, the black/white paradigm helps forge political identities for people of color and allows a "reverse discourse" organized around antisubordination and antisupremacist ideology (74).

The establishment of a strong antisubordination principle is especially important for Asian Americans because they are positioned in the "model minority" middle and could contribute knowingly or unwittingly to the further oppression of African Americans. This buffer position renders Asian Americans especially vulnerable to political manipulation or, even worse, can cause a blindness or amnesia among Asian Americans about discrimination they themselves face. To advocate a coalition among those people of color raced as "black" is not to declare that there are no interethnic conflicts or that the experiences of racism for Blacks, Asians, Latinos, and Native Americans are identical (Calmore 1995).[17] Political alignment and acknowledgment of differences are not mutually exclusive; non-White people of color should "negotiate their common agendas,"[18] one of which must undoubtedly be a broad goal of antisubordination (Calmore 1995, 1233, 1263).

The Historical Dimension

To be sure, the antisubordination principle does not by itself justify the black/white paradigm; that principle could probably be expressed in many different ways. Reliance on the antisubordination principle to legitimate the paradigm would be defeated by arguments offered by Professors Chang and Perea; those scholars may object to the very words "black" and "white" on the grounds that they are indicative of specific races to the exclusion of others. Even if "black" and "white" are not race specific, they may be so construed by people who write or read books on race, or by people who propose or make civil rights legislation. This result could be harmful to non-Black people of color because they may indeed end up marginalized from race discourse and remedies. The next three dimensions of the black/white paradigm that will be discussed —historical, poetic/linguistic, and subversive—will illustrate why the risk we take in preserving the black/white paradigm may be justified.

The historical dimension of the paradigm first and most fundamentally refers to the Black-White struggle since the birth of this nation. The history of the kidnapping, enslavement, and subhuman treatment of Africans by White European Americans is simply the most vivid and terrifying example of white supremacy in American history. The black/white paradigm also serves as a constant reminder of the continued racial oppression of African Americans in the legal, political, and social arenas: mob violence culminating in lynchings, Jim Crow laws, and ghettoization, to name a few of the strategies of subjugation. At the same time that the paradigm evokes this most notorious period in American history, it also recalls the civil rights movement of the 1950s and 1960s and the battle to revolutionize the race hierarchy and power structure of the United States. It brings to mind the inspirational stories of Black activists like Martin Luther King, Thurgood Marshall, and Rosa Parks. In this way, the black/white paradigm not only highlights the longstanding racist ideology of the nation, but it also suggests tactical opposition to that ideology.

Exploring the changing nature and content of the black/white paradigm also offers insights into supremacist ideology as applied to non-Black races. As I have argued above, the paradigm now describes more than the Black and White races; it has developed to articulate a hierarchical vision of racial groups that includes Latinos, Asian Americans, and Native Americans. From this perspective, the black/white paradigm infuses a sense of continuity to the civil rights work of non-Black people of color by revealing the ways in which these groups' histories intersect with the history of Black Americans. One example of historical intersection is the importation of Chinese laborers to replace slave labor during the Reconstruction Era. The Chinese were described as "more obedient and industrious than the negro, [able to] work as well without as with an overseer, and at the same time are more cleanly in their habits and persons than the freedmen" (cited in Wu 1995, 231). This "praise" of Chinese laborers is revealing in that it (1) places the Chinese in an intermediate position between Blacks and Whites; (2) denigrates Blacks further; and (3) subordinates the Chinese as the new "obedient" slave labor force in the place of Blacks (Wu 1995, 229). This example, cited by Professor Wu as the origin of the model-minority myth, demonstrates not only that Asian American history cannot be divorced from the black/white paradigm but also that the legacy of the paradigm remains a vibrant part of contemporary Asian American experience. Another clear moment of historical intersection is the Los Angeles riots, where the histories of at least three non-White racial groups intersected explosively.[19]

These historical examples affirm Neil Gotanda's observation that "[e]ven as the possibilities of racial stratification and the embedded ideological constructions of Orientalism are examined, awareness of the continuation of that basic axis of power and privilege [between Whites and African Americans] must continue" (Gotanda 1996, 246). Any analysis of racial oppression in the United States, including that of Asian Americans, has as its starting point the enslavement and continued subjugation of African Americans. From *Hudgins*[20] in 1806 to the Los Angeles riots in 1992, White privilege and domination over non-Black people of color have been defined and organized within the context of the Black/White relationship. This relationship, as well as subsequent formations, has been expressed specifically through the black/white paradigm.

A failure to acknowledge the significance of the relationship and the origin of the Black/White paradigm has repercussions for Asian American legal scholarship on race.[21] When the acknowledgment is no more than a concession to recorded facts, Asian American civil rights history itself flounders. Harold Koh (1992), for example, has noted the absence of a sense of "movement" and continuity in the Asian American civil rights struggle. Professor Koh's comment supports Professor Perea's argument because the absence of Asian American civil rights history in casebooks and the law school classroom contributes to a "scattered" impression of that history. But this may also be in part due to a failure to recognize the historical intersections among Blacks, Asian Americans, Latinos, and other non-White people of color, leading to a decontextualized and scattered understanding of non–African American civil rights activism.

The Linguistic/Poetic Dimension

Another notable aspect of the black/white paradigm is the vitality of its vocabulary in race discourse. The exchange between the Judge and Steve Biko, as transcribed in Donald Woods's *Biko* (and quoted in the epigraph to part 3), illustrates the hermeneutics of the words "black" and "white" (Woods 1978). In attempting to understand the way in which Biko uses the word "black," the Judge suggests that "black" is an inaccurate description of the physical appearance of Africans.[22] Biko's reply demonstrates that, in fact, the words "black" and "white" are pregnant with negative and positive meanings, respectively.[23] Biko asserts that his embrace of the word "black" is aimed at the black man so that the word may be "elevate[d] . . . to a position where we can look upon ourselves positively; because even if we [Blacks] choose to be called 'brown,' there will still be reference to 'blacks' in an inferior sense in literature and in speeches by white racists in our society" (Woods 1978, 165–66).

Biko's response reveals three crucial insights. The first is that "black" and "white" have developed in opposition to each other in our language. This is not limited to political or racist language; as Biko observed, it exists in literary language. Examples abound: One of the more obvious would be Joseph Conrad's *Heart of Darkness,* where "black" stands for the sinister and unknowable (Conrad 1991). Setting aside whatever political views Conrad might have had, his novella could be interpreted as the story of a man whose descent into madness (and finally death) is caused by his liminal racial position in the jungles of the Congo. In this sense, the pairing of "black" and "white" is almost poetic; its apparent simplicity is, in fact, so expressive of difference and opposition that it approaches the visual.

The second insight is that the black/white paradigm is not one that we can escape through our own will. This indicates not only that we are raced but also that we are raced in specific terms, whether those terms be "black" and "white" or "Black" and "White." This has particular applicability to Asian Americans demanding a third category (perhaps "yellow") that would capture their sense of difference from the black and the white. As Steve Biko observed, we can call ourselves "brown" or "yellow" until we are blue in the face, but it is unlikely that those terms will be adopted or will displace the vocabulary of the black/white paradigm successfully (cited in Wu 1996, 205).

Moreover, it is naive to assume that we can fully control the content of the words that we choose. This leads to Biko's third insight: Rather than attempting to create a parallel racial vocabulary, it may be more effective to undermine the content of the words white racism has chosen. This is a tactic that not only contains the element of surprise but also explodes the assumptions embedded in the current, dominant vocabulary of race. Such explosions happen when Asians in England call themselves "black" (Chang 1996). They also happen when Asians, Whites, and multiracials in South Africa call themselves "black" (Lawrence 1995). This tactic may also explain why the term "African American" is fading out of discourse: it includes West Indians and Muslim Blacks who do not fit neatly under the category of "African American" but share similar experiences and feelings of solidarity.

The Subversive Dimension

The discussion of the linguistic dimension of the black/white paradigm hints at the rich possibility of subversion. Subversion is, in my view, the only way that racialization will progress beyond the black/white paradigm to a discourse that will be not only more inclusive but also more rational. Each of the different dimensions I have discussed in this chapter contains this element of subversion.

The descriptive dimension of the paradigm serves as the foundation for the process of subversion. Scholars such as Omi, Winant, Haney López, and Wu have eloquently argued that race is a social and legal construction, and that race groups in the United States have been defined in relation to blackness and whiteness. This process has been most evident for Asian Americans, whose racial status has shifted from basically "black" to almost "white" over time. The black/white paradigm determines social status and denies free self-definition; this aspect of the paradigm is the most insidious because it creates a self-perpetuating race hierarchy in which the goal is to maintain the status quo for those situated at the top. Understanding the black/white paradigm in this way means that Asian Americans can begin to grapple with both the way racial identity is constructed and the way it can be reconstructed. Such a step requires a critical analysis of the black/white paradigm as a mechanism that situates various racial groups within a structure that restricts access to privileges such as citizenship, education, and employment.

Recognition of the black/white paradigm as an iteration of race hierarchy brings into focus the overarching strategy of domination over all those categorized as "others." But even as the paradigm oppresses, it betrays a small opening for political counteraction in the form of Professor Iijima's "reverse discourse" and through the paradigm's inherent caricature of race relations within its descriptive dimension (Iijima 1997). This also leads to the possibility of coalition among people of color who share the antisubordination agenda. Moreover, the paradigm contextualizes the civil rights agenda, reminding us not only of historical race oppression but also of historical resistance against oppression, especially salient to those who share a sense of intersecting civil rights histories.

In at least one sense, Asian Americans possess greater opportunities to subvert race hierarchy and become agents of change than other people of color. Because Asian Americans have been situated as the model minority, they enjoy greater opportunities in education and occupation. Yet the model-minority status is problematic, especially as it contributes to the maintenance of racist polarity. In the same way that racial categories become destabilized when Asians call themselves black, a rejection of the model-minority status destabilizes racial relationships. This means first that Asian Americans who have achieved financial or political success through the black/white paradigm (and its own unofficial affirmative action) also have the means to effect change by using their position. Second, Asians can subvert race hierarchy by refusing to adopt the politically conservative views that are imputed to the model minority. Both of these decisions require a deep understanding of the paradigm.

The Asian American Civil Rights Agenda: Identifying the Differences

Banishing the black/white paradigm from legal scholarship disconnects it from Asian American civil rights activism. On the other hand, confrontation with, as well as redeployment of, the paradigm by legal scholars has the potential to contribute to activism and further the civil rights agenda. Existing scholarship challenges this notion and argues that the black/white paradigm does not fit the Asian American experience or that community's goals.[24] First, they argue that the discrimination experienced by Asian Americans follows not a color axis but a "foreigner axis." That is, whereas Blacks deal with second-class citizenship, a status repugnant to principles of American democracy, Asian Americans are viewed as outsiders to whom access is rightly denied (Ancheta 1998; Park 1996). The assumption is that because Blacks are assumed to be American citizens, the demand for equal rights, opportunities, and privileges appears more legitimate than when immigrants demand those same things. Second, they argue that some of the most pressing civil rights issues concerning Asian Americans either do not concern Black Americans or affect them differently (Ancheta 1998; Omi and Winant 1994). The logical conclusion to this statement is that a race paradigm that fits the Black civil rights agenda may not necessarily fit the Asian American agenda.

Racism or Nativism?

Angelo Ancheta uses the term "foreigner axis" to explain subordination based on "racial" origin (Ancheta 1998, 64). Therefore, Asian Americans, Latinos, and Arab Americans are categorized as foreigners and immigrants, regardless of actual citizenship status or place of birth. Ancheta calls this mechanism "outsider racialization"

(1998, 64). Outsider racialization closely resembles "nativism," a distinctive type of racism aimed at groups like Asian Americans, Latinos, and Arab Americans. Nativistic arguments about Asian Americans or Latinos are prevalent in political discourse—the controversy over Asian American contributions to the Democratic National Committee in 1996, Proposition 187 in California, the English-only movement, and the myth of the Japanese takeover exemplify the power of nativistic sentiments in the American social and political consciousness. Nativism has, as Professor Chang notes, a certain allure because it tends to express racism and oppression in seemingly race-neutral terms such as "immigrants" and "foreigners" (Chang 1994, 16).

Although nativism is one of the most salient aspects of Asian American experience, Professor Ancheta's argument that Asian Americans are not affected by the color axis seems overstated since nativistic arguments are aimed at those who are classified as non-White.[25] This is why I believe that the term "outsider racialization" is superior to "nativism": It successfully conveys that race and national origin have been combined for discriminatory purposes. Thus, it is curious that Professor Ancheta denies the effect of the color axis in favor of the foreigner axis alone. The assumption of nativist-racists is that the United States is a White nation and that anyone who is not (or does not look) White is a foreigner (Brimelow 1995). As Pat Chew has observed, "Like African Americans, Asian Americans' skin color and other facial features physically distinguish them. . . . As Justice Sutherland noted in *United States v. Bhagat Singh* 'it cannot be doubted that the children born in this country of Hindu parents would retain indefinitely the clear evidence of their ancestry'" (Chew 1994). Thus, nativism properly can be seen as a refined derivative of discrimination based on the color axis.[26]

Notwithstanding the significance of the color axis, the question remains whether outsider racialization "fits" within the black/white paradigm. The role of outsider racialization within the paradigm can be more clearly discerned by examining the way "reverse nativism" is used to discriminate against Black Americans. There is evidence that Blacks who have accents, and are thereby identified as immigrants or foreigners, are treated with less overt discrimination than Blacks who do not have accents. Malcolm Gladwell (1996) argues that the success in New York of West Indians, whom he compares to Korean and Chinese immigrants, is "one last, vicious twist" in the discrimination against Black Americans. He explains,

> Their advantage depends on their remaining outsiders. . . . There is already some evidence that the considerable economic and social advantages that West Indians hold over American blacks begin to dissipate by the second generation, when the island accent has faded, and those in positions of power who draw distinctions between good blacks and bad blacks begin to lump West Indians with everyone else. . . .
>
> In the new racism, as in the old, somebody always has to be the nigger. (79, 81)

While reinforcing the idea that "black" within the paradigm is not specific, reverse nativism sheds light on the interaction between outsider racialization and the black/white paradigm. Comparing the way in which outsider racialization is articulated against Black Americans in New York and against Korean Americans in Los Angeles makes it clear that it is deployed opportunistically between poles of blackness and whiteness. The treatment of Black Americans in New York also suggests that the history of White-on-Black oppression, as well as the accumulation of its signs, may inform the treatment of immigrant groups. It is also plausible to conclude from this example that the treatment of immigrants, in turn, informs the treatment of Black Americans.

Thus, to the extent that racial foreignness contains attributes of whiteness or of blackness, the paradigm captures the subordinated status not only of actual foreigners but more aptly of permanent residents and citizens who happen to be people of color. This is the mode of analysis employed by Professor Iijima in his analysis of the Los Angeles riots, and it can also be usefully employed to examine Proposition 187 in California (Iijima 1997; Haney López 1996). Nonetheless, outsider racialization perhaps does not achieve a perfect "fit" with the black/white paradigm because despite theoretical consistency, the application of the paradigm to the foreigner axis aspect of outsider racialization in the Asian American context remains somewhat counterintuitive.

Items on the Asian American Civil Rights Agenda

The Asian American civil rights agenda encompasses issues such as immigration, welfare, affirmative action, education, and suffrage. Although some of these issues (education, suffrage) coincide with those of the traditional civil rights movement, others (affirmative action, immigration) present newer challenges to civil rights activists.

(1) AFFIRMATIVE ACTION AND THE MODEL-MINORITY MYTH

Asian Americans play a strange and contorted role in the affirmative action debate. Those who would eliminate affirmative action use the Asian American population to exemplify how affirmative action disadvantages non-Whites as well as Whites. This is especially true for affirmative action in higher education, where some Asian Americans have been told—and have come to believe—that the program hurts Asian American students' chances of attending certain universities. Newt Gingrich's warning that "Asian Americans are facing a very real danger of being discriminated against" has been heeded by many Asian Americans as evidenced in their voting pattern on this issue (cited in Wu 1996, 225).

Asian American scholars have expressed concerns about the deployment of Asian Americans as the "example that defeats affirmative action" (Chang 1996; Wu 1995, 225). Frank Wu vigorously attacks the notion that banning affirmative action would actually help Asian Americans:

> The real risk to Asian Americans is that they will be squeezed out to provide proportionate representation to whites, not due to the marginal impact of setting aside a few spaces for African Americans. The linkage of Asian Americans and affirmative action . . . is an intentional maneuver by conservative politicians to provide a response to charges of racism. (Wu 1996, 226)[27]

The discussion of affirmative action is most often bundled with the myth of the "model minority," which has been used to describe Asians in American society. Somewhat reminiscent of Edna Bonacich's groundbreaking sociological theory of the middleman minority (Bonacich 1973), the model-minority myth works to divide the interests of subordinated racial groups. At the same time, it debilitates Asian Americans as individuals (Asians are brainy but lack personality) and as a political entity (Asians are successful and therefore not discriminated against).

The model-minority myth can be fruitfully analyzed within the framework of the paradigm. As I have argued above, situating Asian Americans as a buffer between black and white does not position Asian Americans outside of the black/white paradigm, but rather in a vulnerable place where they can be manipulated to serve the interests of the dominant group. This is most likely what occurred in California when a large percentage of Asian Americans voted to eliminate affirmative action programs in the controversial Civil Rights Initiative of 1996. The myth also ultimately leads to further subordination of Asian Americans, especially by thwarting political mobilization, not only within the Asian American population but also across racial lines. The paradigm can be used to help deconstruct the myth and clarify the subordinated position of Asian Americans in the race hierarchy. Only then can Asian Americans make informed political decisions and meaningfully pursue a civil rights agenda.

(2) IMMIGRATION

The question of immigration is an especially volatile issue within the Asian American community. Although Gabriel Chin has argued that the immigration amendments of 1965 equalized immigration opportunities for Asians as compared with immigrants from the Western hemisphere, the resulting visible increase in the number of immigrants in the United States has precipitated a backlash from White Americans who seek to preserve Anglo-American "culture" (Chin 1996). Demographic anxiety has increased in the face of a growing number of people of color. According to a poll reported in the *New York Times,* White Americans believe that the population of Blacks, Asians, and Latinos in the United States is over twice as large (50.1 percent) as it actually is (24.4 percent).[28]

Demographic anxiety among White Americans can be relieved in two possible ways: The first is to restrict immigration of people of color, and the second is to oppress those people of color who are already in the country (Ancheta 1998). Although both reactions stem from racism, they are distinct phenomena. Therefore, when Asian Americans speak of "immigration," a distinction must be made between *immigration* rights and *immigrants'* rights.[29] The treatment of immigrants presents some serious civil rights issues because under equal protection doctrine, the recent laws that affect immigrants may violate the Constitution (Fiss 1999).[30] One example of such laws is the welfare reform law of 1996, which denies many forms of federal assistance to legal immigrants and their children.[31] Another example is Proposition 187, a measure that denies public education and all nonemergency medical care to undocumented aliens.

Proposition 187 provides fertile ground for analysis using the black/white paradigm. An initiative that was quite obviously directed against illegal immigrants from Mexico, Proposition 187 preyed upon nativist sentiments. Thus, much of the rhetoric of Proposition 187 focused on the idea that illegal immigrants were foreigners taking

American jobs and benefits, entitlements belonging to legal residents only. According to John Park (Park and Park 1996, 177–78),

> Among people of color, the resentment toward undocumented immigrants was especially acute. Kevin Ross, an Inglewood deputy district attorney and political action chairman of the NAACP chapter of Los Angeles, noted that "[f]ifty percent of African American youth are unemployed. When the assertion is made that illegal immigrants do the jobs others wouldn't do in the first place, the black community is offended."

This reaction was not limited to African Americans; many Asian Americans and Latinos voted in support of Proposition 187.[32] The strategy behind Proposition 187 successfully positioned legal residents as "white" relative to illegal immigrants because legal residents possessed the rights to work, to go to school, and to receive medical care.

Proposition 187 should also be understood as a case of outsider racialization against more than just the illegal immigrant community in California, although that community is certainly the law's primary target. The "xenophobic climate" created by Proposition 187 also affects entire Latino and Asian American communities because of its tendency for inclusiveness. As many civil rights workers and scholars have already noted, one major problem with Proposition 187 is its "unintended" effects on all people of color who look or sound foreign (Cervantes et al. 1995; Park and Park 1996).

But extremist propaganda in support of the proposition also makes it clear that the issue was not limited to illegal immigration but intertwined with race and white supremacy:

> Two days before the November 1994 elections . . . flyers were distributed . . . depicting an image of a machine gun firing bullets at a dark skinned man. The flyer reads: "How's this for a new slogan for the U.S. Border Patrol? 'If it ain't white WASTE IT!' Remember, it's stop the Mudslide . . . or drown! 187 Yes! We need a real border. First we get the spics, then the gooks, and at last we get the niggers. They're all going home." (Cervantes et al. 1995, 6)

There can hardly be a clearer representation of the active dichotomy that informs race discourse today.

Conclusion

The increasing visibility of people of color and the much-discussed demographic predictions for the next millennium have led to increased debate about race, law, and resources in the United States. And it is probably safe to conclude that the call for a more complex theory of race relations—one that better incorporates various people of color-has been heeded by the mainstream. This is most lately exemplified by President Clinton's race initiative.

This chapter, however, has sought to demonstrate that the paradigm is a complex theory of race relations and should be recognized as such. An understanding of the paradigm's six dimensions (and there may be more) reveals its capacity both to contextualize race discourse and to express a clear antisubordination agenda. Moreover, the paradigm's persistence in race relations and discourse attests to its continuing relevance and growing complexity. Asian American scholars must resist the temptation to oversimplify or underestimate the paradigm's ability to perpetuate and refine itself by erasing histories, manipulating racial status, and dividing political alliances. Indeed, an alternative theory cannot emerge unless people of color dismantle the current organization and vocabulary of race, which have been articulated through the paradigm.

NOTES

Reprinted by permission of *The Yale Law Journal* Company and William S. Hein Company from *The Yale Law Journal* 108 (1999): 2385–2412.

1. Omi and Winant (1994) also note that the riots "served to focus media attention on generally neglected subjects—Koreans, Central Americans, who were both victims and victimizers" (153).

2. When Angela Oh argued that the commission should look "beyond" the black/white paradigm, John Hope Franklin is reported to have resisted that suggestion by replying that "[t]his country cut its eyeteeth on racism in the black-white sphere." In this chapter, I use the lowercase form of "black" and "white" where the terms are used theoretically, politically, and figuratively.

3. It should be noted that Omi and Winant (1994) do not actually employ the word "paradigm" but alternately use terms such as "model," "conception," "vision," and "theory."

4. Perea's thesis is weak for another reason. Although the early sections of his article seemed to lead to a final, radical demand that the history and experience of groups such as Asian Americans, Latinos, and Native Americans be included in race/civil rights scholarship, Perea ends by merely objecting to the inference that scholarship on the black/white relationship addresses American racism in its totality.

5. For other Asian American legal scholars who take a similar two-tiered approach to the black/white paradigm, see Tamoyo 1995; Wu 1995.

6. Omi and Winant (1994, 70), on the other hand, have suggested that the focus on individual rights and remedies, as well as color-blind racial policy, is a deliberate neoconservative strategy of the 1970s and 1980s.

7. Woods 1978, 165.

8. This conception of "black" and "white" can also be found in Adrienne Davis's analysis of *Hudgins v. Wrights*, 11 Va. (1 Hen. & M.) 134 (1806). In *Hudgins*, three enslaved women sought to be declared free by claiming Native American status. According to Davis (1996a), at the core of the racialized slave system existed White anxiety about being mistakenly enslaved; hence the development of a strong association, and legal presumption, between slavery and blackness, freedom and whiteness.

9. Calmore (1995, 64) identified this as the "matrix of domination and system of oppression" that lies within the black/white paradigm.

10. 4 Cal. 399 (1854).

11. 11 Va. (1 Hen. & M) 134 (1806).

12. Haney López (1996, 79–92) discusses *Ozawa* v. *United States,* 260 U.S. 178 (1927), in which Takao Ozawa, a man of Japanese origin, claimed the right to naturalize on the basis of his assimilated lifestyle and "white" skin color, and *United States* v. *Thind,* 261 U.S. 204, in which Bhagat Singh Thind, a man of Indian origin, claimed the right to naturalize based on his "scientific" classification as "Caucasian."

13. Gingrich has asserted that Asian Americans are facing a very real danger of being discriminated against because they are becoming too numerous at prestigious universities that practice affirmative action (see Wu 1995, 225).

14. It bears repeating that the category "white" is also constructed and that many of those individuals now classified as white were not white less than a century ago (Grant 1924; Jacobson 1998).

15. It would be naive to assert that Asian Americans are not tempted by the advantages of assimilation. Haney López (1996, 63–64) has observed,

> I do believe . . . that dominant America will attempt to situate Asians, Pacific Islanders and Latinos squarely within its efforts to determine who will be "white" in the twenty-first century. . . . It is a call to follow the European immigrant example of groups who, with each generation, have moved into a twilight ethnicity and paid the price of linguistic extinction and cultural loss for the privilege of white racial status.

Wu (1996) has characterized the rise of Asian Americans as "a rise toward whiteness."

16. See Haney López (1996, 166), where he explained that during the Los Angeles riots, Asians-as-victims-of-Black-violence came to stand in for Whites in the racial semiotics of Los Angeles, but Asians-as-victims-of-crime were Black for the purposes of police protection in the same semiotics.

17. We ought to heed Calmore's warning that "it is analytically and strategically wrong to exaggerate the degree of commonality among people of color" (1995, 63).

18. This phrase is used in Calmore 1995.

19. Comparing the histories of Asian Americans and Black Americans is yet another way of understanding the methods of discrimination directed at Asian Americans. Exploring the paradoxes of being Asian American, Pat Chew (1994) describes how Asian Americans "have been victims of lynching, race riots, and slavery," methods of subjugation that are widely known to have been used to oppress Blacks.

20. 11 Va. (1 Hen. M.) 134 (1806).

21. Calmore (1995, 64) states that most advocates of moving beyond the paradigm would reject the importance of understanding Black-White racism. Because there are a few scholars who acknowledge the need for understanding the relationship (Valdes 1997), cautioning against the failure to appreciate the "singular facts and histories [of] the Black experience of slavery and subordination in this country," and because scholarship that focuses on the paradigm is so limited, I am not yet in agreement with Professor Calmore's view.

22. See Woods 1978, 165.

23. Steve Biko refers to the meaning of the word in "black magic," "black market," and "black sheep of the family" (Woods 1978, 164).

24. Ancheta argues (1998) that the axis of the subordination of Asian Americans is not white versus black; Chang (1998) notes that the black/white paradigm treats Asian Americans as interlopers in race discourse; Tamayo (1995) observed that the paradigm is inadequate.

25. This was not always the case. Nativistic sentiment was rampant in the early 1900s when immigration from Eastern and Southern Europe increased. The debate on restricting the immigration influx vacillated between biological arguments based on the racial inferiority of the new immigrants and social arguments based on their ethnic inferiority (see Feagin 1997).

26. Haney López's analysis of the prerequisite cases also reveals that the foreigner axis does not work to the exclusion of the color axis, but rather in conjunction with it (see Haney López 1996, 79–109). Haney López's *White by Law* "provides the crucial link between the analysis of race relations through a black-white paradigm and the treatment of Asian Americans under a citizen-foreigner paradigm" (Wu 1995, 206)

27. Gladwell (1996, 79) notes,

The success of West Indians is not proof that discrimination against American blacks does not exist. Rather, it is the means by which discrimination against American blacks is given one last, vicious twist: I am not so shallow as to despise you for the color of your skin, because I have found people of your color that I like. Now I can despise you for who you are.

28. See Priscilla Labovitz, "Immigration: Just the Facts," *New York Times,* March 25, 1996, A15.

29. The historical bias against Asians in immigration law is by now infamous. Immigration rights complicate the race issue in the United States because a powerful argument for state sovereignty can be made in defense of restricting immigration. The issue of open or fair immigration, while important, is beyond the scope of my chapter.

30. Fiss (1999) argues that laws imposing social disabilities on immigrants create social "pariahs" and violate the Equal Protection Clause.

31. See Personal Responsibility and Work Opportunity Reconciliation Act of 1996, Pub. L. No. 104-193, 110 Stat. 2105; see also Statement by President of the United States, 1996 U.S.C.C.A.N. 2891 (Aug. 22, 1996) ("I am deeply disappointed that this legislation would deny Federal assistance to legal immigrants and their children, and give States the option of doing the same."); Patrick J., "Immigrants to Be Warned of Benefit Cuts," *Los Angeles Times,* Feb. 1, 1997, A1 (reporting on the removal of hundreds of thousands of legal immigrants from the Supplemental Security Income rolls).

32. According to Park (1996), 22 percent of Latinos and almost half of all Asian American and African American voters in California voted in favor of Proposition 187.

REFERENCES

Ancheta, Angelo N. 1998. *Race, Rights, and the Asian American Experience.* New Brunswick, NJ: Rutgers University Press.

Bell, Derrick A. (ed.). 1980. *Civil Rights: Leading Cases.* Boston: Little, Brown.

Bonacich, Edna. 1973. A Theory of Middleman Minorities. *American Sociological Review* 38: 583–94.

Brimelow, Peter. 1995. *Alien Nation: Common Sense about America's Immigration Disaster.* New York: Random House.

Calmore, John O. 1995. Racialized Space and the Culture of Segregation: "Hewing a Stone of Hope from a Mountain of Despair." *University of Pennsylvania Law Review* 143: 1233–63.

Calmore, John O. 1997. Our Private Obsession, Our Public Sin: Exploring Michael Omi's "Messy" Real World of Race. *Law Journal* 15(25): 56–57.

Cervantes, Nancy, Sasha Khoka, and Bobbie Murray. 1995. Hate Unleashed: Los Angeles in the Aftermath of Proposition 187. *Chicano-Latino Law Review* 17(1): 1–21.

Chang, Robert S. 1994. Toward an Asian American Legal Scholarship: Critical Race Theory, Post-Structuralism, and Narrative Space. *Asian Law Journal* 1(1).

Chang, Robert S. 1996. The End of Innocence or Politics: The Fall of the Essential Subject. *The American University Law Review* 45: 687–91.

Chang, Robert S. 1998. Dreaming in Black and White: Racial-Sexual Policing in *The Birth of a Nation, The Cheat,* and *Who Killed Vincent Chin? Asian Law Journal* 5: 41–42.

Chew, Pat K. 1994. Asian Americans: The "Reticent" Minority and Their Paradoxes. *William & Mary Law Review* 36: 1–9.

Chin, Gabriel J. 1996. The Civil Rights Revolution Comes to Immigration Law: A New Look at the Immigration and Nationality Act of 1965. *North Carolina Law Review* 273: 300–303.

Conrad, Joseph. 1899/1991. *Heart of Darkness.* New York: Doubleday.

Davis, Adrienne. 1996a. Identity Notes Part One: Playing in the Light. *The American University Law Review* 45: 695–709.

Davis, Adrienne. 1996b. Race, Law, and Justice: The Rehnquist Court and the American Dilemma. *American University Law Review* 45: 567–615.

Feagin, Joe. 1997. Old Poison in New Bottles: The Deep Roots of Modem Nativism. Pp. 13–43 in Juan F. Perea (ed.), *Immigrants Out! The New Nativism and the Anti-Immigrant Impulse in the United States.* New York: New York University Press.

Fiss, Owen M. 1999. The Immigrant as Pariah. Pp. 3–21 in Owen M. Fiss (ed.), *A Community of Equals: The Constitutional Protection of New Americans.* Boston: Beacon Press.

Gladwell, Malcolm. 1996. Black Like Them. *The New Yorker,* April 19–May 6, 74–79.

Gordon, Avery F. and Christopher Newfield (eds.). 1996. *Mapping Multiculturalism.* Minneapolis: University of Minnesota Press.

Gotanda, Neil. 1996. Multiculturalism and Racial Stratification. Pp. 238–46 in Avery F. Gordon and Christopher Newfield (eds.), *Mapping Multiculturalism.* Minneapolis: University of Minnesota Press.

Grant, Madison. 1924. The Racial Transformation of America. *North American Review* 2(9): 350–52.

Haney López, Ian F. 1996. *White by Law: The Legal Construction of Race.* New York: New York University Press.

Iijima, Chris K. 1997. The Era of We-Construction: Reclaiming the Politics of Asian Pacific American Identity and Reflections on the Critique of the Paradigm. *Columbia Human Rights Law Review* 29.

Jacobson, Matthew Frye. 1998. *Whiteness of a Different Color: European Immigrants and the Alchemy of Race.* Cambridge, MA: Harvard University Press.

Kim, Hyung-Chan. 1992. *Asian Americans and the Supreme Court: A Documentary History.* Westport, CT: Greenwood Press.

Koh, Harold Hongju. 1992. Foreword. Pp. ix–x in Hyung-Chan Kim, *Asian Americans and the Supreme Court: A Documentary History.* Westport, CT: Greenwood Press.

Kuhn, Thomas. 1970. *The Structure of Scientific Revolutions,* 2nd ed. Chicago: University of Chicago Press.

Lawrence, Charles R. 1995. Foreword: Race, Multiculturalism, and the Jurisprudence of Transformation. *Stanford Law Review* 47: 819–26.

Okihiro, Gary. 1994. *Margins and Mainstreams: Asians in American History and Culture.* Seattle: University of Washington Press.

Omi, Michael and Howard Winant. 1994. *Racial Formation in the United States: From the 1960s to the 1990s.* New York: Routledge.

Park, John S. and W. Park. 1996. Race Discourse and Proposition 187. *Michigan Journal of Race and Law* 2(1): 175–204.

Perea, Juan F. 1997. The Binary Paradigm of Race: The "Normal Science" of American Racial Thought. *California Law Review* 85: 1213–15.

Ramirez, Deborah. 1995. Multicultural Empowerment: It's Not Just Black and White. *Stanford Law Review* 47: 957–59.

Tamayo, William R. 1995. When the "Coloreds" Are Neither Black nor Citizens: The United States Civil Rights Movement and Global Migration. *Asian Law Journal* 2(1).

Valdes, Francisco. 1997. Foreword: Under Consciousness, Community, and Theory. *California Law Review* 85: 1087–1104.

Woods, Donald. 1978. *Biko.* New York: Paddington.

Wu, Frank H. 1995. Neither Black nor White: Asian Americans and Affirmative Action. *Boston College Third World Law Journal* 15: 225.

Wu, Frank H. 1996. From Black to White and Back Again. *Asian Law Journal* 3: 185–212.

Are Asian Americans Becoming White?

Min Zhou

> I never asked to be white. I am not literally white. That is,
> I do not have white skin or white ancestors. I have yellow
> skin and yellow ancestors, hundreds of generations of
> them. But like so many other Asian Americans of the sec-
> ond generation, I find myself now the bearer of a strange
> new status: white, by acclamation. Thus it is that I have
> been described as an "honorary white" by other whites,
> and as a "banana" by other Asians . . . to the extent that I
> have moved away from the periphery and toward the
> center of American life, I have become white inside.
> —Eric Liu, *The Accidental Asian* (34)

"Are Asian Americans becoming white?" For many public officials the answer must be
yes, because they classify Asian-origin Americans with European-origin Americans for
equal opportunity programs; neither is an underrepresented group, as blacks, Latinos,
and Indians are. But this answer is premature and based on false premises. Although
Asian Americans as a group have attained career and financial success equated with
being white, and although many have moved near to or even married whites, they still
remain culturally distinct and suspect in a white society.

At issue is how to define "Asian American" and "white." The term "Asian American"
was coined by the late historian and activist Yuji Ichioka during the ethnic consciousness movements of the late 1960s. To adopt this identity is to reject the Western-
imposed label of "Oriental." Today, "Asian American" is an umbrella category that
includes both U.S. citizens and immigrants whose ancestors came from Asia east
of Pakistan. Although widely used in public discussions, most Asian-origin Americans are ambivalent about this label, reflecting the difficulty of being American and
still keeping some ethnic identity: Is one, for example, Asian American or Japanese
American?

Similarly, "white" is an arbitrary label having more to do with privilege than biology. In the United States, groups initially considered nonwhite, such as Irish and Jews,
have attained "white" membership by acquiring status and wealth. It is hardly surprising, then, that nonwhites would aspire to become "white" as a mark of and a tool

for material success. However, becoming white can mean distancing oneself from "people of color" or selling out one's ethnicity. Panethnic identities—Asian American, African American, Hispanic American—are one way the politically vocal in any group try to stem defections; these collective identities may restrain aspirations for individual mobility.

Varieties of Asian Americans

Privately, few Americans of Asian ancestry would spontaneously identify themselves as Asian, and fewer still as Asian American. They instead link their identities to specific countries of origin, such as Chinese, Japanese, Korean, Filipino, Indian, Vietnamese, and so on. In a study of Vietnamese youth in San Diego, for example, I found that 53 percent identified themselves as Vietnamese, 32 percent as Vietnamese American, and only 14 percent as Asian American, and that nearly 60 percent of these youth considered their chosen identity as very important to them.

Some Americans of Asian ancestry have family histories in the United States longer than many Americans of Eastern or Southern European origin. However, they became numerous only after 1970, rising from 1.4 million to 11.9 million, or 4 percent of the total U.S. population, in 2000. Before 1970, the Asian-origin population was largely made up of Japanese, Chinese, and Filipinos. Now, Americans of Chinese and Filipino ancestries are the largest subgroups (at 2.8 million and 2.4 million, respectively), followed by Indians, Koreans, Vietnamese, and Japanese (at more than one million). Some twenty other national-origin groups, such as Cambodians, Pakistanis, Lao, Thai, Indonesians, and Bangladeshis, were officially counted in government statistics only after 1980, and together amounted to more than two million residents in 2000.

The seven-fold growth of the Asian-origin population in the span of thirty-odd years is primarily due to the accelerated immigration subsequent to the Hart-Celler Act of 1965, which ended the national-origins quota system, and the historic resettlement of Southeast Asian refugees after the Vietnam War. Currently, about 60 percent of the Asian-origin population is foreign born (the first generation), another 28 percent are U.S.-born of foreign-born parents (the second generation), and just 12 percent are born to U.S.-born parents (the third generation and beyond). The only exception to this pattern is Japanese Americans, who have a fourth generation and many U.S.-born elderly.

Unlike earlier immigrants from Asia or Europe, who were mostly low-skilled laborers looking for work, today's immigrants from Asia have more varied backgrounds and come for many reasons, such as to join their families, to invest their money in the U.S. economy, to fulfill the demand for highly skilled labor, or to escape war, political or religious persecution, and economic hardship. For example, Chinese, Taiwanese, Indian, and Filipino Americans tend to be overrepresented among scientists, engineers, physicians and other skilled professionals, but less educated, low-skilled workers are more common among Vietnamese, Cambodian, Laotian, and Hmong Americans, most of whom entered the United States as refugees. While middle-class immigrants are able to start their American lives with high-paying professional careers and

comfortable suburban living, low-skilled immigrants and refugees often have to en-
dure low-paying, menial jobs and live in inner-city ghettos.

Asian Americans tend to settle in large metropolitan areas and concentrate in the
West. California is home to 35 percent of all Asian Americans. But recently, other states
such as Texas, Minnesota, and Wisconsin, which historically received few Asian immigrants, have become destinations for Asian American settlement. Traditional ethnic
enclaves, such as Chinatown, Little Tokyo, Manilatown, Koreatown, Little Phnom
Penh, and Thaitown, persist or have emerged in gateway cities, helping new arrivals to
cope with cultural and language difficulties in their initial stage of resettlement. However, affluent and highly skilled immigrants tend to bypass inner-city enclaves and settle in suburbs upon arrival, belying the stereotype of the "unacculturated" immigrant.
Today, more than half of the Asian-origin population is spreading out in suburbs surrounding traditional gateway cities, as well as in new urban centers of Asian settlement across the country.

Differences in national origins, timing of immigration, affluence, and settlement
patterns profoundly affect the formation of a panethnic identity. Recent arrivals are
less likely than those born or raised in the United States to identify as Asian American.
They are also so busy settling in that they have little time to think about being Asian or
Asian American or, for that matter, white. Their diverse origins evoke drastic differences in languages and dialects, religions, foodways, and customs. Many nationalities
also brought to America their histories of conflict (such as the Japanese colonization
of Korea and Taiwan, Japanese attacks on China, and the Chinese invasion of Vietnam). Immigrants who are predominantly middle-class professionals such as the Taiwanese and Indians, or predominantly small business owners such as the Koreans,
share few of the same concerns and priorities as those who are predominantly uneducated, low-skilled refugees, such as Cambodians and Hmong. Finally, Asian-origin
people living in San Francisco or Los Angeles among many other Asians and self-conscious Asian Americans develop sharper ethnic sensitivity than those living in, say,
Latin-dominant Miami or white-dominant Minneapolis. A politician might get away
with calling Asians "Oriental" in Miami but get into big trouble in San Francisco. All
of these differences can create obstacles to fostering a cohesive pan-Asian solidarity. As
Yen Le Espiritu shows in her research, pan-Asianism is primarily a political ideology
of U.S.-born, American-educated, and middle-class Asians rather than of Asian immigrants, who are conscious of their national origins and overburdened with their daily
struggles for survival.

Underneath the Model Minority: "White" or "Other"

The celebrated "model minority" image of Asian Americans appeared in the mid-
1960s, at the peak of the civil rights movement and the ethnic consciousness movements, but *before* the rising waves of immigration and refugee influx from Asia. Two
articles in 1966—"Success Story, Japanese-American Style," by William Petersen in the
New York Times Magazine, and "Success of One Minority Group in U.S.," by the *U.S.
News and World Report* staff, marked a significant departure from the way Asian im-

migrants and their descendants had been traditionally depicted in the media. Both articles extolled Japanese and Chinese Americans for their persistence in overcoming extreme hardships and discrimination to achieve success, unmatched even by U.S.-born whites, with "their own almost totally unaided effort" and "no help from anyone else." The press attributed their winning wealth and respect in American society to hard work, family solidarity, discipline, delayed gratification, nonconfrontation, and of eschewing welfare.

One consequence of the model-minority stereotype is to buttress the myth that the United States is devoid of racism and accords equal opportunity to all, and that those who lag behind do so because of their own poor choices and inferior culture. Celebrating this model minority can help thwart other racial minorities' demands for social justice by pitting minority groups against each other. It can also pit Asian Americans against whites. On the surface, Asian Americans seem to be on their way to becoming white, just like the offspring of earlier European immigrants. But the model-minority image implicitly casts Asian Americans as different from whites. By placing Asian Americans above whites, the model-minority image also sets them apart from other Americans, white or nonwhite, in the public mind.

Let me point to two less obvious effects. The model-minority stereotype holds Asian Americans to higher standards, distinguishing them from average Americans. "What's wrong with being a model minority?" asked a black student in a class I taught on race. "I'd rather be in the model minority than in the downtrodden minority that nobody respects." Whether people are in a model minority or a downtrodden minority, they are judged by standards *different* from those applied to average Americans. Also, the model-minority stereotype places particular expectations on members of the group so labeled, channeling them to specific avenues of success, such as science and engineering, which in turn unintentionally reinforces barriers for Asian Americans in pursuing careers outside these designated fields. Falling into this trap, a Chinese immigrant father might be upset if his son told him that he had decided to change his major from engineering to English. Disregarding his son's passion and talent for creative writing, the father would rationalize his concern: "You have a 90 percent chance of getting a decent job with an engineering degree, but what chance would you have of earning income as a writer?" This rationale reflects more than simple parental concern over career choices typical of middle-class families; it constitutes the self-fulfilling prophecy of a stereotype.

In the end, the celebration of Asian Americans as a model minority is based on the judgment that many Asian Americans perform at levels above the American average, which sets them apart not only from other minorities but also from whites. The truth of the matter is that the larger than average size of the middle and upper-middle class in some Asian-origin groups, such as the Chinese, Indian, and Korean, paves a much smoother path for the immigrants and their offspring to regain their middle-class status in the new homeland. The financial resources that immigrants brought with them to this country also help build viable ethnic economies and institutions, such as private after-school programs, for the less fortunate group members to move ahead in society at a much faster pace than they would do if they did not have access to these ethnic resources.

"It's Not So Much Being White as Being American"

Most Asian Americans seem to accept that "white" is mainstream, average, and normal, and look to whites as their frame of reference for attaining higher social positions. Similarly, researchers often use non-Hispanic whites as the standard against which other groups are compared, even though there is great diversity among whites, too. Like most other immigrants to the United States, many Asian immigrants tend to believe in the American Dream and measure their achievements materially. As a Chinese immigrant said to me in an interview, "I hope to accomplish nothing but three things: to own a home, to be my own boss, and to send my children to the Ivy League." Those with sufficient education, job skills, and money manage to move into white, middle-class, suburban neighborhoods immediately upon arrival, while others work intensively to accumulate enough savings to move their families up and out of inner-city ethnic enclaves. Consequently, many children of Asian ancestry have lived their entire childhood in white communities, made friends with mostly white peers, and grown up speaking only English. In fact, Asian Americans are the most acculturated non-European group in the United States. By the second generation, most have lost fluency in their parents' native languages. David Lopez finds that in Los Angeles, more than three-quarters of second-generation Asian Americans (as opposed to about one-quarter of second-generation Mexicans) speak only English at home. Asian Americans also intermarry extensively with whites and with members of other minority groups. Jennifer Lee and Frank Bean find that more than one-quarter of married Asian Americans have a partner of a different racial background, and 87 percent of intermarried Asians marry whites; they also find that 12 percent of all Asian Americans claim a multiracial background, compared to 2 percent of whites and 4 percent of blacks.

Even though U.S.-born or U.S.-raised Asian Americans are relatively acculturated and often intermarry with whites, they may be more ambivalent about becoming white than their immigrant parents. Many only cynically agree that "white" is synonymous with "American." A Vietnamese high school student in New Orleans told me in an interview, "An American is white. You often hear people say, hey, so-and-so is dating an 'American.' You know she's dating a white boy. If he were black, then people would say he's black." But while they recognize whites as a frame of reference, some reject the idea of becoming white themselves—"It's not so much being white as being American," commented a Korean American student in my class on the new second generation. This aversion to becoming white is particularly common among the well-educated and privileged second-generation college students who have taken ethnic studies courses, or among Asian American community activists. However, most of the second generation continues to strive for the privileged status associated with whiteness, just like their parents. For example, most U.S.-born or U.S.-raised Chinese American youth end up studying engineering, medicine, and law at college, believing that these areas of study will guarantee well-paying jobs and middle-class living and enhance social contact with whites.

Second-generation Asian Americans are also more conscious of the disadvantages associated with being nonwhite than their parents, who as immigrants tend to be optimistic about overcoming the disadvantages. As a Chinese American woman points out from her own experience, "The truth is, no matter how American you think you are or try to be, if you have almond-shaped eyes, straight black hair, and a yellow complexion, you are a foreigner by default. . . . You can certainly be as good as or even better than whites, but you will never become accepted as white." This remark echoes a commonly felt frustration among second-generation Asian Americans who detest being treated as immigrants or foreigners. Their experience suggests that whitening has more to do with the beliefs of white America than with the actual situation of Asian Americans. Speaking perfect English, effortlessly adopting mainstream cultural values, and even intermarrying members of the dominant group may help reduce this "otherness" at the individual level but have little effect on the group as a whole. New stereotypes can emerge and un-whiten Asian Americans anytime and anywhere, no matter how "successful" and "assimilated" they have become. For example, Congressman David Wu was once invited by the Asian American employees of the U.S. Department of Energy to give a speech in celebration of the Asian American Heritage Month. Yet he and his Asian American staff were not allowed into the department building, even after presenting their congressional IDs, and were repeatedly asked about their citizenship and country of origin. They were told that this was standard procedure for the Department of Energy and that a Congressional ID was not a reliable document. A Congressman of Italian descent was allowed to enter the same building the next day with his Congressional ID, no questions asked.

The stereotype of the "honorary white" or model minority goes hand-in-hand with that of the "forever foreigner." Today, globalization and U.S.-Asia relations, combined with continually high rates of immigration, affect the way Asian Americans are perceived in American society. Most of the historical stereotypes, such as the "yellow peril" and "Fu Manchu" have found their way into contemporary American life, as revealed in such highly publicized incidents as the murder of Vincent Chin, a Chinese American mistaken for Japanese and beaten to death by a disgruntled white auto worker in the 1980s; the trial of Wen Ho Lee, a nuclear scientist suspected of spying for the Chinese government in the mid-1990s; the 1996 presidential campaign finance scandal, which implicated Asian Americans in funneling foreign contributions to the Clinton campaign; and most recently, in 2001, the Abercrombie & Fitch tee-shirts that depicted Asian cartoon characters in stereotypically negative ways—slanted eyes, thick glasses, and heavy Asian accents. Ironically, the ambivalent, conditional nature of white acceptance of Asian Americans prompts them to organize panethnically to fight back—which consequently heightens their racial distinctiveness. So becoming white or not is beside the point. The bottom line is that Americans of Asian ancestry still have to constantly prove they are truly loyal American.

NOTE

Originally published in *Contexts* 3.1 (2004): 29–37. © 2004 The Asian Sociological Association, reprint by permission of the University of California Press.

Chapter 17

Diverging Identities

Ethnic and Religious Identities among
Second-Generation Korean Americans

Helen J. Lee

> I think it's like the center in my life because it touches on
> everything that I can do. . . . It's almost like my identity
> almost. Like, this is where I like to be.
> —Mary Soh,[1] age seventeen, discussing the role of the
> Korean Protestant Church in her life

> Nothing really. I mean, well, part of it's just to hang out
> after church and stuff. But, uh, I mean, I just come basi-
> cally because my parents tell me to come, so . . .
> —Charlie Park, age eighteen, also discussing what role
> the Korean Protestant Church plays in his life

Mary Soh and Charlie Park are part of America's "new" second-generation population
—the American-born children of Korean immigrants who came after the enactment
of the 1965 Immigration and Naturalization Act (Portes and Zhou 1993). Both adolescents are also members of the same ethnic/religious institution—a large Korean Protestant Church located in a northeastern city. Yet as the quotations above demonstrate,
these two teenagers have vastly different perspectives on the salience of the ethnic
church in their lives. Mary sees this institution as a place where her ethnic (Korean)
and religious (Christian) identities are crystallized. In contrast, Charlie views this
same institution as playing a minimal role in his life; at most, it serves as a meeting
place to "hang out" with his Korean American friends.

In recent years, there has been a considerable amount of scholarly attention that
examines the role of religion in the formation and maintenance of ethnic identity
among children of immigrants (Bankston and Zhou 1996; Cha 2001; Chai 1998; Chong
1998; Kurien 1998). It is clear from this body of literature that ethnically based religious organizations serve a variety of functions in the lives of ethnic minorities and
are sought out by second-generation individuals for a multitude of reasons. However, much of the descriptive research on the relationship between ethnic and religious identities has focused on second-generation young adults (Cha 2001; Chai 1998;

Chong 1998)—individuals who may be actively seeking a place that reinforces identities crystallized during adolescence.[2] Yet in studying the process of ethnic and religious identity formation, the teenage years—a hallmark time of identity development and exploration—may be one of the most fruitful places to explore this relationship (Erikson 1959).

In this paper, I present findings from a case study of fifteen adolescents in a Korean Protestant church (KPC) in Philadelphia, Pennsylvania, drawing from extensive ethnographic observations and in-depth interviews with second-generation congregation members.[3] This study contributes to the sociological literature on religious and ethnic identity formation by outlining three different typologies of the way religion and ethnic identity are connected among second-generation youth. I extend prior research by using these typologies to descriptively portray the varying kinds and degrees of religious involvement that may be found among children of immigrants within an ethnic/religious institutional setting. I use the term "identity" in the social-psychological sense, examining a person's subjective orientation while recognizing that the conception of the self is shaped and constructed within the larger social environment and through interactions (Nagel 1994). I view ethnicity and religion as two domains of the teenagers' potential identities. The intertwining of the two for these second-generation adolescents is the primary question.

Religion and Ethnic Identity

Sociologists have refined the story of immigrants and their children for decades, examining what motivates foreigners to come and what happens to them and their American-born children after they have arrived. Religious institutions have always been an important part of the story, particularly in understanding how immigrants and their offspring adapt to life in America (Bankston and Zhou 1996; Gordon 1964; Herberg 1955). As once described by Herberg (1955, 24), the dilemma of the immigrant was one of self-identity and self-location. Ethnic/religious institutions became one way to resolve the identity crisis, as they "helped sort out 'who one was' in a bewilderingly complex society" (Greeley 1972, 125).

Following the enactment of the 1965 Immigration Act, immigrants from Asian and Latin American countries became the largest groups to settle in the United States. One consequence of these changes in immigration patterns has been a rich and growing variety of ethnic/religious congregations across the American landscape (Williams 1988). One group that has drawn a fair amount of attention in the study of religion and ethnicity has been the Korean Christian community. It has been estimated that there are over three thousand Korean churches in the United States, mostly of Protestant denomination (Warner 2001). Unlike Sikhism or Hinduism, Protestant Christianity has a long historical presence in America. Yet similar to other immigrant groups, Koreans either joined or established their own ethnic/religious institutions once they were in the United States (Kim and Hurh 1990; Min 1992).

Studies of immigrant congregations, both past and present, have clearly documented a strong relationship between the religious institution and the formation and maintenance of an ethnic community and identity (Williams 1988; Warner 2001). It is less clear what role religion plays in the lives of the children of immigrants. Fifty years ago, Herberg (1955) wrote that in their struggles to assimilate, children of immigrants would retreat from the religious identification of their parents, along with the ethnic/religious institution, as a way to distance themselves from their ethnic heritage. Yet scholars of contemporary second-generation groups have often found that ethnic/religious organizations are salient institutions in the lives of children of immigrants, much as they are for their immigrant parents, and that involvement in these organizations helps to promote or reinforce a sense of ethnic identity and community (e.g., see Bankston and Zhou 1996, Zhou and Bankston 1998 on the Vietnamese; Cha 2001, Chai 1998, and Chong 1998 on Korean Americans; Kurien 1998 on South Asians). Moreover, the ethnic/religious institution may serve as an important place for children of immigrants where "outsider" feelings are diminished—a setting that may sharply contrast with other contexts (work, neighborhoods) second-generation minorities must navigate (Chong 1998).

The extant literature has revealed important insights into how ethnic identity and religious identity formation can become connected. For instance, in a study of two South Asian Hindu organizations, Kurien (1998) found that ethnically based religious congregations informed the second-generation members about their ethnic culture through the use of religious texts and stories. At the same time, these congregations socialized the teenagers into a broader social network of an ethnic/religious community. For the children of Korean immigrants, scholars have also found that religion (typically, Protestant Christianity) is strongly related to their sense of ethnic identity but have also noted distinctions in how the two are connected (Chai 1998; Chong 1998). In an ethnographic study of a young adult congregation in Boston, Chai (1998) found that the opportunity to be with others of the same ethnic and religious background was a motivating factor for second-generation Korean Americans to attend an ethnic church. Yet Chai (1998) also noted that for many of her respondents, the religious aspects of their identity superseded their identity as ethnic Americans. In another study of two Korean American congregations in Chicago, Chong (1998) argued that, due to experiences of racial discrimination and feelings of marginalization, second-generation members sought a place where they could form and express a sense of ethnic identity. The ethnic church provided such a setting, where the traditional beliefs that the members grew up with (e.g., respect for elders, obedience to authority) were fused and "sacralized" with biblical principles and thereby merged together (Chong 1998).

Thus, for some Korean American young adults, the ethnically based congregation provides a setting where their attachments to Korean culture and Christian ideology can coincide. For others, involvement in a second-generation religious institution has meant a stronger development and stricter adherence to theological tenets, where religious identity supersedes ethnic, gender, and other characteristics. Viewed collectively, these studies reveal that the relationship between ethnic and religious identity can vary across and within congregations.

While these studies offer important insight into the role of religion in Korean American communities, they are based on people who willingly seek out and attend an ethnic and religious institution. As young adults who have managed the transition to adulthood, seeking out Korean American Christian groups and holding onto the principles of the ethnic church may be consequences of identities already crystallized in adolescence. Yet it is in adolescence where questions of identity become salient and take on critical importance (Erikson 1959). As noted by Cha (2001), the nature of the relationship between ethnic and religious identity can change throughout the life course of individuals. When it comes to second-generation adolescents, our knowledge of this stage of life remains highly fragmentary (Rumbaut 1994).

The purpose of this study was to explore the intersections of ethnic and religious identity among children of immigrants, using Korean Americans and the ethnic Protestant church as a case study. What, if any, are the identity differences within a group of second-generation adolescents who were all raised by Korean parents, socialized in the United States, and attend a Korean Christian church? Why do they attend an ethnic/religious institution and what role does the ethnic church play in the formation of an ethnic and/or religious identity? How are religion and ethnic identity connected for these teenagers?

The Ethnic Church and the Children of Korean Immigrants

The Korean Protestant Church (KPC) is one of the largest and oldest Korean Christian churches in the Philadelphia area. The church as an institution and as a physical setting has played a crucial role in the Korean community, especially since Koreans in Philadelphia have not concentrated in one particular geographic area. As with other Korean churches, as revealed by prior studies, KPC clearly provides more than just spiritual fellowship (Chai 1998; Kim and Hurh 1990; Min 1992). It also serves as a larger community center, offering Korean-language classes, tae kwon doe (Korean karate) lessons, musical concerts, and other nonreligious offerings. KPC also consists of different congregations and services, including a separate service for the English-speaking junior and senior high school students (separate from the adult service). There are two *jundosanims* (youth pastors) for this group, one pastor for the junior high and one pastor for the senior high school students. Immediately after each service, the adolescents divide into separate Bible studies by grade level, and these studies are further divided by gender.

The youth group also meets on Friday nights for a more "informal" Bible study. These youth group meetings never seem to bring the high turnouts characteristic of Sunday services. On any given Sunday, there are usually between 100 and 120 teenagers who attend. On Friday nights, there is usually only a small group—anywhere from eight to fifteen teenagers.

Overall, the adolescents at KPC appear to be very similar to one another. Most were born in the United States (two came to the United States as young children) and were raised in the Philadelphia area.[4] They are all more comfortable speaking English as opposed to Korean, and told me that they would never want to live in Korea. They come from similar family backgrounds where all but two teenagers are growing up in two-parent homes. Many of their parents are business owners, usually of a dry-cleaning operation, and own a house in the suburbs. According to many of the teen-agers, their schools are predominantly "white." Thus, the contact that they have with other coethnic peers is mainly through the church. All of them have been coming to KPC since they were young children. Lastly, when it comes to their ethnic identifica-tion, every second-generation member I spoke with classifies himself or herself as de-finitively "Korean American."

Yet, when it comes to the role that the ethnic/religious institution plays in their lives, these teenagers defy categorization into one group or one story. In fact, I find that there are three types of Korean American teenagers who attend KPC. The first type, whom I call the ethnic/religious teenager, is actively involved in KPC activities and has a strong sense of both ethnic and religious identities. The second type, whom I call the ethnically identified teenager, comes to KPC for mainly social reasons. This type of teenager has a desire to seek out Korean American friendships, but has not es-tablished a strong attachment to the church or to Christianity as a religion. The third type of teenager has neither a strong ethnic nor a strong religious identity. In fact, this type of teenager either actively questions his/her attachment to the church and to the ethnic community, or rarely contemplates it. For these teens, KPC plays a minimal role in their lives as either a religious or an ethnic institution.[5]

Ethnic/Religious Teenagers at KPC

For one group of teenagers, whom I categorize as the ethnic/religious teenagers, KPC plays an important role in shaping the understanding of both their ethnic and their religious identities. In fact, one of the characteristic markers of the ethnic/religious teenagers is the high level of involvement and participation. This group includes the small handful of teenagers (N = 5) who come for Friday night meetings every week, in addition to the Sunday service, and four of them are officers of the youth group. Most of their parents are actively involved in the church as well and hold leadership posi-tions (e.g., church deacons, elders) and this may partly explain their own high degree of involvement. Yet for some ethnic/religious teens, their active participation in KPC becomes a source of tension in the home. For example, Mary, aged seventeen, spends at least three days a week at church, including almost all day on Sunday:

Q: So what's that like, spending so much time at the church?
A: I like to do it, but my parents are just like, "All right, how come you don't do school work? Why don't you do your, like, homework instead of going to church?" They like yell at me for going to church! What kid's parents yells at them for going to church? Any parent would just like die to have their kids go to church everyday [laughs].

Mary has her priorities, and at times, these priorities do not match what her par-ents think they should be. In her parents' eyes, Mary's strong religious commitment becomes problematic when it supersedes her role as a student. In Mary's eyes, her religious involvement becomes problematic when it conflicts with her parents' wishes or desires.

The ethnic/religious teenagers' attachment to KPC is not solely rooted in their parents' involvement with the church, as the example above demonstrates. Rather, these adolescents emphasize the importance of fellowship and religious teachings. For example, Tracy (another ethnic/religious teenager) states, "The social stuff is just like the extra thing that happens. . . . But I need to hear the sermon and stuff, and the [Bible] studies. Cause when I read the Bible, I don't understand some of things they say, and this is where I learn that stuff." Clearly, the church is more than just a physical meeting place for childhood friends.

However, religious instruction and fellowship are not the only reasons that motivate the ethnic/religious teenagers to come to KPC. Indeed, other non-Korean Christian institutions could fulfill those same functions. Mary, who attends a school with a small number of Korean Americans, explains why KPC is important in her life:

> It's just the fact of the matter that, like, we like to be with people who understand, who know. Like if I'm just like "Dag! I went to school today and I wished I had some kimchee to eat!" And like, if I went to school and said that, they'd be like "What?" But I know that if I'm at the [KPC] retreat, and I'm like, "Yo, don't you feel like eating bulgogi [barbequed beef] right now?" They'd be like "Ah yeah, and mandu [dumplings]." And like, you know? It's the whole like, knowing, cultural knowing. It just feels good. And like, when we hang out here, it's like "Oh, I don't wanna go home." You know?

Mary recognizes the importance of being with fellow coethnic peers who share a bicultural understanding—who balance a hyphenated identity in their lives. The church, as a place for establishing a strong coethnic peer network, may be as important to the ethnic/religious teens as it is for their first-generation parents (Min 1992).

There are other ways through which Korean adolescents can interact with coethnic peers who share the same "cultural knowing." For example, David and Rachel both attend a high school with a sizeable number of Korean American students—enough, in fact, to form an after-school "Korean Club." Yet both are wary of joining Korean cliques and speak of them negatively, as being "too exclusive." These cliques, in the eyes of the ethnic/religious teenagers, stand as insular avenues through which to assert an ethnic identity. In fact, some of the teens state that in the future, it will be more important for them to belong to a religious institution where they feel spiritually fulfilled, as opposed to specifically seeking out a Korean church.

Past studies of second-generation religious congregations have highlighted the way ethnic and religious identities can become intertwined, as religious leaders combine religious doctrines with traditional ethnic values (Chong 1998; Kurien 1998). Thus, pastors can potentially play important roles in helping the KPC teenagers understand how their ethnic and religious identities are connected. The youth pastors, as immigrants themselves, are more in touch with the ethnic culture of the children's parents. At the same time, they know from their own experience some of the pressures these teens may face, as the following testimonial from a Sunday service shows:

Pastor George says, "In high school, I got the most awards for my grade. I was the most awarded person in my class. . . . I really held dear to my grades in high school. But in college, I got grades that I never thought I would get. . . . After college, I applied to twenty-seven medical schools." He then goes on to tell them that all twenty-seven medical schools rejected him, and that he began to question God's love. But he continues by stating, "God needs to shake us out of our comfort zones and shake our foundations if they are not godly."

In this testimony, the pastor is warning the teenagers against placing too much pride and identity in grades and academics, because to do so is not "godly." The KPC teenagers are well aware that their parents hold them to high academic standards. Pastor George sees this academic pressure as a salient problem between parents and children in the church, and through religious interpretations, guides the teenagers away from such pressures. As he expresses during an interview, "These parents always talk about study, study, study. Study is an idol. Study is a god. Harvard is the god that Korean parents worship." Thus, pastors can be important figures because they help KPC teens forge their own identities, separate from their parents' beliefs. Not every Korean value is regarded as congruent with Christian ideals; rather, youth pastors can single them out for being inherently contrary to theological tenets.

The ethnic/religious teenagers regard the pastors as important figures in their lives and view them as important spiritual resources. As respected figures in the eyes of the ethnic/religious teenagers, the pastors are tools that help the teenagers determine what ideals and values make up a Christian identity. The pastors expressed to me that their ultimate job was to guide the KPC teens along a path where their religious identities would encompass other loyalties, including their ethnic identities. The degree to which this is happening for the ethnic/religious teen can be seen in Mary's statement regarding the role that KPC plays in her life:

> I think it's like the center in my life because it touches on everything that I can do. . . . I think that, like, it's kind of different for me because being Christian also adds to the fact that I go to a Korean church, so it's almost like my identity almost. Like, this is where I like to be.

For Mary and other ethnic/religious teens, growing up in a Korean church means that ethnicity and religion are interconnected identities. This fusion of identities may motivate them to continue participating in an ethnic church in the future (Chong 1998). They may also realize, through their involvement in the church, that the goals their immigrant parents emphasize can sometimes contradict their Christian ideals. In these situations, it is their religious identity that may take precedence (Chai 1998).

Ethnically Identified Teenagers at KPC

The ethnic/religious teenagers, who see the church as an important if not central part of their lives, make up one type of congregation member at KPC. During early field observations, I became aware that both the adult leaders and the teenagers recognize that there are different types of Korean Americans, including the "good" and the "bad." One of the ethnic/religious adolescents, Tracy, describes these distinctions:

Um, you got Korean kids who are just like, Korean kids. I guess I'm considered one of those. You just go to school, come home. Maybe like, if your parents own a store, work at the store, go to church, you know, do stuff. . . . Okay, like bad Koreans, who like hang out at *nohlehbang* [Korean karaoke bar] all the time, you know, karaoke bars? Um, they waste mad money, they just hang around at whatever, they smoke, they drink, you know? That kind of thing, like, a lot. And like, then there are Koreans where maybe you hang out with those [bad] kids sometimes, and then maybe you don't. Maybe you have like a cigarette, like whenever.

These definitions were consistent among many of the respondents. "Good" Koreans do not cause trouble and do not get into trouble. "Bad" Koreans engage in more adult behaviors, such as smoking and going to karaoke bars. And then there are those teenagers who float in between.

The majority of the teenagers in the senior high group fall into this "in between" category. They attend church on Sunday, but also might go to a karaoke bar and smoke a cigarette on the previous Saturday night. They are the teenagers (N = 7) that I call the ethnically identified group. Their Korean American status has become increasingly important to them in their adolescent years and is evident in the high priority they place on having coethnic friendships, either within or outside of the KPC youth group. However, in contrast to the ethnic/religious group, the salience of a religious (Christian) identity is minimal. While the ethnic/religious group sees their religious and ethnic identities as overlapping in many respects, the ethnically identified group largely views religion and ethnicity as separate domains.

For the ethnically identified teenagers, weekly church attendance and a strong religious identification are very distinct concepts. While the ethnically identified teenager may come to church every Sunday just as the ethnic/religious teenager does, the ethnically identified teenager attributes primary, if not sole, importance to the social aspects of coming to KPC. For instance, Jason explains how the church is becoming more important to him:

Well, I used to hang out with only school people. . . . and I still do, I mean, I don't dislike them but . . . .(pauses) I don't think I'm any better than them but I just think that we're not on the same level. It's just different interactions. They have different hobbies. We just don't share the same interests. And I think I also just grew kinda closer to my church friends.

Jason attends a small private school where he is the only Korean American in his class. He describes himself as "lower middle class" and feels distant as he contrasts himself with his schoolmates, who "have a lot of money." But class-based differences with his white classmates do not entirely explain why he feels closer to his Korean American peers. When probed further, Jason, like Mary (an ethnic/religious teenager), mentions the importance of being with others who share a sense of "cultural knowing."

In contrast to the ethnic/religious teenagers, some of the ethnically identified teenagers attend KPC because their parents "make them." For example, Charlie describes how coming to church "just didn't mean anything to me" several months prior to our interview:

> A: Well like, a couple months ago I told my parents I didn't want to come any more [to KPC] and they just flipped out. They said, "You're basically going to church until you go to college and there's no question about it."
> Q: Well, did they give you any reasons why they wanted you to keep coming?
> A: Not really. They just said you have to go.
> Q: So then, what role does the church play in your life now?
> A: Nothing really. I mean, well, part of it's just to hang out after church and stuff with my friends. But, uh, I mean, I just come basically because my parents tell me to come, so . . .

Charlie is one of several ethnically identified teenagers who report struggling with forming a religious identity. The fact that kids like Charlie continue to attend KPC can be seen as a sign that they are compliant with their parents' wishes, at least to some extent. It also underscores the point that while religious motivations may be nonexistent for teenagers like Charlie, social relations with other Korean American teens at KPC take on greater importance.

The ethnically identified group of teenagers illustrates how one can have a strong ethnic identity without having a salient religious one. Jennifer attends a high school where there are Korean cliques and although she feels that these groups can be exclusive at times, she also feels that they constitute an important avenue for Korean Americans to get together. Jennifer views her coethnic friends as her "closest" peers, but unlike the ethnic/religious teenagers, some of these friends attend KPC and some do not. When I ask her opinion of the religious teachings at KPC, she reports, "most of the time I hear it, and then I usually forget about it."

The religious leaders at KPC are well aware that some teens place more of an emphasis on socializing in contrast to spiritual growth. For example, after delivering a Sunday sermon, Pastor George finds it necessary to publicly reprimand the teenagers who have tried to "ditch" Bible study. Even when the teenagers attend Sunday school class, there is often a great deal of interaction that does not involve religious instruction. This observation from the boys' Sunday school session illustrates how a Bible study lesson about Abraham becomes a battle over control:

> As Mr. Kim, the Sunday school teacher, starts to talk about the verses they have just read, one boy asks, "What time is it?"
> Then Charlie asks, "Can I get another drink?"
> "After Sunday school," says Mr. Kim. Then he says, "Come on, guys. I need your cooperation." Mr. Kim then asks them, "Okay guys, what is Abraham's occupation?" [In the Bible verses they have just read, Abraham is an owner of livestock.]

"Jeweler," says Charlie, and the rest of the class laughs.

Mr. Kim repeats the question, "Come on, you just read it, what is Abraham's occupation?"

"Carpenter?" asks Donald.

"He owned Microsoft," says John.

"He was a tax collector," Jason responds.

"A prostitute!" shouts John and the class breaks up in laughter again.

Apparently encouraged by the laughter, John goes on to say, "An exotic dancer."

At this point, Donald is laughing so hard that he puts his head down on the table and his body shakes as he laughs.

Whereas the ethnic/religious teenagers also ask questions during Friday night Bible studies, the question asking is mostly driven by curiosity. Frustration on the part of the teacher and free-flowing jokes and laughter on the part of the teenagers characterizes some of the interactions that I observed among the ethnically identified teenagers.

In the eyes of the ethnic/religious teenagers, the congregation members who come solely to socialize are viewed skeptically. As Tracy explains, "a lot of them just go for social reason. . . . I think that at least half of them can't be real Christians, because they go and they do things that are so un-Christianly. It makes me mad. It's like, 'What are you doing? Why did you come here?'" Coming to church for social reasons alone is not only disapproved of by the ethnic/religious teenagers, but in fact stands as a dividing marker between the two groups.

Neither Ethnic nor Religious Teenagers at KPC

There are other teenagers at KPC, whom I call the non–ethnic/religious group, who are uniquely different from the other two types of teenagers described above. While they consider themselves to be Korean American, these three teenagers do not have a strong attachment to KPC as either a religious or an ethnic institution. Unlike the other two types of teenagers, the non–ethnic/religious teenager reports having closest ties to non–Korean American, nonchurch friends. Their interactions with the other KPC teenagers, although friendly, are limited to the few hours that they spend together during Sunday service. For instance, Sal explains to me why he feels closer to his school friends (an ethnically diverse group) as opposed to his church acquaintances:

> Well, my school friends I see everyday. I belong to a certain clique and I'm like really good friends with them. I hang out with them all the time. This [church] is just once a week. I'm not as good friends with the church guys as I am with my school friends.

Sal goes on to explain that because his peer group is school based and racially/ethnically mixed, he stands in contrast to the other teenagers at KPC:

> There are some kids in the church that are really Korean. I would consider myself equal [Korean and American]. . . . Like, I actually don't go out of my way to hang out

with Korean people. There seems to be like a big Philly crowd of Koreans around here, and they like actually go out of their way to hang out with each other. I don't really.

If the non–ethnic/religious teenagers, like Sal, do not come for social or religious reasons, what motivates them to attend KPC? In fact, there is nothing in particular that attaches these teenagers to KPC other than the fact that they come because they have always come. Some of them never really contemplate why they come, and consequently, do not contest coming. For example, when I ask Sal why he attends KPC, he furrows his brow, pauses for a few seconds, and simply replies, "I don't know. I never really thought about it." The non–ethnic/religious teens express the same ambivalence when it comes to their religious identity. As June tells me, "I think if people asked me, I would be like, 'Oh, I grew up Christian. I like have a Bible and stuff. And my family religion is Christian, but I'm not like set in any one way.'"

Elaine, one of the non–ethnic/religious teenagers, states that she comes to church largely as a routine "family thing" and explains, "It's something you have to do on Sundays more so than, like, 'I *really* love God and I *really* need to dedicate some time to Him.'" However, when I ask her if she would continue to come if her parents did not, she replies,

> I mean, it's [coming to KPC] not like a duty or anything. But, uh . . . I'm not sure. If my parents were like, "Do whatever you want," I'm not sure if I would still go. I probably would go, but it's one of those hypotheticals, you know what I mean? You wouldn't really know unless it happened.

Elaine's uncertainty can partly be explained by her lack of religious commitment. However, as I argued earlier, the ethnically identified teenager also does not express a strong identity with Christianity. What makes the non–ethnic/religious teenagers different is that they do not see the social aspects of being with other Korean Americans as a highly salient reason for coming.

In fact, Elaine does not feel comfortable around large groups of Korean Americans, which makes coming to KPC "kinda weird" for her. Elaine is a unique case because, unlike any of the other teenagers I interviewed, "an American [read 'white'] nanny" raised her, while both of her parents were busy running their chain of dry-cleaning stores. Elaine feels fortunate to have had an "American" upbringing and says that as a result, she is more versed (in contrast to other Korean Americans) in "just like, etiquette and politeness and stuff like that." Another consequence of her upbringing is that Elaine feels less comfortable around some of the KPC kids, who have not been brought up in such "American" ways.

The other two non–ethnic/religious teenagers do not express a sense of discomfort around other coethnic teenagers. Rather, they explain that they do not want to limit themselves to having only Korean American friends. For instance, June explains,

> Like, the people I hang out with, um, like if you see me and you see the other Korean kids at school, they'll just hang out with mainly the other Korean kids. Whereas I'll just

hang out with whoever I want to and I've always felt that, really for me, I have more freedom. I don't have to dress like them, speak like them.

The non–ethnic/religious teenagers do not prioritize coethnic friendships, especially when it comes to belonging to a Korean clique. In fact, by not belonging to such groups, they feel that they have more freedom to establish friendships with non–Korean Americans, and are not constrained to act in certain "ethnic" ways.

The non–ethnic/religious teenagers, similar to the ethnically identified teens, see little connection between religion and ethnicity. It is not surprising, given their lack of attachment to Christianity, that there are times when the non–ethnic/religious teenagers seriously question the religious teachings and rhetoric. Elaine provides a good example of this during her interview:

> Okay, like last week the sermon was about not having fear about certain things because they're out of your control. . . . And then he [the pastor] was like, "Don't fear these things because God controls what happens, and he'll take care of you. You won't die until your mission is over." And I was like, "Nooo, I don't think so!" [Laughs.] I mean, people die all the time, and it's not within their control. And you know, it's not because their "mission is over." I mean, like sometimes kids die and you're gonna tell me their mission is over? I mean, I'm like, "I don't think so."

Instead of viewing the KPC pastor as an important authority on what being a Christian means (as the ethnic/religious teenager does), Elaine actively questions and does not accept the pastor's interpretation. Yet in contrast to the ethnically identified teenager, Elaine could *actually recall* what she had heard during the sermon (none of the ethnically identified teenagers seem to remember what pastors say in sermons). Instead of expressing her ambivalence in the form of joking or ditching religious classes, Elaine and the other non–ethnic/religious teenagers sit quietly in their seats and rarely speak during Bible study discussions. If and when they do have questions or even outright disagreements with the religious rhetoric, they do not openly express it. The non–ethnic/religious teenagers are almost imperceptible in their behaviors within the KPC setting. They are also part of the group that is most likely to be missed in studies that focus on second-generation adult congregations, as these teenagers are highly ambivalent about attending *any* church once they leave for college, let alone an ethnic church.

Conclusion

On any given Sunday at Korean Protestant Church, there are Korean American teenagers at the front of the sanctuary, singing contemporary Christian songs with their eyes closed, hands lifted, apparently in deep worship. These teenagers are part of the ethnic/religious group at KPC. And yet, on any given Sunday, without having to look very hard, one can see many other Korean American teenagers in the pews of KPC, some of them not singing at all or barely mouthing the words, and others shifting in and out of the sanctuary. Outside the church, there may be a group of teens playing basketball on the black-tar parking lot at KPC in their Sunday best. These are the adolescents who make up the ethnically identified group and the non–ethnic/religious group.

For the ethnic/religious teenagers, it is clear that the Korean American Christian church is their second home. It represents a place of comfort and belonging that is grounded in being part of an ethnic community that also shares the same religious faith. Yet I have also attempted to show that even for the ethnic/religious teenagers, the second-generation church is not just replicating or reproducing the values and traditions of their parents' culture. These teenagers are learning how to connect what is Korean, what is American, and what overlaps into an identity that is increasingly revolving around what is Christian (Chai 1998). For this reason, it would not be surprising if some of these teenagers end up attending a multiethnic/racial church in the future.

For the ethnically identified teenagers, if given the choice, some of them might not come to KPC if their parents did not "make" them, as long as they could see their friends at a karaoke bar or perhaps in school. But for many of them, KPC is a place where they can easily socialize with a group of other Korean American teenagers. Seen in this light, their participation in the religious institution does involve them in a co-ethnic peer network, but at the same time, may not tie them to a broader ethnic or religious community.

As long as the Korean church continues to provide a place where the ethnically identified teenagers can easily find a network of coethnic friendships, it will still be important to them once they leave their parents' home. Although experiences of racial discrimination or marginalization were not salient themes in the narratives of ethnic/ religious or ethnically identified teens, it is clear that the ethnic church represents one of the few places where second-generation youth can safely and easily identify with others who share a common ethnic heritage. However, once these teenagers enter college, they might find other organizations that can fulfill this social function, such as Korean Student Associations (KSAs) on campus. The Korean Christian church might find itself "competing for the second-generation" with other nonreligious ethnic organizations when it comes to the ethnically identified teenager (Chai 1998).

For the non–ethnic/religious teenagers, coming to KPC is nothing more than a two-hour family routine and holds little social significance. Similar to the ethnically identified teenagers, they also do not see a merging of their ethnic and religious identities. In fact, these teenagers may actively question and criticize the doctrines of the church. For this type of individual in particular, the extent to which the Korean Christian church attempts to "legitimize and sacralize" (Chong 1998) traditional ethnic values with Christian ideology may end up undermining the very thing it is trying to preserve—the ethnic/religious institution.

It is unclear whether the Korean Christian church will take on some degree of importance as the non–ethnic/religious teenagers grow older and start their own families. Both Chai (1998) and Chong (1998) have argued that experiences of marginality in larger society are driving forces for second-generation young adults to seek out and attend an ethnic/religious institution. As these adolescents transition to adulthood, their awareness of differences and discriminatory experiences based on their racial background may indeed be heightened during college or as they enter the labor force. Yet given their lack of attachment to coethnic peers and Christian tenets at this point in their lives, I remain skeptical as to whether they will choose the Korean American church as a vehicle to establish a sense of belonging in the future.

There are several limitations to the study that should be noted. Foremost, the typologies of ethnic and religious identities developed here are based on an exploratory study that draws from interviews with a small sample and ethnographic observations from one congregation. Thus, as with all smaller-scale studies, it is beyond the scope of the paper to say whether these typologies can be found among Korean American teenagers more generally, or to address how they compare to other second-generation ethnic populations. The findings from this study should be viewed within the context of a growing body of work that illustrates the nature of the ethnic and religious identity connection and diversity of experiences found among children of post-1965 immigrants. Further comparative exploration, both across and within second-generation populations, of what these typologies look like during adolescence, how they develop, and how they change over the life course is needed.

Finally, for all of the teenagers at KPC, the story of how they define their ethnicity, their religion, and the salience that these identities hold for them is only just beginning. What this paper has provided is one snapshot of the identity formation and experiences of a group of second-generation adolescents in an ethnic/religious institution. The picture conveyed here cannot delineate the processes by which the teenagers came to differ in the degree of salience they held towards their ethnic and religious identities. Yet this snapshot has described how the role of religion in the formation of ethnic identity, especially for teenagers, can range from minimal to highly salient. Identity formation is a lifelong process, and we need further research to understand how experiences at this crucial stage of adolescence influence identity and adaptation throughout the life course.

NOTES

1. All names have been changed to protect the anonymity of the respondents.

2. By "young adults," these studies often refer to people who are college students or older, such as graduate students and working professionals in their twenties and early thirties.

3. The fieldwork for this study was conducted between September 1999 and April 2000, during which time I became a participant observer at KPC, studying the weekly interactions and religious rhetoric within the church setting and conducting informal interviews with key congregation members. Starting in January 2000, I conducted more formal, in-depth, semistructured interviews with fifteen congregation teenagers who were in their senior year in high school. These interviews were audio recorded with the respondents' and the respondents' parents' consent and lasted about one and a half hours on average. Of the senior high school students I targeted, two could not be reached for an interview and one adolescent declined to be interviewed.

4. In accordance with Zhou and Bankston (1998), I include children who are not U.S.-born but came before the age of five as part of the "second generation."

5. It is important to note that I did not find notable gender differences in terms of what made a teenager more or less likely to be in one typology versus another. See Alumkal (1999), who addresses the role of Protestant Christianity in reinforcing Korean patriarchal ideals among second-generation Korean American women.

REFERENCES

Alumkal, A. W. 1999. Preserving Patriarchy: Assimilation, Gender Norms, and Second-Generation Korean American Evangelicals. *Qualitative Sociology* 22: 127–40.

Bankston, C. L., III and M. Zhou. 1996. The Ethnic Church, Ethnic Identification, and the Social Adjustment of Vietnamese Adolescents. *Review of Religious Research* 38: 18–37.

Cha, P. 2001. Ethnic Identity Formation and Participation in Immigrant Churches: Second-Generation Korean-American Experiences. In *Korean Americans and Their Religions: Pilgrims and Missionaries from a Different Shore* (pp. 141–56). Edited by H. Y. Kwon, K. C. Kim, and R. S. Warner. University Park: Pennsylvania State University Press.

Chai, K. J. 1998. "Competing for the Second-Generation: English-Language Ministry at a Korean Protestant Church." In *Gatherings in Diaspora: Religious Communities and the New Immigration* (pp. 295–331). Edited by R. S. Warner and J. G. Wittner. Philadelphia: Temple University Press.

Chong, K. H. 1998. What It Means to Be Christian: The Role of Religion in the Construction of Ethnic Identity and Boundary among Second-Generation Korean-Americans. *Sociology of Religion* 59: 259–86.

Erikson, E. H. 1959. *Identity and the Life Cycle.* New York: International Universities Press.

Gordon, M. M. 1964. *Assimilation in American Life: The Role of Race, Religion, and National Origins.* New York: Oxford University Press.

Greeley, A. M. 1972. *The Denominational Society: A Sociological Approach to Religion in America.* Glenview, IL: Scott, Foresman.

Herberg, W. 1955. *Protestant-Catholic-Jew: An Essay in American Religious Sociology.* New York: Doubleday.

Kim, K. C. and W. M. Hurh. 1990. Religious Participation of Korean Immigrants in the United States. *Journal for the Scientific Study of Religion* 29: 19–34.

Kurien, P. 1998. Becoming American by Becoming Hindu: Indian Americans Take Their Place at the Multicultural Table. In *Gatherings in Diaspora: Religious Communities and the New Immigration* (pp. 37–70). Edited by R. S. Warner and J. G. Wittner. Philadelphia: Temple University Press.

Min, P. G. 1992.The Structure and Social Functions of the Korean Immigrant Churches in the U.S. *International Migration Review* 26: 1370–94.

Nagel, J. 1994. Constructing Ethnicity: Creating and Recreating Ethnic Identity and Culture. *Social Problems* 41: 152–76.

Portes, A. and M. Zhou. 1993. The New Second Generation: Segmented Assimilation. *The Annals of the American Academy of Political and Social Sciences* 530: 74–96.

Rumbaut, R. G. 1994. The Crucible Within: Ethnic Identity, Self-esteem, and Segmented Assimilation among Children of Immigrants. *International Migration Review* 28: 748–94.

Warner, R. S. 2001. The Korean Immigrant Church as Case and Model. In *Korean Americans and Their Religions: Pilgrims and Missionaries from a Different Shore* (pp. 25–52). Edited by H. Y. Kwon, K. C. Kim, and R. S. Warner. University Park: Pennsylvania State University Press.

Williams, R. B. 1988. *Religions of Immigrants from India and Pakistan: New Threads in the American Tapestry.* New York: Cambridge University Press.

Zhou, M. and C. L. Bankston, III. 1998. *Growing Up American: How Vietnamese Children Adapt to Life in the United States.* New York: Russell Sage Foundation.

1. Kim argues that a discussion of civil rights in the United States naturally invokes a discussion of race as a relationship between whites and blacks. What—according to Kim—are some of the limitations of this model? Why does she urge us to retain it as a mode of analysis? On the basis of Kim's analysis, how would you answer the question "Are Asians Black?" How else might one describe the identities of Asian Americans? In what ways do the experiences of Asian Americans complicate our understanding of civil liberties in the twenty-first century?

2. In discussing the implications of the model-minority hypothesis, Min Zhou writes, "The model-minority image implicitly casts Asian Americans as different from whites. By placing Asian Americans above whites, the model minority image also sets them apart from other Americans, white or nonwhite, in the public mind." Explain what she means and cite evidence from the article to support/refute this idea. When Min Zhou asks the question, "Are Asian Americans Becoming White?" what exactly is she suggesting and why? What criteria does American society use to assess whiteness and judge Asian Americans and members of racial minority groups? Based upon your reading of Kim's article, how might Kim respond to this question? How does Asian America look if the privileges of whiteness are projected upon Asian Americans?

3. Min Zhou notes that many Americans of Asian ancestry are ambivalent about the term "Asian American," preferring instead to identify themselves (typically) by their parents' country of origin. Why do you think they identify themselves in this manner? What effect do class background, education, and immigrant status have on this phenomenon? Under what circumstances do members of Asian-origin groups (Korean American, Filipino American, etc.) embrace a pan–Asian American identity? Under what circumstances do Asian Americans build coalitions with other ethnic and racial groups (including whites)?

4. Discuss the three "types" of Korean American teenagers described by Lee in her study of the KPC church in Philadelphia. How are the three basic typologies similar and how are they different? Thinking of the ethnic/religious typologies, there is another possible type or group of adolescents that might exist that the author does not describe or discuss. What might this be? Why do you think Lee does not describe this group/type? (Hint: think of the study design and sample.) What—if any—are the limitations of Lee's models?

5. What common ground do Korean American adolescents share in their understanding of ethnic identity? What purpose(s) do ethnic/religious institutions play in the lives of second-generation immigrants? What are the benefits of examining religious and ethnic identity formation among adolescents (as opposed to focusing on young adults or older cohorts)? What are the limitations? What other organizations provide comparable experiences for Asian American youth?

6. On the basis of Lee's findings at KPC, what lessons can be drawn about the significance of religious organizations to the social, cultural, and spiritual development of

the second generation? Do you think these experiences are typical of other Asian American groups? How might differences in region (i.e., Los Angeles or New York versus Philadelphia), class, ethnicity, and religious affiliation (Catholic, Buddhist, Hindu, etc.) inform the process of identity formation?

SUGGESTED READINGS

Carnes, Tony and Fenggang Yang (eds.). 2004. *Asian American Religions: The Making and Remaking of Borders and Boundaries.* New York: New York University Press.

Bonus, Rick. 2000. *Locating Filipino Americans: Ethnicity and the Cultural Politics of Space.* Philadelphia: Temple University Press.

Dhingra, Pawan H. 2003. Being American between Black and White: Second-Generation Asian American Professionals' Racial Identities. *Journal of Asian American Studies* 6(2): 117–47.

Espiritu, Yen Le. 1993. *Asian American Panethnicity: Bridging Institutions and Identities.* Philadelphia: Temple University Press.

Jeung, Russell. 2005. *Faithful Generations: Race and New Asian American Churches.* New Brunswick, NJ: Rutgers University Press.

Kibria, Nazli. 2002. *Becoming Asian American: Second-Generation Chinese and Korean American Identities.* Baltimore, MD: Johns Hopkins University Press.

Kim, Rebecca Y. 2006. *God's New Whiz Kids? Second-Generation Korean American Evangelicals on Campus.* New York: New York University Press.

Kurien, P. 2001. Constructing "Indianness" in Southern California: The Role of Hindu and Muslim Indian Immigrants. Pp. 289–312 in Marta Lopez-Garza and David R. Diaz (eds.), *Asian and Latino Immigrants in a Restructuring Economy.* Stanford, CA: Stanford University Press.

Lien, Pei-te, M. Margaret Conway, and Janelle Wong. 2003. The Contours and Sources of Ethnic Identity Choices among Asian Americans. *Social Science Quarterly* 84(2): 461–81.

Liu, Eric. 1998. *The Accidental Asian: Notes of a Native Speaker.* New York: Vintage.

Louie, Andrea. 2004. *Chineseness across Borders: Renegotiating Chinese Identities in China and the United States.* Durham, NC: Duke University Press.

Okamoto, Dina G. 2003. Toward a Theory of Panethnicity: Explaining Asian American Collective Action. *American Sociological Review* 68(6): 811–42.

Park, Kyeyoung. 1999. "I Really Do Feel I'm 1.5!" The Construction of Self and Community by Young Korean Americans. *Amerasia Journal* 25(1): 139–64.

Shah, Soniah (ed.). 1997. *Dragon Ladies: Asian American Feminists Breathe Fire.* Boston: South End Press.

Shankar, L. D. and P. R. Balgopal. 2001. South Asian Immigrants before 1950: The Formation of Ethnic, Symbolic, and Group Identity. *Amerasia Journal* 27(1): 55–84.

Takahashi, J. 1998. *Nisei/Sansei: Shifting Japanese American Identities and Politics.* Philadelphia: Temple University Press.

Tamura, Eileen. 1994. *Americanization, Acculturation, and Ethnic Identity: The Nisei Generation in Hawaii.* Urbana: University of Illinois Press.

Takezawa, Y. 1991. Children of Inmates: The Effects of the Redress Movement among Third-Generation Japanese Americans. *Qualitative Sociology* 14(1): 39–56.

Tsai, J. L., Y. Ying, and P. A. Lee. 2000. The Meaning of "Being Chinese" and "Being American": Variation among Chinese American Young Adults. *Journal of Cross-Cultural Psychology* 31(3): 302–32.

Wong, K. Scott and Sucheng Chan (eds.). 1998. *Claiming America: Constructing Chinese American Identities during the Exclusion Era.* Philadelphia: Temple University Press.

Yang, Fenggang. 1999. *Chinese Christians in America: Conversion, Assimilation, and Adhesive Identities.* University Park: Pennsylvania State University Press.

Zhou, Min and Jennifer Lee. 2004. The Making of Culture, Identity, and Ethnicity among Asian American Youth. Pp. 1–30 in Jennifer Lee and Min Zhou (eds.), *Asian American Youth: Culture, Identity, and Ethnicity.* New York: Routledge.

Zhou, Min and Yang Sao Xiong. 2005. The Multifaceted American Experiences of the Children of Asian Immigrants: Lessons for Segmented Assimilation. *Ethnic and Racial Studies* 28(6): 1119–52.

FILMS

Chien, Windy (producer/director). 1992. *Assimilation/A Simulation* (14-minute experimental).

Grimberg, Sharon and Daniel Friedman (producers/directors). 1997. *Miss India Georgia* (56-minute documentary).

Nakamura, Robert A. (director). 1995. *Something Strong Within* (40-minute documentary).

Ning, Stephen C. (director). 1983. *Freckled Rice* (48-minute documentary).

Riggs, Marlon (director). 1974. *Ethnic Notions* (56-minute documentary).

Soe, Valerie (director). 1986. *All Orientals Look the Same* (2-minute experimental).

Soe, Valerie (director). 1990. *Black Sheep* (6-minute documentary).

Vu, Trac Minh (producer/director). 1997. *Letters to Thien* (57-minute documentary).

Wang, Wayne (director). 1988. *Dim Sum Take Out* (12-minute drama).

Part VII

The Complexity of Ethnicity

Intermarriage and Multiracial Identification

The Asian American Experience and Implications for Changing Color Lines

Jennifer Lee and Frank D. Bean

The 2000 U.S. Census was the first census that allowed Americans to select "one or more races" to indicate their racial identification, reflecting the view that race is no longer conceived of as a bounded category. In 2000, 6.8 million people, or 2.4 percent of the U.S. population (i.e., one in every forty Americans), identified themselves as multiracial. Although one in forty may not appear to be a substantial fraction, by the year 2050, this ratio could soar to one in five (Farley 2001). Asian Americans, however, have a much higher rate of multiracial identification compared to other groups, with 12.4 percent claiming a multiracial background, a figure that is rapidly rising. By the year 2050, sociologists project that 35 percent of Asian Americans could claim a multiracial background (Smith and Edmonston 1997). If this projection proves accurate, more than one in every three Asian Americans would claim a multiracial background in just a few decades. This level of substantial growth in the Asian multiracial population would mostly result from today's high rates of Asian intermarriage, which at present involve more than one out of every four Asians, and more than two out of every five third-and-higher generation Asians, being married to someone of a different race, most commonly someone white.

Coinciding with the rise in intermarriage has been the growth of a new immigrant stream from Latin America and Asia (Zhou 2004). Today, immigrants and their children total more than sixty million persons and account for approximately 22 percent of the U.S. population. The increase in immigration from non-European countries over the past three and half decades has converted the United States from a largely white and black society into one that is composed of several racial and ethnic groups (Bean and Stevens 2003; Waldinger and Lee 2001). Trends in intermarriage and immigration over the past thirty-five years, along with the landmark change in the census allowing Americans to report themselves as belonging to more than one racial group, reflect a significant weakening of the previously strong boundaries among racial groups (Lee and Bean 2003). Combining data from the U.S. Census and Current Population Surveys, we examine the patterns of intermarriage, multiracial identification, and immigration and explore the implications of these findings for the future of Asian American identities and America's changing color lines.

The Rise of Interracial Marriage

The growth of the multiracial population is a result of both the rise in intermarriage between whites and nonwhites and of people's increased willingness to report their multiracial backgrounds. Intermarriage between whites and nonwhites has risen dramatically since the 1967 Supreme Court ruling of *Loving v. Commonwealth of Virginia,* which overturned state laws prohibiting interracial marriage and sex. As recently as 1967, interracial marriage was illegal in sixteen states, but today about 13 percent of American marriages involve partners of different races. Within a thirty-year period alone, between 1960 and 1990, the rate of intermarriage between whites and nonwhites increased tenfold, from 150,000 in 1960 to 1.6 million in 1990 (Jacoby 2001; Waters 1999). If we go back even further to 1880, the rates of intermarriage among Asians and Latinos in this country were close to zero, but now, more than a quarter of all Asians and Latinos marry someone of a different racial background, mostly whites. These intermarriage rates are even higher among younger, native-born Asians and Latinos, and are likely to increase in future generations.

The change in intermarriage rates is significant because sociologists conceive of intermarriage between whites and nonwhites as a measure of decreasing social distance between groups, declining racial prejudice, and changing racial boundaries (Davis 1941; Gilbertson et al. 1996; Gordon 1964; Kalmijn 1993; Lee and Fernandez 1998; Lieberson and Waters 1988; Merton 1941). Hence, a rise in intermarriage between groups indicates a decrease in social distance between those groups, a decline in racial prejudice, and a thawing of racial boundaries. Moreover, the differences in the intermarriage rates between whites and various nonwhite groups provide some indication of the groups' social proximity to whites. In addition, these differences provide a measure of where the white-nonwhite boundary is breaking down most rapidly.

As table 18.1 shows, more than one-quarter of all married Asians and Latinos—27.2 and 28.4 percent, respectively—have a partner of different racial background.[1] An even more striking finding is that two-thirds of young, native-born Asians and two-fifths of young, native-born Latinos marry someone of a different race, and the majority of them marry whites (Qian 1997). The rate of intermarriage among Asians and Latinos is yet more remarkable when we compare them to the intermarriage rate of blacks; only 10 percent of married blacks have a spouse of a different race. Hence, al-

TABLE 18.1
Rates of Exogamy among Marriages Containing at Least One Member of the Racial/Ethnic Group

	White		Black		Asian		Latino		Other	
	Rate (%)	N	Rate (%)	N	Rate (%)	N	Rate (%)	N	Rate (%)	N
Total Marriages	100.0	155,534	100.0	11,593	100.0	7,313	100.0	28,993	100.0	2,342
Same Race	94.2	143,596	89.8	10,190	72.8	5,152	71.6	20,180	25.8	761
Intermarried	5.8	11,938	10.2	1,403	27.2	2,161	28.4	8,813	74.2	1,581
White	—	—	69.1	848	86.8	1,788	90.0	7,949	88.4	1,353
Black	11.0	848	—	—	4.8	85	5.3	432	3.2	38
Asian	20.7	1,788	7.2	85	—	—	3.0	265	1.3	23
Hispanic	55.2	7,949	20.7	432	7.6	265	—	—	7.2	167
Other	13.1	1,353	3.0	38	0.8	23	1.7	167	—	—

SOURCE: Combined U.S. March Current Population Surveys, 1995–2001.

though more than one out of every four married Asians and Latinos has a partner of a different racial background, the comparable figure for blacks is only one in ten.

Not only is intermarriage more common among Asians and Latinos than among blacks, but the rate at which Asians intermarry with whites is also much higher. As table 18.1 shows, among intermarried Asians, 86.8 percent marry whites, 7.6 percent marry Hispanics, and 4.8 percent marry blacks. Among intermarried Latinos, 90.0 percent marry whites, 5.3 percent blacks, and 3.0 percent Asians. Intermarried blacks are also more likely to marry whites, at 69.1 percent, but this figure is far lower than the figures for intermarried Asians and Latinos. Nearly one-fifth of intermarried blacks, or 20.7 percent, marry Hispanics, and 7.2 percent marry Asians. Hence, both Asians and Latinos are considerably more likely to marry whites than are blacks.

The Multiracial Movement

The rise in interracial marriage over the past few decades has resulted in the growth of the multiracial population in the United States. This population became highly visible especially when, for the first time in the nation's history, the 2000 Census allowed Americans to select "one or more races" to indicate their racial identification. The way the U.S. Census measures racial identification, brought about by a small but highly influential multiracial movement, provides a new reflection of changing racial boundaries (DaCosta 2000; Farley 2001; Hirschman et al. 2000; Waters 2000; Williams 2001).

The multiracial movement was composed most prominently of advocates from groups such as the Association for Multiethnic Americans (AMEA) and Project Race (Reclassify All Children Equally). In 1993, these groups criticized the standards of the Office of Management and Budget's (OMB) Statistical Policy Directive Number 15, which asks individuals to mark their "race" on the census. Advocates argued that it was an affront to force them and/or their children into a monoracial category. They elaborated that forced monoracial identification is not only inaccurate because it denies the existence of interracial marriages but also ultimately discriminatory.

A year later, in 1994, the OMB declared that racial categories in Statistical Policy Directive Number 15 were of decreasing value and so the agency considered an alternate strategy—the option to identify with as many races as respondents wished. Hence, the racial options on the 2000 Census included "White," "Black," "Asian," "Native Hawaiian or Other Pacific Islander," "American Indian and Alaska Native," and "Other." While "Latino" or "Hispanic" was not a racial category on the 2000 Census, OMB's directive mandated two distinct questions regarding a person's racial/ethnic background: one about race and a second about whether a person is "Spanish/Hispanic/Latino." Since someone who self-designates as "Spanish/Hispanic/Latino" can be of any race, the Census asks both questions in order to identify the Latino population in the United States.

Although the spokespeople for the multiracial movement wanted a separate "multiracial" category and were not entirely satisfied with this option, they conceded that it was an improvement over forced monoracial identification. On October 30, 1997, the U.S. Census Bureau announced its final decision that, starting with the 2000 Census and extending to all federal data systems by the year 2003, all persons would have the option to identify with two or more races.

America's Multiracial Population

As noted above, 2.4 percent of the U.S. population identified itself as multiracial in 2000. Although this figure may not appear large, a recent National Academy of Science study noted that, because of high levels of intermarriage, the multiracial population could rise to 21 percent by the year 2050, with as many as 35 percent of Asians and 45 percent of Hispanics possibly claiming a multiracial background (Smith and Edmonston 1997). Moreover, the multiracial population is young and twice as likely as other groups to be under the age of eighteen, demonstrating that the multiracial population is likely to continue to grow in future years. Of the multiracial population, 93 percent reported exactly two races, 6 percent reported three races, and only 1 percent reported four or more races.

Although most individuals who reported a multiracial identification reported only two races, multiracially identified individuals are not evenly distributed across all racial groups. As table 18.2 illustrates, the groups with a high percentage of multiracial persons as a percentage of the total group include "Native Hawaiian or Other Pacific Islander (45 percent)," "American Indian and Alaska Native (36 percent)," "Other (16 percent)," and "Asian (12 percent)." The groups with the lowest proportion of persons who claim a multiracial background are "Whites" and "Blacks." However, because whites account for 77 percent of the total U.S. population, most individuals who report a multiracial identity also claim a white background. More specifically, the 5.1 million whites who claim a multiracial background account for only 2.3 percent of the total white population. As with whites, the proportion of blacks who claim a multiracial background is also quite small, accounting for only 4.2 percent of the total black population.

These figures stand in sharp contrast to those among American Indian/Alaska Natives and Native Hawaiian or Other Pacific Islanders, who have the highest percentage of multiracials as a proportion of their populations, at 36.4 and 44.8 percent, respectively. Asians and Latinos are in between with significantly higher rates of multiracial reporting than blacks and whites at 12.4 and 16.4 percent, respectively. In sum, when we compare Asians and Latinos to whites and blacks, we see that Asians have much higher rates of multiracial reporting as a total percentage of their populations compared to Latinos.

If we examine the rates of black-white, Asian-white, and Latino-white multiracial combinations as a percentage of the total black, Asian, and Latino populations, we find these figures equal 1.9, 7.0, and 4.6 percent, respectively. That is, among Asians, the Asian-white multiracial combination is about *three-and-a-half times* more likely to occur, and among Latinos, the Latino-white combination is *more than two-and-a-half times* more likely to occur as the black-white combination among blacks. Why black-white multiracials are far less likely to identify multiracially compared to their Asian-

TABLE 18.2
Multiracial Identification by Census Racial Categories

	Racial Identification* (millions)	Multiracial Identification** (millions)	Percent Multiracial
White	216.5	5.1	2.3
Black	36.2	1.5	4.2
Asian	11.7	1.4	12.4
Other	18.4	3.0	16.4
American Indian and Alaska Native	3.9	1.4	36.4
Native Hawaiian or Other Pacific Islander	0.7	0.3	44.8

SOURCE: U.S. Census 2000.
* Racial/ethnic group totals do not sum to the total U.S. population because multiracial persons are counted here in more than one group.
** Multiracial persons are counted for each race category mentioned.

white and Latino-white counterparts is especially puzzling when we consider that the U.S. Census Bureau estimates that at least three-quarters of the black population in the United States is ancestrally multiracial (Spencer 1997). In other words, while at least 75 percent of black Americans have some white ancestry and thus could claim a multiracial identity on this basis, just over 4 percent choose to do so.

The tendency of black Americans not to report multiracial identifications undoubtedly derives from the legacy of slavery, including lasting discrimination and the legal and de facto invocation of the "one-drop rule" of hypodescent, by which all persons with any trace of black ancestry were labeled racially black. As Davis (1991) argues, the one-drop rule was once used to justify slavery and was later used to support Jim Crow segregation. The one-drop rule applies to no other country and for no other racial or ethnic group, thereby limiting the identity choices and options for multiracial blacks. By stark contrast, the one-drop rule has not been similarly imposed on Asians, Latinos, or American Indians. For example, recent sociological studies reveal that about 50 percent of American Indian/white and Asian/white intermarried couples report a white racial identity for their children (Eschbach 1995; Saenz et al. 1995; Xie and Goyette 1997). In a study of multiracial Hispanic students, the authors find that only 44 percent choose a Hispanic identity (Stephan and Stephan 1989). Hence, unlike the traditional "one-drop rule" that has historically imposed a black racial identity on black Americans, multiracial Asians, Latinos, and American Indians appear to have much more leeway to choose among different racial options, including multiracial and white identities. Historically, multiracial blacks were denied similar options, a constraint that seems to have lasting consequences, even today.

In addition, because a significant proportion of Latinos and Asians in the United States are either immigrants or the children of immigrants, their understanding of race, racial boundaries, and the black-white color divide is shaped by a different set of circumstances than those of African Americans. Most importantly, what sets Latinos and Asians apart from African Americans is that the experiences of the Latinos are not rooted in the same historical legacy of slavery with its systematic and persistent patterns of legal and institutional discrimination and inequality by which the tenacious black-white divide was born and cemented. The unique history and experience of black Americans in this country make the black-white racial gap qualitatively and quantitatively different from the Latino-white or Asian-white racial divides. For these reasons, racial/ethnic boundaries appear more fluid for the newest immigrants than for native-born blacks, providing multiracial Asians and Latinos more racial options than their multiracial black counterparts.

We also need to consider that race is a social and cultural construction rather than a biological category, which means that race is not primordial, rooted in biology, or fixed. Social scientists have even documented the processes by which racial categories have undergone reconceptualization throughout our nation's history (Gans 1999; Gerstle 1999; Omi and Winant 1994; Waters 1990, 1999). For instance, when the Irish, Italians, and Jews first arrived in the United States in the nineteenth century, they were considered racially distinct from and inferior to Anglo-Americans. In essence, they were *not* considered white. However, they successfully achieved whiteness by deliberately and forcefully distinguishing themselves from African Americans (Alba 1985, 1990; Brodkin 1998; Foner 2000; Ignatiev 1995; Roediger 1991). Today, few would contest the claim that Irish, Italians, and Jews are white.

Race and racial boundaries have changed for other groups as well, including Asians. For example, the Chinese in Mississippi changed their racial status from almost black to almost white. Loewen (1988) details how the Mississippi Chinese achieved near-white status by attaining economic parity with whites, emulating their cultural and social practices, and distancing themselves from African Americans and the Chinese who married blacks. The change in racial classification among ethnic groups from nonwhite to white or almost white illustrates that race is a social rather than biological category that has expanded over time to incorporate new immigrant groups. As the historian Gary Gerstle (1999, 289) explains, whiteness as a category "has survived by stretching its boundaries to include Americans—the Irish, eastern and southern Europeans—who had been deemed nonwhite. Contemporary evidence suggests that the boundaries are again being stretched as Latinos and Asians pursue whiteness much as the Irish, Italians, and Poles did before them."

Given the change in racial boundaries over time, it is likely that the boundaries may stretch once again to include newer groups. For instance, some sociologists argue that Asians are the next in line to become white, and whether this hypothesis is correct will depend on a number of factors such as their rate of intermarriage, multiracial identification, continued immigration from Asia, and economic and political incorporation. Considering that 40 percent of third-generation Asians intermarry today and that the children of these unions have the option to identify as "white," Asians may indeed be on the path to whiteness. That many Asian ethnic groups have median household incomes above the national average also bodes favorably for this alternative. However, continued immigration from Asia and the racial stereotypes Asians face as "forever foreign" ensure that this process will be neither inevitable nor smooth. Moreover, "Asian" is a vastly heterogeneous category that masks differences in ethnicity and social and economic status (Zhou 2004). Hence, whether Asians—or at least some Asian ethnic groups—are the next in line to become white still remains to be seen.

The Geography of the Multiracial Identities

Although differences in multiracial reporting across racial groups are readily apparent, it is also noteworthy that rates of multiracial identification are not uniform across the country. For instance, 40 percent of all those who report a multiracial identification reside in the West, a region of the country that has demonstrated substantially more tolerance for racial/ethnic diversity than other parts of the country (Baldassare 2000; Godfrey 1988). As table 18.3 indicates, California leads as the state with the highest number of multiracial persons and is the only state with a multiracial population that exceeds one million. The multiracial population accounts for 4.7 percent of California's population, or one in every twenty-one Californians, about twice the national average. As with the nation as a whole, the multiracial population in California is young. As of 2000, 7.3 percent of Californians under the age of eighteen were identified as multiracial. California's multiracial population appears to be growing rapidly, although we now have only indirect evidence of this growth. To help put this change into perspective, we note that the number of multiracial children born each year in California already exceeds the number of black children born.

Like California, other states with high immigrant populations, and consequently high levels of racial/ethnic diversity, evince larger multiracial populations. In fact, 64 percent, or nearly two-thirds of those who are multiracially identified, reside in just ten states—California, New York, Texas, Florida, Hawaii, Illinois, New Jersey, Washington, Michigan, and Ohio—all of which have relatively high immigrant populations. In essence, states that have higher levels of diversity (as reflected in the percentage of the

TABLE 18.3
State Summaries: Most and Least Multiracial States

Rank	State	Number of Multiracial Persons	Multiracial Population (percent)
1	Hawaii	259,343	21.4
2	Alaska	34,146	5.4
3	California	1,607,646	4.7
4	Oklahoma	155,985	4.5
5	Nevada	76,428	3.8
6	New Mexico	66,327	3.6
7	Washington	213,519	3.6
8	New York	590,182	3.1
9	Oregon	104,745	3.1
10	Arizona	146,526	2.9
.			
.			
.			
42	Tennessee	63,109	1.1
43	Iowa	31,778	1.1
44	Louisiana	48,265	1.1
45	New Hampshire	13,214	1.1
46	Kentucky	42,443	1.1
47	South Carolina	39,950	1.0
48	Alabama	44,179	1.0
49	Maine	12,647	1.0
50	West Virginia	15,788	0.9
51	Mississippi	20,021	0.7

SOURCE: U.S. Census 2000.

population that is *not* non-Hispanic white or non-Hispanic black) boast much larger multiracial populations than states that are less racially diverse.

On the opposite end of the diversity spectrum are states like West Virginia and Maine that have low racial minority populations and thereby exhibit very low levels of multiracial reporting. States such as Mississippi, Alabama, South Carolina, and Louisiana, however, have relatively large black populations and yet evince low levels of multiracial reporting. In these southern states, the traditional dividing line between blacks and whites and the historically constraining "one-drop rule" of hypodescent appear to hinder multiracial identification, leading persons to identify monoracially as either white or black rather than adopting a multiracial identity (Davis 1991; Farley 2001).

The geography of multiracial reporting clearly indicates that the rate of multiracial reporting varies widely across the country, with the highest levels in states that exhibit the greatest racial/ethnic diversity brought about by the arrival of new immigrants to these areas. Hence, although national patterns in interracial marriage and multiracial identification indicate a loosening of racial boundaries, particularly for Asians and Latinos, these shifts appear to be taking place more rapidly in certain parts of the country. Areas of the country that have lower levels of immigration and consequently less racial/ethnic diversity demonstrate the tenacity of the black-white divide. Hence, although some parts of the country like the West may exhibit the softening of racial boundaries, especially between blacks and nonblacks, other areas such as the South prove that the traditional black-white color line endures.

The Emergence of a Black/Nonblack Divide

The Census Bureau's decision to allow Americans to "mark one or more races" to identify themselves is a landmark change in the way the U.S. government collects data on race, reflecting the growth of intermarriages and multiracial births. Perhaps even more importantly, it gives official status and recognition to persons who see their backgrounds as having involved racial mixing—an acknowledgment that speaks volumes about how far the country has come since the days when the one-drop rule enjoyed legal legitimacy. Moreover, such changes may mean that old racial divides are beginning to fade and race may no longer be conceived as rigidly as it was in the past.

What do current trends and patterns in immigration, intermarriage, and multiracial identification tell us about the changing nature of race and racial divides? It appears that increases in intermarriage and the growth of the multiracial population reflect a blending of races and the shifting of color lines. Because interracial marriage and multiracial identification indicate a reduction in social distance and racial prejudice, these phenomena provide evidence of loosening racial boundaries. At first glance, these patterns offer an optimistic portrait, especially considering that interracial marriage was illegal in sixteen states as recently as 1967, and today, about 13 percent of American marriages involve persons from different racial backgrounds. Judging from the past, it appears that as a nation, we have come a long way.

Upon closer examination, however, we find that patterns of intermarriage and multiracial identification are not equally distributed across all racial/ethnic groups. Not only are Latinos and Asians more likely to intermarry than blacks, but they are also more likely to report a multiracial identification. In other words, of the three groups, blacks are the least likely to intermarry and the least likely to claim a multiracial identification. The different rates of Asian, Latino, and black intermarriage and multiracial reporting suggest that while racial boundaries may be fading, they are not eroding at the same pace for all groups.

The crucial consideration here is how we interpret the intermarriage and multiracial identification findings for Asians and Latinos. If we consider Asians and Latinos as racialized minorities (that is, as persons whose race or ethnicity constitutes a basis for substantial discrimination), and thus as persons falling closer to blacks than whites along some scale of social disadvantage, the high levels of multiracial identification in these groups suggest that racial prejudice and boundaries might be fading for all non-white groups. In other words, if these groups are disadvantaged because of their race or ethnicity, but conditions appear to be improving for them, then this suggests the optimistic conclusion that conditions might be improving for all nonwhite groups. If, on the other hand, we consider Asians and Latinos as new immigrant groups whose disadvantage derives from their not yet having had time to join the economic mainstream, but who soon will, then their high levels of intermarriage and multiracial reporting signal that their experience may be different from that of blacks. Furthermore, it suggests that their situations do not necessarily mean that similar improvements can be expected among blacks.

This distinction is critical because it helps us to differentiate whether America's color lines are shifting for all racial/ethnic minorities, or whether they are fading mostly in the cases of nonblack immigrant groups. According to the patterns of inter-marriage and multiracial identification we have described, the color line appears to be less rigid for Asians and Latinos than for blacks. In their cases, Asians and Latinos have high rates of intermarriage and multiracial reporting because they have not been treated like blacks to begin with and because the weakening of racial boundaries that has occurred has not been as fully extended to blacks. Although the color line may be shifting for blacks, this change is occurring more slowly, consequently leaving Asians and Latinos closer to whites than to blacks. As a result, we may be witnessing the emergence of a black-nonblack divide that places Latinos and Asians closer to whites than to blacks. Much of America's racial history to date has revolved around who was white and who was not; the next phase may revolve around the issue of who is black and who is not.

The emergence of a black-nonblack divide in a context where diversity is increasing and racial/ethnic boundaries are diminishing represents a good news-bad news outcome for America. That a white-nonwhite color line does not seem to be emerging is the good news. But that newer nonwhite immigrant groups appear to be jumping ahead of African Americans in a hierarchy divided by race is the bad news. Immigration, intermarriage, and multiracial identification indicate that Asians and Latinos are closer to whites than to blacks and consequently may be participants in a new color line that continues to separate blacks from other groups. Thus, America's new color line may consist of a racial/ethnic divide that places many blacks in disadvantaged positions relatively similar to those perpetuated by the traditional black-white divide.

Conclusion

Over the past few decades, the rate of interracial marriage between whites and non-whites increased tenfold, and its increase went hand in hand with the growth in the multiracial population. Recognizing the growth of America's multiracial population, the 2000 U.S. Census allowed Americans the option to mark more than one race to identify themselves and their children. Coinciding with rising intermarriage between whites and nonwhites over the past thirty-five years was a new immigrant stream from Latin America and Asia, creating a nation that has moved from a largely black and white society to one that is more racially and ethnically diverse. Changes brought about by increasing immigration, interracial marriage, and multiracial identification beg the question of how relevant the traditional black-white color line is for under-standing today's racially diverse cast. If the black-white color line no longer character-izes America's multiethnic society, where will the line be drawn in the twenty-first century?

The trends in intermarriage and patterns of multiracial identification signal that the color line is shifting more readily to accommodate newer immigrant groups such as Latinos and Asians. And while the color line is also shifting for blacks, this shift is occurring much more slowly, demonstrating the tenacity of the black-white divide. Where do Asians and Latinos fit in this divide? At this time, the changing pace of the shifting color lines for these groups points to the emergence of a black-nonblack di-vide that places Asians and Latinos closer to whites than to blacks. This change is most evident in areas with high concentrations of immigrants, high levels of racial/ethnic diversity, and high levels of multiracial reporting.

NOTES

Copyright © 2005 from *Asian American Youth: Culture, Identity, and Ethnicity* by Jennifer Lee and Min Zhou (eds.). Reproduced by permission of Routledge/Taylor & Francis Group, LLC. We would like to thank the Russell Sage Foundation and the Center for Immigration, Popula-tion, and Public Policy at the University of California–Irvine for generous research support on which this chapter is based. This chapter was completed while Lee was a fellow at the Center for Advanced Study in the Behavioral Sciences with financial support provided by the William and Flora Hewlett Foundation, Grant #2000-5633, and while Bean was a Visiting Scholar at the Rus-sell Sage Foundation. For invaluable research assistance, we thank Jeanne Batalova and Sabeen Sandhu.

1. For present purposes, we refer to Latinos as if they were an official "racial" group, al-though government data allows persons indicating that they are Latino to report themselves as belonging to any racial group.

REFERENCES

Alba, Richard D. 1990. *Ethnic Identity: The Transformation of White America.* New Haven, CT: Yale University Press.

————. 1985. *Italian Americans: Into the Twilight of Ethnicity.* Englewood Cliffs, NJ: Prentice Hall.

Baldassare, Mark. 2000. *California in the New Millennium: The Changing Social and Political Landscape.* Berkeley: University of California Press.

Bean, Frank D. and Gillian Stevens. 2003. *America's Newcomers and the Dynamics of Diversity.* New York: Russell Sage Foundation.

Brodkin, Karen. 1998. *How Jews Became White Folks and What That Says about Race in America.* New Brunswick, NJ: Rutgers University Press.

DaCosta, Kimberly. 2000. *Remaking the Color Line: Social Bases and Implications of the Multiracial Movement.* Unpublished Dissertation, University of California–Berkeley.

Davis, F. James. 1991. *Who Is Black?* University Park: Pennsylvania State University Press.

Davis, Kingsley. 1941. "Intermarriage in Caste Societies." *American Anthropologist* 43: 376–95.

Eschbach, Karl. 1995. "The Enduring and Vanishing American Indian: American Indian Population Growth and Intermarriage in 1980." *Ethnic and Racial Studies* 18(1): 89–108.

Farley, Reynolds. 2001. "Identifying with Multiple Races: A Social Movement That Succeeded but Failed?" Research Report No. 01-491. Ann Arbor: Population Studies Center, University of Michigan.

Foner, Nancy. 2000. *From Ellis Island to JFK: New York's Two Great Waves of Immigration.* New Haven, CT, and New York: Yale University Press and Russell Sage Foundation.

Gans, Herbert J. 1999. "The Possibility of a New Racial Hierarchy in the Twenty-first Century United States." Pp. 371–90 in Michèle Lamont (ed.), *The Cultural Territories of Race.* Chicago and New York: University of Chicago Press and Russell Sage Foundation.

Gerstle, Gary. 1999. "Liberty, Coercion, and the Making of Americans." Pp. 275–93 in Charles Hirschman, Philip Kasinitz, and Josh DeWind (eds.), *The Handbook of International Migration.* New York: Russell Sage Foundation.

Gilbertson, Greta, Joseph F. Fitzpatrick, and Lijun Yang. 1996. "Hispanic Intermarriage in New York City: New Evidence from 1991." *International Migration Review* 30(2): 445–59.

Godfrey, Brian J. 1988. *Neighborhoods in Transition: The Making of San Francisco's Ethnic and Nonconformist Communities.* Berkeley: University of California Press.

Gordon, Milton. 1964. *Assimilation in American Life.* New York: Oxford University Press.

Hirschman, Charles, Richard Alba, and Reynolds Farley. 2000. "The Meaning and Measurement of Race in the U.S. Census: Glimpses into the Future." *Demography* 37: 381–93.

Ignatiev, Noel. 1995. *How the Irish Became White.* New York: Routledge.

Jacoby, Tamar. 2001. "An End to Counting Race?" *Commentary* 111.6 (June): 37–40.

Kalmijn, Matthijs. 1993. "Patterns in Black/White Intermarriage." *Social Forces* 72(1): 119–46.

Lee, Jennifer and Frank D. Bean. 2003. "Beyond Black and White: Remaking Race in America." *Contexts* 2(3): 26–33.

Lee, Sharon M. and Marilyn Fernandez. 1998. "Patterns in Asian American Racial/Ethnic Intermarriage: A Comparison of 1980 and 1990 Census Data." *Sociological Perspectives* 41(2): 323–42.

Lieberson, Stanley and Mary C. Waters. 1988. *From Many Strands: Ethnic and Racial Groups in Contemporary America.* New York: Russell Sage Foundation.

Loewen, James. 1988. *The Mississippi Chinese: Between Black and White.* Prospect Heights, IL: Waveland Press.

Merton, Robert K. 1941. "Intermarriage and the Social Structure: Fact and Theory." *Psychiatry* 4: 361–74.

Omi, Michael and Howard Winant. 1994. *Racial Formation in the United States: From the 1960s to the 1980s.* New York: Routledge.

Qian, Zhenchao. 1997. "Breaking the Racial Barriers: Variations in Interracial Marriage between 1980 and 1990." *Demography* 34 (2): 263–76.

Roediger, David. 1991. *The Wages of Whiteness.* New York: Verso.

Saenz, Rogelio, Sean-Shong Hwang, Benigno E. Aguirre, and Robert N. Anderson. 1995. "Persistence and Change in Asian Identity among Children of Intermarried Couples." *Sociological Perspectives* 38(2): 175–94.

Smith, James P. and Barry Edmonston. 1997. *The New Americans.* Washington, DC: National Academy Press.

Spencer, Jon Michael. 1997. *The New Colored People: The Mixed-Race Movement in America.* New York: New York University Press.

Stephan, Cookie White and Walter G. Stephan. 1989. "After Intermarriage: Ethnic Identity among Mixed-Heritage Japanese-Americans and Hispanics." *Journal of Marriage and Family* 51: 507–19.

Waldinger, Roger and Jennifer Lee. 2001. "New Immigrants in Urban America." Pp. 30–79 in Roger Waldinger (ed.), *Strangers at the Gates: New Immigrants in Urban America.* Berkeley: University of California Press.

Waters, Mary C. 2000. "Immigration, Intermarriage, and the Challenges of Measuring Racial/Ethnic Identities." *American Journal of Public Health* 90: 1735–37.

———. 1999. *Black Identities: West Indian Immigrant Dreams and American Realities.* Cambridge, MA: Harvard University Press.

———. 1990. *Ethnic Options: Choosing Identities in America.* Berkeley: University of California Press.

Williams, Kim. 2001. *Boxed In: The United States Multiracial Movement.* Unpublished Dissertation, Cornell University.

Xie, Yu and Goyette, Kimberly. 1997. "The Racial Identification of Biracial Children with One Asian Parent: Evidence from the 1990 Census." *Social Forces* 76(2): 547–70.

Zhou, Min. 2004. "Coming of Age at the Turn of the 21st Century: A Demographic Profile of Asian American Youth." Pp. 33–50 in Jennifer Lee and Min Zhou (eds.), *Asian American Youth: Culture, Identity, and Ethnicity.* New York: Routledge.

Chapter 19

What Must I Be?

Asian Americans and the Question of Multiethnic Identity

Paul R. Spickard

In 1968, Asian American Studies was born out of the Third World Strike at San Francisco State; in 1995, Stanford announced it would finally join the rest of West Coast higher education by offering a major in Asian American Studies. Times and institutions change, as has the definition of what is an Asian American.

When I took the first Asian American Studies class at the University of Washington in 1970, "Asian American" meant primarily Japanese and Chinese Americans, with a few Filipinos allowed a place on the margin. Now "Asian American" includes Koreans, Vietnamese, Thais, Burmese, Laotians, Cambodians, Hmong, Asian Indians, and other Asians and Pacific Islanders. The multiplication of significant Asian and Pacific American populations, and their relative inclusion or lack of inclusion in the pan-Asian group, is the subject of another essay.[1] The topic here is more elusive and perhaps more subtle: the inclusion or lack of inclusion of people of multiple ancestries who are, as some would say, "part Asian," in Asian American Studies.

The Identity Question

Is it possible to have more than one ethnic identity? In *Hunger of Memory*, Richard Rodriguez asserts that members of ethnic minority groups must choose between private and public identities. By this he means that, in order to make satisfactory places for themselves in American society, minorities must either retain the ethnic culture of their youth, family, and community, or they must eschew their ethnicity and adopt the culture, values, and viewpoints of the dominant Anglo-American group. The ethnic, or "private," identity Rodriguez regards as inferior and limiting; the dominant group, or "public," identity he finds superior and liberating, even as he recounts the emotional costs of choosing to flee his own ethnicity.[2] According to Rodriguez and Pat Buchanan and Malcolm X, to name just three examples, a person can have only one ethnic identity and cannot live in more than one community simultaneously. One cannot be Black *and* White, Asian *and* American.[3]

W. E. B. Du Bois had a different view. He contended that every African American possessed and was possessed by a double consciousness, two identities in dialectical conversation. In an *Atlantic Monthly* essay, Du Bois wrote in 1897:

> [T]he Negro is a sort of seventh son, born with a veil, and gifted with second-sight in this American world,—a world which yields him no self-consciousness, but only lets him see himself through the revelation of the other world. It is a peculiar sensation, this double-consciousness, this sense of always looking at one's self through the eyes of others, of measuring one's soul by the tape of a world that looks on in amused contempt and pity. One ever feels his two-ness, an American, a Negro; two souls, two thoughts, two unreconciled strivings; two warring ideals in one dark body, whose dogged strength alone keeps it from being torn asunder.[4]

Such questions of double identity—of ethnicity and nationality—are issues for nearly all people of color in the United States. For no group of people is the dilemma of double identity more pointed than for people of multiple ancestry. They find themselves continually defined by people other than themselves. Regardless of how they construct their own identities, they always find themselves in dialogue with others who would define them from the outside.

Amerasian Santa Cruz poet Douglas Easterly rebels against being defined by Whites, in this excerpt from "Guessing Game":

> Five seconds and they've gotta have you figured
> or it gnaws at them all night in a tiny
> part of their brain till they come up and ask you
> what *are* you?
> like you're from another planet
> * * *
> . . . Leaving you
> a footnote
> in race relation theory
> a symbol
> for the intersection of two worlds,
> one foot in each of them
> so you can be dissected
> stuffed into labeled boxes—
> What *are* you?[5]

Cindy Cordes, a woman of Caucasian and Filipino ancestry raised in Hawaii, puts it this way:

> I have a *hapa* [multiple-identity] mentality. I look white but I don't identify with white culture. I grew up with a Filipino mother in an Asian household. We ate Asian food, had Filipino relationships, Filipino holidays, with Filipino values of family. In Hawaii, I always felt comfortable, so much of our culture is a conglomeration of cultures.

But then she went to Columbia University and found that other Asian Americans "look at me as white." When she went to a meeting of an Asian American student group, "They asked me, 'Why are you here?' "[6]

For multiracial Asians like Cordes and Easterly, one task is to defend themselves against the dominant discourse imposed by White America, in order to establish control of their own identity. But there is a second task that Cordes sees as equally important: to defend herself against the subdominant discourse imposed by Asian Americans. Throughout their history, Asian Americans have also defined people of part-Asian descent,[7] without regard to their actual life-situations or wishes. In thus specifying identities for mixed people of Asian ancestry, some Asian Americans have been as guilty of stereotyping and oppressing, of mythologizing and dominating, as have Whites. Throughout their history, however, multiracial Asian Americans have also chosen identities for themselves. They have created patterns of choosing identities which are the portents for the future.

The Dominant and Subdominant Discourses: Pre-1960s

For most of the history of mixing between Asians and non-Asians in the United States, people of part-Asian ancestry have not had much choice about how to identify themselves. Either the Asian minority or the White majority told them what they must be.

Prior to the 1960s, most Asian American peoples were so opposed to intermarriage that they shunned not only the intermarried couples but also their mixed children. That is in marked contrast to the situation for multiracial people of African American descent, who found at least a grudging welcome among African Americans and who were in any case forced by White Americans to identify as Black. Chinese-Hawaiians in the 1930s, by far the largest group of Amerasians in that era, were far more readily accepted in the Hawaiian community than in the Chinese community.[8] In that same period, Japanese Americans thrust out of their midst most mixed people. The Los Angeles Japanese community ordinarily took care of any of its members who were in need. One result was that only 101 orphans had to be taken care of by the Japanese American Children's Village in 1942. But nineteen of them were people of mixed ancestry. That was far more than their percentage in the Japanese American child population at large. Most of them, probably, were children who had been abandoned and whom no Japanese family would adopt.

White Americans also opposed intermarriage with Asians, and they were not inclined to celebrate the presence in their midst of multiracial people of Asian descent. But the number of Amerasians was so small that Whites could ignore such individuals and let them slide by on the margins of White society.

Strange and vicious ideas about multiracial people of Asian descent have emerged historically from White racism. Those ideas are important because they shaped people's life chances then and now. The fullest exploration of this topic is in a recent essay by Cynthia Nakashima.[9] White ideas about mixed-race people proceeded from biological ideas propounded by pseudoscientific racists in the late nineteenth and early twentieth centuries.[10] Reasoning from the physical properties of plants and animals to the physical and moral qualities of human beings, pseudoscientific racists put on the American intellectual agenda a set of assumptions about multiracial people that still plague mixed people today. Cynthia Nakashima summarizes these ideas:

> [T]hat it is "unnatural" to "mix the races"; that multiracial people are physically, morally, and mentally weak; that multiracial people are tormented by their genetically divided selves; and that intermarriage "lowers" the biologically superior White race . . . that people of mixed race are socially and culturally marginal, doomed to a life of conflicting cultures and unfulfilled desire to be "one or the other," neither fitting in nor gaining acceptance in any group, thus leading lives of confused loneliness and despair.[11]

Most dominant discourse about Amerasians has been in terms of these myths of degeneracy, confusion, conflict, and despair. Edward Byron Reuter, the foremost academic authority on racial mixing in his day, had this to say in 1918:

> Physically the Eurasians are slight and weak. Their personal appearance is subject to the greatest variations. In skin color, for example, they are often darker even than the Asiatic parent. They are naturally indolent and will enter into no employment requiring exertion or labor. This lack of energy is correlated with an incapacity for organization. They will not assume burdensome responsibilities, but they make passable clerks where only routine labor is required.[12]

About the same time, a White California journalist wrote that: "The offspring are neither Japanese nor American, but half-breed weaklings, who doctors declare have neither the intelligence nor healthfulness of either race, in conformity with the teaching of biology, that the mating of extreme types produces deficient offspring."[13] Even Whites who fancied themselves defenders of Asians found themselves debating in terms set by the pseudobiological argument. Sidney L. Gulick, who opposed Japanese exclusion, felt compelled to give evidence that (1) unlike mules, Amerasians were not sterile, and (2) far from being weak and imbecilic, they were stout and smart.[14]

Within popular culture, Amerasians are perceived as sexual enthusiasts. This is related to a mechanism of dominance that attributes lack of sexual control to dominated peoples—women especially—as a way to excuse White male abuses of women.[15] This dynamic, the myth of the erotic exotic," is compounded for women of mixed race.[16] Speaking of Amerasians, Nakashima writes, "The mixed-race person is seen as the product of an immoral union between immoral people, and is thus expected to be immoral him- or herself. . . . [M]ultiracial females are especially likely targets for sexual objectification because of their real and perceived vulnerability as a group."[17]

During World War II, when Japanese Americans were placed into concentration camps on account of their ancestry, a small but significant number of mixed-race people—perhaps 700 Amerasians—also shared that experience. The army and the War Relocation Authority (WRA) ruled that all persons of full Japanese ancestry living on the West Coast had to be imprisoned. Some had non-Japanese spouses; the spouses could choose whether or not to go to the government's prison camps. Amerasians presented a special problem. Were they more Japanese, in which case they should be required to go to prison camp? Or were they more American, in which case they might remain at liberty with their non-Japanese parent? First the government incarcerated all the multiracial people of Japanese ancestry, then it tried to figure out what to do with them.

The WRA eventually made a judgment about each Amerasian's prewar environment. This judgment was made on the basis of the gender of the non-Japanese parent. Amerasian children who had White fathers and Japanese mothers could leave the camps and return to their presumably "Caucasian" (the army's term) prewar homes. Amerasian children who had Japanese fathers and non-Japanese mothers were presumed to have been dominated by their fathers, so while they could leave the prison camp, they were not allowed to return to the West Coast until late in the war. Adult Amerasians could leave the camps, but only if they had "fifty per cent, or less, Japanese blood," and could demonstrate that their prewar environment had been "Caucasian."[18]

Whites were confused about Amerasians and uncertain exactly where to place them. They had a number of stereotypes of multiracial people (Amerasians especially) that were perverse and demeaning. Asians were less confused than whites: generally speaking, they did not want multiracial people of Asian ancestry, and they told them they could not be Asians.[19]

This made life problematic for many multiracial people of Asian descent. Take the case of Kathleen Tamagawa. Born at the turn of the century, she did not like being an Amerasian. She opened her autobiography with the words: "The trouble with me is my ancestry. I really should not have been born." There follows a tale of tortured passage through her young life in America and Japan, undermined rather than supported by parents who had problems of their own. She was, by her own reckoning, a "citizen of nowhere," but by that she meant that she could find no place for herself in Japan. In time, in fact, she married a nondescript, middle-class White American and faded into White suburban life.[20]

Peter, a Japanese-Mexican boy, had a tougher time of it in Los Angeles in the 1920s. His Mexican mother died when he was very young, and he never established ties to any Chicanos. His father remarried, this time to a Japanese woman who did not like Peter. She beat him, ridiculed him, refused to feed him, and finally threw him out of the house. School authorities found him running unsupervised in the streets at age seven. Peter's father told him that "he wished that I had never been born; and at times I have even wished that myself. I have often wished that I were an American and not a Japanese or Mexican." Juvenile court authorities found Peter "an outcast" from both Japanese and Chicano communities. They tried to find a foster home for Peter, but no one would take him because of his mixed ancestry. He finally was sent to the state reformatory.[21]

For every Kathleen or Peter who suffered for their mixed raciality, however, there were others much happier. Kiyoshi Karl Kawakami, a prominent writer and interpreter of Japan to America and America to Japan, married Mildred Clark of Illinois and had two children, Clarke and Yuri. The younger Kawakamis spoke positively of their Eurasianness when interviewed in 1968. They grew up from the 1910s to the

1930s, mainly in the Midwest, well educated and insulated from life's blows by their father's money and status. They had almost nothing to do with Japanese Americans except their father, and in fact looked down on Nisei as people suffering from an "inferiority complex."[22] The common thread is that nearly all mixed racial people of Asian descent prior to the 1960s had to make their way outside of Asian American communities, for Asian communities would not have them.

This was true even for the great Asian American writer Sui Sin Far. Born Edith Maud Eaton in 1865, daughter of an English father and a Chinese mother, she was raised and lived her adult life in several parts of Canada and the United States. She chose to identify with Chinese people to the extent of choosing Chinese themes and a Chinese pseudonym, and she wrote prose sympathetic to the sufferings, fears, and hopes of Chinese North Americans. But she was nonetheless always more on the White side than the Chinese, in relation to where she lived and worked, who were her friends, and the point of view from which she wrote. In Sui Sin Far's writing, there were always people and Chinese. Partly it was because her literary aspirations demanded her work be intelligible to a White audience, partly because Chinese people treated her as an outsider, albeit a friendly one. For example,

> Some little Chinese women whom I interview are very anxious to know whether I would marry a Chinaman. I do not answer No. They clap their hands delightedly, and assure me that the Chinese are much the finest and best of all men. They are, however, a little doubtful as to whether one could be persuaded to care for me, full-blooded Chinese people having a prejudice against the half-white.[23]

Like other part-Asians before the 1960s, Sui Sin Far spent her life racially on the White side.

Winds of Change: Post-1960s

Substantial numbers of Asian Americans began to marry non-Asians in the 1960s. By the 1970s, the numbers of Chinese and Japanese who married outside their respective groups and then had children were so large that Asian American communities were forced to begin to come to terms with and accept the existence of mixed people. There were some limitations on this acceptance, however. Those involved in the Asian American movement of the sixties and seventies seldom had a place for people of multiple ancestry or their distinctive issues. Stephen Murphy-Shigematsu describes the dynamic:

> [I]t has been difficult to include biracial Asian Americans in Asian American communities.
>   The subject of biracial Asian Americans relates directly to interracial couples—an issue that is often seen as threatening to Asian American communities and individuals. There is a feeling that openly discussing this topic amounts to sanctioning interracial marriage and endorsing the death of Asian American ethnic groups.[24]

Today multiracial people of Asian descent take a number of paths to ethnic identity. Very few are inclined or able to identify solely with one part of their inheritance. Many adopt what Amy Iwasaki Mass calls "situational ethnicity." They feel mainly White or Black or Latino (according to their mix) when among White or Black or Latino relatives and friends and act mainly Asian when among Asians.[25]

Joy Nakamura (pseudonym) grew up in Brooklyn. She was in most respects a normal, Jewish girl in a Jewish neighborhood, except that her father was Japanese. Her Nisei father seldom talked about his childhood in California, her Japanese American relatives were far away, and although she felt somehow connected to Japan, she never had an opportunity to explore the connection until she entered a large eastern university. "I met more Asians my first year [in college] than I had ever known. When one Japanese American called me on the phone to invite me to join a Japanese American discussion group, I was very excited. I went to the group meetings a few times, but my 'white-half' began to feel uncomfortable when the others began putting down Whites," so she stopped going. She took classes on Japanese language and culture and enrolled in a seminar on Asian Americans. "I was desperately trying to find myself as an Asian-American woman, but I was not succeeding." She had clashes with her White boyfriend over racial issues, and she tried to ignore her Jewishness. Pressure from an African American activist friend helped Nakamura clarify her feelings. He said,

"You must decide if you are yellow, or if you are White. Are you part of the Third World, or are you against it?" I laughed at his question. How could I possibly be one and not the other? I was born half-yellow and half-white. I could not be one and not the other anymore than I could cut myself in half and still exist as a human being.

At length she decided, "I do not feel guilty about not recognizing my Asianness. I have already done so. I have just readjusted my guilt feelings about ignoring my Jewish half. . . . My Jewishness is something that can be easily hidden. I do not want to hide that fact. I want to tell the world that I am a Jew and a Japanese American."[26]

When I told Joy Nakamura's story at a conference on Jewish history and identity, one member of the audience—a distinguished Jewish scholar—snorted loudly that Nakamura was obviously a sick person. On the contrary, she is healthy and whole. Her choice to embrace both halves of her identity in the mid-1970s is a point of self-understanding which increasing numbers of multiracial people have reached in the two decades since. There is no question that to embrace both (or all) parts of one's identity is a healthier situation than to cling to one and pretend that the other does not exist. The general thinking here is to overturn the idea of a tortured "half-breed," torn between two unreconcilable identities. One has, not a split consciousness, but an integrated identity fused from two—"I am a whole from two wholes," is the way one Japanese-Caucasian man put it.[27]

In recent years a number of organizations of multiracial Asian Americans have sprung up around the country—the Amerasian League in West Los Angeles is an outstanding example—where people can come to explore their multiraciality. There has also grown up a veritable cottage industry of scholarly studies by and about multiracial people of Asian descent.[28]

Asian American Responses

Many mainstream Asian American groups still do not know quite what to do with multiracial Asians. Until very recently, there has been no place for them in Asian American Studies curricula.[29]

Asian Americans have, until recently, merely adopted the biases and boundaries set by White America. In so doing, they internalize the oppression that circumscribes their lives and project that oppressive vision on Amerasians. The 1990–91 controversy over the Broadway version of the hit musical *Miss Saigon* illustrates this point. The play's lead character was a Eurasian pimp. The play's producer and director chose a White person for the role. Asian American actors and community activists protested bitterly, saying the role should go to an Asian. Lost in the shuffle was the fact that, if ethnicity were the casting criterion, the only appropriate actor would be neither a Caucasian nor an Asian, but a person of mixed ancestry.[30] Multiracial Asian Americans exist (and in large numbers), and no amount of ignoring them will cause them to go away.

Increasing numbers of Amerasians are inclined to regard themselves as a variety of Asian American, and increasingly they find that Asians of unmixed ancestry will accept them as fellow ethnics. Across the country, it is hard to find a Japanese American or Chinese American church that does not have interracial couples and biracial children; there are even a few biracial adults. Sometimes, as Nakamura complained, Asian groups will accept Amerasians only if they renounce their non-Asian background. But with increasing frequency Asian American institutions, from athletic leagues to community newspapers to social welfare organizations, seem inclined to admit Amerasians as something like full participants.

Creating Amerasian Culture

In this new era, most Amerasians do not link up primarily with other Amerasians. But in some cultural respects they nonetheless constitute a distinct group. Those who grew up in Japan, for example, the children of American soldiers and Japanese women, have created a social world of their own, different from but not walled off from the Japanese or the Americans around them. They socialize more with each other than with non-Amerasians and have begun to form a third culture that mixes the languages, values, and symbol systems of their two parental cultures.[31]

Intra-Asian Ethnic Variations

In all this, one must remember that there are large differences among multiracial Asians. No one has yet studied the meaning of multiethnicity for multiracial Asians of differing derivations.

A few observations can be made. The community acceptance level for Filipino Amerasians has long been much higher than for other groups. This is because the Filipino immigrant population was so heavily male that, until after World War II, almost any Filipino man who married had to find a non-Filipina mate. The majority of the American-born generation was multiracial.[32]

The situation for multiracial Japanese Americans differs from that of multiracial Chinese Americans, who are fewer in number. The difference has to do not only with the relatively greater numbers of Japanese Amerasians but also with structural differences in the two communities. Japanese Americans are an almost entirely American-born ethnic group. The bulk of the adult population are members of the third or fourth generation. By contrast, over half the current Chinese American population is made up of immigrants. The unmixed Japanese Americans are, as a group, much more assimilated to American society and culture at large, and somewhat more accepting of intermarriage and multiracial people.[33]

A third example of difference is between Korean and Vietnamese Amerasians, on the one hand, and Amerasians whose Asian ancestry is from the other countries mentioned above. Most Amerasians are American-born and -raised, the children of Asian Americans and other sorts of Americans. Nearly all Korean and Vietnamese Amerasians, however, were born in Asia, the children of American GIs and Asian women. Many of the Korean Amerasians were given up for adoption and came to the United States at a very young age. They were raised by people with names like Lund and Anderson in the Midwest. Their life trajectories and their identity issues are quite different from those of other sorts of Amerasians. These frequently revolve around how to connect with their Korean background when they grew up in rural Minnesota knowing only Swedish American culture. Most of the Vietnamese Amerasians, like the Koreans, were born in Asia. But the Vietnamese typically came to the United States only recently, in their teens and twenties. Generally speaking, the Korean and Vietnamese communities have been less eager to include Amerasians than have other Asian groups.[34]

Geographical Differences

If there are intra-Asian ethnic differences, there are also substantial differences depending on one's geographical location. Ethnic dynamics in Hawaii, for example, are quite different from those on the mainland. For over a century, there has been a great deal of intermarriage in Hawaii, and therefore a large number of Hapas, or people of mixed ancestry.

To some extent, in Hawaii the mainland patterns of ethnic acceptance are inverted. Island Chinese these days seem more accepting of multiracial Asians than do island Japanese communities. Hawaii's Chinese community may once have shunned people of mixed parentage, but in the last several decades that community has learned to make room for part-Chinese. One finds people in Chinese churches with Chinese names who look Hawaiian and went to the Kamehameha Schools, which are reserved for people of Hawaiian ancestry. By comparison, island Japanese communities and institutions have less room for multiracial Japanese Americans. There are a substantial number of Japanese Amerasians in Hawaii, but generally they are not tightly connected to Japanese community institutions. They find places in the social system, but usually in a wider, mixed sector that includes Whites, various Asians, some Polynesians, and other mixed people. To be Hapa among Chinese in Hawaii is more acceptable; to be Hapa among Japanese in Hawaii is less acceptable. A Japanese-Caucasian woman recently reported from Hawaii that a Japanese relative twirled the Hapa woman's red hair in her finger and snorted, "What part of you is Japanese—your big toe?"[35]

The reverse is true for most West Coast cities. There, intermarriage by Japanese Americans is more frequent than in Hawaii, and mixed people are more likely to be included in Japanese American communities. By contrast, multiracial Chinese Americans in cities like San Francisco and Seattle are more likely to be treated with suspicion and are less likely to be included in Chinese community institutional life.[36]

Perhaps the biggest difference, however, is between the Pacific states, where there are large Asian communities, and most of the rest of the country, where Asians are more of a novelty. Those large communities keep down the rate of Asian out-marriage.[37] But they also encourage non-Asians to regard Asian Americans as ordinary parts of the social fabric. That acceptance of Asians extends to Amerasians: Amerasians (like unmixed Asians) are less likely to be harassed by Whites in Monterey Park, California, than they are in Columbus, Birmingham, or Boston.[38]

Physical Appearance

Another way in which the experiences of multiracial people of Asian descent vary has to do with their physical appearance. University of Washington professor Jim Morishima tells the story of Kimiko Johnson (pseudonym), whom on the basis of her last name and appearance he took to be a Japanese American married to a Caucasian. When Morishima asked her about her husband, she replied cryptically that she was not married and had never been married but would show him his mistake. Soon she reappeared with an African American youth whom she introduced as her brother. The brother spoke Black English and identified himself as Black. The two Johnsons had the same set of parents—an African American father and a Japanese American mother— yet they identified themselves differently, one as Japanese, one as Black, because that is the way they looked, and therefore the way other people treated them.[39]

Physical appearance, however, does not completely determine one's identity. Christine Hall, Michael Thornton, and Teresa Williams, in studying children of Japanese-American intermarriages, all found some people whose features appeared to favor the Japanese side but who nonetheless identified more strongly with their American heritage (White or Black). Conversely, they found others who appeared physically more American but who for reasons of their upbringing felt more attached to their Japanese identities. Williams found that

> [d]arker-skinned Afroasians did not automatically relate to African Americans, nor did lighter-skinned Afroasians necessarily identify with their Japanese parentage. Eurasians who appeared more Caucasian did not always blend in naturally with Euro-Americans; those who looked relatively more Asian did not always accept their Japanese background willingly and readily.[40]

Only in instances of conspicuous achievement are Asian communities willing to treat mixed people of African American parentage as insiders. This is related to what Cynthia Nakashima calls the "claim-us-if-we're-famous syndrome."[41] It is not likely that many San Francisco Japanese Americans thought of attorney Camille Hamilton as one of their own until she was named by *Ebony* magazine as one of "Fifty Black Leaders of the Future" in 1990. By then *Hokubei Mainichi* was quick to feature her accomplishments.[42]

Implications of Multiple Identities

An increasing number of people who are of mixed ancestry are choosing to embrace multiple identities. Psychological studies by Amy Iwasaki Mass, George Kitahara Kich, and others suggest that a choice of a biracial identity is, for most mixed people, a healthier one than being forced to make an artificial choice.[43] In helping individuals make their way to identity choices, family support is crucial. One must add here, however, that since the pull of the dominant Anglo-American culture is so strong in America, if a child is of mixed Asian and White descent, it is prudent to emphasize the Asian heritage.[44]

In addressing multiracial people of Asian descent, the task for the dominant group in America is to rearrange its understandings to accommodate the reality of biracial identity. Asian Americans must also rearrange their understandings. This means redefining in more inclusive terms what it means to be an Asian American. In the case of some Asian groups—certainly Japanese Americans, and probably Chinese, Koreans, and Filipinos before long—their very survival in an era of high intermarriage depends on coming to terms with and incorporating multiracial Asians.

Asian American Studies programs, to take just one example, ought to do more to include Amerasians. Stephen Murphy-Shigematsu states:

> When biracial people see their concerns expressed as legitimate within the context of Asian American issues, there is a greater opportunity for continued interest and involvement and less chance of alienation. When they are free to acknowledge their non-Asian heritage as an integral part of who they are as a people, without fear of rejection, then their ability to study and work among other Asian Americans will grow.[45]

The good news is that a growing number of Asian American Studies programs—and many other Asian institutions—are doing just that: changing to include issues and persons of multiracial people of Asian descent.

NOTES

Originally published in *Amerasia Journal* 23.1 (1997): 43–60. © 1997 *Amerasia Journal,* reprinted by permission.

1. See Yen Le Espiritu, *Asian American Panethnicity* (Philadelphia: Temple University Press,

1992); William Wei, *The Asian American Movement* (Philadelphia: Temple University Press, 1993).

2. Richard Rodriguez, *Hunger of Memory: The Education of Richard Rodriguez* (New York: Godine, 1982).

3. Buchanan's sentiments on the necessity of obliteration of ethnic differences, and the need to put strict limits on non-northwest European immigrants because they are, in his view, harder to "assimilate," were much in the news during his 1992 run for the U.S. presidency, and they threaten to appear again. See, for example, DeWayne Wickham, "Buchanan Is Mounting a Racist Campaign," *Honolulu Star Bulletin* (December 16, 1991). Malcolm X called on African Americans, most of whom shared his mixed ancestry, to denounce their White background and embrace the Black. In his autobiography he recounted how "I learned to hate every drop of that white rapist's blood that is in me." When he came to self-consciousness as a member of the Nation of Islam, he changed his name: "For me, my 'X' replaced the white slave-master name of 'Little' which some blue-eyed devil named Little had imposed upon my paternal forbears." *The Autobiography of Malcolm X* (New York: Grove, 1965), 2, 199.

4. W. E. Burghardt Du Bois, "Strivings of the Negro People," *Atlantic Monthly* 80 (August 1897), 194–195.

5. Douglas P. Easterly, "Guessing Game," in Asian/Pacific Islander Student Alliance, *Seaweed Soup*, vol. 2 (Santa Cruz, Calif.: University of California, Santa Cruz, Pickled Plum Press, 1990), 26–27.

6. Susan Yim, "Growing Up 'Hapa'," *Honolulu Star-Bulletin and Advertiser* (January 5, 1992).

7. Terminology for mixed-descent people is problematic and cumbersome, and there is no standard. In this paper, I use the term "Amerasian" most frequently, as a label for people who have Asian ancestry on one side and American (White, Black, Native American, etc.) on the other. "Eurasian" refers specifically to people whose non-Asian heritage is European. I also use a number of descriptions, such as "multiracial Asians," "mixed people of Asian ancestry," and "people of part-Asian ancestry," more or less interchangeably. I do not wish here to enter into a discussion of the difference or nondifference between "race" and "ethnicity" (see Paul R. Spickard, *Mixed Blood: Intermarriage and Ethnic Identity in Twentieth-Century America* [Madison: University of Wisconsin Press, 1989], 9–10, for that discussion). Here I use "multiethnic" and "multiracial" interchangeably. By describing a person as having "part-Asian ancestry" I specifically do *not* mean to imply that she is less than a fully integrated personality, nor that she is less than fully entitled to membership in an Asian American community. If in any of this I offend a reader, I can only apologize, plead that the offense is unintentional, and ask that the reader attend to the argument and evidence presented here rather than to taxonomy.

8. Doris M. Lorden, "The Chinese-Hawaiian Family," *American Journal of Sociology* 40 (1935), 453–463; Everett V. Stonequist, *The Marginal Man* (New York: Russell and Russell, 1965; orig. New York: Scribner's, 1937), 41.

9. Cynthia L. Nakashima, "An Invisible Monster: The Creation and Denial of Mixed-Race People in America," in Maria P. P. Root, ed., *Racially Mixed People in America* (Beverly Hills: Sage, 1991), 162–178. Nakashima writes about the images of all sorts of mixed-race people, but her findings apply particularly well to the Amerasian case.

10. On American ideas about race, see Paul R. Spickard, "The Illogic of American Racial Categories," in Root, *Racially Mixed People*, 12–23; James C. King, *The Biology of Race* (Berkeley: University of California Press, 1981).

11. Nakashima, "Invisible Monster," 165.

12. Edward Byron Reuter, *The Mulatto in the United States* (New York: Negro Universities Press, 1969; orig. Ph.D. dissertation, University of Chicago, 1918), 29. See also E. B. Reuter, "The

Personality of Mixed Bloods," in Reuter, *Race Mixture* (New York: Negro Universities Press, 1969; orig. New York: Whittlesey House, 1931), 205–216.

13. Quoted in Kiyoshi K. Kawakami, *Asia at the Door* (New York: Revell, 1914), 71.

14. Sidney L. Gulick, *The American Japanese Problem* (New York: Scribner's, 1914), 153–157.

15. For fuller treatment of this theme, see Spickard, *Mixed Blood*, 35 42, 252 259; Calvin Hernton, *Sex and Racism* (New York: Grove, 1965); Winthrop D. Jordan, *White over Black* (Chapel Hill: University of North Carolina Press, 1968), 154.

16. Elaine Louie speaks of Asian women in general, not specifically of Amerasians, in "The Myth of the Erotic Exotic," *Bridge* 2 (April 1973), 19–20.

17. Nakashima, "Invisible Monster," 168–169.

18. Paul R. Spickard, "Injustice Compounded: Amerasians and Non-Japanese Americans in World War II Concentration Camps," *Journal of American Ethnic History* 5:2 (Spring 1986), 5–22.

19. Rejection of multiracial people of Asian descent was common in China and Japan as well as among Chinese and Japanese Americans. Filipino communities were an exception to this rule of rejection (see below).

20. Kathleen Tamagawa Eldridge, *Holy Prayers in a Horse's Ear* (New York: Long and Smith, 1932), 1, 220.

21. William C. Smith, "Life History of Peter," Survey of Race Relations Papers, Hoover Institution Archives, Stanford University, Major Document 251–A; William C. Smith, "Adjutant M. Kobayashi on the Second Generation," Survey of Race Relations Papers, Major Document 236.

22. Clarke Kawakami and Yuri Morris, interviewed by Joe Grant Masaoka and Lillian Takeshita, May 22, 1968, Bancroft Library, Berkeley, Calif., Phonotape 1050B:10. Other elite Eurasian children inhabited similarly comfortable positions, aware of the Asian aspect to their identities—even trading on it in their careers—but essentially White in outlook and connections. See, for example, the autobiographical portions of Isamu Noguchi, *Isamu Noguchi: A Sculptor's World* (Tokyo: Thames and Hudson, 1967); *The Life and Times of Sadakichi Hartmann* (Riverside, Calif.: Rubidoux, 1970); and (also on Hartmann) Gene Fowler, *Minutes of the Last Meeting* (New York: Viking, 1954). Others in less comfortable circumstances had to struggle— psychically, interpersonally, and financially—to make places for themselves. See, for example, Sui Sin Far, "Leaves from the Mental Portfolio of an Eurasian," *The Independent*, 66:3136 (January 7, 1909), 125–132.

23. Sui Sin Far, *Mrs. Spring Fragrance and Other Writings*, Amy Ling and Annette White-Parks, eds. (Urbana: University of Illinois Press, 1995), 223. The essay is titled, "Leaves from the Mental Portfolio of an Eurasian." See also Paul Spickard and Laurie Mengel, "Deconstructing Race: The Multi-ethnicity of Sui Sin Far," *Books and Culture*, November, 1996.

24. Stephen Murphy-Shigematsu, "Addressing Issues of Biracial/Bicultural Asian Americans," in Gary Y. Okihiro et al., eds., *Reflections on Shattered Windows* (Pullman: Washington State University Press, 1988), 111.

25. Amy Iwasaki Mass, "Interracial Japanese Americans: The Best of Both Worlds or the End of the Japanese American Community?" in Root, *Racially Mixed People*, 265–279. See also Maria P. P. Root, "Resolving 'Other' Status: Identity Development of Biracial Individuals," in L. Brown and M. P. P. Root, eds., *Complexity and Diversity in Feminist Theory and Therapy* (New York: Haworth, 1990), 185–205.

26. Joy Nakamura (pseud.), letter to the author, May 22, 1974.

27. Jean Y. S. Wu, "Breaking Silence and Finding Voice: The Emergence of Meaning in Asian American Inner Dialogue and a Critique of Some Current Psychological Literature" (Ed.D. dissertation, Harvard University, 1984), 173–182.

28. See, for example, Nakashima, "Invisible Monster"; Cynthia Nakashima, "Research Notes on Nikkei Hapa Identity," in Okihiro, *Reflections on Shattered Windows,* 206–213; Barbara Posadas, "Mestiza Girlhood: Interracial Families in Chicago's Filipino American Community Since 1925," in Asian Women United of California, eds., *Making Waves* (Boston: Beacon Press, 1989), 273–282; Murphy-Shigematsu, "Biracial/Bicultural Asian Americans"; Stephen Murphy-Shigematsu, "The Voices of Amerasians: Ethnicity, Identity, and Empowerment in Interracial Japanese Americans" (Ed.D. dissertation, Harvard University, 1986); Christine C. I. Hall, "Please Choose One: Ethnic Identity Choice of Biracial Individuals," in Root, *Racially Mixed People,* 250–265; Christine C. I. Hall, "The Ethnic Identity of Racially Mixed People: A Study of Black-Japanese" (Ph.D. dissertation, UCLA, 1980); Nathan D. Strong, "Patterns of Social Interaction and Psychological Accommodations among Japan's Konketsuji Population" (Ph.D. dissertation, University of California, Berkeley, 1978); Teresa Kay Williams, "Prism Lives: Identity of Bina-tional Amerasians," in Root, *Racially Mixed People,* 280–303; Mass, "Interracial Japanese American"; George Kitahara Kich, "The Developmental Process of Asserting a Biracial, Bicultural Identity," in Root, *Racially Mixed People,* 304–317; George Kitahara Kich, "Eurasians: Ethnic/Ra-cial Identity Development of Biracial Japanese/White Adults" (Ph.D. dissertation, Wright Insti-tute, 1982); George Kitahara Kich, "The Developmental Process of Asserting a Biracial, Bicul-tural Identity," in Root, *Racially Mixed People,* 304–317; Michael C. Thornton, "A Social History of a Multiethnic Identity: The Case of Black Japanese Americans" (Ph.D. dissertation, Univer-sity of Michigan, 1983); Kieu-Linh Caroline Valverde and Chung Hoang Chuong, "From Dust to Gold: The Vietnamese Amerasian Experience," in Root, *Racially Mixed People,* 144–161; Ana Mari Cauce et al., "Between a Rock and a Hard Place: Social Adjustment of Biracial Youth," in Root, *Racially Mixed People,* 207–222; Ronald C. Johnson, "Offspring of Cross-Race and Cross-Ethnic Marriages in Hawaii," in Root, *Racially Mixed People,* 239–249; Cookie White Stephan and Walter G. Stephan, "After Intermarriage: Ethnic Identity Among Mixed Heritage Japanese-Americans and Hispanics," *Journal of Marriage and the Family* 51 (1989), 507–519; Ronald C. Johnson and Craig T. Nagoshi, "The Adjustment of Offspring of Within-Group and Interracial/Intercultural Marriages: A Comparison of Personality Factor Scores," *Journal of Marriage and the Family* 48 (1986), 279–284; Lorraine K. Duffy, "The Interracial Individual: Self-Concept, Pa-rental Interaction, and Ethnic Identity" (M.A. thesis, University of Hawaii, 1978).

29. In just the past few years, Asian American studies programs at the University of Califor-nia campuses at Berkeley and Santa Barbara have begun to teach about Amerasian issues.

30. It has been asserted by some that the part was originally written for an Asian pimp and then transformed into a Eurasian so that a Caucasian could play the part. If that be true, then the situation is similar to the controversy over the *Kung-Fu* television series of the early 1970s, where an originally Chinese leading character was rewritten as a Eurasian so that a White actor could play the part. If that is the situation here, then my analysis must be revised. However, to my knowledge this assertion has never been supported by any hard evidence.

31. Williams, "Prism Lives"; "Strong, Social Interaction and Psychological Accommodation among Japan's Konketsuji Population."

32. Posadas, "Mestiza Girlhood."

33. Spickard, *Mixed Blood,* 61–70; Betty Lee Sung, *Chinese American Intermarriage* (New York: Center for Migration Studies, 1990), 74–86.

34. Kieu-Linh Caroline Valverde and Chung Hoang Chuong, "From Dust to Gold: The Viet-namese Amerasian Experience," in Root, *Racially Mixed People,* 144–161; Nancy Cooper, " 'Go Back to Your Country': Amerasians Head for Their Fathers' Homeland," *Newsweek* (March 18, 1988), 34–35; K. W. Lee, "Korean War Legacy," *Boston Herald Advertiser* (March 24, 1974).

35. Private communication with the author.

36. A unique transition occurred for one group of Amerasians during the period 1930–1960. These were the children of mixed Chinese-Black families in the Delta region of Mississippi. During that period, according to sociologist James W. Loewen, Chinese gradually made a climb in status, from being segregated along with African Americans into the bottom layer of Mississippi life to being granted a kind of acceptance at the lower margin of the White group. In the decades before that transition, quite a few Chinese immigrant men had married African American women. Those mixed couples and their offspring, according to Loewen, were left behind by the unmixed Chinese as they made their ascent; Loewen, *The Mississippi Chinese: Between Black and White* (Cambridge, Massachusetts: Harvard University Press, 1971), 135–153.

37. Spickard, *Mixed Blood*, 73–84.

38. There is also, of course, the enormous difference between the ways multiracial Asians are perceived and treated in the United States and the ways they are treated in various Asian countries. See, for example, Strong, "Social Interaction and Psychological Accommodation among Japan's Konketsuji Population"; Williams, "Prism Lives"; "Court Rejects Japan Nationality for Children of U.S. Fathers," *Japan Times Weekly* (April 4, 1981); Elizabeth Anne Hemphill, *The Least of These* (New York, 1980); Valverde and Chuong, "From Dust to Gold." There is another difference in harassment that is very difficult to express clearly. Insofar as Asians or Whites may be bothered by the presence of multiracial people of Asian descent, Whites are more likely than Asians to be open about their opposition. Whites are more likely to use a racist epithet in public or to snub a person openly. Some of that may be because Asians are more likely to be indirect, even passive-aggressive, in the ways they express disapproval. But also the characteristic—the Asianness of the Amerasian—that sets off a White bigot is perceived by the White to be a disempowering thing. The White person's sense of advantage over the Amerasian may encourage the White bigot to express openly her or his hostility. By contrast, the distinct characteristic—the Americanness of the Amerasian—that sets off the Asian bigot is perceived by the Asian to be an empowering thing. The Asian's sense of threat or disadvantage relative to the Amerasian may encourage the Asian bigot to keep quiet about her or his hostility.

39. James Morishima, "Interracial Issues among Asian Americans" (Panel discussion before the Association for Asian/Pacific American Studies, Seattle, November 1, 1980).

40. Christine Hall finds that Whites and people of color emphasize different characteristics when they consider the physical aspects of racial identity: "It seems that Whites concentrate primarily on skin color, while people of color (who vary tremendously in skin color and ancestry) attend to other features, such as eyes, hair, nose, body build, and stature." Hall, "Please Choose One"; Williams, "Prism Lives"; Thornton, "Multiethnic Identity"; Mass, "Interracial Japanese Americans."

41. Nakashima, "Invisible Monster."

42. That a Japanese American community newspaper would claim a Black Japanese American as one of their own was in itself a remarkable step forward; it could not have happened a decade earlier; *Hokubei Mainichi* (April 1990). Rex Walters, a Eurasian from San Jose, is also an object of the claim-us-if-we're-famous syndrome, on the basis of his basketball exploits for the University of Kansas and National Basketball Association; "Japanese American Athletes," *Hokubei Mainichi* (January 1, 1992).

43. Mass, "Interracial Japanese Americans"; Kich, "Eurasians"; Hall, "Ethnic Identity of Racially Mixed People."

44. Mass, "Interracial Japanese Americans."

45. Murphy-Shigematsu, "Biracial/Bicultural Asian Americans."

Social Construction of Ethnicity versus
Personal Experience
The Case of Afro-Amerasians

Teresa Kay Williams and Michael C. Thornton

There are two significant contributors to ethnicity or racial group identity: a threat of historical experience that is shared by each member of the collectivity, and a sense of potency/strength inherent in the group (see Phinney 1990). In social science research, racial identity, ostensibly feelings toward the group, is rarely examined with explicit measures of group feelings. Usually, a racial label is correlated to psychosocial development of group members. In this regard, racial group membership—and not actual experience—is normally featured.

Thus, race is often used as a proxy for experience, a practice embedded in premises of social science literature (Wilkinson 1984). Deterministic views of race ignore important variations in the way subgroups of Blacks relate to the larger group and to one another. Perhaps no experience better exposes the contradictions regarding the way we view race in America than that of racially mixed individuals and, in particular, those with African heritage (Bonacich 1991; King and DaCosta 1995; Root 1992).

Although a rare occurrence, interracial ties draw much attention because they encapsulate unresolved feelings and attitudes about race (Thornton and Wason 1995). In a society racially stratified, where races are seen to be distinct, racial mixing has always been considered problematic (Spickard 1992). Interracial populations muddy the dualistic view of race (i.e., that each of us is one or another race) and epitomize the inadequacies of this ideology; they lead us to question basic assumptions about how racial life is organized. In this chapter, we elaborate on this point by examining what would normally be considered a subgroup of Black Americans. We explore how Afro-Amerasians situate themselves in an environment that attempts to place them within established racial boundaries.

Literature Review

Black Group Identity

Work on Black group identity is not easy to characterize, in part because of relatively limited research on this issue, especially that which examines ethnic group differences (Porter and Washington 1993). Typically, analysis highlights the influence of social class on identity (e.g., Landry 1987; Farley 1984). Some inquiry suggests that class is only a part of the puzzle. Broman et al. (1988) reveal that older, less-educated respondents in urban areas and highly educated Blacks living outside the West were most likely to feel close to other Blacks. Gurin et al. (1989) show that identity, defined as common fate and as more Black than American, was not simply related to class. Males and those of upper-class status were more likely to feel a common fate with Blacks. Younger Blacks and those who did not work full-time were also more likely to feel more Black than American.

Usually, these studies implicitly assume that group identity is a globally positive (or negative) feeling toward a homogeneous racial referent (Allen et al. 1989). This view fails to recognize that subgroups of Blacks have attitudes about various groups within the racial category (e.g., poor versus middle-class Blacks). It is also common, within this perspective, to treat Blacks as having assimilated and thus not to see identity as an alternate cultural experience (Porter and Washington 1993). These assumptions result in an approach that rarely sees group attitudes as an admixture of positive and negative feelings. This approach does not allow for the possibility that group attitudes may involve an affinity with some aspects of subgroups within the racial category, even while coupled with attempts to disassociate from others (McAdoo 1985; Jackson et al. 1988; Cross 1991).

However, an ambiguity toward the racial group might be expected for minorities who contend with negative images of their group permeating society. Some emerging works identify several reference groups within the overarching racial category. Allen et al. (1989) describe identity as containing two important referents: masses (non-mainstream) and elites (mainstream). They suggest that within the racial category is an array of boundaries and identities prioritized in a variety of ways. For example, case studies show that native Black Americans distance themselves from Black Haitians (Stafford 1985).

Multiracial Identity

Blacks will have different views of Blackness depending on where they are positioned in the social hierarchy. The position we consider here is mixed racial heritage. Historically, this category was simple. "Mixed race" referred to Black-White offspring who were part of a two-tiered system: Whites and Blacks, with racially mixed people viewed as improved versions of Blacks. Changes in the racial composition of the United States have been the catalyst of emerging work accenting race relations as inclusive of Blacks, Asian Americans, and others.

Paralleling work on Black identity that highlights an either/or, strong or weak connection, recent works on multiracial identity depict the phenomenon as a dichotomy: multiracial people maintain stable (i.e., strong), single-heritage identities or multiple-heritage identities (Thornton and Wason 1995). The former position views multiple identities as untenable, while the latter sees them as no less viable than, and often superior to, a single-heritage self-image. Much of this newer work declares that simultaneous membership and multiple fluid identities commonly exist (Root 1992, 1996; Houston and Williams 1997).

A recent review of multiracial identity research found that three paradigms predominate (Thornton and Wason 1995). The first situates "multiracials" as problems, an approach underlying much of the social science research on ethnic identity (Phinney 1990). Racial boundaries are seen as rigid, and between them is a great divide, due in large part to each group holding incompatible attitudes and values. Thus, the problem paradigm argues that multiple identity is inherently troublesome, an emotionally impossible task. Phinney (1990) describes this view as bipolar, a linear model depicting identity as lying along a continuum from strong ethnic to strong mainstream ties. Strengthening one weakens the other. Therein lies the dichotomy: strong in-group identification is negatively related to acculturation, for acculturation is inevitably tied to weakening one's ethnic identity. Studies in this area usually examine clinical populations and Black-White combinations (e.g., Gibbs and Moskowitz-Sweet 1991; Lyles et al. 1985). The struggle for mixed people lies in trying to maintain bonds with incompatible groups.

The second paradigm is the equivalent approach, which describes mixed and mainstream identities as comparable. One theme envisions mixed racial identity development as a process that is similar to monoracial identity development; multiracial identity resembles identities developed among Whites. Another theme within this research argues that all adolescents cope adequately with identity dilemmas, no matter what the racial heritage. This congruence in outcomes reflects good adjustment to the assimilation process by all adolescents.

Unlike the problem paradigm, the equivalent view focuses on cultural (i.e., American) and not racial identity per se. This may in part explain why patterns are similar. These studies may also be limited in that samples are drawn from areas with large minority populations (e.g., the Southwest for mixed-Hispanics and Hawaii for mixed-Asian Americans) (Grove 1991; Johnson and Nagoshi 1986; Cauce et al. 1992; Jacobs 1992). Interestingly, Black-other mixes are rarely examined for this paradigm.

The variant approach is a recent development that has emerged concomitant to multiracials beginning to explore these issues themselves (e.g., see Root 1992; Kerwin et al. 1993; Thornton 1995). Here, mixed racial identity is seen as a new and positive phenomenon. The Stephans (1989, 1991, 1992) find that biracial identity is highly subjective for individuals with similar biological heritages and holding varying identities. Moreover, although these individuals bonded with several groups, few suffered ill effects. While exposure to cultures of origin helped to explain the nature of identification, exposure was not a necessary and sufficient condition for identification. Some with little and others with extensive contact did not identify with the cultures of origin. For Japanese-Whites, experience with a Japanese religion was an important antecedent, while for Hispanic-White combinations, physical appearance was associated with identification. Generally for Amerasians, bicultural socialization is associated with racial tolerance, appreciation of minority cultures, and greater affinity with both single-heritage groups than those groups hold with each other. This was true even for the few studies undertaken on Afro-Amerasians (e.g., Hall 1980).

Models of multiracial identity highlight a two-dimensional process. While acculturation remains the theme, identity may involve strong and/or weak ties with several groups (Phinney 1990). While it is included in emerging works, generally there remains little appreciation of Black identity as multidimensional and involving a variety of reference groups both within and without the racial category. Examining "Black-mixed" subjects tells us more about the nature of group identity within the overall racial (i.e., Black) category. While racial designations are imposed from the outside, in practice the identity that accompanies these labels may be accepted, rejected, or modified among any subgroup. This is particularly the case among those less clearly placed within traditional racial boundaries.

This chapter focuses on Afro-Amerasians and how they situate their experiences and social identities given the popular racial ideology. Here, "Afro-Amerasian" refers to offspring born to Asian (American) women and African American men (Strong 1978; Hall 1980). Amerasians did not appear in Asia in significant numbers until the Spanish American War. Since then, they can be found throughout Asia, including Japan, Korea, Vietnam, Thailand, and Taiwan. There is little known about the number of Amerasians in the United States. The number of Afro-Amerasians is usually estimated to be 10 percent of any overall figure (Thornton 1983).

Historically, this group is seen as having pronounced adjustment problems, in part reflecting the legacy of war, military occupation, poverty, and social devastation in the lands of their birth. These experiences are seen to have irreparable and debilitating effects on racial esteem and ethnic identity development. Emerging works indicate that despite their experiences with marginality, Amerasians have responded to their social circumstances with resilience and have constructed a variety of personal and social identities (Hall 1980; Murphy-Shigematsu 1986; Williams 1992). It is precisely their multiple marginalized status that makes Afro-Amerasians an important Asian American and Black subgroup. The personal identity struggles and resolutions that they undergo parallel experiences of so-called monoracial populations. Afro-Amerasians, however, must cope with an even greater set of contradictory messages.

Methods and Results

Sample

Because Amerasians do not live in recognizable communities, the sample was collected via a snowball technique. The analysis is based on interviews with twenty-seven Afro-Amerasians, who were at the time between the ages of eighteen and thirty-five. Twenty respondents in this sample are of Japanese, two are of Korean, two are of Filipino, and three are of Chinese heritage. Interviews, lasting between two and eight hours, took place in Yokohama and Yokosuka, Japan, in 1988–1989, and in Los Angeles, Santa Barbara, and Oakland, California in 1992–1994. The fourteen informants in Japan were initially contacted by mail or by telephone. These fourteen Japanese Afro-Amerasians had lived in and around military bases in Japan and are bilingual; thus, some interviews were conducted at least in part in Japanese. Several interviews also occurred in the presence of informants' siblings or partners (i.e., spouses and boyfriends). In California, organizations of multiracials and student associations were solicited for participants, resulting in another thirteen interviews; all spoke only English.

Respondents had average education, all having graduated from high school; twenty-four of twenty-seven respondents have at least one year of education after high school.

The experiences identified below reveal the contrast between socially expected identities and experience with those expectations. They show that identity is multidimensional. Given limited space, we can only highlight some of the themes emerging from the interviews.

Racial Identity as a Social Construct

It is through a series of critical moments that the process of racialization takes place, shaping and informing the identities of Afro-Amerasians—identities supposedly in sharp contrast to those found among single racial groups (Williams 1996). "Racialization," argue Omi and Winant (1986, 64), is the "extension of racial meaning to a previously racially unclassified relationship, social practice or group." Some of these critical moments are blatant; others, more subtle. One respondent explains her first memory of having race imposed upon her:

> When I was very little I didn't really think about what my background was, I don't think. But people point it out all the time. Sometimes it's good, but a lot of time it's bad, like they are trying to say, "You don't fit" or "You don't belong." When I was about seven, I was part of a swimming club in Japan. One time when I went to swimming lessons and my father showed up instead of my mom, the Japanese people in my swimming club freaked out because my dad is this big, six-foot Black man. From that time on, my Japanese peers seemed to make jokes or make mostly negative references to my Blackness. They started calling me *kurombo* [a negative word for Black]. Needless to say, I eventually quit. But before my dad showed up that day, I was thought of as "an American" or sometimes a *haafu* [half]. I think that's the moment I realized that it was my Black heritage that most people had a problem with. I mean, both the Japanese and the Whites, maybe even the Blacks themselves all have a problem with Blackness. So, there are times when I just identify as Black to say, "There's nothing wrong with being Black" and other times, I let people know that I'm both Japanese and Black. That's been my experience.

Another respondent describes how this social definition of group membership contrasted with his experience at home:

> You know this race stuff really used to bother me. My parents, even though my mom is Asian and my dad is Black, they didn't racialize their relationship. . . . I know that sounds weird and Black people always get on my case when I say this, but I just don't remember if we ever really said anything about being Black or being Pilipino in our house growing up. It wasn't that we weren't proud or nothing like that. It "just wasn't there." So, when I had to face society outside of my house, I got a pretty heavy dose of race-this and race-that. I knew that I was mixed, Black and Pilipino. Even without mention, you know you're mixed. You just know. But when White people kept treating me like I was Black and when I'd say, "Yeah, my mom, she's Pilipino," they'd ignore

that and would designate me the "Black one" of the bunch, I realized that I was Black to them. I think I had to become more sensitive to racial issues because people were always putting race into who I was. And it was usually not the race I thought I was mixed [sic].

Social encounters that racial Afro-Amerasians experience serve as pieces to puzzles in discerning the social construction of their identities. Most of the respondents resist attempts to force them into one racial category; they choose alternate representations of themselves as "mixed," "biracial," *hapa,* or *haafu.* Previous characterizations of this kind of racial dissonance or crisis (Kich 1982; Thornton 1983) are described as having a negative impact on the experiences of Amerasians. Yet, twenty-five out of the total twenty-seven respondents who identified as "mixed" articulate the personal and social distinctions between the way others perceived and subsequently treated them and the way they understood and identified themselves. The "racial moments" thrust upon the interviewees therefore demonstrate how taken-for-granted assumptions about race and the process by which people racialize their social reality sometimes contradict the way Afro-Amerasians understand and represent themselves. The respondents indicate that they learned to steer their identities around social definitions.

Marginal Status versus Marginal Personalities

Afro-Amerasians, as multiracials, are by definition marginal: they live on the borders of racial boundaries, synthesizing contradictions and meshing dichotomies, as they relate back to the social rules and expectations of the original parent cultures (Hall 1980; Murphy-Shigematsu 1986; Thornton 1983). The marginal-man paradigm observes that, when individuals attempt to move into a new group or cultural setting that is reluctant to accept them, at some time during the process, they will find that they have become strangers to both the old and the new cultures. Caught between two conflicting social groups, such individuals are prone to social ambiguity, divided loyalties, and psychological distress. The marginal person is one in whom the period of crisis is relatively permanent (Park 1928).

Nevertheless, marginality is not inherently crippling or dysfunctional, nor is there only one reaction to it. While works often focus on the negative consequences of this situation, studies usually overlook Park's description of the marginal person as inevitably the one with the wider horizons. There is clearly a difference between occupying a position of a marginal person (e.g., a racial minority)—in other words, experiencing marginality—and exhibiting the characteristics of a psychologically marginal person. If marginality refers to one who is in two incompatible worlds, the definition simply locates the individual in terms of social structure. Hypersensitivity and ambivalence are possible consequences of this experience. Rather than viewing this marginal position as a source of disadvantage, most respondents frame their biracial-bicultural identities as an asset. Eighteen of twenty-seven respondents refer to their biracial/bicultural experience as the "best of both worlds." Many attribute this feeling to their ability to exercise "racial and cultural gymnastics," moving in and out of various social worlds. As a Korean Amerasian explains it,

Everyone tells to me how awful it must be to be Korean and Black during these times of racial tension. Blacks are always saying how Koreans probably don't accept me because they are pretty prejudiced and they don't accept outsiders, especially Blacks. They say I look too Black to be accepted by Koreans. White people and Korean Americans tend to share the belief that the Blacks probably don't accept me because they have developed this kind of racial prejudice toward Koreans out of jealousy and resentment because of . . . economic competition . . . and, that Blacks have this kind of racial pride that excludes everyone else but themselves. . . . I really understand where [they] are coming from, but at a time when people are stressing the superficial importance of multiculturalism, I can proudly say I speak Korean and I understand what Korean people go through. I also know the pain and suffering and stigma of being Black. Blacks and Koreans are more alike than people might think, but only someone who can be inside those communities can know that. . . . I have the best of both worlds where I have one foot in one group and another foot in the other group. How many people can say that? How many people can go home and savor sticky white rice, kimchee, and bulgogi, while listening to and appreciating Gil Scott-Heron rappin 1960's Revolution? It's deep.

A Japanese Amerasian describes how his African American father handled the sometimes-painful assimilation of conflicting worlds:

Japanese kids told me, "Hiroshima *wa omae no sei da zo*" [Hiroshima is your fault] and American kids told me to "Remember Pearl Harbor." Then, White people didn't like my dad. . . . My mother would cry and tell us we'll all go live alone together in an island in the middle of the Pacific Ocean where Japanese and Black and American will melt under the hot sun and live happily ever after. Then, my dad says, "Michi [mother's name], what are you talking about? The boys are a happy melt. *Chotto* cheeseburger special *mitai desho*?" [We're a little like cheeseburger specials, aren't we?]

The cheeseburgers and happy melts represent the privileges accompanying biracial status. Another Afro-Amerasian views multiple heritage similarly, turning society's negativity on its head:

Asians and Blacks are always trying to say how *kawaisoo* I am [pitiful, should feel sorry for] cuz of all the identity crap they assume I'll have to go through. Like other minorities don't ever have to go through it? Give me a break! You know, it's that whole identity crisis argument. "What about the poor little children?" It's a little weird because Whites . . . I don't know if they're guilty or bored or what, but they are the ones who kind of say, "Ooh, how neat, you are so exotic." I guess they are trying to say I'm different, unique, and interesting, although it's kind of coming out racist and all. I respond by saying I have the best of both worlds. I feel lucky to be both and experience both.

Viewing biracial status as a strength is an attempt to counter the tragic depictions of their multiply marginalized heritage. Respondents seem to be saying, "I'm not tragic, I'm not pitiful. I'm more than okay. I'm better than normal. I have the best of both worlds." It parallels the James Brown chant, "Say it loud. I'm Black and I'm proud," or Kid Frost's rap, "Soy Chicano, Brown and proud. This is for the raza."

Paraphrasing W. E. B. Du Bois' idea of double consciousness, Thornton (1983, 207–8) describes Afro-Amerasians of Japanese ancestry as having three warring ideals in one body—one African American, one Asian, and one American. The "best of both worlds" depiction of their reality is articulated by the respondents as a challenge to those who emphasize and highlight the "warring" aspects of multiple identities. This alternative view of their multiple heritage provides a "folk" explanation of how they make sense of, integrate, and synthesize their many "warring ideals in one dark body" (Du Bois 1903/1967).

Multiple Group Identity

The Afro-Amerasian's multiple marginalized social status is assumed to complicate an already troubled identity. Some of the narratives in the previous section clearly refute this claim. These testimonials and newer research suggest that Afro-Amerasians have responded to their social marginality by constructing a variety of personal and ethnic/racial identities (e.g., Hall 1980; Thornton 1983). One respondent reflects,

> I grew up in Gardena [California], you know, that's very Asian and Black and Hispanic, and there are some White people too. So, it was kind of nice growing up in that kind of area especially when you're Black and Asian like me. When there were instances when we had like, racial problems at school and all, I could kind of relate on a personal level, because my parents had their problems of being different and I had to interface with them. If I could have these struggles within myself and in my family even when I understand both sides, I could imagine that people from different races who don't understand each other might run into big ol' racial conflicts.

Another respondent also ties her personal identity to the structural relations between racial groups, mainly Blacks and Chinese. She argues,

> Since I've always felt closest to my Black side and most accepted by the Black community, I mostly identified as Black. I never withheld that I was part Chinese or anything, but I just didn't think it was that important to say it. I don't know, maybe, I did have a hang-up about being Chinese. It wasn't cool or something. Then, I read something on the Black-Chinese in Mississippi. I was so blown away that an entire community like my family existed in the South, of all places. I think that was when I began to see myself in a much larger way. I felt a sense of belonging even though I wouldn't want to move to the South . . . and I also felt that my individual life was a kind of symbol that if I learned to say, "Hey! I'm Black and I'm Chinese," that maybe whatever problems different groups are having could work things out. It was a really important change in the way I started to think about myself.

Similarly, another respondent illustrates how his identity struggles represent society's struggles. He states, "What I go through every day interacting with my Asian and

Black communities and even the Latinos and Whites and Armenians and all, I think the society goes through with it on a grander scale. Maybe this society could learn a thing or two from mixed people."

The identity struggles and resolutions that Afro-Amerasian individuals experience can be seen as analogous to what socially defined racial and ethnic groups face on a structural level. Many of the respondents describe how their ethnic and racialized identities as Afro-Amerasians have been constructed and maintained upon a foundation of negotiations within structural limitations. A particularly salient feature that has affected, informed, and even determined their ethnic identity and racial status has been the birth-ascribed characteristic of race as it has been applied to their African ancestry. Twenty-two of the twenty-seven respondents emphasize a special attention to their African American heritage. Their social interactions with most monoracial groups have affirmed and reaffirmed the need to deal with a particularly negative image presented to this part of their heritage. One Japanese African American man explains,

You know that one inch of Black and you are Black in America, and most Asians and Whites buy into that too. Blacks do too. What is it called? The one-inch or one-drop clause or something like that. I'm aware of that so I'm careful as not to ignore how that way of defining Black people affects me. I feel a special obligation to my Black side because of the history and the degradation of my people. So, if I get a little pro-Black sometimes, it doesn't mean that I don't identify as a *haafu* or anything like that.

Another respondent notes,

When you have Black ancestry, you have to be more in tune to it. The world, thanks to history, has really put down Black people and anything associated with Africa so those of us who are mixed can't hide behind a mixed label to get away from it, even if we look something else and get mistaken constantly for being a race that we aren't part of. I feel an extra "umph" when it comes to my Africanity. It's probably easier for me as an Asian/Black person to claim that I'm mixed because Black people don't mind mixing with other people of color, but I think the half-White mulatto kids have more issues of validation and legitimacy because they are kind of seen as being part of the oppressor and because the history of slavery and White people's deeds. In that sense, when you are a double minority mix, I think it's some ways easier, it's like Third World Unity. Did you notice on "A Different World" [NBC TV sitcom] the mixed character wasn't half-White and half-Black? She was half-Japanese and half-Black. She was acceptable, right?

Because Afro-Amerasians live as multiply marginalized multiracial, multicultural, and even multinational individuals, they cultivate a complex understanding of the sociohistorical positions of the various racial groups to which they belong, and they try to understand the relationships of these groups with society. The sociological lenses through which they experience and process their lives provide for them an identity anchor. In order to manage, manipulate, and present their multiple identities in a world that treats races as distinct, Afro-Amerasians must develop some sort of stable core identity. Most of the interviewees indicate a "mixed" identity as the linchpin to their ethnic and racial affinities. In some cases, Amerasians accept or even defend the heightened boundaries of their parent groups. In other contexts, they challenge and defy those boundaries, creating new meanings of race and negotiating new definitions of ethnicity that include them. Most of the respondents note the conflict between the way society attempts to define them in a variety of situations and their own views about themselves.

Conclusion

Society defines racial experience as homogeneous and distinctive. This has often led researchers to assume that societal definitions define personal experience. This assumption has been reinforced by researchers ignoring subpopulations within racial categories. Nevertheless, individual experience often differs from social expectations of that experience. While society defines race as distinct, Afro-Amerasians experience it as multidimensional.

Past research presumed that a marginal position was concomitant to an ambivalent identity that can turn to turmoil. Afro-Amerasians are estranged in that they are situated between at least two forces: the contrasting push of society to identify as only Black, and the pull of their own personal and unique experience. For them, to listen to social definitions would lead to a marginal personality, for they believe they would ignore important influences unique to their lives. However, instead of succumbing to these forces, they develop a different kind of Black identity that incorporates other parts of their heritage. They choose to situate themselves on the traditional boundaries of racial groups rather than deny important parts of who they are; thus, they choose to be marginal.

Our respondents are unusual in that they grew up in environments (i.e., in California and overseas) where intergroup contact occurred on both the primary and secondary level. Therefore, they had ample opportunity to develop and to nurture an acute awareness about their social location, personal identity, racialized status, and ethnic practices in relationship to other socially defined groups and other mixed-race families. In a rigidly constructed monoracial world, Afro-Amerasians try to make sense of their experiences as racialized peoples. Their struggles with personal and social experiences of identity provide sociological insight into understanding the complexities and contradictions of race and their ever-changing meanings and applications.

NOTES

Originally published in *Journal of Comparative Family Studies* 29.2 (1998): 255–67. © 1998, reprinted by permission.

REFERENCES

Allen, Richard, Michael Dawson, and Ronald Brown (1989). "Schema-based approach to modeling an African American racial belief system." *American Political Science Review* 83: 421–41.

Bonacich, Edna (1991). "Class approaches to ethnicity and race." In Norman Yetman (ed.), *Majority and Minority: The Dynamics of Race and Ethnicity in American Life.* Boston: Allyn and Bacon.

Broman, Clifford, Harold Neighbors, and James Jackson (1988). "Racial group identification among Black adults." *Social Forces* 67: 146–58.

Cauce, Anna, Yumi Hiraga, Craig Mason, Tanya Aguilar, Nydia Ordonez, and Nancy Gonzales (1992). "Between a rock and a hard place: Social adjustment of biracial youth." Pp. 207–22 in M. Root (ed.), *Racially Mixed People in America.* Newbury Park, CA: Sage Publications.

Cross, William (1991). *Shades of Black.* Philadelphia: Temple University Press.

Du Bois, W. E. B. (1903/1967). *Souls of Black Folk.* New York: Macmillan.

Farley, Reynolds (1984). *Blacks and Whites: Narrowing the Gap.* Cambridge, MA: Harvard University Press.

Gibbs, J. and G. Moskowitz-Sweet (1991). "Clinical and cultural issues in the treatment of biracial and bicultural adolescents." *Families in Society* 72(10): 579–92.

Grove, K. (1991). "Identity development in interracial Asian/White late adolescents: Must it be so problematic?" *Journal of Youth and Adolescence* 20: 617–28.

Gurin, Patricia, Shirley Hatchett, and James Jackson (1989). *Hope and Independence: Blacks' Responses to Electoral and Party Politics.* New York: Russell Sage Foundation.

Hall, Christine (1980). *The Ethnic Identity of Racially Mixed People: A Study of Japanese/Black.* Unpublished doctoral dissertation, University of California, Los Angeles.

Houston, Velina H. and Teresa Kay Williams (1997). "No passing zone: The artistic and discursive voices of Asian-descent multiracials." Special Issue of *Amerasia Journal* 1: 23.

Jackson, James, Wayne McCullough, and Gerald Gurin (1988). "Family, socialization environment, and identity development in Black Americans." Pp. 242–56 in H. McAdoo (ed.), *Black Families* (2nd ed.). Beverly Hills, CA: Sage Publications.

Jacobs, James (1992). "Identity development in biracial children." Pp. 190–206 in M. Root (ed.), *Racially Mixed People in America.* Newbury Park, CA: Sage Publications.

Johnson, Ronald and C. Nagoshi (1986). "The adjustment of offspring of within-group and interracial/intercultural marriages: A comparison of personality factor scores." *Journal of Marriage and the Family* 48: 279–84.

Kerwin, C., J. Ponterotto, B. Jackson, and A. Harris (1993). "Racial identity in biracial children: A qualitative investigation." *Journal of Counseling Psychology* 40: 221–31.

Kich, George (1982). *Eurasians: Ethnic/Racial Identity Development of Biracial Japanese/White Adults.* Unpublished doctoral dissertation, Wright Institute.

King, Rebecca and Kimberly DaCosta (1995). "The changing face of America: The remaking of race in the Japanese American and African American communities." Pp. 227–24 in Maria Root (ed.), *The Multiracial Experience: Racial Borders as the New Frontier.* Newbury Park, CA: Sage Publications.

Landry, Bart (1987). *The New Black Middle Class.* Berkeley: University of California Press.

Lyles, M., A. Yancey, C. Grace, and J. Carter (1985). "Race identity and self-esteem: Problems peculiar to biracial children." *Journal of the American Academy of Child and Adolescent Psychiatry* 24: 150–53.

McAdoo, Harriette (1985). "Racial attitude and self-concept of young Black children over time." Pp. 213–42 in Harriette McAdoo and John McAdoo (eds.), *Black Children.* Beverly Hills, CA: Sage Publications.

Murphy-Shigematsu, S. L. (1986). *The Voices of Amerasians: Ethnicity, Identity, and Empowerment in Interracial Japanese Americans.* Unpublished doctoral dissertation, Harvard University.

Omi, Michael and H. Winant (1986). *Racial Formation in the United States: From the 1960s to the 1980s.* New York: Routledge and Kegan Paul.

Park, Robert (1928). "Human migration and the marginal man." *American Journal of Sociology* 33: 881–93.

Phinney, J. (1990). "Ethnic identity in adolescents and adults: Review of research." *Psychological Bulletin* 108: 499–514.

Porter, J. and R. Washington (1993). "Minority identity and self-esteem." *Annual Review of Sociology* 19: 139–61.

Root, Maria (1992). *Racially Mixed People in America.* Newbury Park, CA: Sage Publications.

———. (1996). *The Multiracial Experience: Racial Borders as the New Frontier.* Newbury Park, CA: Sage Publications.

See, Katherine and William Wilson (1988). "Race and ethnicity." Pp. 223–42 in N. Smelston (ed.), *The Handbook of Sociology.* Newbury Park, CA: Sage Publications.

Spickard, Paul (1992). "The illogic of American racial categories." Pp. 12–23 in M. Root (ed.), *Racially Mixed People in America: Racial Borders as the New Frontier.* Newbury Park, CA: Sage Publications.

Stafford, S. (1985). "The Haitians: The cultural meaning of race and ethnicity." Pp. 131–58 in Nancy Foner (ed.), *New Immigrants in New York.* New York: Columbia University Press.

Stephan, C. (1991). "Ethnic identity among mixed-heritage people in Hawaii." *Symbolic Interaction* 14: 261–77.

———. (1992). "Mixed heritage individuals: Ethnic identity and trait characteristics." Pp. 50–63 in M. Root (ed.), *Racially Mixed People in America.* Newbury Park, CA: Sage Publications.

Stephan, C. and W. Stephan (1989). "After intermarriage: Ethnic identity among mixed-heritage Japanese-Americans and Hispanics." *Journal of Marriage and the Family* 51: 507–19.

Stephan, W. and C. Stephan (1991). "Intermarriage: Effects on personality, adjustment and intergroup relations in two samples of students." *Journal of Marriage and the Family* 53: 241–50.

Strong, Nathan (1978). *Patterns of Social Interaction and Psychological Accommodation among Japan's Konketsuji Population.* Unpublished doctoral dissertation, University of California, Berkeley.

Thornton, Michael (1983). *A Social History of a Multiethnic Identity: The Case of Black Japanese Americans.* Unpublished doctoral dissertation, University of Michigan, Ann Arbor.

———. (1995) "Hidden agendas, identity theories, and multiracial people." Pp. 101–20 in Maria Root (ed.), *The Multiracial Experience: Racial Borders as the New Frontier.* Newbury Park, CA: Sage Publications.

Thornton, Michael and Suzanne Wason (1995). "Intermarriage." Pp. 396–402 in David Levinson (ed.), *Encyclopedia of Marriage and the Family.* New York: Macmillan.

Wilkinson, Doris (1984). "Afro-American women and their families." *Marriage and Family Review* 7: 125–42.

Williams, Teresa Kay (1992). "Prism lives: Identity of binational Amerasians." Pp. 280–303 in Maria Root (ed.), *Racially Mixed People in America.* Newbury Park, CA: Sage Publications.

———. (1996). "Race as process: Reassessing the 'What Are You?' encounters of biracial individuals." Pp. 191–210 in Maria Root (ed.), *The Multiracial Experience: Racial Borders as the New Frontier.* Newbury Park, CA: Sage Publications.

1. Lee and Bean's article adds another level of complexity to our understanding of the Asian American population, calling attention to the increasing number of Asians who claim a multiracial background. In what ways has the new immigration contributed to the increasingly racially and ethnically diverse populations in many parts of our country? Why do Asians and Latinos in the United States evince higher rates of multiracial identification than blacks? In what parts of the United States do we find higher rates of multiracial identification, and why?

2. Given the trends and patterns of Asian intermarriage, what implications does the rise in multiracial identification have for the Asian American population and for America's changing color lines? How, as the authors conjecture, may a new divide emerge that separates blacks and nonblacks?

3. What are the obstacles encountered by multicultural Asian Americans in identifying with the Asian American community or the ethnic community into which they marry? How does acceptance of multicultural Asian Americans into the Asian American community differ along ethnic and racial lines, according to Spickard? How has this changed over time? What is situational ethnicity? How does this relate to the experiences of multicultural Asian Americans?

4. Until quite recently, the history of multicultural Asian Americans has been excluded not only from the larger discourse in American history but also from Asian American Studies. Why do you think this is the case? How might this situation be remedied to bring the field of this group into the curriculum? According to Spickard, there are multiple ways in which the identities of multicultural Asian Americans have been historically constructed. Explain.

5. Williams and Thornton's article seeks to show how Afro-Amerasians situate themselves in an environment that attempts to place them within established racial categories. In what ways does the positioning in the social hierarchy affect the way blacks view themselves and their relationships with blacks and with multiracials? How do blacks define blackness in a way that may differ from the way nonblacks define it?

SUGGESTED READINGS

Brunsma, David L. (ed.). 2006. *Mixed Messages: Multiracial Identities in the "Color-Blind" Era.* Boulder, CO: Lynne Rienner Press.

Coronado, Marc, Rudy P. Guevarra, Jeffrey A. S. Moniz, and Laura Furian Szanto (eds.). 2005. *Crossing Lines: Race and Mixed Race across the Geohistorical Divide.* Lanham, MD: AltaMira Press.

Daniel, G. Reginald. 1992. Passers and Pluralists: Subverting the Racial Divide. Pp. 91–107 in Maria P. P. Root (ed.), *Racially Mixed People in America.* Thousand Oaks, CA: Sage.

Kitano, Harry H., Diane C. Fujino, and Jane Takahashi Sato. 1998. Interracial Marriages: Where Are the Asian Americans and Where Are They Going? Pp. 233–60 in Lee C. Lee and Nolan W. S. Zane (eds.), *Handbook of Asian American Psychology.* Thousand Oaks, CA: Sage.

Kibria, Nazli. 2002. Ethnic Futures: Children and Intermarriage. Chapter 6 in Nazli Kibria, *Becoming Asian American: Second-Generation Chinese and Korean American Identities.* Baltimore, MD: Johns Hopkins University Press.

Labov, T. and J. Jacobs. 1986. Intermarriage in Hawaii, 1950–1983. *Journal of Marriage and the Family* 48: 79–88.

Lee, S. M. and K. Yamanaka. 1990. Patterns of Asian American Intermarriages and Marital Assimilation. *Journal of Comparative Family Studies* 21: 287–305.

Qian, Z., S. L. Blair, and S. D. Ruf. 2001. Asian American Interracial and Interethnic Marriages: Differences by Education and Nativity. *International Migration Review* 35(134): 557–86.

Stephan, C. and W. Stephan. 1989. After Intermarriage: Ethnic Identity among Mixed Heritage Japanese Americans and Hispanics. *Journal of Marriage and the Family* 51: 507–19.

Spickard, Paul R. 1989. *Mixed Blood: Intermarriage and Ethnic Identity in Twentieth-Century America.* Madison: University of Wisconsin Press.

Spickard, Paul R. and Rowena Fong. 1995. Pacific Islander Americans and Multiethnicity: A Vision of America's Future. *Social Forces* 73(4): 1365–83.

Sung, Betty Lee. 1990. *Chinese American Intermarriage.* Staten Island, NY: Center for Migration Studies.

Thai, H. 1999. "Splitting Things in Half Is So White!" Conception of Family Life and Friendship and the Formation of Ethnic Identity among Second-Generation Vietnamese Americans. *Amerasia Journal* 25(1): 53–88.

Weisman, Jan. 2001. The Tiger and His Stripes: Thai and American Reactions to Tiger Woods's (Multi-) "Racial Self." Pp. 231–44 in Teresa Williams-Leon and Cynthia L. Nakashima (eds.), *The Sum of Our Parts: Mixed-Heritage Asian Americans.* Philadelphia: Temple University Press.

Williams-Leon, Teresa and Cynthia L. Nakashima (eds.). 2001. *The Sum of Our Parts: Mixed-Heritage Asian Americans.* Philadelphia: Temple University Press.

FILMS

Adolfson, Nathan (producer/director). 1998. *Passing Through* (37-minute documentary).

Gow, William and Sharon Lee (directors). 2003. *More to the Chinese Side* (17-minute documentary).

Fulbeck, Kip (producer/director). 1990. *Banana Split* (32-minute experimental).

Fulbeck, Kip (director). 2003. *Lilo & Me* (10-minute documentary).

Hosly, David (director). 2004. *A Beautiful Blend* (27-minute documentary).

Hwang, Jason (producer/director). 1982. *Afterbirth* (34-minute documentary).

Nair, Mira (director). 1991. *Mississippi Masala* (drama).

Soe, Valerie (producer/director). 1992. *Mixed Blood* (20-minute documentary).

Sperandeo, Midori (producer). 2001. *Hapa* (26-minute documentary).

Yonemoto, Bruce and Norman Yonemoto (producer/director). 1982. *Green Card: An American Romance* (80-minute drama).

Part VIII

Confronting Adversity
Racism, Stereotyping, and Exclusion

Chapter 21

A Letter to My Sister

Lisa Park

It's been almost six years since your suicide. Now when I think about you (and I think about you often), I feel you are somehow with me. My dreams of us together are as vivid and life-composing as any conscious, waking moment. Some like to think that our waking lives are more real, because we believe we can determine them through the choices we make, and that our dreams are merely their epiphenomenal reflections or, worse, expressions of unfulfilled desires. Your presence is more than a memory or a wish. My dreams are ghostly impressions of our collective past, as well as a spontaneous living of experiences I know we never shared before you died, like the dream I had of you and me walking arm in arm. I remembered it as if it was a lost memory, even though I know it never "really happened." I am sometimes grateful for this, because your phantom presence helps me to continue remembering, which I know is important even though it almost rips me apart. No matter how hard I try to subdue, through forgetting, the pain that came with the destruction of our lives, I must bear witness to the crimes committed against you (and against us) that led to your suicide. Conscious memories require constant attention, or else history will erase what happened, and you will disappear as if you had never existed at all. Isn't this why you haunt me to this day, to inscribe what you had learned from living under siege?

I remember the first time, when I found you after you had cut your wrists with a kitchen knife, and later when our father, using his deft surgical skills, sewed you back up in his office. For a while after you had cut your wrists, you undertook to "better" your life and attitude, even though it inevitably meant reinserting yourself into the old vise of conformity. One of the ways you tried to affirm your "new" resolve was to change your physical appearance through plastic surgery, for which our parents willingly put up the money in an effort to keep you happy. They were at their wits' end trying to appease you, but their efforts to pacify you pushed you further into self-hatred. (The annihilation of uniqueness and self-worth is indeed the pacifying aim.) Your obsession with plastic surgery exposed the myth of the whole beauty industry, which portrays plastic surgery as a beautifying, renewing experience, "something special you do just for you." It began with your eyes and nose, and you continued to go back for more. You tried to box yourself into a preconditioned, Euroamerican ideal and literally excised the parts that would not fit. But plastic surgery is irreversible, and so were the twenty-one years of assimilation. You told the doctors in the psychiatric ward, where they placed you just after your second suicide attempt, the reason you took all those pills (which your psychiatrist had given you) was because the plastic surgeons had "ruined" your face. Did you come to a realization (under the advice of your doctors) that you were obsessed with changing your looks, which could only dishearten you further because it medically legitimated your neurosis? Or did you think that the surgery botched up your corporeal plan, which you realized you would have had to live with for the rest of your life? The plastic surgeon referred you to a psychiatrist to help you "work out" your obsession. Help is a four-letter word. You decided death was your only alternative to being stuck with an inescapable body. As soon as you were released from the hospital, you committed yourself to finding a way to kill yourself. Now, on top of what you considered a mistake of a body, you wanted to avoid being thrown into a mental institution, where you were sure you were headed as a consequence of being found out by the psychiatrists.

The first time was different in many ways. First of all, no professional psychologists or mental health experts knew about it. Everyone in our family kept your suicide attempt secret and normalized it as if it had never happened. Secondly, I know you did not want to die, but to get our attention. I remember coming home and discovering you in bed with your wrists bandaged and the bathtub full of blood and water. You thrust your limp arms into the air and cried, pleading for my help. I was devastated, broken-hearted, sickened, and bizarrely nervous all the while about what our parents would do if they had to be interrupted at work! I looked to our brothers for direction, but they acted as if there was no big emergency. I convinced myself that you were not dying, that your slashed wrists were not much worse than a cut finger. When our parents finally discovered you, they became hysterical and burst into wails of anguish—I was so taken aback by their rare show of sympathy that I began crying myself, throwing my body onto yours, because only then did I feel safe enough to reach out to you. Once our mother wondered aloud why I had not told them right away about your suicide attempt. I did not explain myself to her, but it was because all the violence in our lives, both physical and emotional, made your suicide attempt seem normal, everyday. It was not that I was unaware of what a crisis looked like, but that I was used to having to assimilate them into quotidian experience. I was more worried about controlling the "disruption" than about what was actually happening to you. That was the extent of our spiritual and emotional isolation. Do you see how our culture of pain worked? I knew there was an emergency, I was ready to do something! But then I felt I was supposed to walk away, like all the other times when one of us was in distress. Silence was disciplined into us. How did we get to be so utterly ruined? How did we get to the point where we turned our backs on one another?

I feel comfortable placing blame on everyone, and some more than others. We have taken in the values that ultimately hurt and divide us, while some benefit from the suffering of "others." We were too stupid (not innocently, but the result of engineered ignorance) to see it happening to us. Even when it was clear, oftentimes all I could bear was to take care of myself, for my own survival. Most of all, I blame dominant institutions and mainstream society, because of the impossible alternatives they set up for us. They set up what is "good," what is "normal"—everything else is secondary, the "other." And they are very clever about it—they fix it so that the suicide looks like an individual problem, not a social or political matter. Labels of "mental illness" and "madness" are ways of silencing difference and shifting blame from the social to the individual. The social stigma of "dysfunctionality" kept our family secret and prevented us from seeking assistance from those who could offer it. For a long time, I felt we were atypically and inherently flawed, as individuals and as a family, but later learned from other Asian women that our experiences were neither unusual nor indicative of an intrinsic, Asian cultural pathology. However, regardless of any real possibility for collectivity, we had few means for support outside the family. We distrusted social workers and counselors, who had little insight into what we were experiencing.

The Asian "model minority" is not doing well. Do you see what a lie it is and how it is used to reinforce the American Dream and punish those of us who don't "succeed," or who succeed "too much"? It is making me mad knowing the truth of this culture, which is so obvious and yet so strategically dissimulated in the everyday that it becomes invisible, and nothing is left but the violence that results from its disappearance. How do you point out the horror of something that is so fundamentally banal and routine that it ceases to appear traumatic? And when you do point out the lie that is the truth, you feel (and usually are) alone in seeing this and wanting to root it out. It's enough to make you paranoid, because it is such a thorough conspiracy—how can you reform something that is so structural, so absolutely essential to the constitution of this society? Therapy and social work are out of the question, because the point is not to heal or to cope—no token of change can rectify our injury. Why would you want to place yourself into the hands of an institution that seeks to resocialize you into the environment that made a mess of you in the first place? Our inclusion into the American process turned out to be our worst form of oppression. Most people are proud to call themselves Americans, but why would you want to become a productive, well-adjusted citizen when the primary requisite of American-ness is racism? Isn't our madness often the only evidence we have at all to show for this civilizing terror?

I remember when you got arrested for stealing a car in order to escape the nearly all-white university you were attending. A white woman social worker ordered by the courts came to check up on you at home, where you were remanded for probation. Even though you had locked yourself in your bedroom, the social worker tried to break down the door when you refused to see her, despite all of our protests. I was desperate for you to break out of our circle of torment, but I knew my familial and social duty was to defuse the awkwardness and shame of divulging our "personal" problems. As far as our family was concerned, the state was the last place we would look for help, and, according to standards of social acceptability, there was no such thing as a family problem that could not be solved within the family. So I put on a calm, diplomatic facade for the social worker, who had finally given up on making you understand that she was only there to help and decided to interview me instead about our family situation, which her limited thinking deduced to be the problem. I assured her she was wasting her time and that everything was fine. That was enough to satisfy the social worker, and she never came back.

It is a very insidious process that starts when we are young. One of my first memories of the "weeding out" was when we visited our father's place of work. When we were introduced to his co-workers, one of them looked at me and said to our father, "Oh, this one has big eyes." Pretty/normal = big eyes, white. And I at least had relatively "big" eyes. So, did I pass? Can my brothers and sister come, too? Racial passing was impossible for us, even though we were continually pitted against each other according to their racial fantasies.

Another memory: we were on a school bus; our brother broke an implicit rule and occupied one of the rear seats, which one white boy decided he wanted. I burned with rage and humiliation, not knowing what to do, as I watched the white boy repeatedly bang our brother's head against the bus window. (Our brother remembers it a different way, but for a long time I could only recall the young thug's taunting laughter.) Although I pleaded with the bus driver to intervene, which he did only too slowly, I felt helpless. I was afraid to call attention to myself and my already awkward difference. This was only the beginning of our conditioning by their divide-and-conquer strategy.

We became pathetic victims of whiteness. We permed our hair and could afford to buy trendy clothes. Money, at least, gave us some material status. But we knew we could never become "popular," in other words, accepted. It had something to do with our "almond-shaped" eyes, but we never called it racism. You once asked, "What's wrong with trying to be white?" You said your way of dealing with racism was not to let them know it bothered you. But they don't *want* it to bother us. If it did, they would have a revolution on their hands. The "just-convince-them-they-should-be-like-us" tactic. It is so important for the American racial hierarchy to keep us consuming its ideals so that we attack ourselves instead of the racial neuroses it manufactures.

I feel disgusted and angry and so, so sorry when I think of how I participated in the self-hatred that helped to kill you. I did not like to be reminded of my own "Orientalness," and I could not be satisfied with our failure to fit into the white American mold. Our parents were accomplices and victims, too. I remember when our mother once criticized you for cutting off your long, straight, black hair (in your effort to appear less "exotic"). Insulting you, she said, "You have such a round, flat face." She always told us, "You not American. Why you try to be American?" Our father could not understand our dilemma, either: "Your only job is study—Be number one—Do what your father tell you and you never go wrong." When he was challenged, which was usually by you, the one-who-paved-the-way-for-the-rest-of-us, he became a frustrated madman and abuser. We interpreted this as a failure in communication, a clash of cultural values, but the conflict ran deeper than a matter of individual understanding or cultural sensitivity. We did not believe in the possibility of surviving as an Oriental in an American society. Oriental/American. Our only choices. This is what we call a serious identity crisis.

I know people thought they could pick on you because you wore pink Laura Ashley dresses and glasses. Racists think "Oriental" girls never fight back. You told me some white girl, backed by her white thug friends, was threatening to beat the shit out of you. But you were more than this Laura Ashley reflection. The white girl was in for a big shock the day you put on your fighting gear and confronted her in the girls' restroom. You had to "toughen up" just to survive. (What does that entail, what price did you pay?) Our schizophrenia was a conditioned disease. You always and never had a grip on who you were.

You could draw a picture of a tiger springing to attack, frontal view, at the age of nine, and it would be good enough to pass for a *National Geographic* illustration. You were the fastest runner in elementary school and broke the school record for the fifty-yard dash. You made the junior high school track team, but our mother forbade you to run because she thought it would make your legs big and ugly. When our mother told your track coach, you were so embarrassed and humiliated that you never tried to run again. You stopped drawing, too, because you were being groomed by our father to become a doctor. You used to sell your drawings for twenty-five cents each to other classmates in elementary school but soon learned you had no time for art (or "fooling around," as our father would say) because you had to study hard. You broke down one day after having received a B on an exam, because you were afraid it would ruin your straight-A record. Our father told me you had asked your white, male professor to reconsider the grade, but he told you he never gave *foreign* students A's! The real irony was that you were always a capable student, and, more important, an insightful, critical thinker.

I had a desperate feeling something very bad was going to happen. So I wrote a letter to you a week before your second suicide attempt, warning you about my premonition, but the letter never got to you. I wrote that I wanted you to take care of yourself and that, like you, I was barely getting by. (You once wrote a goodbye note to me before you ran away—or was it meant to be read after your death?—that read, "I still don't know how you do it.") I wrote that I would be there for you and to have faith, because no one else was going to do it for us. But mostly, I expressed a deep sense of urgency. I sensed that if you did not do something about the crisis you were living, you would explode.

We spoke on the phone two nights before you took the pills. I was worried and impatient with you, because I wanted you to reassure me that you would not do anything self-destructive, so you told me you were not feeling suicidal. You even said you thought you were "probably the most fucked-up person on this planet" but you felt "good" about how you were going to handle it. I got off the phone feeling relieved, for the moment. Handle it? Was it supposed to be a hint (but I couldn't get it)? Our mother told me you cried, "Mommy, I'm sorry," which she believed signaled your regret for the "mistakes" you had made. "If you can't do anything good for society, you might as well kill yourself." Still, she told me your death took an important part of her, a connection she felt most strongly with you because you had her face. The same face she insulted and helped you to "reconstruct." Our father laughed when you told him the reason you wanted the plastic surgery was because you did not want to look like our mother.

In some ways, your death has shocked this family out of denial. For the first time, our parents owned up to the abuse they inflicted, as well as the suffering they endured from their own social alienation. Imagine how hard it was to maintain their dignity, having to work three times as hard as their white colleagues, who turned up their noses at broken English, and their own kids thinking they were stupid. Our brothers began to rely on me for support they used to get from you. You once told me what our lives would be like if you died. I realize now all the things you told me are true. But without these traumatic changes, I never would have appreciated your wisdom. I wonder if your vision was part of a plan. Did you know what you had to do?

I think you left because you could not live in the world that you knew. It hurts (so much) to imagine your pain and loneliness, . . . but I also know of your courage. You told me you were not afraid to die. *How much you must have known to feel so comfortable with death.* You weren't just a victim. However compromised, your suicide was also a form of resistance, a refusal to carry on under such brutal conditions.

I still have some of your old belongings, including some postsurgery photos that were hidden in a box. I didn't recognize you in the pictures at first. *My* sister is the girl I joked around with, shared a bed with and respected, who cut my hair, let me tag along, took some beatings for me, tolerated my impatience, envied me (too much) and was sometimes proud of me, saved animals with me, spoke Korean more fluently than the rest of us, was the dependable one, the pride of our father, the closest to our mother, the one with the "good heart," the confidant of our grandmother, the toughest one, who could beat us up and occasionally did, our younger brother's favorite sister, the only one who could really talk to our older brother, the one to have my teachers first, and the smart one. My perceptions of you. You said later, "I always feel obligated." Mired in my own worldview, I refused to believe you had it so hard. Your suicide was finally something that belonged to *you.*

I pieced together the events of your suicide through stories told by our family. You pawned a TV set and bought a .38 Magnum. Put blank cartridges into where the bullets should be and sat in bed with the gun hidden underneath the covers. Our mother had spent the day tailing your car around the city, following you from one pawnshop to the next, begging the dealers not to sell you a gun. Eventually she found you at home safely in bed and reassured you that everything was going to be fine. You asked her if you would have to go back there, to the psychiatric place. Our mother tried to comfort you and then left to get you a glass of orange juice, but she had walked no further than the bathroom down the hall when she heard an explosion. You were declared "dead" a few hours later.

So, why am I writing to you, dearest sister? It would be nice to extract an ultimate meaning from all this, to acquire some comfort from analysis, but I am still confronted with the abysmal magnitude of my soullessness. (That is what it feels like, the utter uprootedness of living in this lobotomizing culture.) I cannot hope to achieve a level of wholeness, because my soullessness refuses to be quiescent under this civilizing regime. I am writing to let you know that I still remember, and I will live to tell it regardless of my state of ruin, which means I think it is possible to militate against violence and loss without buying into civility and unity. I am not even calling for anarchy; I cannot allow myself that luxury because we already live in a (nation-)state of organized chaos. Your presence haunts and compels me to recount your death. Maybe my story will be useful in some way—to galvanize a historical or political consciousness—who knows? Maybe through remembering I will even find a patchwork place for myself to take root, just as we do in my dreams.

NOTES

Originally published in *Making More Waves: New Writings by Asian American Women,* edited by Elaine Kim and Lilia V. Villanueva, 65–71 (Boston: Beacon Press, 1997), reprint by permission of Lisa Park.

Chapter 22

"Racial Profiling" in the War on Terror
Cultural Citizenship and South Asian Muslim Youth in the United States

Sunaina Maira

Introduction

Since the attacks of September 11, 2001, and the "War on Terror" waged by the United States at home and abroad, questions of citizenship and racialization have taken on new, urgent meanings for South Asian immigrant youth. Many South Asian Americans, Arab Americans, and Muslim Americans, or individuals who appeared "Muslim," have been targeted for surveillance, detention, and deportation by the state. In the public sphere as well, South Asian, Muslim, and Arab Americans have been the objects of intensified scrutiny and suspicion and, in some cases, have experienced physical assaults and racial profiling as part of the renewed anti-Muslim backlash and demonization of Arabs in the United States.[1] There has been a shift in U.S. race politics after 9/11 where the fault lines are no longer just between those racialized as white Americans/people of color or black/white Americans, but between those categorized as Muslim/non-Muslim, American/"foreign," or citizen/non-citizen. This chapter examines the experiences in the United States of South Asian Muslim youth who emigrated from Bangladesh, India, and Pakistan, in the context of this shifting racial formation and intensified exclusion of Arab and Muslim Americans from national belonging.

The War on Terror

Within six weeks of September 11, 2001, Congress hastily passed the USA-PATRIOT Act, which conveniently stands for United and Strengthening America by Providing Appropriate Tools Required to Intercept and Obstruct Terrorism Act. The new laws to prosecute the "War on Terror" by eroding civil liberties were pushed through under considerable pressure from Attorney General John Ashcroft, who threatened critics of the act "that those who scare peace-loving people with phantoms of lost liberties . . . only aid terrorists."[2] Not so conveniently for Muslim, Arab, and South Asian Americans, the PATRIOT Act gave the government sweeping new powers of investigation and surveillance targeting their communities.[3] It did this by creating an ambiguously defined category of "domestic terrorism"; by granting the government enhanced surveillance powers; and by taking away due process rights from noncitizens who could be placed in mandatory (and in actuality, indefinite and secret) detention and deported because of participation in broadly defined "terrorist activity" (often for minor immigration violations and also in secret).[4] The act's provisions violated basic constitutional rights of due process and free speech and, in effect, sacrificed the liberties of specific minority groups in exchange for a presumed sense of "safety" of the larger majority. Before 9/11, about 80 percent of the American public thought it was wrong for law enforcement to use "racial profiling," popularly used to refer to the disproportionate targeting of African American drivers by police for the offense of "driving while black"; after the shock of the 9/11 attacks, 60 percent favored racial profiling, "at least as long as it was directed at Arabs and Muslims."[5]

It is important to note that discrimination against and suspicion of Arab Americans and Muslim Americans existed in the United States well before 9/11.[6] However, South Asian Americans, particularly Sikh and Muslim males, suddenly found themselves scrutinized as potential "enemy" threats. Surveillance of Arab American communities has always been linked to U.S. foreign policies in the Middle East, and is closely tied to U.S. support of the Israeli occupation of Palestine and military interventions in the region. Arab Americans, and others, who have protested these policies have been monitored at various moments since the 1967 Israeli-Arab war, from the FBI's surveillance of the General Union of Palestinian Students in the 1980s to the attempted deportation of the pro-Palestinian activists known as the "L.A. 8" to the nationwide monitoring and interviews of Arab American individuals and organizations before and during the first Gulf War.[7] Racial profiling must be understood not just as a scrutiny of certain groups because of presumed differences of "racial" or ethnic identity, or just in terms of cultural and social exclusion, but as an everyday practice that is linked to state policies. Racial profiling after 9/11, in particular, highlights the ways in which particular immigrant communities are positioned in relation to the nation-state, domestically and globally.

The shift in racialization of South Asian Americans after 9/11 is significant because South Asians in this country have had a different relationship than Arab Americans to the policies of the national security state. They have generally not been viewed as potentially working against the state's interests, at least not since the early twentieth century when Indian nationalists in the United States who were engaged in transnational activism against British colonialism were subjected to state surveillance.[8] But South Asian immigrants, regardless of their political orientation or class status, have always been positioned within the United States in ways reflecting the state's economic and political interests. The primary influx of immigrants from South Asia came to the United States after the Immigration Act of 1965 as part of an effort by the United States to shore up its scientific and military technology expertise during the Cold War. These graduate students, scientists, and professionals generally did not engage in challenges to their adopted home state's policies. Despite economically strategic lobbying for minority status in the 1970s to avail themselves of civil rights benefits, the first wave of South Asians has for the most part tried hard to live up to the mythic "model minority" image.[9]

The second wave of South Asian immigrants, however, that began coming to the United States in the 1980s through family reunification provisions of the 1965 Act was less affluent than their predecessors, more likely to come from small towns or even villages, and have had a very different exposure to U.S. race politics and the welfare state than those who reside in middle- and upper-middle-class, predominantly white suburbs. These more recent immigrants generally live in urban areas, often in multiethnic communities, and work in service-sector jobs or in small businesses. The civil rights crisis after 9/11 not only affected South Asian, Arab, and Muslim African Americans differently due to their varied histories of arrival and residence in the United States, and the different relationships of the United States with their home nation-states, but it also affected various South Asian American communities unevenly, based on their class status and previous understandings of U.S. racism.

The crisis of civil rights of South Asian Americans after 9/11 is the most virulent example of large-scale scapegoating of South Asians in the United States since the anti-Indian riots on the West Coast in the early twentieth century. As part of the domestic "War on Terror," at least twelve hundred Muslim immigrant men were rounded up and detained within seven weeks in the immediate aftermath of 9/11, none of them with any criminal charges, and some in high-security prisons. Nearly 40 percent of the detainees were thought to be Pakistani nationals, though virtually none of the detainees was identified publicly, and the locations where they were held remained secret.[10] Many Muslim families who experienced the "disappearances" of their husbands, brothers, and sons ended up leaving the country after indefinite separations and loss of the means of family support.[11] There were mass deportations of Pakistani nationals on chartered planes, some leaving in the middle of the night from New York state, that went unreported in the mainstream media.[12]

In June 2002, the National Security Entry-Exit Registration System (also known as "Special Registration") was established, requiring all male nationals over sixteen years from twenty-four Muslim-majority countries, including Pakistan and Bangladesh, as well as North Korea, to submit to photographing and fingerprinting at federal immigration facilities.[13] After news broke of mass arrests of Iranians complying with Special Registration in southern California in December 2002, many undocumented immigrants and those with pending immigration applications tried to flee to Canada. By March 12, 2003, the Canadian immigration service reported 2,111 refugee claims by Pakistanis since January 1.[14] More than fifteen thousand undocumented Pakistanis had reportedly left the country for Canada, Europe, and Pakistan by June 2003, according to the Pakistani Embassy in Washington.[15]

The profiling of Muslim and Arab immigrants affects the composition of communities and the nature of relationships within them, particularly in areas with large concentrations of these populations that have seen an exodus of immigrants, such as Brooklyn's "Little Pakistan" on Coney Island Avenue.[16] Perhaps more alarming, "an unknowable number of immigrants have burrowed deeper underground," creating an even more precarious world of individuals who cannot fully admit they exist, who cannot safely live their lives openly for fear of deportation and so live in the shadows, if not under siege.[17] The "War on Terrorism" has been waged primarily against immigrants, heightening the distinction between citizens and noncitizens and making citizenship a crucible for the post-9/11 crackdown. In fact, the "War on Terror" is an extension of the "war on immigrants," waged since the late 1980s and continuing with the anti-immigrant Proposition 187 passed in California in 1994 and the heightened policing of U.S. borders.[18] The Anti-Terrorism and Effective Death Penalty Act and the Illegal Immigration Reform and Immigrant Responsibility Act of 1996, both passed under the Clinton administration, laid the groundwork for the PATRIOT Act by stripping civil rights from noncitizens in the name of national security. The war on civil liberties did not begin after 9/11 but was accelerated after the Twin Towers tragedy.[19]

The heightened fear and anxiety of those targeted as suspects in the domestic "War on Terror" in the first year after 9/11 seem to have largely diminished in the public sphere, and within South Asian American communities seems to be borne ever more by Muslim and Sikh Americans to the exclusion of those who feel they are not "targets" of the "War on Terror." My own work on issues of immigrant rights with South Asian Americans in Massachusetts revealed that there was, understandably, a heightened sense of fear and vulnerability in Muslim immigrant communities, particularly among working-class immigrants who cannot as easily afford legal counsel to help them if they are harassed or detained. This fear about surveillance, detention, and deportation persists in Muslim American communities around the nation, for Muslims and Arabs continue to be associated with "terrorist" threats to the nation as the "War on Terror" continues to be used by the Bush administration to rally the nation.

South Asian Muslim Immigrant Youth in Wellford

The "war at home" in the aftermath of 9/11 raises questions about what the racial profiling and anti-Muslim backlash mean for South Asian and Muslim immigrant youth coming of age in the United States at a moment when their belonging in the nation is suspect. How do U.S. immigration and "homeland security" policies targeting Muslim immigrants affect the understandings of race, nationalism, and citizenship of South Asian Muslim immigrant youth? This chapter is based on an ethnographic study that I began in fall 2001, focused on working-class Indian, Pakistani, and Bangladeshi immigrant students in a public high school in a town in Massachusetts that I call Wellford. As part of my research, I also interviewed immigrant parents, school staff, community and religious leaders, city officials, and community activists. I argue here that young Muslim immigrants' understandings of citizenship shed light on the ways in which belonging in the United States is defined in relation to transnationalism and globalization, to multiculturalism and polyculturalism, and, increasingly overtly, to the links between domestic and foreign policy that underlie U.S. imperial power.

Wellford is an interesting site for this research, for while media attention and community discussions of racial profiling were primarily focused on South Asians in the New York/New Jersey area, there were hundreds of incidents around the country in places where South Asians have not been as visible in the public sphere or as organized, including incidents in New England. It is also interesting to focus on communities such as Wellford that are known to be politically liberal, to understand what kinds of responses such a setting allows and does not allow, particularly for youth. The Wellford public high school has an extremely diverse student body reflecting the city's changing population, with students from Latin America, the Caribbean, Africa, and Asia. Students from India, Pakistan, Bangladesh, and Afghanistan constituted the largest Muslim population in the school, followed by youth from Ethiopia, Somalia, and Morocco. At the time I did my research, there were about sixty students of South Asian origin, including a few Nepali and Tibetan youth, who were almost evenly split between immigrant students and second-generation youth.

The South Asian immigrant student population in Wellford is predominantly working- to lower-middle class, recently arrived (within five to seven years), and with minimal to moderate fluency in English. These youth generally seemed to socialize predominantly with other South Asian immigrant youth and with other immigrant students in the bilingual education program. The majority of the Indian immigrant youth were from Muslim families, most from small towns or villages in Gujarat in western India. Several of the South Asian students were actually related to one another as their families had sponsored relatives as part of an ongoing chain migration. Whole families had migrated from the same village in Gujarat recreating their extended family networks in the same apartment building in Wellford. The parents of these youth generally worked in low-income jobs in the service sector, and they themselves worked after school, up to thirty hours a week, in fast food restaurants, gas stations, retail stores, and as security guards.

The families of these South Asian (Sunni) Muslim youth are not very involved in local Muslim organizations or mosques that draw a diverse Arab, North African, Asian, and African American population. They tend to socialize mainly with people from their own ethnic community; but they do not seem to affiliate with the Indian American or Pakistani American community organizations in the area either, which tend to involve mainly middle- to upper-middle-class, suburban families.[20] Thus the responses of these immigrant youth are rooted in the specificities of their urban, working-class experience, an experience that is often completely unknown to their more privileged South Asian American counterparts in the area.

Cultural Citizenship

I found that in nearly all my conversations with South Asian immigrant youth, as well as their parents, the discussion would inevitably turn to citizenship, for this was an issue that had profoundly shaped their lives and driven their experiences of migration. There is very little research on youth and citizenship, and much work on young people's understandings of politics is based on a rather narrow definition of the "political" as tied to electoral politics, which is not useful when studying youth who are generally not involved in formal politics. More recent work challenges these assumptions and pays attention to young people's own understandings of politics in different realms of their everyday lives.[21]

Young people may not be interested in voting, but they express their relationship to the state in different ways and develop particular understandings of their role as "citizens." Citizenship has traditionally been thought of in political, economic, and civic terms, but increasingly analyses focus on the notion of cultural citizenship, or cultural belonging in the nation, which is a useful concept when considering the relationship of youth to the nation-state. This notion is very relevant to immigrant communities, as multiethnic societies are forced to confront questions of difference that undergird social inequity. It has become increasingly clear that the rights and obligations of civic citizenship are mediated by race, ethnicity, gender, and sexuality, as well as religion, as has been apparent in the post-9/11 backlash.[22] Cultural citizenship, according to Lok Siu, is the "behaviors, discourses, and practices that give meaning to citizenship as lived experience" in the context of "webs of power relations" and the daily "practices of inclusion and exclusion."[23] Cultural citizenship is an important notion to examine after 9/11 because legal citizenship is clearly no longer enough to guarantee protection under the law with the state's "War on Terror," as is clear from the profiling, surveillance, and detention of Muslim Americans who are U.S. citizens.

The concept of cultural citizenship has been developed by Latino studies scholars such as Renato Rosaldo and William Flores and Rina Benmayor, who are interested in social movements for immigrant and civil rights. They employ the concept of cultural citizenship in such a way as to analyze "how cultural phenomena—from practices that organize the daily life of individuals, families, and the community, to linguistic and artistic expression—cross the political realm and contribute to the process of affirming and building an emerging Latino identity and political and social consciousness."[24] The concept has also been developed by cultural theorists such as Aihwa Ong who are concerned with citizenship as a process by which the state regulates and disciplines citizens. Ong defines cultural citizenship as "a dual process of self-making and being-made within webs of power linked to the nation-state and civil society."[25] Some scholars, such as Toby Miller, are somewhat skeptical about the possibility of using citizenship as the collective basis for political transformation, for it is increasingly individualized and privatized in neoliberal capitalist states, such as the United States, where being a citizen is more akin to being a consumer of services or social goods offered by the state. My work, in a sense, bridges these two approaches: I am interested in the critical possibilities of cultural citizenship for galvanizing struggles for civil and immigrant rights as suggested by the work of Latino studies scholars. At the same time, I view citizenship as a limited basis for social transformation, given that it is tied to the state and is often based on a model of consumer citizenship.[26]

In my research, I found that there are three major ways in which South Asian immigrant youth understand and practice cultural citizenship: *flexible citizenship, multicultural or polycultural citizenship,* and *dissenting citizenship.* These terms are drawn from the ways in which the young immigrants in my study expressed and practiced cultural citizenship. It is also important to note that legal citizenship still remains very important, especially given that the "War on Terror" has used citizenship as a major weapon in its crackdown on undocumented immigrants and noncitizens and that less affluent immigrants were generally the ones most severely affected. Cultural citizenship always has to be considered in relation to questions of formal documentation and economic citizenship, as my research shows.[27]

The forms of citizenship that emerged from this study—flexible, multicultural and polycultural, and dissenting—are responses that these immigrant youth expressed simultaneously. They are not exclusive of one another nor do they exist in some kind of hierarchy of political or social development. I view these modes of citizenship not as static categories in a typology but as processes that are dynamic and cross different spheres: social, economic, and political. These citizenship practices are performed by adults as well, but it is clear that young people have to negotiate particular concerns due to their positioning in the family and social structure, and their participation in education. While immigrant youth have to deal with the migration choices of their parents and the demands of being both students and workers, it is clear that their lives are deeply shaped by the state and economic policies that drive their parents to cross national borders. Young people, too, grapple with the meaning of the state's role in their lives and with the implications of war, violence, and racism for an ethics of belonging.

Flexible Citizenship

"Flexible citizenship" describes the experience of migrants who use transnational links to provide political or material resources not available to them within a single nation-state, as has been argued for affluent Chinese migrants by Aihwa Ong.[28] It is different from traditional notions of dual citizenship, which imply an actual legal status as citizen of two nation-states, for it leaves open questions of national loyalty or strategic uses of citizenship status. The Muslim immigrant youth in my study display modes of flexible citizenship, for they understand citizenship in relation to the United States as well as one or more nations in South Asia. For them, national affiliations (such as "Indian" or "Bangladeshi") as well as linguistic-regional identities such as Gujarati or Pathan were very important, and they viewed all these identifications as compatible with national belonging in the United States. They came to the United States sponsored by relatives who are permanent residents or citizens, in some cases fathers who migrated alone many years earlier, so they grew up in transnational families spanning two continents. Transnational marriages and social ties are common in their families. However, their experiences of flexible citizenship were often more difficult than those of the elite Asian immigrant families studied by Ong and others. At least two boys had been separated from their fathers for about fifteen years; Faisal said his father had left Pakistan for the United States right after he was born, and in effect missed his son's childhood while he was working in the United States to support him and his family till they could be reunited. By the time Faisal came to the United States, however, his older brother was too old to enroll in high school and had to struggle to get a GED and find a job with limited English skills, so this flexible citizenship had its costs for these working- and lower-middle-class migrant families.

Most of these young immigrants desired and had applied for U.S. citizenship, because of what they perceived as its civic and also economic benefits: a few stated that they wanted to be able to vote, and several said that they wanted to be able to travel freely between the United States and South Asia, to be mobile in work and family life. About half of these South Asian Muslim immigrant youth have green cards already; the remaining are a mix of citizens and undocumented immigrants. After 9/11, of course, citizenship has become less a matter of choice for immigrants, particularly Muslims and South Asian/Arab Americans, than a hoped-for shield against the abuses of civil rights. In fact, a few youth I spoke to were surprised that I myself had not obtained citizenship yet in the fall of 2001, and were in some cases concerned that I seemed to have taken so long to obtain this vital document!

Citizenship for these immigrant youth is part of a carefully planned, long-term, family-based strategy of migration undertaken in response to economic pressures on those living in, or at the edge of, the middle class in South Asia. Some of these youth in Wellford imagine their lives spanning national borders and speak of returning to South Asia, at least temporarily, once they have become U.S. citizens and perhaps when their parents have retired there. For example, Ismail, who worked as a computer assistant after school, wanted to set up a transnational hi-tech business so that he could live part-time in Gujarat and part-time in Boston while supporting his parents. He saw this as a strategy for Non-Resident Indians (or NRIs, a term used by the Indian government) to fulfill their obligations to the home nation-state, using the benefits of U.S. citizenship. It seems to me that these young immigrants' notions of flexible citizenship are based on at least two linked processes of "self-making and being-made" as citizens in relation to multiple nation-states.[29] First, their identification with India or Pakistan is based largely on transnational popular culture, on Bollywood films, South Asian television serials, and Hindi music that they access through video, DVDs, satellite TV, and the Internet. In the interest of space, I cannot delve into an analysis of transnational popular culture here, but it is clearly an important arena for the expression of transnational cultural citizenship by immigrant youth.

Second, flexible citizenship is intertwined with labor and education, areas that are interrelated for working-class, immigrant youth. These youth have come to the United States with their families, in some sense, as migrant workers. They work in low-wage, part-time jobs in retail and fast-food restaurants and struggle in school to get credentials for class mobility. These service-sector jobs are generally occupied by young people of diverse ethnic backgrounds in the United States.[30] However, unlike nonimmigrants who provide this flexible labor, immigrant youth can perform economic citizenship, which is based on individual productivity in the capitalist state, and they may aspire to the American Dream, but they cannot win cultural citizenship because they are nonwhite, because they are immigrant, and, currently, because they are identified as Muslim, so they are excluded from full national belonging. Their participation in U.S. public culture, in fact, occurs largely through work; their relations outside the school and community are mainly with other immigrant or young workers and with employers. For example, Walid, a Pakistani immigrant boy, lamented that he could never go out into the city with his friends because they all worked on different schedules and it was almost impossible for them to have a night off together, given that he worked night shifts at his weekend job as a security guard.

Compared to more affluent South Asian immigrants, these working-class youth are more ambiguously positioned in relation to what Ong calls the U.S. neoliberal ideology that emphasizes "freedom, progress, and individualism."[31] They see the limits of this model of the self-reliant consumer-citizen—and of the American Dream—in their own lives, and that of their families. Soman, who worked in his family's Bengali restaurant after school and who often waited on more affluent South Asian immigrant students from the prestigious university down the street, said, "Here, you live in a golden cage, but it's still a cage. . . . [M]y life is so limited. I go to school, come to work, study, go to sleep." Soman's comment about being imprisoned by the "golden cage" of the American Dream is profound because in a single image it points to the glittering appeal of American capitalism and the confining imprisonment of belief in this illusion. It also suggests that young immigrants and their families may acknowledge the self-delusion, but continue to participate in it because at least, for immigrant youth, there is little alternative now that they are in the United States.

The idea of productive citizenship is tied to the need for a low-wage, undocumented/noncitizen labor pool by employers who wish to depress wages and keep labor compliant. Citizenship requirements discipline workers and keep immigrants vulnerable to exploitation and fear of dissent, as is very evident after 9/11 with the ongoing arrests and deportations of immigrant workers for visa violations.[32] There continues to be fear among noncitizens who have transnational ties, political or familial, that are increasingly suspect when the "threat" to national security is attributed to specific foreign nations.

Yet, in the face of such regulations of citizenship and national boundaries, it became apparent to me that these young Muslim immigrants thought about citizenship in ways that were themselves flexible, shifting, and contextual. In some cases, it seems that religious identity actually prompts youth to think of themselves as belonging to the United States or at least identifying with its concerns, if not identifying as "American." Ismail said to me in the fall of 2001, "Islam teaches [us that] what country you live in, you should support them. . . . See, if I live in America, I have to support America, I cannot go to India." This of course is the same boy who said that he ultimately wanted to return to India and support its development. But these statements are not as contradictory as they first appear; Ismail is able to frame his relationship to Islam in a way that will help him think through questions of loyalty at a moment in the United States when Muslims are being framed as noncitizens *because* of a particular construction of Islam. Ismail instead uses Islam to counter this exclusion of Muslims from the nation-state, both officially and unofficially, and to develop a flexible definition of citizenship. Flexible citizenship is clearly an economic/family strategy for these youth but also part of a cultural strategy that allows them to manage diverse national affiliations.

Multicultural/Polycultural Citizenship

Not surprisingly, some of these immigrant youth talked about ideas of cultural difference and relationships with others in terms of multicultural citizenship, since multiculturalism is such a pervasive discourse of cultural belonging in the United States, particularly in the arena of education. Multicultural citizenship is based on the idea of minority cultural rights, or the rights of minority groups within multiethnic nations to express their cultural identity. The high school, implicitly and explicitly, promoted this notion of multicultural citizenship through visual symbols and support for ethnic-based student activities. Outside the high school's main office was a display case with changing exhibits that often focused on the theme of cultural diversity, among other issues, acknowledging the different ethnic groups in the school through artistic and cultural products, often tied to ethnic heritage month celebrations.

For South Asian immigrant students, multicultural citizenship was expressed through everyday understandings of pluralism embedded in the social fabric of their relationships. Most of them emphasized that they had friendships crossing ethnic and racial boundaries, as Walid did in commenting on his black, Egyptian, Moroccan, and Gujarati Indian friends. In their daily lives, these youth did, in fact, hang out with Latino, Caribbean, African American, and Asian students, and especially with Muslim African youth from Somalia, Ethiopia, or Egypt, potentially forming a pan-Islamic identity. Yet it was also apparent that students in the school, as in most American high schools and even colleges, tended to cluster by ethnic group in the cafeteria and on the playground. Ismail commented that his friendships with non–South Asian students were sometimes questioned by "*desi*" (South Asian) youth, but he defended this by arguing for a more expansive conception of community:

> I hang out with different kids but even I heard it from a lot of *desis* who say, "Why you go with them?" They don't like it, but I say if you want to live in a different world, you have to exist with them. . . . Sometimes you have to go outside [your group] and say, yeah, alright, we are friends too, we are not going to discriminate [against] you, because . . . we don't look like you. . . . [Y]our relationship is gonna be bigger, right. But if you're gonna live in the *desi* community, you're only going to know *desi* people, not the other people.

Ismail traced the value he places on multiculturalist coexistence to a notion of India as a multiethnic nation. He said, "India is a really good place to live in . . . because they've got a lot of religions, different languages, different people." But this was before the massacre of Muslim Indians during the Gujarat riots in spring 2002 shook the belief in the reality and depth of Indian secularism for many Indians, especially Muslims, even though the Indian Muslim youth I spoke to continued to cling to their belief in Indian pluralism after the riots.

Coexisting with this idea of multicultural inclusion were moments of tension among different groups of youth in the school, as there are in any school or community. After September 11, some of the South Asian immigrant youth, particularly the Muslim boys, felt targeted by other high school youth. Accusations of "you're a terrorist" or "you're a bin Laden" entered into fights among boys who flung these new racial epithets at one another as part of a national discourse about Muslims and Arabs as the "enemy threat" that was intensified after 9/11. The South Asian Muslim boys, and girls, felt this acutely: did this mean *they* were the enemy, and how could they live as such?

One of the anti-Muslim incidents in Wellford after 9/11 occurred in the school, when an African American girl accused two Pakistani boys, Amir and Walid, of "killing people" and reportedly called them "Muslim niggers." The girl was eventually suspended but Amir was, in fact, a friend of the girl's brother and said he tried to intervene to soften her punishment. Both boys emphatically refused to portray the incident as a Black/South Asian or Black/Muslim conflict; they insisted that this was the case of a lone individual who Walid half-jokingly said must have been "drunk" or "high." Amir, in fact, said that he thought African Americans were less likely to have an uncritically nationalist response to the events of 9/11 than white Americans, even though he was hesitant to extend this generalization to their responses to the military campaign in Afghanistan.

For Walid and Amir, 9/11 prompted a heightened self-consciousness about racialization that seemed, if anything, to reinforce the black-white racial polarization. Walid felt that African Americans were not as shattered by the attacks on the United States because, in his view, black Americans feel alienated from the nation-state due to the legacy of slavery. While this racialized difference after 9/11 is more complex than Walid suggests, what is important is that he *believes* that African Americans share his experience of marginalization within the nation. But Walid does not completely dismiss the renewed nationalism of Americans after 9/11, saying, "The first thing is they're born here in the USA, so that's their country. . . . We are immigrants. . . . If something happens in back home, like, and someone else did something, we're gonna be angry too, right?" Yet it is also apparent that 9/11 seems to have drawn him into an understanding of citizenship that is based on racialized fissures in claims to national identity and affiliation with other youth of color.

For Walid and others, the response of African Americans seems more significant than that of Latinos or even Arab Americans because on the one hand they are the largest group of students of color in the school, and on the other hand, they stand for a particular manifestation of contested U.S. citizenship to these youth, even if not all are actually U.S.-born. The responses of these Pakistani boys suggests to me a potentially *polycultural citizenship,* based not on the reification of cultural difference that multiculturalism implies, but on a complex set of political affiliations and social boundary crossings. Robin Kelley's notion of polyculturalism suggests that "we were multi-ethnic and polycultural from the get-go." A polycultural approach to difference suggests that cultures are inevitably already hybridized, and that there are no discrete, "pure" cultures.[33] Polycultural citizenship is embedded in the messiness and nuances of relationships of different groups with one other and with the state, and is based on a political, not just cultural resonance, based on particular historical and material conjunctures.

Polycultural citizenship is not an idealization, however, of the complexities of race politics. I do not want to suggest that polyculturalism exists in the absence of antiblack racism in this community, or that racialized antagonisms and suspicion in the school are not imbibed at all by immigrant youth; in getting to know these youth over a period of time, I have found that these tensions do indeed exist. Rather, there is room in my notion of polycultural citizenship to acknowledge the resentment and competition bred by daily struggles for turf or resources. These young immigrants simultaneously invoke a multiculturalist discourse of pluralist coexistence and a poly-culturalist notion of boundary crossing and affiliation, embedded in political experience but also in popular-culture practices shared with youth of color. These young people are not involved in formal political organizations or in traditionally defined activism, but their deepened understanding of racism is based on a political, not just cultural, resonance with other youth of color in the school based on their shared experiences after 9/11.

Muslim immigrant youth sense a connection with other youth of color and with African Muslim youth in the city, even as they struggle with the challenges that Muslim identity has posed to liberal multiculturalism. Multiculturalist responses to the assault on the civil liberties of Muslim and Arab Americans have tended to consider racial profiling within a racialized framework of minority victimhood. "Muslim Americans," or the trio of "Arab, Muslim, and South Asian Americans," are constructed as just another culturally (and religiously) distinct ethnic category whose problems can be contained within a discourse of domestic racism. The assumption is that "racial profiling" can be addressed simply by "cross-cultural understanding" or interreligious "dialogue" that leads to inclusion within the multicultural nation. However, the "War on Terror" has highlighted the limitations of multicultural citizenship as a response to state policies targeting Muslim and Arab Americans after 9/11, for these were based not just on racial or religious but on political profiling. "Muslim" identity has been ethnicized since 9/11, but it is not an ethnic or racial category at all, even within the ambiguous construction of race in the United States, although Muslims have certainly experienced an intensified racialization as a demonized "other." But it is important to keep in mind that "racial profiling" and Islamophobia after 9/11 are at root tied to imperial policies that drive the global "War on Terror," particularly U.S. interests in dominating the Middle East. However, liberal multiculturalism suppresses a critique of the state and evades discussions of political injustice through a discourse of cultural difference.

After 9/11, it also became apparent that minority groups who had traditionally borne the brunt of racial profiling were not completely resistant to the anti-Arab and anti-Muslim suspicion and paranoia of the "War on Terrorism." There are many reasons for the failure of interracial alliances among these groups, historically and politically, that could be clarified in a longer discussion. Such a discussion would have to include the resistance of some South Asians to affiliate with marginalized groups of color in their desire to achieve model minority status and the hyper-nationalism that emerged in the United States after 9/11 and that absorbed even marginalized groups. The U.S. empire uses difference and consumption, in its domestic subordination of marginalized groups, to divide struggles against racism at home from movements for justice and against imperialism abroad.

Dissenting Citizenship

Muslim Americans and Arab Americans are defined, particularly after 9/11 but also at other moments, such as the Iran hostage crisis and the Gulf War, as political scapegoats and *therefore* cultural aliens.[34] Their presumed cultural difference is highlighted as part of a political and cultural doctrine that defines American interests and national identity in opposition to a "foreign enemy" and an "enemy within." Syed Khan, an Indian immigrant who was on the Board of Religious Directors of the Islamic Center of Sharon, was the founder of Muslim Community Support Services, an organization that held forums on issues of civil rights and cultural citizenship for Muslim Americans after 9/11. Khan commented in the fall of 2002 on the White House's early public embrace and then neglect of Muslim American leaders after 9/11: "Initially leaders including Bush had spoken up [against racial profiling], but afterwards, when it wasn't as critical, outreach to Muslim Americans has stopped completely. Now, it's bashing time." Other South Asian Muslims I spoke to were quick to point to the outpouring of support offered by neighbors and friends after 9/11. The two perspectives are, of course, both true. Individual acts of solidarity have coexisted with acts of discrimination, private and state-sponsored, on a mass scale.[35] The two processes often work together in racial profiling that works through contradictions of official rhetoric, which emphasized multicultural inclusion, and state policy, which continued to target Muslim and Arab Americans through surveillance, detention, deportation, and programs such as Special Registration.

Khan worried, as others in the community did, that Muslim Americans were not speaking up enough against the prospect of social and political, if not physical, internment, given the specter of the mass internment of Japanese Americans as "enemy" threats during World War II that loomed in historical memory when the mass detentions of Muslim and Arab Americans took place after 9/11. However, my research demonstrated that some Muslim immigrant youth were willing to voice political views, even publicly, that most South Asian middle-class community leaders were afraid of expressing. The Muslim immigrant youth I spoke to had an analysis of 9/11 and the U.S. war in Afghanistan that drew on a notion of international human rights and resisted the nationalization of the Twin Towers tragedy. Amir said to me in December 2001,

> You have to look at it in two ways. It's not right that ordinary people over there [in Afghanistan], like you and me, just doing their work, get killed. They don't have anything to do with . . . the attacks in New York, but they're getting killed. And also the people in New York who got killed, that's not right either.

Aliyah, a Gujarati American girl who could very easily pass for Latina, chose to write the words "INDIA + MUSLIM" on her bag after 9/11. For her, this was a gesture of defiance responding to the casting of Muslims as potentially disloyal citizens; she said, "Just because one Muslim did it in New York, you can't involve everybody in there, you know what I'm sayin.'" Issues of innocence, culpability, justice, and collective punishment were uppermost in the minds of the South Asian Muslim students when discussing this topic, even for new immigrants such as Zeenat. She thought that the bombing of Afghanistan in response to the attacks of 9/11 was "wrong" because the United States was attacking people who were not involved in the terrorist attacks and, echoing Ayesha's remark, said, "After September 11, they [Americans] hate the Muslims. . . . I think they want the government to hate the Muslims, like, all Muslims are same."

After the anti-Muslim incident in the high school, the International Student Center organized a student assembly featuring two Arab American speakers who criticized the "War on Terrorism" and the attack on civil liberties. Amir, Walid, and a Gujarati Muslim girl, Samiyah, delivered eloquent speeches condemning racism to an auditorium filled with their peers. Amir said that when he was threatened by some young men in Boston, "I could have done the same thing, but I don't think it's the right thing to do." Amir is a muscular young man and his call for nonviolent response was a powerful one at that assembly, one that could also be taken to be a larger political statement about the U.S. response to the attacks. Samiyah stood up in her *salwar kameez* and said, "We have to respect each other if we want to change society. You have to stand up for your rights." Muslim immigrant youth were being publicly drawn into race politics and civil rights debates in the local community, although it is not clear yet what the impact of this politicization will be over time. But a year later on the anniversary of September 11, when the International Student Center organized another student assembly, Samiyah's younger sister and another Gujarati Muslim girl, Mumtaz, voluntarily made similar speeches that were reported in the local press. Mumtaz spoke of her sadness at the events of 9/11 and also said "that it's not right to go after Pakistan and Afghanistan and all Muslims who had nothing to do with it."

Even though these working-class youth do not have the support of, or time to participate in, community or political organizations, they have become spokespersons in the public sphere willing to voice a dissenting view. Other Muslim American youth have been forced to play the role of educators as well, giving speeches at their schools and in community forums about Islam, though a coordinator of a Muslim youth group at the Central Square mosque says that it is a role not without pressure or fatigue for young Muslim Americans. Understandably some of them are also hesitant to speak publicly about political issues given that even legal citizens are worried about expressing political critique or dissent in the era of the PATRIOT Act. Repression works on two levels to silence dissent, as Corey Robin points out: on a state level, and also on the level of civil society, where individuals internalize repression and censor themselves.[36] Robin argues that "fear does the work—or enhances the work—of repression," noting that the "effects of "Fear, American Style" are most evident today in immigrant, Middle Eastern, and South Asian communities, as well as in the workplace where "suppression of dissent" is evident since 9/11.[37]

In the face of such repression, I have found these Muslim immigrant youth to be engaged in a practice of dissenting citizenship based on a critique of state policies, both privately and publicly. Their expression of dissenting citizenship means they stand apart from the dominant perspective in the nation at some moments, even as they stand together with others outside the borders of the nation who are affected by U.S. foreign policy. Jamila, a Bangladeshi girl, said of the war in Afghanistan, "I felt bad for those poor people there. Because America didn't have no proof that they actually did it, but they were killing all those innocent people who had nothing to do with it." Amir and other youth emphasized the importance of political justice and respect for international human rights, denouncing both the terrorist attacks and militarized state aggression as a means of retribution. Dissenting citizenship captures some of the ambivalence toward the United States that these youth experience, for America is simultaneously a place invested with their parents' desire for economic advancement and security and their own hopes to belong in a new home, and also the site of alienation, discrimination, and anxiety about belonging.

The perspective of Muslim immigrant youth is very much rooted in their identities *as* Muslims, for they are targeted as Muslims by the state, and it also sheds light on the links between U.S. policies at home and abroad. These young immigrants are subjects of both the "Wars on Terror" *and* the war on immigration. The dissenting views of Muslim immigrant youth implicitly critique U.S. imperial power through their linking of warfare *within* the state to international war. It is this link between the domestic and imperial that makes their perspective an important mode of dissent because the imperial project of the new Cold War works by obscuring the links between domestic and foreign policies. The United States has had a long history, since its wars in Cuba, Puerto Rico, and the Philippines in 1898, of "imperialism without colonies" or of "informal empire" and of neocolonial occupation, as in Iraq.[38] The conceptualization of U.S. empire is a project that has drawn renewed attention now that the term "empire" has come out of the closet, in the academy and mass media. Despite the different forms that U.S. empire has taken in exercising direct or indirect control, such as through proxy wars or client states (such as Israel, Jordan, and now Afghanistan), the dominance of U.S. military, economic, and political power, the three major aspects of imperial power, is still paramount.[39] The war at home and the war abroad, the two fronts of empire, actually work in tandem with each other at the expense of ordinary people everywhere.

Conclusion

It is important to remember that there are important continuities before and after 9/11 that are often not acknowledged enough in discussing the "War on Terror." My use of "post-9/11" is not meant to signify a radical historical or political rupture in U.S. politics but rather a moment of renewed contestation over ongoing issues of citizenship and transnationalism, religion and nationalism, civil rights and immigrant rights. This state of emergency, the crisis of civil rights and warfare, is in fact not exceptional in the United States,[40] for the post-9/11 moment builds on measures and forms of power already in place. This is a state of everyday life in empire. The research here is an attempt to craft an ethnography of the new empire in order to understand the everyday struggles of those, such as immigrants and youth, whose lives have been transformed by this ongoing crisis and who have found subtle and complex ways to express their dissent.

NOTES

Originally published as "Youth Culture, Citizenship and Globalization: South Asian Muslim Youth in the United States after September 11," in *Comparative Studies of South Asia, Africa, and the Middle East* 24.1 (2004): 219–31. © 2004 *Comparative Studies of South Asia, Africa, and the*

Middle East. All rights reserved. Used by permission of the publisher. The research on which this paper is based was funded by the Russell Sage Foundation and supported by my research assistants, Palav Babaria and Sarah Khan. Thanks to Louise Cainkar for her editorial feedback on an earlier version of this article.

1. There were seven hundred reported hate crimes against South Asian Americans, Arab Americans, and Muslim Americans, including four homicides (two involving South Asian American victims), in the three weeks following 9-11-01 (Jeff Coen, "Hate Crimes Reports Reach Record Level," *Chicago Tribune*, October 9, 2001). At least two hundred hate crimes were reported against Sikh Americans alone (Jane Lampan, "Under Attack, Sikhs Defend Their Religious Liberties," *Christian Science Monitor*, October 31, 2001). The Council on American-Islamic Relations reported that it had documented 960 incidents of racial profiling in the five weeks after 9/11/01, with hate crimes declining and incidents of airport profiling and workplace discrimination on the increase (Associated Press, San Jose, CA, "Hate Crime Reports Down, Civil Rights Complaints Up," October 25, 2001).

2. Nancy Chang, *Silencing Political Dissent: How Post–September 11 Anti-Terrorism Measures Threaten Our Civil Liberties* (New York: Seven Stories/Open Media, 2002), 94.

3. Ibid., 29–32.

4. Ibid.

5. David Cole and James Dempsey, *Terrorism and the Constitution: Sacrificing Civil Liberties in the Name of National Security* (New York: New Press, 2002), 168.

6. CAIR (Council on American-Islamic Relations), *The Status of Muslim Civil Rights in the United States: Patterns of Discrimination* (Washington, DC: Council on American-Islamic Relations Research Center, 1998); Jack G. Shaheen, "Hollywood's Reel Arabs and Muslims," pp. 179–202 in *Muslims and Islamization in North America: Problems and Prospects,* ed. Ambreen Haque (Beltsville, MD: Amana Publications, 1999).

7. Cole and Dempsey, 35–48; Louise Cainkar, "No Longer Invisible: Arab and Muslim Exclusion after September 11," *Middle East Report* 224 (Fall 2002). Accessed through website: http://www.merip.org/mer/mer224/224_cainkar.html; Jordan Green, "Silencing Dissent," *ColorLines* 6.2 (2003): 17–20.

8. Joan Jensen, *Passage from India: Asian Indian Immigrants in North America* (New Haven, CT: Yale University Press, 1988).

9. Vijay Prashad, *The Karma of Brown Folk* (Minneapolis: University of Minnesota Press, 2000).

10. Stephen J. Schulhofer, *The Enemy Within: Intelligence Gathering, Law Enforcement, and Civil Liberties in the Wake of September 11* (New York: Century Foundation Press, 2002,) 11.

11. Chang, 69–87.

12. Oliver Ryan, "Empty Shops, Empty Promises for Coney Island Pakistanis," *ColorLines* 6.2 (2003): 14–16; see p. 16.

13. The re-registration component of the program was officially ended by the Department of Homeland Security in December 2003, after protests by immigrant/civil rights and grassroots community organizations, while other aspects of the program remained in place, and the detentions and deportations put in place by the program continue.

14. Ryan, "Empty Shops," 16.

15. Rachel L. Swarns, "More Than 13,000 May Face Deportation," *New York Times*, June 7 2003, Internet posting.

16. Ryan, "Empty Shops."

17. Swarns, "More Than 13,000."

18. Bill O. Hing, "No Place for Angels: In Reaction to Kevin Johnson," *University of Illinois Law Review* 2000 (2): 559–601; Bill O. Hing, "The Dark Side of Operation Gatekeeper," *UC Davis Journal of International Law & Policy* 7.2 (2001): 123–67.

19. Kathleen Moore, "A Closer Look at Anti-Terrorism Law: *American Arab Anti-Discrimination Committee v. Reno* and the Construction of Aliens' Rights," in *Arabs in America: Building a New Future,* ed. Michael Suleiman (Philadelphia: Temple University Press, 1999), 84–99; see p. 95. From 1996 to 2000, the government sought to use secret evidence to detain and deport two dozen immigrants, almost all of them Muslims, but ultimately the government evidence was thrown out and the accused were released (Cole and Dempsey, *Terrorism,* 127).

20. The 2000 Census reported 2,720 Indian immigrants (2.7 percent of the population), 125 Pakistanis, and 120 Bangladeshis in Wellford, a city that is 68.1 percent White American, 11.9 percent African American, 11.9 percent Asian American, and 7.4 percent Latino (U.S. Census Bureau, 2000). This, of course, does not include undocumented immigrants. The "native" population is 74.1 percent and foreign-born is 25.9 percent; 17.7 percent are not citizens and 31.2 percent speak a language other than English.

21. Kum-Kum Bhavnani, *Talking Politics: A Psychological Framing for Views from Youth in Britain* (Cambridge: Cambridge University Press, 1991); David Buckingham, *The Making of Citizens: Young People, News, and Politics* (London: Routledge, 2000).

22. Lauren Berlant, *The Queen of America Goes to Washington City: Essays on Sex and Citizenship* (Durham, NC: Duke University Press, 1997); Kathleen Coll, "Problemas y necesidades: Latina Vernaculars of Citizenship and Coalition-Building in Chinatown, San Francisco," Paper presented at Racial (Trans)Formations: Latinos and Asians Remaking the United States, Center for the Study of Ethnicity and Race, Columbia University, March 2002; Toby Miller, *The Well-Tempered Subject: Citizenship, Culture, and the Postmodern Subject* (Baltimore, MD: Johns Hopkins University Press, 1993); Renato Rosaldo, "Cultural Citizenship, Inequality, and Multiculturalism," in *Latino Cultural Citizenship: Claiming Identity, Space, and Rights,* ed. William. F. Flores and Rina Benmayor (Boston: Beacon Press, 1997), 27–38.

23. Lok Siu, "Diasporic Cultural Citizenship: Chineseness and Belonging in Central America and Panama," *Social Text* 69 (2001): 7–28; see p. 9.

24. William V. Flores and Rina Benmayor, eds., *Latino Cultural Citizenship: Claiming Identity, Space, and Rights* (Boston: Beacon Press, 1997), 6; Renato Rosaldo, "Cultural Citizenship, Inequality, and Multiculturalism," in Flores and Benmayor, eds., *Latino Cultural Citizenship,* 27–38.

25. Aihwa Ong, "Cultural Citizenship as Subject-Making," *Current Anthropology* 37.5 (December 1996): 738.

26. Gill Jones and Claire Wallace, *Youth, Family, and Citizenship* (Buckingham, UK: Open University Press, 1992).

27. T. H. Marshall, *Citizenship and Social Class* (Cambridge: Cambridge University Press, 1950).

28. Aihwa Ong, *Flexible Citizenship: The Cultural Logics of Transnationality* (Durham, NC: Duke University Press, 1999); Linda Basch, Nina Glick Schiller, and Cristina Szanton Blanc, eds., *Nations Unbound: Transnational Projects, Postcolonial Predicaments, and Deterritorialized Nation-States* (Amsterdam: Gordon and Breach, 1994).

29. Ong, "Cultural Citizenship," 737; Ong, *Flexible Citizenship.*

30. Katherine S. Newman, *No Shame in My Game: The Working Poor in the Inner City* (New York: Knopf and the Russell Sage Foundation, 1999); Stuart Tannock, *Youth at Work: The Unionized Fast-Food and Grocery Workplace* (Philadelphia: Temple University Press, 2001).

31. Ong, "Cultural Citizenship," 739.

32. Manu Vimalassery, "Passports and Pink Slips," *SAMAR (South Asian Magazine for Action and Reflection)* 15 (2002): 7–8, 20; see Ong, "Cultural Citizenship," for a fuller discussion.

33. Robin D. Kelley, *Yo' Mama's Disfunktional! Fighting the Culture Wars in Urban America* (Boston: Beacon Press, 1997).

34. Cole and Dempsey, *Terrorism*; Fereydoun Safizadeh, "Children of the Revolution: Transnational Identity among Young Iranians in Northern California," in *A World Between: Poems, Short Stories, and Essays by Iranian-Americans,* ed. Persis Karim and Mohammad M. Khorrami (New York: George Braziller, 1999), 255–76.

35. Bill O. Hing, "Vigilante Racism: The De-Americanization of Immigrant America," *Michigan Journal of Race and Law* 7.2 (2002): 441–56; Vijay Prashad, "The Green Menace: McCarthyism after 9/11," *The Subcontintental: A Journal of South Asian American Political Identity* 1.1 (2003): 65–75; Corey Robin, "Fear, American Style: Civil Liberty after 9/11," in *Implicating Empire: Globalization and Resistance in the 21st-Century World Order,* ed. Stanley Aronowitz and Heather Gautney (New York: Basic Books, 2003), 47–64.

36. Robin, "Fear," 47–64.

37. Ibid., 48, 53.

38. Amy Kaplan, "Where Is Guantánamo?" In *Legal Borderlands: Law and the Construction of American Borders,* ed. Mary Dudziak and Leti Volpp, special issue of *American Quarterly* 57.3 (2005): 831–58; Harry Magdoff, *Imperialism without Colonies* (New York: Monthly Review Press, 2003); Ediberto Román, "Membership Denied: An Outsider's Story of Subordination and Subjugation under U.S. Colonialism," in *Moral Imperialism: A Critical Anthology,* ed. Berta Esperanza Hernández-Truyol (New York: New York University Press, 2002).

39. Alain Joxe, *Empire of Disorder* (Los Angeles: Semiotext(e), 2002).

40. Keya Ganguly, *States of Exception: Everyday Life and Postcolonial Identity* (Minneapolis: University of Minnesota Press, 2001).

Chapter 23

Without a Trace

*Asian Americans and Pacific Islanders in
Prime-Time Television*

*Christina B. Chin, Noriko Milman, Meera E. Deo,
Jenny J. Lee, Nancy Wang Yuen*

Introduction

Television creates a kind of hyper-reality, a shared fantasy world that merges with and sometimes overshadows the more mundane world of real life for millions of Americans. (Lichter et al. 1994, 13)

While prime-time television is often considered mere "fantasy," it is one of the most pervasive agents of socialization and, consequently, demands critical examination. This is particularly pertinent given that the world of prime time often fails to present an accurate portrait of reality. Past studies of television reveal discrepancies by group statuses, such as race and gender (Children Now 2004; Entman and Rojecki 2001; Gray 1995; Hoffman and Noriega 2004). White males tend to dominate the world of prime-time television while all other groups remain severely underrepresented compared to their population percentages (Children Now 2004; Hoffman and Noriega 2004; Hunt 2002, 2003) and/or restricted to particular networks associated with "ethnic" programming, as in the case of African Americans (Hunt 2002, 2003).

Asian Americans and Pacific Islanders (AAPIs) are consistently underrepresented numerically and especially missing from lead roles (Asian American Justice Center et al. 2006; Children Now 2004; Hoffman and Noriega 2004; National Asian Pacific American Legal Consortium et al. 2005). The estimated number of AAPIs living in the United States in 2004 approximated fifteen million, or about 5 percent of the total U.S. population (U.S. Census Bureau 2006). AAPI fictional characters in the world of prime-time television are consistently underrepresented at less than half of their actual U.S. population (Asian American Justice Center et al. 2006; Children Now 2004; National Asian Pacific American Legal Consortium et al. 2005; Screen Actors Guild 2004). AAPI actors are typically relegated to supporting and marginal roles, portraying only 1.3 percent of all lead roles in film and television in 2003 (Screen Actors Guild 2004). In contrast, white actors dominated in 2003, with 74.8 percent of the total lead roles (Screen Actors Guild 2004). When examining prime-time television, the difference in quality of roles between groups is even more startling. According to a study of the fall 2003–2004 prime-time season (Children Now 2004), "significant percentages of African American (25%), white (23%) and Latino (20%) characters appeared in opening credits roles, yet just one in ten Asian/Pacific Islander characters (11%) played a starring role" (3).

This lack of representation and prominence of AAPI characters is problematic given that people are more likely to use popular images when making assumptions about groups with whom they have little or no contact (Entman and Rojecki 2000). As a result, the limited images of AAPIs not only restrict the actors who portray them but also narrow the popular perceptions of AAPIs in the United States. While people use both real-world examples and typifications, such as stereotyped characterizations from the media, to represent groups to which they belong, only typifications are used to conceptualize groups to which they do not belong (Entman and Rojecki 2000).

This chapter, based on data collected for the fall 2004 and fall 2005 seasons of prime-time television, demonstrates how Asian Americans and Pacific Islanders continue to be marginalized in terms of both numbers and the quality of characters.[1] We examine prime-time shows, paying particular attention to numerical representation by race, gender, network, program, and geographic setting. Furthermore, focusing on only those shows featuring AAPI actors, we explore character quality by discussing screen time, genres, relationships, occupations, and status.

Our findings show that from the 2004 to the 2005 season, there have been improvements in character depth. This increased prominence has resulted in some pioneering award nominations and wins for AAPI actors, as well as for some prime-time programs that showcase complex AAPI characters. However, despite the growing recognition of AAPIs among audience and industry members, because of lack of numerical representation onscreen, they remain marginalized in the world of prime-time television.

Methodology and Sample

This study examines both network websites and episodes of prime-time programming on the six national broadcast networks. Since the study focuses on recurring characters that develop in depth and complexity over time, news magazine programming, reality shows with no regular hosts, animated series, and movie specials were excluded from the sample. Regular characters were determined by using the program's opening credits along with the network websites and self-reports. In addition, this study also examines diversity within the AAPI community by distinguishing between monoracial[2] and multiracial[3] AAPI actors. Both monoracials and multiracials were identified by coding websites for actor phenotype and name, as well as character name. For ethnically ambiguous actors, reliable internet databases, such as www.imdb.com, were used to investigate race or ethnicity. Table 23.1 provides an overview of all the AAPI regulars in the fall 2004 and fall 2005 prime-time seasons.

To maximize the data from recorded episodes, we intentionally coded only first-run episodes (not reruns) in which the AAPI regulars appeared. Consequently, if the AAPI

TABLE 23.1
AAPI Regulars by Network, Season, Program, Ethnicity, and Gender

Network	Season	Program	Actor	Character Name	Actor Ethnicity	Character Ethnicity	Character Gender
ABC	2004	*Boston Legal*	Rhona Mitra	Tara Wilson	Multiracial AAPI (Indian-white)	White	Female
ABC	2004	*NYPD Blue**	Mark-Paul Gosselaar	John Clark, Jr.	Multiracial AAPI (Indonesian-white)	White	Male
ABC	2005	*Grey's Anatomy*	Sandra Oh	Cristina Yang	Korean	Korean	Female
ABC	2005	*Hot Properties***	Amy Hill	Mary	Multiracial AAPI (Japanese-white)	Ambiguous	Female
ABC	2004/2005	*Lost*	Naveen Andrews	Sayid Jarrah	Indian	Iraqi	Male
ABC	2004/2005	*Lost*	Daniel Dae Kim	Jin-Soo Kwon	Korean	Korean	Male
ABC	2004/2005	*Lost*	Yunjin Kim	Sun Kwon	Korean	Korean	Female
FOX	2005	*Bones*	Michaela Conlin	Angela Montenegro	Multiracial AAPI (Chinese-white)	Ambiguous	Female
FOX	2004/2005	*MADtv*	Bobby Lee	(Various)	Korean	Various Asian	Male
FOX	2004	*North Shore*^	Jason Momoa	Frankie Seau	Multiracial AAPI (Hawaiian-white)	Ambiguous	Male
FOX	2005	*That '70 Show***	Tommy Chong	Leo	Multiracial AAPI (Chinese-white)	Ambiguous	Male
NBC	2004/2005	*Crossing Jordan*	Ravi Kapoor	"Bug"	Indian	Indian	Male
NBC	2004	*ER*	Ming-Na	Jing-Mei	Chinese	Chinese	Female
NBC	2004/2005	*ER*	Parminder Nagra	Neela Rasgotra	Indian	Indian	Female
NBC	2004	*Hawaii**	Aya Sumika Tamiya	Linh	Multiracial AAPI (Japanese-white)	AAPI	Female
NBC	2004	*Hawaii**	Cary-hiroyuki Tagawa	Terry Harada	Japanese	Japanese	Male
NBC	2004	*Hawaii**	Peter Navy Tuiasosopo	Kaleo	Samoan	Pacific Islander	Male
NBC	2005	*Inconceivable***	Ming-Na	Rachel Liu	Chinese	Chinese	Female
NBC	2004/2005	*Law and Order: Special Victims Unit*	B.D. Wong	George Huang	Chinese	Chinese	Male
NBC	2005	*Surface*	Ian Anthony Dale	Davis Lee	Multiracial AAPI (Japanese-white)	Ambiguous	Male
NBC	2004	*Third Watch*	Anthony Ruivivar	Carlos Nieto	Multiracial AAPI (Filipino, Chinese, white)	Ambiguous	Male
UPN	2004	*Enterprise**	Linda Park	Hoshi Sato	Korean	Japanese	Female
UPN	2005	*Half and Half*	Alec Mapa	Adam Benet	Filipino	Filipino	Male
WB	2004/2005	*Gilmore Girls*	Keiko Agena	Lane Kim	Japanese	Korean	Female
WB	2004/2005	*Smallville*	Kristin Kreuk	Lana Lang	Multiracial AAPI (Chinese-white)	White	Female

* Show canceled in 2004; ** Show canceled in 2005

regular(s) did not appear in episodes, the recording schedule was extended to capture episodes in which the AAPI regular(s) did appear.[4] As a result of this coding process, the presence of AAPIs may be overrepresented. While the data collected for the fall 2004 season uses only one recorded episode, the 2005 season includes averaged data collected from two episodes of each show. Excluding commercial time, the average total show time for hour-long programs is forty-one minutes; the average for half-hour-long programs is twenty-one minutes.

All data were subjected to two levels of analysis. First, a macro-level analysis examined general program characteristics that included genre, network, and program setting. This information was obtained from network websites; where information was lacking, actual episodes were reviewed. Second, a micro-level analysis identified more detailed characteristics for each regular character on shows featuring at least one regular AAPI actor, such as race, gender, occupation, intimate relationships, character setting, language, character name, screen time, and plot summary. The race and gender of characters were obtained from network websites while all remaining information was obtained from coding recorded episodes. To ensure reliability between coders, 8 percent of the sample was coded by each of the coders independently. The observed frequency of agreement, based on the calculation of kappa, was at 95 percent or higher.

Numerical Representation

How are AAPIs numerically represented on prime-time television, and how do those figures compare with the number of AAPIs in the U.S. population? To answer these questions, this study explored the numerical representation of AAPI regulars by race, gender, television network, individual program, and program setting. Using this data, we reveal a clearer picture of how AAPIs are represented in the world of prime-time television and how this may not be an accurate reflection of the world in which we live.

AAPI Regulars by Race and Gender

For both the fall 2004 and fall 2005 seasons, the dominance of white male characters persisted in prime-time television. Whites remained the principle subjects of shows in 2004 and 2005, constituting 77.9 percent and 70.6 percent of all regular characters, respectively. In fall 2004, only 16.8 percent, or eighteen out of the 107 total regular characters, were portrayed by AAPI actors, twelve of whom were AAPI monoracial and six, AAPI multiracial. By 2005, this percentage declined to 13.8 percent, or sixteen AAPI regulars out of 116 total regulars; eleven were AAPI monoracial and five were AAPI multiracial.

Despite the slightly higher population percentage of females (51 percent) compared to males (49 percent) in the United States, in fall 2004, male regular characters were

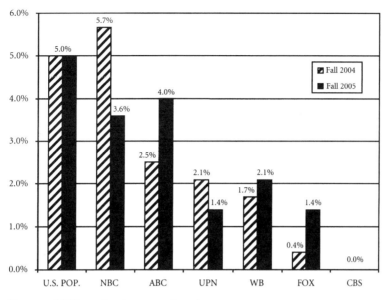

Fig. 23.1. AAPI regulars by network and season.

overrepresented compared to females across every major racial group (white, African American, Latino, and AAPI).[5] The following season, gender representation improved only for AAPIs and Latinos, with an equal number of male and female AAPI regulars featured on prime-time television.

AAPI Regulars by Network and Program

For both prime-time seasons, some networks and programs featured more AAPIs than others, though most fell short of reflecting the actual AAPI population in the United States (see figure 23.1). In fall 2004, NBC was the only network to feature a percentage of AAPI regulars (5.7 percent) that generally mirrored the U.S. AAPI population (5.0 percent).[6] But for both seasons, all other networks fell below this percentage, with three networks (UPN, WB, and FOX) at less than half and one network (CBS) with no representation at all.

In fall 2004, among the 113 prime-time programs, only thirteen featured at least one AAPI actor; three programs (NBC's *ER* and *Hawaii* and ABC's *Lost*) included more than one AAPI actor. There was virtually no change by the following season, with fourteen of the 102 prime-time shows featuring at least one AAPI actor. While the ratio of shows with at least one AAPI actor increased marginally, there was only one show that had more than one AAPI actor among its regular cast: ABC's *Lost,* with three AAPI regular actors. This wide dispersal of AAPI actors among programs suggests a "tokenism" of AAPIs in some shows, especially as these actors received limited screen time and character prominence, both discussed below.

Missed Opportunity Programs

In both 2004 and 2005, the nationwide AAPI population stood at 5.0 percent of the total U.S. population. However, in some U.S. cities and counties, AAPI population percentages were much higher. For both seasons, there were fifty-one shows set in locations densely concentrated[7] with AAPIs, yet the majority of them failed to feature a single AAPI regular character. We thus consider these "missed opportunity programs."

Shows located in U.S. cities on the West Coast, which contain much higher concentrations of AAPIs than the nationwide figure, consistently underrepresented AAPIs in their casts. For example, of the five programs set in San Francisco, CA, where AAPIs constitute over 30 percent of the city's population (U.S. Census Bureau 2004), no AAPI regulars were featured, with the exception of the 2005 season of *Half and Half* on UPN. All twenty programs set in Los Angeles County, which is more than 10 percent AAPI, completely excluded AAPIs from their collective casts. Even on the two shows set in Honolulu, HI, where over 60 percent of the residents are AAPI (U.S. Census Bureau 2004), AAPI regular characters constituted less than a quarter of the regular cast members.

Accurate AAPI representation on programs set on the East Coast did not fare any better. Aside from NBC's *Law and Order: SVU*, all twenty-four programs set in New York City featured no AAPI regulars even though the city has a nearly 10 percent AAPI population (U.S. Census Bureau 2004). An especially glaring omission was *King of Queens* on CBS, which is set in the borough of Queens, NY, where AAPIs constitute around 20 percent of the total population (U.S. Census Bureau 2004).

Examining the numerical representation of AAPI regular characters reveals how prime-time television grossly underrepresents AAPIs, particularly in cities with high AAPI concentrations. Consequently, this lack of representation perpetuates the invisibility of AAPIs on the television screen, directly contributing to a perception of AAPIs as "foreigners" who have not established prominent communities within the United States.

Character Representation

How do those few AAPI regulars fare in character representation compared to their non-AAPI counterparts? To assess this, we explored character prominence as indicated by screen time and qualitative indicators including featured genre, relationship, and occupational status. Our findings suggest that the majority of AAPI regulars on prime-time television are rendered largely invisible; they may be seen, but generally remain unnoticed.

Character Screen Time: Fifteen Minutes of Fame?

The extent to which a character's personality, background, and relationships can be well developed is directly affected by the amount of screen time allotted to that char-

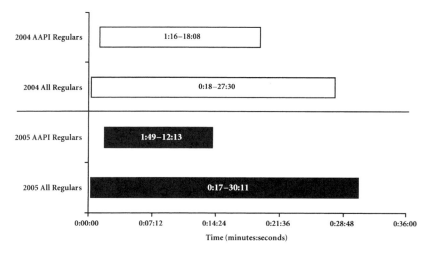

Fig. 23.2. 2004–2005 screen-time ranges for all AAPI/non-AAPI regulars on one-hour programs.

acter. Thus, screen time reflects the prominence of regulars in their respective programs by making it clear which characters are central to the show and which are peripheral.

To evaluate character screen time, several factors were considered to enable as many meaningful comparisons as possible. AAPI actor screen times were not only compared against non-AAPIs but were also disaggregated to provide a comparison between AAPI monoracial and AAPI multiracial screen times. Further comparisons were made between female and male AAPI regulars.

In general, AAPI regulars featured less prominently than non-AAPI regulars, as indicated by their significantly lower screen times (see figure 23.2). In 2004, the highest AAPI screen time (18 minutes 8 seconds) was only two-thirds of the highest non-AAPI screen time (27 minutes 48 seconds). In 2005, the highest AAPI screen time (12 minutes 13 seconds) was less than *half* of the highest non-AAPI screen time (30 minutes 28 seconds). In half-hour sitcoms (not shown here), the highest AAPI screen time ran 4 minutes 12 seconds, less than *one-third* the highest non-AAPI screen time of 15 minutes 47 seconds. The absolute lowest screen time for any regular character on either one-hour or half-hour shows totaled a mere 27 seconds, and was held by an AAPI actor.

Figure 23.3 shows the screen-time ranges across various groups in one-hour programs, and indicates significant differences across monoracial and multiracial AAPI status, as well as gender. In 2004, multiracial AAPIs had noticeably better screen-time presence than their monoracial counterparts. The highest monoracial AAPI screen time (8 minutes 57 seconds) was less than *half* the highest multiracial AAPI screen time (18 minutes 8 seconds). Also, the lowest multiracial AAPI screen time was above five minutes whereas the lowest monoracial time was less than two minutes. Another overall trend from the 2004 screen-time data was that male AAPIs fared better than female AAPIs.

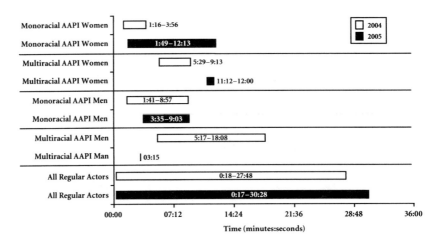

Fig. 23.3. 2004–2005 screen-time ranges for one-hour programs.

The distinction between monoracial and multiracial AAPIs was less clear in 2005, in part because there were fewer multiracial AAPI regulars in this season. Instead, the most remarkable distinction among AAPI actors in 2005 was across gender groups. AAPI women in the 2005 lineup had much higher average screen times than AAPI men, with a high of 12 minutes 13 seconds. In contrast, the highest male AAPI screen time was just over 9 minutes.

To further evaluate the prominence of AAPI regulars relative to others *within* their respective shows, each AAPI character's screen time was ranked against the screen times of all other regular cast members on that show. For example, if an AAPI regular ranked first in her program, she had more screen time than any other regular on her show. This type of evaluation revealed nuances that may have been missed if only the actual screen time measurements were examined. That is, an AAPI character screen time of 5 minutes 40 seconds is very low if the character is also last in screen time rankings for that show (i.e., every other regular has more screen time). However, it may *not* necessarily indicate poor screen time if the character is also ranked second in screen time (i.e., only one regular has more than 5 minutes and 40 seconds of screen time). This is particularly true for shows with large ensemble casts (such as ABC's *Lost*) in which screen time is distributed more widely among many characters.

No AAPI regulars ranked first in either season while only two had the second highest ranking within their respective programs. Interestingly, in 2004, two male AAPI regulars had the second highest rankings in their respective program whereas two female AAPIs ranked the second highest in 2005. Despite these highlights, most AAPIs still remain largely overshadowed by their fellow cast members. In 2004, 50 percent of AAPI regulars ranked either last or second-to-last in their respective programs. There was notable improvement in 2005; only four out of 16 AAPI regulars ranked last or second-to-last. Thus, despite the presence of AAPIs as regulars on prime-time shows, their low screen-time rankings indicate their peripheral status and that there is still room for much improvement.

Genres and Relationships: Exclusion from the "American" Family

Genres serve as important navigational tools for television audiences.[8] Viewers often expect certain plot and character conventions based on the type of show they are watching. For example, dramas tend to include serious subjects while situational comedies ("sitcoms") focus on humorous characters. Given the fact that most sitcoms revolve around families and domestic settings, the presence of characters on these types of programs are particularly salient; whether it be the Cleavers on *Leave It to Beaver* or the Cosby family on *The Cosby Show,* quintessential "American" television families are those featured on sitcoms.

While invisibility may define AAPI presence on prime-time television, exclusion generally characterizes those AAPIs featured on television sitcoms (see figure 23.4). In 2004, AAPI actors were present only in television dramas, with the exception of Bobby Lee, who starred in the sketch comedy *MADtv* (FOX). A notable improvement, AAPI actors were featured on three sitcoms in the 2005 season: *Hot Properties* (ABC), *That '70s Show* (FOX), and *Half and Half* (UPN). AAPI presence on sitcoms can allow actors to explore role options and audiences to view AAPIs in varied situations and settings; however, the actors on these shows portrayed only peripheral characters, so these goals were not truly realized. Unlike their non-AAPI counterparts, who were all family members or close friends, all of the AAPI regulars were simply acquaintances. In fact, since the cancellation of *All American Girl* (ABC) in 1995, there have been no sitcoms that focus primarily on AAPIs or their families. Their marginal presence on television sitcoms implies a unidimensionality to AAPI characters.

Another indicator that AAPI families are missing from prime-time television is the

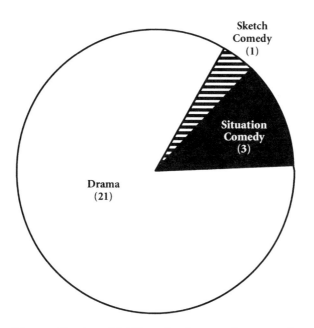

Fig. 23.4. Number of AAPI regulars by genre (2004–2005).

lack of familial relationships among AAPI regulars. When featured in relationships, AAPIs tend to be in romantic rather than familial relationships. In fact, in comparison to the 2004 prime-time season, AAPI regulars in 2005 were even more likely to be involved in romantic relationships.[9] Of the ten definitively AAPI characters, seven were shown to be closely linked to other characters. Even though AAPI romantic relationships may pique audience interest in the character's development throughout the episode and series, the relationships tend to be fleeting and rarely develop into long-term "family" arrangements. Perhaps speaking to the dearth of AAPI characters on prime-time television more generally, "Jin-Soo" and "Sun" of ABC's *Lost* were the only AAPI regulars featured as a married couple. All other AAPI regulars featured in relationships were involved in shorter-term pairings with non-AAPI characters. Thus, as in television sitcoms, most other AAPIs were excluded from meaningful, long-term domestic partnerships, especially those featuring children. Stated succinctly, AAPIs are still not considered to constitute an "American" family.

Occupation and Status: Still the "Model Minority"

Identifying the occupations of characters in a program increases their multidimensionality by revealing their status and background, while also offering a glimpse into their everyday lives. In both the 2004 and 2005 seasons, the majority of AAPI-identified characters on prime-time television had high-status occupations (see table 23.2). Of these, at least half held advanced degrees, most often in the medical sciences.

TABLE 23.2
Occupation of AAPI-Identified Characters by Network and Program (2004–2005)

Network	Program	Season	Actor	Character	Occupation
ABC	*Grey's Anatomy*	2005	Sandra Oh	Cristina Yang	Medical intern
	Lost	2004–2005	Daniel Dae Kim	Jin-Soo Kwon	Mobster/ Businessman
	Lost	2004–2005	Yunjin Kim	Sun Kwon	(Unknown)
NBC	*Crossing Jordan*	2004–2005	Ravi Kapoor	"Bug"	Medical examiner
	ER	2004	Ming-Na	Jing-Mei	Medical doctor
	ER	2004–2005	Parminder Nagra	Neela Rasgotra	Medical doctor
	Hawaii	2004	Aya Sumika	Linh Tamiya	Police officer
	Hawaii	2004	Cary-Hiroyuki Tagawa	Terry Harada	Police captain
	Hawaii	2004	Peter Navy Tuiasosopo	Kaleo	Police officer
	Inconceivable	2005	Ming-Na	Rachel Liu	Attorney
	Law & Order: SVU	2004–2005	B.D. Wong	George Huang	Forensic psychiatrist
UPN	*Enterprise*	2004	Linda Park	Hoshi Sato	Linguistic specialist
	Half and Half	2005	Alec Mapa	Adam Benet	Administrative assistant
WB	*Gilmore Girls*	2004–2005	Keiko Agena	Lane Kim	"Brainy" student/ Drummer for a rock band

Once again revisiting the issue of genre, the high status of most AAPI characters may be a reflection of the genre in which they were featured; regardless of race, most characters on one-hour dramas tend to have high-status professions. However, the absence of AAPI characters from other genres and, as a consequence, their exclusion from a varied range of occupations, may contribute to generalizations about AAPI individuals and obscure group diversity, particularly with regard to social class and educational attainment. Indeed, the "model minority" stereotype, that AAPIs represent "the model worker, the overachiever, the math maniac, or the science/computer nerd . . . [distorts] images of Asian-origin Americans and characterizes them as anything but 'normal'" (Lee and Zhou 2004, 10). Additionally, the label restricts AAPIs to complacency, silencing voices of dissent and political activism. Though some racial stereotypes may imply a "positive" characteristic about a group, these are still problematic because they generalize attributes of some members of the group and assume they are true for all. In this regard, the portrayals of high-status AAPIs on prime-time television may be reinforcing the euphemistic "model minority" myth.

Exemplary Programs

Of all television programming in the 2004 and 2005 seasons, two series stood out as exemplary in their inclusion and portrayal of AAPIs. These two shows, *Lost* and *Grey's Anatomy*, were both on ABC and among the most popular of all prime-time programs. *Lost* was the only show to feature three AAPI actors: Naveen Andrews ("Sayid"), Yunjin Kim ("Sun"), and Daniel Dae Kim ("Jin"). Although these actors had relatively low screen times, their characters were well developed and multifaceted. For example, all were involved in friendships as well as romantic relationships. Additionally, *Lost* was the only program to feature AAPI characters speaking in a foreign language; "Sun" and "Jin" frequently spoke Korean with each other while English subtitles were displayed to translate the dialogue for non-Korean speaking audiences.

The other exemplary program, *Grey's Anatomy*, highlighted AAPI actor Sandra Oh's character "Dr. Cristina Yang" through significant character depth and screen time. Her character is not simply that of a "token Asian" in the workplace; in addition to images of her on the job, viewers also catch glimpses of her in a variety of settings outside the hospital, revealing insights into her professional and her personal life. For example, viewers followed her involvement in an interracial relationship with a fellow doctor and learned she was pregnant with their child. It is no surprise that such a multifaceted character also ranked second in screen time among all regular characters on her program, averaging 10 minutes 57 seconds. For her compelling portrayal, Sandra Oh received both a Golden Globe award and a Screen Actors Guild award.

Significantly, both of the exemplary programs discussed above are consistently ranked within the top five of all prime-time television programs. For the week of October 10–16, 2005, during which we coded both shows, *Lost* captivated 14.1 million viewers and ranked fourth according to Nielsen ratings while *Grey's Anatomy* ranked fifth, drawing in an audience of 13.4 million. With such wide viewership, these programs have the most potential to explore and expand the roles of AAPI regulars, while also influencing the largest audience.

Conclusion

> I'm really proud to be on a show whose casting is a little more representative of how I think the world is. So to all my fellow Asian Americans out there, I share this with you. And be encouraged and keep shining.
>
> —Sandra Oh (acceptance speech, Screen Actors Guild Award for Outstanding Performance by a Female Actor in a Drama Series, 29 January 2006)

The state of AAPIs on prime-time television is perhaps best summed up by the above words, spoken by Sandra Oh as she accepted her 2005 Screen Actors Guild award. Clearly Sandra Oh and others enrich television programming with their acting abilities, yet few shows provide outlets to showcase their talents.

The findings based on the fall 2004 and fall 2005 prime-time seasons paint a complex picture of growing prominence amid a general landscape of invisibility. Beginning with quantitative indices, AAPIs are still significantly underrepresented on prime-time programs; 93 percent of prime-time shows completely exclude AAPI regulars from their casts. The findings reveal a lack of numerical representation by race and gender and by network, most pointedly in densely populated AAPI settings. This is particularly the case for those "missed opportunity" programs, set in locations densely populated with AAPIs, but not featuring a single AAPI regular. Moreover, analyses of character representation reveal a lack of screen time for AAPIs compared to their non-AAPI counterparts.

However, this study shows that AAPIs have made some strides in the 2005 prime-time season, as compared to the year before, especially in regards to character depth and complexity. AAPIs are now included in a variety of television genres, though the data demonstrate that AAPI regulars remain concentrated in television dramas. AAPI regulars are more likely to be featured in intimate relationships, but generally lack familial ties compared to their non-AAPI counterparts. Finally, our examination indicates some diversity among AAPI regulars' occupations, though the majority continues to occupy high-status positions. However slight, these improvements culminated in a discussion of two exemplary shows: *Lost* (ABC) and *Grey's Anatomy* (ABC).

Overall, despite some progress in character prominence and quality, the lack of numerical representation renders AAPIs largely invisible on prime-time television. We can conclude that prime-time television continues to underrepresent AAPIs, ignoring this population's presence in America. Hence, any strides made with regard to character representation tend to be obscured. Given that audiences may use these popular television images to make assumptions about various racial and ethnic groups, AAPI invisibility during prime time does little to counteract or dispel existing stereotypes. In this sense, prime-time television fails to create a diverse (and realistic) lens through which to view the world.

NOTES

1. The data is published in two reports: (1) National Asian Pacific American Legal Consortium, Nancy Yuen, Christina Chin, Meera Deo, Jenny Lee, and Noriko Milman, "Asian Pacific Americans in Prime Time: Lights, Camera, and No Action" (Washington, DC: National Asian Pacific American Legal Consortium, 2005), and (2) Asian American Justice Center, Christina Chin, Meera Deo, Jenny Lee, Noriko Milman, and Nancy Yuen, "Asian Pacific Americans in Prime Time: Fall 2005 Season" (Washington, DC: Asian American Justice Center, 2006).

2. Person of a single or multiple Asian ethnic or Pacific Islander heritage.

3. Person of Asian or Pacific Islander descent plus one or more non-Asian race.

4. The sampled episodes aired between September 29 and November 19, 2004, and September 26 and December 22, 2005, between the standard prime-time television hours of 8:00 P.M. and 11:00 P.M. PST, with the exception of FOX's *MADtv,* which aired at 11:00 P.M. PST.

5. Percentages compiled from the report on the Annual Demographic Supplement to the March 2002 Current Population Survey: U.S. Census Bureau.

6. Percentages compiled from the report on the Annual Demographic Supplement to the March 2002 Current Population Survey: U.S. Census Bureau.

7. Defined here as constituting at least 10 percent of the total population.

8. While a few AAPIs act as hosts on news, sports, and reality programs, we did not examine these genres because we wanted to analyze characters that developed in depth and complexity over time.

9. All romantic relationships involving AAPIs were heterosexual, with the exception of a skit involving Bobby Lee on FOX's *MADtv.*

REFERENCES

Asian American Justice Center, Christina Chin, Meera Deo, Jenny Lee, Noriko Milman, and Nancy Yuen. 2006. *Asian Pacific Americans in prime time: fall 2005 season.* Washington, DC: Asian American Justice Center.

Children Now. 2004. *Fall colors, 2003–2004: prime time diversity report.* Oakland, CA: Children Now.

Entman, Robert M. and Andrew Rojecki. 2001. *The black image in the white mind: media and race in America.* Chicago: University of Chicago Press.

Gray, Herman. 1995. *Watching race: television and the struggle for "Blackness."* Minneapolis: University of Minnesota Press.

Hoffman, Alison and Chon Noriega. 2004. *Looking for Latino regulars on prime-time television: the fall 2004 season.* Los Angeles: UCLA Chicano Studies Center.

Hunt, Darnell. 2002. *Prime time in black and white: making sense of the 2001 fall season.* Los Angeles: UCLA Ralph J. Bunche Center for African American Studies.

———. 2003. *Prime time in black and white: not much is new for 2002.* Los Angeles: UCLA Ralph J. Bunche Center for African American Studies.

Lee, Jennifer and Min Zhou (eds.). 2004. *Asian American youth: culture, identity, and ethnicity.* New York: Routledge.

Lichter, Robert S., Linda S. Lichter, and Stanley Rothman. 1994. *Prime time: how TV portrays American culture.* Washington, DC: Regnery Publishers.

National Asian Pacific American Legal Consortium, Nancy Yuen, Christina Chin, Meera Deo, Jenny Lee, and Noriko Milman. 2005. *Asian Americans in prime time: lights, camera, and little action.* Washington, DC: National Asian Pacific American Legal Consortium.

Screen Actors Guild. 2004. *Casting Data Report 2003.* Screen Actors Guild.

U.S. Census Bureau. 2004. American Community Survey. http://www.census.gov/acs/www/ (accessed 1 May 2006).

———. 2006. Facts for features: Asian/Pacific American heritage month: May 2006. vol. CB06-FF.06: Census Bureau's Public Information Office.

1. Park illustrates, through a letter to her sister, how the model minority myth is a destructive force in the Asian American community today. She presents a dismal view of mental health and its relationship to the community, even asking, at one point, "Why would you want to place yourself in the hands of an institution that seeks to resocialize you into the environment that made a mess of you in the first place?" What are the social forces in the larger society and within the community that pushed her sister toward multiple suicide attempts? What obstacles prevented her sister and her family from seeking mental health counseling? To what extent does her sister's tragic experiences mirror the experience of young people growing up in the Asian American community? What lessons can we draw from this tragedy?

2. Maira argues in her essay that "[r]acial profiling must be understood not just as a scrutiny of certain groups because of presumed differences of 'racial' or ethnic identity, or just in terms of cultural and social exclusion, but as an everyday practice that is linked to state policies." What does she mean by this? Can you think of any conditions under which racial profiling is an appropriate law enforcement tool? Why or why not? What are the origins of racial profiling as applied to Arab Americans? What are your arguments for or against racial profiling based on the following criteria: (a) national security; (b) civil rights; and (c) foreign relations? What are the implications of racial profiling for Americans of Middle Eastern descent in the post-9/11 era?

3. Discuss the differences between "civic citizenship" and "cultural citizenship" as these terms apply to the experiences of the South Asian immigrant youth studied by Maira. How do the youth in Maira's study understand these concepts of citizenship?

4. How is the issue of Asian American representation in TV and film informed by issues such as screen time, genre of program in which Asian American actors appear, TV occupations, and "missed opportunity" programs? How do the experiences of "monoracial" Asian American actors compare with their multiracial counterparts? Why is this significant?

5. What are some stereotypical representations of AAPIs on prime-time television? What are some of the positive or neutral representations of AAPIs that you've seen? How do the representations of AAPIs compare to those of other racial groups? Why do you think there are discrepancies?

6. What are your thoughts about AAPI actors portraying characters with ethnicities and races different from their own? Why do you think there are differences between female and male AAPI actors and their television representation? What implications might this have on shaping racialized and gendered AAPI images?

7. What strengths/weaknesses have you seen in programs with plots that focus on AAPIs? What positive or negative impacts can the representations of AAPIs in prime-time television have on society as a whole? What changes, if any, do you think need to be made in order to more accurately represent AAPIs? Other racial

minorities? Do you think networks have a responsibility to include more AAPIs on prime-time television? Why or why not?

SUGGESTED READINGS

Ancheta, Angelo N. 1998. *Race, Rights, and the Asian American Experience.* New Brunswick, NJ: Rutgers University Press.

Du, Phuoc Long, and Laura Ricard. 1996. *The Dream Shattered: Vietnamese Gangs in America.* Boston: Northeastern University Press.

Das Gupta, M. 2004. A View of Post-9/11 Justice from Below. *Peace Review* 16(2): 141–48.

Green, Donald, Dara Strolovitch, and Janelle Wong. 1998. Defended Neighborhoods, Integration, and Racially Motivated Hate Crime. *American Journal of Sociology* 104.2: 372–403.

Hamamoto, Darrell Y. 1994. *Monitored Peril: Asian Americans and the Politics of TV Representation.* Minneapolis: University of Minnesota Press.

Hyun, Jane. 2006. *Breaking the Bamboo Ceiling: Career Strategies for Asian Americans.* New York: HarperCollins.

Kurashige, S. 2000. Beyond Random Acts of Hatred: Analyzing Urban Patterns of Anti-Asian Violence. *Amerasia Journal* 26(1): 208–31.

Lien, Pei-te. 1997. *The Political Participation of Asian Americans: Voting Behavior in Southern California.* New York: Garland.

McClain, Charles J. 1996. *In Search of Equality: The Chinese Struggle against Discrimination in Nineteenth-Century America.* Berkeley: University of California Press.

Ngai, Mae. 1998. Legacies of Exclusion: Illegal Chinese Immigration during the Cold War Years. *Journal of American Ethnic History* 18.

Ngai, Mae. 2002. From Colonial Subject to Undesirable Alien: Filipino Migration, Exclusion, and Repatriation, 1920–1940. In Josephine Lee, Imogene Lim, and Yuko Matsukawa (eds.), *Re/Collecting Early Asian America: Readings in Cultural History.* Philadelphia: Temple University Press.

Rana, Junaid Akram. 2006. *Forced Return: U.S. Deportations to Pakistan after 9/11.* Madison, WI: American Institute of Pakistan Studies.

Salyer, Lucy E. 1995. *Law Harsh as Tigers: Chinese Immigrants and the Shaping of Modern Immigration Law.* Chapel Hill: University of North Carolina Press.

Sethi, Rita C. 1994. Smells like Racism: A Plan for Mobilizing against Anti-Asian Bias. Pp. 235–50 in Karin Guillar-San Juan (ed.), *The State of Asian America: Activism and Resistance in the 1990s.* Boston: South End Press.

Shih, Johanna. 2006. Circumventing Discrimination: Gender and Ethnic Strategies in Silicon Valley. *Gender & Society* 20(2): 177–206.

Shimabukuro, Sadamu. 2001. *Born in Seattle: The Campaign for Japanese American Redress.* Seattle: University of Washington Press.

Takagi, Dana Y. 1992. *Retreat from Race: Asian-American Admissions Policies and Racial Politics.* New Brunswick, NJ: Rutgers University Press.

Watanabe, M. E. 1995. Asian American Investigators Decry Glass Ceiling in Academic Administration. *Scientist* 9.11 (May 29): 1.

Woo, Deborah. 2000. *Glass Ceilings and Asian Americans: The New Face of Workplace Barriers.* Lanham, MD: AltaMira Press.

Xiong, Yang Sao and Min Zhou. 2005. Selective Testing and Tracking for Minority Students in

California. In Daniel J. B. Mitchell (ed.), *California Policy Options*. Los Angeles: UCLA Lewis Center.

FILMS

Cho, Michael (producer/director). 1996. *Another America* (56-minute documentary).

Choy, Christine and Renee Tajima (producers/directors). 1988. *Who Killed Vincent Chin* (87-minute documentary).

Ina, Satsuki Ina (producer). 1999. *Children of the Camps* (57-minute documentary).

Nakamura, Tadashi (director). 2007. *Pilgrimage* (25-minute documentary).

Nakasako, Spencer and Vincent DiGirolamo (coproducers/codirectors). 1982. *Monterey's Boat People* (29-minute documentary).

Okazaki, Steven (producer/director). 1989. *Days Waiting* (28-minute documentary).

Omori, Emiko and Chizuko Omori (coproducers). 1999. *Rabbit in the Moon* (85-minute documentary).

Siegel, Taggart (director). 1988. *Blue Collar and Buddha* (57-minute documentary).

Soe, Valerie (producer/director). 1986. *All Orientals Look the Same* (2-minute experimental).

Takagi, J. T. and Hye Jung Park (producers/directors/writers). 1996. *The Women Outside* (53-minute documentary).

Vu, Trac Minh (producer/director). 1997. *Letters to Thien* (57-minute documentary).

Part IX

Behind the Model Minority

Chapter 24

The Cold War Construction of the Model Minority Myth

Robert G. Lee

Racist Love

The elevation of Asian Americans to the position of model minority had less to do with the actual success of Asian Americans than to the perceived failure or worse—refusal—of African Americans to assimilate. Twenty years ago the writer Frank Chin expressed it this way: "Whites love us because we're not black" (Chin 1974). Asian Americans were "not black" in two significant ways—they were politically silent and ethnically assimilable.

The Cold War construction of Asian America as a model minority that could become ethnically assimilated despite what the *U.S. News and World Report* euphemistically called its "racial disadvantage" reveals the contradiction between the continuing reproduction of racial difference and the process of ethnic assimilation. The representation of Asian Americans as a *racial* minority whose apparently successful *ethnic* assimilation was a result of stoic patience, political obedience, and self-improvement was a critically important narrative of racial liberalism that simultaneously promoted racial equality and sought to contain demands for social transformation. The representation of the Asian American as the paragon of ethnic virtue who should be emulated by "Negroes and other minorities" reflected not so much Asian success as it did the triumph of an emergent discourse of race in which culture difference replaced biological difference as the new determinant of social outcomes. Although the deployment of Asian Americans as a "model minority" was made explicit in the mid-1960s, its origins lay in the triumph of liberalism and the racial logic of the Cold War (Lee 1999).

The narrative of Asian ethnic assimilation fit the requirements of Cold War containment perfectly. Three specters haunted Cold War America in the 1950s: the red menace of communism, the black menace of race mixing, and the white menace of homosexuality. On the international front, the narrative of ethnic assimilation sent a message to the Third World, especially to Asia, where the United States was engaged in increasingly fierce struggles with nationalist and Communist insurgencies, that the United States was a liberal democratic state where people of color could enjoy equal rights and upward mobility. On the home front, it sent a message to "Negroes and other minorities" that accommodation would be rewarded, while militancy would be contained or crushed.

The successful transformation of the Oriental from the exotic to the acceptable was a narrative of Americanization, a sort of latter-day *Pilgrim's Progress,* through which America's anxieties about communism, race mixing, and transgressive sexuality might be contained and eventually tamed. The narrative of Asian ethnic assimilation helped construct a new national narrative for the atomic age that Walter Lippman had dubbed "the American Century."

World War II as Prelude

Ironically it was Japan's attack on Pearl Harbor and America's entry into the Second World War that began unraveling the Yellow Peril myth. The Second World War was a watershed event for Asian Americans. The differential treatment of Asian American ethnic groups brought into sharp focus the contradiction between their exclusion as a racial subjects and the promise of their assimilation as ethnic citizens.

America's entry into the war against Nazi Germany and Imperial Japan made it increasingly difficult to sustain national policies based on theories of white racial supremacy. After Dunkirk, the United States and its allies depended on support from their colonial subjects in India, China (not, strictly speaking, a colony), Southeast Asia, and North Africa. The very nationalist movements whose representatives had been summarily dismissed by Woodrow Wilson at Versailles were now actively courted by the United States as allies against the Axis powers. In August of 1941, four months before the United States entered the war, Roosevelt and Churchill signed the Atlantic Charter recognizing the right of "peoples" to decide their own form of government. Later that year, in response to the threat by civil rights leader A. Phillip Randolph to lead a massive protest march on Washington, Roosevelt signed an executive order outlawing racial discrimination by companies doing business with the federal government and established a Committee on Fair Employment Practices.

Official pronouncements of racial equality notwithstanding, the wholesale and brutal incarceration of the Japanese American population on the West Coast underscored, in no uncertain terms, the willingness of the U.S. government to invoke race as a category of subordination to achieve its goals.[1] This willingness to use racial categories would result in physical hardship, economic ruin, family disintegration, and psychological trauma for more than 120,000 Japanese Americans, men and women, elderly and infant, citizen and immigrant.

After Pearl Harbor the United States found itself allied with a weak and divided China. The Yellow Peril, that alliance of Japanese brains and Chinese bodies that had fired the racial nightmares of turn-of-the-century strategists of empire, from Kaiser Wilhelm to Sax Rohmer, had remained in the imagination. Japan's plans for empire, though couched in a Pan-Asian anticolonial rhetoric, met with resistance in China and elsewhere in Asia. For the first time, being able to tell one Asian group apart from another seemed important to white Americans. Two weeks after the Japanese attack on Pearl Harbor brought the United States into the war, *Life* magazine ran a two-page pictorial entitled "How to Tell Japs from the Chinese." The reporter for *Life* magazine wrote,

U.S. citizens have been demonstrating a distressing ignorance on the delicate question of how to tell a Chinese from a Jap. Innocent victims in cities all over the country are many of the 75,000 U.S. Chinese, whose homeland is our stanch [sic] ally....

To dispel some of this confusion, *Life* here adduces a rule of thumb from the anthropomorphic conformations that distinguish "friendly Chinese" from enemy alien Japs. ("How to Tell Japs from the Chinese" 1941, 14)

On the right side of the article, two facial portraits of Orientals are juxtaposed one above the other. The top picture (of the minister of economic affairs of the Chinese Nationalist government) is captioned "Chinese public servant" while the one below (of Admiral Tojo, the Japanese prime minister) is captioned "Japanese Warrior." Although the pictures are the same size and the proportions of the facial features virtually identical, the notes tell a vastly different story. The Chinese, *Life* told its readers, has "parchment yellow complexion, more frequent epicanthic fold, higher bridge, never has rosy cheeks, lighter facial bones, longer narrower face and scant beard." Tojo, on the other hand, as a

representative of the Japanese people as whole ... betrays aboriginal antecedents, had an earthy yellow complexion, less frequent epicanthic fold, flatter nose, sometimes rosy cheeks, heavy beard, broader shorter face and massive cheek and jawbone.

In addition, the *Life* article showed two pictures entitled, respectively, "Tall Chinese Brothers" and "Short Japanese Admirals." *Life,* taking no chances with its racial taxonomy, supplied the following "field" notes: The Chinese brothers were "tall and slender" with "long legs" while the Short Admirals were "short and squat" with "shorter legs and longer torso." Had *Life* only added blonde hair and blue eyes, it might have created the perfect Aryan Chinaman.

Not wanting to appear unlearned in the matter of racial anthropology, *Life* pointed out that its illustrations were drawn from northern Chinese. Southern Chinese (at that time the overwhelming majority of Chinese residents of the United States), the magazine noted, were short and "[w]hen middle aged and fat ... look more like Japs." The *Life* editors went on to tell the reader that

Southern Chinese have round, broad faces, not as massively boned as the Japanese. Except that their skin is darker, this description fits the Filipinos who are [also] often mistaken for Japs. Chinese sometimes pass for Europeans, but Japs more often approach the Western types. ("How to Tell the Japs from the Chinese" 1941, 14)

Lest this confusing racial taxonomy fail Americans in this time of crisis, *Life* reassured its audience that cultural difference could also be identified visually. "An often sounder clue is facial expression, shaped by cultural, not anthropological, factors. Chinese wear the rational calm of tolerant realists. Japs, like General Tojo, show the humorless intensity of ruthless mystics" (ibid.).

Aware that readers might be suspicious that this exercise in racial cataloguing was similar to that practiced by Nazi social scientists, *Life* assured its audience that American physical anthropologists were "devoted debunkers of race myths." Debunking notwithstanding, *Life* asserted that the ability to measure the difference between the Chinese and Japanese "in millimeters" enabled American scientists to "set apart the special types of each national group." To lend an air of precision, scientific objectivity, and authority to the photos and the accompanying text, *Life's* editors festooned the pictures with handwritten captions and arrows that simulated anthropological field notes.

The same disjuncture between the newly articulated ideals of racial egalitarianism and the practice of racial discrimination can be seen in the Supreme Court's decisions in the Japanese American internment cases. In the case of Gordon Hirabayashi, a student at the University of Washington who had challenged the right of military authorities to establish a curfew applicable only to persons of Japanese ancestry, the Court stated that discrimination on the sole basis of race was "odious to a free people." Nevertheless, the court refused to curb the authority of the military in times of national emergency and upheld Hirabayashi's conviction. Likewise, in the case of Fred Korematsu, a house painter from Oakland who had evaded relocation by disguising his appearance, the Court held that while race was an "inherently invidious" category for discrimination by the state and subject to "strict scrutiny," the court accepted the state's claim of military necessity for the incarceration of Japanese Americans.[2]

Despite its massive mistreatment of Japanese Americans, the still rigidly enforced segregation of African Americans throughout most of American society (not least of which was in the armed forces) and the deadly antisemitic policy of denying refuge to Europe's Jews, the U.S. government condemned the Nazi's doctrine of racial superiority and identified the defeat of racism as one of the reasons "Why We Fight." While Japanese Americans were singled out on the basis of their "race," other Asian American ethnic groups received favorable treatment from the federal government.

In 1943, Congress voted to repeal the Chinese Exclusion Act, which had for sixty years forbidden Chinese, with few exceptions, from entering the United States. Repeal of exclusion had been a foreign policy goal of successive Chinese governments for over a half-century. Repeal was pushed through the U.S. Congress on the grounds that it would keep the wavering Nationalist Chinese government of Chiang Kai-shek in the war against Japan (Riggs 1950).

In the next year, legislators introduced two bills in Congress to establish immigration quotas for India and the Philippines. Congress passed these bills in 1946 on the eve of Philippine independence. The repeal of Chinese Exclusion and the effective dismantling of the Asiatic Barred Zone of 1917 had greater symbolic value than immediate demographic effect since the number of visas issued to Asian countries was still severely restricted. Nevertheless, the ideological statement implied by the dismantling of racially specific barriers signaled an erosion of white supremacy as a national doctrine.[3]

Making the Model Minority Myth

In January 1966, the *New York Times Magazine* published an article with the title "Success Story: Japanese-American Style," and in December the *U.S. News and World Report* published an article focusing on Chinese Americans entitled "Success Story of One Minority in the U.S." As their titles suggested, both articles told the story of Asians in America as a narrative of triumphant ethnic assimilation.

This new popular representation of Asian Americans as America's model of successful "ethnic assimilation" was created in the crisis of racial policy that had surfaced at the highest levels of the federal government during the previous year. The policy debate that emerged in 1965 reflected deep ideological division over responses to the demands for racial equality that had developed in the two decades since the end of the Second World War.

The Watts riot in the summer of 1964 and the growing demands of African Americans for economic equity as well as formal political rights, along with the gradual dismantling of Jim Crow segregation in the South, plunged racial policy into crisis. The contours of the crisis can be seen in the conflicting responses of the Johnson administration to black demands for racial equality. In March of 1965, the assistant secretary of labor, Daniel Patrick Moynihan, published a *Report on the Black Family* that laid much of the blame for black poverty on the "tangle of pathology" of the black family and admonished African Americans to rehabilitate their dysfunctional families in order to achieve economic and social assimilation. In June of that same year, at Howard University's commencement, President Johnson articulated a vision of racial equality through sweeping social reconstruction in a massive War on Poverty. Both genuinely claimed to support racial equality and civil rights, but the two speeches could not have been further apart in their analysis and proposed solutions. The conflict between Johnson's response and Moynihan's response forms the specific ideological context in which the Model Minority representation of Asian America emerged.

Johnson's speech emphasized the historical reality of race in America as compelling logic for extending civil rights into the economic sphere. Referring to the disadvantaged position of many blacks in the American economic structure, Johnson declared, "You do not take a person who for years has been hobbled by chains and liberate him, bring him up to the starting line of a race and then say[,] 'you are free to compete with all the others' and still justly believe that you have been completely fair" (Rainwater and Yancey 1967, 79). The president went on to lay the principal responsibility for black poverty on white racism, both historical and present, and he outlined an agenda of government-sponsored social changes to ameliorate discrimination and poverty.

Moynihan took a radically different political tack. Quoting his former Harvard colleague, sociologist Nathan Glazer, Moynihan complained that "the demand for economic equality is now not the demand for equal opportunities for the equally qualified: it is now the demand for equality of economic results. . . . The demand for equality in education . . . has also become a demand for equality of results, of outcomes" (124).

Moynihan left implicit Glazer's ominous threat that American society, despite a commitment towards equality of opportunity, would be "ruthless" in suppressing equality of results. Moynihan went on to describe a black culture of poverty as a "tangle of pathology" born in slavery but "capable of perpetuating itself without assistance from the white world" (49).[4] In particular, Moynihan identified the prevalence of female-headed households as a barrier to economic success. For Moynihan, the key to both racial integration and economic mobility was not in structural changes or social reorganization that might correct past injustice, but in the rehabilitation of "culturally deprived" black families.

The *U.S. News* article was quite explicit about the political context of its report when it asserted, "At a time when it is being proposed that hundreds of billions be spent on uplifting Negroes and other minorities, the nation's 300,000 Chinese Americans are moving ahead on their own with no help from anyone else" ("Success Story" 1996, 73–78). Foreshadowing an obsession that was to shape Richard Nixon's campaign rhetoric a year later, the writer of the *U.S. News* article described America's Chinatowns as "havens for law and order" and made no fewer than six references to low rates of delinquency among Chinese American youth (ibid.).

Making the Silent Minority

The construction of the Model Minority was based on the political silence of Asian America. An oft-cited example of Asian American self-reliance was the underutilization of welfare programs in 1970. Despite the fact that 15 percent of Chinese families in New York City had incomes below the federal poverty level, only 3.4 percent had enrolled to receive public assistance. This statistic has often been used as an example of a cultural trait of self-reliance and family cohesion. An alternate explanation, grounded in recent Asian American history, would stress apprehension and mistrust of the state's intentions towards Asian immigrants and their families.

The wartime incarceration of Japanese Americans left deep wounds within this ethnic community. The removal to fairgrounds and racetracks, the relocation to remote barbed-wired camps, the uncertainty of loyalty oaths, the separation of family members, all traumatized the Japanese American community. The Japanese American Citizens League's policy of accommodation with the War Relocation Authority and its role in suppressing dissent within the camps had left bitter divisions among many Japanese Americans. Japanese Americans, for the most part, were anxious to rebuild their lives and livelihoods and reluctant to relive their experience. In particular, the nisei generation remained remarkably silent about their camp experience until the emergence of the Asian American movement in the 1970s and the Redress Movement of the 1980s. Social psychologists have likened the response of Japanese Americans who had been unjustly incarcerated to that of victims of rape or other physical violation. They demonstrated a complex of anger, resentment, self-doubt, and guilt, all symptoms of post-traumatic stress syndrome (Takezawa 1995).

While postwar Japan became America's junior partner, the People's Republic of China became its principal enemy. After the Korean War broke out in 1950, and especially after China entered the war in 1951, the United States made every effort to isolate Communist China, economically and diplomatically, and embarked on a military policy of confrontation aimed at "containing" the expansion of Chinese influence throughout Asia and the Third World. The fear of Red China extended to the Chinese American community. In 1949, Chinese communities in the United States were divided in their attitudes toward the Communist revolution. Although the number of Communists in Chinese American communities was few, many who were not Communists or even leftists nonetheless found some satisfaction in the fact that a genuinely nationalist, reputedly honest, and apparently more democratic government had finally united China after a century of political chaos, weakness, and humiliation. On the other hand, Chiang Kai-shek's Kuomintang Party had long enjoyed the support of the traditional elites in the larger Chinatowns (Lai 1992, 3–82).

When the Korean War broke out in 1950, Congress passed the Emergency Detention Act, which vested the U.S. attorney general with the authority to establish concentration camps for any who might be deemed a domestic threat in a national emergency. The mere authorization of such sweeping powers of detention served as a stark warning to Chinese Americans that what had been done to Japanese Americans a decade earlier could also be done to them without effort.

The pro–Chiang Kai-shek Chinatown elite, working with the FBI, launched a systematic attempt to suppress any expression of support for the new Communist regime in China. The Trading with the Enemy Act, which prohibited any currency transfers to the People's Republic of China, including remittances to family, was used as a tool to attempt to deport suspected Communist sympathizers. Although only a few leftists and labor leaders actually were deported, the threat of deportation had a deeply chilling effect, since many hundreds of Chinese had come to the United States as "paper sons" during the long decades of exclusion and were in the United States under false pretenses.

In 1952 Congress passed the McCarran-Walter Immigration and Nationality Act, which dismantled racial prohibitions on immigration and established an Asian-Pacific Triangle with an immigration quota cap of two thousand visas. Even though McCarran-Walter still strictly limited Asian immigration, the Red Scare that was its impetus was contagious. In 1955 Everett F. Drumwright, the U.S. consul in Hong Kong, issued a report warning that Communist China was making use of "massive" fraud and deception to infiltrate agents into the United States under cover as immigrants. Drumwright's hysterical and largely unsubstantiated report provide the rationale for massive FBI and INS raids into Chinatowns around the country to search out pro-China subversives. Chinatowns were flooded with public notices and street flyers warning of potential spies and subversives, while "innocent residents" were encouraged to report suspected subversives to the FBI.

In 1957 Congress authorized the Chinese Confession Program. Chinese Americans who had come as paper sons were encouraged to confess their illegal entry. In return for consideration for an appropriate (but not guaranteed) adjustment of their status, the applicant had also to make a full disclosure on every relative and friend. The government used the gathered information to try to deport those who were identified by the FBI's informants as supporters of China or as domestic troublemakers. Membership in leftist organizations, in labor unions, and in "patriotic" organizations melted away in the face of the sustained harassment and attack from the conservative elite within Chinatowns, and the FBI and INS from without (Hing 1993; Lee 1996).

Containing the Red Menace: The Fordist Compromise

At the close of the Second World War, American workers infused the labor movement with a renewed militancy. During the war years union membership had grown from nine million in 1940 to about fifteen million in 1945. This represented almost 36 percent of the nonagricultural workforce, the highest proportion of unionized labor in the country's history. During the war years, organized labor had agreed to a no-strike policy and to curb wage demands as a patriotic obligation to the war effort. However, at the war's end, pent-up wage demands and the problems of reabsorption of millions of men leaving the service led to a resurgence of demands for wages and a reassertion of control over work conditions. Labor strife soon boiled over at General Motors and in the oil industry. In 1945, forty-five hundred work stoppages, mainly wildcat strikes and sitdowns, involved five million workers. Some of these work stoppages took the form of hate strikes aimed at driving women and black workers from the factory positions they had earned during the war (Lipsitz 1994). In 1946, the steelworkers went on strike, then the miners. Strike fever spread: in 1946 a general strike was called in Stamford, Connecticut; in 1947 militant labor called general strikes to shut down business in Houston, Rochester, Pittsburgh, and Oakland.

In May 1946, President Truman seized the railroads to prevent a strike. Altogether Truman would seize and operate nine industries under powers granted the executive branch by the War Labor Disputes Act. Management launched a massive attack on radical, particularly Communist Party, leadership within the labor movement. Their most effective tool was the Taft-Hartley Act passed in 1948, which outlawed the closed shop, secondary boycotts, jurisdictional strikes in violation of NLRB decisions, and jointly administered welfare funds, and made unions suable in federal courts for violation of contracts. The Taft-Hartley law stripped collective bargaining rights from unions having Communists among their leadership and resulted in successive purges of the labor movement. Employers and employees could petition for decertification elections and federal employees were forbidden to strike. State right-to-work laws were legalized and the president was given power to enforce eighty-day cooling off period during which labor would be compelled to return to work.

The long period of economic growth that sustained America's rise to hegemonic power depended on a sustained labor-management accord. This pattern of cooperation has been called the Fordist Compromise, since it seemed to usher in that stage of capitalism that Henry Ford had envisioned, one in which working-class demand for durable consumer goods would drive economic growth. The Fordist Compromise permanently institutionalized many of the features of "scientific management" that had been introduced during the war. Under the new production-oriented union leadership, labor contracts developed a pattern of close collaboration between labor leadership and management on issues of supervision, productivity, and work rules (Gordon, Edwards, and Reich 1982, 170). In return, management and the state worked together to create a working class that had the social characteristics of a middle class. Real income rose by 30 percent between 1945 and 1960. The Fordist Compromise also called for a relatively high degree of state intervention, from the mediation of labor relations through the National Labor Relations Board to the regulation of working conditions through agencies such as OSHA to the organization of a "welfare state" of permanent entitlements for the new "middle" class, such as Social Security, subsidized housing, educational financing, unemployment insurance, and increased public higher education. The state also took on an expanded role in intervening in the economy through an ever wider range of fiscal control policies and by exercising its economic power as the purchaser of last resort.

The sustained economic growth on which the Fordist Compromise depended was fueled by several sources, but initially it was $40 billion in wartime personal savings and a pent-up demand for durable consumer products that drove production. This required the reinvigoration of the patriarchal nuclear family. Wartime production had increased the number of women in the labor force from just under fourteen million in 1940 to just over nineteen million in 1945 (Goldin 1990, 152). Both management and federal agencies worked to encourage and sometimes force women back into the home while work assignments in many plants were resegregated along racial lines (Lipsitz 1994, 69–95). As men returned from war and started families, the birth rate in the United States grew for the first time in several decades, leading to the sustained growth of a domestic market for housing, education, and durable consumer goods. The nuclear family was the necessary social unit of consumption for durable goods, the automobiles (fifty-eight million in the decade of the 1950s), refrigerators, toasters, and televisions whose production drove the economy.

The realization of the Fordist Compromise could only be imagined in a world in which the United States had reconstructed a sphere of influence based on free trade and open markets. In the late 1930s and '40s, American policy planners in the State Department and the Council on Foreign Relations had initially imagined a "Grand Area" of American influence to include the Western Hemisphere and the Asia-Pacific area. By the end of the war, the United States was in position to supplant Britain, France, and the Netherlands in many, if not all, of their colonial territories (Shoup and Minter 1977). The American postwar project of global transformation supplanted European colonial administration with nationalist elites whose economic interests and political allegiances were aligned with American interests. By the end of the 1940s, one-third of all manufactured goods in the world were made in America, and U.S. officials emphasized the theme of maintaining a high level of exports as a critical factor in avoiding a postwar depression.[5] American policymakers therefore took as an article of faith that the reconstruction of a stable, multilateral, capitalist economic system would rely on the unobstructed movement of capital and labor.

America's strategy for global reconstruction required the reconstruction of both Western Europe and Japan as major industrialized trading partners. In Europe, the Marshall Plan funneled millions of dollars into the rebuilding of Western Europe. Financing the reconstruction of Europe could not be funded solely through European-American trade, however; imports from Europe only amounted to one-third of 1 percent of the U.S. gross national product. The United States therefore looked to Asia and the Pacific to close the "dollar gap." The development of a Pacific Rim strategy thus became a central requirement for American policy planners directly at the war's end. Although MacArthur had begun to dismantle prewar cartels such as Mitsui and Mitsubishi as a means of democratizing the Japanese economy along with its political system, by 1947 the decision was made to reconstruct Japan's prewar economic machine as a foil to a possible revolutionary China. Japanese manufacturing was to become "the Workshop of the American Lake." Japan was to play a critical role as a junior partner in the Pacific Rim Strategy. After the "loss" of China, Japan, with American encouragement, focused its economic attentions on Southeast Asia. In its report on Asian economic development in 1952, the Institute for Pacific Relations spelled out the role that Japan was to play between the United States and the Southeast Asian market.

> There can be little question that . . . the best area for Japanese economic expansion is in Southeast Asia, with its demands for capital and consumer goods, its raw materials and rice surplus. . . . It would seem that Japan should be encouraged to develop trading outlets there in the interest of the overall structure of Pacific security. Japan has herself shown keen interest in these trade possibilities, especially in Thailand, Malaysia, Indonesia, and India. (Kent 1983, 95)

The Pacific Rim was not only a crucial market for American goods, but it was also a highly profitable region for export of capital. In addition to the redeployment of Japanese capital, direct U.S. investment in the Pacific Rim was a major source of profits for American corporations. While overseas investments grew at about 10 percent per annum, twice the growth rate of domestic investment, American investment in the Pacific Rim outside of Japan brought a 25.5 percent return on investment, and investment in the Japanese economy brought in 11.3 percent. Between 1951 and 1976, the book value of American investments in the Pacific Rim grew from $16 billion to $80.3 billion (97).

Containing The Black Menace: Ethnic Assimilation

In 1944, the same year in which the Supreme Court heard the Japanese internment cases, Gunnar Myrdal published *An American Dilemma: The Negro Problem and Modern Democracy,* a massive collaborative study of American race relations. Drawing on the work of a generation of American liberal social scientists, notably sociologist Robert E. Park and his students, *An American Dilemma* signaled the intellectual discrediting of biological theories of racial superiority and the triumph of the concept of ethnicity as the dominant paradigm for explaining and transforming race relations. Myrdal's report to the Carnegie Foundation focused on the disparity between the egalitarian ethos articulated in the nation's founding documents and the practice of racial discrimination in American society. Myrdal was clear about the implications of the "American dilemma" for America's role as the principal organizer of the postwar world order: "If America in actual practice could show the world a progressive trend by which the Negro finally became integrated into modern democracy, all mankind would have reason to believe that peace, progress, and order are feasible" (Myrdal 1944, lxxii). Myrdal's hope was a statement of liberal faith. The triumph of liberalism, including racial liberalism, was made possible by the victory of the United States and its allies over the Axis powers and was necessary to the rise of a Pax Americana in the postwar era.

The Cold War provided a national security dimension to the "race problem." Although Soviet communism was perceived as the greatest threat to the established order, after the Soviet Union exploded its own atomic bomb in 1949, the struggle against the Soviet Union was limited to a war of containment (Schurman 1974, 16–19, 91–114, and passim). Since the establishment of relatively stable opposing blocs in Europe in the mid-1950s, the struggle between the United States and the Soviet Union was played out principally in Asia, Africa, and Latin America. In 1954, the term "Third World" was coined as India, the People's Republic of China, and Indonesia (with the tacit support of the Soviet Union) sponsored a conference of nonaligned nations at Bandung, Indonesia. The demands of the Third World nations, largely peoples of color, for independence, self-determination, and economic development became the ideological arena in the contest between the Soviet Union and the United States.

It is not surprising, then, to find federal intervention on behalf of civil rights expressed in the language and logic of the Cold War. As early as 1948, in *Shelley v. Kraemer,* a case involving restrictive covenants in real estate, the federal government's brief supporting the dismantling of racial restrictions on housing "relied" on the State Department's view that "the United States has been embarrassed in the conduct of foreign relations by acts of [racial] discrimination in this country" (Dudziak 1988, 105).

In the most significant postwar desegregation case, *Brown v. Board of Education,* both the Justice Department and the NAACP briefs emphasized the important foreign policy implications of the case. The Justice Department's *amicus* brief stated the foreign policy case explicitly:

> The existence of discrimination against minority groups in the U.S. has an adverse effect upon our relations with other countries. . . . Racial discrimination furnishes grist for the Communist propaganda mills and it raises doubts even among friendly nations as to the intensity of our devotion to the democratic faith. (Dudziak 1988, 110)

A decade later, in the aftermath of the Watts riots, both President Johnson's Howard University speech and the preface to Moynihan's *Report* referred to this ideological struggle and framed the problem of civil rights and social justice in the United States within the global context of the Cold War. Both initially emphasized the need to provide the world with a model of the "true American revolution" as an alternative to communism. The president opened his speech by declaring,

> Our earth is the home of revolution. . . . Our enemies may occasionally seize the day of change. But it is the banner of our movement which they take. And our own future is linked to this process of change in many lands in the world. But nothing in any

country touches us more profoundly, nothing is freighted with meaning for our own destiny, than the revolution of the Negro American. (Rainwater and Yancey 1967, 79)

Moynihan (1965) opened his report with the observation that "the [black] movement has profound international implications, . . . [and] it was not a matter of chance that the Negro movement caught fire in America at just that moment when the nations of Africa were gaining their freedom" (47).[6] He went on to invoke the threat of perceived separatist black Muslim doctrines or the "attractiveness of Chinese communism" to American blacks.

Anxious to replace the invidious category of race, for which there was little scientific justification and significant political cost, liberal theorists subsumed race relations to ethnicity. Ethnicity theory was grounded in the belief that, while certain historically anachronistic patterns of racial segregation persisted, modern American society was open to the full participation of all who were willing to participate. Liberal social scientists who promoted the ethnicity paradigm argued that the desired assimilation of blacks into modern American society could be achieved in two steps. The barriers of Jim Crow segregation had to be dismantled (over the objections of "premodern" segregationists like the Klan, the White Citizens Councils, and an entrenched southern power structure), and nonwhites had to accommodate themselves to the "universal" demands of modernity.

The blueprint for ethnic assimilation was Robert Park's theory of a four-stage Ethnic or Race Relations Cycle. Park identified four stages in a natural and irreversible process of ethnic assimilation. The stages were initial contact between the outsider and the host society, economic and political competition, economic and cultural accommodation of the ethnic to the host society, and, finally, assimilation into the host society. These patterns of cultural assimilation and integration were assumed to be universally applicable to all "newcomers" into the modern city and applicable to racial as well as ethnic relations. This was a narrative of modernization drawn from studies of the historical experiences of European immigrant groups in American cities. The ethnic component of cultural identity was identified with the Old World. Seen as premodern and dysfunctional, ethnic differences of language, custom, and religion were transcended as the immigrant became modern and American.

Since the stages of assimilation were based on a narrative of universal modernization and not on a theory of subordination, the burden was on the "latecomer" to modernization to accommodate to the "host" society. It did not occur to assimilation theorists that racially subordinated people might be reluctant to abandon cultures of survival that had been developed over centuries of oppression. The black sociologist, E. Franklin Frazier, a student of Park and one of the most important contributors to *The American Dilemma,* wrote,

> Since the institutions, the social stratification, and the culture of the Negro community are essentially the same as those of the larger community, it is not strange that the Negro minority belongs among the assimilationist rather than the pluralist, secessionist, or militant minorities. It is seldom that one finds Negroes who think of themselves as

possessing a different culture from whites and that their culture should be preserved. (Frazier 1957, 681)

Assimilationists supported the civil rights movement in the dismantling of southern Jim Crow segregation and encouraged voting-rights and electoral-political participation. Assimilation theory, however, suggested that the duty of the state was limited to the dismantling of formal, legislated barriers to participation. Since the greater part of assimilation rested on the accommodation of the minority to the "host" society, state regulation of "private" activity in the interest of equal condition was seen to have little positive and possibly greater negative effect. The sociologist Milton Gordon, who in the early 1960s elaborated and refined Park's Race Relations Cycle into a seven-stage theory of ethnic assimilation, warned explicitly,

> The government *must not* use racial criteria positively in order to impose desegregation upon public facilities in an institutional area where such segregation is not a function of racial discrimination directly, but results from discrimination operating in another institutional area or from some other causes. (Gordon 1964, 259; emphasis added).

In the 1950s and early 1960s, liberalism, with its universalist claims on science and progress, became the hegemonic ideology of the American imperium. The political requirements of the Cold War and the logic of liberal universalism required an adherence to a doctrine of racial equality. Liberal social scientists articulated a theory of modernization that could be deployed as an ideological alternative to communism in resolving the problem of the Third World. Its domestic version, ethnic assimilation, would provide a similar nonradical solution to the "Negro problem."

Ethnicity theory met the requirements of liberalism by articulating a doctrine of individual competition in a "color-blind" society, or, in Milton Gordon's view, a society in which the state played a neutral role. Ethnicity theory articulated a vision of the color-blind society but evaded a critique of the historical category of race altogether. Ethnicity theory offered a promise of equality that could be achieved, not through political organization and community empowerment, but only through individual effort, cultural assimilation, and political accommodation. For liberals who sought both to develop the Negro and to contain black demands for the systematic and structural dismantling of racial discrimination, the representation of Asian American communities as self-contained, safe, and politically acquiescent became a powerful example of the success of the American Creed in resolving the problems of race.

In 1955, less than a year after the Supreme Court had shocked the system of southern segregation by declaring separate but equal education inherently unequal and unconstitutional, the torture and lynching of Emmett Till, a black fourteen-year-old who was accused of flirting with a white woman, shocked the world. The exoneration of Till's killers by a jury of their white peers signaled a strategy of "massive resistance" to racial equality in the South. The murder of Emmett Till served as the counternarrative of racial intolerance and violence that threatened to undermine the liberal narrative of Myrdal's American Creed so painstakingly assembled and elaborately articulated.

Containing the White Menace: The Nuclear Family as Civil Defense

In 1948, Alfred Kinsey shocked America by reporting that a third of American men had engaged in some homosexual activity during the course of their lives and that a majority had experienced homoerotic desire. The news should not have come as a surprise, as the 1940s had witnessed a marked expansion of sexual freedom and experimentation with new definitions of gender relations. During the war years, millions of young men went into the armed forces and millions of young women went into the factories. These young people established new patterns of dating, and had a more relaxed attitude toward premarital sex than did their parents. During the same period, gay and lesbian public cultures emerged in cities around the country (D'Emilio and Freedman 1989, 282).

Kinsey's study, *The Sexual Behavior of the Human Male,* a dry sociological survey of twelve thousand respondents, became an immediate best seller. It also drew the ire of conservative churchmen and politicians. For reporting these activities of Americans, Kinsey was accused of aiding and abetting the Communist cause and was investigated by the House Committee on Un-American Activities.

In the Cold War search for traitors and subversives, homophobia and anticommunism went hand in hand. Following on the heels of Senator Joe McCarthy's search for Communist agents, the Senate launched investigations to root out homosexuals in the federal government. Nonreproductive sexuality, homosexuality in particular, was seen as a threat to the national security. Anticommunist crusaders warned that homosexuality weakened the nation's "moral fiber," making it susceptible to both sexual and political seduction. Just as communism was considered a perversion of the natural economic order, homosexuality was considered a perversion of the natural biological order. In an era when the sudden turn from American triumph in the Second World War to the high anxiety of the Cold War could only be explained by treason, homosexuals were seen to have secret lives much likes spies or foreign agents. Shortly after his inauguration as president in 1953, Dwight Eisenhower issued an executive order barring gay men and lesbians from federal employment (D'Emilio and Freedman 1989, 292–93).

The link between anticommunism and homophobia was not merely psychological or metaphorical; in the atomic age reproducing the nuclear family was understood to be the key to national survival. In the 1950s and early 1960s, seeking to capitalize on America's advantage in nuclear weapons, strategic planners stressed the survivability of nuclear war. This strategic doctrine relied on a program of civil defense, the mass mobilization and education of the civilian population regarding their duties during nuclear war. At the heart of civil defense was the belief that the nuclear family was the primary social unit through which the American Way of Life could be preserved or resurrected (May 1988, 102–4; Oakes 1994). Talcott Parsons, perhaps the most influential American sociologist between 1940 and the 1960s, argued that the middle-class family, with its "natural" gendered division of labor, was the most efficient and implicitly the highest form of social organization. In the absence of a state apparatus that might be obliterated or cut off from its people by nuclear war, the nuclear family was a "natural" social unit that would reproduce America.

NOTES

Excerpt from "The Cold War Origins of the Model Minority," pp. 145–61 in *Orientals: Asian Americans in Popular Culture* by Robert G. Lee. Used by permission of Temple University Press. © 1999 by Temple University. All rights reserved.

1. In this case, the goal was not to meet a real threat to national security but to ease anxieties about the government's preparedness and to mobilize support for policies of austerity and sacrifice. See Weglyn (1976) and Irons (1983), for example.

2. See *Korematsu v. United States* in Kim (1992, 833–67). Under "strict scrutiny," discrimination by the state on the basis of race is held to be illegitimate unless the state can show an overriding national interest. This ruling, that race is a "suspect category," became a much cited justification of subsequent rulings against racial discrimination. Under *coram nobis* Korematsu, Hirabayashi, and Yasui were granted a new trial in 1984. In 1986, Hirabayashi was vindicated, and the government decided not to contest the other cases. Also see Takezawa (1995).

3. Reference to Asiatic Barred Zone of 1917. Asian immigration was "normalized" under the provisions of the Immigration Act of 1924, which had established a system of national quotas. Each country was assigned a quota of visas equivalent to 5 percent of the total number of immigrants from that country of origin who resided in the United States in 1905. The resulting quota for Chinese visas was a mere 105 per year, and Indian and Philippine visas were limited to one hundred for each country.

4. The likelihood that Moynihan also drafted Johnson's speech does not negate the point that the speech and the report reflect two quite different ideological tendencies.

5. In 1960 the United States still enjoyed a favorable balance of trade of $6 billion.

6. See Glazer (1975) for the full text.

REFERENCES

Chin, Frank, ed. (1974) *Aiiieeee! An Anthology of Asian American Writers.* Washington, DC: Howard University Press.

D'Emilio, John and Estelle B. Freedman (1989) *Intimate Matters: A History of Sexuality in America.* New York: Perennial Library.

Dudziak, Mary L. (1988) "Desegregation as a Cold War Imperative," *Stanford Law Review* 41 (November): 61–120.

Frazier, E. Franklin (1957) *The Negro in the United States,* rev. ed. New York: Macmillan.

Glazer, Nathan (1975) *Affirmative Discrimination: Ethnic Inequality and Public Policy.* New York: Basic Books.

Goldin, Claudia (1990) *Understanding the Gender Gap.* New York: Oxford University Press.

Gordon, David M., Richard Edwards, and Michael Reich (1982) *Segmented Work, Divided Workers: The Historical Transformation of Work in the United States.* New York: Cambridge University Press.

Gordon, Milton (1964) *Assimilation in American Life.* New York: Oxford University Press.

Hing, Bill Ong (1993) *Making and Remaking of Asian America through Immigration Policy, 1850–1990.* Stanford, CA: Stanford University Press.

"How to Tell Japs from the Chinese" (1941) *Life Magazine,* 19 December.

Irons, Peter H. (1983) *Justice at War: The Story of the Japanese American Internment Cases.* New York: Oxford University Press.

Kent, Noel J. (1983) *Hawaii: Islands under the Influence* New York: Monthly Review Press.

Kim, Hyung Chan, ed. (1992) *Asian Americans and the Supreme Court.* New York: Greenwood Press.

Lai, Him Mark (1992) "The Chinese Marxist Left in America to the 1960s," in *Chinese America: History and Perspectives.* San Francisco: Chinese Historical Association of America.

Lee, Rainwater and William Yancey (1967) *The Moynihan Report and the Politics of Controversy.* Cambridge: Massachusetts Institute of Technology Press.

Lee, Robert G. (1999) *Orientals: Asian Americans in Popular Culture.* Philadelphia: Temple University Press.

———(1996) "The Hidden World of Asian Immigrant Radicalism," in *The Immigrant Left in the United States,* eds. Paul Buhle and Dan Georgakas. Albany: SUNY Press.

Lipsitz, George (1994) *Rainbow at Midnight: Labor and Culture in the 1940s.* Urbana: University of Illinois Press.

May, Elaine Tyler (1988) *Homeward Bound: American Families in the Cold War Era.* New York: Basic Books.

Moynihan, Daniel P. (1965) *The Negro Family: The Case for National Action.* Washington, DC: U.S. Labor Department.

Myrdal, Gunnar (1944) *An American Dilemma: The Negro Problem and Modern Democracy.* New York: Harper & Brothers.

Oakes, Guy (1994) *The Imaginary War: Civil Defense and American Cold War Culture.* New York: Oxford University Press.

Petersen, William (1966) "Success Story: Japanese American Style," *New York Times Magazine,* January 9.

Rainwater, Lee and William Yancey (1967) *The Moynihan Report and the Politics of Controversy.* Cambridge, MA: MIT Press.

Riggs, Fred Warren (1950) *Pressures on Congress: A Study of the Repeal of Chinese Exclusion.* New York: King's Crown Press.

Schurmann, Franz (1974) *The Logic of World Power: An Inquiry into the Origins, Currents, and Contradictions of World Politics.* New York: Pantheon Books.

Shoup, Laurence H. and William Minter (1977) *Imperial Brain Trust: The Council on Foreign Relations and United States Foreign Policy.* New York: Monthly Review Press.

"Success Story of One Minority in the U.S." (1966) *U.S. News and World Report,* 26 December.

Takezawa, Yasuko (1995) *Breaking the Silence: Redress and Japanese American Ethnicity.* Ithaca, NY: Cornell University Press.

Weglyn, Michi (1976) *Years of Infamy: The Untold Story of America's Concentration Camps.* New York: William Morrow.

Chapter 25

From Model Minority to Economic Threat
Media Portrayals of Major League Baseball Pitchers Hideo Nomo and Hideki Irabu

David Tokiharu Mayeda

Introduction

In 1947, Jackie Robinson suited up in a Brooklyn Dodgers uniform, becoming the first African American ever to play major league baseball outside of the established Negro leagues (Anderson 1997). Robinson's story is fairly well known among American sports fans. Like any pioneer who breaks racial barriers in American institutions, Robinson experienced extreme racism while promoting social change. For the most part, however, Robinson's story is one of both struggle and success. Enduring extreme racism from fans, opponents, and even some teammates, Robinson proved to be one of the most accomplished baseball players of his time, Black or White, and further proved to some skeptical Americans that African Americans could succeed in traditionally White institutions.

Fast-forward to 1964, when major league baseball drafted a second pioneer in terms of racial (and national) integration. At this time, a twenty-year-old baseball player from Japan, Masanori Murakami, began pitching for the San Francisco Giants. Murakami's history in the American major leagues was far shorter than Robinson's and much less publicized. Due to homesickness and a more lucrative contract offer, Murakami returned to Japan to play professional baseball in 1965 (Murray 1995). Perhaps due to Murakami's short stay with the San Francisco Giants, American sports fans know virtually nothing about this young Japanese pitcher's success in America and the social impact he might have had for Japanese nationals and Japanese Americans.

Today in the 1990s, American baseball is experiencing a more significant influx of pitchers from Asia, predominantly from Japan. Unlike Robinson, these players are not forced to encounter violent and overt racism while fulfilling their athletic dreams of playing in the American major leagues. Still, their integration into American baseball has hardly gone unnoticed by the American press, which also makes their experience different from that of their Japanese predecessor, Murakami.

The two Japanese pitchers who have drawn the most attention from American sports media are Hideo Nomo, formerly of the Los Angeles Dodgers and currently with the New York Mets, and Hideki Irabu of the New York Yankees. Nomo first arrived on the American sports scene in February 1995 when he signed with the Dodgers (Nightengale 1995a). Just over two years later in April 1997, the Yankees acquired exclusive rights to negotiate with Irabu (Moran 1997). This article will argue that American media portrayals of these two Japanese pitchers have mirrored stereotypical images of Asian Americans and Asian nationals, thereby perpetuating a national culture that already unfairly categorizes Asian Americans and Asian nationals as model minorities and economic threats.

Model Minorities and Economic Threats

One of the most common and damaging stereotypes of Asian Americans is that of the model minority. According to Wong, Lai, Nagasawa, and Lin (1998), the model minority stereotype inaccurately "suggests that Asian Americans conform to the norms of society, do well in school and careers, are hard working and self-sufficient" (100). Although these qualities may seem positive on the surface, positive stereotypes can be harmful in their own way. Taylor and Stern (1997) argue that the model minority stereotype "can lead to hostility on the part of other minorities and the majority culture. It can inhibit assimilation by reinforcing the public perception of the minority as generic and unidimensional" (55–56). For example, documenting some of the harsh resentment displayed toward Asian American college students for "taking over" America's elite universities, Takagi (1992) states, "Articles in the popular press reported that some white students claimed that M.I.T. stood for Made in Taiwan and that U.C.L.A. stood for University of Caucasians Living Among Asians" (60). Furthermore, viewing Asian Americans as model minorities distracts individuals from the diversity that exists within Asian America. Although on average it may be true that more Asian Americans have higher educational and occupational status than other ethnic minorities, the model minority myth allows for serious problems within Asian American communities to be easily overlooked and dismissed as trivial. Finally, the model minority myth can be used to control Asian Americans and other minority groups. As expressed by Wong et al. (1998), "The 'success' of the minority is offered as proof that the American dream of equal opportunity is valid for those who conform and who are willing to work hard" (100). The myth implies that if one racial minority group buys into the American dream, where any individual can succeed via determination and sacrifice, then other minorities should be able to do the same; in turn, the hurdles of racism, sexism, and classism are discounted as significant influences in society. Ultimately, the model minority myth is a conservative tool that falsely debunks any notions of systematic discrimination.

A second common stereotype of Asian nationals (in particular Japanese nationals) is that of the economic threat. In the post–World War II era, Japan evolved into a capitalistic power respected, and in some cases feared, on a global level. On November 21, 1991, *Newsweek* headlined its cover by observing the Japanese bombing of Pearl Harbor as its fiftieth anniversary approached. A series of articles was published in this issue, one entitled "Coming to Terms with Japan." In this story, Japanese industrial plants and their leaders are designated as the new army striking the United States (Watson, Powell, and Thomas 1991):

> Fifty years later, many Americans wonder who won the war after all. They see Japan's business-suited legions conquering worldwide markets, wiping out entire U.S. industries and planting their flag on blue-chip properties all over America. The Japanese thrive by dint of virtues once considered distinctively American: hard work, thrift, ingenuity. But they sometimes appear to grasp success by underhanded means. (46)

In essence, Japanese businessmen are portrayed as Japan's new soldiers. The authors do go on to say that Americans and Japanese are experiencing cultural misunderstandings because "[e]ach country's national character is almost a mirror image of the other's" (46), and if the United States is to come to terms with Japan, the two countries must learn to understand one another more accurately on a cultural level. Nonetheless, Japan is still cast as a legitimate threat to the United States's economy if both countries fail their cultural sensitivity tests.

Sadly, this is only one of many articles that have appeared in popular media that characterize Japan as an economic menace to America. Just over one year later, *Newsweek* again published an article (Schwartz et al. 1992) on Japan in their business section, entitled "The Push to 'Buy American': Will the Latest Form of Japan-Bashing Work?" Again, the authors attempt to show both sides of the story. Perspectives of American protesters (who have lost jobs to Japanese industry) and Japanese business (that claims to practice fair capitalism) are both explained. However, a subsection of the article (Thomas 1992) attempts to explain "Why Japan Must Share the Blame" in this economic conflict. Briefly acknowledging that Americans are using racism as a means to confront the issue, the bulk of the section blames Japan's "stubborn" trade policies for America's economic anguish. On May 18 that same year, *Fortune* headlined its cover story, "Why Japan Will Emerge Stronger," with a subarticle that questions, "What If Japan Triumphs?" (Kirkland 1992). American minds were primed to perceive the Japanese as an economic threat.

Within this economic discourse, sports were not an unrelated subject. Likening the global economy to a sporting arena, a Japanese legislator was quoted in *Newsweek* as saying, "In economics, as in sports, you cannot make excuses, because the results show up in the scores," to which the author replies, "When Bush hears this argument, he'd best call time out" (Powell 1992, 33). In 1992, Japanese businessmen also offered to purchase the Seattle Mariners, which further stirred American emotions (Schwartz et al. 1992).

As the global economy has expanded, making national boundaries less rigid, the United States has experienced a new wave of Asian immigration. Today, American baseball is buying Japanese, and a new wave of athletic immigrants are playing on American soil.

Before Nomo: Asian Athletes in American Minds

Hideo Nomo was the first high-profile pitcher from Asia to pitch in the American major leagues, but he was not the first Asian or Asian American athlete to play professionally in the United States. Asian American athletes such as tennis star Michael Chang and Olympic figure skater Kristy Yamaguchi had reached the spotlight prior to Nomo's arrival in Los Angeles. However, the media portrayals of these Asian American athletes have differed from depictions of Asian nationals who compete in American athletics. As will be illustrated, when Asian nationals attempt to play in "America's national pastime," it appears that stereotypical images often become more frequent and harmful.

In the March 28, 1994, issue of *Sports Illustrated,* Tom Verducci's article, "Orient Express," introduces the Los Angeles Dodgers' Chan Ho Park and the Seattle Mariners' Mokoto Suzuki to American sports fans. Verducci's (1994) article includes a description of Park's pitching motion:

> One, two, three, four, five seconds passed—an eternity charged with the tension of utter stillness. Suddenly he jerked his hands down, kicked his left leg above his head, drew back his right arm, thrust himself forward, brought his arm around as furiously as if he were cracking a whip and let loose another pitch toward . . . what, exactly? Recognition as a trans-cultural phenomenon? Or homogenization into the great American pastime?
>
> That might as well have been a flying saucer on the mound, the way the baseball establishment has reacted to Chan Ho Park and the unique method by which he sometimes delivers a baseball. No one knew what to do about it. No one wanted to touch it. It was just so—well, so foreign. (24)

Is Park performing some kind of Oriental ritual, summoning mystical powers in the midst of his pitching motion? Verducci (1994) goes on to explain that Park's hesitation in his pitching technique evoked a stir of controversy among opposing major league teams who felt that the pitching style was illegal. In South Korea, this hesitation in pitching is commonly used among pitchers to distract batters. In America, however, Park is objectified by his critics into a "flying saucer" who uses unfamiliar and illegal tactics to trump his opponents.

Using more threatening language, Verducci (1994) goes on to state that "[a] two-man Asian invasion has hit baseball" (24). The integration of two Asian pitchers into American baseball should hardly be considered an "invasion." There are literally thousands of players in the American major and minor leagues, yet Park and Suzuki are still labeled invaders. Wong (1994) argues that the "Asian invasion" cliché is commonly used among journalists and criticizes the term, stating that "[i]ronically, these headlines' 'Asian invasion' imagery, which reinforces the stereotype of Asians as hostile foreigners, detracts from what were otherwise balanced articles about some aspect of the Asian American experience" (55). According to Verducci (1994), not only are Park and Suzuki tagged as invaders in America's national pastime, but Park is further orientalized and opposed by American players and teams.

Though it does not focus on American major league baseball, one of the most damaging accounts of Asian baseball players is found in Pico Iyer's *Video Night in Kathmandu: And Other Reports from the Not-So-Far East.* Iyer (1988) is extremely critical of the Japanese culture, claiming it is far too serious and therefore inappropriate for American baseball. Using baseball as a metaphor for America, Iyer suggests to readers that Americans should be wary of Japan's success—for if the Japanese can contaminate America's national pastime, surely they have the potential to impose their "deleterious" culture on America. Iyer writes that

> Japanese baseball, in fact, was driven by the same unbending will to succeed, the same single-minded determination, the same almost inhuman commitment to industry that had made the entire country a world leader in industry. . . . If the country could lower its birthrate, increase its average height by four inches in four decades and solve what had been the worst pollution problem in the world, why could it not also conquer a game? (329–30)

According to Iyer (1988), the Japanese culture has watered down one of America's most meaningful cultural institutions. Moreover, Iyer uses baseball to turn Japan into a perceived national threat, invading America's cultural space. Iyer ends his section on Japan with a recount of the 1984 Los Angeles Olympic Games, in which America's baseball team lost to Japan:

> "The Gold is ours," said one American pitcher, speaking for the entire country. "They'll need an army to take it away from us." In the final, however, . . . the Japanese decisively trounced the Americans at the American national sport, by a score of 6-3. (355)

Since when did America own baseball? Is the game itself a commodity that has been bought and patented by America? And there is further confirmation that Japan's succession over baseball is an omen that Japan will soon take over America, if not by militaristic force then via economic force and cultural appropriation.

A final way in which Asian athletes have been damaged in the media is by their being displayed as physically inferior. Though not used in regard to baseball yet, it is this Asian stereotype, portraying the Asian and Asian American athlete as physically inept, that is most pervasive and accepted in American media. *Runner's World* journalist Amby Burfoot (1992) attempts to explain why Japanese athletes have not flourished on an international level in track and field. In a brief section of his article subtitled "Sport: The Illusion of Fairness," Burfoot claims that

> Japanese are passionate about sports and surely rank among the world's most disciplined, hardest-working and highest-achieving peoples. These qualities have brought them great success in many areas and should produce the same in sports. Yet the Japanese rarely succeed at sports. They fall short because, on average, they are short. Most big-time sports require size, speed and strength. A racial group lacking these qualities must struggle against great odds to excel. (90)

Burfoot (1992) focuses almost exclusively on physical and racial perceptions of Japanese (as well as African and African American) athletes, devoting none of his article to the issue of perceived competence, which many sports theorists have said is a key to athletic performance. Similar to Iyer (1988), Burfoot (1992) briefly discusses Japanese cultural values that should make Japanese triumphant in any athletic endeavor. Yet, unlike Iyer (1988), Burfoot (1992) claims that Japanese are constrained by their bodies, which inhibits them from achieving what their culture should enhance. Taking this biologically oriented approach is especially dangerous because it works in tandem with other biological and cultural stereotypes. Asians and Asian Americans are stereotyped as less athletic but hard working and more intelligent (hence, they are the model minority). In comparison, Africans and African Americans are stereotyped as more athletic (Hoberman 1997) but lazy (Lapchick 1991, 276–78) and less intelligent (Lapchick 1995).

In the early 1990s, when an unusually high number of Chinese female athletes (in particular runners and swimmers) broke world records, they were denounced for using performance-enhancing steroids. Whether or not the allegations were true, it seemed incomprehensible to journalists that a Chinese athlete could break a world record without steroid assistance. As Hoberman (1997) attests, "Westerners are prepared to accept the idea of Chinese deceit, but we do not associate Asians with supernormal athletic ability" (139). In a 1995 *Los Angeles Times* article, "The Crooked Shadow,'" Almond and Tempest report on the pervasive use of steroids throughout a number of sports in China. Nowhere in the article is there even a question that some of the Chinese competitors, who broke world records, may have been clean. In all fairness, it is very unlikely that so many world records would be broken in such a short time span without the assistance of performance-enhancing drugs. Yet, the ease with which Americans seemed to accept the Chinese athletes' fraud is equally disturbing.

There has been an extreme dearth of literature written on Asian athletes in America. Among the sparse literature that is available, Asian athletes have been depicted as anything but normal. They are either mysterious competitors, cultural appropriators, cheaters, or simply athletically inept. In February 1995, Hideo Nomo signed to pitch for the Los Angeles Dodgers, initiating what would soon become "Nomomania" in Los Angeles. How Nomo and, later, Hideki Irabu would be presented to the American public would again prove to be stereotypically Asian.

Methodology

Taking a content analysis, articles from the *Los Angeles Times* sports section (January 1995 through November 1995) and the *New York Times* sports section (December 1996 through October 1997) were read and analyzed. The period of time in which each newspaper was studied represents the time when negotiations began for each athlete to pitch for his respective team until each pitcher's first major league season ended. The *Los Angeles Times* and *New York Times* were chosen because Nomo, pitching for the Los Angeles Dodgers, would obviously receive the most media coverage in Los Angeles and Irabu, pitching for the New York Yankees, would likewise receive the most coverage in New York.

This study does not intend to compare the *Los Angeles Times* and the *New York Times*. Although the argument can be made that the newspapers serve different target audiences and have different writers and editors, they are two of the most widely distributed and well-known newspapers in the United States and in the world. Thus, the two newspapers do serve as adequate representatives of American media. Most importantly, the two newspapers are major American newspapers depicting Japanese athletes in America. Therefore, the compared presentations of the two pitchers are useful in understanding how American readers perceive Asian athletes. Anderson (1991) argues that communities are bonded by print media and that print media serve as one of the primary factors that shape national sensibilities. Articles in the magazine *Sports Illustrated* are also examined, but they will only serve as supplemental data because there were so few articles dedicated specifically to the two Japanese pitchers.

Results

Hideo Nomo: The Model Minority

In March 1995, American major league baseball players were on strike, and it would seem that another "Asian invasion" into America's national pastime could not have worse timing. How would American players, who were previously striking for more money, receive the first Japanese national to play in the major leagues since 1965? Apparently, Nomo did something right, as American media, American fans, and American baseball players partook in an international phenomenon of Nomomania. Was Hideo Nomo an athletic model minority?

It was no secret that Nomo was not satisfied playing professional baseball in Japan, although he was one of the country's most famous and successful pitchers (Nightengale 1995b). It had always been Nomo's ultimate goal to play baseball in the United States. Flattering the American major leagues, Nomo made American baseball the standard by which international players must measure their skills. After his second major league start, Nomo was quoted as saying, "I'm so glad I got to pitch in a real major league game. . . . This is what I always wanted. My dream was realized" (Nightengale 1995c, C4). Here, Nomo defines the American major leagues as the real major leagues, again making professional baseball in Japan subpar to the American standard. Whether baseball in America is in fact superior or inferior to baseball in Japan is inconsequential here. What is important to demonstrate is Nomo's implicit comparison between baseball in the two countries, and furthermore the way Nomo is then presented by American sports media.

Nomo also set guidelines on and angered Japanese media that followed him, causing one Japanese reporter to reply, "He keeps saying how he's going to do everything like the major league players, but he doesn't do interviews in the clubhouse. If he likes American ways, he should do what Americans do" (Nightengale 1995b, C7). An article in *Sports Illustrated* even went so far as to say, "Pitcher Hideo Nomo turned his back on Japan and now faces batters for the Dodgers" (Verducci 1995a, 45). Resisting the Japanese media, attempting to emulate American players, and turning his back on Japan, Nomo conformed as the quintessential model minority. The rhetoric used by Verducci (1995a)—that he "turned his back on Japan"—is strikingly similar to that used by the Japanese American Citizen's League (JACL) during the early 1920s and even during the Japanese American internment of the 1940s. Spickard (1996) states, "From the start, these progenitors of the JACL emphasized the American citizenship of the Nisei generation, loyalty to the United States, and disavowal of connections with Japan" (91). It is precisely this type of discourse—rejecting Japan and whole-heartedly accepting America while disregarding America's realities of racism—that serves as the foundation for the model minority myth.

Nomo's immediate success also made him one of the Dodgers' primary advertising tools. Prior to Nomo's first start at Dodger stadium, the slogan "Nomo Mr. Nice Guy!" emerged in the *Los Angeles Times,* and Nomo attained the moniker "The Tornado" due to his "unique windup and delivery." Nomo's success even helped him surpass being orientalized as a mysterious Japanese entity. Following a sparkling performance against the Pittsburgh Pirates, Nightengale (1995d) wrote,

> Nomo is no longer considered a novelty merely because he's the first Japanese player in 30 years to pitch in the major leagues. These days, he simply is being recognized as one of the finest pitchers in the National League. (C1)

Even some of the major leagues' top players from other teams openly admired Nomo's success. Though Nomo was advertised as having a "unique" pitching style, he was quickly assimilated into the American major leagues as simply a great pitcher.

By early July 1995, a story entitled "Nomomania Grips L.A. and Japan" ran on the *Los Angeles Times*'s front page (Nightengale 1995e), making Nomo a household name in southern California. And responding to fans who were boycotting baseball because of the players' earlier strike, *Sports Illustrated* ran their July 10, 1995, issue with Hideo Nomo gracing the cover, which read "What's Right about Baseball: Rookie Ace Hideo Nomo Is Just One Reason the Game Is Better Than You Think" (Verducci 1995b).

Always humble in his success and glory, Nomo surpassed all expectations and became one of baseball's primary icons. Dodger executive vice president said of Nomo (Nightengale 1995f),

> Here's a guy who had everything. He put everything on the table—fame, fortune, and all of the conveniences anyone would ever want. What he was saying was, "I'm willing to risk everything just to go against the best." Perhaps the most memorable thing he said is, "I haven't proven anything. I've done nothing." That impressed me. That impressed me a lot. (C6)

Again the prototypical model minority, Nomo graciously embraced his success while sacrificing personal comforts for his American team. Though Nomo did not carry the Dodgers to the World Series, he did earn Rookie of the Year honors (Nightengale 1995g) and expanded the possibilities that other Japanese pitchers could play baseball in the United States (MacGregor 1995).

Certainly, it was Nomo's pitching success that garnered him positive media attention and the ability to surpass being orientalized and labeled an economic risk. But in the process, Nomo was also presented as a very typical model minority. Hard-working, self-sacrificing, and quiet as (he was rarely quoted in newspapers), Nomo reaffirmed to readers that Asian nationals and Asian Americans were model minorities. It should be noted here that although Hideo Nomo is a Japanese national and not Asian American, he and Hideki Irabu can still affect the way mainstream America views Asian Americans. White Americans often fail to differentiate between Asian nationals, Asian Americans, and different Asian American groups. Thus, the inaccurate or stereotypical portrayal of one Asian (Nomo or Irabu) and/or Asian American can falsely represent diverse groups of Asians and Asian Americans for dominant American audiences. How would a Japanese pitcher not so successful and more expensive be received and presented in the American media?

Hideki Irabu: The Economic Threat

With the success of Nomo, the New York Yankees sought their own Japanese pitching star in Hideki Irabu. Less than two months after America celebrated the fiftieth anniversary of Jackie Robinson being the first African American to play major league baseball and less than two months after Tiger Woods became the first African, Asian, and Native American to win golf's prestigious Masters title, Hideki Irabu signed to play ball for the Yankees. With the media frenzies that surrounded both Robinson's anniversary and Woods's victory, it would seem that America should be prepared to accept minority athletes without prejudice, even if they were from another country. Yet, Irabu's agreement to play in America did not come without controversy.

Heralded as a better pitcher than Nomo while pitching in Japan, Irabu demanded to play only for the Yankees, although he was initially under the San Diego Padres' rights. Furthermore, when Irabu was finally traded to New York, his pitching value allowed him the leverage to attain a $12.8 million contract to be paid over four years with an $8.5 million signing bonus. The $12.8 million contract was the most ever given to a player who had never pitched in the American major leagues (Chass 1997a).

Despite initial support for Irabu from most Yankee teammates, skepticism regarding Irabu's market value did emerge. Yankee pitcher David Wells was quoted as saying in regard to Irabu (Chass 1997a) that

> I don't think it's right that one of us who has been busting his butt for the organization has to go. Maybe it will work out. He's one of our teammates so I have no bad feelings about the guy. (B9)

Wells's initial comments seem fair enough. However, criticism regarding Irabu's signing from Wells and other Yankee players intensified to such an extent that the

Yankees' owner, George Steinbrenner, publicly denounced those players chastising Irabu (Diamos 1997a). Throughout his minor league starts, Irabu became known as the Japanese pitcher who signed for $12.8 million: "For $12.8 million, Hideki Irabu will be expected to deliver more than laser fastballs, savage splitters and victories for the Yankees" (Sandomir 1997, B13); "Steinbrenner, who gave the Japanese pitcher a $12.8 million contract, said before the game that he had no such concerns" (Chass 1997b, 4); "So the Yankees summoned Girardi to the Bronx on a rare day off, and he helped tutor the $12.8 million pitcher for two hours" (Curry 1997, B13). Irabu's identity was not one of an athlete but more of a risky economic investment, and although Irabu's first major league start silenced most skeptics, he soon fell prey to a media barrage of criticism that consistently mentioned his high-priced contract. And criticism was exacerbated by the fact that Irabu did not pitch well in subsequent outings.

Irabu also was identified in relation to the White American pitcher, Nolan Ryan. Sports writer Harvey Araton (1997) said of Irabu that

> [i]n the interests of accuracy, fair expectation and proper respect, it is not soon enough to wipe the term "Japanese Nolan Ryan" from the Hideki Irabu glossary. Drop it. Strike it. . . . Irabu is not Ryan or the young Dwight Gooden or today's Mariano Rivera. He should not be held to those unrealistic standards of high hard heat. (B9)

Why was Irabu being compared to an American standard in the first place? Did he intend to be the next "Japanese Nolan Ryan"? Or did Irabu simply want to be a successful American major league pitcher who happened to come from Japan? Because Irabu was set up in relation to an American standard, he was fighting an uphill battle to gain acceptance from the beginning. Being Japanese definitely resulted in extra and unnecessary criticism. Even an opposing batter, David Justice, was aware of the additional condemnation being cast upon Irabu and remarked that "[h]e's just a regular pitcher. If his name wasn't Irabu, we wouldn't even be talking about him. If it was Jaret Wright or somebody, there wouldn't be this much hoopla about him. But it's not his fault" (Chass 1997c, B11).

As Irabu continued to pitch poorly, his $12.8 million contract became more and more noticeable. After losing in his third start, Irabu was referred to as "[t]he $12.8 million man [who] lost to someone named Scott Karl (a Milwaukee Brewers pitcher)" ("Irabu Is Rocked" 1997, C2). Following a third consecutive lackluster performance, sports journalist Jason Diamos (1997b) claimed, "This is clearly not what George Steinbrenner had in mind when he signed Irabu to a $12.8 million deal" (7). As expressed by Smith (1997), Irabu became known as a $12.8 million financial disaster:

> One year after George Steinbrenner signed a supposed known quantity in Rogers for $20 million only to see the veteran left-hander flop in New York, the Yankee owner turned around and signed an unknown quantity in Irabu for an astounding $12.8 million.
>
> The Yankees, it seems, concede that Irabu, at 2-2 with a burgeoning earned run average and the look of a deer caught in the headlights, currently had no idea of what to expect in the major leagues. (B7)

Criticism of Irabu, strictly as an overpaid pitcher not producing wins, is certainly warranted. What readers can potentially digest, however, is another Japanese entity that is financially threatening an American institution. Irabu's Japanese heritage and national status were displayed prominently by the *New York Times* (Weber 1997) and therefore a cultural sensitivity should have accompanied any articles, positive or negative, on Irabu. As noted previously, the American media had already conditioned its readers to view Japan and Japanese nationals as economic threats. Although Japan has generally been cast as a threat to America's economic base and Irabu was cast in an opposite light as an economic disaster, both Japan and Irabu were depicted as economic dangers. The *New York Times*'s constant mentioning of Irabu as a \$12.8 million, Japanese, and failing pitcher could only reinforce notions of Japanese as economic perils for America.

Conclusion

Presently, Nomo, although not pitching as well as in his rookie season, continues to play in the American major leagues for the New York Mets, and Irabu has improved his game, still pitching for the New York Yankees. The media cannot control the success or failure of an athlete. Neither can the media control whether an athlete is overpaid, or whether an athlete presents him- or herself as self-sacrificing. But at a time when cultural sensitivity is imperative, the media must reach a higher consciousness in terms of cultural awareness. Because athletics are not independent from politics, sports writers need to be aware of the political circumstances surrounding their stories. This study does not intend to berate the *Los Angeles Times*'s and the *New York Times*'s sports sections. Rather, this study is an attempt to illustrate how images in sports can reify injurious stereotypes if cultural sensitivity is not applied. There are more constructive ways to discuss an overpaid Japanese pitcher without losing important content in the story.

Asian nationals and Asian Americans, like other foreign nationals and racial minorities, have endured years of stereotyping in the United States. Sports, as popular and powerful as they are in America, should be used to break down faulty images, not to reinforce them. For decades, African American athletes have been tracked out of "thinking positions" in sports, such as the quarterback in football and the pitcher in baseball (Lapchick 1995, 92). It should not go unnoticed that all of a sudden Asian nationals (stereotypically viewed as less athletic but more intelligent) are specifically recruited to play in the "thinking position" of pitcher. If this positional racialization goes on without scrutiny, unproven and false images of both Asian and African Americans will be further essentialized in American minds.

The answer, however, is not to present or view sport as a color-blind institution. In fact, it is important to promote athletes' ethnicities and national origins. As one Japanese American fan from San Francisco said, "I'm a Giants fan, and always will be a Giant fan, but like a lot of people here today, I'm a Nomo fan" (Nightengale 1995c, C1). More recently, many Latin Americans have taken a great deal of pride watching Sammy Sosa compete with Mark McGwire in breaking Roger Maris's single-season home-run record ("It's a Slugger's Race" 1998). To dismiss athletes' ethnicities would be to take away ethnic pride fans find in their athletic heroes. It is especially important that further research regarding Asian and Asian American athletes investigates the additional factor of gender, as Asian and Asian American women are so frequently stereotyped as passive and subservient. In fact, research has affirmed that the model minority myth is particularly damaging to Asian and Asian American women because it enables a perception that views Asian and Asian American women as easy targets for sexual harassment. Depictions of Asian and Asian American women in athletics can be very effective in dispelling these racialized and gendered stereotypes. For Asian nationals and Asian Americans (both male and female) who are so often categorized as resigned and athletically inferior, finding athletic heroes could be very useful not only in dissolving racial stereotypes but also in promoting ethnic pride. At the same time, other stereotypes of Asians and Asian Americans should not be supported in the process.

NOTES

Originally published from *Journal of Sport & Social Issues* 23.2 (1999): 203–17. © 1999 Sage Publications Inc., reprint by permission.

REFERENCES

Almond, E., & Tempest, R. (1995, February 12). "The crooked shadow": Chinese swimmers, under a drug cloud, today are expected to be banned from Pan-Pacific championships. *Los Angeles Times*, pp. C1, C12.

Anderson, B. (1991). *Imagined communities.* New York: Verso.

Anderson, D. (1997, March 30). The days that brought the barrier down: Fifty years later, Robinson's first manager recalls the integration of the majors. *New York Times*, sec. 8, pp. 1, 12.

Araton, H. (1997, July 16). Let's face it, Irabu is not Nolan Ryan. *New York Times*, p. B9.

Burfoot, A. (1992, August). White men can't run: Why Black runners win every race from the sprints to the marathon. *Runner's World*, pp. 89–95.

Chass, M. (1997a, July 6). Irabu agrees to Yankees' offer of $12.8 million. *New York Times*, pp. B7, B9.

Chass, M. (1997b, July 6). Irabu hurls shutout: Will debut Thursday. *New York Times*, sec. 8, p. 4.

Chass, M. (1997c, July 16). Once praised to the skies, Irabu falls somewhat closer to earth. *New York Times*, p. B11.

Cho, S. (1997). Asian Pacific American women and racialized sexual harassment. In E. Kim, L. Villanueva, & Asian Women Unified of California (eds.), *Making more waves: New writing by Asian America women.* (pp. 164–73). Boston: Beacon.

Curry, J. (1997, July 9). Irabu plays game of catch with Yankees' Girardi. *New York Times*, pp. B13, B15.

Diamos, J. (1997a, June 11). Steinbrenner is irked by players' criticism. *New York Times*, sec. 8, pp. 1, 7.

Diamos, J. (1997b, July 27). Irabu is knocked out: Maybe out of the rotation. *New York Times*, sec. 8, pp. 1, 7.

Espiritu, Y. L. (1992). *Asian American panethnicity: Bridging institutions and identities.* Philadelphia: Temple University Press.

Hoberman, J. (1997). *Darwin's athletes: How sport has damaged Black America and preserved the myth of race.* New York: Houghton Mifflin.

Hudson, M. A. (1995, April 28). Dodger verdict is yes on Nomo's first start: Japanese pitcher allows two earned runs and six hits in 5 1/3 innings, while striking out six. *Los Angeles Times,* pp. C1, C5.

Hurh, W. M., & Kim, K. C. (1989). The "success" image of Asian Americans: Its validity, and its practical and theoretical implications. *Ethnic and Racial Studies, 21*(4), 512–38.

Irabu is rocked and riled by Brewers. (1997, July 21). *New York Times,* p. C2.

It's a slugger's race, but it is also about race. (1998, September 20). *New York Times,* pp. 37, 38.

Iyer, P. (1988). *Video night in Kathmandu: And other reports from the not-so-far East.* New York: Vintage.

Kirkland, R. (1992, May 18). What if Japan triumphs? *Fortune,* pp. 60–65.

Klint, K., & Weiss, M. (1987). Perceived competence and motives for participating in youth sports: A test of Harter's Competence Motivation Theory. *Journal of Sport Psychology, 9,* 55–65.

Lapchick, R. (1991). *Five minutes to midnight: Race and sport in the 1990s.* New York: Madison.

Lapchick, R. (1995). Race and college sport: A long way to go. *Race & Class: A Journal for Black and Third World Liberation, 36*(4), 87–94.

Los Angeles Times. (1995a, May 12). Advertisement, p. C4.

Los Angeles Times. (1995b, May 12). Advertisement, p. C8.

MacGregor, H. (1995, October 9). A hit with players, agent is screwball to owners in Japan. *Los Angeles Times,* pp. C1, C12.

Marchetti, G. (1993). *Romance and the "yellow peril": Race, sex, and discursive strategies in Hollywood fiction.* Berkeley: University of California Press.

Moran, M. (1997, April 23). Yankees get rights to Irabu in deal with Padres. *New York Times,* pp. B9, B11.

Murray, J. (1995, September 24). Murakami mania was ocean away. *Los Angeles Times,* pp. C1, C11.

Newman, R. (1995, March 26). It may be now or never for baseball. *Los Angeles Times,* pp. C3, C14.

Nightengale, B. (1995a, February 14). East meets west for pitcher Nomo. *Los Angeles Times,* pp. C1, C3.

Nightengale, B. (1995b, April 22). The Dodgers' Asian armistice: After keeping Japan's Hideo Nomo at arm's length, Korea's Chan Ho Park decides to extend his hand. *Los Angeles Times,* pp. C1, C7.

Nightengale, B. (1995c, May 3). Nomo debut great, Dodger finish isn't: Japanese pitcher throws five strong innings, but bullpen blows 3-0 lead in 15th against Giants. *Los Angeles Times,* pp. C1, C4.

Nightengale, B. (1995d, June 15). Nomo looks just as good as 16-K-gold: Dodger rookie not having much trouble the second time around. Pirates fall, 8-5. *Los Angeles Times,* pp. C1, C9.

Nightengale, B. (1995e, July 4). Nomomania grips L.A. and Japan. *Los Angeles Times,* pp. A1, A24.

Nightengale, B. (1995f, August 6). Nomo comes close to no-no: Pitcher gets two hits, one more than Giants, who get only an infield single in seventh. *Los Angeles Times,* pp. C1, C6.

Nightengale, B. (1995g, November 10). In Nomo's biggest windup yet, he winds up rookie for the year: Pitcher becomes fourth consecutive Dodger to receive the honor by outpolling the Braves' Chipper Jones. *Los Angeles Times,* pp. C1, C8.

Noe, N. (1998, May). Fists of fury: Asian American women are making deep impressions in the world of boxing. *A. Magazine,* pp. 12–13.

Ong, P., Bonacich, E., & Cheng, L. (1994). *The new Asian immigration in Los Angeles and global restructuring.* Philadelphia: Temple University Press.

Osajima, K. (1988). Asian Americans as the model minority: An analysis of the popular press image in the 1960s and1980s. In G. Okihiro, S. Hune, A. Hansen, & J. Liu (eds.), *Reflections on shattered windows.* (pp. 165–74). Pullman: Washington State University Press.

Padres' Gwynn becomes member of the Nomo admiration society. (1995, June 29). *Los Angeles Times,* p. C7.

Powell, B. (1992, January 6). Japan's trade charade: What it will tell Bush is part truth, part nonsense. *Newsweek,* p. 33.

Roberts, G., Kleiber, D., & Duda, J. (1981). An analysis of motivation in children's sport: The role of perceived competence in participation. *Journal of Sport Psychology, 3,* 206–16.

Rudisill, M. (1981). Influence of perceived competence and casual dimension orientation on expectations, persistence, and performance during perceived failure. *Research Quarterly for Exercise and Sport, 60*(2), 166–75.

Sandomir, R. (1997, June 25). Arriving on a t-shirt near you: Hideki Irabu. *New York Times,* p. B13.

Schwartz, J., Powell, B., Washington, R., & Yoffe, E. (1992, February 3). The push to "buy American." *Newsweek,* pp. 32–35.

Smith, C. (1997, July 29). For Yankees and Irabu, hype and big plans backfire. *New York Times,* p. B7.

Spickard, P. (1996). *Japanese Americans: The formation and transformations of an ethnic group.* New York: Twayne.

Takagi, D. (1992). *The retreat from race: Asian-American admissions and racial politics.* New Brunswick, NJ: Rutgers University Press.

Taylor, C., & Stern, B. (1997). Asian-Americans: Television advertising and the "model minority" stereotype. *Journal of Advertising, 26,* 47–60.

Thomas, R. (1992, February 3). Why Japan must share the blame. *Newsweek,* p. 35.

Verducci, T. (1994, March 28). Orient express: A pair of young Asian pitchers, the Dodgers' Chan Ho Park and the Mariners' Makoto Suzuki, have thrown baseball for a loop. *Sports Illustrated,* pp. 24–27.

Verducci, T. (1995a, May 15). He's over here: Hideo Nomo turned his back on Japan to pitch for Los Angeles. *Sports Illustrated,* pp. 44–46.

Verducci, T. (1995b, July 10). What's right about baseball: Rookie ace Hideo Nomo is just one reason the game is better than you think. *Sports Illustrated,* pp. 16–22.

Vincenti, J. (1997). The relationship between female status and physical strength in a Japanese university athletic club. *Journal of Sport & Social Issues, 21*(2), 189–210.

Watson, R., Powell, B., & Thomas, R. (1991, November 25). Coming to terms with Japan: With the cold war over, the relationship has to change. It can be made better. *Newsweek,* pp. 46–47.

Weber, B. (1997, July 11). Cultures blend in stands as Irabu takes the mound. *New York Times,* pp. B1, B9.

Wong, P., Lai, C., Nagasawa, R., & Lin, T. (1998). Asian Americans as a model minority: Self-perceptions by other racial groups. *Sociological Perspectives, 41,* 95–118.

Wong, W. (1994). Covering the invisible "model minority." *Media Studies Journal, 8,* 49–60.

1. What are the origins of the model minority thesis? How does this compare with previous depictions of Asian Americans? What, if anything, is significant about the evolution of these images over time? What, in your opinion (and Lee's) has prompted these changes in the model minority myth? Is it still utilized with the same political agenda in mind?

2. Bob Lee talks at length about the Cold War conditions that gave rise to the model minority myth. Based upon the evidence he provides, to what extend to you agree or disagree with this assessment? In what ways—if any—do discussions of sexuality factor into the construction of the model minority myth?

3. To what extent—if any—does the model minority myth factor into contemporary debates about Asian American identity? Can you think of any ways in which the media continues to perpetuate this stereotype? What negative effects does it continue to perpetuate for contemporary Asian Americans?

4. Through examining the media portrayals of two Japanese pitchers playing in American major league baseball, Mayeda interrogates the dual image of Asians as both model minorities and economic threats. In what ways do the American media and the public homogenize Asian Americans and Asian nationals, and in what ways does such homogenization affect the way Asian Americans are viewed in their own country? What are the effects of the model minority stereotype and what lies behind this seemingly positive image? What do you think are the key mechanisms for stereotyping Asian Americans? How would Asian Americans and the society as a whole act to counter the negative effects of stereotyping?

SUGGESTED READINGS

Ecklund, Elaine H. 2005. "Us" and "Them": The Role of Religion in Mediating and Challenging the "Model Minority" and Other Civic Boundaries. *Ethnic and Racial Studies* 28(1): 132–50.

Fung, Richard. 1994. Seeing Yellow: Asian Identity in Film and Video. In Karin Aguilar-San Juan (ed.), *The State of Asian America: Activism and Resistance in the 1990s.* Boston: South End Press.

Hing, Bill Ong. 1997. *To Be an American: Cultural Pluralism and the Rhetoric of Assimilation.* New York: New York University Press.

Ho, Pensri. 2003. Performing the "Oriental": Professionals and the Asian Model Minority Myth. *Journal of Asian American Studies* 6(2): 149–75.

Ima, Kenji. 1995. Testing the American Dream: Case Studies of At-Risk Southeast Asian Refugee Students in Secondary Schools. Pp. 191–208 in Rubén G. Rumbaut and Wayne A. Cornelius (eds.), *California's Immigrant Children: Theory, Research, and Implications for Educational Policy.* San Diego: Center for U.S.-Mexican Studies.

Lee, Robert. 1999. *Orientals: Asian Americans in Popular Culture.* Philadelphia: Temple University Press.

Lee, Stacey J. 1996. *Unraveling the "Model Minority" Stereotype: Listening to Asian American Youth.* New York: Teachers College, Columbia University.

Lee, Wen Ho with Helen Zia. 2001. *My Country versus Me: The First-Hand Account by the Los Alamos Scientist Who Was Falsely Accused.* New York: Hyperion.

Louie, Andrea. 2004. *Chineseness across Borders: Renegotiating Chinese Identities in China and the United States.* Durham, NC: Duke University Press.

Marchetti, Gina. 1994. *Romance and the "Yellow Peril."* Berkeley: University of California Press.

Ng, Wendy. L. 2002. *Japanese American Internment during World War II: A History and Reference Guide.* Westport, CT: Greenwood Press.

Ono, Kent A. 2005. Guilt without Evidence: Informal Citizenship and the Limits of Rationality in the Case of Wen Ho Lee. Pp. 76–88 in G. Thomas Goodnight (ed.), *Proceedings of the Twelfth NCA/AFA Conference on Argumentation.* Annandale, VA: National Communication Association.

Park, Jung-Sun. 2004. Korean American Youth and Transnational Flows of Popular Culture across the Pacific. *Amerasia Journal* 30(1): 147–69.

Petersen, William. 1966. Success Story: Japanese-American Style. *New York Times Magazine,* January 9.

Pyke, Karen and Tran Dang. 2003. "FOB" and "Whitewashed": Identity and Internalized Racism among Second-Generation Asian Americans. *Qualitative Sociology* 26(2): 147–72.

Sue, Stanley, and Sumie Okazaki. 1990. Asian American Educational Achievement: A Phenomenon in Search of an Explanation. *American Psychologist* 45: 913–20.

Takagi, Dana Y. 1990. From Discrimination to Affirmative Action: Facts in the Asian American Admissions Controversy. *Social Problems* 37: 578–92.

Trueba, H. T., L. R. L. Cheng, and K. Ima. 1993. *Myth or Reality? Adaptive Strategies of Asian Americans in California.* London: Falmer Press.

Tuan, Mia. 1998. *Forever Foreigners or Honorary Whites? The Asian Ethnic Experience Today.* New Brunswick, NJ: Rutgers University Press.

Walker-Moffat, Wendy. 1995. *The Other Side of the Asian American Success Story.* San Francisco: Jossey-Bass Publishers.

Wolf, Diane L. 1997. Family Secrets: Transnational Struggles among Children of Filipino Immigrants. *Sociological Perspectives* 40(3): 457–82.

Wollenberg, Charles M. 1995. "Yellow Peril" in Schools (I & II). Pp. 3–29 in Don T. Nakanishi and Tina Yamano Nishida (eds.), *The Asian American Educational Experience: A Source Book for Teachers and Students.* New York: Routledge.

FILMS

Berges, Paul Mayeda (producer/director). 1991. *En Ryo Identity* (23-minute documentary).

Ding, Loni (producer/director). 1982. *On New Ground* (30-minute documentary).

Dong, Arthur (director). 1989. *Forbidden City, U.S.A.* (56-minute documentary).

Gee, Deborah (director). 1988. *Slaying the Dragon* (60-minute documentary).

Huang, Renanta (director). 2003. *Tribute and Remembrance: Asian Americans after 9/11* (69-minute documentary).

Lee, Joyce (producer/director). 1993. *Foreign Talk* (11-minute drama).

Nakamura, Robert A. (director) and Karen Ishizuka (producer). 1996. *Looking like the Enemy* (52-minute documentary).

Nakasako, Spencer (producer/director). 1984. *Talking History* (30-minute documentary).

Okazaki, Steven (producer/director/writer). 1994. *American Sons* (28-minute documentary).

Soe, Valerie (director). 1992. *Picturing Oriental Girls* (15-minute experimental).

Tajiri, Rea (producer/director/writer). 1991. *History and Memory* (30-minute documentary).

Tanaka, Janice (director). 1999. *When You Are Smiling: The Deadly Legacy of Internment* (60-minute documentary).

Part X

Multiplicity, Citizenship, and Interracial Politics

Chapter 26

Heterogeneity, Hybridity, Multiplicity
Marking Asian American Differences

Lisa Lowe

In a recent poem by Janice Mirikitani, a Japanese-American nisei woman describes her sansei daughter's rebellion.[1] The daughter's denial of Japanese American culture and its particular notions of femininity reminds the nisei speaker that she, too, has denied her antecedents, rebelling against her own more traditional issei mother:

> I want to break tradition—unlock this room
>   where women dress in the dark.
>   Discover the lies my mother told me.
>   The lies that we are small and powerless
>   that our possibilities must be compressed
>   to the size of pearls, displayed only as
>   passive chokers, charms around our neck.
> Break Tradition.
>   I want to tell my daughter of this room
>   of myself
>   filled with tears of shakuhatchi,
>
>   poems about madness,
>   sounds shaken from barbed wire and
>   goodbyes and miracles of survival.
>   This room of open window where daring ones escape.
> My daughter denies she is like me . . .
>   her pouting ruby lips, her skirts
>   swaying to salsa, teena marie and the stones,
>   her thighs displayed in carnivals of color.
>   I do not know the contents of her room.
> She mirrors my aging.
> She is breaking tradition. (9)

The nisei speaker repudiates the repressive confinements of her issei mother: the disciplining of the female body, the tedious practice of diminution, the silences of obedience. In turn, the crises that have shaped the nisei speaker—internment camps,

505

sounds of threatening madness—are unknown to, and unheard by, her sansei teenage daughter. The three generations of Japanese immigrant women in this poem are separated by their different histories and by different conceptions of what it means to be female and Japanese. The poet who writes "I do not know the contents of her room" registers these separations as "breaking tradition."

In another poem, by Lydia Lowe, Chinese women workers are divided also by generation, but even more powerfully by class and language. The speaker is a young Chinese American who supervises an older Chinese woman in a textile factory.

> The long bell blared,
> and then the *lo-ban*
> made me search all your bags
> before you could leave.
> Inside he sighed
> about slow work, fast hands,
> missing spools of thread—
> and I said nothing.
> I remember that day
> you came in to show me
> I added your tickets six zippers short.
> It was just a mistake.
> You squinted down
> at the check in your hands
> like an old village woman peers
> at some magician's trick.
> That afternoon
> when you thrust me your bags
> I couldn't look or raise my face.
> *Doi m-jyu.*
> Eyes on the ground,
> I could only see
> one shoe kicking against the other. (29)

This poem, too, invokes the breaking of tradition, although it thematizes another sort of stratification among Asian women: the structure of the factory places the English-speaking younger woman above the Cantonese-speaking older one. Economic relations in capitalist society force the young supervisor to discipline her elders, and she is acutely ashamed that her required behavior does not demonstrate the respect traditionally owed to parents and elders. Thus, both poems foreground commonly thematized *topoi* of diasporan cultures: the disruption and distortion of traditional cultural practices—like the practice of parental sacrifice and filial duty, or the practice of respecting hierarchies of age—not only as a consequence of immigration to the United States but as a part of entering a society with different class stratifications and different constructions of gender roles. Some Asian American discussions cast the disruption of tradition as loss and represent the loss in terms of regret and shame, as in the latter poem. Alternatively, the traditional practices of family continuity and hierarchy may be figured as oppressively confining, as in Mirikitani's poem, in which the two generations of daughters contest the more restrictive female roles of the former generations. In either case, many Asian American discussions portray immigration and relocation to the United States in terms of a loss of the "original" culture in exchange for the new "American" culture.

In many Asian American novels, the question of the loss or transmission of the "original" culture is frequently represented in a family narrative, figured as generational conflict between the Chinese-born first generation and the American-born second generation.[2] Louis Chu's 1961 novel *Eat a Bowl of Tea,* for example, allegorizes in the conflicted relationship between father and son the differences between "native" Chinese values and the new "westernized" culture of Chinese Americans. Other novels have taken up this generational theme; one way to read Maxine Hong Kingston's *The Woman Warrior* (1975) or Amy Tan's recent *The Joy Luck Club* (1989) is to understand them as versions of this generational model of culture, refigured in feminine terms, between mothers and daughters. However, I will argue that interpreting Asian American culture exclusively in terms of the master narratives of generational conflict and filial relation essentializes Asian American culture, obscuring the particularities and incommensurabilities of class, gender, and national diversities among Asians; the reduction of ethnic cultural politics to struggles between first and second generations displaces (and privatizes) intercommunity differences into a familial opposition. To avoid this homogenizing of Asian Americans as exclusively hierarchical and familial, I would contextualize the "vertical" generational model of culture with the more "horizontal" relationship represented in Diana Chang's "The Oriental Contingent." In Chang's short story, two young women avoid the discussion of their Chinese backgrounds because each desperately fears that the other is "more Chinese," more "authentically" tied to the original culture. The narrator, Connie, is certain that her friend Lisa

> never referred to her own background because it was more Chinese than Connie's, and therefore of a higher order. She was tact incarnate. All along, she had been going out of her way not to embarrass Connie. Yes, yes. Her assurance was definitely uppercrust (perhaps her father had been in the diplomatic service), and her offhand didacticness, her lack of self-doubt, was indeed characteristically Chinese-Chinese. (173)

Connie feels ashamed because she assumes herself to be "a failed Chinese"; she fantasizes that Lisa was born in China, visits there frequently, and privately disdains Chinese Americans. Her assumptions about Lisa prove to be quite wrong, however; Lisa is even more critical of herself for "not being genuine." For Lisa, as Connie eventually discovers, was born in Buffalo and was adopted by non–Chinese American parents; lacking an immediate connection to Chinese culture, Lisa projects upon all Chinese the authority of being "more Chinese." Lisa confesses to Connie at the end of the story: "The only time I feel Chinese is when I'm embarrassed I'm not more Chinese—which is a totally Chinese reflex I'd give anything to be rid of!" (176). Chang's story portrays two women polarized by the degree to which they have each internalized a cultural definition of "Chineseness" as pure and fixed, in which any deviation is constructed as less, lower, and shameful. Rather than confirming the cultural model in which "ethnicity" is passed from generation to generation, Chang's story explores the "ethnic" relationship between women of the same generation. Lisa and Connie are ultimately able to reduce one another's guilt at not being "Chinese enough"; in one another they are able to find a common frame of reference. The story suggests that the making of Chinese American culture—how ethnicity is imagined, practiced, continued—is worked out as much between ourselves and our communities as it is transmitted from one generation to another.

In this sense, Asian American discussions of ethnicity are far from uniform or consistent; rather, these discussions contain a wide spectrum of articulations that includes, at one end, the desire for an identity represented by a fixed profile of ethnic traits and, at another, challenges to the very notions of identity and singularity which celebrate ethnicity as a fluctuating composition of differences, intersections, and incommensurabilities. These latter efforts attempt to define ethnicity in a manner that accounts not only for cultural inheritance but for active cultural construction, as well. In other words, they suggest that the making of Asian American culture may be a much "messier" process than unmediated vertical transmission from one generation to another, including practices that are partly inherited and partly modified, as well as partly invented.[3] As the narrator of *The Woman Warrior* suggests, perhaps one of the more important stories of Asian American experience is about the process of receiving, refiguring, and rewriting cultural traditions. She asks: "Chinese-Americans, when you try to understand what things in you are Chinese, how do you separate what is peculiar to childhood, to poverty, insanities, one family, your mother who marked your growing with stories, from what is Chinese? What is Chinese tradition and what is the movies?" (6). Or the dilemma of cultural syncretism might be posed in an interrogative version of the uncle's impromptu proverb in Wayne Wang's film *Dim Sum*: "You can take the girl out of Chinatown, but can you take the Chinatown out of the girl?" For rather than representing a fixed, discrete culture, "Chinatown" is itself the very emblem of fluctuating demographics, languages, and populations.[4]

I begin my chapter with these particular examples drawn from Asian American cultural texts in order to observe that what is referred to as "Asian America" is clearly a heterogeneous entity. From the perspective of the majority culture, Asian Americans may very well be constructed as different from, and other than, Euro-Americans. But from the perspectives of Asian Americans, we are perhaps even more different, more diverse, among ourselves: being men and women at different distances and generations from our "original" Asian cultures—cultures as different as Chinese, Japanese, Korean, Filipino, Indian, and Vietnamese—Asian Americans are born in the United States and born in Asia; of exclusively Asian parents and of mixed race; urban and rural; refugee and nonrefugee; communist-identified and anticommunist; fluent in English and non–English speaking; educated and working class. As with other diasporas in the United States, the Asian immigrant collectivity is unstable and changeable, with its cohesion complicated by intergenerationality, by various degrees of identification and relation to a "homeland," and by different extents of assimilation to and distinction from "majority culture" in the United States. Further, the historical contexts of particular waves of immigration within single groups contrast with one another; the Japanese Americans who were interned during World War II encountered quite different social and economic barriers than those from Japan who arrive in southern California today. And the composition of different waves of immigrants differs in gender, class, and region. For example, the first groups of Chinese immigrants to the United States in 1850 were from four villages in Canton province, male by a ratio of ten to one, and largely of peasant backgrounds; the more recent Chinese immigrants are from Hong Kong, Taiwan, or the People's Republic (themselves quite heterogeneous and of discontinuous "origins"), or from the Chinese diaspora in other parts of Asia, such as Macao, Malaysia, or Singapore, and they are more often educated and middle-class men and women.[5] Further, once arriving in the United States, very few Asian immigrant cultures remain discrete, impenetrable communities. The more recent groups mix, in varying degrees, with segments of the existing groups; Asian Americans may intermarry with other ethnic groups, live in neighborhoods adjacent to them, or work in the same businesses and on the same factory assembly lines. The boundaries and definitions of Asian American culture are continually shifting and being contested from pressures both "inside" and "outside" the Asian origin community.

I stress heterogeneity, hybridity, and multiplicity in the characterization of Asian American culture as part of a twofold argument about cultural politics, the ultimate aim of that argument being to disrupt the current hegemonic relationship between "dominant" and "minority" positions. On the one hand, my observation that Asian Americans are heterogeneous is part of a strategy to destabilize the dominant discursive construction and determination of Asian Americans as a homogeneous group. Throughout the late nineteenth and early twentieth centuries, Asian immigration to the United States was managed by exclusion acts and quotas that relied upon racialist constructions of Asians as homogeneous;[6] the "model minority" myth and the informal quotas discriminating against Asians in university admissions policies are contemporary versions of this homogenization of Asians.[7] On the other hand, I underscore Asian American heterogeneities (particularly class, gender, and national differences among Asians) to contribute to a dialogue within Asian American discourse, to negotiate with those modes of argumentation that continue to uphold a politics based on ethnic "identity." In this sense, I argue for the Asian American necessity—politically, intellectually, and personally—to organize, resist, and theorize *as* Asian Americans, but at the same time I inscribe this necessity within a discussion of the risks of a cultural politics that relies upon the construction of sameness and the exclusion of differences.

The first reason to emphasize the dynamic fluctuation and heterogeneity of Asian American culture is to release our understandings of either the "dominant" or the emergent "minority" cultures as discrete, fixed, or homogeneous, and to arrive at a different conception of the general political terrain of culture in California, a useful focus for this examination since it has become commonplace to consider it an "ethnic state," embodying a new phenomenon of cultural adjacency and admixture.[8] For if minority immigrant cultures are perpetually changing—in their composition, configuration, and signifying practices, as well as in their relations to one another—it follows that the "majority" or dominant culture, with which minority cultures are in continual relation, is also unstable and unclosed. The suggestion that the general social terrain of culture is open, plural, and dynamic reorients our understanding of what "cultural hegemony" is and how it works in contemporary California. It permits us to theorize about the roles that ethnic immigrant groups play in the making and unmaking of culture—and how these minority discourses challenge the existing structure of power, the existing hegemony.[9] We should remember that Antonio Gramsci writes about hegemony as not simply political or economic forms of rule but as the entire process of dissent and compromise through which a particular group is able to determine the political, cultural, and ideological character of a state (*Selections*). Hegemony does not refer exclusively to the process by which a dominant formation exercises its influence but refers equally to the process through which minority groups organize and contest any specific hegemony.[10] The reality of any specific hegemony is that, while it may be for the moment dominant, it is never absolute or conclusive. Hegemony, in Gramsci's thought, is a concept that describes both the social processes through which a particular dominance is maintained and those through which that dominance is challenged and new forces are articulated. When a hegemony representing the interests of a dominant group exists, it is always within the context of resistances from emerging "subaltern" groups.[11] We might say that hegemony is not only the political process by which a particular group constitutes itself as "the one" or "the majority" in relation to which "minorities" are defined and know themselves to be "other," but it is equally the process by which positions of otherness may ally and constitute a new majority, a "counterhegemony."[12]

The subaltern classes are, in Gramsci's definition, prehegemonic, not unified groups, whose histories are fragmented, episodic and identifiable only from a point of historical hindsight. They may go through different phases when they are subject to the activity of ruling groups, may articulate their demands through existing parties, and then may themselves produce new parties; in *The Prison Notebooks*, Gramsci describes a final phase at which the "formations [of the subaltern classes] assert integral autonomy" (52). The definition of the subaltern groups includes some noteworthy observations for our understanding of the roles of racial and ethnic immigrant groups in the United States. The assertion that the significant practices of the subaltern groups may not be understood as hegemonic until they are viewed with historical hindsight is interesting, for it suggests that some of the most powerful practices may not always be the explicitly oppositional ones, may not be understood by contemporaries, and may be less overt and recognizable than others. Provocative, too, is the idea that the subaltern classes are by definition "not unified"; that is, the subaltern is not a fixed, unified force of a single character. Rather, the assertion of "integral autonomy" by not-unified classes suggests a coordination of distinct, yet allied, positions, practices, and movements—class-identified and not class-identified, in parties and not, ethnic-based and gender-based—each in its own not necessarily equivalent manner transforming and disrupting the apparatuses of a specific hegemony. The independent forms and locations of cultural challenge—ideological, as well as economic and political—constitute what Gramsci calls a "new historical bloc," a new set of relationships that together embody a different hegemony and a different balance of power. In this sense, we have in the growing and shifting ethnic minority populations in California an active example of this new historical bloc described by Gramsci; and in the negotiations between these ethnic groups and the existing majority over what interests precisely constitute the "majority," we have an illustration of the concept of hegemony, not in the more commonly accepted sense of "hegemony-maintenance," but in the often ignored sense of "hegemony-creation."[13] The observation that the Asian American community and other ethnic immigrant communities are heterogeneous lays the foundation for several political operations: first, by shifting, multiplying, and reconceiving the construction of society as composed of two numerically overdetermined camps called the majority and the minority, cultural politics is recast so as to account for a multiplicity of various, nonequivalent groups, one of which is Asian Americans. Second, the conception of ethnicity as heterogeneous provides a position for Asian Americans that is both ethnically specific, yet simultaneously uneven and unclosed; Asian Americans can articulate distinct group demands based on our particular histories of exclusion, but the redefined lack of closure—which reveals rather than conceals differences—opens political lines of affiliation with other groups (labor unions, other racial and ethnic groups, and gay, lesbian, and feminist groups) in the challenge to specific forms of domination insofar as they share common features.

In regard to the practice of "identity politics" within Asian American discourse, the articulation of an "Asian American identity" as an organizing tool has provided a concept of political unity that enables diverse Asian groups to understand our unequal circumstances and histories as being related; likewise, the building of "Asian American culture" is crucial, for it articulates and empowers our multicultural, multilingual Asian-origin community vis-à-vis the institutions and apparatuses that exclude and marginalize us. But I want to suggest that essentializing Asian American identity and suppressing our differences—of national origin, generation, gender, party, class—risks particular dangers: not only does it underestimate the differences and hybridities among Asians, but it also inadvertently supports the racist discourse that constructs Asians as a homogeneous group, that implies we are "all alike" and conform to "types"; in this respect, a politics based exclusively on ethnic identity willingly accepts the terms of the dominant logic that organizes the heterogeneous picture of racial and ethnic diversity into a binary schema of "the one" and "the other." The essentializing of Asian American identity also reproduces oppositions that subsume other nondominant terms in the same way that Asians and other groups are disenfranchised by the dominant culture: to the degree that the discourse generalizes Asian American identity as male, women are rendered invisible; or to the extent that Chinese are presumed to be exemplary of all Asians, the importance of other Asian groups is ignored. In this sense, a politics based on ethnic identity facilitates the displacement of intercommunity differences—between men and women, or between workers and managers—into a false opposition of "nationalism" and "assimilation." We have an example of this in recent debates where Asian American feminists who challenge Asian American sexism are cast as "assimilationist," as betraying Asian American "nationalism."

To the extent that Asian American discourse articulates an identity in reaction to the dominant culture's stereotype, even to refute it, I believe the discourse may remain bound to, and overdetermined by, the logic of the dominant culture. In accepting the binary terms ("white" and "nonwhite," or "majority" and "minority") that structure institutional policies about ethnicity, we forget that these binary schemas are not neutral descriptions. Binary constructions of difference use a logic that prioritizes the first term and subordinates the second; whether the pair "difference" and "sameness" is figured as a binary synthesis that considers "difference" as always contained within the "same," or that conceives of the pair as an opposition in which "difference" structurally implies "sameness" as its complement, it is important to see each of these figurations as versions of the same binary logic. My argument for heterogeneity seeks to challenge the conception of difference as exclusively structured by a binary opposition between two terms by proposing instead another notion of difference that takes seriously the conditions of heterogeneity, multiplicity, and nonequivalence. I submit that the most exclusive construction of Asian American identity—which presumes masculinity, American birth, and speaking English—is at odds with the formation of important political alliances and affiliations with other groups across racial and ethnic, gender, sexuality, and class lines. An essentialized identity is an obstacle to Asian American women allying with other women of color, for example, and it can discourage laboring Asian Americans from joining unions with workers of other colors. It can short-circuit potential alliances against the dominant structures of power in the name of subordinating "divisive" issues to *the* national question.

Some of the limits of identity politics are discussed most pointedly by Frantz Fanon in his books about the Algerian resistance to French colonialism. Before ultimately turning to some Asian American cultural texts in order to trace the ways in which the dialogues about identity and difference are represented within the discourse, I would like to briefly consider one of Fanon's most important texts, *The Wretched of the Earth* (*Les damnés de la terre*, 1961). Although Fanon's treatise was cited in the 1960s as the manifesto for a nationalist politics of identity, rereading it now in the 1990s we find his text, ironically, to be the source of a serious critique of nationalism. Fanon argues that the challenge facing any movement dismantling colonialism (or a system in which one culture dominates another) is to provide for a new order that does not reproduce the social structure of the old system. This new order, he argues, must avoid the simple assimilation to the dominant culture's roles and positions by the emergent group, which would merely caricature the old colonialism, and it should be equally suspicious of an uncritical nativism, or racialism, appealing to essentialized notions of precolonial identity. Fanon suggests that another alternative is necessary, a new order, neither an assimilationist nor a nativist inversion, which breaks with the structures and practices of cultural domination and which continually and collectively criticizes the institutions of rule. One of the more remarkable turns in Fanon's argument occurs when he identifies both bourgeois assimilation and bourgeois nationalism as conforming to the same logic, as responses to colonialism that reproduce the same structure of cultural domination. It is in this sense that Fanon warns against the nationalism practiced by bourgeois neocolonial governments. Their nationalism, he argues, can be distorted easily into racism, territorialism, separatism, or ethnic dictatorships of one tribe or regional group over others; the national bourgeois replaces the colonizer, yet the social and economic structure remains the same.[14] Ironically, he points out, these separatisms, or "micro-nationalisms" (Mamadou Dia, qtd. in Fanon 158), are themselves legacies of colonialism. He writes: "By its very structure, colonialism is regionalist and separatist. Colonialism does not simply state the existence of tribes; it also reinforces and separates them" (94). That is, a politics of ethnic separatism is congruent with the divide-and-conquer logic of colonial domination. Fanon links the practices of the national bourgeoisie that has assimilated colonialist thought and practice with nativist practices that privilege one tribe or ethnicity over others; nativism and assimilationism are not opposites but similar logics both enunciating the old order.

Fanon's analysis implies that an essentialized bourgeois construction of "nation" is a classification that excludes other subaltern groups that could bring about substantive change in the social and economic relations, particularly those whose social marginalities are due to class: peasants, workers, transient populations. We can add to Fanon's criticism that the category of nation often erases a consideration of women and the fact of difference between men and women and the conditions under which they live and work in situations of cultural domination. This is why the concentration of women of color in domestic service or reproductive labor (child care, home care, nursing) in the contemporary United States is not adequately explained by a nation-based model of analysis (see Glenn 1981). In light of feminist theory, which has gone the furthest in theorizing multiple inscription and the importance of positionalities, we can argue that it may be less meaningful to act exclusively in terms of a single valence or political interest—such as ethnicity or nation—than to acknowledge that social subjects are the sites of a variety of differences.[15] An Asian American subject is never purely and exclusively ethnic, for that subject is always of a particular class, gender, and sexual preference and may therefore feel responsible to movements that are organized around these other designations. This is not to argue against the strategic importance of Asian American identity, nor against the building of Asian American culture. Rather, I am suggesting that acknowledging class and gender differences among Asian Americans does not weaken us as a group; to the contrary, these differences represent greater political opportunity to affiliate with other groups whose cohesions may be based on other valences of oppression.

As I have already suggested, within Asian American discourse there is a varied spectrum of discussion about the concepts of ethnic identity and culture. At one end, there are discussions in which ethnic identity is essentialized as the cornerstone of a nationalist liberation politics. In these discussions, the cultural positions of nationalism (or ethnicism, or nativism) and of assimilation are represented in polar opposition: nationalism affirming the separate purity of its ethnic culture is opposed to assimilation of the standards of dominant society. Stories about the loss of the "native" Asian culture tend to express some form of this opposition. At the same time, there are criticisms of this essentializing position, most often articulated by feminists who charge that Asian American nationalism prioritizes masculinity and does not account for women. At the other end, there are interventions that refuse static or binary conceptions of ethnicity, replacing notions of identity with multiplicity and shifting the emphasis for ethnic "essence" to cultural hybridity. Settling for neither nativism nor assimilation, these cultural texts expose the apparent opposition between the two as a constructed figure (as Fanon does when he observes that bourgeois assimilation and bourgeois nationalism often conform to the same colonialist logic). In tracing these different discussions about identity and ethnicity through Asian American cultural debates, literature, and film, I choose particular texts because they are accessible and commonly held. But I do not intend to limit *discourse* to only these particular textual forms; by *discourse,* I intend a rather extended meaning—a network that includes not only texts and cultural documents but social practices, formal and informal laws, policies of inclusion and exclusion, and institutional forms of organization, for example, all of which constitute and regulate knowledge about the object of that discourse, Asian America.

The terms of the debate about nationalism and assimilation become clearer if we look first at the discussion of ethnic identity in certain debates about the representation of culture. Readers of Asian American literature are familiar with attacks by Frank Chin, Ben Tong, and others on Maxine Hong Kingston, attacks which have been cast as nationalist criticisms of Kingston's "assimilationist" works. Her novel/autobiography *The Woman Warrior* is the primary target of such criticism, since it is virtually the only "canonized" piece of Asian American literature; its status can be measured by the fact that the Modern Language Association is currently publishing *A Guide to Teaching "The Woman Warrior"* in its series that includes guides to Cervantes's *Don Quixote* and Dante's *Inferno.* A critique of how and why this text has become fetishized as the exemplary representation of Asian American culture is necessary and important. However, Chin's critique reveals other kinds of tensions in Asian American culture that are worth noting. He does more than accuse Kingston of having exoticized Chinese American culture; he argues that she has "feminized" Asian American literature and undermined the power of Asian American men to combat the racist stereotypes of the dominant white culture. Kingston and other women novelists such as Amy Tan, he says, misrepresent Chinese history in order to exaggerate its patriarchal structure; as a result, Chinese society is portrayed as being even more misogynistic than European society. While Chin and others have cast this conflict in terms of nationalism and assimilationism, I think it may be more productive to see this debate, as Elaine Kim does in a recent essay ("'Such Opposite'"), as a symptom of the tensions between nationalist and feminist concerns in Asian American discourse. I would add to Kim's analysis that the dialogue between nationalist and feminist concerns animates precisely a debate about identity and difference, or identity and heterogeneity, rather than a debate between nationalism and assimilationism; it is a debate in which Chin and others stand at one end insisting upon a fixed masculinist identity, while Kingston, Tan, or feminist literary critics like Shirley Lim and Amy Ling, with their representations of female differences and their critiques of sexism in Chinese culture, repeatedly cast this notion of identity into question. Just as Fanon points out that some forms of nationalism can obscure class, Asian American feminists point out that Asian American nationalism—or the construction of an essentialized, native Asian American subject—obscures gender. In other words, the struggle that is framed as a conflict between the apparent opposites of nativism and assimilation can mask what is more properly characterized as a struggle between the desire to essentialize ethnic identity and the fundamental condition of heterogeneous differences against which such a desire is spoken. The trope that opposes nativism and assimilationism can be itself a colonialist figure used to displace the challenges of het-erogeneity, or subalternity, by casting them as assimilationist or anti-ethnic.

The trope that opposes nativism and assimilation not only organizes the cultural debates of Asian American discourse but figures *in* Asian American literature, as well. More often than not, however, this symbolic conflict between nativism and assimilation is figured in the *topos* with which I began, that of generational conflict. Although there are many versions of this *topos,* I will mention only a few in order to elucidate some of the most relevant cultural tensions. In one model, a conflict between genera-tions is cast in strictly masculinist terms, between father and son; in this model, moth-ers are absent or unimportant, and female figures exist only as peripheral objects to the side of the central drama of male conflict. Louis Chu's *Eat a Bowl of Tea* (1961) ex-emplifies this masculinist generational symbolism, in which a conflict between na-tivism and assimilation is allegorized in the relationship between the father, Wah Gay, and the son, Ben Loy, in the period when the predominantly Cantonese New York Chinatown community changes from a "bachelor society" to a "family society."[16] Wah Gay wishes Ben Loy to follow Chinese tradition, and to submit to the father's author-ity, while the son balks at his father's "old ways" and wants to make his own choices. When Wah Gay arranges a marriage for Ben Loy, the son is forced to obey. Although the son had had no trouble leading an active sexual life before his marriage, once mar-ried, he finds himself to be impotent. In other words, Chu's novel figures the conflict of nativism and assimilation in terms of Ben Loy's sexuality: submitting to the father's authority, marrying the "nice Chinese girl" Mei Oi and having sons, is the so-called traditional Chinese male behavior. This path represents the nativist option, whereas Ben Loy's former behavior—carrying on with American prostitutes, gambling, etc.—represents the alleged path of assimilation. At the nativist Chinese extreme, Ben Loy is impotent and is denied access to erotic pleasure, and at the assimilationist American extreme, he has great access and sexual freedom. Allegorizing the choice between cul-tural options in the register of Ben Loy's sexuality, Chu's novel suggests that resolution lies at neither pole but in a third "Chinese American" alternative, in which Ben Loy is able to experience erotic pleasure with his Chinese wife. This occurs only when the couple moves away to another state, away from the father; Ben Loy's relocation to San Francisco's Chinatown and the priority of pleasure with Mei Oi over the begetting of a son (which, incidentally, they ultimately do have) both represent important breaks from his father's authority and from Chinese tradition. Following Fanon's observa-tions about the affinities between nativism and assimilation, we can understand Chu's novel as an early masculinist rendering of culture as conflict between the apparent op-posites of nativism and assimilation, with its oedipal resolution in a Chinese Ameri-can male identity; perhaps only with hindsight can we propose that the opposition it-self may be a construction that allegorizes the dialectic between an articulation of es-sentialized ethnic identity and the context of heterogeneous differences.

Amy Tan's much more recent *The Joy Luck Club* (1989) refigures this *topos* of gener-ational conflict in a different social context, among first- and second-generation Man-darin Chinese in San Francisco and, more importantly, between women. Tan's *Joy Luck* displaces *Eat a Bowl* not only because it deviates from the figuration of Asian

American identity in a masculine oedipal dilemma by refiguring it in terms of mothers and daughters but also because *Joy Luck* multiplies the sites of cultural conflict, positing a number of struggles—familial and extrafamilial—as well as resolutions, without privileging the singularity or centrality of one. In this way, *Joy Luck* ultimately thematizes and demystifies the central role of the mother-daughter relationship in Asian American culture.

Joy Luck represents the first-person narratives of four sets of Chinese-born mothers and their American-born daughters. The daughters attempt to come to terms with their mothers' demands, while the mothers simultaneously try to interpret their daughters' deeds, expressing a tension between the "Chinese" expectation of filial respect and the "American" inability to fulfill that expectation. By multiplying and subverting the model of generational discord with examples of generational concord, the novel calls attention to the heterogeneity of Chinese American family relations. On the one hand, mothers like Ying-ying St. Clair complain about their daughters' Americanization:

> For all these years I kept my mouth closed so selfish desires would not fall out. And because I remained quiet for so long now my daughter does not hear me. She sits by her fancy swimming pool and hears only her Sony Walkman, her cordless phone, her big, important husband asking her why they have charcoal and no lighter fluid.
>
> . . . because I moved so secretly now my daughter does not see me. She sees a list of things to buy, her checkbook out of balance, her ashtray sitting crooked on a straight table.
>
> And I want to tell her this: We are lost, she and I, unseen and not seeing, unheard and not hearing, unknown by others. (67)

The mother presents herself as having sacrificed everything for a daughter who has ignored these sacrifices. She sees her daughter as preoccupied with portable, mobile high-tech commodities which, characteristically, have no cords, no ties, emblematizing the mother's condemnation of a daughter who does not respect family bonds. The mother implies that the daughter recognizes that something is skewed and attempts to correct it—balancing her checkbook, straightening her house—but, in the mother's eyes, she has no access to the real problems; being in America has taken this understanding away. Her daughter, Lena, however, tends to view her mother as unreasonably superstitious and domineering. Lena considers her mother's concern about her failing marriage as meddlesome; the daughter's interpretation of their antagonism emphasizes a cultural gap between the mother who considers her daughter's troubles her own and the daughter who sees her mother's actions as intrusive, possessive, and, worst of all, denying the daughter's own separate individuality.

On the other hand, in contrast to this and other examples of disjunction between the Chinese mothers and the Chinese American daughters, *Joy Luck* also includes a relationship between mother and daughter in which there is an apparent coincidence of perspective; tellingly, in this example the mother has died, and it is left to the daughter to "eulogize" the mother by telling the mother's story. Jing-mei Woo makes a trip to China, to reunite with her recently deceased mother's two daughters by an earlier marriage, whom her mother had been forced to abandon almost forty years before when fleeing China during the Japanese invasion. Jing-mei wants to fulfill her mother's last wish to see the long-lost daughters; she wishes to inscribe herself in her mother's place. Her narration of the reunion conveys her utopian belief in the possibility of recovering the past, of rendering herself coincident with her mother, narrating her desire to become again "Chinese."

> My sisters and I stand, arms around each other, laughing and wiping the tears from each other's eyes. The flash of the Polaroid goes off and my father hands me the snapshot. My sisters and I watch quietly together, eager to see what develops.
>
> The gray-green surface changes to the bright colors of our three images, sharpening and deepening all at once. And although we don't speak, I know we all see it: Together we look like our mother. Her same eyes, her same mouth, open in surprise to see, at last, her long-cherished wish. (288)

Unlike Lena St. Clair, Jing-mei does not seek greater autonomy from her mother; she desires a lessening of the disparity between their positions that is accomplished through the narrative evocation of her mother after she has died. By contrasting different examples of mother-daughter discord and concord, *Joy Luck* allegorizes the heterogeneous culture in which the desire for identity and sameness (represented by Jing-mei's story) is inscribed within the context of Asian American differences and disjunctions (exemplified by the other three pairs of mothers and daughters). The novel formally illustrates that the articulation of one, the desire for identity, depends upon the existence of the others, or the fundamental horizon of differences.

Further, although *Joy Luck* has been heralded and marketed as a novel about mother-daughter relations in the Chinese American family (one cover review characterizes it as a "story that shows us China, Chinese-American women and their families, and the mystery of the mother-daughter bond in ways that we have not experienced before"), I would suggest that the novel also represents antagonisms that are not exclusively generational but are due to different conceptions of class and gender among Chinese Americans.

Toward the end of the novel, Lindo and Waverly Jong reach a climax of misunderstanding, in a scene that takes place in a central site of American femininity: the beauty parlor. After telling the stylist to give her mother a "soft wave," Waverly asks her mother, Lindo, if she is in agreement. The mother narrates:

> I smile. I use my American face. That's the face Americans think is Chinese, the one they cannot understand. But inside I am becoming ashamed. I am ashamed she is ashamed. Because she is my daughter and I am proud of her, and I am her mother but she is not proud of me. (255)

The American-born daughter believes she is treating her mother, rather magnanimously, to a day of pampering at a chic salon; the Chinese-born mother receives this gesture as an insult, clear evidence of a daughter ashamed of her mother's looks. The scene not only marks the separation of mother and daughter by generation but, perhaps less obviously, their separation by class and cultural differences that lead to different interpretations of how female identity is signified. On the one hand, the Chinese-born Lindo and American-born Waverly have different class values and opportunities; the daughter's belief in the pleasure of a visit to an expensive San Francisco beauty parlor seems senselessly extravagant to the mother whose rural family had escaped poverty only by marrying her to the son of a less humble family in their village. On the other hand, the mother and daughter also conflict over definitions of proper female behavior. Lindo assumes female identity is constituted in the practice of a daughter's deference to her elders, while for Waverly, it is determined by a woman's financial independence from her parents and her financial equality with men and by her ability to speak her desires, and it is cultivated and signified in the styles and shapes that represent middle-class feminine beauty. In this sense, I ultimately read *Joy Luck* not as a novel which exclusively depicts generational conflict among Chinese American women but rather as a text that thematizes the trope of the mother-daughter relationship in Asian American culture; that is, the novel comments upon the idealized construction of mother-daughter relationships (both in the majority culture's discourse about Asian Americans and in the Asian American discourse about ourselves), as well as upon the kinds of differences—of class and culturally specific definitions of gender—that are rendered invisible by the privileging of this trope.[17]

Before concluding, I want to turn to a final cultural text which not only restates the Asian American narrative that opposes nativism and assimilation but articulates a critique of that narrative, calling the nativist/assimilationist dyad into question. If *Joy Luck* poses an alternative to the dichotomy of nativism and assimilation by multiplying the generational conflict and demystifying the centrality of the mother-daughter relationship, then Peter Wang's film *A Great Wall* (1985)—both in its emplotment and in its very medium of representation—offers yet another version of this alternative. Wang's film unsettles both poles in the antinomy of nativist essentialism and assimilation by performing a continual geographical juxtaposition and exchange between a variety of cultural spaces. *A Great Wall* portrays the visit of Leo Fang's Chinese American family to the People's Republic of China and their month-long stay with Leo's sister's family, the Chao family, in Beijing. The film concentrates on the primary contrast between the habits, customs, and assumptions of the Chinese in China and the Chinese Americans in California by going back and forth between shots of Beijing and Northern California, in a type of continual filmic "migration" between the two, as if to thematize in its very form the travel between cultural spaces. From the first scene, however, the film foregrounds the idea that in the opposition between native and assimilated spaces, neither begins as a pure, uncontaminated site or origin; and as the camera eye shuttles back and forth between, both poles of the constructed opposition shift and change. (Indeed, the Great Wall of China, from which the film takes its title, is a monument to the historical condition that not even ancient China was "pure," but coexisted with "foreign barbarians" against which the Middle Kingdom erected such barriers.) In this regard, the film contains a number of emblematic images that call attention to the syncretic, composite quality of all cultural spaces: when the young Chinese Liu finishes the university entrance exam his scholar-father gives him a Coca Cola; children crowd around the single village television to watch a Chinese opera singer imitate Pavarotti singing Italian opera; the Chinese student learning English recites the Gettysburg Address. Although the film concentrates on both illustrating and dissolving the apparent opposition between Chinese Chinese and American Chinese, a number of other contrasts are likewise explored: the differences between generations both within the Chao and the Fang families (daughter Lili noisily drops her bike while her father practices tai chi; Paul kisses his Caucasian girlfriend and later tells his father that he believes all Chinese are racists when Leo suggests that he might date some nice Chinese girls); differences between men and women (accentuated by two scenes, one in which Grace Fang and Mrs. Chao talk about their husbands and children, the other in which Chao and Leo get drunk together); and, finally, the differences between capitalist and communist societies (highlighted in a scene in which the Chaos and Fangs talk about their different attitudes toward "work"). The representations of these other contrasts complicate and diversify the ostensible focus on cultural differences between Chinese and Chinese Americans, as if to testify to the condition that there is never only one exclusive valence of difference, but rather cultural difference is always simultaneously bound up with gender, economics, age, and other distinctions. In other words, when Leo says to his wife that the Great Wall makes the city "just as difficult to leave as to get in," the wall at once signifies the construction of a variety of barriers—not only between Chinese and Americans but between generations, men and women, capitalism and communism—as well as the impossibility of ever remaining bounded and impenetrable, of resisting change, recomposition, and reinvention. We are reminded of this impossibility throughout the film, but it is perhaps best illustrated in the scene in which the Fang and Chao families play a rousing game of touch football on the ancient immovable Great Wall.

The film continues with a series of wonderful contrasts: the differences in the bodily comportments of the Chinese American Paul and the Chinese Liu playing ping pong, between Leo's jogging and Mr. Chao's tai chi, between Grace Fang's and Mrs. Chao's ideas of what is fitting and fashionable for the female body. The two families have different senses of space and of the relation between family members. In one subplot, the Chinese American cousin Paul is outraged to learn that Mrs. Chao reads her daughter Lili's mail; he asks Lili if she has ever heard of "privacy." This later results in a fight between Mrs. Chao and Lili in which Lili says she has learned from their American cousins that "it's not right to read other people's mail." Mrs. Chao retorts: "You're not 'other people,' you're my daughter. What is this thing, 'privacy'?" Lili explains to her that "privacy" can't be translated into Chinese. "Oh, so you're trying to hide things from your mother and use western words to trick her!" exclaims Mrs. Chao. Ultimately, just as the members of the Chao family are marked by the visit from their American relatives, the Fangs are altered by the time they return to California, each bringing back a memento or practice from their Chinese trip. In other words, rather than privileging either a nativist or assimilationist view, or even espousing a "Chinese American" resolution of differences, *A Great Wall* performs a filmic "migration" by shuttling between the various cultural spaces; we are left, by the end of the film, with a sense of culture as dynamic and open, the result of a continual process of visiting and revisiting a plurality of cultural sites.

In keeping with the example of *A Great Wall*, we might consider as a possible model for the ongoing construction of ethnic identity the migratory process suggested by Wang's filming technique and emplotment: we might conceive of the making and practice of Asian American culture as nomadic, unsettled, taking place in the travel between cultural sites and in the multivocality of heterogeneous and conflicting positions. Taking seriously the heterogeneities among Asian Americans in California, we must conclude that the grouping "Asian American" is not a natural or static category; it is a socially constructed unity, a situationally specific position that we assume for political reasons. It is "strategic" in Gayatri Spivak's sense of a "strategic use of a positive essentialism in a scrupulously visible political interest" (205). The concept of "strategic essentialism" suggests that it is possible to utilize specific signifiers of ethnic identity, such as Asian American, for the purpose of contesting and disrupting the discourses that exclude Asian Americans, while simultaneously revealing the internal contradictions and slippages of Asian American so as to insure that such essentialisms will not be reproduced and proliferated by the very apparatuses we seek to disempower. I am not suggesting that we can or should do away with the notion of Asian American identity, for to stress only our differences would jeopardize the hard-earned unity that has been achieved in the last two decades of Asian American politics, the unity that is necessary if Asian Americans are to play a role in the new historical bloc of ethnic Californians. In fact, I would submit that the very freedom, in the 1990s, to explore the hybridities concealed beneath the desire of identity is permitted by the context of a strongly articulated essentialist politics. Just as the articulation of the desire for identity depends upon the existence of a fundamental horizon of differences, the articulation of differences dialectically depends upon a socially constructed and practiced notion of identity. I want simply to remark that in the 1990s, we can afford to rethink the notion of ethnic identity in terms of cultural, class, and gender differences, rather than presuming similarities and making the erasure of particularity the basis of unity. In the 1990s, we can diversify our political practices to include a more heterogeneous group and to enable crucial alliances with other groups—ethnicity based, class based, gender based, and sexuality based—in the ongoing work of transforming hegemony.

NOTES

Originally published in *Diaspora* 1.1 (1991): 24–44. © 1991 University of Toronto Press, reprint by permission. Many thanks to Elaine Kim for her thought-provoking questions and for asking me to deliver portions of this essay as papers at the 1990 meetings of the Association of Asian American Studies and of the American Literature Association; to James Clifford, who also gave me the opportunity to deliver a version of this essay at a conference sponsored by the Center for Cultural Studies at UC Santa Cruz; to the audience participants at all three conferences who asked stimulating questions which have helped me to rethink my original notions; and to Page duBois, Barbara Harlow, Susan Kirkpatrick, George Mariscal, Ellen Rooney, and Kathryn Shevelow, who read drafts and offered important comments and criticism.

1. Nisei refers to a second-generation Japanese American, born to immigrant parents in the U.S.; Sansei, a third-generation Japanese American. *Issei* refers to a first-generation immigrant.

2. See Kim, *Asian,* for the most important book-length study of the literary representations of multigenerational Asian America.

3. Recent anthropological discussions of ethnic cultures as fluid and syncretic systems echo these concerns of Asian American writers. See, for example, Fischer; Clifford. For an anthropological study of Japanese American culture that troubles the paradigmatic construction of kinship and filial relations as the central figure in culture, see Yanagisako.

4. We might think, for example, of the shifting of the Los Angeles "Chinatown" from its downtown location to the suburban community of Monterey Park. Since the 1970s, the former "Chinatown" has been superseded demographically and economically by Monterey Park, the home of many Chinese Americans as well as newly arrived Chinese from Hong Kong and Taiwan. The Monterey Park community of 63,000 residents is currently over 50 percent Asian. On the social and political consequences of these changing demographics, see Fong.

5. Chan's history of the Chinese immigrant populations in California, *Bittersweet,* and her history of Asian Americans are extremely important in this regard. Numerous lectures by Ling-chi Wang at UC San Diego in 1987 and at UC Berkeley in 1988 have been very important to my understanding of the heterogeneity of waves of immigration across different Asian-origin groups.

6. The Chinese Exclusion Act of 1882 barred Chinese from entering the U.S., the National Origins Act prohibited the entry of Japanese in 1924, and the Tydings-McDuffie Act of 1934 limited Filipino immigrants to fifty people per year. Finally, the most tragic consequence of anti-Asian racism occurred during World War II when 120,000 Japanese-Americans (two-thirds of whom were American citizens by birth) were interned in camps. For a study of the anti-Japanese movement culminating in the immigration act of 1924, see Daniels. Takaki offers a general history of Asian-origin immigrant groups in the United States.

7. The model minority myth constructs Asians as aggressively driven overachievers; it is a homogenizing fiction which relies upon two strategies common in the subordinating construction of racial or ethnic otherness—the racial other as knowable, familiar ("like us"), and as incomprehensible, threatening ("unlike us"); the model minority myth suggests both that Asians are overachievers and "unlike us" and that they assimilate well and are thus "like us." Asian Americans are continually pointing out that the model minority myth distorts the real gains, as well as the impediments, of Asian immigrants; by leveling and homogenizing all Asian groups, it erases the different rates of assimilation and the variety of class identities among various Asian immigrant groups. Claiming that Asians are "overrepresented" on college campuses, the model minority myth is one of the justifications for the establishment of informal quotas in university admissions policies, similar to the university admission policies which discriminated against Jewish students from the 1930s to the 1950s.

8. In the last two decades, greatly diverse new groups have settled in California; demographers project that by the end of the century, the "majority" of the state will be composed of ethnic "minority" groups. Due to recent immigrants, this influx of minorities is characterized also by greater diversity within individual groups: the group we call Asian Americans no longer denotes only Japanese, Chinese, Koreans, and Filipinos but now includes Indian, Thai, Vietnamese, Cambodian and Laotian groups; Latino communities in California are made up not only of Chicanos but include Guatemalans, Salvadorans, and Colombians. It is not difficult to find Pakistani, Armenian, Lebanese, and Iranian enclaves in San Francisco, Los Angeles, or even San Diego. While California's "multiculturalism" is often employed to support a notion of the "melting pot," to further an ideological assertion of equal opportunity for California's different immigrant groups, I am, in contrast, pursuing the ignored implications of this characterization of California as an ethnic state: that is, despite the increasing numbers of ethnic immigrants

apparently racing to enjoy California's opportunities, for racial and ethnic immigrants there is no equality but uneven development, nonequivalence, and cultural heterogeneities, not only between but within groups.

9. For an important elaboration of the concept of "minority discourse," see JanMohamed and Lloyd.

10. This notion of "the dominant"—defined by Williams in a chapter discussing the "Dominant, Residual, and Emergent" as "a cultural process . . . seized as a cultural system, with determinate dominant features: feudal culture or bourgeois culture or a transition from one to the other"—is often conflated in recent cultural theory with Gramsci's concept of hegemony. Indeed, Williams writes: "We have certainly still to speak of the 'dominant' and the 'effective,' and in these senses of the hegemonic" (121), as if the dominant and the hegemonic are synonymous.

11. See Gramsci, "History." Gramsci describes "subaltern" groups as by definition not unified, emergent, and always in relation to the dominant groups:

> The history of subaltern social groups is necessarily fragmented and episodic. There undoubtedly does exist a tendency to (at least provisional stages of) unification in the historical activity of these groups, but this tendency is continually interrupted by the activity of the ruling groups; it therefore can only be demonstrated when an historical cycle is completed and this cycle culminates in a success. Subaltern groups are always subject to the activity of ruling groups, even when they rebel and rise up: only "permanent" victory breaks their subordination, and that not immediately. In reality, even when they appear triumphant, the subaltern groups are merely anxious to defend themselves (a truth which can be demonstrated by the history of the French Revolution at least up to 1830). Every trace of independent initiative on the part of subaltern groups should therefore be of incalculable value for the integral historian. (54–55)

12. "Hegemony" remains a suggestive construct in Gramsci, however, rather than an explicitly interpreted set of relations. Contemporary readers are left with the more specific task of distinguishing which particular forms of challenge to an existing hegemony are significantly transformative and which forms may be neutralized or appropriated by the hegemony. Some cultural critics contend that counterhegemonic forms and practices are tied by definition to the dominant culture and that the dominant culture simultaneously produces and limits its own forms of counterculture. I am thinking here of some of the "new historicist" studies that use a particular notion of Foucault's discourse to confer authority to the "dominant," interpreting all forms of "subversion" as being ultimately "contained" by dominant ideology and institutions. Other cultural historians, such as Williams, suggest that because there is both identifiable variation in the social order over time, as well as variations in the forms of the counter-culture in different historical periods, we must conclude that some aspects of the oppositional forms are not reducible to the terms of the original hegemony. Still other theorists, such as Ernesto Laclau and Chantal Mouffe, have expanded Gramsci's notion of hegemony to argue that in advanced capitalist society, the social field is not a totality consisting exclusively of the dominant and the counterdominant but rather that "the social" is an open and uneven terrain of contesting articulations and signifying practices. Some of these articulations and practices are neutralized, while others can be linked to build important pressures against an existing hegemony. See Laclau and Mouffe, especially pp. 134–45. They argue persuasively that no hegemonic logic can account for the totality of "the social" and that the open and incomplete character of the social field is the precondition of every hegemonic practice. For if the field of hegemony were conceived according to a "zero-sum" vision of possible positions and practices, then the very concept of hegemony, as plural and mutable formations and relations, would be rendered impossible. Elsewhere, in "Hegemony and New Political Subjects," Mouffe goes even further to elabo-

rate the practical dimensions of the hegemonic principle in terms of contemporary social movements.

13. Adamson reads *The Prison Notebooks* as the postulation of Gramsci's activist and educationalist politics; in chapter 6, he discusses Gramsci's two concepts of hegemony: hegemony as the consensual basis of an existing political system in civil society, as opposed to violent oppression or domination, and hegemony as a historical phase of bourgeois development in which class is understood not only economically but also in terms of a common intellectual and moral awareness, an overcoming of the "economic-corporative" phase. Adamson associates the former (hegemony in its contrast to domination) with "hegemony-maintenance," and the latter (hegemony as a stage in the political moment) as "hegemony-creation." Sassoon provides an excellent discussion of Gramsci's key concepts; she both historicizes the concept of hegemony and discusses the implications of some of the ways in which hegemony has been interpreted. Sassoon emphasizes the degree to which hegemony is opposed to domination to evoke the way in which one social group influences other groups, making certain compromises with them in order to gain their consent for its leadership in society as a whole.

14. Amilcar Cabral, the Cape Verdean African nationalist leader and theorist, echoes some fundamental observations made by Fanon: that the national bourgeoisie will collaborate with the colonizers and that tribal fundamentalism must be overcome or it will defeat any efforts at unity. In 1969, Cabral wrote ironically in "Party Principles and Political Practice" of the dangers of tribalism and nativism: "No one should think that he is more African than another, even than some white man who defends the interests of Africa, merely because he is today more adept at eating with his hand, rolling rice into a ball and putting it into his mouth" (57).

15. I am thinking here especially of de Lauretis; Spivak; and Minh-ha. The last explains the multiple inscription of women of color:

[M]any women of color feel obliged [to choose] between ethnicity and womanhood: how can they? You never have/are one without the other. The idea of two illusorily separated identities, one ethnic, the other woman (or more precisely female), partakes in the Euro-American system of dualistic reasoning and its age-old divide-and-conquer tactics. . . . The pitting of anti-racist and anti-sexist struggles against one another allows some vocal fighters to dismiss blatantly the existence of either racism or sexism within their lines of action, as if oppression only comes in separate, monolithic forms. (105)

16. For a more extensive analysis of generational conflict in Chu's novel, see Gong. Gong asserts that "[t]he father/son relationship represents the most critical juncture in the erosion of a traditional Chinese value system and the emergence of a Chinese American character. Change from Chinese to Chinese American begins here" (74–75).

17. There are many scenes that resonate with my suggestion that generational conflicts cannot be isolated from either class or the historicity of gender. In the third section of the novel, it is class difference in addition to generational strife that founds the antagonism between mother and daughter: Ying-ying St. Clair cannot understand why Lena and her husband, Harold, have spent an enormous amount of money to live in a barn in the posh neighborhood of Woodside. Lena says: "My mother knows, underneath all the fancy details that cost so much, this house is still a barn" (151). In the early relationship between Suyuan Woo and her daughter, Jing-mei, the mother pushes her daughter to become a success, to perform on the piano; we can see that such desires are the reflection of the mother's former poverty, her lack of opportunity as both a poor refugee and a woman, but the daughter, trapped within a familial framework of explanation, sees her mother as punishing and invasive. Finally, the mother-and-daughter pair An-mei and Rose Hsu dramatize a conflict between the mother's belief that it is more honorable to keep personal problems within the Chinese family and the daughter's faith in western psychother-

apy: the mother cannot understand why her daughter would pay a psychiatrist, a stranger, to talk about her divorce, instead of talking to her mother: the mother who was raised believing one must not show suffering to others because they, like magpies, would feed on your tears says of the daughter's psychiatrist, "really, he is just another bird drinking from your misery" (241).

REFERENCES

Adamson, Walter. *Hegemony and Revolution: A Study of Antonio Gramsci's Political and Cultural Theory.* Berkeley: University of California Press, 1980.

Cabral, Amilcar. *Unity and Struggle: Speeches and Writings of Amilcar Cabral.* Trans. Michael Wolfers. New York: Monthly Review, 1979.

Chan, Sucheng. *Asian Americans: An Interpretive History.* Boston: Twayne, 1991.

———. *This Bittersweet Soil: The Chinese in California Agriculture, 1860–1910.* Berkeley: University of California Press, 1986.

Chang, Diana. "The Oriental Contingent." In *The Forbidden Stitch,* edited by Shirley Geok-Lin Lim, Mayumi Tsutakawa, and Margarita Donnelly. Corvallis: Calyx, 1989. 171–177.

Chu, Louis. *Eat a Bowl of Tea.* Seattle: University of Washington Press, 1961.

Clifford, James. *The Predicament of Culture: Twentieth Century Ethnography, Literature, and Art.* Cambridge: Harvard University Press, 1988.

Daniels, Roger. *The Politics of Prejudice.* Berkeley: University of California Press, 1962.

Fanon, Frantz. *The Wretched of the Earth.* Trans. Constance Farrington. New York: Grove, 1961.

Fischer, Michael M. J. "Ethnicity and the Post-modern Arts of Memory." In *Writing Culture,* edited by James Clifford and George Marcus. Berkeley: University of California Press, 1986.

Fong, Timothy. 1990. "A Community Study of Monterey Park, California." Dissertation, University of California, Berkeley.

Glenn, Evelyn Nakano. "Occupational Ghettoization: Japanese-American Women and Domestic Service, 1905–1970." *Ethnicity* 8 (1981): 352–386.

Gong, Ted, "Approaching Cultural Change Through Literature: From Chinese to Chinese-American." *Amerasia* 7 (1980): 73–86.

Gramsci, Antonio. "History of the Subaltern Classes: Methodological Criteria." *Selections* 52–60.

———. *Selections from the Prison Notebooks.* Edited and translated by Quinton Hoare and Geoffrey Nowell Smith. New York: International, 1971.

Great Wall, A. Dir. Peter Wang. New Yorker Films, 1985.

JanMohamed, Abdul, and David Lloyd (eds.). *The Nature and Context of Minority Discourse.* New York: Oxford University Press, 1990.

Kim, Elaine. " 'Such Opposite Creatures': Men and Women in Asian American Literature." *Michigan Quarterly Review* (1990): 68–93.

———. *Asian American Literature: An Introduction to the Writings and Their Social Context.* Philadelphia: Temple University Press, 1982.

Kingston, Maxine Hong. *The Woman Warrior.* New York: Random House, 1975.

Laclau, Ernesto, and Chantal Mouffe. *Hegemony and Socialist Strategy.* London: Verso, 1985.

Lauretis, Teresa de. *Technologies of Gender.* Bloomington: Indiana University Press, 1987.

Lowe, Lydia. "Quitting Time." *Ikon 9, Without Ceremony: A Special Issue by Asian Women United.* Special issue of *Ikon* 9 (1988): 29.

Minh-ha, Trinh T. *Woman, Native, Other: Writing Postcoloniality and Feminism.* Bloomington: Indiana University Press, 1989.

Mirikitani, Janice. "Breaking Tradition." *Without Ceremony.* 9.

Mouffe, Chantal. "Hegemony and New Political Subjects: Toward a New Concept of Democracy." In *Marxism and the Interpretation of Culture,* edited by Cary Nelson and Lawrence Grossberg. Urbana: University of Illinois, 1988. 89–104.

Sassoon, Anne Showstack. "Hegemony, War of Position and Political Intervention." *Approaches to Gramsci,* edited by Anne Showstack Sassoon. London: Writers and Readers, 1982.

Spivak, Gayatri. *In Other Worlds.* London: Routledge, 1987.

Takaki, Ronald. *Strangers from a Different Shore: A History of Asian Americans.* Boston: Little, Brown 1989.

Tan, Amy. *The Joy Luck Club.* New York: Putnam's, 1989.

Williams, Raymond. *Marxism and Literature.* Oxford: Oxford University Press, 1977.

Yanagisako, Sylvia. *Transforming the Past: Kinship and Tradition Among Japanese Americans.* Stanford: Stanford University Press, 1985.

Chapter 27

"Obnoxious to Their Very Nature"
Asian Americans and Constitutional Citizenship

Leti Volpp

[T]he American of Asian descent remains the symbolic
"alien," the metonym for Asia who by definition cannot
be imagined as sharing in America. (Lowe 1996, 6)

Introduction

The terms "Asian American" and "American citizenship" stand in curious juxtaposition. It might be thought that the latter easily embraces the former, but historically
this has not been the case. For more than a century and a half, Asian Americans were
barred from naturalization; and they continue to be viewed as a group whose loyalty to America remains in doubt. Recent controversies involving Asian Americans,
namely, the "Asian connection" in the campaign finance scandal of 1996 and the pros-
ecution of nuclear scientist Wen Ho Lee, raise important questions as to whether
Asian Americans are considered unsuited to participate in democratic engagement,
and how such a perception might shape different discourses of citizenship. This is
an understudied area, and this essay constitutes an initial attempt to think through
the contradictory relationship of Asian American racialization and theories of citizenship.

As described by Lisa Lowe (1996), the Asian immigrant functions as a phantasmic
site on which the United States as a nation projects a series of anxieties regarding internal and external threats to the coherence of the national body. "American Orientalism" is the term some have devised to describe the way the national identity of the
United States has been constructed in opposition to Asians and Asian Americans—
who are categorized as "foreigners," in contrast to "citizens" (Aoki 1996; Gotanda 1985,
1992). Defined antithetically against those who enjoy citizenship, the fitness of Asian
Americans for integration into our national body becomes suspect. But what is meant
by the term "citizenship" bears elaboration.

In a recent writing, Linda Bosniak (2000a) untangles the ways in which notions of
citizenship implicate several distinct discourses, namely, citizenship as legal status, citizenship as rights, citizenship as political activity, and citizenship as identity/solidar-

ity. Citizenship as legal status means who can possess the legal status of a citizen—in the United States, as granted by the Constitution or by statute. Citizenship as rights signifies the rights necessary to achieve full and equal membership in society. As described by T. H. Marshall (1964), this approach tracks efforts to gain the enjoyment of civil, political, and social rights in Western capitalist societies. In the context of the United States, citizenship as rights is premised on a liberal notion of rights, and the failure to be fully enfranchised through the enjoyment of rights guaranteed under the Constitution is often described as exclusion or as "second-class citizenship" (Black 1970; Karst 1989). Citizenship as political activity posits political engagement in the community as the basis for citizenship, as exemplified both by republican theories that played a key role in the founding of American democracy, as well as by a recent renaissance of civic republicanism (Michelman 1977–78; Sunstein 1985). Lastly, citizenship as identity, or citizenship as solidarity, refers to people's collective experience of themselves, their affective ties of identification and solidarity (Bosniak 2000a).

Race cuts against the promise of each of these citizenship discourses, and the racialization of Asian Americans[1] seems at odds especially with the latter two discourses of political activity and identity. By focusing on the experience of Asian Americans vis-à-vis each of these citizenship discourses, we can begin to theorize why this is the case. In examining the relationship of these discourses to each other, we can differentiate them through understanding the first two—citizenship as legal status and citizenship as rights—as sites where the citizen functions as an object, the passive recipient of rights. The third discourse, citizenship as political activity, requires the citizen to function as an active subject,[2] and the fourth discourse, citizenship as identity, refers to the citizen's sense of subjectivity.

Citizenship for Asian Americans in the form of legal status or rights has not guaranteed that Asian Americans will be understood as citizen-subjects or will be considered to subjectively stand in for the American citizenry. We could understand these different discourses as temporally ordered. While in the contemporary moment Asian Americans may be perceived as legitimate recipients of formal rights, there is discomfort associated with their being conceptualized as political subjects whose activity constitutes the American nation. There is, perhaps, even more discomfort associated with the idea that Asian Americans can represent the U.S. citizenry as a matter of identity. What follows sketches in more detail the relationship of each of these different citizenship discourses to the racial identity of Asian Americans.

Citizenship as Legal Status

A historical overview indicates how racial exclusion has shaped the ability of Asian Americans to formally acquire citizenship. Citizenship in the United States is granted through birth, or through naturalization. The U.S. Constitution initially included no definition of citizenship, although Congress was given the authority to adopt "an uniform Rule of Naturalization." The first federal citizenship statute, passed by Congress in 1790, limited naturalization to "free white" aliens. Following the Civil War, Congress discussed the wisdom of striking racial restrictions to naturalization, but concerns about granting the privileges of citizenship to Native Americans and Chinese immigrants precluded such a shift. Thus, the statute was amended to permit naturalization of "aliens of African nativity or African descent." From 1870 until 1952, the racial bars led to much litigation. The reasoning by courts as to who was allowed to be "white" for these purposes variously followed rationales of "scientific evidence," "common sense" (Haney López 1996), and the noncitizen's ability to perform characteristics associated with whiteness (Tehranian 2000).

Inability to naturalize established the basis for upholding alien land laws, which prevented "aliens ineligible to citizenship" from owning land (Aoki 1998). These laws were explicitly passed for the purpose of disenfranchising Asian immigrants from the right to own, rent, or devise agricultural property. The racially defined inability to own property, to naturalize, and to immigrate, created a triple burden that constituted, in opposition to the citizen, the "alien": one unable to engage in the basic functions of the citizen, and therefore politically powerless.

Racial eligibility for naturalization intersected with gender. From 1855 until 1922, noncitizen women who married U.S. citizens or legal permanent residents who naturalized acquired U.S. citizenship.[3] However, these rules did not apply to women subject to the racial bars to naturalization. This meant that until 1870 the only wives welcomed into the American polity were free white wives. The logic of dependent citizenship was extended in 1907 to U.S. citizen wives as well, so that U.S. citizen women—of any race—who married noncitizen men were stripped of their citizenship, since the wife was to take the nationality of her husband. The law was partially repealed in 1922, but it continued to take away U.S. citizenship from women who married men ineligible to naturalize. This primarily affected women who married Asian men, and was the law until 1931 (Bredbenner 1998).

Racial restrictions on naturalization were selectively lifted in the twentieth century, first, in the 1943 Magnuson Act, when Congress, for foreign policy reasons during WWII, allowed Chinese to become naturalized citizens (Gotanda 1996). This was followed in 1946 when Filipinos and Indians were allowed to naturalize. In 1950, the racial bar was lifted for those from Guam, an act followed two years later by the removal of the racial criteria for naturalization altogether.

At the same time that racial exclusion was codified in the laws governing naturalization, the United States deviated from the common-law rules inherited from England regarding birthright citizenship[4] based on territory, since not all persons born in the United States were deemed citizens. Chief Justice Taney's opinion in *Dred Scott v. Sandford* (1857)[5] held that free blacks born in the United States were not citizens. Taney reasoned that

> [t]he words "people of the United States" and "citizens" are synonymous terms, and mean the same thing. They both describe the political body, who, according to our republican institutions, form the sovereignty, and who hold the power and conduct the government through their representatives. They are what we familiarly call the "sovereign people," and every citizen is one of this people, and a constituent member of this sovereignty.[6]

In equating "citizens," the "people of the United States," and the "political body," Justice Taney chose to define the sovereign body of the people as consisting of only one class of citizens, explicitly excluding blacks.

The first sentence of the Fourteenth Amendment, of course, was written to reject Taney's judgment. It provides that "all persons born or naturalized in the United States and subject to the jurisdiction thereof, are citizens of the United States and of the State wherein they reside." Brook Thomas has suggested that a second founding moment of the republic has been considered the Civil War and the amendments that reconstituted the nation. At this second founding moment, blacks may have been considered by some to be included in the sovereign body of the people, but the Chinese still were not (Thomas 1998, 705), as shown by the naturalization statute.[7]

The exclusion was lifted, to some degree, by the Supreme Court's 1898 decision in *Wong Kim Ark,* which held that Chinese born in the United States would be entitled to birthright citizenship. The Court found that the Fourteenth Amendment was plain in its application as to "all persons"—aside from "children of members of the Indian tribes, standing in a peculiar relation to the National Government."[8] It is doubtful that *Wong Kim Ark* represented any significant shift in the acceptance of the Chinese as citizens. The consequences of holding otherwise would have been severe, since, as the Court observed, a contrary result would cast doubt on the citizenship of "thousands of persons of English, Scotch, Irish, German or other European parentage, who have always been considered and treated as citizens of the United States."[9] Furthermore, with the restrictions on the immigration of Chinese in place since the 1880s, the Court's decision would recognize birthright citizenship for relatively few Chinese Americans.

Citizenship as Rights

Classic liberalism holds that the government is created by the people to protect inalienable rights supposedly possessed by all individuals. Citizenship defines the class of full rights holders; to be designated a citizen means that one has become conscious of one's identity as a free subject destined to be given state protection of certain rights.

As described by T. H. Marshall (1964), the rights that citizenship protects have followed a particular order in Western capitalist democracies. First are civil rights—born of the classic liberal concern to protect individuals against state power; these rights, in effect, police the state, and are primarily championed or vindicated in the courts. Second are political rights—the formal ability to participate as full and presumptively autonomous members in the governance of polities, primarily by broad extension of the suffrage. Last to come have been social rights, which impose affirmative legal-constitutional obligations on the state in the form of economic welfare and security, the right to share in full in the social heritage, and the right to live the life of a civilized being according to the standards prevailing in the society.

In the United States, discussions of rights-based citizenship focus on the promise of protection guaranteed by the Fourteenth Amendment and full membership in the community of rights. Every individual is presumptively entitled to be treated by the organized society as a respected, responsible, and participating member; equal citizenship forbids an inferior or dependent caste, or treatment of some as nonparticipants (Karst 1988; Sunstein 1994). Some constitutional theorists such as Kenneth Karst (2000) and William Forbath (1999) have recently pushed for the recognition of material equality as fundamentally constitutive of equal and effective citizenship, although most attention has focused on what Marshall called political and civil rights.

Liberalism promises the progressive incorporation of previously excluded social groups through expansion of "the circle of belonging" (Karst 1989). This is not obsolete as a strategy when one, for example, considers the condition of noncitizens (Bosniak 2000b). The requirement that the subject of liberalism be the "abstract citizen" of the political state, where all "citizens" are accorded "equal rights," is worth something to those who have not been accorded rights in the past.

But at the same time, for racialized subjects, the fiction of "equal citizenship" can mean denying the continuing effects of racial exclusion through the government's failure to protect civil, political, and social rights for persons of color. "Equal citizenship" and racial exclusion from such were not thought to contradict each other at the nation's founding, for liberalism conditioned eligibility of universal rights upon one's possession of a particular subjectivity. Those designated as being unable to exercise reason were deemed incapable of consent. The world was split into two: those who had attained the capacity to guide themselves to their own improvement and those outside history, mired in stagnation and despotic custom (Mahmud 1999). For African Americans, for example, exclusion from citizenship was rationalized through the argument that blacks lacked the capacity for rational thought, independence, and self-control that was essential for self-governance (Roberts 1996). Even after formal legal citizenship was granted to African Americans, the belief was that citizenship had to be cultivated, so that they could learn to live in the United States as "responsible free men" (Franke 1999).

The historical contradictions at the core of America's liberalism continue to be replicated in the present day. Liberal notions of citizenship suppress particular and local differences, separating one's abstract will from the specifics of social conditions, such as the racialized body. The liberal state stands apart from the differences in civil society, permitting it to ignore the ways in which structures of exploitation have been sedimented in the United States (Prashad 2000). Jurisprudentially, this has been accomplished in the modern era through a discourse of colorblindness, which mandates formal equality but not substantive equality, guaranteeing equality of process, without attention to unequal effects. This discourse also equates the acknowledgment of race with racism, so that race-conscious attempts at mediating racial discrimination are met with charges of racism. More recently, the discourse of liberal multiculturalism has been used to manage difference through highlighting cultural specificity, while minimizing the role of race and racism in maintaining white privilege.[10] Neither colorblind universality nor the depoliticized aestheticization of difference can satisfactorily address existing subordination.

Liberal theory cannot explain why Asian Americans can be cast "both as persons and populations to be integrated into the national political sphere," and thus deserving of the protection of rights, and "as the contradictory, confusing, unintelligible elements to be marginalized and returned to their alien origins" (Lowe 1996, 4). While there is no question that American law mandates that Asian Americans be afforded the rights of all citizenry under abstract principles of egalitarian plurality, their racial location still functions to disrupt the enjoyment of full political and social equality.[11]

Citizenship as Political Activity

The idea that citizenship is defined through political engagement is important both historically and for its recent renaissance in legal theory.[12] Against monarchism and feudalism, classic civic republicanism maintained that the protection of the common good was the goal of society; that citizens had to be virtuous, through subordinating their private ends to this public good; that to be virtuous, citizens had to exercise their own political will and be active in political life; and that they were entitled to equality under a representative, democratic system of laws. The integrity of the republican order was fragile, and perpetually threatened by corruption.

At the founding of the republic, ownership of property was considered a fundamental prerequisite to the making of the good citizen. Owning property tied the citizen's fate to that of the larger polity. This gave the citizen a stake in the important political controversies of the day but also provided a shield against the state and private parties. As we know, Asian Americans were made racially ineligible to participate in the citizen's prerogative of property ownership.[13]

In the 1970s and 1980s, legal theorists such as Cass Sunstein and Frank Michelman began to embrace the idea of civic republicanism as a model of how citizens could come together to decide matters of the public good in a process of self-government, so that citizenship would manifest itself in broadly guaranteed rights of participation (Sunstein 1985; Michelman 1977–78). In a much cited essay on constitutional citizenship, Paul Brest (1986) advocated a turn from a liberal, consumer conception of democracy to one where participation is considered an essential human good. The idea that civic participation in the political community constitutes the core of what we mean by "citizenship" remains popular.[14]

In response to the interest in civic republicanism, Derrick Bell and Preeta Bansal (1988) have criticized the assumption that a social consensus can emerge from reasoned deliberation by individuals who think rationally and who can abstract from their private experiences to collectively determine the common good. They argue that any consensus ideology in America will inevitably be one of racial domination, whereby the interests of blacks are suppressed to promote the common good. Racial reforms have come about not through civic virtue, but through the convergence of minority interests with those of whites (Bell 1980). This skepticism about the promise of neo-civic republicanism is lent force by its historical origins. The founders of the republic cast onto African Americans and Indians those qualities they felt republicans should not have, so that they were devoid of virtue in a society that required such (Takaki 1979).[15] Who was to participate in the republic was also limited along gender lines. Linda Kerber (1998) has examined how freeing women from civic obligations that men were to fulfill—treating them as "ladies" without obligations, such as military service—served to legitimate their disenfranchisement from rights, such as voting.

What has not been a focus of inquiry are the particular ways in which Asian Americans have historically been thought incapable of membership in a civic republic, and the extent to which these historic assumptions still hold sway in the contemporary stereotyping of Asian American communities. Doubt that the Chinese were fit for citizenship in a republic is evident in early debates about their citizenship. In discussing whether the racial bar on naturalization should be completely lifted, prior to the 1870 legislation, Senator Cowan warned,

> Whether this door [of citizenship] shall now be thrown open to the Asiatic population. . . . [For the Pacific Coast this would mean] an end to republican government there, because it is very well ascertained that those people have no appreciation of that form of government; it seems to be obnoxious to their very nature; they seem to be incapable either of understanding or carrying it out.[16]

Similarly, the 1877 Report of the Joint Special Committee to Investigate Chinese Immigration stated,

> [T]he Chinese do not desire to become citizens of this country, and have no knowledge or appreciation of our institutions. Very few of them learn to speak our language. . . . To admit these vast numbers of aliens to citizenship and the ballot would practically destroy republican institutions on the Pacific coast, for the Chinese have no comprehension of any form of government but despotism, and have not the words in their own language to describe intelligibly the principles of our representative system.[17]

As Rogers Smith has described, the survival of "republican institutions" was for some the primary threat posed by Chinese immigration, since republics required "a homogenous population," not what one representative called an "ethnological animal show" (Smith 1997, 362). Chinese immigrants were thought incapable of assimilation into American understandings of republican government. They were believed to understand only despotic government and political absolutism, not democratic principles. Chinese immigrants were constructed as a foreign group whose deep-seated, ineradicable cultural, political, and religious differences rendered them undesirable as prospective members of the polity (Torok 1996).

At that time, while Chinese immigrants were thought to be under the yoke of despotic control, China was not perceived as an imminent military threat to the national military security of the United States. By contrast, from the early 1900s onward, Japanese immigrants were so perceived, which led to new forms of Asian American stereotypes, namely, the idea of disloyalty and allegiance to a threatening foreign military power. Japanese Americans were portrayed as an imminent "fifth column" threat within the United States, waiting to be activated at the emperor's command, so that the plowshares of Japanese immigrant farmers would transform into swords at the whim of a foreign power (Aoki 1998).

This portrayal of Chinese and Japanese Americans as under the sway of their foreign sovereigns presaged Japanese American internment, when nearly 120,000 persons of Japanese descent, including U.S. citizens, were swept up into remote camps for the duration of World War II. It was considered too administratively onerous to distinguish those who were loyal from those who were not; so Japanese ancestry served to signify presumptive disloyalty to the United States. Here, race fundamentally contradicted the purported promise of citizenship as rights, in the form of racial ancestry trumping the fact of U.S. citizenship.

The subsequent importance of assumptions of disloyalty, and pressure to demonstrate loyalty to the United States in order to be perceived as incorporated in the national body, as "American," cannot be understated. During World War II, in his capacity as executive secretary for the Japanese American Citizens League, Mike Masaoka proposed a "suicide battalion" of Japanese Americans whose loyalty would be assured by their having families and friends held by the government as hostages. He also recommended to the U.S. government in 1942 that Japanese Americans be branded, stamped, and put under the supervision of the federal government. As Chris Iijima (1998) has documented, "super-patriotic" narratives in the form, for example, of the 442nd regiment—the Japanese American regiment that sustained the most injury during WWII—grounded the subsequent successful movement for Japanese American redress from the U.S. government.

With the advent of "Red China" as a military threat to the United States, the political loyalty of Chinese Americans also became suspect. Stereotypes that once were projected onto Japanese Americans were now projected onto Red China—that "the Chinese" were fanatical, cruel, militaristic, devious, inhuman, and inscrutable (Aoki 1996). For Filipino, Korean, Cambodian, and Vietnamese Americans, U.S. colonialism, neocolonialism, and war directly led to their location in the United States—shaping their racialization sharply in relation to U.S. imperialism as "little brown brothers" and enemy aliens.

With the repeal of race-based limits on immigration and the removal of racial bars to citizenship, Asian Americans could begin building citizenship through political activity. Whether contemporary racialization of Asian Americans still bars full civic participation deserves critical attention. The recent election of Gary Locke as the first Asian American governor of a state on the U.S. mainland and the recent appointment of Norman Mineta to be secretary of commerce for the remainder of the Clinton administration might seem to signify that all is well. However, only three of the 435 members of the House of Representatives are Asian American, and there are only two senators who are Asian American—roughly a quarter of the numbers that might be expected if there were a form of proportional representation.[18]

In addition, there are disturbing echoes of historical stereotypes in recent controversies involving Asian Americans. The "Asian connection" in the campaign finance scandal of 1996 centered on two men, John Huang and Charlie Yah-lin Trie—both naturalized U.S. citizens—who were donors and fundraisers for President Clinton's reelection and the Democratic National Committee. In the months before the 1996 election, the media and Clinton's challengers attacked Clinton for using Huang to raise money from illegal foreign sources, particularly from James Riady, the owner of the Indonesia-based Lippo Group. Soon the idea that there was a foreign Asian plot to buy influence in Washington, DC, became major news. The *National Review* created an infamous cover, featuring Clinton, Hillary Rodham Clinton, and Al Gore with buck teeth, and in putative "Asian" dress. "Asian" and "Asian American" became conflated with each other and with political corruption and foreign subversion (Wang 1998; Wu and Nicholson 1997). This concern still rages, as exemplified by the use of repeated shots of Gore fundraising at the Hsi Lai Buddhist Temple in California in an attempt to discredit him.

Whether or not illegal fundraising was conducted, the coverage of these events by the media and their use by both political parties have been racist.[19] The Democratic National Committee, for example, decided to only accept money from U.S. citizens, and audited its roll of donors for "dirty money," which was equated with Asian and Asian American donations. In a frightening linkage to the Chinese being driven out of West Coast communities a century ago, Michael Lewis of the *New York Times* wrote, "This fear of Asians isn't all bad. If riding a few Asians out of Washington on a rail helps to generate public support for campaign finance reform, well then, hitch up the ponies, giddyap!" (Chen and Minami 1998, 373).

More recently, Wen Ho Lee, a physicist with the Los Alamos research laboratories, was indicted for negligent handling of secret data, in the form of downloading data on his home computer. Born in Taiwan, Lee is a naturalized U.S. citizen. While Lee was terminated from Los Alamos because of allegations that he gave data to the People's Republic of China as a spy,[20] the government now admits he did not provide classified information to any foreign government, and has only alleged that he mishandled classified information. While Lee was indicted on more than fifty counts under the Atomic Energy Act—the only person ever charged under this act—and was subsequently held in solitary confinement without bail in federal prison for nine months, the federal government ultimately dropped all but one charge of downloading data, to which Lee pled, followed by an apology by the federal district judge for the way Lee had been treated. Former counterintelligence chiefs of the Los Alamos lab and the Energy Department have said that Lee became a suspect because of ethnicity, and there is a strong argument that he is the victim of racial profiling.[21] The search warrant was obtained on the U.S. attorney's affidavit that he was "overseas ethnic Chinese" (Gotanda 2000).[22]

While the "Asian connection" and the treatment of Wen Ho Lee might seem isolated incidents, the media attention they have garnered has been both enormous and suggestive of a particular racialization of Asian Americans. This racialization is constituted through the implication that Asians and Asian Americans are indistinguishable, creating the presumption that Asian Americans enter the republic with a continuing allegiance to their country of origin, rendering them subject to corruption and disloyalty, and foreclosing their ability to function as subjects. While there is a reluctance in this color-blind era to recognize the role of historical racialization in shaping present-day realities, it seems clear that earlier constructions of Asian Americans continue to exert a powerful influence. The perception that the political activity of Asian Americans is somehow at odds with "American" political interests serves to deny Asian Americans the effective political subjecthood essential to full citizenship.

Citizenship as Identity

Citizenship is also understood as people's collective experience of themselves, in terms of their belonging to a particular community as expressed on the terrain of culture. In this manner, as well, citizenship has served as a proxy for race, so that "American" is equated with being white, and Asians are perceived to stand in for those who are excluded from national membership. Thus the infamous headline, "American beats out Kwan" reported by MSNBC in 1998, suggesting that the white American skater, Tara Lipinski, was victorious over the purportedly non-American Michelle Kwan. Asian Americans are racialized both as nonwhite and as noncitizens, foreign and unassimilable (Chang 1999; Gotanda 1985). From the advent of Asian immigration, there has been a persistent view that the racial identity of Asians who are U.S. citizens by birth or naturalization is characterized by their being distinctly foreign.[23] In fact, "citizen" and "Asian" could be said to function as antonyms in the U.S. context.

This dissonance can begin to be explained as a product of the discourse of Orientalism. Edward Said (1978) described Orientalism as a master discourse of European civilization that constructs and polarizes the East and the West. Western representations of the East serve not only to define those who are the objects of the Orientalizing gaze, but also the West, which is defined through its opposition to the East, so that, for example, the West is defined as "modern," "democratic," and "progressive," through the East being defined as "primitive," "barbaric," and "despotic." In the context of the United States, while American Orientalism has turned to North Africa, the Middle East, and Turkey, it has also focused heavily on East Asia in defining "America" in contradistinction to the "East."

Earlier fears of a "yellow peril" that would eat away the American nation from within have now publicly been replaced with a new, ostensibly favorable characterization of Asian Americans as the "model minority." The final lifting of racial exclusion in immigration in 1965, and the eradication of racial bars to naturalization and to property ownership did correlate with a large turn in perceptions of Asian Americans. The idea of the "model minority" is that a strong work ethic and family cohesion have led to Asian American economic success, without the need to rely on government welfare. As many have documented, the idea of the model minority is a myth that belies poverty and disenfranchisement, including high welfare use by certain Asian American communities. It is also used to discipline other persons of color in the United States. For the purposes of this essay, the most salient fact to note is that the success touted here is economic success—not political. In other words, the idea that Asian Americans somehow constitute a model minority is not incompatible with the idea that Asian Americans are still largely incapable of democratic engagement. Many have argued that the yellow peril still lurks, that the idea of the model minority has always coexisted with the idea of the Asian American as the "gook" (Lee 1999, 11). Thus, even while the model minority is promised the putative ability to assimilate easily into the nation, Asian Americans continue to serve as agents of foreign or multinational capital in the U.S. imagination.

Through the lens of the Asian American experience, we can begin to perceive how the fourth category of citizenship, citizenship as identity, is not created through the enjoyment of the first three categories of citizenship, but rather appears ontologically separate. While many scholars approach citizenship as identity as if it were derivative of citizenship's other dimensions, it seems as if the guarantees of citizenship as status, rights, and politics are insufficient to produce citizenship as identity.[24] In fact, the relationship citizenship as identity appears to bear to the first three kinds of citizenship is more complicated. I would argue that it is not only nonequivalent to the citizenship produced through political and legal activities; also, sentiments concerning the identity of citizenship can reduce the ability to exercise citizenship as a political or legal matter. Thus, the general failure to identify Asian Americans as constituting American national identity reappears to haunt the access of Asian Americans to the first three categories of citizenship.

This should not surprise. Race has always fundamentally contradicted the promise of liberal democracy. The racially exclusive origins of liberalism and civic republicanism were starkly at odds with their purported goals. While membership in the citizenry has been widened, simply adding rights with an accompanying logic of color-blindness will not translate into substantive enjoyment of citizenship. Ideas about race will continue to disrupt the ability of Asian Americans to function and be identified as citizens. To be Asian American suggests in the American imagination the idea that one acts according to cultural dictates somehow fundamentally different from those known in the United States. One's Asianness seems to be the difference one must suppress in order to be a full citizen. There is a danger to trying to define citizenship in isolation from identity, since particularities will determine how successfully such citizenship can be accessed and enjoyed. It is imperative to address all four citizenship discourses if one is truly in search of the guarantee of constitutional citizenship, for only with access to all four forms of citizenship can one be deemed a full citizen.

Conclusion

While much has been written about the presumption of Asian American disloyalty, what has not been previously examined is the manner in which assumptions about Asian American character are particularly at odds with the requirements for the member of the civic republic. This dissonance explains the particular site of recent controversies involving Asian Americans.

That the political engagement of Asian Americans in the American republic will inevitably be accompanied by concerns about their loyalty, their trustworthiness, and their ability to prioritize national as opposed to foreign interests is a form of cultural racism. To be seen as primarily governed by group loyalty to one's country of origin suggests a limited capacity for agency, will, or rational thought. This is obviously dehumanizing, since our beliefs as to what is "human" rest on such capacities.[25] The differentiation of who is allowed to be "human," through discourses about racial inferiority, has been fundamental to the creation of many modern democracies. The American rights-bearing subject was allowed to consolidate through the very exclusion of certain racialized subjects.[26]

The boundaries of the nation are constructed through excluding certain groups. The "imagined community" of the American nation, peopled by "citizens," has relied on difference from the Asian alien to fuse its identity. Discourses of democracy rest on an image of antidemocracy, in the form of despotic societies whose members are incapable of civic activity. The idea that there are "Asian values" that are antithetical to "Western values" of liberty and equality helps solidify this conclusion. The fusion of antidemocratic with Asia, and Asian with Asian American suggests that Asian Americans are somehow fundamentally incapable of taking part in the democratic political processes. To the extent that Asian Americans and Asians are fungible in the American imagination, the fact that neo-Confucianism is used to explain economic development in Asia at the expense of "Western values" of individualism and freedom encourages the perception that Asian Americans are somehow unable to grasp the principles of Western political engagement.

The discourse of constitutional citizenship claims that all citizens ought to be treated equally. But, as I have suggested, there are particular assumptions about Asian Americans that have forever rendered their presumptive fitness for citizenship suspect. The frequent responses to assaults on the citizenship of the Asian American—namely, the assertion that "I am an American!" (Chang 1999) and attempts at demonstrating patriotism and loyalty—have been inadequate. Such attempts fail to recognize why particular stereotypes are thrust upon Asian Americans, and the connection of these stereotypes to the legacy of contradictions in citizenship. What is called for are new forms of struggle that understand the limits of solely seeking membership in the national political body, and that instead undertake its transformation through the creation of political solidarities across racial and national boundaries.

NOTES

Originally published in *Citizenship Studies* 5.1 (2001): 57–71. © 2001 Taylor & Francis, reprint by permission.

1. I am aware that in this essay, I am primarily using the experiences of Chinese and Japanese Americans to define what I am calling "Asian American" experiences. This is a source of concern because of the frequent and problematic use of Chinese and Japanese Americans to function as metonymous for all of Asian America, which is an extremely heterogeneous entity. There are enormous differences within the identity category "Asian American" along lines of class, gender, immigration history, and sexuality, as well as along lines of ancestry. The term has been used to encompass people with origins in countries as diverse as China, Japan, the Philippines, India, Bangladesh, Pakistan, Sri Lanka, Vietnam, Thailand, Cambodia, Laos, Singapore, Malaysia, East Timor, Indonesia, Burma, and Tibet. Nonetheless, I think there is some salience in the experiences I am using to represent this category, since—despite the heterogeneity within the category—"Asian American" has often been homogenized to mean Chinese and Japanese Americans vis-à-vis the state and national culture.

2. I am using the subject/object distinction here differently than the distinction has traditionally been invoked in jurisprudence, which has contrasted the object of rights—the fetus, the child, the slave—with the subject—the person, the adult, or the citizen. Legal liberalism has

used the subject/object distinction to distinguish the rights-bearing subject from the object who does not. I am making a different distinction, suggesting, instead, that the idea of citizenship through political activity constructs the citizen-subject, while the idea of citizenship as liberal rights assumes a more passive recipient of rights.

3. For an important analysis of the relationship between citizenship and marriage, see Cott (1998).

4. Two doctrines govern citizenship by birth: *jus soli*—citizenship by soil, which confers citizenship to a person on the basis of the place of birth; and *jus sanguinis*—citizenship by blood or descent, that confers citizenship based upon the citizenship of the person's parents at the time of birth. *Jus sanguinis* is principally an issue for children born abroad of U.S. citizen parents and is not a focus here.

5. *Scott v. Sandford,* 60 U.S. (19 How.) 393 (1857).

6. Id. at 404.

7. Contemporaneously, in *Plessy v. Ferguson,* Justice Harlan referred to "a race so different from our own that we do not permit those belonging to it to become citizens of the United States"—which he contrasted with "citizens of the black race in Louisiana, many of whom, perhaps, risked their lives for the preservation of the Union," 163 U.S. 537, 561 (1896). For a discussion, see Chin (1996).

8. 169 U.S. 649, 682 (1898). Native Americans continued to be barred from birthright citizenship until federal legislation was passed in 1924. Whether U.S. citizenship was desired or should be considered regressive is a subject of controversy and not addressed here.

9. Id. at 694.

10. I would distinguish liberal multiculturalism from a stronger multiculturalism that questions the fundamental premises of what are considered to be core values. Importantly, I would also differentiate multiculturalism from a crude cultural relativism to which it is often analogized and suggest that there may be a way to accompany the value of multiculturalism with a critical perspective espousing antisubordination. See Volpp (2000).

11. As a concrete example, there are serious questions as to why Wen Ho Lee was imprisoned in solitary confinement for nine months—which would constitute a grave violation of his civil rights—when former CIA director John Deutsch received no punishment for similarly downloading computer data.

12. In separating liberal theory from civic republicanism, I recognize that there has been concern that the difference between these two theories has been greatly overblown. See, for example, Stolzenberg (1998) and Williams (1998). Nonetheless, I have found it useful to separate liberalism from republicanism for the purposes of this essay in order to differentiate the way each theory implicates notions of citizenship.

13. Race played a fundamental role in also shaping the entitlement to property of other groups: African Americans were themselves considered property, and Native Americans and Mexican Americans were dispossessed of their property. See Luna (1999).

14. The impulse to reinvigorate citizenship, through reviving the civic republican ideal, has been called a romantic one (White and Hunt 2000, 94).

15. Later, common assumptions about the unique fitness of the "Anglo-Saxon race" for self-rule were used to justify the failure to extend constitutional citizenship to the inhabitants of U.S. territories (Smith 1997, 434). I am not examining here the decision to only accord statutory and not constitutional citizenship to Puerto Ricans. For a discussion of that point, see Roman (1998).

16. Statement of Senator Cowan, *Cong. Globe,* 42nd Cong., 1st sess., 1866, 57:499.

17. 44th Cong., 2nd sess., 1877. S. Rept. 689, quoted in Torok (1996, 55–56).

18. I am including Representatives Matsui, Mink, and Wu, and Senators Akaka and Inouye in this calculation and am not including nonvoting delegates Underwood and Faleomavaega of Guam and American Samoa. The current Asian American population is estimated at 4 percent of the total U.S. population.

19. For the fundraising affair, the implication has been that Huang and Trie represent all Asian Americans, and that all Asian Americans who participate in politics are somehow linked to the scandal (Wu and Nicholson 1997).

20. As has been noted, the idea that a Taiwanese would spy for the People's Republic of China makes little sense.

21. For example, Robert Vrooman, the former chief of security at Los Alamos, has stated publicly that Lee was singled out because of his ethnicity.

22. For information about the campaign on behalf of Wen Ho Lee, see http://wenholee.org.

23. As Kevin Johnson (1997, 354–57) describes, Latinas and Latinos have also consistently been perceived as foreigners to the United States.

24. See Bosniak (2000a, 479), making this point, asserting that the sentiment of citizenship has independent sources other than the way citizenship is conceived and practiced in our legal and political worlds.

25. The differentiation of "Asian" from "human" was exemplified through a story that likened Chinese people to insects. The *Washington Post* ran a story in 1999, describing the arrest of Lee:

> China's spying, they say, more typically involves cajoling morsels of information out of visiting foreign experts and tasking thousands of Chinese abroad to bring secrets home one at a time like ants carrying grains of sand. The Chinese have been assembling such grains of sand since at least the fourth century BC, when the military philosopher Sun Tzu noted the value of espionage in his classic work, *The Art of War*. (*Washington Post* 1999, sec. A7).

26. Gender-based exclusion also created the rights-bearing subject. See Kerber (1998), Smith (1997).

REFERENCES

Aoki, K. 1996. "Foreign-Ness" and Asian American identities: Yellowface, World War II propaganda, and bifurcated racial stereotypes. *Asian Pac. Am. L.J.* 4:1–61.

———. 1998. No right to own? The early twentieth-century "alien land laws" as a prelude to internment. *B.C. L. Rev.* 40:37–72.

Bell, D. 1980. Brown v. Board of Education and the interest-convergence dilemma. *Harv. L. Rev.* 93:518–33.

Bell, D., and Bansal, P. 1988. The republican revival and racial politics. *Yale L.J.* 97:1609–21.

Black, C. 1970. The unfinished business of the Warren Court. *Wash. L. Rev.* 46:3–45.

Bosniak, L. 2000a. Citizenship denationalized. *Ind. J. of Global Legal Stud.* 7:447–509.

———. 2000b. Universal citizenship and the problem of alienage. *Nw. U. L. Rev.* 941:963–82.

Bredbenner, C. 1998. *A nationality of her own: Women, marriage, and the law of citizenship.* Berkeley: University of California Press.

Brest, P. 1986. Constitutional citizenship. *Clev. St. L. Rev.* 34:175–97.

Chang, R. 1999. *Disoriented: Asian Americans, law, and the nation state.* New York: New York University Press.

Chen, E. M., and Minami, D. 1998. Petition for hearing. *Asian L.J.* 5:357–82.

Chin, G. J. 1996. The Plessy myth: Justice Harlan and the Chinese cases. *Iowa L. Rev.* 82:151–82.

Cott, N. 1998. Marriage and women's citizenship in the United States, 1830–1934. *Am. Hist. Rev.* 103:1440–74.

Forbath, W. 1999. Caste, class, and equal citizenship. *Mich. L. Rev.* 98:1–75.

Franke, K. 1999. Becoming a citizen: Reconstruction-era regulation of African American marriages. *Yale J.L. & Human.* 11:251–309.

Gotanda, N. 1985. "Other non-whites" in American legal history: A review of justice at war. *Colum. L. Rev.* 85:1186–92.

———. 1992. Asian American rights and the "Miss Saigon syndrome." In *Asian Americans and the Supreme Court,* ed. H. Kim, 1087–103. Westport, CT: Greenwood Press.

———. 1996. Towards repeal of Asian exclusion: The Magnuson Act of 1943, the Act of July 2, 1946, the Presidential Proclamation of July 4, 1946, the Act of August 9, 1946, and the Act of August 1, 1950. In *Asian Americans and Congress: A documentary history,* ed. H. Kim, 309–28. Westport, CT: Greenwood Press.

———. 2000. Racialization of Asian Americans and African Americans: Racial profiling and the Wen Ho Lee case. *UCLA L. Rev.* 47:1689–1703.

Haney López, I. 1996. *White by law: The legal construction of race.* New York: New York University Press.

Iijima, C. 1998. Reparations and the "model minority" ideology of acquiescence: The necessity to refuse the return to original humiliation. *B. C. Third World L.J.* 19:385–427.

Johnson, K. 1997. Racial hierarchy, Asian Americans and Latinos as "foreigners" and social change: Is law the way to go? *Or. L. Rev.* 76:347–68.

Karst, K. 1988. Citizenship, race, and marginality. *Wm. & Mary L. Rev.* 30:1–49.

———. 1989. Belonging to America: Equal citizenship and the Constitution. New Haven, CT: Yale University Press.

———. 2000. The bonds of American nationhood. *Cardozo L. Rev.* 21:1141–82.

Kerber, L. 1998. *No constitutional right to be ladies: Women and the obligations of citizenship.* New York: Hill and Wang.

Lee, R. G. 1999. *Orientals: Asian Americans in popular culture.* Philadelphia: Temple University Press.

Lowe, L. 1996. *Immigrant acts: On Asian American cultural politics.* Durham, NC: Duke University Press.

Luna, G. 1999. On the complexities of race: The treaty of Guadalupe Hidalgo and Dred Scott v. Sandford. *U. Miami L. Rev.* 53:691–716.

Mahmud, T. 1999. Colonialism and modern constructions of race: A preliminary inquiry. *U. Miami L. Rev.* 53:1219–46.

Marshall, T. H. 1964. *Class, citizenship, and social development.* Garden City, NY: Doubleday.

Michelman, F. 1977–78. Political markets and community self-determination: Competing judicial models of local government legitimacy. *Ind. L.J.* 53:145–206.

———. 1988. Law's republic. *Yale L.J.* 97:1493–1537.

Prashad, V. 2000. *The karma of brown folk.* Minneapolis: University of Minnesota Press.

Roberts, D. 1996. Welfare and the problem of Black citizenship. Review of *Pitied but not entitled: Single mothers and the history of welfare,* by L. Gordon and *The color of welfare: How racism undermined the war on poverty,* by J. Quadagno. *Yale L.J.* 105:1563–1602.

Roman, E. 1998. The alien-citizen paradox and other consequences of U.S. colonialism. *Fla. St. U. L. Rev.* 26:1–47.

Said, E. 1978. *Orientalism.* New York: Pantheon.

Smith, R. 1997. *Civic ideals: Conflicted visions of citizenship in U.S. history.* New Haven, CT: Yale University Press.

Stolzenberg, N. 1998. A book of laughter and forgetting: Kalman's "strange career" and the marketing of civic republicanism. Review of *The strange career of legal liberalism,* by L. Kalman. *Harv. L. Rev.* 111:1025–84.

Sunstein, C. 1985. Interest groups in American public law. *Stan. L. Rev.* 38:29–87.

———. 1994. The anticaste principle. *Mich. L. Rev.* 92:2410–55.

Takaki, R. 1979. *Iron cages: Race and culture in nineteenth-century America.* Oxford: Oxford University Press.

Tehranian, J. 2000. Performing whiteness: Naturalization litigation and the construction of racial identity. *Yale L.J.* 109:817–48.

Thomas, B. 1998. China men, *United States v. Wong Kim Ark,* and the question of citizenship. *Am. Q.* 50: 689–717.

Torok, J. H. 1996. Reconstruction and racial nativism: Chinese immigrants and the debates on the Thirteenth, Fourteenth, and Fifteenth Amendments and civil rights laws. *Asian L.J.* 3:55–103.

U.S. officials may never learn how China got warhead secrets. *Washington Post.* Reprinted in *Augusta Chronicle,* 22 March 1999, sec. A7.

Volpp, L. 2000. Blaming culture for bad behavior. *Yale J.L. & Human.* 12:89–116.

Wang, L. 1998. Race, class, citizenship, and extraterritoriality: Asian Americans and the 1996 campaign finance scandal. *Amerasia* 24:1–21.

White, M., and Hunt, A. 2000. Citizenship: Care of the self, character, and personality. *Citizenship Stud.* 4:93–116.

Williams, J. 1998. The rhetoric of property. *Iowa L. Rev.* 83: 277–361.

Wu, F., and Nicholson, M. 1997. Have you no decency? An analysis of racial aspects of media coverage on the John Huang matter. *Asian Am. Pol'y Rev.* 7:1–37.

Chapter 28

Interracial Politics

Asian Americans and Other Communities of Color

Claire Jean Kim and Taeku Lee

The Los Angeles rebellion of 1992 was a flashpoint in which the struggles of Blacks, Latinos, and Asian Americans converged with explosive consequences. Dubbed the nation's first "multiracial" riot, it drove home the point that racial dynamics in the United States cannot be understood through a simple black-white framework. But events in L.A. were only the most dramatic example of interminority conflicts that have emerged in many American cities during the post-1965 era as economic restructuring and global migration flows have brought racial/ethnic groups into more extensive contact with one another, reshaping their identities and relationships and creating new pressure points for conflict among them. Of course, rapid economic and demographic change has also opened up new possibilities for coalition and cooperation among racial/ethnic groups, from electoral politics to grassroots community activism. Asian Americans, often depicted as an "interstitial" group and a potential "swing vote," have played and will continue to play a key role in interracial conflicts and coalitions in American politics.[1]

Political scientists have studied majority-minority relations and black-white dynamics for some time, but they have only recently turned their attention to interactions between Asian Americans and other communities of color. As a result, there are relatively few political science works on this topic. However, there is a growing body of scholarship, much of it explicitly interdisciplinary, written by scholars in sociology, ethnic studies, law, and history. We review and assess this literature in this chapter, with an emphasis on the thematic content of the works rather than on the disciplinary membership of the authors.

In the first section, we discuss works that focus on overt conflict and cooperation between Asian Americans and other communities of color in the electoral arena, as well as works that explore racial/ethnic group attitudes that have clear implications for the prospects of conflict and cooperation. In the second section, we discuss works that look more broadly at how ideology, power dynamics, and racial hierarchy shape patterns of conflict and cooperation among these groups, particularly outside of formal political institutions. This is not a perfect dichotomous classification: some works span both categories, and some defy both. Still, it helps us to recognize the distinction between those works that focus primarily on observable intergroup behaviors and attitudes and those that are explicitly concerned with contextualizing group interactions within the American racial hierarchy. We conclude with some suggestions about future directions for research on this topic.

Electoral Politics, Policy Issues, and Attitudes

Historically, there has been little written on Asian American participation in the formal institutionalized arena of electoral and policy competition among elite actors, in large part because Asian Americans have been few in number, relatively inactive in electoral politics, and underrepresented among policy elites. However, with the rapid growth of the Asian American population in recent years and the deepening and diversifying of Asian American modes of political participation, a growing number of scholars have started asking questions about Asian Americans' acquisition of partisanship, voting behavior, and political participation (Cho 1999; Lien 1997; Ong and Nakanishi 1996; Uhlaner, Cain, and Kiewiet 1989; Cain, Kiewiet, and Uhlaner 1989). Some predict that because of their rapid growth, geographical concentration in key electoral states, and weak partisanship, Asian Americans may become a "swing vote" that plays a pivotal role in American politics (Cho and Cain 2001; Nakanishi 1991).

This burst of interest in Asian American politics has also produced works that examine Asian American collaborations with other groups of color in the realm of electoral politics. This is not to say that Asian Americans have been meaningfully incorporated into all of the literature on cross-racial conflict and cooperation. Many of the leading works on bi/multiracial coalitions in urban politics continue to focus primarily if not exclusively on two or more of the following groups: white liberals, Blacks, and Latinos (Browning, Marshall, and Tabb 1997; Gilliam 1996; McClain and Stewart 1995; Sonenshein 1993; Henry and Muñoz 1991; Mladenka 1989; Falcon 1988). Still, there are several recent works that do highlight Asian Americans' political interactions with other communities of color, exploring empirical cases of and prerequisites for coalition building.

For example, scholars have written about Asian-Latino political cooperation in the San Gabriel Valley of Los Angeles County during the past decade. Recognizing their shared interest in fighting discrimination and political exclusion, these two groups have joined forces to defeat discriminatory local ordinances and secure favorable state assembly and senate redistricting plans (Saito 1998; Horton 1995; Fong 1994; Saito 1994). Similarly, in New York City in the early 1990s, Asian Americans, Latinos, and Blacks formed a multiracial coalition to promote a redistricting plan that linked Chinatown to the predominantly Puerto Rican and Black Lower East Side. Although the plan was defeated, and the redrawn District 1 ended up linking Chinatown to white areas to the west, the coalition's cross-racial, working-class emphasis was embraced by the victorious candidate, Kathryn Freed (Saito 2001; Saito and Park 2000). The multiracial coalition of Blacks, Latinos, Asian Americans, and whites that formed in Houston in the late 1990s was more successful: it was instrumental in getting Lee Brown elected as mayor and in defeating Proposition A, an anti-affirmative-action measure (Saito and Park 2000).

Scholars have also analyzed instances in which Asian Americans' experiences with interracial electoral politics were difficult and clearly unsuccessful. Both Michael Woo's failed bid for mayor of Los Angeles in 1992 and Ted Dang's unsuccessful campaign for mayor of Oakland in 1994 indicated that Asian American candidates could not necessarily count on strong support from non-Asian people of color (Saito 2001; Fong 1998; Sonenshein 1994).

Reviewing the available empirical evidence, Saito and Park (2000) argue that bi/multiracial political alliances are most likely if (1) racial/ethnic groups can set aside short-term, group-specific considerations to address fundamental issues related to social change; (2) they can resist narrow, race-based politics while at the same time recognizing the importance of race in American society; (3) individuals and organizations have built and sustained relationships across group boundaries over time as a basis for promoting collaborative efforts; and (54) each group contains organizations that can serve as vehicles for community mobilization, leadership training, resource building, etc. Oliver and Grant (1995), who argue that bi/multiracial coalitions are only feasible on the local level and are likely to be issue oriented and temporary rather than enduring, identify different prerequisites. In their view, residential propinquity (local spaces of interaction in which individuals from different groups can develop relationships and trust) and relative parity in status and resources (e.g., citizenship and education) are the most important factors. By these measures, Asian Americans are most likely to form alliances with whites, Latinos, and Blacks, in that order.

In addition to the works on electoral alliances, a substantial literature now exists on the leading policy issues affecting Asian Americans and other groups of color. Many of these works examine the contours of public opinion about immigration and affirmative action as general issues and in the form of specific initiatives such as California's Proposition 187 and Proposition 209 (Cho and Cain 2001; Lien and Conway 2001; Bobo and Johnson 2000; Lee 2000; Ong 2000; Ong 1999; Citrin et al. 1997; Chin et al. 1996; Hing and Lee 1996). They suggest clear points of commonality and difference between Asian Americans and other communities of color. On immigration, for example, Blacks tend to be closer to whites in viewing it negatively, while Asian Americans and Latinos tend to view it more positively. Strong Black support for Proposition 187 prompted Black leaders to engage in a national-level debate about how to protect Black jobs without fanning the flames of anti-immigrant agitation (Park and Park 1999). On affirmative action, on the other hand, Asian Americans tend to be less negative than whites but also considerably less positive than Blacks and Latinos. These points of contact and difference have clear implications for the likelihood of cross-racial collaboration on these issues.

On at least one occasion, Chinese Americans have clashed directly with other groups over the issue of race-based remedies in education. In the renowned case, *Brian Ho v. San Francisco Unified School District,* Chinese American plaintiffs seeking to increase Chinese American enrollments at Lowell High School successfully challenged school desegregation practices (that had been instituted pursuant to a lawsuit by the NAACP in the 1980s) that had benefited not only Blacks and Latinos but also certain other Asian-descent groups such as Korean Americans and Filipino Americans

(Ong 2000; Yamamoto 1999; Dong 1995). This case reminds us that the Asian American panethnic rubric can obscure as much as it reveals, depending upon the circumstances.

Studies that examine interracial contact also help us to understand the prospects for and barriers to cooperation between Asian Americans and other communities of color. Numerous sites of interracial contact have been intensively studied, including residential areas, workplaces, networks of friends, and public spaces (Lien et al. 2001; Massey 2000; Umemoto 2000; Hum and Zonta 2000; Bobo, Johnson, and Suh 2000; Lee 2000; Lee and Fernandez 1998; Green, Strolovich, and Wong 1998; Massey and Denton 1993). These studies indicate a distinct structuring of interracial contact and racial attitudes in the United States: Blacks and whites are the most distant from one another in terms of daily contact, material conditions, and attitudes toward racism, with Asian Americans and Latinos falling somewhere in between. Importantly, both Asian Americans and Latinos show considerable internal heterogeneity here along ethnic or national origin lines (Lee 2000; Bobo et al. 1994; Uhlaner 1991). Blacks live the most "hypersegregated" lives of any racial/ethnic group in the United States (Massey and Denton 1993). Asian Americans live significantly less segregated lives than African Americans, and are also somewhat less segregated from whites than Latinos are (Massey 2000; Hum and Zonta 2000).[2] Once again, Asian Americans and Blacks, in particular, appear to lack the extensive contact and shared experiences that facilitate coalition building.

Group perceptions of discrimination and identity also shape the prospects for conflict and cooperation between Asian Americans and other groups of color. Studies show that most Americans think that Blacks face the highest level of discrimination of any racial/ethnic group and that both Blacks and Latinos face the greatest barriers to opportunity and advancement. While roughly 40 percent of Asian Americans report having personally experienced discrimination (Lee 2000; Lien et al 2001; Bobo et al. 1994, Uhlaner 1991), few Americans (Asian Americans included) believe that Asian Americans as a group face special obstacles (Bobo, Johnson, and Suh 2000; Lee 2000; Uhlaner 1991). This data suggests that Asian Americans, on the one hand, and Blacks and Latinos, on the other, may not readily identify with each other or perceive strong common interests, despite their shared experience of racial discrimination in the United States.

While opinion studies find that Blacks express a stronger sense of sharing a racially linked fate than do other groups (Bobo and Johnson 2000; Cain, Citrin, and Wong 2000), panethnicity is an increasingly important theme in Asian American politics and analyses of Asian American politics (Lien 2001; Lai 2000; Tuan 1999; Kibria 1997; Lien 1997; Espiritu 1992).[3] Scholars have shown that a sense of shared fate or collective identity shaped Asian American political opinions about Proposition 187 and Proposition 209 (both initiatives of profound concern and interest to communities of color), and that it shapes their views of education and employment issues more generally (Cho and Cain 2001; Bobo and Johnson 2000; Cain, Citrin, and Wong 2000; Lien 1997). However, the development of a strong racial identity can be seen as a double-edged sword when it comes to cross-racial coalition building: on the one hand, group identities can politicize people and awaken them to their shared interests with members of other racial groups; on the other hand, they can prevent people from seeing past their own group boundaries.

Racial Hierarchy, Power, and Ideology

The second type of scholarship on conflict and cooperation between Asian Americans and other groups of color seeks to situate group interactions within the context of racial (and/or economic) hierarchy. Rather than focusing on and describing overt intergroup behaviors and attitudes alone, these works allude to groups' differential positioning in society and the economy in order to explain why they interact with each other the way that they do.

Apart from a few scholars who characterize Asian Americans as virtually "white" in terms of their status in American society (Ignatiev 1997; Hacker 1992), most concur that Asian Americans occupy a distinctive "third" position in the American racial hierarchy, somewhere in between Black and white.[4] Characterizations of this "third" position vary somewhat: Ancheta (1998) discusses how Asian Americans have been subordinated by whites but differently than Blacks—i.e., via the denial of citizenship; C. Kim (1999) argues that Asian Americans have been "triangulated" vis-à-vis whites and Blacks through simultaneous processes of relative valorization and civic ostracism; others worry that Asian Americans might serve as a "buffer zone" between whites and Blacks (E. Kim 1997) or as a "racial bourgeoisie" (Matsuda 1993). What these scholars agree on is that the Asian American experience has been at once distinct from the white and Black experiences and importantly conditioned by them. Even though the answer to Gary Okihiro's (1994) now-famous question—"Is yellow black or white?"—is "neither," it is important that the question be posed in just this way. Asian American politics must be understood as deriving from the uniquely liminal, ambivalent position(s) that Asian Americans occupy in the American racial order.

Only recently have scholars begun to address the intermediate or buffer position that Asian Americans occupy between whites, or *haoles,* and Native people in Hawai'i (Trask 1999).[5] A recent issue of *Amerasia Journal* (26.2 [2000]), guest edited by Candace Fujikane and Jonathan Okamura, contains a breakthrough collection of articles that contend that the Asian American experience in Hawai'i has not been one of immigrant success against all odds but rather one of "settler colonialism" (Fujikane 2000). While Asian Americans in Hawai'i frequently complain about anti-Asian discrimination on the part of *haoles,* these articles argue, they are much less willing to acknowledge their own role in dispossessing Native people of their resources and benefiting from the latter's political, economic, and social subjugation. An important caveat: as on the mainland, statements about Asian American positionality in Hawai'i should be strongly qualified by attention to intragroup national origin (and other) differences. For instance, Japanese Americans are the most powerful Asian American group in Hawai'i and stand in a hierarchical relationship to Filipinos there, just as Asian Americans as a whole do to Native people.

How do racial hierarchies get constructed and reproduced? In the post-1965 era, no single myth has done more work in this regard than the model minority myth, which holds that Asian Americans are hard-working, law-abiding, thrifty, family-oriented, education-revering people who have made it in American society and should serve as a "model" for other, less virtuous minorities, especially Blacks.[6] As Asian Americanists have been saying for more than a generation, the model minority myth functions ideologically to reproduce racial hierarchy in America by essentializing and homogenizing Asian American experiences, exaggerating Asian American prosperity and downplaying Asian American needs, arousing Black resentment towards Asian Americans, delegitimating Black demands for social programs, and legitimating racially discriminatory arrangements (Lee 1999; Chun 1995; Osajima 1988). Despite this persistent critique, major opinion makers such as politicians, the media, and business elites continue to embrace this myth. Indeed, studies have shown that institutional powerholders sometimes cite the model minority myth as a justification for giving preferential treatment to Asian Americans over Blacks (Gotanda 1995; Hatamiya 1993). To the extent that Asian Americans themselves buy into this myth and evince feelings of superiority toward Blacks, the racial hierarchy becomes that much more entrenched (K. Park 1997; E. Kim 1997).

Several scholars have examined the calculated representation of Asian Americans for particular political purposes around the issue of affirmative action (Omi and Takagi 1996). During the controversy over Asian American admissions quotas at selective universities in the 1980s, conservatives depicted Asian Americans as victims of pro-Black affirmative action programs, when they were actually being harmed by quotas intended to preserve the whiteness of student bodies (Takagi 1992). Similarly, proponents of Proposition 209 in California insisted that "preferential treatment" for Blacks and Latinos rendered Asian Americans victims of "reverse discrimination" (Park and Park 1999), and Republican Governor Pete Wilson publicly cited the *Brian Ho* case discussed above as a source of his doubts about affirmative action. Asian Americans have a very complicated relationship to affirmative action (Ong 2000), but that reality is obscured by the ideological maneuverings of conservatives bent on eliminating these programs.

The scholarship on Black-Korean conflict—or conflict between Korean immigrant merchants and Black customers/neighborhood residents—explores the way in which racial/economic hierarchy shapes intergroup conflict.[7] Adapting Bonacich's middleman-minority framework (1973), much of this literature focuses upon the proximate urban economic formation within which Korean merchants (middlemen) come into contact with poor Blacks (the masses) and end up bearing the brunt of the latter's frustrations (K. C. Kim 1999; Min 1996; Light and Bonacich 1988; Ong et al. 1994). Some works, however, theorize more broadly about the impact of power relations, racial ideology, the social construction of racial categories and meanings, and patterns of racial hierarchy upon Black-Korean conflict (C. Kim 2000; K. Park 1997; Abelmann and Lie 1995; Ikemoto 1993; Cho 1993). The implications of Black-Korean conflict for Korean American political mobilization and incorporation in various cities has received considerable scholarly attention (J. S. Park 1999; E. Park 2001; W. Park 1994).

While Black-Korean conflict has been memorialized in popular films and television programs, Latino-Korean conflict remains a relatively obscure phenomenon. Aside from a few works on Latino-Korean tensions in the Los Angeles garment industry (Bonacich 1994) and Latino participation in the Los Angeles rebellion of 1992 (Navarro 1994), scholars have paid little attention to the matter, reinforcing the popular perception that Latinos and Asians do not experience the kinds of conflicts that Blacks and Korean Americans do. Yet the sustained conflict between Latino store employees and Korean-owned produce stores that is occurring in New York City at the time of this writing belies this perception and suggests the need for more research on Latino-Korean interactions.

Scholars have analyzed the influence of racial hierarchy on conflicts between Asian Americans and Native Hawaiians. At issue between the two groups is whether Asian Americans have benefited from Native Hawaiian subjugation, and if so, what should be done about it. As the Native Hawaiian sovereignty movement has gained momentum in recent years, it has become increasingly critical of the role that ascendant Asian American (especially Japanese American) politicians, business elites, and intellectuals play in thwarting Native Hawaiians claims to land, water, and other natural resources (Trask 2000; Trask 1999). In response to the movement, some Japanese Americans and other Asian Americans have issued apologies and called for reparations for Native Hawaiians, while others have strongly denied any wrongdoing (Yamamoto 1999). Clearly, there is dissension within the Japanese American community in Hawai'i over what stand to take regarding the sovereignty question (Yoshinaga and Kosasa 2000).

Racial hierarchy generates differential group experiences that make coalition building difficult and creates fault lines along which intergroup conflict is likely to occur. However, scholars have shown that processes of racial subordination can also encourage cross-racial alliances by subjecting racial/ethnic minorities to similar forms of mistreatment or disempowerment and convincing them that they share certain short-term and long-term interests. In New York City, the Coalition Against Anti-Asian Violence has built a thriving multiracial grassroots alliance dedicated to fighting racially motivated violence and police brutality. Perhaps the most notable and successful cross-racial coalitions between Asian Americans and other groups of color outside of the electoral arena have been in the area of labor organizing. On more than one occasion, Korean Immigrant Workers Advocates has joined forces with the predominantly Latino Local 11 of the Hotel Employees and Restaurant Employees Union to pressure Korean conglomerates to renew labor contracts with union workers in Los Angeles (Saito and Park 2000; Omatsu 1995), thus extending the historical tradition of Latino-Asian labor cooperation in California (Almaguer 1994). In these instances, class commonalities decisively overrode the fragmenting pull of racial/ethnic identities. Although a few individual activists such as Grace Lee Boggs and Yuri Kochiyama have worked to link the Black and Asian American struggles through their writings and personal activism, instance of Black-Asian cooperation have been few (Choi 1999; Boggs 1998; Kochiyama 1994), in part because of the reasons discussed above.[8] Despite the difficulties of cross-racial collaboration, many scholars urge Asian Americans to persist in this path in the interest of justice for all (C. Kim 2000–2001; Yamamoto 1999; E. Kim 1997; Omatsu 1994; Matsuda 1993).

Conclusions

The scholarship discussed above, generated by scholars in various fields, lays an indispensable foundation for our understanding of conflict and cooperation between Asian Americans and other communities of color. But much remains to be done. We need to know more about the connection between Asian American panethnicity and cross-racial conflict and collaboration. Under what circumstances does panethnicity promote or hinder alliances? Do cross-racial conflict and collaboration, in turn, promote or hinder panethnicity? It would also be useful to complicate the picture with more systematic attention to intra-Asian diversity along the lines of national origin, generation, class, gender, etc. Does it make sense to talk about "Latino-Asian" conflict or does that broad label obscure more than it reveals? In addition, we need to theorize more fully the relative positions of Asian Americans and Latinos in the racial hierarchy. Are Asian Americans closer to Latinos than to Blacks in the racial order? Does this help us to explain why Asian-Latino conflict has been relatively infrequent and Asian-Latino cooperation relatively common?

We might also think about investigating further the now-familiar notion that Asian Americans may become a powerful swing vote in American politics. Is this happening as expected or has something gone awry? What role might Asian American voters be expected to play in coming years? Studies of grassroots mobilizations and alliances around particularly salient issues such as Proposition 187 and Proposition 209 would complement nicely the kinds of public opinion data that we currently possess. Finally, it might be useful to try to lower the barrier between the two main categories of scholarship identified above. For instance, scholars might consider undertaking the unorthodox task of tracing the impact of patterns of racial hierarchy upon electoral activities and outcomes or policy attitudes.

These are just some of the possible directions in which future research on this topic might go. Clearly, this is an exciting time to do work in this area. Ongoing demographic changes both heighten the intellectual challenge (by making the subject matter a moving target) and raise the political stakes of doing such scholarship. In addition, there are important new data sources on the horizon, including a five-city Pilot National Asian American Politics Study that will yield long-awaited information about cities inside and outside of California. We hope that political scientists will take up this challenge and move to the forefront of future efforts to understand interracial conflict and cooperation in American politics.

NOTES

Originally published in *Political Science and Politics* 34.3 (2001): 631–37. © 2001 Cambridge University Press, reprint by permission of Cambridge University Press.

1. Although we focus on the post-1965 period in this article, conflict and cooperation between Asian Americans and other communities of color date back into the 1800s.

2. This was not always the case. Historically, whites used restrictive covenants, terror, landlord discrimination, local decrees barring business and land ownership, and various other means to ghettoize Asian immigrants (Hing 1993; Chan 1991).

3. In a five-city study of Asian Americans, Lien et al. (2001) found that roughly 60 percent of respondents claimed to have a sense of shared ethnic-group fate and more than half expressed a sense of racial or panethnic shared fate.

4. Not all scholars agree that Asian Americans are advantaged relative to Blacks. For instance, a few argue that Asian Americans (specifically Korean Americans) stand in a horizontal relationship with Blacks insofar as Korean Americans have economic power but lack political power and Blacks have political power but lack economic power (K. C. Kim 1999; Chang 1994).

5. Although Native Hawaiians justly consider themselves an indigenous people rather than a racial/ethnic minority, they have also been racialized by whites in ways that make their inclusion in this article reasonable.

6. Apparently, there is a fine line between being successful and being too successful: a 1993 *Los Angeles Times* poll of southern Californians shows that Asian Americans are widely viewed as having achieved too much economic success and as trying too hard to achieve that success (Lee 2000; McClain and Stewart 1995).

7. Note that naming this "Black-Asian" conflict would obscure the fact that of all Asian American groups, Koreans alone occupy the small-business niche in Black urban neighborhoods, which places them in a precarious, tension-ridden position of racial and class superiority over their customers and makes intergroup conflict likely.

8. The Black-Korean Alliance in Los Angeles, which shut down following the rebellion of 1992, was ill conceived from the start in that it involved Black clergymen, politicians, and community leaders—but *not* the Black activists who were leading the boycotts and protests against Korean-owned stores. As a result, the Alliance had no leverage against these activists at all. The same problem was replicated in Black-Korean cooperative alliances in other cities, with the same results.

REFERENCES

Abelmann, Nancy and John Lie. 1995. *Blue Dreams: Korean Americans and the Los Angeles Riots.* Cambridge, MA: Harvard University Press.

Almaguer, Tomás. 1994. *Racial Fault Lines: The Historical Origins of White Supremacy in California.* Berkeley: University of California Press.

Ancheta, Angelo N. 1998. *Race, Rights, and the Asian American Experience.* New Brunswick, NJ: Rutgers University Press.

Bobo, Lawrence D. and Devon Johnson. 2000. "Racial Attitudes in a Prismatic Metropolis: Mapping Identity, Stereotypes, Competition, and Views on Affirmative Action." In Lawrence D. Bobo et al., eds., *Prismatic Metropolis: Inequality in Los Angeles.* New York: Russell Sage Foundation.

Bobo, Lawrence D., Devon Johnson, and Susan A. Suh. 2000. "Racial Attitudes and Power in the Workplace: Do the Haves Differ from the Have-Nots?" In Lawrence D. Bobo et al., eds., *Prismatic Metropolis: Inequality in Los Angeles.* New York: Russell Sage Foundation.

Bobo, Lawrence et al. 1994. "Public Opinion before and after a Spring of Discontent." In Mark Baldassare ed., *The Los Angeles Riots.* Boulder, CO: Westview.

Boggs, Grace Lee. 1998. *Living for Change: An Autobiography.* Minneapolis: University of Minnesota Press.

Bonacich, Edna. 1994. "Asians in the Los Angeles Garment Industry." In Paul Ong et al., eds., *The New Asian Immigration in Los Angeles and Global Restructuring.* Philadelphia: Temple University Press.

———. 1973. "A Theory of Middleman Minorities." *American Sociological Review* 5(37): 583–94.

Browning, Rufus P., Dale R. Marshall, and David H. Tabb. 1997. *Racial Politics in American Cities,* 2nd ed. New York: Longman.

Cain, Bruce, Jack Citrin, and Cara Wong. 2000. *Ethnic Context, Race Relations, and California Politics.* San Francisco: Public Policy Institute of California.

Cain, Bruce, Roderick Kiewiet, and Carole J. Uhlaner. 1989. "The Acquisition of Partisanship by Latinos and Asian Americans." *American Journal of Political Science* 35: 390–422.

Chan, Sucheng. 1991. *Asian Americans: An Interpretive History.* Boston: Twayne.

Chang, Edward T. 1994. "Jewish and Korean Merchants in African American Neighborhoods: A Comparative Perspective." In Edward T. Chang and Russell C. Leong, eds., *Los Angeles— Struggles toward Multiethnic Community.* Seattle: University of Washington Press.

Chin, Gabriel, Sumi Cho, Jerry Kang, and Frank Wu. 1996. *Beyond Self-Interest: Asian Pacific Americans toward a Community of Justice; A Policy Analysis of Affirmative Action.* Los Angeles: LEAP Asian Pacific American Public Policy Institute and UCLA Asian American Studies Center.

Cho, Sumi. 1993. "Korean Americans vs. African Americans: Conflict and Construction." In Robert Gooding-Williams, ed., *Reading Rodney King/Reading Urban Uprising.* New York: Routledge.

Cho, Wendy Tam. 1999. "Naturalization, Socialization, and Participation: Immigrants and (Non-)Voting." *Journal of Politics* 61(4): 1140–55.

Cho, Wendy Tam and Bruce E. Cain. 2001. "Asian Americans as the Median Voters: An Exploration of Attitudes and Voting Patterns on Ballot Initiatives." In Gordon H. Chang, ed., *Asian Americans and Politics: Perspectives, Experiences, Prospects.* Washington, DC: Woodrow Wilson Center and Stanford University Press.

Choi, Jennifer Jung Hee. 1999. "At the Margins of the Asian American Political Experience: The Life of Grace Lee Boggs." *Amerasia Journal* 25(2): 19–40.

Chun, Ki-Taek. 1995. "The Myth of Asian American Success and Its Educational Ramifications." In Don Nakanishi and Tina Yamano Nishida, eds., *The Asian American Educational Experience.* New York: Routledge and Kegan Paul.

Citrin, Jack et al. 1997. "Public Opinion toward Immigration Reform: The Role of Economic Motivations." *Journal of Politics* 59: 858–81.

Dong, Selena. 1995. " 'Too Many Asians': The Challenge of Fighting Discrimination against Asian-Americans and Preserving Affirmative Action." *Stanford Law Review* 47: 1027–57.

Espiritu, Yen Le. 1992. *Asian American Panethnicity: Bridging Institutions and Identities.* Philadelphia: Temple University Press.

Falcon, Angelo. 1988. "Black and Latino Politics in New York City." In F. Chris Garcia, ed., *Latinos in the Political System.* Notre Dame, IN: Notre Dame University Press.

Fong, Timothy P. 1998. "Why Ted Dang Lost: An Analysis of the 1994 Mayoral Race in Oakland, California." *Journal of Asian American Studies* 1(2): 153–71.

———. 1994. *The First Suburban Chinatown.* Philadelphia: Temple University Press.

Fujikane, Candace. 2000. "Asian Settler Colonialism in Hawai'i." *Amerasia Journal* 26(2): xv–xxii.

Gilliam, Frank D., Jr. 1996. "Exploring Minority Empowerment: Symbolic Politics, Governing Coalitions, and Traces of Political Style in Los Angeles." *American Journal of Political Science* 40: 56–81.

Gotanda Neil. 1995. "Re-Producing the Model Minority Stereotype: Judge Joyce Karlin's Sentencing Colloquy in *People v. Soon Ja Du.*" In Wendy Ng et al., eds., *ReViewing Asian America: Locating Diversity.* Pullman: Washington State University Press.

Green, Donald P., Dara Z. Strolovitch, and Janelle X. Wong. 1998. "Defended Neighborhoods, Integration, and Racially Motivated Crime." *American Journal of Sociology* 104: 372–403.

Hacker, Andrew. 1992. *Two Nations: Separate, Hostile, Unequal.* New York: Scribner's.

Hatamiya, Leslie. 1993. *Righting a Wrong: Japanese Americans and the Passage of the Civil Liberties Act of 1988.* Stanford, CA: Stanford University Press.

Henry, Charles P. and Carlos Munoz, Jr. 1991. "Ideological and Interest Linkages in California Rainbow Politics." In Bryan O. Jackson and Michael B. Preston, eds., *Racial and Ethnic Politics in California.* Berkeley, CA: Institute for Governmental Studies.

Hing, Bill Ong. 1993. *Making and Remaking Asian America through Immigration Policy, 1850–1990.* Stanford, CA: Stanford University Press.

Hing, Bill Ong and Ronald Lee eds. 1996. *The State of Asian Pacific America, Volume III: Reframing the Immigration Debate.* Los Angeles: LEAP Asian Pacific American Public Policy Institute and UCLA Asian American Studies Center.

Horton, John. 1995. *The Politics of Diversity: Immigration, Resistance, and Change in Monterey Park, California.* Philadelphia: Temple University Press.

Hum, Tarry and Michela Zonta. 2000. "Residential Patterns of Asian Pacific Americans." In Paul M. Ong, ed., *The State of Asian Pacific America, Volume IV: Transforming Race Relations.* Los Angeles: LEAP Asian Pacific American Public Policy Institute and UCLA Asian American Studies Center.

Ignatiev, Noel. 1997. "Treason to Whiteness Is Loyalty to Humanity." In Richard Delgado and Jean Stefancic, eds., *Critical White Studies: Looking behind the Mirror.* Philadelphia: Temple University Press.

Ikemoto, Lisa. 1993. "Traces of the Master Narrative in the Story of African American/Korean American Conflict: How We Constructed 'Los Angeles.'" *Southern California Law Review* 66: 1581–98.

Kibria, Nazli. 1997. "The Construction of 'Asian American': Reflections on Intermarriage and Ethnic Identity among Second-Generation Chinese and Korean Americans." *Ethnic and Racial Studies* 20(3): 523–44.

Kim, Claire Jean. 2000–2001. "Playing the Racial Trump Card: Asian Americans in Contemporary U.S. Politics." *Amerasia Journal* 26(3): 35–65.

———. 2000. *Bitter Fruit: The Politics of Black-Korean Conflict in New York City.* New Haven, CT: Yale University Press.

———. 1999. "The Racial Triangulation of Asian Americans." *Politics & Society* 27(1): 105–38.

Kim, Elaine. 1997. "Korean Americans in U.S. Race Relations: Some Considerations." *Amerasia Journal* 23(2): 69–78.

Kim, Kwang Chung ed. 1999. *Koreans in the Hood: Conflict with African Americans.* Baltimore, MD: Johns Hopkins University Press.

Kochiyama, Yuri. 1994. "The Impact of Malcolm X on Asian-American Politics and Activism." In James Jennings, ed., *Blacks, Latinos, and Asians in Urban America: Status and Prospects for Politics and Activism.* Westport, CT: Praeger.

Lai, James. 2000. "Asian Pacific Americans and the Pan-Ethnic Question." In Richard A. Keiser and Katherine Underwood, eds., *Minority Politics at the New Millennium.* New York: Garland.

Lee, Robert. 1999. *Orientals: Asian Americans in Popular Culture.* Philadelphia: Temple University Press.

Lee, Sharon and M. Fernandez. 1998. "Trends in Asian American Racial/Ethnic Intermarriage: A Comparison of the 1980 and 1990 Census Data." *Sociological Perspectives* 41(2): 323–42.

Lee, Taeku. 2000. "Racial Attitudes and the Color Line(s) at the Close of the Twentieth Century." In Paul M. Ong, ed., *The State of Asian Pacific America, Volume IV: Transforming Race Relations.* Los Angeles: LEAP Asian Pacific American Public Policy Institute and UCLA Asian American Studies Center.

———. 1999. "The Backdoor and the Backlash: Campaign Finance and the Politicization of Chinese Americans." *Asian American Political Review* 9: 30–55.

Lien, Pei-te. 2001. *The Making of Asian American through Political Participation.* Philadelphia: Temple University Press.

———. 1997. *The Political Participation of Asian Americans.* New York: Garland.

Lien, Pei-te and M. Margaret Conway. 2001. "Comparing Support for Affirmative Action among Four Racial Groups." In Yvette M. Alex-Assensoh and Lawrence J. Hanks, eds., *Black and Multiracial Politics in America.* New York: New York University Press.

Lien, Pei-te et al. 2001. "The Pilot Asian American Political Survey: Summary Report." In James Lai and Don Nakanishi, eds., *The National Asian Pacific American Political Almanac, 2001–2002.* Los Angeles: UCLA Asian American Studies Center.

Light, Ivan and Edna Bonacich. 1988. *Immigrant Entrepreneurs: Koreans in Los Angeles, 1965–1982.* Berkeley: University of California Press.

Massey, Douglas S. 2000. "The Residential Segregation of Blacks, Hispanics, and Asians, 1970–1990." In Gerald Jaynes, ed., *Immigration and Race.* New Haven, CT: Yale University Press.

Massey, Douglas S. and Nancy A. Denton. 1993. *American Apartheid: Segregation and the Making of the Underclass.* Cambridge, MA: Harvard University Press.

Matsuda, Mari. 1993. "We Will Not Be Used." *UCLA Asian American Pacific Islands Law Journal* 1: 79–84.

McClain, Paula D. and Joseph Stewart, Jr. 1995. *"Can We All Get Along?" Racial and Ethnic Minorities in American Politics.* Boulder, CO: Westview.

Min, Pyong Gap. 1996. *Caught in the Middle: Korean Communities in New York and Los Angeles.* Berkeley: University of California Press.

Mladenka, Kenneth D. 1989. "Blacks and Hispanics in Urban Politics." *American Political Science Review* 83: 165–92.

Nakanishi, Don T. 1991. "The Next Swing Vote? Asian Pacific Americans and California Politics." In Bryan O. Jackson and Michael B. Preston, eds., *Racial and Ethnic Politics in California.* Berkeley, CA: Institute for Governmental Studies.

Navarro, Armando. 1994. "The South Central Los Angeles Eruption: A Latino Perspective." In Edward T. Chang and Russell C. Leong, eds., *Los Angeles—Struggles toward Multiethnic Community.* Seattle: University of Washington Press.

Okihiro, Gary. 1994. *Margins and Mainstreams: Asians in American History and Culture.* Seattle: University of Washington Press.

Oliver, Melvin L. and David M. Grant. 1995. "Making Space for Multiethnic Coalitions: The Prospects for Coalition in Los Angeles." In Eui-Young Yu and Edward T. Chang, eds., *Multiethnic Coalition Building in Los Angeles.* Los Angeles: Institute for Asian American and Pacific American Studies.

Omatsu, Glenn. 1995. "Labor Organizing in Los Angeles: Confronting the Boundaries of Race and Ethnicity." In Eui-Young Yu and Edward T. Chang, eds., *Multiethnic Coalition Building in Los Angeles.* Los Angeles: Institute for Asian American and Pacific American Studies.

———. 1994. "The 'Four Prisons' and the Movements of Liberation: Asian American Activism from the 1960s to the 1990s." In Karin Aguilar-San Juan, ed., *The State of Asian America: Activism and Resistance in the 1990s.* Boston: South End Press.

Omi, Michael and Dana Y. Takagi. 1996. "Situating Asian Americans in the Political Discourse on Affirmative Action." *Representations* 55: 155–62.

Ong, Paul M. 2000. "The Affirmative Action Divide." In Paul M. Ong, ed., *The State of Asian Pacific America, Volume IV: Transforming Race Relations.* Los Angeles: LEAP Asian Pacific American Public Policy Institute and UCLA Asian American Studies Center.

————, ed. 1999. *Impacts of Affirmative Action: Policies and Consequences in California.* Walnut Creek, CA: AltaMira Press.

Ong, Paul and Don T. Nakanishi. 1996. "Becoming Citizens, Becoming Voters: The Naturalization and Political Participation of Asian Pacific Immigrants." In Bill Ong Hing and Robert Lee, eds., *The State of Asian Pacific America, Volume III: Reframing the Immigration Debate.* Los Angeles: LEAP Asian Pacific American Public Policy Institute and UCLA Asian American Studies Center.

Ong, Paul et al. 1994. "The Korean-Black Conflict and the State." In Paul Ong et al., eds., *New Asian Immigration in Los Angeles and Global Restructuring.* Philadelphia: Temple University Press.

Osajima, Keith. 1988. "Asian Americans as the Model Minority: An Analysis of the Popular Press Image in the 1960s and 1980s." In Gary Okihiro et al., eds., *Reflections on Shattered Windows: Promises and Prospects for Asian American Studies.* Pullman: Washington State University Press.

Park, Edward J. W. 2001. "The Impact of Mainstream Political Mobilization on Asian American Communities: The Case of Korean Americans in Los Angeles, 1992–1998." In Gordon H. Chang, ed., *Asian Americans and Politics: Perspectives, Experiences, Prospects.* Washington, DC: Woodrow Wilson Center and Stanford University Press.

Park, Edward J. W. and John S. W. Park. 1999. "A New American Dilemma? Asian Americans and Latinos in Race Theorizing." *Journal of Asian American Studies* (October): 289–309.

Park, Jung Sun. 1999. "Identity Politics: Chicago Korean-Americans and the Los Angeles 'Riots.' " In Kwang Chung Kim, ed., *Koreans in the Hood: Conflict with African Americans.* Baltimore, MD: Johns Hopkins University Press.

Park, Kyeyoung. 1997. *The Korean American Dream: Immigrants and Small Business in New York City.* Ithaca, NY: Cornell University Press.

Park, Winnie. 1994. "Political Mobilization of the Korean American Community." In George O. Totten III and H. Eric Schockman, eds., *Community in Crisis: The Korean American Community after the Los Angeles Civil Unrest of April 1992.* Los Angeles: University of Southern California Center for Multiethnic and Transnational Studies.

Saito, Leland T. 2001. "Asian Americans and Multiracial Political Coalitions: New York City's Chinatown and Redistricting, 1990–1991." In Gordon H. Chang, ed., *Asian Americans and Politics: Perspectives, Experiences, Prospects.* Washington, DC: Woodrow Wilson Center and Stanford University Press.

————. 1998. *Race and Politics: Asian Americans, Latinos, and Whites in a Los Angeles Suburb.* Urbana: University of Illinois Press.

————. 1994. "Asian Americans and Latinos in San Gabriel Valley, California: Interethnic Political Cooperation and Redistricting, 1990–92." In Edward T. Chang and Russell C. Leong, eds., *Los Angeles—Struggles toward Multiethnic Community.* Seattle: University of Washington Press.

Saito, Leland T. and Edward J. W. Park. 2000. "Multiracial Collaborations and Coalitions." In Paul M. Ong, ed., *The State of Asian Pacific America, Volume IV: Transforming Race Relations.* Los Angeles: LEAP Asian Pacific American Public Policy Institute and UCLA Asian American Studies Center.

Sonenshein, Raphael J. 1994. "Los Angeles Coalition Politics." In Mark Baldassare, ed., *The Los Angeles Riots.* Boulder, CO: Westview.

———. 1993. *Politics in Black and White: Race and Power in Los Angeles.* Princeton, NJ: Princeton University Press.

Takagi, Dana Y. 1992. *The Retreat from Race: Asian-American Admissions and Racial Politics.* New Brunswick, NJ: Rutgers University Press.

Trask, Haunani-Kay. 2000. "Settlers of Color and 'Immigrant' Hegemony: 'Locals' in Hawai'i." *Amerasia Journal* 26(2): 1–24.

———. 1999. *From a Native Daughter: Colonialism and Sovereignty in Hawai'i.* Rev. ed. Honolulu: University of Hawai'i Press and the Center for Hawaiian Studies.

Tuan, Mia. 1999. *Forever Foreigners or Honorary Whites? The Asian Ethnic Experience Today.* New Brunswick, NJ: Rutgers University Press.

Uhlaner, Carole J. 1991. "Perceived Discrimination and Prejudice and the Coalition Prospects of Blacks, Latinos, and Asian Americans." In Bryan O. Jackson and Michael B. Preston, eds., *Racial and Ethnic Politics in California.* Berkeley: Institute for Governmental Studies.

Uhlaner, Carole J., Bruce Cain, and Roderick Kiewiet. 1989. "Political Participation of Ethnic Minorities in the 1980s." *Political Behavior* 11: 195–231.

Umemoto, Karen. 2000. "From Vincent Chin to Joseph Ileto: Asian Pacific Americans and Hate Crime Policy." In Paul M. Ong, ed., *The State of Asian Pacific America, Volume IV: Transforming Race Relations.* Los Angeles: LEAP Asian Pacific American Public Policy Institute and UCLA Asian American Studies Center.

Yamamoto, Eric K. 1999. *Interracial Justice: Conflict and Reconciliation in Post–Civil Rights America.* New York: New York University Press.

Yoshinaga, Ida and Eiko Kosasa. 2000. "Local Japanese Women for Justice (LJWJ) Speak Out against Daniel Inouye and the JACL." *Amerasia Journal* 26(2): 143–57.

1. What is Lisa Lowe's core argument in her article? What kinds of essentializing themes in Asian American culture does she try to subvert? How are the emergent themes in her discourse, which are framed in a post-1965 context, relevant to the historical experiences of pre–World War II immigrants to the United States from Asia?

2. What is Lowe's purpose in invoking the debate that emerged around Maxine Hong Kingston's *Woman Warrior*? To what extent is this argument cast about issues pertaining to "nationalisms" and "assimilation"? What, according to the author, is a more appropriate reading of this text? What are the implications of these lessons for the development of an Asian American identity?

3. Define the four categories of citizenship discussed by Volpp in her article and provide examples for each of ways in which the American government (or its public) have historically excluded Asian Americans from enjoying their citizenship rights. How prevalent is this exclusion today? What challenges face contemporary Asian Americans as they attempt to combat the notion of being "forever foreigners" in American society? How—according to Volpp—is it possible for Asian Americans to be perceived at once as "model minorities" and at the same time as foreigners incapable of fully exercising the rights of U.S. citizens?

4. Discuss the notion of "equal citizenship" as it applies to Asian Americans (see Volpp's discussion of "citizenship as rights"). In what ways have liberal notions of citizenship proscribed the rights of racialized subjects? What lessons can be drawn from Volpp's discussion of citizenship in the wake of 9/11? How does the "War on Terror" complicate notions of race and citizenship in the United States? Are there any parallels that can be drawn from Asian American experiences?

5. Kim and Lee note that the 1992 Los Angeles rebellion complicates the way we understand race in the United State. The authors argue that the black-white framework is outdated and inadequate for explaining race relations in contemporary America. Based on your own reading of the existing literature and your own empirical observation, do you agree with their argument? Or would you think that the black-white dynamic continues to dominate America's race relations? What are the sources of interracial conflict and what is the basis for interracial coalition? How is the positioning of Asian Americans, who are internally diverse, in the racial hierarchy affect their political participation and the effectiveness of interracial politics?

SUGGESTED READINGS

Aoki, Andrew L. and Don Nakanishi. 2001. Asian Pacific Americans and the New Minority Politics. *PS: Political Science and Politics* 34(3): 605–10.

Chang, Jeff. 1994. Race, Class, Conflict, and Empowerment: On Ice Cube's "Black Korea." Pp. 87–107 in Edward T. Change and Russell C. Leong (eds.), *Los Angeles: Struggles toward Multiethnic Community.* Seattle: University of Washington Press.

Chung, Angie. 2001. The Powers That Bind: A Case Study of the Collective Bases of Coalition Building in Post–Civil Unrest Los Angeles. *Urban Affairs Review* 37: 205–26.

Diaz-Veizades, J. and E. Chang. 1996. Building Cross-Cultural Coalitions: A Case-Study of the Black-Korean Alliance and the Latino-Black Roundtable. *Ethnic and Racial Studies* 19(3): 680–700.

Fujita, Rony. 2000. Coalitions, Race, and Labor: Rereading Philip Vera Cruz. *Journal of Asian American Studies* 3(2): 139–62.

Hirabayashi, Lane. 1995. Back to the Future: Reframing Community-Based Research. *Amerasia Journal* 21(1–2): 103–18.

Horton, John. 1995. *The Politics of Diversity: Immigration, Resistance, and Change in Monterey Park, California.* Philadelphia: Temple University Press.

Joyce, Patrick. 2003. *No Fire Next Time: Black-Korean Conflicts and the Future of America's Cities.* Ithaca, NY: Cornell University Press.

Kim, Claire. 2000. *Bitter Fruit: The Politics of Black-Korean Conflict in New York City.* New Haven, CT: Yale University Press.

Kim, Elaine H. 1995. Beyond Railroads and Internment: Comments on the Past, Present, and Future of Asian American Studies. Pp. 11–21 in Gary Y. Okihiro, Marilyn Alquizola, Dorothy Fujita-Rony, and K. Scott Wong (eds.), *Privileging Positions: The Sites of Asian American Studies.* Pullman: Washington State University Press.

Lien, Pei-te. 2002. The Participation of Asian Americans in U.S. Elections. *Asian Pacific American Law Journal* 8.

Lowe, Lisa. 1996. *Immigrant Acts: On Asian Cultural Practices.* Durham, NC: Duke University Press.

McGregor, Davianna Pomaika'i. 2004. Engaging Hawaiians in the Expansion of the U.S. Empire. *Journal of Asian American Studies* 7(3): 209–22.

Naber, Nadine. 2002. So Our History Doesn't Become Your Future: The Local and Global Politics of Coalition Building Post September 11th. *Journal of Asian American Studies* 5(3): 217–42.

Nakanishi, Don and James S. Lai (eds.). 2003. *Asian American Politics: Law, Participation, and Policy.* New York: Rowman & Littlefield.

Omi, Michael and Howard Winant. 1994. *Racial Formation in the United States: From the 1960s to the 1990s* (2nd ed.). New York: Routledge.

Ong, Paul. 2003. The Affirmative Action Divide. Pp. 377–406 in Don Nakanishi and James Lai (eds.), *Asian American Politics: Law, Participation, and Policy.* New York: Rowman & Littlefield.

Park, Edward. 1998. Competing Visions: Political Formation of Korean Americans in Los Angeles, 1992–1997. *Amerasia Journal* 24: 41–57.

Park, Kyeyoung. 1996. Use and Abuse of Race and Culture: Black/Korean Tension in America. *American Anthropologist* 98(3): 492–99.

Rodriguez, Robyn and Nerissa S. Balce. 2004. American Insecurity and Racial Filipino Community Politics. *Peace Review* 16(2): 131–40.

Saito, Leland. 1993. Asian Americans and Latinos in San Gabriel Valley, California: Interethnic Political Cooperation and Redistricting, 1990–92. *Amerasia Journal* 19(2): 55–68.

Seshagiri, Urmila. 2003. At the Crossroads of Two Empires: Mira Nair's Mississippi Masala and the Limits of Hybridity. *Journal of Asian American Studies* 6(2): 177–98.

Takahashi, Jere. 1997. *Nisei/Sansei: Shifting Japanese American Identities and Politics.* Philadelphia: Temple University Press.

Vo, Linda. 2004. *Mobilizing an Asian American Community.* Philadelphia: Temple University Press.

Wang, L. Ling-Chi. 1995. The Structure of Dual Domination: Toward a Paradigm for the Study of the Chinese Diaspora in the United States. *Amerasia Journal* 21(1–2): 149–69.

Wong, Janelle S. 2005. Mobilizing Asian American Voters: A Field Experiment. *Annals, AAPSS* 601: 102–14.

Yamamoto, Eric. 1999. *Interracial Justice: Conflict and Reconciliation in Post–Civil Rights America.* New York: New York University Press.

FILMS

Ding, Loni (producer/director). 1987. *The Color of Honor: Japanese American Soldiers in World War II* (101-minute documentary).

Kim-Gibson, Dai Sil (director). 2003. *Wet Sand: Voices from L.A. Ten Years Later* (documentary).

Nakamura, Tadashi (director). 2007. *Pilgrimage* (25-minute documentary).

Sakya, Sapana, Donald Young, and Kyung Yu (directors). 2003. *Searching for Asian America* (90-minute documentary).

About the Contributors

Frank D. Bean, Ph.D., is Professor of Sociology at the University of California, Irvine.

Carl L. Bankston III, Ph.D., is Professor of Sociology at Tulane University.

Christina B. Chin is a doctoral student of sociology at the University of California, Los Angeles.

Meera E. Deo is a doctoral student of sociology at the University of California, Los Angeles.

Yen Le Espiritu, Ph.D., is Professor and Chair of the Department of Ethnic Studies at the University of California, San Diego.

Lynn H. Fujiwara, Ph.D., is Assistant Professor of Women's and Gender Studies and Sociology at the University of Oregon.

J. V. Gatewood is a doctoral student in the Department of American Civilization at Brown University.

Danielle Antoinette Hidalgo is a doctoral student in the Department of Sociology at the University of California, Santa Barbara.

Alice Y. Hom is Director of Intercultural Community Center at Occidental College and a doctoral student in the American Studies and History program at Claremont Graduate University.

Claire Jean Kim, Ph.D., is Associate Professor of Political Science at the University of California, Irvine.

Janine Young Kim, J.D., is Associate Professor of Law at Southwestern Law School.

Helen J. Lee, Ph.D., is a researcher at the Public policy Institute of California.

Jennifer Lee, Ph.D., is Associate Professor of Sociology at the University of California, Irvine.

Jenny J. Lee is a doctoral student of sociology at the University of California, Los Angeles.

Robert G. Lee, Ph.D., is Associate Professor of American Civilization at Brown University.

Taeku Lee, Ph.D., is Associate Professor of Political Science at the University of California, Berkeley.

Wei Li, Ph.D., is Associate Professor of Asian Pacific American Studies at the Arizona State University.

Lisa Lowe, Ph.D., is Professor of Comparative Literature at University of California, San Diego.

Daryl J. Maeda, Ph.D., is Assistant Professor of Ethnic Studies at the University of Colorado at Boulder.

Martin F. Manalansan IV, Ph.D., is Associate Professor of Anthropology at the University of Illinois at Urbana-Champaign.

Sunaina Maira, Ed.D., is Associate Professor of Asian American Studies at the University of California, Davis.

David Tokiharu Mayeda, Ph.D. is Assistant Professor in the Department of Psychiatry, University of Hawaii.

Noriko Milman is a doctoral student of sociology at the University of California, Los Angeles.

Anne Mulvey, Ph.D., is Professor of Psychology at the University of Massachusetts, Lowell.

Glenn Omatsu is Senior Lecturer in Asian American Studies at California State University Northridge.

Rhacel Salazar Parreñas, Ph.D., is Professor of Asian American Studies at the University of California, Davis.

Lisa Park (pseudonym) is a mixed-heritage Asian American writer.

Tuyet-Lan Pho, Ph.D., is Director Emerita, Center for Diversity and Pluralism University of Massachusetts, Lowell and a visiting professor of Ethnic Studies at University of California, San Diego.

Emily Skop, Ph.D., is Associate Professor of Geography and Environment at the University of Texas at Austin.

Paul R. Spickard, Ph.D., is Professor of History and Asian American Studies at the University of California, Santa Barbara.

Ajantha Subramanian, Ph.D., is Assistant Professor of Anthropology and Social Studies at Harvard University.

Michael C. Thornton, Ph.D., is Professor of Afro-American Studies and Asian American Studies at the University of Wisconsin.

Karen Umemoto, Ph.D., is Associate Professor of Urban and Regional Planning at the University of Hawaii at Manoa.

Leti Volpp, Ph.D., is Professor of Law at the University of California, Berkeley.

Teresa Kay Williams, Ph.D., is Professor and Chair of the Department of Asian American Studies at California State University Northridge.

Nancy Wang Yuen is a doctoral student of sociology at the University of California, Los Angeles.

Min Zhou, Ph.D., is Professor in the Department of Sociology and the founding chair of the Department of Asian American Studies at the University of California, Los Angeles.

Index